The World Seen from the Distance of a Small Village

The World Seen from the Distance of a Small Village

The house call - to the world

To Tony Blair

Sending this book I want by this to express to you and to your country my deep sympathy.

In a struggle for a better world every idea should be taken seriously and be counted

I send you my best wishes

T. [signature]

Tadeusz Maciejczyk, M.D.   July 8/2005

WINEPRESS WP PUBLISHING

© 2004 by Tadeusz Maciejczyk, M.D. All rights reserved.

Printed in the United States of America

Packaged by WinePress Publishing, PO Box 428, Enumclaw, WA 98022. The views expressed or implied in this work do not necessarily reflect those of WinePress Publishing. Ultimate design, content, and editorial accuracy of this work are the responsibilities of the author.

No part of this publication may be reproduced, stored in a retrieval system, or transmitted in any way by any means—electronic, mechanical, photocopy, recording, or otherwise—without the prior permission of the copyright holder, except as provided by USA copyright law.

Unless otherwise noted, all scriptures are taken from the King James Version of the Holy Bible.

Verses marked NKJV are taken from the *New King James Version*. Copyright © 1979, 1980, 1982 by Thomas Nelson, Inc. Used by permission. All Rights Reserved.

ISBN 1-57921-407-X
Library of Congress Catalog Card Number: 2001094163

DEDICATION

To my father, who never preached about how to live, but who lived with responsibility and integrity every day of his life.

And

To my mother, who shaped my spirit and my soul.

Contents

Foreword 9
Book One: I Was Forced to Write
    June 1983 – January 1987 11
Book Two: Life and Work in the Shadow
    of a Malpractice Suit
    January 1987 – June 1990 119
Book Three: Involvement: Feeling of Mission
    June 1990 – May 1995 375
Book Four: "My *Sen O Szpadzie*"
    (My Dream About a Sword)
    June 1995 – August 2002 575
Notes 735

Foreword

This book, to some degree is a reflection of my life. Without realizing it, it was inspired by advice my mother gave me long ago. She said, "a man never stops being a soldier in his lifetime. He always should be ready to defend his convictions and his beliefs." Such a message doesn't promise an easy life, nevertheless, they are wise words. Now I realize more and more that holding to my mother's advice has given me an inner peace even though I have often been surrounded by turmoil.

This book is involved in the search for truth and for the meaning in everyday happenings, both inside of us as individuals and in the world surrounding us. Every chapter of this book was written as I found my own road through the problems and conflicts of life. It was written to create in me a vision, a path that guided me into my future.

This book was written not as a theoretical, distant, and post facto dissertation about problems, difficulties or challenges, but instead it was

The World Seen from the Distance of a Small Village

written in the heat of ongoing battles. Testimonies born out of such an involvement have a special force that penetrates the soul. They never lose their freshness and are never outdated or obsolete. They can touch deeply into the soul of the listener lifting the spirit and mobilizing him to action. Several times I have observed the expressions on the faces of those who were reading one or another segments of this book and I could see they were touched.

Unique in many ways, this book is a sincere testimony of our time bordering on a documentary. It can be meaningful, appealing and challenging to any age, both to those who feel important and to those for whom life has seemingly been unkind. It has a special call to all those who still have a dream. In this aspect it can be compared to the *Diary of Anne Frank*, given that the circumstances are different.

Sincerity is the strength of this book. I invite you to participate as you read and thus form your own opinions.

Tadeusz Maciejczyk, M.D.

BOOK ONE

I WAS FORCED TO WRITE

Dear Darryl Wahler,

    I received your certified letter and I was surprised. In your previous letter you were demanding I carry malpractice insurance prior to consideration of my reappointment for 1984, which is still far away. Today you are giving me an ultimatum to comply within ten days.
    I was planning to come with this insurance next fall, after I had time to check and see the conditions. I do not like to act in the situation of panic or when I am put against the wall.
    About the subject, my position is clear. I consider this insurance a disgrace. It is not helping medicine. It is depriving it. On one side, it protects the doctors who are alienating patients by cold, distant, economically and emotionally abusive practices. On the other side of the spectrum, it feeds the resentments and disappointments and opens the

avenue for revenge. It gives an open field to easy fortune hunters. In between, it inflates all those institutions and practices that scavenge on such a delicate ground. In this way, the medicine is getting more anxious, more rigid, and enormously more expensive. Everybody feels the weight of this insurance. It is a burden, which produces nothing. It is a dead weight. It merits a nationwide debate and rejection.

In conclusion, unwillingly, I will try to get malpractice insurance before the end of the year, if, after this letter, I will get any. I hope you will reconsider your ultimatum. If not, I will stop my contacts with Sterling Hospital on June 15.

I am sorry that my almost twenty years of practice in this hospital has to end because of such an important medical priority—a new pressure from somewhere, and anxiety.

Sincerely,

Tadeusz Maciejczyk
Milledgeville, June 6, 1983

Book One

June 16, 1983
Tadeusz Maciejczyk, M.D.
Box 788
Milledgeville, IL 61051

CESSATION OF HOSPITAL PRIVILEGES
We are indeed sorry to notify you, Dr. Maciejczyk, that as of 01/01 this date you will no longer be able to admit patients to Community General Hospital. You may continue to treat any patients already in the Hospital until they are discharged or until their care is transferred to another staff physician.

As you know, the reason for this discontinuation is that you have chosen not to submit proof of your professional liability insurance because, as we understand, you have chosen not to have any.

Should you change your mind, Dr. Maciejczyk, please contact the office of the Chief Executive Officer to obtain the necessary papers to reapply for staff privileges.

Again, Dr. Maciejczyk, we are indeed sorry about this turn of events. We are sympathetic to your position and hope that you will be equally understanding to ours.

> Ron Smeltzer, President
> Board of Directors
> pr

copy to: Medical Staff President, Board Chairman, Department of Family Medicine Divisional Director, Nursing Services.

Ron Smeltzer, President
Board of Directors
Community General Hospital in Sterling

Thank you for your letter and notification of my status. I lost my medical privileges in Sterling Hospital not because of malpractice, but because of an ever-increasing hunger of malpractice insurance to engulf more contributors. Suddenly the hospital became uncertain of its existence. If the doctors are not covered—I was told—the hospital could lose all its assets in case of litigation.

The World Seen from the Distance of a Small Village

This atmosphere of fear did not exist a few years ago. Who is creating it? Who is blackmailing the hospital? A situation is created in which the State is still issuing the licenses, but to really practice medicine you have to pay the malpractice insurance for permission. What will be next? Terror is omnipotent if it meets nothing else but submission.

Medical care is a very special institution. It requires enormous confidence between the doctor and the patient in order to give the best. It cannot give this best in the environment of staged confrontation, suspicion, accusation and ever-present intimidation, which are the tools malpractice insurance needs to prosper.

Malpractice insurance imposes a ransom on the doctors or hospitals to pay and in this way is giving them its OK to work under increasingly tougher and more costly conditions. Those deals are transferred immediately to the average patient in the form of an extra fee added to every office visit or any hospital service. For this reason, those deals should not be done secretly, in a closet, but should be made public each year and open to discussion. As with every other tax, ultimately the people should have the voice as to where the limit is. The malpractice insurance should make public its income; how it was used; what the operation expenses were and it should give a clear account from the previously closed period.

The height of taxation for malpractice insurance should never be determined by a showcase of a trial with enormous awards, which I see in no other way, but as a club directed against anybody who would dare to oppose them. You pay what we want or you can be destroyed next. Some just regulation of those problems has to be established. A search should be started for some alternative body that would attend to all the elements of social justice that are now dominated by malpractice insurance.

I hope that I will still have a chance to join the Sterling Hospital in a new atmosphere where I will be able to contribute to its noble purpose with pride—not with a feeling of shame—that I am here because I paid the bribe.

Sincerely,

Tadeusz Maciejczyk, M.D.
Milledgeville, June 23, 1983

Book One

The Village Board of Milledgeville

As you know, I am no longer on Staff of the Community General Hospital in Sterling, and this creates a special situation for my patients from Milledgeville and around. My letters to Sterling Hospital never were publicized completely and at this point, I feel I should report my situation, my arguments and my stand to the Village Board.

I opposed a precipitous buying of malpractice insurance, because I would have to pay for it by increasing my office fee. I consider such an artificial expense a drain from the people who are already sick and in need—an immoral act. To buy this insurance, I would have to have a mandate for it from my patients.

For this reason I would like to ask these questions to all interested:

1. Are you aware that the malpractice insurance is paid by you during each visit or hospital service?
2. Should the malpractice insurance mechanism (cost, who is paying, how the money is spent, what is the product of this institution) be explained and discussed publicly in clear terms?
3. Should you be told exactly how much you pay for malpractice insurance each time you have a visit or a hospital service, or even when you buy medicine?
4. Should a public debate and independent analysis bring a limit to this enormous exploitation of the people in need?
5. Should I buy this insurance at the cost of increasing fees for each visit?
6. Should I rather, because of my obstinacy, leave Milledgeville, or will the people help me in this—my search for the way out from the trap of malpractice insurance?

Thank you.

Tadeusz Maciejczyk, M.D.
Milledgeville, July 7, 1983

The World Seen from the Distance of a Small Village

The Carroll County Review

I thank you very much for you article about my stand against the malpractice insurance. Apparently your newspaper is reaching many people because I felt their reaction. They were expressing understanding and desire to cooperate. In response, I was telling them that my voice alone would do very little. If one thousand people will start to ask questions, demand information and explanations, it will be a good beginning. If one million will do this, it would be a force that would have the power to ask for change.

And—there are many unanswered questions about this insurance.

Really—How much an average person in the U.S. is paying for malpractice taxation (added to all visits, to all hospital services, nursing home stays, even the nurses visitations and medications).

It would be very revealing to know how this burden is distributed in different age groups, i.e., for people in their twenties, forties, sixties, eighties. The problem is that the distribution of this taxation is very unfair. The more chronically sick a person is, the older and more fragile he become, the more he is victimized because he has to pay more. It would be very good, if the organizations of the aged people would start to investigate this situation and put a stop to such an abuse and exploitation because it will not get better. It will get worse. If somebody can get 100 dollars without any effort or opposition the next time he demands 200. Greed has no limit.

Another question: How much the malpractice insurance is collected annually from all the corners where its versatility can reach.

Also: What happens to the treasure the malpractice is accumulating? Who is the beneficiary? How is this money spent? This money is public money, obtained by taxation even if this taxation is indirect. It should be publicized, studied and scrutinized. It is the treasure taken away from the poorest, from the sick and especially from the old.

It would be very interesting to look into the show trials and big rewards giving lavishly from money collected in such a painful way to many people. Was it really a trial or was it really a show? How much were the collections up after each one of them?

It would be interesting to point out those people who organize this kind of exploitation and ask them questions from the public forum. They should define exactly what they are giving back to the people in exchange for such an enormous sacrifice. What is their product? What are their achievements?

It would be interesting to make a meticulous study to clarify how much malpractice insurance increased the cost of medical treatment by

Book One

its byproduct, by introducing into medicine an element of fear. How many unnecessary tests, duplications, consultations are done just to be on safe ground, to avoid possible accusations? How much of this is a benefit? How much is simply a costly waste?

The malpractice insurance affects everybody. It has without a doubt an enormous influence and it will fight back. But the malpractice insurance has a weak spot. It pretends it is taxing the rich doctors and hospitals for the protection of poor and victimized, while exploiting without mercy the poor and serving only itself. It is like a repetition of Hans Christian Anderson's story of *The Emperor's New Clothes*. The people have the right to take another look and to ask questions.

>Tadeusz Maciejczyk, M.D.
>Milledgeville, July 20, 1983

Dear Mayor General John Singlsub,

Yes, I remember your reaction and your stand against the policy to reduce our defenses in S. Korea. At that time I gave you for this a plus mark. Obedience is a big virtue. The courage to stand, even alone, in defending a principle, is something supreme in the human soul and only this is making the best turns in our destiny.

I affirm a need of this country for strong defenses and I consider that the MX Missiles program is a necessary evil to curtail the Soviet appetite. Goodwill not convince them. Strength will. MX Missiles are necessary to contain the Soviet's aggressiveness.

But, it would be very sad if our program would remain reduced to weaponry of containment. Then, there would be no other hope but to build later another defense system, really to build one such a system after another. It would be a grim perspective.

My view is that while building strong defenses to contain now, we should not pass one day without attacking, attacking those positions in Russia where they are weak, where there is an obvious or potential vacuum or hunger for something the Soviet State cannot give their citizens. Every vacuum is waiting for something to fill in.

A few months ago, Catholic bishops published a letter asking for nuclear disarmament. Once, I was discussing this with our deacon, an active and good man. I told him that I would sign such a declaration only if together we would collect money, not from Catholics, but from all Believers in the U.S. and in the world, to build a system of radio

The World Seen from the Distance of a Small Village

stations that would inform the Soviets all the time and in all dialects of Soviet Russia about the true picture of the world here, about our anxieties, about the manifestations for peace and about the reasons why there is pressure here to build up defenses and a pressure for disarmament.

In Russia there is a big conscious or unconscious hunger for something more transcendental than slogans. There is a need for a truth. I noted such a thing in 1945 in Poland. For about ten days one Russian captain was coming to our home to sleep. Really he saved my life when the security police came to take me. That captain was constantly returning the conversation to the same questions: whether there is a God and if so, how can he know this? How can he find it? For so many years he was taught atheism. He was searching for a truth. About God, not Catholic, not Protestant, just about marvelous God, audiences to Russia should not cease. Sure, there will be an audience there.

America has freedom created by a free society. Without speaking exactly about America, there should be a constant talk to Russia about freedom, about freedom of a person, freedom of soul, freedom of conscience, about justice without which freedom cannot exist, about freedom to be different and to express the differences, about the freedom to take a stand dictated by the conscience.

There should be constant information about Afghanistan, about Poland, about all the injustices there; the morality, the human aspects, all about what the authorities do not want to reveal. There should be constant talk to Lithuanians, Latvians, Estonians. The Ukraine and Belorussia should be studied and should have constant audiences not only about what happens but about their history, their culture created inside and outside, about their free human needs. The free world should not be intimidated to be silent about it. The Muslim world in Russia should be given all the attention. No one atrocity done in Afghanistan should be omitted there.

The Soviet laws should be scrutinized. Soviet justice for the political offenders should be discussed, without any trial to make conclusions. Not a partisan, not national, and not sectarian, but just a human and teaching approach would be the most effective.

To win the battle for peace in the world, we cannot lose one day. I agree that MX Missiles are necessary, but without aggressively fighting for the change of soul and conscience in Russia, it would have a hollow effect.

I am sorry I cannot contribute much. Never have I had a talent to get rich and now I am a little like Gen. Singlaub years ago. I opposed the malpractice insurance in our hospital and I lost my privileges. I lost my privileges now when I have four children in college to support. I am

Book One

struggling but I am an optimist. I include my letters to the hospital and to local newspapers for you to take a look at because the malpractice insurance is a problem of our whole society. America cannot build a missile defense system and not strive for real justice inside. The malpractice insurance is depriving and is weakening our country.

I hope President Reagan will get the missiles system and I hope also that America will not stop with such a security but will engage in an active fight for the soul of Russia and for the real freedom of the world.

If I could contribute anything it will be always to your disposition.

Sincerely,

Tadeusz Maciejczyk
Milledgeville, August 4, 1983

Dr. S. Patel
President of the Medical staff
Community General Hospital of Sterling

Thank you for your call and for the expression of friendship and goodwill from the medical staff. Also thank you for the invitation to return to work in the hospital and for assurances that the reinstatement would not be difficult and the amount of malpractice insurance required from me would be only the minimum.

I am sending to you copies of my first letter to the Administration and of the letter to the *Carroll County Review*. The last one was published entirely and had a fairly good response. With the help of them I want to clarify my way of thinking and my objections not only to the financial part of the malpractice insurance, but also to its moral aspect, which to me is important. I would like you to explain to me and to convince me that I am wrong in my evaluations and that such insurance and subsequent hardship put on the sick to pay for it, is beneficial for medicine and for them, that morally it is sound. If I get such an explanation I will return to my old place in Sterling Hospital and I will feel really happy.

A few days ago, I received a letter from Dr. Leonard Berlin. (He had a malpractice process, but he took to the court the accuser and he won. *Time Magazine* even wrote about him.) This time his letter was conciliatory. He appeared to put his arms down. His conclusion was: "So, sadly, it seems the hospital has a right to demand that you carry malpractice

The World Seen from the Distance of a Small Village

insurance. The whole malpractice system is bad for medicine, bad for the people, and bad for the country. But we have, I'm sorry to say, virtually no choice in the matter. I guess we have to live with it."

This conclusion I cannot accept. Whoever evaluates anything of importance in such a way cannot just give up and live with it. Such an evaluation brings an obligation to concentrate and to work for change—a change for the good of medicine, for the good of the people, for the good of the country, as he put it. We all have some debt to them. If the undertaking has the appearance of pure impossibility, then that is still not an excuse. One sentence in the last booklet of Robins Reader says, "To believe an undertaking is impossible is the surest way to make it so. Many worthwhile projects are strangled by a cowardly imagination. After all, how can you know it can't be done until you try it?"[1]

I hope I will return to Sterling one day. Milledgeville naturally belongs to Sterling and I have there many attachments, but for now, before I buy the minimum of malpractice insurance to satisfy the readmitting authorities, I do not like to lose the principle that dictates to me the stand I took. I am sorry. I am as I am.

Best wishes to everybody.

Tadeusz Maciejczyk
Milledgeville, September 1, 1983

Book One

The Carroll County Review

    Through your paper I want to thank our Village Board for standing on my side in the dispute over malpractice insurance. I also want to give my many thanks to all those who signed so many pages of the petition to Sterling Hospital requiring revision of my condition. Responding to the invitation of the president of the medical staff of Sterling Hospital to give up the resistance fulfill the requirements and come back to work there, I wrote to him a letter. Its copy I include here to complement what I am telling now. There, I expressed again my position and my view of the system of malpractice.

    Solutions to this problem will not be easy. It forms a vicious circle of greediness, threats, fear, submission to the manipulations of those who are harvesting from this circle and general passivity in admitting ever-increasing burdens that this circle is imposing. The September 21, 1983 *Wall Street Journal* estimated that the only defensive procedures aimed at protection from persecution are increasing the cost of medical treatment by 30%; that means by about 20 billion dollars a year, more than the whole crop of this country. The people are bearing the cost.

    How to break this circle and its consequences? This would be a program that should start with an open discussion and wide participation on the pages of this newspaper, in meetings, in the approaching year of election. To such a discussion, I invite everybody. Only a strong popular voice of popular opinion with pressure from all parts of the country can bring the ever-widening wheel of this circle to some kind of halt and transformation in a system of justice not so destructive and abusive.

                                     Tadeusz Maciejczyk
                                     Milledgeville, September 25, 1983

The World Seen from the Distance of a Small Village

Establishment of Martin Luther King Day

Another lazy day without aim. As designed, it would be a day of a dance around a magnificent, but already cold monument. It would be a day for politicians who have nothing to offer but speeches. In no way it would be a day of MLK's dream.

The nature of Martin Luther King's dream is dynamic, requiring action and involvement. As such, it should be a day of commitment at every level, from personal reexamination: who am I? How can I be better? Through striving for peace in the families, among neighbors, between neighborhoods. For such a day the homes, houses and streets could be cleaned and beautified by voluntary work to add splendor to the occasion and the disputes could be resolved in a different, very special spirit. In such a day the achievements toward realization of MLK's dream could be publicized and some kind of "Oscar" could be rewarded to the most outstanding. That day the authors, the artists, theater groups and film companies could present their new creations and the school children, instead of staying home, could have a day of deliberation on how the dream of ML King could be put into action and stay alive in hearts.

Because of a dynamic nature of such a day, the dream day should not be placed in the winter when the communications are limited by the weather. More appropriate would be a warm spring day. Such celebrations should be spontaneous. No official approval to hold them is necessary and if turned into tradition, it could be the biggest day in the U.S., and it could spread beyond the U.S. to the world, wherever hate and indifference make life miserable and dangerous.

Tadeusz Maciejczyk
Milledgeville, October 27, 1983

Book One

The Problem of Aging

The problem of aging and the consequences it creates is hanging over our society, solved only partially and frequently neglected. As it is now, it is crying for some additional thinking, planning and action. The advancing age is changing people's capacity to cope. It was always so, but the fast-growing new patterns of social structures, the speed of changes are leaving the aged more perplexed and helpless. The world known to them is disappearing; the new one they look on with anxiety. Dispersed and struggling to survive, they have no time or energy to transfer to society the experiences of their lives.

The old age approaches in many ways. It has many phases and many faces. For this reason the approach to the problem of aging cannot be standardized, nor left only to them to resolve.

Until now the old people had three main forms of arrangements to organize their lives. The first, and the best solution, was to stay with the extended family, sharing with them the obligations and the joys. Of course, there was a condition to this. Without harmony and understanding, it could be very unpleasant.

The second solution, very frequent in our society, was to live alone, struggling to maintain independence and dignity, frequently at the cost of isolation, loneliness, growing deterioration of self-image, inadequate personal care and nourishment and finally, depression and anxiety.

The third way was something that years ago looked like a perfect solution: admission to the nursing home. This solution now remains a very good arrangement for the completely disabled, but to put there those who still have a need and a will to live is social injustice. Many of the old people fear such a placement and reject it until the last cry for help because to them such a "deportation" has a meaning of pre-grave existence and of a definitive rejection from life.

As always, there are people who adjust well to the lonely life or to the seclusion of the nursing homes where gradually, and many times quickly, they lose their personalities. A large segment of the old remains that need a "better" arrangement. They want to maintain their independence and they want to be active, but at the same time, they need basic services and the company of others. This segment, dispersed and intimidated by daily problems, form no more than a mute and silent force. Giving them proper conditions, they could become a balancing element for the exuberance, the mistakes and the push of the young. Their lives' experiences could have a more forceful voice in the opinion shaping and in the preservation of traditions.

The World Seen from the Distance of a Small Village

If this is so, is such a solution possible? Is it affordable? Is it practical enough to try?

I imagine that the basic unit of such a plan would be a home with a homely appearance (different from hotels and motels). Such a home should be big enough to support a centralized administration, kitchen and laundry, and give the residents an adequate space for social activities. A supervising nurse to attend to all basic needs of the members would be a good idea. If possible a garden around for all those interested in gardening and maybe a nursery where working mothers could leave their small ones in the hands of volunteering grandmothers and grandfathers under the supervision of the nurse. In such a home all inside chores would be done by the residents, both to decrease the cost of living and to create a feeling of togetherness, or caring for one another; a feeling of belonging and of being wanted and appreciated. Nobody can buy those values with money. Without them any home is cold and inhospitable. After the chores, everybody would be encouraged to develop their own interests and activities. A home of this kind shouldn't stay in isolation. They should be the centers of social, cultural, religious and political activities. They should resound with life.

Anybody whose strong spirit is resisting the limitations imposed by a declining body would be a candidate. Each member should accept that all other residents belong to his new family.

Would such an enterprise be practical economically? The initial capital could be raised with bonds by each particular locality. The investment could be secure in the sense that we will always have old people with the same human needs among us. Advantages would be many. Common management could bring the prices from the suppliers down. Communication with other places could be easier. Safety would improve. If such homes would appear in many places, a resident of one home could be a guest in some other distant home while traveling.

Each person, each society needs adventures to test themselves. Can we take this idea as a kind of our adventure and test?

Tadeusz Maciejczyk, M.D.
Milledgeville, January 15, 1984

Book One

Northwestern Steel and Wire Company
Sterling, Illinois

 I am the only doctor in Milledgeville and because of this, I see several of your workers. The remark that I want to make is about the stress of those patients. The main cause of this stress is the weekly change of shifts in your factory.
 From the medical point of view, this arrangement is keeping your workers in a permanent state of stress. Just when they are starting to adjust to a new schedule of work and sleep, the change is forcing them to another strain of adjustment. This is a very potent factor that can breed in the workers a feeling of dissatisfaction, restlessness or apathy.
 Such an arrangement also creates frequent days when the workers are more tired, more distracted, less careful, more prone to accidents and much less productive than they would be under other conditions.
 All those factors should be taken into account. In my judgment, a change of shift every two months would be much healthier and more advantageous to the factory and to the workers, even if in the beginning they would appose it.
 It may be true that factory arrangements are not my business, but I sincerely believe that it would bring many improvements for everybody and this is the only reason I am writing this letter.

           Tadeusz Maciejczyk, M.D.
           Milledgeville, March 12, 1984

The World Seen from the Distance of a Small Village

Whether Solidarity is weaker or stronger, suppressed or growing and giving fruits, history will tell.

In a poem "Dziady," Adam Mickiewicz writes about students, imprisonment, tortures and deportation in chains to Russia in 1824 for belonging to a student organization of Filomats and Filarets. One of the prisoners in the prison cell, trying to explain the meaning of that madness to his friends, told them this story.

When God expelled the sinner from the paradise
He didn't want him to die from hunger
And He ordered the angel to prepare wheat
And to throw it along the way of the man.
Adam came, found it, looked on from the distance
And left, because he didn't know what to do with the wheat.
Then at night a wise devil came, and told to himself:
"Not in vain did God scatter this grain here.
It has to be that this grain contains a special power.
We will hide it before Man finds out that power."
He made a ditch with a horn in the ground and put the wheat in there.
He spat on it, covered it with the earth, and stomped it with the hoof.
Proud and satisfied that he had crossed God's intentions
He began to laugh and roar, and he disappeared.
And then in the spring—to the great surprise of the devil—
Grew grass, blossoms, spikes and seeds.
Oh, you who walk into the world only at midnight,
Calling cunningness an understanding, and a malice a might,
You who find faith and the freedom and bury them:
You can think that you deceived God and you are deceiving yourselves.
The grains of Solidarity did not disappear just because they were buried.[2]

> Tadeusz Maciejczyk, M.D.
> Milledgeville, May 10, 1984

Book One

This letter was sent to:

TV Channel 4 Rock Island, Illinois
Tom Davis, WSDR, Sterling, Illinois
The National Republication Congressional Committee
U.S. News and World Report
Time Magazine
Newsweek
The White House

The anomaly of the disarmament talks is that while trying to ease the ultimate consequence of the process, it avoids seeing or speaking about the whole problem. The problem, the real cause of the arms race, is the injustice done and perpetuated to whole nations. The only right the perpetrator has to do is his big fist. It is very unlikely that he would weaken this fist just because of talks or treaties. Oh yes, he can act and speak like the wolf from the children's books about the wolf and the sheep, and he can even sign documents, but he will always find 1000 ways to arm himself up to the teeth, because by some strange logic of guilt and punishment, he is living in a permanent real fear. This fear of his cannot be alleviated in other ways, but only by domination and subjugation of everybody around him. Only then he would have some peace of mind.

Is it a utopia to think about real freedom and independence of all nations of the world and to work for it?

The Soviet Union, the strong supporter of so many independence movements and the inspiration of so many freedom fighters in so many lands of the world, should have no objection to discussing this problem openly and to starting action. Free plebiscites could be an instrument for such a project. In this way the satellite nations could express freely their love for the present system. Lithuania, Latvia and Estonia are nations and should have the right to be free. Of course, Bielorussia and Ukrania are nations. Nobody else but the Soviets recognized this when they asked for an independent nation status for them in ONU and in UNESCO. There are many other nations in the West and in the East that have the right to be heard.

With the freedom for every nation, free uncensored communication between people, may be with arbitrations between conflicting wills, but always recognizing the dignity of each society, the arms race would be finally something of the past. It would be simply unnecessary.

The World Seen from the Distance of a Small Village

Without freedom for every nation, any disarmament talks will be practically a waste of time.

Tadeusz Maciejczyk, M.D.
June 7, 1984

The (Phil) Donahue Show

On July 13, I watched a part of your show discussing the issues of peace and disarmament. On the podium were three activist ladies from the peace movement.

I was in complete agreement with them that an action for peace is urgent. I disagreed with the plan they were suggesting. The only insinuations they were giving, in the part I saw, were to press our government for a "bold" initiative to talk to the Soviets and to make a peace. Apparently they were washing their hands from any harder, personal involvement and commitment that could parallel and reinforce they cry for peace.

Our government can deal mainly with the Soviet government, which at present seems to be unapproachable. In this condition a diplomacy, which would not mean surrender, has a limit. And our government has also an obligation to defend somehow our freedom.

I would like to suggest to all peace activities, if they are sincere in their readiness for sacrifice, to develop a different strategy, a strategy whose main aim would be to promote contacts, mutual language without distortions, mutual understanding, and mutual goals between the people of the West and of the East, using as an instrument a constant "people-to-people" talk. In such talks, no governments should be involved. All financing, planning and realizations would be done by volunteer contributions of money, time and skills throughout the world. A talk to people living in the Soviet empire could be done through all existing and future radio stations. The broadcasts would be twenty-four hours a day and in all languages of the European and Asiatic Soviet territories. To attain this would require an enormous effort, constant planning, alertness, boldness and intellectual mobilization, but as I see it, only such an action could lead to real unity, understanding and peace. I hope that in the meantime, our government would be strong enough to protect such a movement from intimidation.

To complement this letter, I am sending you my previous letters dealing with this problem.

Book One

Tadeusz Maciejczyk, M.D.
July 15, 1984

I would be very grateful to you for doing copies of my letters and sending them to those ladies on the podium. Thank you.

The World Seen from the Distance of a Small Village

Charles H. Percy
United States Senator

Dear Sir:

I thank you for your letter and for the discussion of U.S. policy in Central America. In this matter I agree entirely that the U.S. has to stand firmly to prevent formation of the strategic Soviet client states in that region because such states could later destabilize all the continent. Therefore, even a prolonged presence of U.S. troops in Honduras makes sense and is justified.

The U.S. policy in Central America should be something more than a mere ramification of its global confrontation with the Soviets or a reflex to the Soviet pressure. Our policy there should be very special, and very responsive to the deepest layers and roots of the Salvadoran tragedy. The Soviets, as usual, are entering through the back door wherever injustice and consequent bitterness have grown into explosive moods. Their meddling exacerbates such a mood still more, deepens the hate and creates forces for which the Soviet empathy appears sincere and natural and the domestic situation intolerably and requiring a drastic, even violent change. This way an idealistic sincere man can change into a pawn of the Soviet game.

How to respond to such a situation?

Obviously the government should be helped to preserve law and order. This would be a first step. A simultaneous and more importantly, more promising U.S action should be an effort to create the best conditions for a dialogue between all factions of the Salvadoran society. I do not see any substitution for a dialogue. True peace has to grow from inside; it cannot be imposed. The long-range victory in San Salvador will not depend on the suppression of the rebels, but on their genuine reintegration into a real and active life stream. This would be the ultimate victory of the free world in Central America. Only such an arrangement could terminate there for good any further Soviet subversion.

The Salvadorian dialogue cannot take place in San Salvador. There, on the battleground, the tempers, the fears, the apprehensions are too high to talk calmly. For such talks, a Washington location would be more convenient and more proper.

The nature of such a dialogue should be very special. Political accommodation shouldn't be its only objective. This dialogue should reach the depth of that nation. John Powell, the author of a small, but very

Book One

good book, *Why Am I Afraid to Tell You Who I am?* would call such a dialogue a "gut level talk."[3] In such talks everybody should participate: the government, the rebels and everybody in between. Whoever has an idea and cares should have a right to speak. Nobody should be too big or too small to tell his view, his testimony. A truth would have to emerge from such a discussion and on its foundation, a future could be built and new rules could be created, which would be respected by all.

In the Salvadorian case, a conference like the one in Paris with Viet Nam, or recently in Geneva for Lebanon, would be worthless. Here such a conference has to have different dimensions. The mediator in such a talk should be very special. It should not be a politician, or a journalist, or an expert of Communism or on Central America, but a person of a category and the spirit of John Powell. Such a person could be accepted and could be trusted by all, and under his mediation, solutions could be found that could heal not only the Salvadorian illness, but could teach many other sick spots of the world, and could bring for all of us a little more of peace.

Cyprian Norwid, the XIX century Polish poet wrote once about a man afflicted by many tragedies, bad luck, self-deprecation and pain. That man was ready to give up when one day he got an idea that he could use all those adversities to work for him. As the poet tells it, it was at that point all those adversities escaped from him and he became free.

Maybe like him, we could use our mistakes and our adversities in San Salvador to create a new means to overcome such situations. Maybe this new way could have not only local, but also universal value and could help us to look into the future with more confidence.

Tadeusz Maciejczyk, M.D.
August 5, 1984

It was very late in my office when I was writing this letter, but I hope that my general idea will remain clear. Together with this letter, I send you my other letters, which were dealing with problems of this our world. I wish you the best in your campaign.

The World Seen from the Distance of a Small Village

The Justice Department of Ogle County

I received a letter from the Sheriff of your county with the wide-open eyes.

I was made a criminal and a warrant was issued to the police to take me. If the system of justice of your county works with such finesse, it really can create problems.

I had a car accident on January 17, 1984. I was for this in the Ogle County Court twice. I admitted my guilt already during the first session. Indicating the need for the second trial, the judge said that maybe the stop sign was not there, and the police officer telling me so was not telling the truth. This way maybe I was innocent and his obligation was to check, to verify this. My protests didn't change anything. Both trials consisted mainly of the intimidating monologue of the judge with little chance to respond.

I went to the courtroom with the checkbook. When I raised the checkbook to pay, the judge stopped me. "Not now, not here," he said. He very rapidly enumerated different positions of my fine and he asked me to leave the courtroom. On the way out, I went to the clerk to pay. He didn't know how much it was and told me to do this later.

Later, I expected a notification from the court office indicating how much my fine was. In any civilized country this would be a logical attitude. This letter never came. After awhile I concluded that in Ogle county hurry was not a vice, and then I forgot about the problem. I have my own daily obligations that absorb my attention.

Then, on September 8, I received a letter from the Sheriff's Department with the warrant. I was really offended. I didn't feel guilty of any negligence. I was always ready, and I am, to obtain notification of how much my fine is and to pay it immediately.

I take the present court action not only as molestation, but also as a blow to my faith in American institutions—faith I do not want to lose. A judge above all should be just. I need this faith in American institutions probably more than others because I came from the place where the courts were the instrument to break the opposition and the will of the nation. The real justice didn't count there. In 1945/46 in Poland, I was condemned to death as a bandit because I belonged to the polish Home Army and to the unit that regrouped against Communists. I had the luck to escape. I want to stress that the present petty kind of molestation, like in my case, is not improving society. If it is applied to somebody who still is not formed morally and emotionally, it can help to create monsters.

Book One

For all those reasons, I protest. I admit that I am guilty of passing the stop sign. The sun blinded me and I was on an unknown country road. I strongly feel that all that followed my first trial was expensive and unnecessary.

> Tadeusz Maciejczyk, M.D.
> Milledgeville, September 12, 1984

The World Seen from the Distance of a Small Village

John J. Rapp
Judge of the Circuit Court of the 15th Judicial Circuit
(that included the Ogle County Court)

I am sending this letter to you not to complain, but to stress my belief that the institutions that deal with the public should not harm carelessly. The court is, and should be, a place of reverence and of the confidence of the society. If it acts like a despot and punishes without guilt through the petty rules, it creates doubt about values and can create an atmosphere of mistrust and sarcasm. I feel that the judge doesn't need to be clever. He should be wise and just.

          Tadeusz Maciejczyk, M.D.
          Milledgeville, September 16, 1984

Book One

John Hughes
Assistant Secretary for Public
Affairs and Department Spokesman

I thank you for your letter and for the explanation of the most recent situation in Central America. I recognize that a considerable work was done there. The Soviet influence was restricted. The falling structures of different countries were supported and modified towards more democratic form. In El Salvador the people started to have some hope.

And yet . . . the end of the tunnel is still too far to see and the difficulties to bring the conflict to a conclusion are multiplying. In the U.S. there is already a restlessness and erosion of will. The funds for continuation of the present policy in C. America are harder to get, and the outside friends are looking the American intervention in this region with uneasiness and suspicion. Finally, the house of El Salvador is still divided and the civil war is going on.

It looks, that in the planning for renewal in C. Am. some very important element is missing. We are trying to build there a beautiful house, from up—down, with a hope that this structure somehow will stabilize the ground, so, that the house would be durable and would resist the outside storms. Until now only the strength of the U.S. is preventing this structure from collapsing.

To obtain a real peace, it would be logical to prepare first the minds of the people. The past, and especially the last years of civil war, with the atrocities from the left and from the right, made, that the emotions became bottled up inside of each person separately paralyzing them. It is true, that the people are going to the polls, expressing in this way their hunger for some positive change, but to speak, to open the embottled emotions, they are afraid. It looks to me, that unless they have a chance to open their inside, to feel the ears of the world with their testimonies, they will be unable to see clearly their way beyond the present. Only afterwards, they would be able to start a constructive vision of the future. Such an outcry would provide also all the symptoms for the diagnosis—and then the medicine that the U.S. is trying to give them for years, would be the most appropriate and would have the maximum healing power. It looks to me extremely important, to find a way to the minds of the Salvadorian people, especially to those who formed the previous establishment, and to the rebels.

Who really an ordinary rebel is? Their leaders can be the orthodox Communists, probably with some special Central American flavor. The young volunteers most probably are not. They joined the Communist cause, because it was the only strong and active opposition to the hated oligarchic oppression. I do not think that the arm shipments from Cuba and from Nicaragua are the central element of the guerilla strength. The arms have to be given to the hands of the faithful, of the believers, to be lethal. Those faiths and those beliefs are the central problem there. We will not move forward without opening them and without neutralizing them. To win, their beliefs have to be taken into account, to be acknowledged as important, and discussed loudly before the audience of the world. Such a public satisfaction could be the more important element and a turning point in the rebellion.

In the guerilla war much more than in wars between countries each bullet, each act of terrorism or of destruction, is a substitution for a word that had no chance to be told, or which was not listened to. It could be very well, that listening to the words, would have a calming effect, and could produce a necessary relaxation.

The optimal end story to the present El Salvador situation, would be, that all sides of the conflict would get some kind of satisfaction and a common goal, while the Soviets would lose their influence on minds.

What are the other possible scenarios?

1. Continue the present situation: something, but not enough to prevail definitively, dragging this tragic conflict for years.
2. Withdraw—It is not our business. We should not impose our view on others. This fire is far from our home.
3. Or the most desired solution. With a massive support, the rebellion would be crashed, all the resistance centers broken, and an order imposed. If all this would be done without communication, without reaching the minds of the guerilas, it could be that the end of the war would not mean the end of the struggle. The struggle would descend into underground, and a legend would be born—a beautiful legend, exciting to each new generation, conquering what the guerrilla could not conquer. The Soviets in such a legend would be seen as a friends, the U.S. an aggressor and a collaborator of the old exploitating class. In such a situation the Soviet investment in Central America would not be lost even after guerrilla defeat. For them the back door would be always open, and the Soviets love such a situation, and they know, as nobody else, how to use it. In meantime for the U.S., would be impossible to reach the hearts of many for long time.

Book One

So, maybe a continuation of the present policy, together with the opening of a serious and honest dialogue would be the best what we can do.

If this line of action would be accepted, the persons of authority on such a dialogue should be consulted. I think especially about John Powell. I do not know him. I cannot tell what his reaction would be. I only feel that he would be enormously useful in giving the substance and the spirit to such a dialogue. He could be influential in creating the patterns for the debate, and in mobilizing the people who could be prepared for the realization of such a plan.

Such a plan never should be rigid and prefabricated. Its general idea should be clear, but it should have a maximal flexibility to respond to any unexpected problem or to any sudden change in situation. The aim of the dialogue should be a creation of a democracy in essence, but the regional characteristics, and near to heart traditions, should have all the room for expression. If on the ashes of the past, the new order would be able to inspire a pride in all the population, because this would be their own best creation (not just a copy from somebody else) the better would be. It would assure a better durability and resistance to erosions. In this way also it would remain open to grow, to necessary innovations, because it would be a part of the life there.

The terms of the dialogue probably should be determined by somebody more competent than me. I have an impression that in such talks everybody should speak as an individual. It should not be a meeting of leaders. An individual can feel more free to discuss all the aspects of problems without restrictions which a leader of a group could feel. The authenticity of each voice should be its biggest value. Confrontation of persons from different circles could come later in the next step of group discussion. The persons considered as important should be invited to Washington, and helped to come there. If their dialogue would create a special climate of openness, and a need for more dialogue centers in different places of Latin America, such centers could be organized later.

It is probably, that such a dialogue would have an enormous echo in all Latin America, but also in U.S. and in Europe. General reaction except in Communist countries probably would be positive. Consequences? Hard to say. But the risks are minimal. Maybe the interest in dialogue would grow and substitute the fighting, and open the way to the true peace.

I cannot imagine that U.S. would lose anything by carrying this plan out. It would not contradict American spirit, or American tradition. It would sublimate them. The smallness of El Salvador would make it an

The World Seen from the Distance of a Small Village

excellent testing ground for such a project. And maybe, that other places of eternal conflict, like in Lebanon, could take an inspiration from it.

I believe, that the peace of the world depends on frank discussion of existing differences through the gut level talks of the people. The more of such talks, the better. Such discussions should not be a show for ambitious leaders. It should reach the people, reach the deepest layers of their emotions, and make them ready for reconciliation. From such a zero point of their inner state, a building of peace could start, and maybe a new friendship.

Tadeusz Maciejczyk, M.D.
Milledgeville, October 1, 1984

Book One

George Bush
Vice-President of the United States

Dear Sir:

I was watching your debate with Mrs. Ferraro, and I felt well listening to your arguments. Then, at one point, I became uneasy and ashamed. It was, when did you collectively described the 13,000 Palestinian soldiers as terrorist, whose defeat, with the blessing of the U.S., was just, and good.

I felt uneasy, because if I would be a Palestinian, I would fight in those units. Every nation has a right to express its will to exist and to have conditions necessary for self-respect. The Israelis didn't give the Palestinians any other way to react. For them they were non-existent. When they directed publicly their attention to them, persistently they were adding derogatory epithets, degrading them at every occasion. In such a situation the Palestinian refugees, living in miserable camps from the mercy of the world, had to identify themselves, to survive the shock of destitution, and somehow make their vision of the future.

During the war of 1967 I felt all the sympathy for Israel. The young state was fighting to survive. After a victory I expected from Israel a moral example that would shine, and would teach the rest of the world. I expected them to open their arms, to be generous, to understand and to share. They themselves were the victims of brutality and hate. The opportunity for such a gesture was excellent.

Instead, I was dismayed by the growing arrogance of the glorious victors, whose hearts became harder, and the appetite bigger. The relations between Israelis and the subdued Arabs acquired similarity to what I saw in Poland during German occupation. An Arab became a kind of *Untermensch* from that era. The talks were only from masters to servants. The desperate acts of resistance, including the shelling through the border, were responded in the eye for the eye policy, with the blind bombardment of open Palestinian settlements. The shellings were the act of terror, the bombardments were not.

The Palestinians had to live, to grow and to look the world around through such an open wound. They were condemned for looking to the Soviets for help—and in the same time they were negated any sympathy even from the West. The U.S. was looking on them through the Israeli eyes. They were pushed into a pit, they were spit on, and their frustration was even bigger, because all who were passing by, were trying not to see them there, down, in the pit. To see them so, would be impolite to

The World Seen from the Distance of a Small Village

that, who was above the pit. The world felt uneasy and somehow responsible for their condition, and the world preferred not to hear their plea.

We should have a justice equal to everybody whether he is influential in our political process, or no. Your description of the Palestinians can have some political advantage, but will not build the future of the world. And will not enhance the respect of the U.S. Surely, it will not bring the peace. The Israel of the last decades was promoting its selfish dreams, using U.S. and everybody else. Israel will not obtain its fullness, its fulfillment on this pathway. It will only drag itself, and the rest of the world into uneasy times, and maybe into a catastrophe.

I expect, that this my opinion will be labeled by Israelis as anti-Semitism. They use this bullet epithet, against anybody who doesn't like their attitude, with the same seriousness, as the Soviets when they condemn any opposition to them, as an act against peace-loving forces.

But I do not wish the Israelis ill. I only would like them to be what all their history was trying to prepare them for: an example, and a moral force. They exchanged those values for the material goods. That is, what looks to me, a pity.

Sincerely,

Tadeusz Maciejczyk
Milledgeville, October 15, 1984

P.S. An *untermensch* and terrorist in the eyes of the Nazis, and the Communist regime that followed them, but a fighter for freedom, and a better world in my own understanding.

cc: The White House
    Embassy of Israel
    Embassy of Jordon

Book One

Dear Dr. Maciejczyk:

Thank you for your recent letter concerning U.S. policy in the Middle East. It was thoughtful of you to write, and I appreciate your having taken the time to share your views.

Commitment to Israel's security and well-being has been a cornerstone of American policy in the Middle East since the creation of Israel in 1948, in which the United States played a key supporting role. Israel and the United States are bound closely by historic and cultural ties as well as concrete interests. Our continuing economic and security assistance to Israel is an acknowledgement of these ties and a signal of our commitment.

At the same time, the United States maintains close cooperative relations with moderate Arab states, such as Egypt, Jordan, Lebanon, and Saudi Arabia. These ties rest on mutual interests in achieving a just and lasting Middle East peace, limiting Soviet influence in the region and, in the case of the oil-producing nations, in maintaining stability in the world financial markets, as well as consulting on the international energy situation.

I certainly did not mean to infer in my public remarks that all Palestinians were terrorists or that Palestinians do not have the right to peacefully coexist in the Middle East. The right of Israel to live in peace and security and the attainment by the Palestinians of their legitimate rights are basic to our policy in the Middle East. Only by broadening the peace process to include Israelis, Jordanians, the Palestinians, and other Arabs can we best guarantee a just and lasting peace in the Middle East. I will, however, continue to speak out vociferously against those who use terrorism as a means to express their political, religious, or personal views.

With best wishes,

                        Sincerely,
                        George Bush
                        Vice-President of the United States

The World Seen from the Distance of a Small Village

Dear Sir,

I thank you for your letter. It gave me a strange impression of hopelessness in the Middle East. The fundamental problems there are not changing. Your letter could be written ten years ago, or maybe even ten years from now, and still be as actual, as today. With the passage of time, only the erected barriers became higher and more impenetrable. A fresh air is coming from nowhere.

It is a strange, pathologic condition, which appeared with the creation of the Israeli state. And I think, that the creation of Israel could be accomplished without this devastating tale. It could, but—it was easier this way.

It looks to me, that the cause of the present malady in the Middle East was not a fact of creation of the Israeli state. It was not even the expulsion and the dispossession of the Palestinians from their homes. It was the way the Israelis related to those Palestinians afterwards. They could come to them giving them a helping hand, helping them to start a new life, in a new situation to which the Palestinians were not prepared at all. They could still remain friends, and even prosper together. If the Israelis would react this way, the Good Samaritan way, the Middle East could be a happy place today, and the Israeli influence could be spreading far beyond their borders.

Instead, Israel reacted with a complete denial, making from this issue a blind spot in their conscience. They were looking on the Palestinians denying to see anything. They started to refer to them only after different acts of resistance, but then, they pictured them as inhuman, inferior, despicable and worthless terrorists. It is very consoling and absolving to the inside, to injure and to hate somebody, who is so obviously villain. It almost looks, that years ago, the SS men created for themselves similar consoling and absolving feelings, doing what they were ordered to do. Apparently, the condition of the Palestinians became such a trauma to the subconscious of Israel, that they, being unable to react to it with the healthy, open, human way, reacted with such a pathological devastation. It didn't bring them happiness. It gave them a guilt feeling, feeling of estrangement in place, of being endangered, and needing constant protection.

It was a very special spectacle: Israel, the nation with the recent history of persecution which culminated in a holocaust, being so merciless to its own victims, voicing this kind of methodical, unchanging anger and hate to them, and using a Soviet style demagogue for a cover up. The anger and the hate produced escalation of reactions to Palestinians fighting back: from the massacres of bombardments of the Palestinian settlements, which were explained as a lesson teaching retaliations, to lunging a total war against Palestinians, with a not well hidden desire to give them a definitive holocaust.

Never during their existence did Israel show enough civil courage to acknowledge Palestinians, to sit together in a human way, to talk, and to search together for solutions. The blind spot in their conscience, with all its negative compensation became the second nature.

All considered, it appears to me, that it is only one perfect way to bring a just and lasting peace to the Middle East. It can be done by shaking off the apprehensions, the fears, and break the legacy of the blind spot, sitting the Israeli and the Palestinians across the table to negotiate. I am thinking: all Palestinians, including the PLO. Give the Palestinians independence, and freedom from Israeli interference from the start. Those negotiations would deal mainly with the problem how to create trust and harmony after all those decades of hate. To force such a solution, U.S. has to be firm, and take a lead, because, no doubt, Israel will oppose such a plan vigorously. They would rather play their game indefinitely.

Obviously, to start such a move, all should be prepared carefully with other Arab states. Such a broadening of the peace process would have for purpose to create conditions and environment in the Middle East in which the newly created peace would be able to mature and acquire vitality. Opening of diplomatic relations with all other states of the region, study for the mutual economic and cultural cooperation, student exchange, opening of tourism, all those things would help to assure, and to encourage, to dissolve the accumulated ice. From the distance U.S. would maintain equal relations with Palestinians and with Israel, giving them additional assurance, helping in passing the difficult moments. Such a solution would be probably a powerful instrument to change the today's terrorists into peace workers. Long before anybody heard about Palestinian terrorism, the Prime Min. Menachim Begin was a terrorist himself with the price put on his head, and—later he even was awarded with the Nobel peace prize.

And really—I do not see any other solution that would give the Israeli its rights to live in peace and security. Passing the painful moment to decide for trust and reconciliation, Israel would get infinitely more. They would become a natural part of the tissue of the Middle East, not just an implant pressed by the forces of rejection.

The World Seen from the Distance of a Small Village

What are the other possibilities?

1. Making from Israel an encircled, almost besieged fortress, would set there a climate of war, with all its consequences, as a permanent condition.
2. To encircle the Israel with international peace-keeping forces, would create a ghetto, reminiscent of the times of World War II. It would be difficult to sustain economically, always in fear, unstable emotionally, deepening in the state of paranoia. The atmosphere of hate would escalate on both sides of such borders. The anger against Israel would be directed towards its protectors, multiplying the casualty, producing a second thought in the countries, which such a force would provide. The friendly Arab states would be increasingly uneasy. The Soviet meddling would become more provocative than ever. And how such a development would end? Who knows?
3. Giving the Palestinian a partial autonomy, with Israel controlling practically everything would satisfy nobody. It would create an increasing tension inside and outside. The whole system would be like an imitation of the Soviet empire, with the satellite states on its periphery, but in a wrong place, and with different capabilities. Such an arrangement would not work forever. The bitterness, and the hate would be difficult to control, and Israel would never know a real peace.

In all such situations only the Soviet Union would benefit. It would give them a chance to enter into the Arab body each time deeper.

The situation in the Middle East, with all its conflicts, passions, and divisions, requires a lot of good will and of wisdom, to resolve. Speaking vociferously will not help, will correct nothing. It will only produce a vociferous reaction from the other side, producing more victims, and making the abyss between actions and the reason enormously more distant. Vociferousness never was a synonym for wisdom.

To obtain a real peace, Israel will have to show imagination, and civil courage, and will have to take risks. And the actions taken by them have to be sincere, without any hidden malice. This has to be a price for being admitted, for becoming a part.

If Israel insists in playing its present game, its future will be uncertain forever. Even a day can come when America, counting its casualties, can come to a conclusion, that the cornerstone of its Middle East policy was wrong, and for Israel can come a time of despair. Already

Book One

now, I have an impression, that the death of so many Americans in Lebanon, was not exactly a very glorious one. In spite of all assurances, they didn't die protecting the peace. As until now, they died to preserve the status quo, to perpetuate the Israeli game, and the unhappiness of the region. Their death puts a moral obligation on the U.S. government to act for the true solutions and true peace.

And I hope, that the Middle East will get finally such a definitive solution. The boil of the Israeli-Palestinian relations has to be cut open and the wound healed. I hope that the U.S will have enough stamina and determination to make a real peace a reality.

Sincerely,

Tadeusz Maciejczyk
Milledgeville, December 2, 1984

The World Seen from the Distance of a Small Village

Council for Inter-American Security and American Defense Institute

I received in almost immediate succession three letters, all of them asking for help to Central America.

I was reading them with conflicting feelings. On one side I recognized the importance of the problem, and the intentions of the authors of those letters, on the other hand, I was embarrassed by the way those letters were presented. All those letters were looking like fabricated in the same factory. All were weepingly pessimistic in tone, and were trying to create fear. For those pictured fears, they were proposing only one remedy: give us money, and we will use it without any control, and without any responsibility to the donors. For this money we will support lobbying, make advertisements and we will mail more letters. How such a self-serving bureaucracy and self-propaganda could help to save Central American—it was not very clear to me.

During the last year or two, I received many such letters seeking each time for bigger donations for different purposes. All those letters gave me an impression that they were written by the same person, who permanently was in the same depressed, uninspiring mood. Even my impression was worse. I had a feeling that the author wished to coax out money from the naïve and idealistic, while blinking with the other eyes, that he did this again.

It looks to me that these letters, these kinds of activities, are not helping the cause. In fact they are enormously harmful to the real problem. They are not mobilizing. They are giving no field to get involved, to show creativity, to invent new ways, and to extend the circles of involvement. Somebody, who receives such a letter, nagging for money, and a complete, uncontrolled confidence even if he gives, he doesn't want to be nagged again. Such activities really are isolating the cause. They even create a feeling that nothing else can be done. The negative backlash of such pseudo-activities should be seriously reevaluated.

After reading all those three letters, I didn't see in them any promising solution to the problem of Central America. How to save Nicaragua? Should we send there American troops? Are the Contras our only hope to prevent transformation of that country into a Soviet stronghold?

It is absolutely clear to me that the men who oppose the Sandinista regime should continue to receive our help. To deny them, would create a good example how risky it is to put the faith in America, how superficial and whimsy are our commitments, and how much safer it is not to rise head against tyranny. Not the usefulness of the Contras, but the value of our credibility and purpose is at stake. After actively helping to create "Contras" suddenly changing the heart, would make Contras defenseless and exposed to government ruthlessness.

But what are the other options? Really—can't we count on anything else, but on old style military maneuvers, and diplomatic activities, maybe with the giving or restricting the economic aid, as a way to solve the problem of Central America?

We are witnessing now a very important moment in the life of Central America, especially of Nicaragua. This is the moment of the awakening of the masses. A social, educational, cultural, even religious transformations are producing there new realities. New formulas, new orders, new alignments established now can dominate the future, and the old methods of pacification and governing are not applying to them easily. The Soviets are trying to use the convulsions of this transformation to Sovietize the region. They are playing well on the anti-American sentiments of the people, and they are putting their figures strategically. They know what they want.

So—how big are our possibilities in this different, new, rapidly changing battlefield for Central America? Do we know this field? How, and how much can we increase our chances of winning? I hope, that we will take very seriously those considerations. If we do, the weapons the Soviets are trying to accumulate in Nicaragua will have a secondary importance. If not, the seriousness of the situation will be real. For this reason we have to know what way and how to walk there. A superficial, unprepared, only diplomatic or military activity to win the population there will not be enough. Radio and TV advertisements will do nothing. Only serious studies, discussions and explanations could give true remedies and solutions. Such an interest could even spark an enthusiasm and create a new "Peace Corps" like excitement, involving especially the young on both sides.

But we have to know the field. We should know how to walk there, and not to make blunders. The lines of this kind of front in Central America will be always delicate and uncertain. Even in each person there can exist many such lines. Knowing the field we can more easily set off those elements favorable to us, and dissipate and calm the others.

In Central America, conflicting feelings towards U.S. are everywhere. They admire Americans for one, and they dislike them for other reasons. They have a benevolence towards us, but also jealousy and envy. They have a pride and warmth, but in the same time they suffer from inferiority complex, which hampers the closeness. There are old attachments, because of good deeds of America, and old suspicions because of previous American abuses. The trends towards nationalism are strong, but it is also an awareness that the nationalisms are closing and dividing, while the common cause of mankind is broad, and is breaking the national boundaries. In the present convulsions of C. America the fears, the cautions, the hurrahs, the hopes, the experimentations and the uncertainties are marking every day.

For this stage, for this time of transformation in C. America more than at any time before, gut level talks are necessary to find the way. I was speaking about them writing about problems and solutions in San Salvador. The U.S. should provide a frame and a stage for such talks. The actors should be mostly the Central Americans themselves. I feel, that such a serious, true talk, unrestricted, over all the aspects of life and dreams there could be accepted and patronized by many Americans, and the donors would be not excluded from involvement. Such a struggle, such a search, would make a unity of our globe much more possible. In such gut level talks, which echo would reach every corner of C. America, more probably the Soviets would lose the ground.

It is true, that the battle for Central America is a part of the Soviet global strategy. Because of this, the U.S. should respond to this challenge with the global response. Afghanistan at the present could be the place to start this kind of answer. The Afghans should be trained and equipped not only for the use of military weapons, but also with radio stations with the trained personnel to spread their message, their testimonies and feelings to the whole Moslem population in the Soviet Union, which is like a sleeping giant, waiting for awakening. A religious fervor is already on the increase among them. A constant talk to them about Afghans and by the Afghans, can introduce a new element to the struggle for Afghanistan liberation, and also to the global defenses of freedom. It would introduce a new uncertainty for the Soviets, and a threat of erosion in a Soviet apparent monolith. Those gut level talks should be also extended to Ukrainians, to Bielorussians, to Baltic States nations, and even to ethnic Russians, trying to separate them from the elements of Sovietization of their personnel, and even national life.

In such a war for the souls, and for the convictions of the people, America's strength should be high. It would be not a "cold war." It would not test the will of one government by another government. It would be tedious work to get an access and to liberate the deposits of good will and of common sense, which exist everywhere, but frequently are dampened and pressed down by the different layers of hate, prejudices, distrust and fears accumulated by history and propaganda. Such a public

Book One

talk and a search for solutions and remedies could spark enthusiasm and interest and could create a new edition of the Peace Corps that could involve especially the young on both sides.

                                      Tadeusz Maciejczyk, M.D.
                                      Milledgeville, December 31, 1984

The World Seen from the Distance of a Small Village

Ronald Reagan
President of the United States
And the leader of the Republican Party

Dear Mr. President:

I read your last letter with the feeling of perplexity. Not even the newly elected officers could start its work, and already you are proclaiming a new 1985 GOP Victory Fundraiser. It is true, that with all the tuitions hanging in the immediate future, it is not easy for me to "kick off" 100 dollars—but this is not a main reason for my uneasiness. What is bothering me is the dissonance of this announcement, the readiness of the party bosses for a new easy spending, without a moment of reflection, and the mood of the countryside. As far as I could sound it out speaking with many people, I felt, that in general the people were sick and tired of the last, long campaign of the Democratic Party. campaign. More. Behind that early rush and campaigning fever, the people sensed anxiety, weakness, and the emptiness of the Democratic Party. The party rhetoric, the money spent, didn't penetrate to the hearts of the people. The long campaign was considered wasteful, and was not convincing. It didn't show any advantage, produced bitterness by its free spending and by escalation of easy promises, which almost nobody could take seriously. It was a lesson, which the Republicans should keep in mind.

After the last fall election, I was expecting, that the following year would be dedicated to the real work: that means to analysis, to study, to prepare well the agenda. I was expecting also intense activity in the countryside, also there analyzing their experiences, finding new talents, new men of action with the leadership qualities, with understanding of the issues, dedication, and warmth. If such men would be found, the party should preserve for them also a chance to be elected. In this way, this coming year could be a year of excitement for the party of gaining new blood, new strength and new ideas. Pushing now the names of the candidates will prevent such a miracle to happen. No time would be given to rejuvenate. The members joining the party for work in such elections would be rather persons with the spirit of servants. For the real talents with creativity and greatness the room would be closed and the attraction vanished.

If I were a leader, I would dedicate this year to spread the messages of goals, giving to them a vision of a mission, which would be practical, but also eternally human, and somehow touching the souls. Then I would ask everybody to join in the effort. It is sure, that such a purpose and such a vision should be clear and elevating. If the party would elaborate such a task, and present it to the people, the resonance of the country would be great. Really, it looks to me, that the people are hungry for such a cause and such a leadership. If the party would direct its lead in such a way, the fear of the liberal special interest competition would be not threatening at all.

In contrast, your "National Agenda Survey" is not a goal. It is a tactical adjustment to certain situations, and to resolve specific problems. It cannot produce excitement. It is not touching the human spirit and cannot satiate that special human hunger. Its only attraction is a calculated advantage. It has not strength to gather the forces around.

And still I want to repeat that reading for the first time your letter about the money urgently needed to spend it in the first critical phase of the plan, my first thought was, that that money was not for the well-being of the country, but for the comfortable chairs for the Party dignitaries and workers. I cannot tell what was the reaction of others. My reaction I felt almost like a pain. What other conclusion could appear in me? The letter was telling, that those party dignitaries would dedicate themselves to select the candidates for the price of 680,000 dollars in the first phase of the plan only. And apparently they expected another flow of cash for this purpose later. And above this amount they would have money to spend for campaign school, for voter research, and for special funds.

But it looks to me, that the campaign training for candidates would be best done in the field while working on the practical matters, showing there their knowledge and their dedication. Such an approach would be much more effective than those special schools preparation and tricks learning. Those candidates, who would need such a help to pass the test, should not be supported by the party. Also the issues, and the voter research would come to the central offices of the party from the countryside reports. Such a confidence and this arrangement would surely vitalize the bases of the party. The central should have through such a plan enough material to digest to classify and to interpret—to make this first post election year a time really well spent for the good of the party and for the whole country. If in the countryside, the men chosen in such a natural selection, would speak for the program, no doubt, the press and the other news media would turn to them to listen to them, and to spread their message. It would be much more valuable than the paid advertisements, and the organizational support only.

I did not like to write this letter. I would rather prefer to find in your message elements of excitement and mobilization. But at this point, my best service cannot be more than this sad letter.

Tadeusz Maciejczyk, M.D.
Milledgeville, January 13, 1985

The World Seen from the Distance of a Small Village

Guy Vander Jagt
Chairman of the National Republican Congressional Committee

I received your cablegram, learning from it that in your evidence, the only remnant from my answer to the President's letter was a short statement: "No record of response."

In light of this, I am wondering whether it has a sense to bother, to concentrate and to try to present any different idea or different view. Apparently the party managers have no time to read and no reason to descend to the rank level to think together. They are too busy in their automatic performance not only to respond to somebody's serious letter but also even to register it.

I was imagining that a functioning party would have an institution which I could call a "Bank of Ideas," which would be placed somewhere between the leadership and the body of the party. The new ideas would flow to such a center from both directions being there registered, classified, correlated with other similar thoughts, digested and evaluated from different angles to find for them the best application. Such an institution would be a center and the heart of the party, its real treasury, and its road to greatness and to the true service. It would be also a place to test new talents, and a school to teach the meaning and the way of service. It could be even a modern version of the legendary fountain of youth for the party.

In my letter, I was trying to discuss all points of the President's message. Generally I am not satisfied with a mere marking of a prepared, short questionnaire, which I consider a worthless simplification because each problem is much more complicated to put it off with a simple yes or no. Sorry. I am still not a computer automaton. I need to believe in the cause before I give it my wholehearted support.

I want to tell you also that I am not a rich man—if that would be your only need for me. I am an M.D., but I have no talent to transfer it into a wealth of gold. Generally I see people in need and I am soft. Almost two years ago I was kicked out from the staff of the hospital because I refused to buy malpractice insurance. In my understanding it was immoral to raise my fees to pay for such a protection. I include here the copies of my two letters to the hospital because the problem didn't disappear. It got worse. (Of course—if you have the time to read them.)

Because of this, because of three tuitions, because I feel I should help my family in Poland, which is in hardship because of Solidarity, because I feel that the hungry should be helped first, I have to count my

Book One

possibilities in other areas. But I am willing to sacrifice. Nevertheless, before the sacrifice, I want to believe in its purpose.

My questions were not answered by the Party. From your cablegram I saw, that they were even not perceived, that I was speaking to a deaf organization apparatus, which only looks for one important thing: the money.

To some degree, your cablegram served me as a cold shower.

Tadeusz Maciejczyk, M.D.
Milledgeville, February 21, 1985

The World Seen from the Distance of a Small Village

Send to: The White House
        Vice President Bush
        Newsweek
        Time Magazine
        U.S. News and World Report
        Foreign Policy
        Foreign Affairs
        The Saudi Arabian Embassy

As a previous member of the Resistance movement during World War II, I am uneasy and confused reading today's news from Lebanon. Who was I? Was I a resistance fighter or was I a terrorist? Where is the boundary between the two? Who is the judge? How was I supposed to behave?

The recent events in Zrariyeh made me very pessimistic about the possibility of a true peace between Israel and the rest of the people of the Middle East. What happened there was an emotional outburst based in the dominating Israeli policy of "teaching a lesson." I see very little difference between Zrariyeh and the massacre of Lidice in the Nazi occupied Czechoslovakia. In both the "iron fist" policy dominated and the good will or communication were absent. What is in the character of the Israeli? What makes them so shortsighted? Why did they not restrain from creating this kind of monument, which just on their border will teach the generations of Arabs to look into Israel and to hate? The desire of revenge, the superiority complex of the "lesson teachers," can be attractive and sweet while tasted. It bears a very bitter fruit afterwards. Or maybe that this kind of behavior was a sign not of strength, but of deep rooted insecurity and an inability to respond with anything more noble, but with the more primitive of all arguments: with the iron fist.

In 1941 in the Ukraine, the approaching German troops were greeted as saviors with joy and with flowers. In 1944 only hate remained from that warm welcome. What it exactly is, what makes the Israeli presence in Lebanon similarly irritating and impalatable? Nothing happens in a vacuum. A careful study of all those questions would help all sides, would clarify the air, and would be the first step towards peace.

Today in Lebanon the dominating factor is chaos. All political maneuvering to prevent it has failed. The confusion is deepening. The future holds nothing promising.

It looks to me that the first step to introduce in Lebanon some kind of law and order, would be a rediscovery of a common language and a proper meaning for the words. Following this, a real effort should be made to use the communication to the fullest.

The communication, the increase of discussions, has to have a place and environment. Would it not be useful to create in Lebanon a "Forum for Public Discussions," which could be reached by all, where arms would be forbidden, but the doors would be open to anyone? The discussions on the Forum could be monitored by eminent, highly prestigious personalities from the Arab world, or maybe from the West also. A safety of such a place and of everybody attending could be provided by the U.N. Peace-keeping units.

Surely a Forum alone would not be enough to make a break. A serious effort should be done to create a general opinion, which would condemn any gun shelling or any other form of fighting before its objective would be discussed on the Forum. Every leader has an obligation to defend the rights of his people, but he also should be able to present his claim to the public and to defend his reasons in a public debate. It should be stressed once and again, that using guns, without being able to justify it in a public debate, is not only a crime and a descent to a Mafia level, but above all it is a show of public incompetence and of civil cowardice. The leaders generally are not killed in such a battle. The young and idealistic, sent by the leaders, and the innocent bystanders, are.

If such a public opinion would become strong enough and the authority of the Forum on the increase, a miracle could happen and the peace gradually could be re-established and fortified. A dialogue and a more relaxed relationship between different fighting groups could be established and maybe also a trust and appreciation.

There has to be some turning point. And the turning point cannot be imposed. It has to teach and has to mobilize the people, to involve them. Maybe a "Forum" could create a momentum.

Tadeusz Maciejczyk, M.D.
Milledgeville, March 24, 1985

The World Seen from the Distance of a Small Village

The Health Department
Section for Social Security Payments
Washington, D.C.

I have a complaint, which in my judgment is legitimate and should be taken into consideration.

At the time when the Deficit Reduction Act of 1984 was established, I accepted the assignment and I signed the Reduction Participation act.

Since then, I found out that those acts were tailored for those who knew how to prize themselves. Consequent limitations and adjustments of the act were for them a confirmation that their attitude was right. They learned the lesson. With any new opportunity they will demand a new obtainable maximum. It looks to me that this law is producing an effect contrary to its aim. It creates a climate of conformance to the control while watching the competition and waiting for a moment to press their prizing harder than ever to outsmart everybody else. I see this very clearly in the escalation of prizes of the pharmaceutical products.

In the same time those acts didn't do anything to reward those who voluntarily were keeping their fees at the minimum level seeing in their job rather a mission than a business. It is more. Those acts punished them without mercy, bringing their voluntary low fee to the ridiculous low. According to those acts my fee for a visit was reduced to between $8.32 and $10.40 after adjustment from the voluntary contribution of the patient. From this fee I am required still to spend money and time to maintain a constant correspondence with the agencies and with the patients.

A law that teaches only to be clever, that creates rather than prevents, the competition in rising prices, a law which is not rewarding those who were trying to live by them even before it was created, but punishes them, bringing them to the limit of bankruptcy, such a law is not a good law. It will not invite restraint. It will not heal the situation.

I am trying to do a good work and I have a right to be paid by the average of the area and not by the minimum bottom. For my intentions, I should feel that my attitude was good, right and appreciated, that I was not a naïve fool.

In the logic of your law, there is no place for a genuine restraint. There is only a pause of waiting and watching, of an anticipation of the right moment to squeeze again. The naïve will have no other choice but to be eliminated.

I think that the Deficit Reduction Act should be discussed again and it's inadequacies corrected.

Book One

Tadeusz Maciejczyk, M.D.
Milledgeville, April 11, 1985

Cc: The White House
   Health Department of Illinois
   Area Senators and Congressmen
   Blue Cross-Blue Shield of Illinois

The World Seen from the Distance of a Small Village

Alan J. Dixon
U.S. Senator from Illinois

Dear Sir:

I read your last bulletin about rights and options for the health care for Medicare patients. My general impression was that it was a useful paper, full of practical information. All those new laws are generous to the elderly. I understand, because I was practicing such a protective approach to all my patients in all the years of my work. What was a surprise to me was that this my past was used against me in the applications of the new Medicare legislation. I wrote about it in my letter to Congressman Guy Vander Jagt, which copy I include.

In your bulletin I have a serious objection to your declaration that unless the family agreed in writing, they are not responsible for the medical bills after the death of the parent.

It looks to me that this kind of preaching from the pulpit of the U.S. Senatorial position will not increase the moral strength of the nation. In the time when America desperately needs to strengthen the family ties and tradition, the mutual care and responsibilities in the family circles, and the decency and a conscience in the life of each individual, you, in your authority—you are declaring that all those things are a burden, and should be considered an attic souvenir, because the new law absolves the families from this kind of inconveniences. Whether the moral law absolves—I am not certain. Such a law is not changing according to the convenience and the opportunism of the lawmakers.

Every stick has two ends. How would the health providers react? And also what an effect such a law would have on the next generation? The education, the moral strength and the moral standards, the personal dignity and responsibility are acquired at home in the early childhood from the examples of the parent's attitudes and actions. A preaching of selfishness and opportunism is easy and can increase the popularity of such a preacher. It is so tempting to be excused, to take advantage, to relegate the responsibilities, but such an attitude is leaving in the soul, and consequently in the life, a bitter taste of guilt to cope and a self deprecation which saps the integrity of such a person in all other aspects of his life. If multiplied, it can make the future of the whole society guilt-ridden, unsatisfied and weak.

All particular situations are different. A common sense should dictate to what point the children bear the responsibilities for very special,

Book One

costly treatments—but those special cases should not influence the general principle and the natural law.

Voting, or not for you in the next election, I would prefer to know that your decisions as a Senator are not done for the popularity contest, but for the long into the future look, to create a more healthy, more morally robust society.

> Tadeusz Maciejczyk
> Milledgeville, May 16, 1985

The World Seen from the Distance of a Small Village

Judy G. Bradford
Assistant Executive Director of the Mid State Foundation for Medical Care, Inc.

Because of your verdict in the case of admission of Mrs. Mildred De Jonge to the Morrison Hospital on December 9, 1984 H.R #09-69-47— I have a question, which is important to me for my work in the future. Without your clear-cut answer, I would feel uneasy and abusive while admitting most of the Medicare patients to the hospital.

My question is: At what point of treatment at home, do I have a right to do the admission?

Mrs. De Jonge was sick for about two years and the spells of diarrhea each time more prolonged and more exhausting, were returning frequently in the last half year in spite of continuous treatment at home. The anxiety, the apprehension were growing, closing the vicious circle and contributing to perpetuation of her symptoms. The cause of this was not known. The blood test, the stool test didn't give the answer. In this condition, I admitted her to go to the bottom of the problem. In my conscience I was doing a right thing. I was not abusing.

Because no organic lesion was found, because the patient responded with a spectacular change just to the fact of admission and hospital evaluation—this admission was condemned by the distal experts on medical evaluations and treatment conducts.

It appears to me that the post facto judgments based on paper evidence and computer classifications are not exactly the best way to evaluate human needs. I know that the battle of Waterloo, which Napoleon lost in 1815, would be easily won, even by no genius, after all the facts and consequences were known from the history, but in the heat of the struggle, emotions and fears, the weight of the realities was different.

In this situation, to be able to work, in the presence of constant big brother eye of the experts of scrutiny, I ask you to give me a clear answer: how to make a decision to admit a patient when it is not an obvious, undisputed and easy diagnosis to make admission justified and still the patient is in agony?

Tadeusz Maciejczyk, M.D.
Milledgeville, June 8, 1985

Book One

Ronald Reagan
President of the United States

Dear Mr. President:

I am writing this letter in an hour of a national anguish and sorrow. Many people are trying now to find a solution to the present crisis, to the tragedy in Lebanon as well as in San Salvador. If my opinion would differ from the others, or even if it would sound strange, it would be probably because it was the result of my own deliberations. They passed not only through my mind, but also through my heart.

I believe that the seizure of TWA 847 and kidnapping and brutalizing of its passengers with the murder of one of them should be answered not with the force or vengeance, but with the talks and communications. The idea of talks under such circumstances should not be threatening to our ego. There is always a way to communicate openly with a dignity, wisdom and long-range results. Secret, bashful hidden contacts and pressures cannot heal much. Surely such a tactic cannot change our disaster into a victory for everybody. Only such an end result would truly calm and heal. Yes, it is much more easy, much less compromising to speak with indignation and to open all the pressure devices behind the scene, but such an action would be shortsighted. Such a policy would hold only a promise of perpetuation and worsening of the unhealthy, inflamed condition, which originated the present incident and could multiply them in the future.

I always believed that the U.S. has some kind of mission. Somehow we have an obligation to the forefathers of America to spread their democratic ideas. This spread can be accomplished only through the communication marked by sincerity and an effort to understand. It looks to me that in the present day's world we have an abundance of talks with a scarcity of communication and consequently of understanding each other. We created, or for us were created, many taboos, which restrict our free contacts. We behave as prudes. We restrain from talking to some groups or some organizations because we consider them unclean. The Pharisee in the old times behaved similarly. And yet. Already Jesus, in one of His confrontations with them, told that it is the sick, not the healthy who need the doctor. We should be always ready to go with our democratic ideas and principles to the sick and display them in our words and in our deeds, i.e., immediate problems and blows should never preclude from our vision the long distance goals. Only in this way

The World Seen from the Distance of a Small Village

we can mobilize the people of the world behind us, and confront the danger of Soviet Communism with the united effort of all. Our contact with others, our actions, should give us a possibility to grow and the others to grow with us. Contrasting with such an attitude, a posture of a holy indignation was always a bad building material.

The U.S. has only one way to improve the emotional climate of the world. It can do this only while being itself. Such work never can be done if the U.S. continues to be a satellite of Israel tied up by different promises or previous good will gestures, conscious of every rise of their eyebrow, yielding to every pressure of their lobbyists. Behaving in such a way, U.S. will never be able to create a healthy equilibrium between Israel and other Arab nations and ultimately help Israel in a long range.

In today's world there are many people, many groups, many nations, with a wounded, soaring ego, with a broken self-image and no condition to develop a healthy self esteem. They are restless and they feel a need to fight for their rights, for their place, for their restitutions. As they have no other means, terrorism appears to them a way. Because of a deep feeling of injustice, they mobilize even the more noble and idealistic who in other conditions could be a treasure to build a peaceful world. If nobody speaks to those groups, understand them, help them to resolve their conflicts, there will be no peace. The Soviets will have always advantage using them for their purposes.

Against all those "enemies of mankind," the ultimate answer lays in openness and communication, in showing them our respect to their problems, in listening to them, while maintaining our principles and our values. This kind of war cannot be won with the antiterrorism squads.

When I read that the bomb, which in Beirut killed more than eighty innocent people, was used from the inspiration of America, and with the approval of our Secretary of State, I couldn't believe. I never imagined that the U.S. could fall so low, becoming a terrorist in its own way. Such a myopic bravery was only a testimony of our lack of vision and a distant ultimate purpose. I feel that after such a revelation, Mr. Schulz should step down as a Secretary of State. If the U.S. allows to lose its moral standard, its fall will be deeper in its consequences.

The present crisis, like every other crisis, represents a danger, but also an opportunity. It is during the crisis when we have to think things again and in the process we grow, we mature. In this way the present episode could be changed into an improvement and strength. If we do not use the opportunity of the crisis to grow, we will be on the way to shrink. The ideas of the forefathers of America will be seen by many only in the crazy mirror of the carnivals.

Book One

True greatness can have many faces and forms, but it always has to be true to the inner self. America, in the present world should make an effort to find this inner self again; because it looks to me that it became lost.

Our defense against terrorism should be not our fist, but the best of our hearts and the best of our minds. In some special way we should be the leader. We cannot escape from this. We have to lead the people of the earth towards a better future. All the people. Not only the saints, the just or the submissive. Anything less for America would mean no greatness.

>Tadeusz Maciejczyk
>Milledgeville, June 27, 1985

The World Seen from the Distance of a Small Village

Mid State Foundation for Medical Care, Inc.

Re: Case: Lillian Smith
   Morrison Community Hospital
   334-05-8054-A

   As the hospitalization of this patient was not approved and the explanation for the rejection in my view, was very vague, useless for acquiring any kind of criteria how to handle such a case in the future, I have to ask you: what would be the perfect way to handle this case?
   I ordered ambulance transportation to the hospital after I got a call that the patient fell and became immobilized; could not put weight on the leg, and complained about pain in the groin area.
   The distance from my office to the nursing home is nineteen miles. The distance from the nursing home to the hospital is about twenty miles. The ambulance refuses to wait, has to go home immediately after bringing patient. Patient is senile, confused, very weak and scarcely responding to questions. The X-ray technicians notify me that patient has a fracture of the left pubic bone. The radiologist is absent. He comes to this hospital only every other day in the morning. I ordered rest and accommodation of the ailing leg. The next day, after examination, I recognized an incomplete fracture of the left superior public ramus. Patient had undisputed pain in this area during examination. In this situation the ambulance was called again and patient was sent back to the nursing home with instructions.
   I have to insist again that after your declaration, I have no choice but to ask: How you would handle this case? Without such teaching instructions, I would have to conclude that your work is very superficial and serves not the needs of medical care, but solely the bureaucracy and its tyranny.

Tadeusz Maciejczyk, M.D.
Milledgeville, July 7, 1985

Book One

Allen Weinstein
President of the Center for Democracy
Professor of History at Boston University

Dear Sir:

I am an immigrant, an outsider and maybe because of this, I didn't know about the approaching bicentennial of the Constitution. Because of this, and maybe also because in my recent letter to the President I touched somewhat similar theme, I read your article with interest. It was a revelation to me, that a special commission of the bicentennial was created and that already many groups are engaged in studies, conferences and events of the celebration, which could reach beyond concerns of bureaucrats, lawyers and scholars and involve the broader American public in reaffirming the constitutional heritage.

But I was baffled by the limits put on such an involvement. The public would be used mainly to provide money and resources to build a monument to the Constitution—a Democratic Hall. Then, in that Hall, new generations would get an inspiration and understanding, would be touched, and convinced by the genius of the creators of the Constitution. In this way, those generations would produce new scholars, new experts, and new analyzers of the vast field this constitution can cover. In addition, such celebration would attract an international attention and fascination from friends, as well as from the enemies.

Somehow, such a frame for celebration gave me a feeling of disappointment. In my mind, it would be not a party, which would be as worthy and as imaginative, as the Constitution itself. It would not change the life in the present, nor in the future. It would not generate strength, movement and new realities. It is true—it would give us a magnificent mausoleum, but without warmth, and without that special spark, which penetrates into the hearts, opens the eyes, fills the spirit and transforms the present into a better tomorrow. The fathers of the Constitution would feel probably uncomfortable inside the palace of marble, which would be too cold, to be a place of a wide-open spirit. The sound of piling of new doctoral works about their creation could make feel uneasy those practical men of wisdom.

The American constitution was made from the materials of the 18th century to serve and to last. It passed many tests and it remained as sharp and as precious as ever because it was done without a need to adjust it to any pre-existing system, but as a general framework for co-

The World Seen from the Distance of a Small Village

existence and cooperation of any free people. It was done by men who knew well the human nature.

If the bicentennial celebration wants to be truly worthy of the Constitution itself, it has to find a way, and also the means to use this Constitution in our troubled time as an instrument for peace on earth. Instead of closing it in a magnificent mausoleum, it should be brought to light in every corner of the globe. Make this celebration not just a family birthday, but also an object of hope and interest of every human on earth. Maybe such a design looks like a fantasy, but this fantasy is better than the grim fantasy of the future wars.

At present we are striving to create a strong military force to resist the Communist threat. But until now the biggest strength asset of the Soviets is not their ever-expanding army but their ideology, which enabled them to penetrate and to dominate minds of millions. Their ideology, based on a few 19th century prophets became completely outdated. It proved to be wrong in practice, and yet, it continues to be a holy shrine of the Soviet Empire without which all their power would be much less threatening. Artificially and stubbornly, they keep their dead ideology animated and alive in the imagination and in the spirit of many in every country of all continents. Through this ideology, they are giving themselves the right and the mission to conquer and to dominate the world.

Against such a Soviet threat, we cannot oppose a military force only, even if it would be equipped with the most advanced weapons. Against the ideological offensive of the Soviets, we should organize an equivalent peace offensive using as an arm the treasure we have—the American Constitution. The bicentennial provides an opportunity to open such an offensive and to bring it even to the Russian people itself. In this way also, the peace movements of the West would get a choice between the surrendering for the sake of peace, or fighting to create peace without surrender. Many people who today fall into apathy and resignation, would stand up to think, to imagine, to develop new ways, and to work.

We have in our hands a great gift, great treasure. But any gift, any talent somebody has is not his exclusive property. Closed and hidden, it will remain fruitless and increasingly sterile. Only when operated and used to its fullness, it can surprise by its unexpected possibilities. Such a gift—as the Constitution is—should not be stored in the museum for magnificent vegetation there.

Not long ago, in our church, a parable was read about a landlord who gave his assets to his servants for the time of his absence. One of those servants, fearful that he can damage or lose the treasure, buried it in the ground and after the lord's return, gave it him back as it was: undiminished and unchanged. And the lord condemned that man because the talents we have, we have to use, to operate with them, and to multiply them.

Maybe we are such a tenant. We want to preserve the Constitution inside of our home and to admire it in the museum, even if the air there would be cemetery, instead of going ahead, and make through it new reaches, new realities, a new future.

So? Instead of building a monument and a home for scholars or a Mecca for pilgrims, why not build a simple utilitarian type of structure, not in Washington, but in Philadelphia, which could be called an International Center for Constitutional Studies. Such an Institute would have many different sections for different related problems and geographically for all the corners of the world. It would be filled with people from everywhere, boiling with activities, adjusting, creating, knowing each other in cooperation. It would be a monument that would give opportunity to grow to everyone. And the old men, the fathers of this country, would feel well in such a simple, but fully alive center.

Tadeusz Maciejczyk
Milledgeville, August 8, 1985

The World Seen from the Distance of a Small Village

Allen Weinstein
Newsweek

RE: My response to "My Turn"
Afghanistan - A new Soviet offensive
August 5, 1985

    Whoever considers himself a civil rights defender takes part in popular manifestations whether it would be on the University Campus, before the U.N. or on the streets in any place, then looks this article, turns the page, and goes to sleep without any action, he is a fraud and a falsificate of the frontshield image of himself he is trying to show to others. He has a double set of reactions, a double standard of ethics. He will never bring true peace to any place.

                              Sincerely,

                          T.S. Maciejczyk, M.D.
                          Milledgeville, September 6, 1985

Book One

To: The American Family Physicians
RE: The Malpractice Phenomenon

Not long ago, few people knew about the malpractice insurance. It existed, but it was a private problem. It was not imposing, not threatening, not breaking the conscience of anybody, and not changing the soul of the nation. Then the news media showed the possibility malpractice was presenting: the spectacular suits with enormous rewards. And the life in the U.S. changed. A new phenomenon appeared and multiplied fast: a 20th century gold rush for the treasures emerging from the malpractice opportunity. A new cast of managers and organizers, who discovered this gold mine and were growing in number, were working to keep the mine open and filled with gold. More and more people were looking for an opportunity to accuse, to sue, to get rich, to succeed in life this way. To them was unimportant what they were destroying on the way, whom and how they were hurting. No scruple became a virtue. A consciousness and integrity—a burden. The minority engaged in this chase succeeded in terrorizing the active part of the society and added enormously to the misery of the normal, honest people.

And the miseries were coming. The businessmen, the manufacturers, the health related institutions became insecure and anxious. The unpredictability of the threat became a real factor. How the malpractice threat contributed to bankruptcies, to closure of places, to shyness even to open the new enterprises, to the sluggishness of recovery and the slam and gloom many people feel overwhelmingly at present, would be a material for a very interesting and very necessary studies. If we want to recover, we have to count every adverse health problem of the nation, and the malpractice spirit surely is one of them.

The field of medicine, and medical-related institutions and industries became a primary target of those treasure hunters. People in grief, people dissatisfied, insecure, and emotionally unstable, were used by ever-increasing number of malpractice managers, and medicine which by nature is working on the thin edge between health, illness and death, where the unexpected changes are common and cannot be avoided, was always, and always will be vulnerable. There is no way to measure there the depth of suffering, and the eloquence on the accuser could be the only stick to measure them in courts.

The problem was that the gold mine was emptying rapidly and new resources pressures and enforcements were necessary to fill them up. The trials and the rewards served to blackmail the resistant. The payments were going up. The pressure was made to make everybody pay. The doctors who were opposing such pressure were losing their privileges. And the payments always were passing through the chain of contributors. Ultimately, not the hospitals, not the insurance companies, not the doctors were paying. They were put only in somewhat uncomfortable and ethically false situations. The ultimate source of those treasures for the gold seekers were the old, the sick, those who frequently could less afford such a burden. They had to pay higher fees for visits or hospital services, higher payments for insurance, and buy more expensive medicines. The general mass of population became robbed in view of everyone and with the blessing of the courts and legislations. The biggest organized robbery was taking place and the robbers were giving themselves an aureole of fighters for the rights of those who suffered.

The malpractice phenomenon merits an effort to clarify all their aspects: the causes, the actions, and the consequences. The consequences are multiple. They are material. The malpractice helps to deplete the resources of the old and sick, and to bring almost to the brake such institutions as Medicate and Medicaid. It also affected many enterprises by its threatening property. Emotionally, it created and reinforced a feeling that in today's time an honest work is not rewarding, gives no security, nor prosperity. In this way the attention of many deviated from anything creative to a pursuit of opportunities of easy solutions through big malpractice gains.

Spiritually? It dulled the distinction between what is moral and amoral and in such a way opened the way to all other unethical activities because: why not? Only an entrance on such a pathway is shocking and self-restrictive. In general the malpractice as it is, is weakening and dividing the society and is creating negative factors in personality and whole society development whose consequences can be still more disastrous in the future, than at present.

In any way, the malpractice phenomenon is one of the problems that require attention, study and new decisions.

Tadeusz Maciejczyk, M.D.
Milledgeville, September 29, 1985

Book One

Darryl Wahler, C.E.O.
Director of the Community General Hospital
Sterling, Illinois

Dear Sir:

Thank you for your call and for the offer to readmit me to the medical staff of the Sterling Hospital. I wanted this for a long time and I am grateful to you for your proposition. Nevertheless, there are two problems, which make this new switch uneasy for me.

1. As you know, I gave up my resistance and I took the malpractice insurance, but it was not an easy step for me. I did this to be able to continue to serve, but against my conviction, and with an idea to drop this insurance whenever possible. I include here a copy of my letter to the insurance company where I expressed my feelings about the problem and also how I understand the malpractice phenomenon, and consequently, why I am opposing it. I would not like to mislead you that I am already converted and repentant.
2. My other problem is that during those thirty months, I developed a kind of loyalty to the Morrison Hospital. In the time when I was cast out from the Sterling Hospital, Morrison gave me a hand on and opportunity to practice and kept me as long as it was possible, even under pressure. I would feel very uneasy to shove them aside now, just because in a better place I got a smile again. I just do not know how to do this kind of swinging.

To resolve those problems I need more time. I want to think about them to observe and to understand people's will.

Regardless what will be my decision, I thank you for your call and I wish you the best. Also, I would like to ask you transmit my salute to all whom I knew in Sterling Hospital.

Sincerely,

Tadeusz Maciejczyk, M.D.
Milledgeville, November 24, 1985

cc: Village Board of Milledgeville, Illinois

The World Seen from the Distance of a Small Village

Hijacking again?

The last hijacking was more brutal, more dehumanized, and more despicable than any previous and it finished in a tragedy bigger than anybody would like to predict. Anger and a condemnation from all over the world was natural, and was just.

And yet—I was uneasy when our Secretary of State, speaking to reporters, recommended only fighting back, closing the routes of escape for the hijackers, prosecuting them, and in this way intimidating other potential offenders. I was uneasy because his strategy summarized in the contemptuous epithet, that the hijackers were animals, was not addressing the real problem, and consequently could not cure the situation, and could not bring peace. It was only dehumanizing more this very special war.

It looks to me, that our real adversary in all that series of acts of terror in the Middle East were not the men executing them, not the acting terrorists. Our main adversary to be addressed and dealt with was so in the past, as it will be in the future, the idea, the beliefs that are moving those men. While the idea is alive, elimination of few men will not improve anything. Their place will be taken by others and one more element will be added to make the next encounter still more explosive and possibly more brutal.

As I can see, those men, who are attacking and disorganizing our civil life arrangements in the name of their ideas, are not animals. In not one of their attacks was their objective personal gain, robbery, or some selfish advancement or satisfaction. In all instances those men were ready to die, to sacrifice themselves for their cause. In this sense, I feel for them my deep respect.

In this sense also, I was hurt very deeply when Mrs. Klinghoffer put a price on her grief, changing a world moral issue into a financial affair. With this act she put a very special crown on today's western civilization, and denigrated it in the eyes of many people.

The ideas and idols always had a very special place in human history. A brute force and terror never was a good weapon against them. All the might and brutality of the Roman Empire did not suppress the idea of Christianity. From the graves of the martyrs, from their torture places, new believers were getting faith and strength, which the next persecution and martyrdom could not break.

More recently in history, the opposition to the Czarist Russia of Nineteenth century was getting strength in spite of the omnipotence of the police. From the Decabrists movement, down the road, new men were willing to risk their lives for the image of justice. With only contra ter-

Book One

ror, without any dialog, and with the growing anger and hate, this opposition degenerated into a violent Bolshevik revolution.

Each case in the history of such struggles was different. I do not want to compare the posture of the first Christians with the terrorists of today. I only want to tell that ideas have a special life, special nourishment, and special way of mobilization of men, which the strategy of our Secretary of State is not taking into account. Or—maybe we are afraid to face those ideas, because we are involved differently. But if we are so uneasy, it can be, that our involvement has an element of participation to injustice. If this is a case, the longer we play this our special role, the more suffering we will provoke.

If the U.S. wants to build a safer, more peaceful world, it cannot do this by playing a super policeman, planting our spies in every place, watching constantly to be on time, and in the right place to prevent the next attack, using force, and professing an attitude of terror against terror.

All those elements could be necessary to some extent, but our main effort towards normalization should be directed towards understanding of the ideas, and the forces, which are motivating our adversaries, engaging them primarily and in this way neutralizing its explosiveness. While opposing each act of terror, we should have ready special working teams, specialized in a given region and given problem. Such teams should be prepared and ready at any time to engage the other side in discussion, clarification, searching for just solutions, calming emotions and researching the situation in which the people could live again together in harmony.

We all can behave as animals, biting each other; or we can use our human mind and good will to promote understanding. The taboos, which would forbid us to speak directly to the bad guys, to the unclean, leaving them permanently out of our "Noble Us" circle, will perpetuate that nasty war of attrition, and the suffering of the innocent. Breaking those taboos would mean a liberation from the smallness of spirit, which created them. The "Teams Keeping Peace Through Discussion of Ideas" national or international, specialized in the specifics of each conflict, probably would be a more decisive step towards a better future than all the maneuvering of forces against forces separated by walls of silence and hate.

And, if I would have to add something to this letter, I would like to tell, that for the Secretary it is easy to speak his inflaming for the attackers observations about their nature. He will be well protected during all of his travels. The ordinary U.S. citizen is not so lucky. He can pay a bitter price for the Secretary's "frankness and candor."

Tadeusz Maciejczyk
Milledgeville, December 5, 1985

The World Seen from the Distance of a Small Village

Mid-State Foundation for Medical Care, Inc.

Case: Cross Hester
01-7799
Morrison Community Hospital

    I was reading your verdict in the case of Mrs. Hester Cross with a kind of dismay. The final diagnosis in this case was probably an acute gastritus. But how was I supposed to treat a patient who was fainting, had no strength to speak, was nauseated and was vomiting. Before admission, patient had an acute epigastric pain, was sitting bent forewards, and had a history of previous attack of pancreatitis. At the time of decision for admission she was looking like in the state of shock, and was very anxious. This patient always was strong, and she was not trying to impress. She was not kept in the hospital longer than necessary to clear the situation. Without hospitalization, I would not have lab results, which you are citing so wisely.

    I am sorry that I am responding after your 5 days term (counting from the day I received that letter.) It is the end of the year. Everybody needs the insurance papers to have done and we have different activities usual for the time of Christmas. I think also, that this very short term was calculated to serve further your purpose of saving, of avoiding payment and so stress to the authorities your usefulness. Sorry that I got such an opinion about you.

    During all my years of practice I was always trying to be honest and to serve. I never was trying to make a frivolous hospitalization and I am very aware of the financial stress of Medicare. I know that freedom has a price and a wasteful attitude leads to dependence and one or another type of slavery, but the art of leading towards a better future is to convince and to inspire, not to police and to enforce artificial regulations.

    I wish you luck in your work of a gendarme. I will not bother you anymore. I want to use my time to somewhat better purpose. And I will do always as my conscience and the impression of the moment dictate me to do. I do not know how to behave otherwise.

                                   Sincerely,

                                   Tadeusz Maciejczyk, M.D.
                                   Milledgeville, December 16, 1985

This letter's copies were sent also to Morrison Hospital, to Rep. Lynn Martin, to Senators Dixon and Simon and to Washington Department of Health.

Book One

Explanation for the letter to Mid-State Foundation for Medical Care, Inc.

    Maybe I am overreacting. Maybe I should bend my head and gracefully accept all the absurd regulations and controls. But, I do not know how to bow if I feel that I have a point and I should speak. For this reason I protest.

    I send this letter to you not to complain, or to look for compassion and consolation, but to revise all this situation and to rethink the solutions. Is the establishment of the Foundation for Medical Care procedures the best answer to the problem? How much it costs to create and to maintain such an office, and what it gives in return? Are there not better, more positive ways to influence the doctors, and to get from them results, making them participants in the effort of saving, without degrading care?

                                     Tadeusz Maciejczyk, M.D.
                                     Milledgeville, December 16, 1985

The World Seen from the Distance of a Small Village

Editor of *U.S. News and World Report*
Discussion of the editorial "The Christmas Massacre"

"He who is merciful to the cruel is cruel to the merciful" would be true, if its consequence, that he who is cruel to the cruel is merciful to the merciful, would have any sense.

Those qualities do not come from the mercantile measuring of how much for how much and of what? They come from the inside of self. Cruelty comes from the visible or invisibly inside torture of spirit. The mercifulness from inside order and peace.

Not long ago I saw a picture of a group of armed Israeli braves walking the road in south Lebanon. They were on the mission to inflict more cruelty for less cruelty in order to prevent cruelty. And I was wondering why they were laughing. The most cruelty they were inflicting was to their own children and grandchildren. They will have to live in a prison country surrounded by a sea of hate and desire for vengeance. The dosification of cruelty is producing only one result: a humiliation and hate, which have a very long life. They are creating a breeding ground for terrorism.

Tadeusz Maciejczyk, M.D.
Milledgeville, January 12, 1986

Book One

To: The Republican Party

Is the defense strategy = peace strategy?
Last week I received two letters. One, an Official Survey on Reagan Administration Defense Strategy was composed of 8 questions, and a usual request for donation. The other was a National Referendum on the United Nations, and was signed by Congressman Stan Parris.

The questionnaire of the first letter was easy and clear on the surface. My answer in the "yes or no" column were identical with the viewpoint of the Republican Party. But they were identical only in a very broad sense. Being in agreement with its general intentions, I felt uneasy, because the survey was suggesting that the strong military defenses were the ultimate answer towards the creation of peace. With the umbrella of the military, the diplomacy could do the rest.

Nevertheless, the history holds many examples of the fragility of peace based on military strength and diplomatic maneuvering. Such a peace, while giving an anxious sense of security, always was subject to changes in balance, to sudden shifts in pressures, or to eruptions from below the surface. The essential element for lasting peace was always an idea—big enough, clear and warm enough to touch a wide array of common people, giving them a sense of unity and of common purpose. Such an idea would give a strength to assure continuity, to produce a rebirth after cataclysms and to reappear in every new generation in spite of changing times.

Looking around it is easy to see, that today's big countries were not created by sword or diplomacy alone. Each of them had a special, magnetic idea, which gave them a power to inspire and to spread among people.

The Soviet empire began with the idea of the "Third Rome" in an obscure, small principality of Moscow. Their insistence, that the prince of Moscow, after his marriage to the last princess of Byzantium, was the head of all Orthodox churches, was a pretext for ruthless expansion, with merciless and brutal elimination of opponents, as was the case of Novogorod. The religious character of czars gave them a right to interfere and to subvert in every place with the orthodox population.

In the 19th century, this religious expansion was not enough for the political ambitions of Russia, and they invented a new idea—idea of Panslavism. This idea was proclaiming to all Slav nations, that Russia, the only free and great Slav country, was feeling a brotherly love for all other Slavic nations under foreign occupation, and would help them to get free. This propaganda was taking place in the time, when in Poland, also a Slav country, but already absorbed by Russia, reigned a continuous state of terror. The Poland's then-governor was nicknamed by Russians themselves, the *Muraviev-Vieshatiel* (somebody who hangs men).

The 20th century brought another example of Russian inventiveness in finding ideas, which could give them a pretext to expand. Only one year after the Bolshevik revolution, in 1919, they formed Komintern, which was supposed to prepare ways for the spread of the Russian Revolution all over the world. And something incredible happened. They succeeded in establishing that the Russian Communist Party was representing all the underprivileged and oppressed people in the world. With this title they started to interfere in the affairs of everybody, mobilizing their agents and their faithful in every country on earth. And millions believed. They were blind to the realities of life in the Soviet Union. Their eyes were fixed in the painted mirage of the Soviet paradise. In the time when so many were dying in Soviet prisons and Gulags, when in the Ukraine millions died in a few months after forced confiscations of all food, just to break the resistance there, all over the world, the image of happiness which the life under communism would bring, was holding, was not diminishing.

The Soviet prominence of today was not a military or diplomatic success. It was a living example how mighty an idea can be, if common people can relate to it. The Soviets understand the value of an idea. They assign to its cultivation and spread their best talents. Not the army, not the diplomacy gives them a compass, a persistence and a certainty, that in a final account they will impose their kind of peace over all the nations of the world.

I will only mention shortly, that China was spreading from a small country on the banks of the yellow River through the ideas of Confucius, and the Chinese ability to print them. The U.S. maintained its unity from the inspiration of the Constitution.

Today U.S. and the Soviets are confronted in shaping the future of the world. The present moment is very special. The Reagan administration did a big effort to modernize U.S. defenses. The Soviets, realizing that they are behind in modernization, decided that the period of friendship, of exchange, of flirt, would serve them better than their usual bad mood and bad manners. And so, we have the present smiles since Geneva. But from behind the smiles continue a thunder. The 4th program of the Soviets to be accepted next spring as a guide for the Soviet policy until the end of the present century, speaks clearly about the inevitable transformation of all the earth into a reign of communism. The present friendship did not stop the planning, and a gradual accumulation of strength for the realization of the *Pax Sovietica* in the world. To this goal, they tend with the persistence and a flexibility of an excellent chess player. For the first time the present Soviet program speaks about Pacific, and a fighting front of the communism in the Philippines.

Against such a formidable enemy and their ideology, the U.S. is building a military wall. From behind this wall our diplomats are looking the world, are arranging military alliances, are forcing rebels to get quiet and are showing a carrot to promote obedience or an enthusiasm for our way of life.

About building a real, lasting peace thinks nobody. Nobody is doing any studies, surveys, exploration, subject or men selection to create a durable peace based on a common, popular and great idea, which would be like a compass for a long planning, and like a monitor for short term activities and distractions. Without such a compass of an idea, our behavior and our diplomacy lack continuity and lack strength to inspire and to lead.

And so where are we now? Who is winning?

In the Philippines, we are paralyzed and unable to separate from a selfish, inefficient regime for fear of our bases. By prolonging our indecisiveness we are giving more and more people to the influence of the communist propaganda and organization. This way, we can lose there everything.

In Central America we care about military and diplomatic games, and we dominate over the vacuum of ideas. We have a chance now to put there true seeds, from which a lasting peace would grow, but we show no capacity, nor willingness. One day it can be too late.

Recently our Secretary of State went to Eastern Europe with a goodwill mission. He was speaking only to governments. In Romania he was too delicate to spend a night in a poorly heated room, and in this way share the difficulties of the common people there. In Yugoslavia, when confronted with the remark that the terrorists want to tell something by their actions, he hit the table with the fist and shut everybody. Did he have to do this precisely there where the people are so sensitive to a similarly delicate treatment from their Soviet bosses? For this performance, Mr. Shultz should obtain the highest Soviet commendation. He did for them more than they ever expected. He depressed the spirit of the people; he undermined people's faith in America, and he increased the Soviet chances for Sovietization. In this trip the public money was spent very badly.

Finely the show of force around Libya. I felt not proud. I felt embarrassed. It all was like a game without conclusion. Only the Arab extremists gained more influence, and more of the Arab soul was given away to the communist propaganda.

The World Seen from the Distance of a Small Village

Without a leading idea, without its compass, we are bouncing from one crisis to another, losing our advantage, time and probably friends. Preoccupied with small obstacles, we have no patience to look calmly at the horizon.

Really—it is time for reflection; a time to start the search for our "compass."

But how to find it? I do not know what the "idea" should be. I am only convinced that such an idea should be very universal, very Christian in spirit and very democratic. It should be very tolerant and very redeeming. It should be open to everybody without preconditions, without taboos, without pharisaic postures or a vengefulness of the eye for an eye policy. Without such a unifying idea, our free world can be lost. Appearance and acceptance of such an idea should be done in a very honest and sincere discussion of all existing problems. From local discussions to global accord, it should inspire and motivate the common man and the highest leaders. It should create a new era.

Finally, I want to tell, that the U.N. should continue as it is. Only our approach to the U.N. should change. We should assign to the posts there not just diplomatic technicians, but our more prominent and more dedicated leaders, who under the influence of the "idea" could transform the present U.N. opportunism into a body truly dedicated to the free world greatness.

Tadeusz Maciejczyk. M.D.
Milledgeville, January 12, 1986

Book One

January 23, 1986
Tadeusz Maciejczyk, M.D.
Box 788, 444 Main Street
Milledgeville, IL 61051

Dear Dr. Maciejczyk:

Thank you for your letter about my January 13 editorial, "The Christmas Massacre."

It is always helpful to learn the views of others, and I read yours with interest.

Reader letters have not been eliminated, but appear toward the back of the book in our "Voices of America" section.

I appreciate your taking the time to write.

                         Sincerely yours,

                         Mortimer B. Zuckerman
                         Chairman and Editor-in-Chief
                         U.S. News and World Report

The World Seen from the Distance of a Small Village

To: Readers of *The Daily Gazette*

I thank you for your letters in response to the article about me and my viewpoints. I understand that such a discussion, if sincere, can help the understanding and a finding of a way out from the uneasiness of today.

I have to confess, that I didn't watch too closely the birth of the Israeli state. My attentions of that time were elsewhere. During the war of '68 I was with all my heart with the Israelis. I saw them as the fighters defending their rights to survive. What turned me off later was not the Arab propaganda. I never saw much of it. It was the Israeli retaliatory bombardments of open Palestinian settlements. I could understand the bitterness of Palestinian offenders who lost everything and couldn't resist to make a shooting attack through the border. I couldn't find in my mind any justification for the retaliatory killing of the innocent, including many women and children. I considered those air raids as a most ugly terrorism of all: a terror of the mighty against the defenseless. During all my life, I considered that the victor should be magnanimous, and should give a hand to the opponent to help him to rise. I want to stress again that I do not blame all the Israelis for those killings of innocents. But I consider that those who ordered and implemented the bombardments were terrorists. A poetic expression of the late Golda Meir that she could never forgive the Arabs for causing Israeli boys to kill was only a nice self-indulgent self-absolution.

I never was thinking about participating in Israeli-Palestinian discussions. I reacted when Vice-Pres. Bush in his debate with Mrs. Ferraro described the 13,000 Palestinian soldiers as terrorists, whose defeat with the blessing of the U.S. was just and good. I wrote to him, that his statement offended me, because if I would be a Palestinian, I would fight in those units. I was telling him my belief that each nation has a right to express its rights to exist and to have conditions necessary for self-respect. The Israelis did not give the Palestinians any other way to react. (In include the copies of both my letters to Vice-President.) Maybe the *Gazette* could send its copies to those who would be interested to read them.)

Another main point raised in discussion was a statement that Israel will not negotiate with the PLO until it recognizes Israel. In my view, discussion with that part of the society that already surrendered never brings peace. It only potenciates the reaction of those who stand firm. Israel did many heroic deeds defending themselves—including the success of the Entebbe. What makes me perplexed is, that all that bravery was done in order to avoid the supreme heroism of face-to-face confrontation with all the Palestinians, without selecting them, and in this way find a possibility of coexistence, and maybe even of reconciliation and friendship. Are the Israelis not mature enough for such heroism? I do not believe this. I know many good qualities of the Israelis. I read about "good fence" and the Ethiopian emigration. I hope that Israelis will stretch those good qualities in a final reconciliation with all the Palestinians, without preconditions with whom they want to talk.

Finally, I have to tell, that I am not an expert on the bible. My faith in God is simple. I believe that He is the father of all of us: of the Jews, of Christians, of Moslems, and even of those who negate His existence. What I was saying in my previous letters, and now, is not an anti-Semitism. It is only an indication, that I see a solution for Israel and for Middle East peace in a different way, and that I care. Otherwise some few niceties, complete agreement, or just silence would be much more easy and much less compromising.

Sincerely,

Tadeusz Maciejczyk
Milledgeville, January 23, 1986

The World Seen from the Distance of a Small Village

Lynn Martin
Congress of the United States

Dear Mrs. Lynn Martin:

In your last letter—Febr. 4, you are telling, that terrorism is an important issue, that it poses a foreign policy problem of immense proportions, that this terrorism is directed against U.S. citizens and U.S. interests, and that terrorists are trained by certain governments. You are further telling, that we should be willing to consider a whole range of options in dealing with the terrorist threat.

The first and fundamental option should be a talk—a sincere, gut-level talk, performed publicly in front of the world audience about all grievances of the movement against America. I hope, that America has enough moral strength to take such a risk. It would be the less costly, but radical, and probably the most effective measure.

In their special way, the terrorists are very rational. Surely, they are not irrational. They are only very desperate, and they cling to their last option of keeping the attention on their cause alive. They use all the training and financing opportunities they can get, and very likely they are used by other forces with all the premeditation, in order to shrink our sphere of influence. I believe that terrorists behind that ferocious face preserve at the bottom a true sympathy towards America. Our kindness to their cause could be like a spring sun to the ice covers, and America could see suddenly a change in the situation. This would be the most effective action, not only against terrorism, but also against those forces, which use the terrorists to weaken America.

Considering the other variants, if we swallow a hook, and we want to show that we are "macho," we will change ourselves only into the partners in a general, deepening madness, we will increase divisions in our camp and we will lose our biggest asset: the moral strength. In such a situation, maybe not the terrorists, but somebody else, would smile with satisfaction, that they got what they wanted for almost no cost.

I send you my best wishes.

Tadeusz Maciejczyk
Milledgeville, February 20, 1986

Book One

431 Park Place
Kalamazoo, MI 49001
March 5, 1986

T. Maciejczyk, M.D.
Box 788
Milledgeville, IL 61051

Dear Dr. Maciejczyk,

My father, Robert Reiff, shared with me copies of letters that you have written to President Reagan, vice-President Bush, and Allen Weinstein. I want to commend you for the time and effort you have put into such correspondence. Letting our government officials know our thinking on issues is very important and often overlooked or shrugged off as useless by many citizens.

I am going to send your letters on to the Washington Office Representative for the Church of the Brethren, Mr. Leland Wilson. I was in a meeting with him Monday and told him about your and he was interested in reading your letters. He has recently gotten involved in a Mid-East working group of several religious leaders. I thought he may have some information to share with you.

Best wishes to you.

Peggy Reiff Miller

The Dilemma of Central America

The problem of Central America is not getting its proper solution. After years of trials, it remains a basket of uncertainties.

The history prepared this region to be a trouble spot. Divided in small states, governed by the old oligarchy that was not interested in progress and evolution, Central Am. came to the late 20th century economically poor, socially divided and emotionally explosive. With almost no positive communication between the classes, the climate for collision was inevitable. The wakening of masses, a rebellion, murders, a general anxiety, fears and hate, became a new landscape of the land.

This explosive situation in a region of such strategic importance as Central America could not remain without calling attention. The U.S. was considering this region vital to its security and economy. The Soviets looked there to gain influence, foothold, maybe a stronghold in its incessant march to subjugate the globe.

The methods of the two superpowers of dealing with the potential dangers and opportunities in C. Am. were different.

The U.S. was trying to stabilize the existing regimes and to obey the legal rules of each country. Its relation was only touching the surface, without bothering to understand the people. The diplomacy was applying pressure, or giving favored treatment to reach its objectives. By acting in this way, the U.S. frequently was perceived by the population, as the part of the oppressive system, interested merely in exploitation. Those perceptions were softened by the activities of various American church or secular organizations, sincerely dedicated to the people.

The Soviet tactics were different. Their agents were entering in darkness, avoiding light, acting below the ground. They were working out the territory. They were identifying the leaders, organizing the unsatisfied, convincing, pointing at the U.S. as the evil supporter of the oppressive oligarchy. Their purpose was clear. They were sending the outstanding to Russia for training and indoctrination, they were providing arms to the organized groups; they were indicating how to seize the power. When they succeeded, like in Cuba or Nicaragua, they were incorporating that country into their global system, imposing their laws, breaking the opposition, using a skillful propaganda and nationalistic feeling to their advantage. Once dominated, such country had little chance to escape their embrace.

This is a situation of today's Nicaragua—country in the center of Central America—located only one good jump from the vital Panama Canal. The people's revolution against the U.S. sponsored Somosa dynasty, was stolen and twisted by Soviet-chosen men who were in the right place at the right moment. Instead of intended democracy, the country was transformed into another Soviet satellite, and the nationalistic and anti-American feelings were used for consolidation.

The Contras, if they would try to liberate their country, would have to fight not only against the Soviet-equipped army, but also against the Soviet propaganda machine. And whatever our evaluation, the Soviets are the artists and the true masters in using this machine. They would be not softened by any kind of scruples. Pushing the contras into such a fight without psychological preparation of the world is a frightening decision. They would have poor chances in this fratricidal war. And even a victory of the Contras would not bring a peace to Nicaragua, nor to the region. It would be only one more fragment of changing fortunes in a struggle for something that would be as elusive as ever.

What appears to be a center of dilemma in Central America, is a collision of the past with the dreams for the future. The past is known and rejected. The dreams are fuzzy, unformulated, scattered in thousands of different images, which never had a chance to be brought completely to the surface and discussed to its depth. The bottled up emotions are coloring the past and the future. Hate and suspicion make barriers. In such a mutilating situation, a creative free spirit has not much chance to develop. At the present the orientations there are divided. On the extreme there are pro-American and pro-Soviet wings. The vast majority in the middle would like to have their own model. As long as this prevalent model is not worked out, the instability and the agitation will continue. The domination of one or another extreme will only deepen the genuinely longing for something that would be not imported, but truly theirs, born from their own style, feelings and flesh. Only such an evolution would give the region stability, peace and pride.

The Contras can help to realize such a plan. As a standing force, they would not permit to transform Nicaragua in a full Soviet outpost. They would stand like a symbol and as an alternative. But their primary purpose should not be a shooting war.

While the Contras would provide a physical support, a real battle for the destiny of C. Am. should take place. This could be done by a confrontation of all complaints, perceptions, dreams and ideas in a public debate transmitted to all C. Am. through the network of radio stations. Organization, direction, planning of such debates should be done by people who understand the psychology of a man as an individual and a man in society. Previously I was suggesting for such a job the name of John Powell, author of *Why Am I Afraid to Tell You Who I Am?* This book

The World Seen from the Distance of a Small Village

is describing very well an emotional and spiritual buildup of a person, but it also describes the emotional and spiritual forces in societies of any size. John Powell could be influential in creating the patters for the dialogs, and could indicate people in the U.S. and in C. Am. who are prepared for such an undertaking. Such a work should never be done by the politicians because they are eager to bend the problems to their convenience, nor by journalists, because they are after sensation. Such work should be completely neutral, and done disinterestedly. It should be done this way to create a resonance in all Latin America and maybe in the world. It would be a battle to create a peace through a climate of openness, of liberation of energy and involvement. It would lead to the transformation of C. Am. into a completely different structure that would be conscious of its purposes and immune to Soviet subversion.

Help for the Contras should not depend on a progress of talk with the present Nicaragua regime. This regime can be very cooperative until the disappearance of Contras. Afterwards who could dictate them anything? New Contras would not be rebuilt easily. Who with common sense would trust the new promises of the U.S.?

Tadeusz Maciejczyk
Milledgeville, March 27, 1986

Book One

A serious illness, which is not responding to present treatment

Last week three leading weekly magazines: *Time, Newsweek* and *U.S. News* brought articles about the situation in the Middle East. Each of the stories was different and each of them was complementing the other two, giving altogether a picture of a vicious circle in the land where life stopped being normal long ago.

The circle can be entered with the U.S. News description of the life in the West Bank. Two nations, two religions, the same God seen in a different way. There is no physical distance between both camps. They can walk on the same street. The frightening reality is a complete lack of any meaningful communication between them. They look at each other with a dreadful silence. The 20 years of such a coexistence only increased the separation and deepened mutual tension and hate. Army patrols are patrolling the streets and searching the houses that for one reason or another appear suspicious to them. The law is dictated by one side and rejected by the other. The young Arab generation, born already during the occupation, is determined intensely to fight Israel. Searches, round-ups, blowing up homes of suspects, confiscation of land, are the background in which those youngsters are growing emotionally. What would be a reaction of Americans if they would be put in a similar situation? The Israelis feel the sentence that hangs over them. Chaim Bibowski summarizes this feeling with a confession, "I keep my gun closer to me than my wife." How long can such a tension last before it explodes into convulsion?

The second fragment of the circle was reported in *Time*. A *Katyusha* (Russian bomb) explosion in a school yard. Four children, one teacher wounded. The offender? Somewhere in the hills on the other side of the border. In 90 minute Israeli fighter planes bombed two buildings on the side of the Palestinian refugee camp. At least ten people were killed and 25 wounded. There was no court, no judgment, no communication, no evidence that the people there were really guilty. Who were those who were killed? Were among them innocent civilians? Perhaps women? Perhaps children? Between one episode and another it was only a deadly silence—like on the streets in the West Bank, and then a lynch-type murder called nicely a "retaliation." This crime was committed with the American made planes and bombs, perhaps with an approval or even with an applause of the American authorities. Of course, the Katyusha shooting was obvious terrorism. The bombardment—a lynch murder— a noble fight against terrorism. A double standard was a frequent phenomenon in the history of mankind. But it is necessary to tell also, that

The World Seen from the Distance of a Small Village

those double standards never gave good solutions and never were bringing true peace. The Arabs have now all its rights to retaliate with another act of terror. Please—explain—why not? The blind bombardment of a house on the side of the crowded refugee camp has without a doubt characteristics of terrorism, even by the Israeli standard, and Israel believes in 'eye for an eye' responses.

The last segment of the circle is brought by *Newsweek*. The author is asking very interesting questions: Why they hate? Why they kill? Terrorists are not born, they are made. Muhammad Sarhan survived Israeli bombardments of the Sabra camp. His father was killed during the massacre in 1982 by Christian militiamen while Israeli troops stood by. Sayid also lost relatives. Obeida's husband says his wife, and small daughter were killed in Shatila refugee camp in an Israeli air raid. Sayid angrily jumps to the American reporter indicating to himself: Do you see it? No tail. No hair on my face. I am a man, not an animal. Churlish observation of our Secretary of State apparently did not help to bring a sanity, and only put salt to the wounds.

Two months ago, discussing an editorial that concluded that Israelis understand the ancient proverb, that he who is merciful to the cruel is cruel to the merciful, and so must they, the Israelis, I responded that those qualities do not come from the mercantile measuring of how much for how much and of what, but from the inside of self. The cruelty comes from the visible or invisible inside torture of spirit, while the mercifulness from inside order and peace. Israeli behavior, Israeli policy created a torture of spirit to millions of human beings. We are starting to collect the harvest from this policy.

Once, a long time ago, it was told, that the good tree would be known by its fruits. A good tree is bringing good fruit. As until now, the fruit, which the world obtains from the tree of modern Israel is poisonous.

How to repair the Middle East? Its illness requires medicine completely different from that used until now. The more urgent remedy would be a policy that could heal the tortured spirit of all men there: the spirit of the Arabs, and also the spirit of the Israelis. Will Israel be able to transform its policy towards such an objective? Will the U.S.?

Tadeusz Maciejczyk
Milledgeville, April 6, 1986

Book One

Editor
The Daily Gazette

    For the second time I saw in your column "Voice of the Reader" a letter of Mr. Fred Turk, voicing his opinion about our relation with Nicaragua. I agree with him that the method "might makes right" is wrong, and is feeding only the hate, promising more complications in the future. As I also was trying to influence our Representative Mrs. Lynn Martin about this problem, and my ideas are somewhat different, I feel an obligation to share my views with our readers.

    I expressed those my views in an article, "The Dilemma of Central America." It is an idea completely original, born in the territory of *The Daily Gazette*, and being so should be supported and publicized in our paper. The ideas and influences should have not only one way: from the centers down, but also from the down of the ranks up. Such a discussion would surely serve our country.

    I hope *The Daily Gazette* will publish this my article and will ask the readers for discussion.

                    Sincerely,

                    Tadeusz Maciejczyk, M.D.
                    Milledgeville, April 13, 1986

The World Seen from the Distance of a Small Village

Gary G. Kreep
Executive Director of U.S. Justice Foundation (USJF)

Dear Sir:

Sorry that I had an uneasy time to make my mind as quickly as you were recommending and to vote for a death penalty for anyone convicted of spying against the U.S. My answer to your suggestion is a definitive "No."

This doesn't mean that I want to be mild on traitors, especially those who are doing this for money. I believe they deserve a punishment, but I am not brave enough to condemn them to death.

In your letter you are turning to me as to the fellow "conservative," and I am uncertain what exactly such a term means. In my life, I was always trying to be just rational. Anyway, looking conservatively on the problem, looking into the past for solutions, I see a kind of punishment that would fit just perfectly for this type of offense. I am thinking about the punishment of public pillory. A prisoner would be taken out from his cell early in the morning to spend the day at the pillory and would be taken back to the prison late at night. To serve the pillory, he would be put at the entrance to his factory or other place of his work, facing the bypassing of old friends. He would have his breakfast and supper in the prison. During the day he would eat, if the bypasser would have a mercy to give him something. He would spend at the pillory six days a week. On Sunday he could stay home to digest his impression.

I consider that the person guilty of this type of crime against his own country and his society should feel the public reaction, and the public condemnation not in the isolation of the prison cell or even at his death place, but in direct confrontation with those whom he betrayed.

Whether such a punishment would be more or less effective than the death penalty would be something to see and to study. At least certain countries would have not one more pretext to point at the U.S. as a villain and barbarous and use it for its own political games.

I cannot give you my contribution for the establishment of the death penalty that I do not approve. I will be willing to contribute if the pillory punishment would take a serious consideration as a remedy for this type of crime.

Tadeusz Maciejczyk, M.D.
Milledgeville, April 19, 1986

Book One

Ronald Reagan
President of the United States

Dear Mr. President:

In the last days I received several letters from your different supportive organizations demanding agreement with your policy, loyalty and contributions. Some of them were written in a very panegyric form to you as a leader and to me as a wise, thoughtful follower. In one I was reading pages trying to find a concept or direction and I was wondering how somebody could talk so much without telling nothing except flattery and self-adoration. I was told in another that if I do not contribute now to elect proper candidates, I will be destroyed next year by taxation. All those letters were pointing at the liberal Democrats as a number one enemy.

Reading those letters I was thinking that they were not building a harmonious, strong, cooperative society. I know that those letters were nothing else but an election time cunningness. They were intended to produce in the receiver a feeling of importance and enough fear in order to open widely his pocket. They were acting on the worst instincts in the society: a shallow pride, fear with apprehension and hate.

I am not used to panegyrics. I am trying to see to understand and from the facts elaborate my own approach. If I would see, that you are fighting for a right cause with wisdom and vision, I would stand with you whether your policy would be popular or not. I voted for you with this kind of devotion.

Today this my devotion is lost. Responding to those letters, I do not want to put there signs of yes or no to general and obvious questions. I want to explain why my devotion vanished. This could be also a part of surveys.

I am not an expert in economical problems. As other ordinary citizens here, I do not believe any more in the promises of the balanced budget in 1990. I saw other terms passing by while the borrowing was producing enormous payments on loans that will hang as a memory for the next generations.

So much was told in those letters about present and future prosperity. I do not see its symptoms here around. I see foreclosures, disappearance of factories, lack of security in the people and an anxious expectation of what will be the next to hit them.

About bureaucracy and bureaucratic waste I can only tell that never until now I was so deep in senseless paperwork. As you, I also believe that the traditional values and "work ethics" incentive are what would

The World Seen from the Distance of a Small Village

keep America strong, but the labyrinths of paper regulations that are multiplying from one day to another surely will not help to produce such a miracle.

But economic realities for me were always secondary in importance. They are the basic, but not the essence of life. The economic success alone never really satisfies. We always want more and more and having everything in the material sense, a person can be still very unhappy and empty. We cannot worship an economic success alone. An economic success is not the principal objective of true leadership. Frequently it is a byproduct of an emotional and soul-fulfilling environment created by the leader.

It can be debated whether America's pride had been restored. When talking about this with different people, old or young, I found a vacillation and a lack of conviction. Except for very a superficial approach, I found widespread doubt and unfulfilling, yes, probably it is, but . . . something very essential was lacking.

Our national defenses were rebuilt in a sense of numbers of arms and units efficiency—while at the same time we are losing a support of many people abroad. It may be that we do not care about such a support, but from the point of global policy a human factor is very important as an ingredient of a general defense system. Our policies are not gathering, not unifying, not building a unity that could extend above the level of the national communities. Our policies frequently are repelling such a tendency. Nowhere American leadership of today is producing an echo of enthusiasm and admiration, as it was in Pres. Kennedy's days. Our policies have no far seeing, global, genuinely human projections. We have no time or patience for them.

Our policies are dictated by the popularity slogans necessary for the next election. Re-election strategies dominate above all other elements in an approach to the problems of the country or of the world. Debts to the outstanding contributors and supporters is putting chains on the hands of administrations and has to be paid with something that doesn't belong to the elected official, or to his party, but to the country or to the world. More and more frequently a jittery, very early start of the political campaign downgrades the effectiveness of the government, signaling to all friends and adversaries that the lame duck period had already begun. Those early races are not a result of a love or care for the country. They indicate rather a selfishness and a complete disregard for the country on one side and a deep insecurity on the other. Such politicians behave like those card players who cannot resist but to show their cards before time, counting on some kind of advantage. Can a destiny of all the country be trusted in such jittery hands?

In such a situation we are bouncing from one event to another following them rather than dominating them.

In two regions that are more inflamed at the present time, this our stagnation is very visible.

In Central America what we really want is to have safe and subservient states. We do not care about the people there. We would like to be loved by them, but a confidence and communication we have only with the governments that we are able to manipulate. We have no program for a transformed new Central America with which we could deal as an equal with the equal. If we could, we would like to bring everything there to the previous normal.

In the Middle East everything would be smooth and as usual, if not for terrorists, the appearance of hostile states and Soviet infiltration. Without them we would quietly forget about the injustice that was done and perpetuated there. To make our stand it is much more easy, much more comfortable for us to take a shallow look on terrorism and to produce a theory that they are doing this just to entertain themselves.

We are reacting to the terrorism with holy indignation and anger because in dealing with the Middle East we have no vision of ours. We are only a stamp for the Israeli policy that assured of the U.S. unconditional assistance and protection is persisting in its unyielding, chauvinistic and vengeful attitude, creating in this way a pot burning with emotions, frustration, humiliation, anger and a desire for vengeance. The overflow from this mixture is visible in the form of terrorism that is directed especially against the U.S. Israel, transformed into a fortress by American arms shipments and by other generous subsidies, has no intention to create conditions for a definitive reconciliation and peace. The time is working for them. In the meantime, we became a target and we became engaged in the war with the Israeli terrorism. We are starting to do the job that Israel would not dare to do.

Our adventure in Libya was not a heroic act. It was not a wise act. It produced negative reactions even among friends and more condemnation. It gave Khadafy a new strength. It endangered the moderate Arab leaders. It restricted our political and economical relations with the Arab world and increased the Soviet penetration. It left a stigma on us and created memories among many young people to the point that they were burning the American flag. It happened even in England. It also improved the image of the Soviets by a simple contrast, and made their maneuvering in the future much more easy. It showed that in this world, we behave like a small kid with a new toy. We spent millions to modernize our military equipment and we couldn't resist showing it to every-

The World Seen from the Distance of a Small Village

body, nullifying in this way our advantage. The Soviets were just watching and taking notes. It came to them completely gratis.

It is still true that America is the richest and the strongest nation on earth, but America is not a leader. Whoever in history was leading was doing so with the ideas that had a mobilizing effect on the people. Strength alone is sterile, is blind and it is used and abused by others, the way we are used by Israel. One can wonder why it is so. Are our politicians so deep in obligations to the Jewish capital and influence to sacrifice for this the real interests of this country? And to betray the idealism of the forefathers of America who believed in the justice and liberty for all? There is no justice and no liberty for Palestinians and we guarantee this injustice.

The history will judge your presidency. Generally the panegyrics are disappearing rapidly from the pages of the history books. The men with the panegyric tendencies will prize quickly somebody else. They have souls of slaves. They sell themselves. In posterity each new generation will cast its own judgment and its own evaluation of the legacy let for them from your time.

I still think that it could be a great legacy.

As for now, I will give whatever I can to the cause of the Afghan people. In the present time, not America, but they are giving the world a testimony of an eternal need of men to be free. Today they are the leaders of men with a free soul.

Tadeusz Maciejczyk
Milledgeville, May 11, 1986

Book One

Freedom vs. Terrorism—Differently
(Discussion of an editorial, "Freedom vs. Terrorism" in *U.S. News and World Report,* June 2, 1986)

It looks to me that those two notions are not opposing each other. In different circumstances, in different ways, with different emotional charges, they go in the same direction.

Freedom is something that cannot be described and lived fully and easily. It is not something static or unchanging. Freedom is like perfection. We tend to it. By our action we can expand it or shrink it. It can grow. Or it can be lost because of our misbehavior, or because or external aggression. Freedom should be never taken for granted. It requires a constant watch, constant effort, constant self-discipline. Freedom can have different boundaries, different depths, different intensities, different flavors. It can flourish in the more improbably places—even in a concentration camp where the internal freedom cannot be taken away from certain individuals, although their external chains are heavy. In contrast, it can be absent or be evaporating in the midst of an apparently free society. Freedom has not a clear stick to be measured and compared. Maybe a degree of openness in expression, action and creativity could be one of such measurements. Freedom cannot develop in places where emotional strain is surpassing the human resistance. It requires a certain internal harmony and internal peace. Above all it requires a domination by mind of our emotional responses.

When those conditions are violated, a special illness is appearing that can lead up to a violent, vicious terrorism.

It is because Terrorism is born from the lack of freedom that produces an intense emotional building up. In a certain way, it is a violent hammering into a door of freedom because they become closed to them, and reinforced by the soundproof devices to prevent their cry for freedom to be heard by others. Terrorism is a result of long torture of spirit when finally even the hope started to disappear.

As freedom, terrorism can have many forms, many stages. It can be organized inside a suppressed, tense society, or it can appear in some autistic personality who became unable to cope with his imagined problems and starts his own terrorism against the surroundings.

Juvenile delinquency is something different from terrorism. It appears within the emotional and spiritual boredom, inside emptiness and lack of purpose. To such a life a flavor can be added only with some kind of kicks. But a transition between juvenile delinquency and terrorism exists. When those kicks are getting cruel and calculated, it can give

The World Seen from the Distance of a Small Village

a signal of an excess of emotions that torture the soul of such a person pushing him to terrorism.

I would never tell that terrorism is a "method of choice." It is the last method to which a person or a society is growing, when everything became obscure, without hope and the pain of existence is intolerable.

I do not think either that the terrorism is a "gangsterism of politics." Gangsterism is an infighting of certain groups for the material luxuries of life acquired by the illegal means. Terrorism should never be put in the service of any cause because it represents a wrong, destructive pattern, destroying something it is so passionately looking for: destroying the freedom. But, in a very special way, the terrorism is not an enemy of freedom. It is the ultimate cry for freedom.

Mr. Zuckerman is charging that by telling all those problems the way I told them here would corrupt our language and our morals. But I still maintain that this my voice to resolve the problem of terrorism with communication and justice instead of fighting it with a bigger and bigger stick from behind the wall of silence will not corrupt our existence. In the name of freedom, freedom of thinking, acting and looking for solutions, my obligation is to speak and not to worry how my view of the true would collide with somebody else's designs.

Concluding those deliberations about the nature of terrorism, I have to still stress my view that against all other affirmations, terrorism is a kind of freedom fighting. It is the fighting for the freedom from the nightmare of life. And like in a nightmare, in the terrorist acts, the symbols acquire enormous proportions. The small girl gunned down in the Rome airport was for the attacker a symbol of all those forces that changed a centuries old normal existence of Palestinians into the present tragedy. In the moment of pulling the trigger to kill, that terrorist could feel the highest sublimation of putting his life also as a noble offering for his country. Such a paradox exists and we, whom life has put into a different situation, sparing us from years of tortures, we have no unlimited rights to be their judges, applying for them standards from outside of the realities of their existence, at the same time still keeping the door of communication tightly closed, and the soundproof devices in full action and consequently do not change anything in the life of those who became the pariahs of our 20th century to a great degree due to our policies.

As Mr. Zuckerman, I also fully subscribe to the idea that not doing something about terrorism is morally unacceptable. Nevertheless, force against them should be tempered, military strikes excluded, but minds and communication should be open.

Book One

I am appalled by the preventive suggestions of Mr. Zuckerman: preemptive actions, coordinated, well-financed secret efforts, devise and carry out concerted operations; all democracies must have their own trained antiterrorist units; a succession of blows and counterblows; all out attacks against the targets.

What would be the consequences of all those actions? Did ever anger and fist resolve any real problem properly? What would the world look like after an apparent victory? Would it be safer? Wiser? Richer?

Probably the world would emerge from such a war enormously tense, highly emotional, with sharp divisions and without any true promise of peace. It would be a world of constant surveillance and readiness because terrorism would be suppressed, but more than ever terrorists would be sworn in waiting for the moment of relaxation to strike. Who would really benefit from such a war? This is not hard to imagine.

Israel was using the tactics recommended by Mr. Zuckerman for a long time and it did not bring peace to the region. It only produced more chaos, more hatred, more uncertainty. The unrest extended beyond the boundaries of the Middle East striking the West, that brought the Israeli State to its existence and is supporting everything that Israel is doing to its neighbors.

It would be much better for the successful conclusion of the upcoming battle with terrorism if Israel would not take any part in it. They did already enough and gave the world the present convolutions. Israel is not impartial in this world tragedy. Israel is the part of the drama—its main cause. Israel's behavior frequently acts as a slap in the face of all Arabs, the radical and the moderates, the wealthy and the poor, the educated and the ignorant. Some of them, like Saudis, understand the greater purposes and are trying to keep calm and neutral. Some, like Syria quietly, consequently are preparing themselves for the moment and sell their soul to the Soviets. Some, like Libya express loudly their hatred. But all of them feel provoked and under pressure.

Except for this, Israel has its own aims. The last Israeli arms deal with Ayatolla's Iran, one of the main sponsors of terrorism, has its own significance. Was it just a business arranged behind their so-called friends? Or maybe that Israel welcomes the Palestinian's terrorism against the Western nations? It puts the Arab's wrath away from them, and mobilizes the world against their enemies. Being small, surrounded by the Arab sea and behaving as they do, the Israelis have to use everybody for protection.

It is necessary to oppose each act of terrorism, but in the same time it is necessary to open serious discussions to heal the wounds of the Middle

The World Seen from the Distance of a Small Village

East. This healing should be done not on the surface through the governmental treaties because treaties will not bring peace, but from the bottom, opening and cleaning all the cracks of those wounds, producing gradual reconciliation of the people and a new order in the region.

Israel could contribute to this operation in a special, very important way. It could stop the insulting for the Arabs patrolling the streets in the Arab cities and give this duty to the International Peace Keeping units. It would decrease enormously the tension and give more chances to the good will discussions.

In the long range, a definitive reconciliation, not through the governments' signature on the piece of paper, but by a freely-admitted peace among the common people from the streets—Israeli and Arab—is what would give the Israeli the true victory and a peace of spirit that in turn would permit them to flourish their real talents, with the benefit for them, for the Arabs and for the world.

Because I understand a solution to the Middle East problem this way, I welcome the interview with Abu Abbas. Somebody finally has to open the separating door and to take from them the soundproof devices.

> Tadeusz Maciejczyk
> Milledgeville, June 15, 1986 (Father's Day)

P.S. Because my view is so much different from all others that I had the chance to read, for the sake of freedom that always gains from true discussions—it should be published. TM

Book One

June 25, 1986
U.S. News and World Report
2400 N. Street, N.W.
Washington, DC 20037
Mortimer B. Zuckerman, Chairman and Editor-in-Chief

Tadeusz Maciejczyk, M.D.
444 Main Street, Box 788
Milledgeville, IL 61051

Dear Dr. Maciejczyk:

Thank you for taking the time to read and comment on my June 2 editorial, "Freedom vs. Terrorism."

I hope you will find yourself more in agreement with the other things that I write, and I appreciate your interest.

                Sincerely,

                Mortimer B. Zuckerman
                Chairman and Editor-in-Chief

                MBZ/fmf

The 4th of July Celebration

I was watching the 4th of July celebrations and I liked them. They were elevating the spirit, they were unifying, they wee healthy and they were well done.

Nevertheless, I felt that it was not everything. The meaning of 4th of July is much bigger. It is a symbol of freedom. As such, this day should find a place and time to present the last year state of freedom here and in the world.

It is important because freedom is a very special commodity. It is eternally the same and yet, it is constantly changing. It is changing here in this country, and it is changing in the world. Freedom has an extremely complex structure. It is adjusting to conditions and stages of life. It can be dressed differently. It can be bent, used or abused. The technological or material progress, changing morals, changing social structures—all those factors can make a special print even on the essence of freedom. Many gradual changes in our perception of freedom cannot be seen by a casual observation, but they can make currents in the subsurface that would be good to know, to watch and to guide.

Pres. Reagan in his New York address told that freedom should be never taken for granted. In the past we paid for it with blood. At present, to preserve this freedom we maintain our military strength and we are expressing our readiness to use it if necessary.

For all those reasons we should know very well what the freedom really is and how it works. We should strive to know all its anatomy, physiology and also its pathologic changes. It is so because without a doubt, we can give the best care to those problems we know best. To serve well freedom, we should work constantly to know it. To preserve, to expand freedom it is not enough to be strong. First of all, it is necessary to know its substance. It would be good to keep a sharp eye on all the current changes in the elements of freedom here and in the world, make order in them, understand its significance, analyze them, keep a record of all changes and maybe on each 4th of July present an inventory of all aspects of freedom during the last year to the people of the U.S. as well as to the people of the world.

Such a report would mean hard year-round work. A sporadic consideration when a special problem arises would be not enough. Preparation of such a report would require constant attention, teamwork, specialization in the subject, dedication and a high moral standard of everybody involved. Only then, this kind of work would become an

Book One

accomplishment and could earn prestige and authority almost equal to that of the Nobel Prize Institution. If such a level would be reached, such work could become a world's center for guidance. It would be necessary in serene times, like a special laboratory in the service for health preservation and in the time of crises for a clearer, unemotional orientation. It could prevent bloodshed or another world convulsion. It would promote in a special way our knowledge of ourselves.

Such an institution could be called "Academy for Observation and Analysis of Freedom." Obviously it should be completely independent of any government or from any political affiliation. It should exist and work solely for the sake of freedom here in this country and in the world. It should be able to speak the truth even in the situations when the political considerations and realities would prefer to close the eyes. It should show and potentiate the noble aspects of humanity.

I think that such a project can be realized and if done, I think that its investments would pay back generously.

Tadeusz Maciejczyk
Milledgeville, July 10, 1986

The World Seen from the Distance of a Small Village

USIF
United States Justice Foundation
2091 East Valley Parkway
Suite 1-C
Escondido, California 92027

July 15, 1986
Tadeusz Maciejczyk, M.D.
Box 788
444 Main Street
Milledgeville, IL 61051

Dear Dr. Maciejczyk:

    I would like to take this time to thank you for your letter dated April 19, 1986, which this office received May 20, 1986, expressing your views.
    We are at all times receptive to both requests and suggestions concerning our present and future projects. Please feel free to contact us at any time.
    Again, thank you.

                                  Sincerely,

                                  Gary G. Kreep
                                  Executive Director
                                  United States Justice Foundation

GGK:mlw

Book One

Cocaine Plague. Crack Addiction

It hit at once a large segment of the nation, and if it is so destructive as the newspapers are telling, it should shake everybody as the appearance of AIDS shook the gay society.

The news about this new menace is really alarming. In the past few months every city, country and almost every little town has been hit by the crack epidemic. It crosses all racial, social and economic boundaries. It has an exponential growth. The authorities are indicating an abundant supply of cocaine as a root of the problem. The DEA's interdiction campaign has so far failed to make much headway against major traffickers. The justice system has been unable to thwart the cocaine trade at any level. Courts are too lenient . . . and so on.

Such is the news from the besieged city, hopelessly indefensive and lacking of its own immunity system to such a danger. The defenses applied until now only increase the feeling of hopelessness. The Peruvian adventure of helicopter search and destroy missions, like in Vietnam; the failure to stop the trafficking from entering the U.S.; a police "crack down" on the streets; a sleepy performance of the Justice, which apparently cares very little about human destruction by crack in this country; the White House theatrical gesture of urine testing, which probably will be a measure as effective as the washing of hands by Pontius Pilate.

What is intriguing me in this serious situation is that while exterior applications of those plasters are discussed, nobody looks into ourselves. Why are we so vulnerable? What are we lacking, what unfulfilled needs we have, that we are so eager to try any surrogate with a promise of a moment of happiness and pay such an enormous price for it?

It has to be a special hunger left within us, unsatisfied, unanswered, ignored by those who were supposed to satiate our needs. It looks that this hunger is not material. It is produced not by a possible racial uneasiness. It is not a problem of education or employment. Somewhere below our happy or tragic face, external success or failure, hectic activities or leisure, lays a huge vacuum, which our society is unable to fill up.

What can this vacuum be? It is not a lack of entertainment. The U.S. is saturated, as no other country, with "entertainers." Being an entertainer is a lucrative occupation. It is an occupation that leads easily to becoming an idol, a semi-god for many. Is this entertainment so shallow that it never reaches the soul and never can penetrate more than just below the skin? Or maybe this entertainment is interfering, is blocking

The World Seen from the Distance of a Small Village

something, that otherwise would enter us as a part of our preparation for life? Or could it be that this entertaining system, which saturates us from every TV screen, from every corner of our lives, is pushing us deeper into internal despair, because its attractiveness has a short span, gives no fulfillment, no joy of a new, positive discovery, no deeper experience? Maybe in that longing for the highs, the users are pushing their desire for entertainment to the extreme? Or maybe they are hunting those selves they would like to be, if the inner vacuum they have would be occupied by something able to give them a pride in themselves in their inner self-evaluation.

In this country we have political leaders of our choice. We have also very large amounts of spiritual leaders, many schools teaching about social environment and social behavior. We have here more social workers than any other nation on earth. How it happened that all of them somehow failed to inspire, to lead and to guide?

Our political leaders generally are too busy managing the mechanics of administration, conducting countless plots to impress, to get votes, to repeat once again some very important pool. It looks that they lost the ability to lead to a distant, great objective the only satisfying goals of human dreams. But the distant goals are not popular. We want everything at once and now. And the politicians do not dare to reach into unpopular remedies. Most frequently they are the high priests of the goddess of "Popularity." Popularity has a special cheap shine and smile. It has very little depth and it is a very bad teacher of men. But it gives vote victories. Because of this, today's political leaders of the U.S. are not inspiring. They are only managing and plotting to be elected or re-elected. Definitively, they cannot fill up the vacuum left in the human soul.

Our spiritual leaders became muffled under the heavy overcast of entertainment and amusement needs. There are too many temptations and desires unlatched, which when tried, are only widening the vacuum feeling. The spiritual leaders have to go against the popularity current and even they are trying to adjust, to compromise, and are disorienting.

And finally there is another painful fact of life in this country, or perhaps as also in other countries of advanced economy. This country is unable to give its small children a continued presence and care of their mothers. The mothers have to go to work because of economic necessities, or maybe because of the new ambitions of some women. Their babies are neglected, not in their material needs, but by a very special starvation that leaves in them very special scars that cannot heal completely during their lifetime. The substituting remedies: the babysitters, the day care centers, cannot give the children that very special loading of that special force and strength the mother does. If the extended family is close and cooperative, this immediate lack of mother can be substituted by a loving care of others, but it is not a frequent condition in today's life in America, where families are more and more dispersed. There is a potential tragedy built into our society that extends increases each year and that became revealed to a certain point by the present "crack epidemic" test. In the long range, it would be very helpful if a law would be created and enforced that a mother should remain home until her youngest child reaches the school age. Perhaps a development of a home-done parts for factories, like in Switzerland, could help to overcome the economic family needs. Otherwise I do not see avoidance of such, like the present, or other future catastrophes.

Within the family problems, another issue is also outstanding: the issue of divorces. In this aspect, if the matrimony has children—the needs of children should have all the priority, not the whims of the parents. Such is the law in the nature—an whoever is breaking the natural law always has to pay a high price. The divorces are like an escape from uneasiness, unhappiness, frictions, growing apart of the parents, potentiated by their own self-concentration or selfishness, and also by those institutions that benefit from this kind of discord. If there is a threat of divorce in the matrimony with children, every effort should be done to delay, to reconcile, to avoid final breaking apart, and to keep children in the family of both parents together. It can be done. It never will be easy. But otherwise, even the best social workers, best foster homes, will not correct the damage done to the children.

Then what? Where is the best strategy to conduct the war against cocaine, crack and other attempts against the integrity and health of a person?

Obviously, the effort to limit the flow of drugs is important. The police surveillance has to continue. The Judiciary has to finish their neglect, or almost lack of participation. If the war on drugs is declared, a martial law would be beneficial. If anybody dies from the drug abuse—it should be clearly stated—it would be judged as a murder in the martial law time. It would mean a death penalty without appeal for the pusher and for all the line of his drug suppliers to the top. Also, as the purpose of drug smuggling is money, all the property of the accused should be confiscated completely. This money could go to the rehabilitation centers.

The politicians probably will continue as they are. The real leaders with a talent to inspire are appearing not frequently and if they would exist, they would have probably little chance in the American elective

The World Seen from the Distance of a Small Village

system. This system favors popularity, promises or solutions without sacrifices and an external shine.

The entertainment, the TV shows, should finally start to try to upgrade the society, instead of tearing it down. They also are following the criteria of popularity as the only indicator of what should appear or not on the screens. It looks that the price the nation is paying for such an arrangement is catastrophic and cannot continue. Positive programs can also be enormously entertaining. The test of the public can be changed. Why not try?

In conclusion, while immediate drastic containment of the cocaine flow is necessary, a long-range measure should be introduced that would give the nation greater resistance to this, or another danger of addiction.

Tadeusz Maciejczyk
Milledgeville, August 21, 1986

Book One

Explanation of My Letter

I wrote this letter of protest because medical work of today gives no joy. It is a free man who works most effectively and imaginatively. President Reagan told this on one of his speeches.

But—the actual medicine became not free. In a hard time for financing the Medicare programs, instead of an approach, discussions, leadership actions among the free men, we got a number of rigid babysitters who are supposed to watch, to direct and to spank.

An institution of babysitters can be questionably useful for babies. If it is imposed upon adults, it produces only one effect: it kills the personality, the imagination and the initiative. In its place it sharpens only one skill—the skill of how to cheat the babysitter.

The babysitter program will not bring a happy solution to the future of medical care in America. It reflects sadly upon the present, supposed-to-be leaders of our nation who are unfit for a hard time man-to-man talks with their own countrymen and instead looking from above, from their high places hidings, they are creating monsters and watchdogs that are supposed to reach the objectives and rule the unruly with the flow of paper *ukases* (directives requiring obedience without discussion) and a power of sanctions.

Every person, every institution, every great team to live and to develop requires a certain amount of warmth and sincerity with sincere talks that can bring understanding and calm. There is no trace of all those things in the present policy of this administration towards medical family. It is there only a contempt and bureaucratically-increasing tendency to mold everything to a robot level and to use a whip if necessary.

The history will judge those methods and those ways to solve the problem, those brave approaches to the looming disaster, those two faces used for talk, one with the public, another with the medical institutions; those unrestrained desires to masquerade and to look well before the electorate, whatever the consequences.

This letter reflects my sincere feelings and I know that sincerity many times doesn't pay: it breaks the rules of the game and it is unpopular.

Tadeusz Maciejczyk, M.D.
Milledgeville, September 1, 1986

Medicare Participating Physician Program

Before I consent to continue my participation of my third year in your organization, I need to discuss with you my apprehensions and my doubts. I formulated them in a number of problems and questions and I expect concrete answers from you.

1. Participation in your program requires such a paperwork that the normal activity of the office is suffering. It almost created an absurd situation in which a paperwork becomes more important than the real treatment of patients.
2. Your paperwork requirements made from the office an agency of your organization that is expected to function without pay, without adequate for the purpose equipment and frequently with very little of your cooperation. The bureaucratic machine, created by you, doesn't bother to try to understand and to adjust to the condition of small medical offices like mine that nevertheless are the outposts of medical care and are important.
3. I cannot keep my office open with your payments, reduced by different arbitrary cuts, hard to understand rejections, delays of payments and your self-declared act of wisdom and generosity that what you declare rejected or reduced is valid also for the patient, making my loss irrevocable. On the other hand, the hardship you impose on the function of the office requires more clerical hours, more time lost explaining, clarifying, arguing.
4. Your customer charges base system is rewarding those who have no scruples to make high charges and is punishing and destroying those who worked rather to fulfill their mission and were modest or more than modest in their fees. You are proving that it pays to be smart and abusive and that those who are modest and merciful can be bitten twice: before your appearances, restricting themselves voluntarily and afterwards because you used this opportunity to exploit them completely.
5. I want to stress that the "customary charges" are not the only criteria of the quality of care. I want also to remind you that for usual citizens, there exists something called "minimum wage."
6. I was told that if I would install a computer in my office connected with Marion, the handling of my problems would be quicker and more accurate. In relation to this suggestion, please help me to understand. Who should pay for this installation? I have no capital necessary. I never knew how to charge adequately.

I always had an impression that the patient is in a need and I always was handing him the smallest bill, always with a kind of embarrassment. Finally, answer, who is supposed to pay for this extravagance?
7. I came to a conclusion that your main inclination is not a just, imaginative and flexible medical care system that could last and serve, but to impose a bureaucratic, rigid rule over something, what should be inspired by an idea, but as loose and as individual as possible.
8. I was told that those who break out from your organization will be punished by enforcing on them unrealistic fee schedules and some other sanctions. Strange—how our democracy is evolving. Years ago, in another system, I was condemned to death for being a rebel. I hope that your punishment will not go to such an extreme. I also hope that I will provoke discussion that would give us an understanding and consequently, for me, some kind of inspiration to continue to serve in your organization, not because of threat of sanctions, but because I would understand, appreciate and believe in your actions.

Bureaucratic pressure, with all its ruthlessness will not mobilize me, and will not inspire. Surely, it will not make this nation go through the uneasy time smoothly and in harmony.

Sincerely,

Tadeusz Maciejczyk, M.D.
Milledgeville, August 28, 1986

cc: The White House
U.S. Department of Health and Human Services
U.S. Senators and Representative
Major newspapers and magazines
Some civic organizations

The World Seen from the Distance of a Small Village

Rep Mark Siljander
United States Congress

Dear Sir:

I agree with you. There is a danger. It existed for a long time and it will not subside until the Soviets get their prey: world domination, or until some miracle changes their soul. They will do everything, even the military concessions, to disarm the U.S.—emotionally inside, and to discredit it in the eyes of the world. In the final account, not the military clash, but the moral strength, the strength of the spirit and the influence over the minds of the people of the world, will decide about the outcome of this mortal struggle. In this subsurface war, the Soviets will have no moral, not any other human restraint. Their brain-team is mapping the strategy of what to do on the surface and what should be obtained under the coverage of the exterior smiles or temporary concessions. I would not be surprised at all, if they would stay, somewhere in the deep shadow, behind the present crack epidemic. It is working so wonderfully for their purposes. And I have no doubt that they study everything inside the U.S. very carefully. Everybody of importance is measured. Everybody can be used by them one way or another, not knowing it. It is enough to develop some emotional issue and the hints of easy, popular solutions. The flies always come then.

Not other, but just this was a cause of the fall of Poland in 18th century. In January 84, I was writing in my letter that it would be a useful experience to do a good study of the fall of Poland to Russia. Useful, because analyzing the Russian methods of 200 years ago, after adjustment of time and circumstances, one can find there all the elements of the present Soviet global strategy. The 18th century Poland, after devastating wars of the 17th century and after more than 60 years of foreign kings on Polish thrones, had no moral strength to resist.

I send you my letters in which I was writing about the problem of peace and freedom. I believe that the military strength is important, but it is a secondary and only supportive factor. The real outcome will come not from the military build-up, but form the creation, sublimation, spreading in the world of a great idea that could win the human hearts, mobilize them not on our side, because against this can be resistance of pride, or some old resentments, but on the side of a common good and justice. Building up institutions and structures that would work in this direction should have as much priority as the military. Otherwise, a time can come, when to make the last military battle, could be too late.

Tadeusz Maciejczyk
Milledgeville, September 4, 1986

Book One

Patrick G. Gray
Medical Manager
St. Paul Fire and Marine Insurance Company
Chicago, IL

RE: Professional Liability Policy 512TG2001

Dear Sir:

I thank you for your answer and explanation of reasons for a sharp increase in my liability insurance cost. It reflects the cost of society's expectations and demands. And—it is the basic responsibility of society to correct the social ills that affect this insurance.

The price became hardly affordable for me. But more than this, I have difficulties of a different order. I understand differently the meaning of justice and morality. I refuse to look at each of my patients as a potential enemy, whom I have to strike first, charging him more to buy protection for me. This is immoral. Except this, such an approach is impairing development of the special closeness, special resonance and touch that generates the warmth, the trust and the confidence.

I believe also that such conflicts, such barriers, forced and put between sides of contact, if multiplied by thousands or millions across the nation are producing a micro trauma that is not benign any more. It affects not only the economy, but the character, the strength. A society torn by internal mistrust, without warmth, is a weak society that will not stand the test of time.

In every nation it is a passive majority and within it an energetic, enriching minority that drives and pushes forward. This minority can be put on a special pillory in the name of justice. Such situations will benefit some. Some will flourish and use it as a tool. A parasitic way to get rich will start to make sense. In the long range, the majority will suffer from direct and multiplying indirect consequences. In my case, the direct consequence for majority would be a higher fee for my services.

I was thinking intensely during those days of vacillation. Finally I concluded that if I have to be a doctor for those who put confidence in me, I cannot become toothless, i.e., without access to a hospital.

For this reason I will buy from you the necessary insurance. I hope that I will be able to pay for it in December. If you agree, I can pay half in November and half in December. I am sorry that I cannot pay it at one time.

Please notify me about your decision.

Tadeusz Maciejczyk, M.D.
Milledgeville, November 16, 1986

The World Seen from the Distance of a Small Village

NATIONAL CONSERVATIVE DEFENSE SURVEY
American Defense Committee
Washington, D.C. 20069

For each of the questions below, check the answer that best expresses your position
Choose either: Yes, No or Undecided.

1. I believe America must remain strong in order to be safe from the Soviet Union's threat.

    YES

2. I believe that it is the goal of the Soviet Union to bring the entire world under its political influence and dominance.

    YES

3. I believe that the Sandinista takeover of Nicaragua is but one more step in the plan for a Marxist Caribbean that began with the takeover of Cuba.

    YES,

but I have a doubt. The Marxists took the opportunity that the U.S. was refusing to see and to take. They preached the ideas of Marxism in places where the old beliefs and orders were crumbling leaving an ideological vacuum. The U.S. did nothing in this sense. Even now, the Contras are preparing for a military action alone. They have no one leading, inspiring idea that could convince the masses. In Central America, not a military action, but such an inspiring idea will win. In the absence of anything else, the Marxists ideology will conquer the hearts and the Contras will fail.

4. I believe that it is still the will of the American people to remain FREE from Communism.

    YES,

but I do not see any crusade-like conviction behind. The biggest asset we have, the freedom, is not felt until it is lost. A lack of a convincing, living idea is making the free world weak. The today's armed forces are like a shield to hide behind—not as an outpost to advance.

Book One

5. I believe that it is the specific responsibility of President Reagan and the United States Congress to uphold the will of the American people by giving America as strong a national defense as possible.

YES

The strongest national defenses, but including non-military elements with diversified purposes. The best scenario for the armed forces is to stabilize the existing confrontation, preventing surrender. On the other fronts an appalling social, humanistic, economic ideas, transmitted directly to populations should be a part of our arsenal. Not military, but those contra-ideas, would weaken the Marxist grip. A naked military strength has its perils. It was best illustrated in Iran where a modern and well-equipped army of the Shah disintegrated when confronted by a physically weak, but armed with a popular idea Ayatollah. The urgent obligation of the President and the congress is to give America and the world an idea for a just, better world. An idea capably to inspire and to lead. The U.S. is practically sitting on the wealth of ideas that are not used. They are abundantly present in the programs of the Fathers of this country, in the symbol of the Statue of Liberty, in Abraham Lincoln pronunciations, in the "dream" of Martin Luther King, in the ideas of John F. Kennedy. The arsenal of the U.S. against Marxism should have not only the strong military. This is only an insurance. U.S. should have also the missionaries of ideas actively fighting for freedom. Only such a fight could give a promise of peace.

Tadeusz Maciejczyk
Milledgeville, November 22, 1986

(The dream of Martin Luther King could be transformed into the best policy toward S. Africa; could help to heal the wounds there and decrease hate that is always a perfect fishing ground for the Soviets.)

The World Seen from the Distance of a Small Village

Medicare B
Marion, IL

I was notified that at the end of the year, I have to decide whether to stay with you or get out.

I was thinking about getting out from your Participation program. I felt bitter and I felt abused. As never before, I started to be uncertain economically. I worried whether I could survive and continue to keep my office open.

A few weeks later, speaking with another doctor, I told him that I was participating. He looked on me with a kind of pity and I felt embarrassed. I had nothing to tell him that would indicate my moral or economical motivation. I understood that in your organization my contribution was completely unilateral. I felt used, exploited. I felt like a fool sucker.

I understand that in hard times there is a need for sacrifices, but a sacrifice calls also for togetherness and mutual help. I need to feel not only your demands and the limitations imposed by you on me, but also your support and care for me when I am in need.

Such a peril I feel now more than ever. Feeling already an economical squeeze, I got a news that my malpractice insurance was increased four times above the last year's level. I need this insurance to be able to admit my patients to the hospital. I want nothing more from them. As a consequence of this increase, for every hospital admission I did last year, I would have to pay $141 just to this insurance. This is more than I collected for those hospitalizations.

The insurance company explaining those increases indicated that it reflects the cost of social expectations and demands. And, it is the basic responsibility of society to correct the social ills that affect this insurance.

In this situation, considering that most of those admissions were for the patients on Medicare, I feel that I have the right to ask you for help.

1. Can you pay half part of that insurance? (Considering all factors, I consider that it would be completely fair.)
2. Or maybe you would advise me officially that I should raise my fees?
3. Would you be ready to use all your influence and the authority of the Federal and State Health Departments to bring down the cost of Malpractice insurance?

4. In the same way could you work out a law that would establish a clear line between doctors and hospitals' responsibility in litigations?
5. By belonging and bearing the sacrifices can we earn some kind of consideration and help for our retirement age needs?

I hope that you can make feel all participating doctors that they are used, but also that they are not left on the side and ignored when they cannot cope with the imposed burden.

Signing this new document of "participation" I went to feel that you are not an imposer of a new version of medieval serfdom without our rights. I do not like to feel ashamed by confession that I participate. I want to be proud from my work and my actions.

Sincerely,
Tadeusz Maciejczyk, M.D.
Milledgeville, December 18, 1986

The World Seen from the Distance of a Small Village

Darryl Wahler, C.E.O.
Community General Hospital in Sterling, Illinois

I write to you now asking for medical privileges in your hospital. I reevaluated the situation that is changing rapidly. The issue, which produced my conflict with the Sterling Hospital, became wider and deeper. It is now threatening not only to individual persons, but probably to the whole country. My lonely protest against you lost its sense. The strategy should be different now.

Meanwhile, in Milledgeville, the people are asking me more and more frequently whether I would return and when. Also in Morrison, the direction of the hospital changed and I feel less in debt with them. And finally, as I told before, Milledgeville, by its location belongs to Sterling.

For all these reasons, I ask you, if you have no objections, to send me application forms for privileges.

To explain better my present situation, I send you the copies of my last two letters written to the insurance company and to the Medicare.

I thank you for your patience with all these my problems.

                    Sincerely,

                    Tadeusz Maciejczyk, M.D.
                    Milledgeville, January 8, 1987

BOOK TWO

LIFE AND WORK IN THE SHADOW OF A MALPRACTICE SUIT

Williams & McCarthy
A Professional Corporation
Attorneys at Law
400 Talcott Building
P.O. Box 219
Rockford, Illinois 61105
February 5, 1987
Dr. Tadeusz Maciejczyk
Milledgeville, IL 61051

RE: Macchi v. Maciejczyk
Dear Dr. Maciejczyk:

The World Seen from the Distance of a Small Village

This letter confirms my understanding that you have elected not to retain my services nor those of Williams & McCarthy in the above-captioned case. You have also rejected my offer to list for you other attorneys from whom you might seek representation. Presumably, you are at the point pursuing your case pro se. If you should desire legal representation in the future, I suggest that you contact the Carroll County Bar Association or the Bar association of a neighboring county and ask for a lawyer referral.

While I acknowledge your rejection of Williams & McCarthy's services, I take this opportunity to reiterate my recommendation that you employ legal counsel rather than proceed pro se. An attorney would be helpful at the pleading stage, in the pretrial discovery process and at the trial itself should your case proceed that far. Regardless of the course you choose, I wish you good fortune in the resolution of this matter.

                              Very truly yours,
                              WILLIAMS & McCARTHY
                              Lynn A. Williams
                              1C165pc

Book Two

Clerk of the Court of the Carroll County
Case No. 87 L 2; dated January 22, 1987

Dear Sir:

Your notification about the trial against me took me by surprise. The accusations of the act are telling that Mrs. Wilma P. Macchi came to me for the treatment of her decubitus ulcerations and I refused; I let her down in some other way, or I mismanaged the treatment and in this way I provoked some kind of catastrophe for this patient's condition. All accusations are very unspecific, repeating impressive to the public words, but unclear and fuzzy in descriptions, never counting the problem accurately, counting apparently on the emotions and ignorance of the jury and not on its integrity and wisdom.

I will follow here point by point all the accusations giving them my answer.

Point 1: Yes, I am licensed to practice medicine in Illinois and I am doing the general practice work in Milledgeville in the last 22 years.

Point 2: As my record shows, I was a family doctor of Mrs. Wilma P. Macchi from April 7, 1969 to February 12, 1971. Then, she moved with all her family somewhere South.

I saw Mrs. Wilma Macchi again on January 3, 1977 (after six years) when she made a visit to her old place, She had a flu for five days and she had signs of an acute sinusitis.

The next time I saw Mrs. Macchi was six and one-half years later in September of 1983. This was already the period of my supposedly criminal or unethical behavior. She came that time for the treatment of her urinary infection. Because I did not see her for so long, at the end of the visit I asked her about her family, her life, how she was organizing her life in spite of her paraplegia. In the course of this conversation, Mrs. Macchi told me, as a kind of confession, that she developed decubitus (bed sores). I did not feel that she had any intention to start any treatment for this condition with me. Decubitus is a very slow process with the long time, when the conditions mature to produce finally a break and open into a chronic lesion. I did not feel that her sporadic visit, after more than six years of absence, was giving me any right to start such treatment. The objective of her visit was the acute urinary infection, nothing more.

Her next visit in my office was one year later in September, 1984. At that time, she was complaining of a painful, swollen right knee with effusion in the articulation. During that visit there was no mention of the decubitus.

That was the last time I saw Mrs. Macchi.

Point 3: Tells that during 1983–1984, I rendered conservative treatment for a sore in the sacral area of Mrs. Macchi.

My Answer: I never was involved in the treatment of her sores. She never asked me to do this. (As a collateral, I would like to ask the accusing party what they understand by the expression "conservative treatment" in this kind of problem.)

Point 4: On February 1, 1985, Mrs. Macchi entered the Community General in Sterling. On February 6, 1985 surgery was performed for extensive debridement of the sacral decubitus ulcer.

Point 5: This point is very interesting and should be explained to the Jury with all details. It tells that on February 1, 1985, the day she entered the Sterling Hospital "for the first time Mrs. Macchi had reasonable grounds to believe or learn of any possible negligence on my part."

In this aspect the Jury should be informed with all details:

Subpoint A. Why she was not thinking this way before?

Subpoint B. What were the events that impressed her and changed her mind?

Subpoint C. What arguments were used to change her mind?

Subpoint D. Who was the person who produced this change of her mind?

Because that person was so instrumental in preparation of the ground for this judicial action, he should be called before the Jury to explain this again to all the parties of the conflict.

Point 6: This point is very hazy. What is means, that the plaintiff Mrs. Macchi, "was in the exercise of ordinary care for her own safety." Exactly what was she doing to describe it this way?

Point 7: This is a central point of accusation and my guilt of one or more negligent acts is formulated here.

Subpoint A: is telling that "I failed to properly diagnose the sacred decubitus ulcer."

My Answer: I did not need to diagnose this. The patient told me this in conversation after the visit. But she did not ask me for any treatment of her decubitus. In none of the two visits in 1983–84, the decubitus ulcer was an object of her visit. In both occasions, this patient had one acute, immediate condition that required treatment and this I did apparently well. It was all she consulted me for. The chronic problem in the best of my understanding of the medical ethic, belonged to her family doctor of that time, whoever and wherever he was.

Subbpoint B: is telling that I failed to properly treat her decubitus ulcer.

My Answer: I never even saw that ulcer. I never was asked, never it was objective of her visits. Because her visits were so sporadic (after 12-1/2 years of living in the South) I didn't consider that she was or could be my patient for all her problems or that I had any right to force on her my treatment. She was just a sporadic visitor for an acute situation of that moment.

Subpoint C: is charging that I failed to refer this patient to a specialist.

My Answer: Again, I was not her family doctor at that time and I was never involved in the treatment of this patient's decubitus. Even with my best desires to help her to approach this problem, I did not know at that time and I still do not know any such specialist in the South.

In relation to this point of the accusation I have to tell that in about the same time, I had in Morrison Hospital, a patient who was diabetic, almost blind, with urinary and fecal incontinence and with the cancer of the right lung. His condition was critical. He had very low serum albumin, which is necessary for healing and building of a new tissue. That man had enormous, infected, necrotic to the bone decubitus all over the sacral area. He also had decubitus over the thoracic vertebrae, on both heels and on the elbow. I was doing several debridments (cutting off the dead tissue) and when after all the winter long treatment he was transferred to the Good Samaritan Nursing Home, all those enormous lesions were closed. The chart of that patient can be obtained from the Morrison Hospital on request and be presented to the court as an evidence that a treatment of a decubitus is not a mystery to me.

Because of a very special flavor of the present accusation, I would like also to present here the case of a lady in her eighties, a diabetic, who in November 1982 developed a sudden and rapidly progressing gangrenous lesion of her right foot. According to the rules of hospital in such cases, I had to consult the specialist in infectious diseases. I was notified about this obligation after one week of hospital treatment when the patient was already better. That doctor, after seeing my patient once, recommended amputation of the affected foot. I refused and I resisted all pressures. Today, after more than four years, this lady is walking on her two feet and her right foot is the better one. The medical hospitalization chart of that lady should be a party of material for the Jury for their decision.

That case of that lady had a special continuation. About two months after I discharged her, I participated in the meeting of the Internist of the hospital. I was there as a delegate from General Practitioners. At the end of the meeting, the doctor specialist in the infectious diseases left discreetly the room and the doctor who was presiding over that meeting announced a presentation of a case of medical mismanagement and a non-professional behavior of one member of the staff asking for judgment. It was the case of my fight to save the foot of that lady from amputation. The uneasy atmosphere of that part of the meeting broke Dr. J. Erickson, when after looking at the chart, he declared that he didn't see there anything wrong, that the cat can be skinned many ways.

It is very likely that the same infectious diseases specialist was consulted on February 1, 1985 in the case of Mrs. Macchi. The record of the clinic visit and of all time of hospitalization of Mrs. Macchi should be a part of material in disposition of the Court.

At this point, I want to stress that I feel no hostility toward Mrs. Macchi. I do not see her very guilty. She is only an instrument in somebody else's hands. If she would be in need and come to me, I would treat her as any other patient.

Point 8: Here the act of accusation is defining my guilt "as a direct and proximate result of one or more of the foregoing negligent acts or omissions done by me. Wilma P. Macchi was directly injured thereby:

Subpoint A: She sustained permanent injuries both internal and external.

My Answer: I do not see any relation between me and Mrs. Macchi's decubitus problems, but because of accusations, I demand precision:

a) What were the internal injuries?
b) What were the external injuries?

Subpoint B: She sustained prolonged pain and complications that required extensive surgery.

My Response: Again, in no way I was involved in the history of this patient's decubitus. But to verify the statement of prolonged pain and complications, a day-by-day Clinic and Hospital record should be presented to the Jury, translated into clear graphics and sketches and plain language explanation of symptoms and surgical procedures that could be understood by laymen in the Jury.

Subpoint C: That she incurred and will incur large sums for hospital and medical expenses.

My Response: I never was involved and I was not a cause of her expenses, but because this point has a meaning, all the statements and receipts from the doctors, clinic or hospital should be a part of the acts of the Court. My cost for the visit of 1983 for urinary infection was $13.00. For the visit in 1984, for the treatment of the acute arthritic inflammation of the knee was $15.00. This second visit was still not paid until now.

Subpoint D: She endured and will endure great pain and suffering.

Book Two

My Answer: I was not involved in any stage of her decubitus.

Subpoint E: This patient was otherwise permanently injured.

My Answer: And I was thinking from all previous comments, that she was in the hands of experts. Please explain exactly what kind of permanent injuries? I am asking because still can happen that this lady can come to me one day for help.

Concluding my answers to each of the points of accusations, I have a right to demand precise answers to the following questions:

1. What all those accusations have to do with me and those two very separated visits that were both for an acute, immediate problem of a completely different nature?
2. Why Mrs. Macchi didn't come to me, presented her decubitus problem and asked for help? I have no reason to believe that I would treat her with less dedication than when I was treating for decubitus the diabetic and cancer patients in the Morrison Hospital.
3. Why she never had complained or claimed against me until she went to Sterling Hospital for treatment? Surely, it had to be a great deal of persuasion and ill will involved if it changed Mrs. Macchi so radically. Who was the doctor who injected into her this kind of hate? If he has something to tell and he has a minimum of integrity, he should step forward and tell this openly. He should not hide. Only cowards behave in this way.

The last page of the accusation act brings a copy of an official statement from the expert-specialist. In this document he is naming me twice by name, charging that in his medical opinion, based upon reasonable medical probability, I deviated from the standard of care of a reasonable, prudent physician and because of this, I failed and I became a cause of all the suffering of Mrs. Macchi. After such a solemn and official statement, after his fuzzy prescription for a perfect behavior, he was not a man enough to sign that act of accusation that remained anonymous.

Are we going to be a nation that has to live permanently under the constant watch of this kind of anonymous experts and informers? I do not believe that the American Justice needs anonymous informers to function. I want to believe in American Courts.

Tadeusz Maciejczyk, M.D.
Milledgeville, February 5, 1987

The World Seen from the Distance of a Small Village

Clerk of the Court of the Carroll County
Mt. Carroll, IL
(Case No. 87 L 2; dated January 22, 1987)

Dear Sir:

With this letter I confirm the delivery to me of the trial notification and I send to you my responses to each of the points of the accusation act. I want to be over with this obligation because I need the inside peace to be able to concentrate in my present work. I owe this to my patients. As much as I can, I have to finish the situation of suspension and until the time of the trial not to think about this assault any more.

Many friends were advising me to tell nothing and so to deny the ammunition to the other side. But I have nothing to hide. I accept the challenge of the truth. The other side can do the same, if they wish so.

Many very good friends were advising me not to go into this trial without the lawyer. I was surprised when a person, who really was wishing me well, after looking into history and substance of this case was convincing me that I need not only a lawyer, but the very best one if I want to be saved from all clever traps of the other side. The people were telling me that here in this country in the court, I should not expect a search for the justice or for the truth, but a merciless fight for the dollar. I was told that with my English, I will convince nobody and I will be an easy prey. The oratory from the other side will dominate and win. In the decisive moment of questioning, I will be given a tricky, well-prepared question to answer in one word: yes or no, and I will be destroyed, torn apart in an emotional scene. The poor, accusing lady in her wheelchair will be rolled into the room and I will be painted as a beast who abused such an innocent creature.

From TV shows I knew already all this. And I knew that forbidding full answer to any question has more to do with burying the truth than with bringing it to light. Such a forced shortcut never added glory to American Justice.

In spite of all that, I decided to go to the trial alone. On one side I have no money to pay for such a defense. Most American people would be unable to afford it. Except this, I feel that a process against me is not because of any criminal act, not because of a civil abnormal behavior, but because of differences in interpretation of my professional, medical work. Here I know better than the lawyer what obligations I took while deciding to be a physician and what the ethics of a physician should be. Questioning of those principles requires my direct answer, without intermediary.

Book Two

There is no doubt in my mind that I would be never standing here in the defendant's place in this Court, if that would be not because of a very special climate in this country, created and cultivated by special circles. This climate is tempting the people with easy money. If only you have a pretext, you should try. You are losing nothing and you can get rich with more certainty than playing the lottery. The gold mine was discovered and its exploitation was put into a full swing. The managers, the organizers, the ideologists gathered to work together to squeeze out from this mine everything they could. The ideologist justified and made palatable the game to anybody who could have moral objections. You have the right and you are helping the justice that is already long overdue was the general line. Every human tyranny, since the beginning of time, was hiding its true face behind such a wandering frontal façade.

In my life, I have witnessed the terror of the Gestapo. Immediately afterwards came the terror of the imposition of Communism in Poland. At that time I was condemned to death. I was charged to be a bandit. There was a period when I was never sure whether the next day I would still be free. I survived. The people were helping. But I couldn't stay there. I had to go west. At that time I was imagining that the next spring would be a big push back. I didn't come here to get rich.

Today, I have to live again in an environment of terror—terror produced by an organized greed. Again I find myself in the situation in which I never can be sure whether the next day the anonymous expert of perfection would point his finger at me and the inquisition expert, this or another Mr. Cacciatore, will be ready to tear me apart, my good name would be smeared, my work interrupted, my family exposed to suffering and strain and our feeling of even relative security would be destroyed. At this point I am on trial for something that whoever was looking until now into it was considering it absurd and abusive.

When will be the next time?
What is the purpose to work in such an abusive condition?
In other times, when the people were different, in the Declaration of Independence, its first point was affirming that every person had a right to live, to be free, to work and to search for happiness. Happiness, informers, inquisition and a constant need to not deviate from the standard of a reasonably prudent person as the anonymous perfection expert put it in the letter of accusation, are not living together well. Was the Declaration revoked? Is it reserved now only for some? Apparently for my misfortune, I have a wrong profession. I can be kicked in the back with impunity. I should be rich and an easy prey.

The World Seen from the Distance of a Small Village

But I am not rich. I never had a talent to be one. I never even had a desire to be one. I see the richness of life not exactly in the money.

For this reason, I am sorry, but I cannot afford to pay the ransom requested in this assault. If I am convicted, I am ready to go to jail. I would go there with the feeling that I was fighting for such a U.S. in which I would be proud to live.

I expect from the present trial not only a decision whether I am guilty or not. I need a guidance for the future. I expect a definition when a professional, an institution or any entity could be sued for malpractice. Exactly what the malpractice is? Is it primarily a goldmine? Is it an absolution given to everybody for all their personal responsibility because Mr. Cacciatore always will find somebody else to blame and pay? Is this an instrument to convert this nation into a cripple, because nobody will dare to take any risky decision? Is this a school for the society at large to grow opportunistic and cynical?

The climate created by malpractice is perversive. Not long ago we all witnessed how the highest officials of this nation were refusing to take responsibility-something very fundamental of any leadership. On TV before the world, they were standing, looking to the sides, trying to point to somebody else, giving excuses that were hard to believe. How those officials want to continue to represent and to be respected, it is beyond my comprehension. A high moral standard means much. Frequently it means more than the best arms.

In my work I have to concentrate maximally on the problems of each patient who comes from sometimes full and uneasily waiting in the waiting room. I have to understand them; I have to decide, to explain, to convince, to warn, or to calm down. All this in a short time given me by circumstances. I cannot be there for the sake of a perfect record keeping for every possible litigation. My purpose there is different. There I should be free from such a worry. Only in this way I can give my best from me. And I should be permitted to do a mistake. It goes together with being human. I cannot renounce my humanity. Nobody can seriously claim that he is always right, never wrong. What I can promise only is that I will always do the best of my capacities in any given moment. The second opinion is available to everybody.

While working, I also want to be free from the rigid standards of some "expert," as in the case of the diabetic lady with the gangrenous lesion in her foot. I have a big respect for experts, but I do not think that the history was made by the "prudent" men who always were obedient to them. History was made by men who had a dream, and were ready to break the standards to reach to them.

Book Two

The Supreme Court should finally break its silence in the subject as hot as the malpractice is, and should clearly tell at which point a punishable malpractice begins and what is the decisive element that is making a change and without which there is no guilt. The country cries for such a declaration.

Concluding—because those accusations of malpractice are not harmless and never should be taken lightly—just because there is no risk for the accusing party, I am asking the Court for compensation. I am asking for $100,000 (one hundred thousand dollars) from the plaintiff's attorney, William T. Cacciatore and from the anonymous doctor, to be paid to the American Medical Association for the fund to fight abusive malpractice accusations, whether they would be medical or of any other nature.

I also ask another compensation of another $100,000 (one-hundred thousand dollars) from Attorney William T. Cacciatorre and the doctor paid to the American Red Cross for the Fund of Homeless of America and for the creation of a network of volunteers who would solve this problem their own unique way in each community. This compensation is for the undeserved suffering of my family, for the tears of my daughter and for the sleepless nights of my wife.

Please, notify me about the day of the trial.

Sincerely,

Tadeusz Maciejczyk, M.D.
Milledgeville, February 13, 1987

NOTE: This letter was published in the *Carroll County Review*, Thomson, Illinois on February 25, 1987 with the following editor's note.

"The following letter was written by Dr. Tadeusz Maciejczyk to the Clerk of the Court of Carroll County following his notification of a malpractice suit filed against him by Wilma Macchi. Another letter received from Dr. Maciejczyk answered the accusations of the suit point by point, but due to the length of the letter and limited space, it will not be printed. The letter indicates Maciejczyk's feeling that he is not guilty of negligence in Mrs. Macchi's case."

The World Seen from the Distance of a Small Village

Arliss Andresen
809 20th Avenue
Fulton, IL 61252

March 1, 1987

Dear Dr. Maciejczyk,

When Dad died in October, 1985, I was going to write you to thank you for the many good things you did for him while you were his doctor. I didn't. The thought occurred to me occasionally, but I never took the time. When I read your letter in the *Review* this week, I said, "I must write that note!" It must be a trying time, but don't give up.

I will never forget the day I stood in your office and you told me Dad didn't have much longer to live. I wouldn't believe it and he *did* live *much* longer, but I know, too, they *weren't* the most enjoyable years of his life. I'm sure your care had something to do with him living beyond your expectations.

Thanks again and I'm sorry I've been so long getting around to saying it to you.

                                      Sincerely,
                                      Arliss Andersen

Book Two

Dear Dr. Maciejczyk:

I wanted to drop you a few lines to let you know that I am behind you 100%. You are doing the right thing just as you did fighting the malpractice insurance. If more people would stand up for what is right this world would be a much better place to live. If there is anything that I can do as a friend, village trustee or any other capacity I would be very honored to help you.

I had the pleasure of meeting and visiting with your wife and daughter when she came over to Chadwick to take her drivers exam for her license. I can understand your anguish over this whole affair. I truly feel for all of you.

I also want to thank you for all the care and concern you had and your visit with Fay when he was at Good Samaritan Nursing Home. We did appreciate your concern.

I will close for now, but just wanted you to know how I feel, and as I stated before if there is anything I can do to help, I will be happy to.

Take care and God Bless all of you.

                        Your Friend
                        Jane Fossett

The World Seen from the Distance of a Small Village

Leida J. Gonzales
Staff Assistant to Alan J. Dixon, U.S.S.

I thank you for your very clear answer.

I want only to tell that I want help from the Senator not for myself. I can go to jail. Never I was there before and it is good to widen the life's experience.

What I want from the Senator is his attention to the problem of malpractice that is wrecking this country and is creating an atmosphere in which a feeling of suffocation and frustration on one side and cynicism and abuse on another are colliding more and more frequently, making the life uncertain and painful. Such an environment will dump the necessary enthusiasm and will multiply inner conflicts. It will drain the biggest asset and resource any nation can have: the faith of the people in a common cause and common destiny. Nothing stable can be built on an increasingly shaky ground. Such an inner illness of a nation will prepare an open road for the Soviets to come here more likely, than even the most faulty arms limitation treaty. How are we seen? How is this inside environment shaping us? In a letter that I received today from my wife's brother from Spain I read: "*Lastima que las actuaciones de un dirigente mundial como el Pres. Reagan aparezcan—desde aqui—tan poco limpias.*" (It is a pity that the activities of such world's leader, as President Reagan, are appearing from here so little clean.)

The laws that are permitting the judicial system to enact them in an irresponsible, abusive and selfish way were created by the legislation branch and they reached a pathological proportion during the time of Sen. Dixon's service in the Senate.

I am not asking Senator Dixon to help me. I am asking him to look into this whole problem and not to close his eyes because the lobby for malpractice is enormously powerful and can even break his career. I ask him to serve this country long range vital health and interest and not his present day advantage.

I am sorry that I disturbed the peace of mind of the Senator.

Tadeusz Maciejczyk, M.D.
Milledgeville, March 12, 1987

Book Two

The Daily Gazette
Sterling, Illinois

Editor:

Not long ago did you ask to write the reader's opinion about Governor Thomson's tax hike. In this matter I would like to ask you for a tabulation:

1. How many times during the campaign counting all proclamations did the Governor say that the taxes would not be raised?
2. How many times did he admit such a possibility?
3. How many times did he really contemplate an increase?

If Governor Thomson had been reelected because he was deceiving the people and simply lied to them, in such a situation he may become a living proof to some that in order to succeed in life, it is necessary to lie, to be dishonest and that by telling the truth, without being "clever," the road up is closed without opening.

By this action he also can become a living proof to others that it was once more and again confirmed, that all politicians are dirty liars and all the democratic process is not more than a farce and a joke done to those who still believed in it. Such a perception of democracy could make from its living tissue a dead phraseology as it happened to the communist ideology in Russia.

For this reason, this case of controversy should be clarified. If it would be apparent, if the opinion would prevail, that Governor Thomson was lying repeatedly to the people across the state, that he had no confidence in the people and that the people became distrustful of him—Governor Thomson should resign and the new election should be called. For the future of democracy, for the confidence in the democratic process and the people's whole-hearted commitment to it, it would be the best solution.

The worst enemies of democracy are those, who being in positions of importance, and holding power, are bad teachers to the people.
Tadeusz Maciejczyk, M.D.
Milledgeville, March 12, 1987

P.S. If you wish, I can give you one hundred signatures below this letter.

The World Seen from the Distance of a Small Village

March 7, 1987

Dear Dr. Maciejczyk,

I have read your letter in the *Carroll County Review* with deep concern. You have my sympathy in this stressful situation. I admire your courage and strength of purpose. I'm sure that you have some of the traits that the founding fathers of our Constitution had.

It is a shame that their intent of justice for all has been eroded. Hopefully the tide will turn.

Have you contacted Mr. Calvin Schueneman Of Sterling and Mr. Harlan Rigney of Hanover, who are representatives of your area? Even a copy of your letter to the *Carroll County Review* and Circuit Court would arouse their interest to sponsor a bill in the state. Perhaps Lynn Martin might be contacted on the national level. A bill addressing this situation would generate much interest. I've enclosed clippings of what has been done in Missouri to amend this serious problem.

I intend to write my Congressman and Senator on the national level using a copy of your letter to get their interest in amending this unjust situation.

                                          Sincerely,

                                          Mrs. Ervin (Alberta) Loos
                                          P.S. Enclosed Dec. *Reader's Digest* article.

Book Two

Madeleine Edmondson
Office of Editor of *Newsweek*

    I thank you for your letter. It has no dating. I presume that it refers to my malpractice problem. I agree and I understand that you cannot help me directly.
    But this my problem is also a serious problem of this country and in this sense it should be an object of a study and scrutiny, not at one time, but periodically because malpractice malady is a very dynamic process; it is relatively recent and its consequences are only in the appearance stage. This malady is changing the present, but it is also projecting a big shadow on the future. The field of malpractice is enormous; the effects are complex, not always easy to be seen, reaching even the deep layers of life.
    My case is a testimony of how lightly, how frivolously it is used. My letter about the issue of malpractice was printed in the Carroll County Review and I observed that the people were very receptive, very sensitive to this problem.
    I send you my two last letters.
    I hope they would be interesting to the editor.

                          Sincerely,
                          Tadeusz Maciejczyk, M.D.
                          Milledgeville, March 19, 1987

My Evaluation of the "Balanced Budget/Tax Limitation Amendment"

I received your invitation to take part in a massive petition to the President and to congress to make a passage of the "Balanced Budget/Tax Limitation Amendment." It presented a puzzle to my mind and I do not know how to resolve it logically. However, I am trying to understand its meaning, I am coming to a conclusion that it is nothing else but one more act of deceiving ourselves. It looks to me as another gesture done with a specific purpose to change nothing in the substance of our reality, but to create an impression that we are acting, fighting, correcting. Please, correct me if I am wrong.

In this strange situation, the President and many of our leaders are repeating that we are on the "threshold of an unprecedented prosperity" and we do not like to lose privileges that come from looking the scene of our life from this point of view. We also know that the shadow of the enormous debt created to fuel this "prosperity" is getting bigger each day and we are approaching the precipice. But, I was told that the Congress voted salary increases for themselves. So did our Governor. Bureaucracy and paperwork is getting suffocating. Euphoria is not disturbed. Very few are looking for a true remedy, for a full acknowledgement of reality and for some austerity program. Instead, we are making a gesture. We are demanding a new amendment that is supposed to solve all those problems by a magic force and without any hardship to us.

In this situation of double talk and a subcutaneous feeling of being in a false spot, we are harvesting from the decades of a special training to which our society got to be used to. We select mostly those candidates who are full of promises. We know that they are lying. How many times I heard such a crude description of their campaign love songs. But nevertheless, one time after another, we fall into the same trap. We vote for them. It would be very interesting to make a good study of this phenomenon.

There is something basically wrong in our campaign system. Our campaigns generally are not clarifying the issues. They are creating a chaos in which nobody can see clearly.

Each time, or maybe each time more, our costly campaigns are filled with misinformation, disinformation, distortions, flattening of issues, proliferation of slogans—and after all this expensive orgy, we are approaching the voting places still in the dark, voting for our illusion, blindly following a group or party or even marking a name that sounds to us nicer.

Maybe it would be much better to organize those campaigns and its spending in a different way.

A central body of judges and biographers would make an initial, official book of candidates from national, down to more local levels that could be reprinted by all newspapers. On the basis of those descriptions, during campaigns, these candidates would build their images, correcting or completing its statements. At the end of the campaigns, the same group of official body of judges and biographers would present changes of their initial information about candidates produced by campaigns, drafting the final characteristic of each of them. The candidates could have the last word to the public in the last stage.

Such an arrangement could be much less costly and more informative. It would put into an orderly frame the present chaos, decrease abuses of campaigns, force the candidates to speak more concretely, stimulate the public, activate interest, increase the questions from the people and by this make the campaigning more lively without enormously boring repetitions of the same slogans over and over again. Such a campaign would present better to the electorate the problems, the directions and the needs of the time.

As for the present, earnestly, I do not feel in the mood to write or to sign a petition for the "Balanced Budget/Tax Limitation Amendment." Making a theater where the life should be real is not my inclination.

I hope that we will take steps to put our feet in a real world without empty gestures and without escaping from true responsibilities. And I hope that we would start to build our future and a future of our children on such a basis.

Tadeusz Maciejczyk
Milledgeville, March 26, 1987

Meg Greenfield
(My comment to "The Political Debt Bomb," *Newsweek,* April 6, 1987)

Dear Ms. Greenfield:

In conclusion of this article you are formulating a number of statements:

The World Seen from the Distance of a Small Village

1. We have developed a presidential-nomination system that is programmed for inefficiency and waste.
2. The ability to raise money is often much too important a factor in the final success or failure.
3. The present way of doing those things is "nuts" and should be reformed.

The main danger of this situation is not as much its financial consequence. The real danger is the devastation it is producing to many people in their approach to life's problems, to its moral rules and their relation to democracy, which we are supposed to be the main bearer of in the world. Our elections are teaching a very visible and very convincing lesson to our population and to everybody else. It is important to teach this lesson well because it will have inevitable repercussions.

I am sending you my two last letters. Both of them are dealing with the election problems. One of those letters I sent to the local newspaper, but as always, it was not printed.
If you would read them, I would like to have your opinion, your impression about the remedies that I was proposing.
My best wishes in your work, which I consider is very important. And I think that you are doing it well.

Sincerely,

Tadeusz Maciejczyk
Milledgeville, April 3, 1987

April 5, 1987

Dear Dr. Maciejczyk:

We want you to know that you are in our thoughts and prayers as you pursue these problems in court that have fallen upon you. Altho' we cannot and do not know all of the details, only having read the accounts in the newspapers, we do know that our faith and trust in you definitely assures us of your innocents. We also trust the Lord that truth will prevail.

Book Two

I know that you have definite connections Dr. Maciejczyk, and certainly admire you for them.

Sincerely,

Phillis and Russell Wagenknecht

Medicare B
Office of Complaints of the Personal

Again I am discouraged and bitter.
On one side I am pressed to participate in your program. Periodically I receive warnings of what would happen if I would not. In return you are practicing a continuous, merciless and premeditated robbery of what I rightfully earned with my work. This is supposed to be a service aiming towards a solution for the health of the elderly and a social justice.

But, all my life I was trying to be just to all my patients. I saw they were human beings in need of help. I understood my profession not as a business, but as a mission. I never abused anybody by charging too much. I would be most happy if I could not charge at all.

Nevertheless, I have to life, to keep my office functioning and to provide for my family. The balance, which I archived between this my mission and my needs, became strained by your policies. My income went down. Last year for the first time I was unable to save money for the IRA deposit. My youngest daughter soon will go to the university and I do not know how I can pay the tuition in the present circumstances.

And so, here I am. At 63, after so many years in practice, I have no savings, no retirement, no coverage for a moment if I became disabled.

Previously I was not thinking about those problems. I was happy. While working, I felt entertained and fulfilled. I felt a need to give myself.

Your intrusion made me fill the bitterness of the exploited. I started to feel like somebody, who is kept in bondage by a huge invisible, deaf force. I have nothing to tell, when my small, never excessive charges are reduced or not approved at all, and then still diminished by a discount. I cannot ask the patient to pay if something was not approved by you. This is a newly-defined, punishable crime. An urgent house call at night was not approved by your justice or savings-minded wisdom. So there were many other services. My nurse, who is in charge of dealing with you, told me that lately those non-approvals and reductions became more frequent.

In this abnormal situation of exploitation, I have no clear way to fight for my rights because in this "free, democratic society" not one of my letters to you was responded to and letters sent to other instances produced only vague promises that those my observations and complaints would be kept in mind for the future occasions. For now, the rigid and cold bureaucracy is continuing its dictatorship. I didn't observe that the supposed-to-be beneficiary—the old people—are happy with its reign.

A work can be done with joy and in this way it is bringing life and vitality. It stimulates the drive for excellence. The same work can be done under the whip. It will come out shabby and in the worker will create a feeling of being denigrated and exploited. Such a condition will create in him dissatisfaction and tension that in time can degenerate into hate. If our dealings with other nations, which in one way or another depends on us, is conducted with similar "skillfulness" and intuition, it is a small wonder that America is losing the battle for the hearts of the people of the world in spite of their natural sympathy and that the atmosphere in the United Nations is as it is. True leadership is the art of showing the objectives, finding out the way toward them and lifting the spirits and the wills even in the circumstances of gloom. A squeezing out to the point of destroying of everything that starves to be independent, by a cold bureaucratic system with computerized rules, will not lead this country to greatness.

In your letters and directives, I was told that the basis for your payment evaluations is the national or regional averages for given services. Clearly, I am evaluated below the average and in this letter I ask you to correct this injustice.

I ask you to send me information about average payments to doctors for the work I am doing. If I participate, I should have the right to be informed and to be treated without perpetuated discrimination just, because to start, I was not smart enough and I kept my fees low. I can take the limitations imposed by hard times, but only if they are distributed justly.

What I am asking in this letter is just a justice.

> Tadeusz Maciejczyk, M.D.
> Milledgeville, May 3, 1987

Book Two

Medical Economics - Editor

Your article, "Malpractice Suits Are a Family Affair," was for me like a confirmation of my own experiences. An accusation, even as groundless as the one against me is producing suffering and trauma. This its aspect should be emphasized and should be dealt with all seriousness. I understand the need to bring to justice the negligence or the actions with the malicious purposes. The frivolous suits have nothing to do with justice. They are like a highway assault with a gun to get money. The only difference is in the nature of the gun.

In dealing with my problem, I did not ask a lawyer to defend me. It looks to me that they play a ping-pong game. One lawyer is giving the other occasion to get a big premium and he expects a return of such a favor. This chain should be somehow broken.

And also, the lawyer of the frivolous suit should know that he can pay a price for his careless jumping around. The philosophy that I should try because anyway I can lose nothing, should be stopped. I do not blame the victims. The emotional or mental state can explain their readiness or agreement to the suit. The lawyer has a special training and should use his judgment carefully. The first obligation for them should be the same as for the doctors: do not harm needlessly.

Also, I consider that the problem of malpractice became ripe enough, produced enough pain and tears in this country, produced enough emotional and economical damage to be finally taken into consideration by the Supreme Court. This modern version of the "wild west" in the judicial field, should be brought to its true proportions.

I send you the copies of my two letters to the Court Clerk. I would be grateful if you would give me your advice in how to proceed with this, my personal problem, to use it as an instrument to correct the whole issue of malpractice.

If you are not tired of me, I should send you the copies of my letters to Medicare B.

Again, I thank you for your article.

Tadeusz Maciejczyk, M.D.
Milledgeville, May 7, 1987

The World Seen from the Distance of a Small Village

B. Lee Wilson
Internal Revenue Service

Your letter, with the news of federal tax deposit penalty is still puzzling me and your second letter didn't clear the reasons or give me any hint how to handle this problem in the future.

I went to the bank where until now I was making my tax deposits, and they gave me photocopies of corresponding papers. They also scratched their heads and wondered.

In general, the life in the U.S. is getting more and more frightening. Stable values and norms are collapsing. New complicated forms are appearing every day. The trust into our suppose-to-be-leaders is vanishing under the heavy bombardment of scandals appearing in front pages of every newspaper. In Illinois, we have a governor who was elected not in a clean contest, but because he had no restraint whatsoever to lie shamelessly and persistently. The taxation authorities are looking for any pretext to scratch some extra money to improve the deficit that anyway cannot be repaired this way. The people with whom I speak look to the future with gloom. Under all those blows, without anybody to stand up and really lead, the spirit of enterprise, which gave the U.S. its strength in the past, is moribund. People are looking for some easy shortcuts, for a lottery or suit luck, maybe for some kind of shelter or for dependence and stagnation. I do not see a leader who would inspire them. Those, who call themselves the "leaders" are not more than political manipulators with a selfish, myopic vision, just until the next election. I was trying to analyze them. I have my hope that Paul Simon is different.

Last week I read in our local newspaper, *The Daily Gazette*, a thought for today. It was telling: "The more corrupt the state, the more numerous the laws." It was told by Tacitus, Roman senator and historian who lived between 56 and 115 A.D.

Because of the special skepticism and distrust with which I am looking for this extra help that the IRS is doing now for the government, maybe it would be appropriate to tell the story from the past that was also about an extra taxation for a special purpose. To some extent, it touched the life in the U.S.

About 100 years ago, German Chancellor Bismark decided that it was unthinkable that in one hour ride east from Berlin, people didn't speak and frequently didn't understand German. The remedy he invented was effective. New laws were created, frequently conflicting. Whatever people were doing—a watching policemen was writing them a penalty. Soon a situation was formed in which they were approached by the authorities telling them that what they had was not enough to pay that penalty. Nevertheless, the authorities were merciful. They didn't put them in jail. They gave them free tickets in cattle wagons to Hamburg then they packed them to the bottoms of the ships and sent them to America. This way, those simple men, knowing only Polish, without education, because the schools were in German language, without any familiarity with life other than the remote village life, were left in New York on the streets without any help. Maybe in addition, behind them the "Polish jokes" were spread. For the conscience of the executors of that plan apparently it was easier if everybody could see that those their victims were nothing more but imbeciles. And, whatever can be told about that fragment of history, nobody can deny that it was done in a perfectly legal manner.

I do not know how to judge your penalty now. I would like to understand the reasons. Technicalities can be manipulated and tend to be artificial, frequently with bad intentions. I want to understand what I did wrong to merit a punishment and ask that it be explained to me. Otherwise, such punishment will leave me only with the bitter taste and a feeling that I am submerged each time more in a dirty water that suffocates the life.

Tadeusz Maciejczyk, M.D.
Milledgeville, IL May 31, 1987

P.S. I know that if I would be smart, I would keep my mouth shut and I would hold my thoughts to myself as many do. But I feel that I have an obligation to a true democracy to speak clearly, because democracy is made from a very delicate substance that spoils easily and can for long time cover its stench with perfumes and with an appropriate cover. The old story of the naked king tends constantly to get a new life.

The World Seen from the Distance of a Small Village

Robert Dole
Senator of the United States

Dear Sir:

I found the questions in your "Urgent Issues Survey" interesting and worthy of an effort to be answered as accurately as possible.

In beginning I want to make clear that I do not consider you as my candidate for Presidency. I recognize you as a very gifted senator and mediator. Here is your talent that you have an obligation to use for a common good. I do not see in you the material for a lonely post at the top. There the talents have to be different. Such a post should not be considered as a coronation of other successes in the political career or to fulfill somebody's ambitious ego. The leadership qualities required for presidency have a completely different nature. Service in Congress gives only a marginal preparation for such a job. Even as I see this, too long a stay in Congress can hamper the ability to be a good, creative leader in the White House and to preserve open vision on the nation's and humanity's destiny and a personal strength to raise the wills and morally mobilize the people to co-labor in a big task of shaping the future.

Question 1. Do you think America's federal budget deficit threatens our economic stability?

Answer: Absolutely, yes. Nobody who is distracted and limited by such an enormous debt can be economically stable. This is especially true if the reality of such a burden is consciously downgraded and, as much as possible hidden from the public's attention.

Considering this enormous debt, presidential proposal for the substantial increase of the salaries for the Congress was more than irresponsible. It looked like a bribery temptation by the President that was accepted by the Congress. It gave no good image either to the President, nor to the Congress, especially in the eyes of those from here around, who were asked to renounce part of their paycheck in order to preserve their jobs. Everybody else, as I know, was looking this congressional show with a feeling of frustration. To the average man from here, it was obvious that the present Congress lost the contact with those whom they represent and the comprehension of their struggles and emotions. They put themselves above them.

If behind this temptation and its acceptance was a philosophy that the posts for the public service should have the monetary power to attract the most able from the candidates, then even a very superficial look on the last year's stories tells that such a selection gives no guarantee. Those men frequently use the public office as a best arena to attract the attention of the potential highest bidders for their brains. The society would be much better if those posts would go to the more modest who prize themselves less, but who keep in their hearts a love and a need to serve, to fulfill their lives in a mission to the nation, to humanity and to God.

Question 2: Can America's trade deficit be solved without protectionist legislation?

Answer: I have no clear answer to this question. The reality is that the world is aiming to a global, economical integrity. Building now the walls of protectionism would delay this process, would anger and embitter many, would be used by others who always wait for any discord to take advantage. It would not change the direction of life.

It would be much wiser to create ways for an orderly progress into this global integrity, already now building structures and institutions that would facilitate cooperation and prevent abuses and frictions. Such a work now even could be counted as building fundamentals for a safer and more peaceful world in the future.

On the other side, America should not be a dumping place for indiscriminate foreign production. If any foreign industry is helped by its government with the tax money to export cheaper, it should be calculated and taxed at the entrance to the U.S.

Question 3: Has President Reagan's Strategic Defense Initiative forced the Soviet Union to come back to the bargaining table?

Answer: yes, but without a victory for the U.S.

Reagan's S.D.I. neutralized to a high degree the Soviet game of Soviet threats and intimidation. It unveiled long known Soviet weaknesses. It brought a relief, but also new anxieties to the West. It forced the Soviets to a change of tactics, not of the essence of their policies.

Maybe it helped to bring to power the charismatic Gorbachev more suited for the new tactics.

In the same time, the Chernobyl disaster made the nuclear arms less attractive even to Soviet bosses. It showed clearly what a nuclear victory would be even for the victors and those who would survive. Reagan's S.D.I. also exacerbated in the Soviet high circles the feeling of lagging behind in economy and in necessary technology.

In this sense, the S.D.I. brought the Soviets to the bargaining table. But they came there not in a defeated mood, but in the mood of looking at America and at the West and calculating how much they could gain for themselves from such a turning point of the situation.

The World Seen from the Distance of a Small Village

From beginning of this phase, they bombarded the world with propositions, stressing their good will and the U.S. obstinacy and gradually they produced a feeling that they are the hope for the conflicting world—not the U.S. I had the impression that when Gorbachev was speaking (not Reagan) the world was listening, was interpreting each of his expressions, giving him credit of hope and even trust and a readiness to help him one way or another, just to fortify those magnificent prospects. In the depth of the S.D.I. defeat, the Soviets were winning in a field much more important than the military. Somehow they became the champions of peace. Below this winning surface, the Soviets were doing not one step back in their march toward global domination. Still more extensively than before, they were building their subterranean structures, reaching the territories where they never tried before. In spite of all evidence, their bankrupt ideology somehow survived and continues to be a central element and tool for the Soviets to penetrate and conquer.

In the meantime, on our side, during all the years of Reagan in power, the U.S. did nothing to promote true democracy, except defending or bending the local rulers to be on our side in the alliance. Nothing was done to help the local, native democratic seeds and tendencies to grow into a healthy democratic system. During all those years, Reagan gave the world not one stimulating idea for human growth, for humankind. His policy was a policy of reacting to Soviet moves or intentions. He never had a plan for independent, conscious and long-range creative building of the world's human bounds that in this way would grow with time into a new, better future for everybody. He never formulated any civil, social, cooperative long-range program for Central America, for the MidEast, for Africa or for any place. He never presented to America or to the world a vision of the future for which it would be so wonderful to dedicate life's effort. Somehow, below the surface of our lives here in the U.S., the feeling of emptiness of shallowness, of living for today, is more and more distressing. WE are not looking into an exciting tomorrow. The scandals, cropping from the most unexpected sides, are tips of the iceberg, the extreme visualization of this inside emptiness. It is sad to observe that when Reagan speaks now, nobody listens; nobody takes him too seriously. Not long ago, I received a letter from a friend of mine in Spain, a lifetime friend of America. He was writing: "It is a pity that the actions of such a world's leader as president Reagan is appearing—from here—so very little clean."

The emptiness that Reagan's America brought to the world made that the Reagan S.D.I. ultimately gave no victory for us and in the present world, rewarded the Soviets with bigger acceptance and a bigger role in

Book Two

the world's destiny. With America's prestige at the lowest level in a long time, we have very little moral strength.

In this sense the bringing of the Soviets to the bargaining table was not more, but a hollow victory.

Question 4: Should the President have the useful power of a "Line Item Veto?"

Answer: yes, it looks completely logical to me.

Tadeusz Maciejczyk, M.D.
Milledgeville, June 14, 1987

P.S. Because your questions were so timely, I sent the copies of this letter to other candidates and to newspapers.

The World Seen from the Distance of a Small Village

To Forgive or Not Forgive?

The Papal audience for Austrian President Kurt Waldheim provoked strong Jewish reaction and a world controversy. Was it appropriate? Was it wise? Was it justified?

The audience was called irresponsible. It produced Jewish anger and indignation, embellished by remarks about the Vatican's spotty record in opposing fascism and about the legacy of anti-Semitism in the Polish church. The frequently expressed Jewish "anti-Polonism" (anti-Polish) gives them apparently a necessary emotional outlet. Who cares what this "legacy in the Polish church" was? I have no idea what they have in mind. Obviously, it was intended to make the Pope feel uneasy and guilty. It was the same pressure instrument that was used during the Jewish invasion of Lebanon when voices were appearing about rising anti-Semitism in America.

In order to force a recall of this papal audience, threats were used. The Jewish leaders would boycott the meeting with the Pope here in America. Protestors in concentration camp uniforms appeared on St. Peter's Square. A concession was expressed that the reaction to the audience would be mitigated if President Waldheim would at least publicly deplore his past. Otherwise, the irresponsible gesture of forgiveness by the pope would carry unwelcomed consequences.

Who is right? How should we act to push the future of the world in the right direction?

If the calculations are right, that Abraham lived in Babylon during the time of Hammburabi before he left for his big journey to the Promised Land, then the Jewish eye-for-an-eye policy could be traced to the Hammburabi Code. One thousand years later, during the Babylonian captivity, the Talmudic code of the Jews was written and brought to Jerusalem after their liberation. On the Jewish ground, this code acquired a pharisaic style of relating to God, to their countrymen and to other people.

Today, after so many years of experience, Jews did not change their views on justice. The eye-for-an-eye policy is shaping their policy to their neighbors. They are unanimous in unforgiveness, in a permanent, frozen dwelling in the painful past and in using this past as a kind of weapon, as an arm-twister, even as a sort of blackmail to press others to be in agreement with them and with whatever they do.

But, we are Christians and Christ did not teach us to be just in accordance to the Hammburabi code, or to the Talmudic norms. He was stressing something completely opposite. He taught forgiveness. He was speaking about forgiveness in the prodigal son parable. He showed its practical application when confronted with the angry crowd, ready to stone a woman caught in adultery and He elevated forgiveness to the maximum human virtue in one of His last acts, when He assured the criminal hanging on His side, that still the same day he would be with Him in paradise.

He forgave and He never asked anybody who was forgiven to deplore publicly their past. Generally, the deepest transformation produced by forgiveness occurs in a silent, inner self-search, as it happened to Mary Magdalene. The exteriorization of the fruit of forgiveness comes later, not especially in the form of a spectacle.

The older I get, the more of human life I see, the more I value those quiet acts to forgive. Forgiveness clears the mind. It gives a lasting relief from anxiety. It helps free our inner and our public life and in this way it is creative and fruitful.

On the contrary, strong, unforgiving postures are not the mark of greatness or heroism. Unforgiveness dwells in the shadow of fear and weakness, of unwillingness for self-examination or generosity. Yet, unforgiveness attracts. It dresses itself in splendid robes to hide the despair inside, but it closes the horizons. It pretends to stop the time and a normal evolution of emotions and feelings in humans.

I think that the Jews and the Israeli state would be much more secure if they would help to create a forgiving world. Nobody can be forced to true repentance and change by making him a pariah. This would be the best way to create monsters, smiling when forced to smile and waiting for an occasion. We all know this from history.

I do not know what were the motivations of the Pope to grant Mr. Waldheim an audience. I only feel that the present world needs a spirit of forgiveness more than at any time in the past. And also, I feel that it was more appropriate for the Christian religious leader to initiate this move. In this field, every one of us can contribute because we all have our conflicts.

And, if the Jewish leaders are threatening with reprisals and vengeance, maybe it indicates that the talk with them would have very little depth and sincerity anyway.

Tadeusz Maciejczyk., M.D.

Also an *Untermensch* (Nazi concept of an "inferior man") during the time of war and madness

Milledgeville, July 1, 1987

The World Seen from the Distance of a Small Village

Internal Revenue Service

I received a second penalty in less than one month for failure to made deposits for 941 in the presently required terms. What previously was normal, now is punishable. How many more penalties will I receive?

I am bitter. I am very bitter and dispirited. If I could, I would like to apply for any monthly paid job, because America, without hesitation, is preparing a grave for small enterprise and for those, who until now were trying to be independent. In the last few years, one blow comes after another. How long can I still fight them without collapsing? I am getting tired.

I spent the night without sleep, caught by anxiety. My small solo practice in the countryside, where I was thinking that I was needed, cannot bear more burdens. The Medicaid never paid much and now is not paying. The government payments for Medicare are out of my control. They are delayed, diminished, discounted or completely denied. I do not understand the logic in their assessments. A house call to a dying man, after midnight and over two hours long, was rejected and not paid at all. Under the present law, I couldn't ask the family to pay those thirty dollars. It would be considered a crime. It could tarnish the government's smile to the patients. And it is only one of the flowers in the garden of America planted by the current lawmakers. And all this is aggravated by an amount of paperwork that is not easy to keep up with.

In this situation, frequently, I have no ready money to meet my payments. I pray, and somehow, frequently in the last moments, a miracle happens. But it is nerve wracking. To pay the 941 deposits, previously I had a certain flexibility in time. Now, with the imposed rigidity and frequency of terms, I cannot cope. I am not used to borrowing money and I will not go to rob a bank. But, the government is more hungry each day and it is merciless.

Why struggle? America is not America any more. America became a paradise for bureaucracy, for big businesses that can buy their way out, for different types of Bakkers and for the people with the spirit of dependence, but not for independent working men.

A few months ago, I received a letter from Rep. Lynn Martin, in which she told me that the small enterprises are an asset and the biggest potential providers of the additional jobs in America. This statement sounded to me like a painful joke. America under this government is not thinking about tomorrow. It is using all its imagination to look well today. And it never was brave enough to be sincere and open with the people. And so, it is painting with bright colors something as ugly as a public sale out of the nation's assets and calling this a "privatization." It poses hidden taxation; it arranges an Iranian deal; it produces enormous debt and in the same time it gives themselves large increases of salaries. Tomorrow? Tomorrow will be somebody else's headache. This government is devaluating this country economically, but also it squanders away its moral prestige, it's prestige as a symbol and its prestige as a hope for the world.

I do not blame the IRS. The IRS has to do what the government and Congress decide and they live in their artificial and closed world and are lacking any big breaking idea for leadership. Their ideal is just to be popular today.

In this letter, I want to ask the IRS for one favor. You have to calculate the amount of my penalty anyway, so please put this entire process on the paper that you send to me: how you arrived at the original amount and how much it was, then how much it increased by adding a percentage to this original sum to make the final amount. I should have the right to know all the details of my punishment. Even a criminal is present at his trial, instead of receiving a final sentence with the back page general explanation. Without this complete information, I can have more doubts about its fairness.

I have to tell you also that I am unable at the present time to make the 941 deposit for the last quarter as the present law requires. I will do this as soon as I can, anyway, before the end of this month as I was doing for year. The time is slow now in the office and I have no reserves.

So, if you have to, you will punish me again. My wife is worrying that you can take our home and put us on the street. You have the power. What can I do? I write this letter of protest against the people's advice. They consider that to talk to you is a waste of time. I can only tell you that I will pay as soon as I can.

In a way, I am rebellious, but I am an American patriot. I have my own vision of the mission America has in the world. But your pressure and squeeze I see as a kind of American edition of the Soviet Gulag for a crime of trying to remain independent and for trying to keep my prices for patient's visits as low as possible.

I will try to preserve my independence as long as it is possible in this country today.

Sincerely,

Tadeusz Maciejczyk, M.D.
Milledgeville, July 12, 1987

The World Seen from the Distance of a Small Village

Robert H. Harner, M.D.
President of the
Swedish American Hospital Medical Staff

Dear Dr. R.H. Harner:

I thank you sincerely for your interest and persistence in looking into my case of malpractice, for reading through all my arguments and even looking for help for me, contacting especially your lawyer-friend. Not even my closest friends did as much for me.

Regarding my pending malpractice suit, I realize the danger. I will be in there in the courtroom in a place never tested by me. There I will face a man trained in legal argumentation and there I will feel alone.

Nevertheless, I will go there to face him and the situation. Now, in the same way as before, I feel that I was not accused, but assaulted and that what is against me is not a search for justice, but a disrespect and disregard for even the fundamentals of justice. To me, this trial looks like a modern-time highway piracy by somebody who used his school training in place of a gun, but because of this, in the same way, or even more, he is destructive to society. If he succeeds, no person will be safe and the law will serve only as a fig leaf to serve their tyranny.

The opinion of your lawyer friend didn't help my apprehension. It only gave me a feeling that I was chosen as a kind of toy or sucker in the lawyer's game called "justice." In this game one attorney accuses somebody, gives an opportunity for other attorneys to defend and expects him to accuse somebody else to return the favor. It is a very profitable game. In this game also, of course, the defendant's attorney has to be "most excellent." It is a beautiful and useful term. It permits there to be no limit for charges. It is an excellent money-squeezing instrument. It also gives a kind of justification and a social tolerance for even the most absurd accusations. The accusation had to have something if it requires such an excellence for defense. But, it serves, and it elevates, not the justice, but a "justice game."

Because of this, I think that it would be morally wrong for me to support such a game. Your attorney-friend somehow denigrated in my eyes his whole profession. I am sorry, because my father in law, whom I respected very much, was a lawyer.

A long time ago, during the occupation, I was given an assignment that from all the evidence looked like a certain trap and I was afraid. In that situation, I prayed. I went to confession and communion and I did what I was supposed to do. I will go into this trial with the same spirit. I do not give the accusing party much more moral value than I gave the

Book Two

Nazi occupants. In this confrontation, I do not intend to hide behind somebody—whom, especially after your friend's opinion, I can suspect to be a co-profiteer in the big nationwide game of lawyers.

I do not know what will happen to me. I am ready to go to jail. I would go there with my head high. I always felt that I was like a soldier in a big battle for a better world. Probably I will be such a "Don Quixote" until the last day of my life. And probably I will not regret to be so impractical or maybe even so stupid.

Also, I want to tell that whatever will be the result of my present troubles, I see in them a painful experience, but not a punishment. They are for me like one more lesson in the school of life. I do not know. Maybe it is a necessary preparation for something that is still ahead of me. Really, it gave me an occasion to see many things with a completely new eye.

When the time comes, I will notify you about the day of my trial. Maybe then I would see you and thank you personally for your help. For that occasion, I would like to invite to the courtroom everybody who would like to carry on the fight for a true justice, a condemnation of a "justice game," and a clear presentation of the consequences of such a game to all the society.

Sincerely,

Tadeusz Maciejczyk, M.D.
Milledgeville, July 30, 1987

P.S. This is my situation and my problem to resolve. But, because of its epidemic spread, it is also a serious national illness.

The time is coming when it will be more and more urgent to make a detailed inventory of the consequences of this a "Wild West "edition of justice that without any control from above, lost all its limits for greed and has no more place for an old time conscience or common sense.

The inventory of the consequences of malpractice frenzy should take into account all its aspects: economic, jobs, moral, ethics, distrust among people, an apprehension, passivism, dependence, slow death of the American spirit of independence and enterprise, etc.

And, of course, this should be balanced against the idealistic, positive principles of malpractice.

Tadeusz Maciejczyk, M.D.

The World Seen from the Distance of a Small Village

Walt Disney Production Office
Director of the new projects evaluations
Hollywood, California

Dear Sir:

I am writing this letter because yesterday, in my office, while doing a check-up for two 5th grade twin brothers and talking with them, I told them the story from my childhood.

The story was about a book that I read when I was probably ten years old. One time, late at night, when I was still reading, my father came and put the light down telling me that it was time to rest.

But I couldn't sleep. I was thinking about the adventure of the two twin brothers who felt badly at home with their widowed mother and they decided to escape into the big unknown world. Their adventures in that world was a fantasy reaching very deep into the imagination of a ten year old boy. In spite of the effort, I couldn't sleep. Finally, when I felt that everybody else at home was in a deep sleep, I got up and went outside. Standing below the street lamp, I continued my reading.

The book's Polish name was "*O dwoch co ukradli ksiezyc,*" that means "About two who stole the moon" and it was written by Kornel Makuszynski.

While telling that story to my young patients, it came to me that I should tell you about that book. You have the talent, the power and the capacity to make from the story of that book a real gift to the children of America and to the children of the world. Probably it would be as interesting to them as it was to me, because the story is timeless in character, is very human and can be understood in every culture. That story would teach and its influence would be good. It could direct children's fantasies, preparing them in a very special way to enter years later into the world of adults.

I do not know how to send this letter, even I do not know whether such an office exists, but I would like to let you know about that my story and about that book.

Sincerely,

Tadeusz Maciejczyk, M.D.
Milledgeville, August 6, 1987

Book Two

Chief Justice of the Supreme Court of the United States

Dear Sir:

I have a problem with many aspects: economic, justice, ethics, moral that gives me a feeling of frustration and of hopelessness. This problem is not only mine. It has a capacity to be not only damaging, but even destructive to the whole society. I hope that you will take it seriously and help.

My problem: My premium for malpractice insurance increased more than twice since last year (almost ten times since the Fall of 1985) and this time it was given to me only for six months; its end hanging in an uncertainty.

I cannot afford this rise, nor this uncertainty. No institution can develop in a healthy way on such a foundation. My income last year dropped to $32,000 and I have still one daughter who should go to university soon. The education is the only thing that I can give her for life.

In this situation and feeling no protection from any authorities that apparently prefer to look the other way, while the orgy of malpractice litigations is destroying the economy and the character of the people of this nation, I have questions, and I need answers for them from you.

What should I do in my situation?

1. Should I squeeze the people who are already frequently poor in order to collect the requested additional tribute to the insurance company?
2. Should I refuse to pay this insurance and consequently be excluded from an access to hospitals for those patients who consider me their doctor?
3. Should I expect and require that Medicare, which controls payments to me and to the hospitals for a substantial number of patients, bear also a part of the burden of the malpractice cost because, in a sense, it is both my and the hospitals' employer?
4. Should I expect from the Supreme Court to put finally some order in a completely wild field of malpractice suits that terrorize and immobilize many of the initiatives of this nation?

Should the Supreme Court finally break its silence in a subject as hot as the malpractice is? And should the Supreme Court firmly establish what is the fundamental element of malpractice at which point a punishable malpractice begins and which is the decisive element that is making a change and without which there is not guilt?

During last year, my conscience and my sense of decency had been violated. I was forced to collect even bigger amounts of money from my patients in order to feed the beast that anyway never will be satisfied until it sucks out the last drop of blood from its direct and indirect victims. By not complying, without an access to hospitals, my service to people would be mutilated. But a person who day-by-day violates his conscience and his convictions, even if he gets rich and important, he will be a weak and unhappy person inside of himself. Are we going to create a nation with such a soul? This is supposed to be a country that in the past was proud to free the people from tyranny and to be a bearer of freedom, giving a hope to the oppressed of the world. But we created, we tolerate and we pretend not to see the terror born here from the greed of some and organized into a seemingly unbreakable ring by those who by education should be protectors and guardians of the true law. They organized their terror well and they carefully closed all doors for escape. They were trained in law.

All terror is getting fat and bold when the people are losing hope and confidence in any other alternative, in their leadership. In the days of the pre-Hitlerian Germany, the people pretended not to see and not to hear when somebody was violated and was screaming for help. It was easier to survive this way. And for some it was a signal and an opportunity to get rich and important. In some way this country is getting to this point. A terror is on the rise. Everybody feels it and everybody is trying to survive, or even to get from it a profit. We live today. Tomorrow???

My work hangs in uncertainty. What will be after those six months even if I agree to squeeze the people more and I pay the beast? The government, the judiciary, the legislature give an impression that for them this problem is not existing. I heard from some that they are well paid off. I do not know. But the economic marasmus in which we are sinking will not improve if the climate for independent work and enterprise will not get free from an indiscriminate terror of the malpractice axe that swings without any kind of restraint.

I heard from many places that many people who need attention are not going to the doctor because they are squeezed out to pay for malpractice insurance costs and to compensate for the Medicare cuts and refusals. The selfishness and the greed are omnipotent. I wonder whether here, in this country, the government is really for the people as I was learning from the textbooks. If it was true long ago, it would be worth all the effort to bring it back to life.

The tyranny has many forms. In Russia it is a political doctrine and a requirement for a blind physical and moral obedience. In America, apparently, it is an unrestrained abuse and exploitation not as much by hoodlums as by those, who by education, should be the guardians of the true law.

Maybe the Ayatollah Khomeni's stress on returning to fundamentals has some sense, if it would be not for his cruelty and hate. Also the Christian churches are calling for a spiritual renewal. An unrestrained world with the decreased sense of what is moral is living just for today and is leading us into a very dark and fearsome tomorrow. It is a time to strive to make a change.

Can I expect any answer and any action from you?

Tadeusz Maciejczyk, M.D.
Milledgeville, August 9, 1987

The World Seen from the Distance of a Small Village

Senator R. Dole,

As I told, I sent you the copies of my letters that are dealing with the problems of some importance for the campaign. They represent different views the views of an outsider, who in his very limited way is fighting for a better America because he believes that America has a destiny to bring the world to safety.

But such a destiny requires more than military force, technical superiority, diplomatic skills and capital. Above all, it will require spiritual ability that could inspire the people of the world.

If America loses this quality and it seems America does, no material power will save us from internal corrosion by greed and selfishness and ultimately by the exterior forces.

I would like for America a leadership that would take the spiritual heritage of this country seriously as a principal material and weapon to build a better world.

Tadeusz Maciejczyk
August 19, 1987

Book Two

St. Paul Fire and Marine Insurance Company
Chicago Service Center

General Manager

Dear Sir:

I wanted to write this letter to Mr. Jost, but after looking over your "Physicians' and Surgeons' Update," I decided to write directly to you.

In the last notice from Mr. Jost, I was told that my premium for the next year will be more than double and it will be extended only for six months. I can hardly afford such an increase. All my life I had no talent to make business for me. I felt in my work a mission and materially I was just surviving. I have no resources.

I agree to drop the deliveries and in this way diminish your responsibilities. Doing effort, maybe I could pay even a 50% increase, but not the over 150%.

I agree with you that the time is strange. I started to hate to be a doctor, even if I feel the dedication and I enjoy the opportunity of helping others that this profession brings. But I know already what the accusation of malpractice is doing. I lived and I still am living under its strain. It is a social illness that is progressing, and worsening the prognosis for the nation's well-being. As Iacocca said: "Other countries don't spend their time looking for Mr. Deep Pockets.' They're too busy beating our brains out in the marketplace."

The hysteria of malpractice suits is a clear sign of something in the soul of this nation that will lead directly to its downfall. It is a pity that the government and the Supreme Court are looking the other way because apparently they do not care and it is more convenient for them not to see.

I send you my correspondence with the court and other letters about my lawsuit and my practice. They will show you my efforts to preserve my convictions about what is decent and what is right in my relations with my patients.

I ask you again to reevaluate my premiums. As I said, I can drop the deliveries, but I have to preserve for my work a right to admit my patients to the hospitals.

Tadeusz Maciejczyk, M.D.
Milledgeville, August 20, 1987

The World Seen from the Distance of a Small Village

Paul Simon
United States Senator

Dear Sir:

I thank you for your letter in which you are evaluating differently the Papal audience for President Kurt Waldheim. I write to you again because I believe that this audience, in some way, is one of the central problems that we have to face. It shows how to pass from one era of the past into another one of the future and to give that new era strong foundations and more human principles. Depending on how we do this passage, we can inject into the life of the future completely different characteristics.

In this aspect the Jews are determined to remember, to hunt the guilty, to stage them trials, to keep them constantly in disgrace, to build mausoleums of the past horrors and in this way avoid repetition of that dark age.

On the other hand, the Pope, by his act, indicated a different way: the way to forgive, to create and to build new spirit and brotherhood, and to make from them a foundation for the future in which a holocaust would have no emotional ground to appear.

To forgive doesn't need to mean the same as to forget. Forgiveness remembers, but while remembering, it responds with positive remedies to prevent the wrong. It builds a special spirit, creates images of better ways to deal with our conflicts. Forgiveness is imaginative, is optimistic and is elevating. It elevates those who forgive and those who are forgiven.

On the contrary, the non-forgiveness knows only how to build the roadblocks, fortresses, how to enter into isolation and an anxious dissatisfaction. The non-forgiveness is nothing more than reversed hate. It is not a conquering force.

Writing to you, I should indicate that St. Paul, your namesake, was hating and persecuting Christians. He was an activist, an initiator. For him, the local persecution was not enough. He was on his way to extend and to organize those persecutions elsewhere when he experienced a sudden change. If the Christian community would decide to reject him, not to forgive, casting him away, the Christianity would not be as strong and its vitality not so enduring to win in spite of repeated holocausts of Roman persecutions. During those persecutions, not infrequently, the torturers were becoming Christians and they were accepted by them as brothers. If they died in the next wave of persecution, they were venerated as martyrs and as saints. To forgive for the first Christians was not a sign of weakness. By forgiving, they were conquering. To forgive and to win is not something easy. It requires character, dedication and a spiritual strength. The non-forgiveness requires nothing. It is a cheap product of a lost spirit that makes men not free, but enslaved to the memories filled with hate and anxiety.

If by forgiving, we would produce some international harm, I would risk doing this harm without hesitation.

I know that you are running for the Presidency. I know also the potential of those who could turn against you, if you would dare to introduce forgiveness and its consequences in your campaign. Somehow, in this free country, the voice of real freedom is suppressed by pressure groups that would withhold support and would, or could, turn all the press against you. But, as a proverb says, "The one who is not taking a risk is not going to jail." (I learned this proverb form my street friends in my childhood.) Who knows?

Such a decision could be a test of a man for many and who knows how the country would respond in spite of the pressure forces? The country today is hungry for a leader with character, with spirit, with his own strong convictions based on wisdom, which because of those qualities could indicate to all of us the best way into the future.

I want to tell also that the leader who will emerge from the coming election will have not an easy glorious term, if that is what he is looking for. The U.S. is still a leader of the free world, but its prestige is washed away by scandals, its money is spent, the debt will be like chains around the legs and the different types of crises will multiply. You can add in addition that the spirit of the people of this country is already very low and the anxiety is high. Whoever will be the next leader should be able and ready to make fundamental decisions, looking wisely into the future, and filling the present emptiness with the new spirit. Not a showman leadership, but an ability to renew, to break the old harmful clichés, will make the new leader's greatness or nullity. The lukewarm, shallow, uncompromising present day debates, even if loaded with hidden stings, are not a promise of such a leadership. The country wants more. Those discussions and debates are a wonderful opportunity not only to test the candidates, but also to test the people and the visible and the hidden needs of the time.

In this letter, I wanted to stress that I have my reasons to never want to witness a time that creates a potential for holocaust. I wanted to tell about my grade school friend whose brother and father were shot on the spot for helping the Jew to survive; about the priest who baptized me,

The World Seen from the Distance of a Small Village

who was killed in a similar circumstance just outside the church, about my two classmates who died in a monthly public execution (only in July 1943, 160 people were executed on the streets of Kielce, Poland); about my two sisters who died from TB a few years after the war from the war miseries, and so on. But I do not think it is necessary. I overcame the bitterness and I would like to help to create a world based on different principles.

When I read that the Jewish children, in great majority, consider the Arabs inferior to them, I feel a deep uneasiness. Is this what the Jews learned from their past? It was precisely such a conviction that gave birth to the Nazi movement.

Again, I thank you for your answer. It was the only one that I received from my letter about the Papal audience for Mr. Waldheim.

I send you my best wishes.

Tadeusz Maciejczyk
Milledgeville, August 27, 1987

cc: Dole
    Bush
    Senator Dixon
    Newsweek
    Time
    U.S. News & World Report
    Chicago Council

Book Two

Clerk of the Court of Carroll County

Dear Sir:

I notify here that I received a copy of a letter of the plaintiff's attorney in which he is asking to transfer the trial against me to Winnebago County Court. His main and only motivation for this transfer was that, since two articles about my trial appeared in *The Carroll County Review*, the people of this county became "prejudiced against the plaintiff and I obtained an undue influence over the minds of the inhabitants of this county." (One of those articles was a simple notification that the trial against me was registered in this county court, the other contained my comments about the nature of the accusation.) I indicated in my letter that if the plaintiff would like to write about her point of view, it would be completely O.K. with me.

Expressing my gratefulness for the compliment about my ability to influence the minds of the people, I am asking not to exaggerate my capability. It should not be considered as a reason and justification to deny me the right to be judged in my home county. Bernard Goetz, from the New York subway, was not judged in Alaska, but in a New York court, in spite of thousands of local and national editorials and public commentaries. The capacity of the people from the Carroll County for a sound and honest judgment should not be degraded by this kind of discrimination.

To substantiate my point, I want to indicate that the issue of my trial is not of an emotional nature, where the anger or indignation could blind an impartial vision of my crime.

Secondly, I want to stress that the accusation against me has a strong ingredient of being a public and social problem and menace that can have importance to the people of this place. My malice, my bad professional judgments, my misconduct, could be a potential hazard to the people who are, or could be, my patients and they are living here, not in Winnebago.

The problem of a completely different category is another aspect of this petition for venue. It implies that my letter, which was published, impaired an impartiality of judgment here.

In this aspect, I want to indicate my firm conviction that in a search for true justice, every light, even the smallest, even given in an inconvenient time, should not be rejected, but welcomed. A search for justice per se is a search for a perfect, more complete vision and understanding

The World Seen from the Distance of a Small Village

that needs all the illumination it can get. In fact, that my letter should be beneficial not for me, because I was exposing my cards prematurely, but to Mr. Cacciatore, who can see me better through this letter and in this way, shape his attack more efficiently. Every expression contains and gives some clues. And even, if that letter would give me some point, Mr. Cacciatore, being a professional in the courtroom, will have enough advantage over me, even if he has a fragment of equity on his side. Or, is he so worried precisely because he has any?

In opposition to a need for light in a search for true justice, is a desire for obscurity, secrecy and intolerance even for a louder whisper, if the primary objective of the trial has no solid ground and is primarily intending to produce a kind of legal robbery and extortion. If this would be the case, then the transfer of this trial to Rockford, to the attorney Cacciatore's hometown and his environment could represent a special danger to the cause of justice. It could create a temptation for behind-the-scenes manipulations and arrangements, over which I would have no control at all.

In this aspect, I want to add that I see the jury primarily as a representation of the forum, which means of all the local people, who directly, or potentially are interested in the subject of judgment. They should be not just any people from far away.

Each trial, except for its primary objective, should include a secondary, wider purpose: it should serve as a lesson and as an occasion for an awareness of our social needs and ills. In this way, the court can influence and guide. Such a purpose cannot be obtained if the trial is taken out of its place, transplanting it to a location where it has no echo at all.

Concluding, I ask the authorities of this court to permit for this trial to be performed in its native place and among the people truly interested in what it could tell and teach.

Centuries ago, St. Paul said that it is the love that never does wrong to the neighbor and hence it is a true fulfillment of the law. Let us make the deliberations of this court to be guided not by hate and stratagems, but by a love for a common good.

Tadeusz Maciejczyk, M.D.
Milledgeville, September 17, 1987

Book Two

American Medical Association
Chicago, Illinois

In this letter I want to inform you about a common now days problem that I am involved in: a malpractice suit. The reason I am writing about this to you is that consequently I involved you in this process.

What I am telling is explained better in the final part of my letter, dated February 13, 1987 to the court authorities. In that segment of my letter I wrote: "Concluding—because those accusations of malpractice are not harmless and never should be taken lightly—just because there is no risk for the accusing party, I am asking the Court for compensation. I am asking for $100,000 (one hundred thousand dollars) from the plaintiff's attorney, William T. Cacciatore and from the anonymous doctor, to be paid to the American Medical Association for the fund to fight abusive malpractice accusations, whether they would be medical or of any other nature."

I have still the court battle before me. For information about my way of reacting and thinking, I am sending you my correspondence related to this trail from the beginning until the present moment.

In this letter I want to ask you for your support. The plague of malpractice suits that impoverish the nation in so many aspects should be dealt not only as a legal dilemma, but increasingly as a pathologic devastation of the legal system that lost in its judgments the distinction between justice, goodness, common sense, greed and malice and became a bad teacher for society.

For all those reasons, I ask the American Medical Association to support with all its authority and its influence this my battle and my determination to find another way to bring some sanity to the present malpractice situation.

I would like to have some answer from you.

> Tadeusz Maciejczyk, M.D.
> Milledgeville, October 22, 1987

P.S. I include also my letter to the Supreme Court in another way related to the malpractice crisis.

The World Seen from the Distance of a Small Village

American Medical Association
Chicago, Illinois

Attention: Miss Betty Jane Anderson

Dear Miss Betty:

    I thank you for your kind answer, explanation and evidence of care given to my case.
    Asking for AMA support, I thought about your approval of my different way of reacting to the reckless malpractice accusations, maybe your presence as an observer during the trial and your acceptance of the compensation from the attorney and the anonymous doctor as a legitimate counter arm and satisfaction for an abusive suit.
    I know that I have no knowledge, nor experience in the present day legal complexities, but I have a strong feeling of what is right and what is wrong. All my life I had a need for compassion and a feeling of mission in life. The medical preparation is only supporting those central elements of my life. Those elements are guiding me now in my fight.
    In this my trial, in my unorthodox way, I intend to defend myself, but also with the big emphasis, the mission of medicine and the interests of the sick. I do not want to increase charges to my patients, to pay artificial charges, even if Medicare would approve it. It is clear to me that all legal arguments and means changed nothing in the malpractice abuses. The number of litigations each year is bigger. The sophistication in those accusations is constantly farther reaching. The cost of this "sport" is constantly going up and it has to be paid ultimately by the sick who truly should have more consideration and protection.
    I sincerely reject what in one recent letter I was offered. "Are you tired and sick of the present malpractice and Medicare situation? Do you desire to close and give up? You do not need to do this. We will do the unpleasant work for you and you will dedicate yourself only to medicine."
    It looks like an additional body put between the doctor and the patient and additional squeeze on him or the patient for money while the doctor could do this work closing eyes on the patient's miseries that would follow his treatment. I cannot continue forever an exploitation of the normal, honest patients to finance big premiums for the sake of a small minority that many times show the qualities of social parasites. A formula has to be found in the judicial system that would define more clearly what the malpractice is. As long as this work is not done, because

Book Two

of an excuse of a complexity of the subject, the indiscriminate treasure hunting in such a jungle will intensify and the nation will suffer.

Today I received a notification from the plaintiff's attorney who demands now to strike my answer to his petition to change venue. If you would like to help me, please inform me what is required in Ch. 110 #2-603 III Rev. Status 1986. What tells Ch. 110 #2-604, ILL Rev. Statues and also what are the requirements in Ch. 110 #2-610.

I hope you will do all you can to help me. Thank you. I need those explanations as soon as it can be.

Tadeusz Maciejczyk, M.D.
Milledgeville, November 1, 1987

The World Seen from the Distance of a Small Village

DePaul University, Chicago
Thomas D. Abrahamson, Director of Admissions

Dear Sir:

I thank you for your letter to Cristina, for inviting her to study in your school and for inviting us to visit DePaul today, on November 1.

We were planning to come and to write afterwards to Cristina because she is in the Philippines and will remain there until next June. This is the reason why she is not contacting you directly.

But suddenly I couldn't go. I was confronted with another problem and I cannot neglect the preparations and work related to it. I have a pending malpractice suit. It looks to me that it was more than frivolous. It was malicious. Because of this I decided to fight it my own unorthodox way. Three days ago, I received a notification from the plaintiff's attorney that on December 1, he would come to the court to present a motion to strike my answer to his request for a change of venue. On September 21, I won in my first in my life appearance before the judge. At that time the venue was denied. Now, I am confronted with a repeated attack for the same.

I write this letter to justify my absence in the visitation in your school. And, it came to my mind that maybe someone interested in this kind of small battle could look into this my case. Because my reaction is unusual, it could be interesting. And I need all the advice I can get. My intentions are not selfish and I think they are noble. Maybe because I believe so, I do not shrink to ask you for such help. I send here the copies that refer to this trial. I will be grateful for your observations.

Maybe also, because you are a Catholic school and I do not know how to judge my arguments, I will send you also my two letters where I defended the pope's audience for Mr. Waldheim. It was how I understood the meaning of that audience.

I will send the application sheets that I received from you to Cristina. She didn't write since September 21 and we worry. The place where she is now as a Rotary exchange student is primitive, but because of this she is not spoiled there. And she was writing about that place with a lot of sympathy. I think that such a place is a good eye opener. It looks like Cristina matured in those last few months.

Book Two

Again, I ask your pardon for writing about my problems that should not belong here and I send you our gratefulness for what you offer to Cristina.

> Tadeusz Maciejczyk
> Milledgeville, November 1, 1987

The World Seen from the Distance of a Small Village

American Red Cross
17th & D Street N.W.
Washington, D.C. 26666

In this letter I want to inform you not as much that I have a malpractice suit as that consequently I involved you in this suit without previous communication.

To explain better the situation, I am sending you my correspondence related to this trial from the beginning until the present moment. There, in my letter to the court, dated February 13, I was writing:

> Concluding—because those accusations of malpractice are not harmless and never should be taken lightly—just because there is no risk for the accusing party, I am asking the Court for compensation. I am asking for . . . .
>
> I also ask another compensation of another $100,000 (one-hundred thousand dollars) from Attorney William T. Cacciatorre and the doctor paid to the American Red Cross for the Fund of Homeless of America and for the creation of a network of volunteers who would solve this problem their own unique way in each community. This compensation is for the undeserved suffering of my family, for the tears of my daughter and for the sleepless nights of my wife.

I this letter I want to ask you for your support. I would like to have your moral and philosophical approval of my way of dealing with the problem of reckless accusations, maybe also a presence of your observer at the trial and an acceptance of the compensation that I specified in my letter to the court.

I am sorry, but I have no faith any more that the normal discussion between both sides of the conflict would bring any improvement. The temptations are too big. And I do not want to continue to increase charges to my patients to pay the each time bigger tribute to the malpractice inquisition overlords. The sick, the already afflicted, have to pay ultimately the bill for this nation-wide game and they should have finally more consideration and protection. Here, in this aspect, I see an additional mission for the Red Cross. If you could raise your voice in their protection asking for justice for them, it would have an enormous significance.

I have a big respect for your continuous humanitarian work and I would not like to dilute your prestige for something small and unim-

Book Two

portant, but it looks that the extent of resentment and even hatred created by malpractice overindulgence is something serious and requires preventative efforts.

I hope I will get from you some answer and I wish you all the best.

Tadeusz Maciejczyk, M.D.
Milledgeville, November 5, 1987

The World Seen from the Distance of a Small Village

Pete Dupont
Rockland, De

Dear Sir:

I thank you for your letter and for the questionnaire. They impressed me as important and interesting. For this reason I want to give them full answers, instead of marking the YES or No column.

Similar to you, I distrust the Soviet sincerity. I saw them. I was "liberated" by them. I know also the roots from which their methods were developing. They started this way a long time ago in the Imperial Russia. Because of this, without a deep moral transformation, and truly democratic revolution, the Soviets will follow their dream of world domination.

To oppose this Soviet drive, your survey has one simple answer: to be stronger militarily. To build the S.D.I. To exercise more pressure, you are asking not to vote for a presidential candidate who would answer "NO" to those two propositions.

But from history and from observation, I learned that the military superiority and a confidence in the more advanced weaponry are very uncertain and fragile instruments for lasting peace. The most guarded secrets of technical advancements were stolen in the past and can be stolen again. The balance of military strength can be reversed before we realize it. As I see this, the long-range security and the ultimate victory of the free world cannot be obtained by a military power alone. Such a purpose will require from us much more.

I know that the military strength is necessary. It should protect us from pressures and blackmail from the other side.

While this protection lasts another task should start and continue developing without interruptions: the task to build the unity of the people of the world. It would be an uneasy task. It would require giving the world a very special and potent inspiration, to produce new spirit and new hope. It would require from the leaders and from all participants a great vision, new skills for dialogues and a lasting dedication to the cause. It would require a special mobilization of the best we have. For this, wisdom would be more necessary than diplomacy. To progress and to succeed, it would need sincerity and openness. Only such work and leadership directed in this way could bring finally a *Pax Mundi* (peace of the free world) instead of *Pax Sovietica*. (Peace inside the Soviet domination.)

Book Two

For those reasons, responding to your questionnaire, my views are that:

1. Yes, I favor the research and development of S.D.I., but not as a principle objective of our policy. It should only give a protection for a main work to build the structures for world unity and world peace.
2. I would avoid demonstrative gestures and bellicosity. I would just do quietly what would be obviously necessary.
3. I do not know whether I would not vote for a candidate who would oppose S.D.I. and a stress on the military, but without hesitation, I would vote for somebody who would undertake the mission of world unity, preserving its rich diversity and traditions, including in this drive even the people of Russia.

Finally, I would favor an aid to all freedom fighters, but with a condition that their main objective would be not an engagement in military activity, but a protection for an uninterrupted dialogue, not as much with the opposing government as with the population at large. The purpose of fighting, a vision of the future, a planning in details of the situation and of the social structures after eventual settlement, a mobilization and the education of the intellectually competent personal that could serve and guide in the lasting peace would qualify the movements whether to receive help. Just readiness for harassment and fighting could lead to a substitution of one bad regime by another. Such "freedom fighters" would not help the cause of world stability and peace.

                        Tadeusz Maciejczyk
                        Milledgeville, November 15, 1987

P.S. I am sorry that my letter is coming late. I am distracted. I have a malpractice suit. In late September I was before the judge to speak against the transfer of my trial to Rockford. Now I have to go again on December 1 because the opposing lawyer asked to strike my answer to his petition for venue. I have no lawyer. I want to respond to the accusations personally. It looks to me that in the field of malpractice the legal system lost the balance and shows clear pathological abnormalities. It lost in its judgment the distinction between justice, goodness, common sense, greed and malice and became a bad teacher for society.

The World Seen from the Distance of a Small Village

Later I will send you the copies of my other papers about the objectives of leadership.

I wish you luck.

Tadeusz Maciejczyk

I am including my letter with arguments against the transfer of my suit to Rockford. I think that it is different way of my fighting for a better America.

Editor of *U.S. News & World Report*
To "Kramer at Large"

Fiddling with rationale usually was not well tolerated and generally was ridiculed and resisted by "wise" men, entrenched in the established world's concepts. But such a fiddling also was a redeeming force that was showing new openings and was introducing in a new era.

The rationale of Mr. Kramer, which while counting the money, calculates the future situations by today's standards, also can be questionable. An inspiring leadership has a power to touch many unknown forces in the spirit of men that are never discovered or even suspected by professional administrators. Look into history. Or even in our reaches, we all know men or societies who succeeded where others, more experienced, failed.

We never should discourage the forces and the spirit for change, even for an apparent return to old patterns, because it always was so that in dimensions eternally the same, man was carving constantly different shapes and realities.

Tadeusz Maciejczyk
Milledgeville, Illinois, November 26, 1987

Book Two

Clerk of the Court of Carroll County

Dear Sir:

I obtained a copy of Mr. Cacciatore's new demand to strike my answer to his petition for a change of venue, a petition that was denied.

As before, in this motion, Mr. Cacciatore is formulating charges that lack substance and apparently are intending to make me feel the pressure.

Charge No. 1: that "my answer failed to state a plain and concise statement of my defense."

My Answer: I told my reasons against the change of venue clearly and in simple language. But, if Mr. Cacciatore doesn't understand, I will put them more plainly:

1. Numerous legal antecedents indicate that a trial can and should be held in its original place even in spite of extensive publicity.
2. Mr. Cacciatore's statement and main reason for a transfer of this trial, that my letter in *The Carroll County Review* caused "my undue influence over the minds of the inhabitants of this county" is a direct insult to all the people of this county. It insinuates that the people here are so primitive and their minds are so feeble that my one letter was enough to brainwash them.
3. The people from this county and not from any other place are exposed to my acts and should be warned.
4. Only the crimes of unusual emotional impact are those that can distort the local judgment by anger or indignation. My "guilt" does not belong to this category.
5. The excess of explanation never hurts a search for a truth.
6. The insistence on obscurity and secrecy and intolerance for an appearance of an independent public opinion are not an indication of good intentions, but of a desire for abusing and twisting justice.
7. The jury is a representation of local people who should be involved, not just any people from far away.
8. Each trial should be a lesson of life for the community. If the court abandons this its obligation for the sake of manipulation and legal tricks, it will lose its great status and will fail its mission.

Charge No. 2: that my answer contains a "prayer for relief." Here I have to ask Mr. Cacciatore to:

The World Seen from the Distance of a Small Village

A. Make a definition of a prayer
B. Compare this definition with any part of my answer explaining his charge.

I want to make clear that the citation of St. Paul is not a prayer. St. Paul was a living, historical personality who through his writing and actions molded the world in which we are living today. His quotation impressed me for its wisdom that knows to put eternal never-changing truths in one simple sentence. Citing St. Paul should not be taken differently than any other citation from Caesar, Machiavelli, Descartes or Marx, who also made a deep influence on the world's development.

And as before, here again, I hope that the judgment of this court will be guided not by anything else, but by a love for a common good. This certainly is not a prayer.

Charge No. 3: My answer to Mr. Cacciatore's petition to change venue failed to contain an explicit admission of denial of each allegation of the complaint.

My Answer: My explicit admission or denial of allegations of the complaints was not required in the petition to change venue. But, at this point, I have a right to ask Mr. Cacciatore what is his explicit charge against me? I ask him to express this in one clear sentence: What exactly is the nature of my guilt or crime? What did I do wrong? What law did I transgress or break? The accusation act from last January was anything but explicit.

In conclusion: because my name was correlated with the charge of malpractice in this county newspaper and consequently the confidence of the local people in my work could suffer, it would be only an act of justice to hold all the hearings against me here, where I was publicly accused. Mr. Cacciatore has to prove here before the local people, that his accusation and his charge was real; that it was not libel.

Considering all those factors, I am asking again the court to keep this trial here and to dismiss the present Mr. Cacciatore's motion to strike my previous answer.

Tadeusz Maciejczyk, M.D.
Milledgeville, November 30, 1987

Book Two

U.S. News & World Report
Editor

Two weeks ago, I read M. Kramer's report about Sen. Simon's Pinocchio problem and because I felt that it was unfair, I wrote a letter to the editor. Today, in the reader's comments and under a changed and more negative title of "Simononics," I found two letters identical to Mr. Kramer's in tone, range and level.

I do not pretend to write better letters and I do not blame you for not printing my answer, but I have a right to expect from you a presentation of all the spectrum of readers' views.

I am not in Sen. Simon's camp. I am neutral. I am constantly looking for the best person for the presidency. But I would like tolerance and some degree of impartiality in a paper of your category. I do not think that Mr. Kramer's article was so bad that it needed all this kind of support to stick.

If, among all the answers, only mine would differ from the general tone of condemnation, then, my answer should be printed. Otherwise, in my eyes, your paper is not much different from the Soviet's *Pravda*.

Tadeusz Maciejczyk, M.D.
Milledgeville, December 7, 1987

The World Seen from the Distance of a Small Village

Alan J. Dixon
Senator of the United States

A few days ago, I received a telephone call from your secretary. She was asking whether you could be of some help to me. I am grateful for this your kindness.

I have now a malpractice suit that changed my life. Its accusation is strange. Still now I would act the same way, as I did. But Mr. Cacciatore, the accusing lawyer, is pressing. Even if his knowledge of medicine is somewhere next to zero, he is ready to blame, to prosecute, to condemn and of course, to collect.

I do not want any accommodation or settlement. I do not want another lawyer to represent me and this way to create a situation in which two blind men would judge the third one for color blindness. I want to personally respond to the charges, discuss them before the jury and clear my name. For this reason, I am going now through the nightmare of previously unknown to me legal maneuverings. I know that I can lose everything I have, including my home and maybe a prospect of university for my youngest daughter, but I do not know how to act differently. In our home now, uncertainty lingers behind every smile.

And I am tired. I think now that after it is all over and if there would be no change in the working condition, I would leave the U.S. and go to some other country. I do not know how to work under Mr. Cacciatore's whip. I do not like the rapidly spreading Mafia type grip that is trying to control and to exploit all active America under the banner of justice.

Five years ago, I rebelled against the obligatory malpractice insurance because it would automatically raise the prices for a patient's visit. Consequently I lost my privileges in Sterling General Hospital.

In the last two years, I was forced to take this insurance and I became a "tax collector" for the malpractice fund. I took the lowest coverage. My practice became reduced. I even cannot deliver babies. But without this insurance, I would have no access to any hospital.

I feel deeply the injustice and the immorality that the malpractice fever and over-practicing is producing. The sicker, the more disabled and more hopeless is the person, the higher is his malpractice taxation. On the other side, the more parasitic is the nature of this justice recipient, the more abusive are his claims and bigger expectations of reward, the bigger his desire to terrorize. And this or another Mr. Cacciatore will be always ready and willing for the inquisition role.

In this way the independent work in the U.S. became not very attractive. People's ambition became to hang to some stable place that pays well and requires a minimum of responsibility. It is something not very promising for America.

Not long ago, I was speaking with a man from the highway engineering office who got a promotion and more responsibility. He refused. He explained this to me this way: "If I accept, I would have insurance coverage while working, but twenty years from now, I could lose everything." Such an undercurrent in attitude and in thinking is something that has to be taken seriously by the U.S. planners of the future. To make a drive for a strong military and to ignore those symptoms of a malady within the society would be not a sign of genius.

I hope that my resistance to be subdued by my malpractice suit will be a fight not only for my cause, but also for a general realization that some healthy reforms in the present malpractice situation have to be introduced for the good of the country as a whole.

Tadeusz Maciejczyk, M.D.
Milledgeville, December 10, 1987

P.S. I include two photocopies of two documents that illustrate the present malpractice grip

1. Frequent now advice how to be protected from the malpractice long arm.
2. A consequence of malpractice to any family with a child for immunization.

   a. Price of a vial $55.00
   b. After malpractice surcharge . . . . $146.63 (a vial before malpractice was about $4.50)

Is it how the U.S. wants to perpetuate their justice?

The World Seen from the Distance of a Small Village

Pete Dupont
Rockland, Delaware

I received your questionnaire about the welfare system and I delayed my answer. I wanted to think about it. A quick, precipated, guided by impulse only and not revolved in mind answer on a subject of such an importance would be more than thoughtlessness. I t would have a potential for bad consequences.

Yes, I believe that our current welfare system is a failure. It lost the realization of what should be its purpose and its limits. It also lost its ability to inspire, to motivate and to guide. Its actions frequently are promoting just hanging around and decaying. The welfare's self-serving bureaucracy overgrew around the original mission and distorted many good intentions. I think that the society rebellion against such a welfare is justified.

Yes, I would think twice before replacing this agency by something else. This something else quickly could become the same, changing only its name. We cannot eliminate welfare in a society. Even Christ told that we always will have the poor among us.

The best solution to the present problems of welfare would be a complete reform of the existing system. It would be necessary to come to the bottom of those problems and restructure them, making them work according to the changing needs and means. It can be that such a reform would require more courage, determination and wisdom than just liquidation.

The questions to answer would be:

1. Who should be helped by welfare?
2. Who should never be on welfare?
3. What are the situations between:

   a. What circumstances would decide?
   b. What would be a time limit?
   c. Whether to require partial or total reimbursement later.

Such a welfare should have close connections with the employment services. And here is a very uneasy problem. Can the U.S. create enough work? How to encourage private initiative and self-employment? I am self-employed and I am a so-called able body and in the last years, many

Book Two

times I am so discouraged and so disaffected that welfare in some moments looks to me attractive. Why to bother?

Tadeusz Maciejczyk, M.D.
Milledgeville, December 13, 1987

*My letters to Sen. A. Dixon explain the causes of my disaffection. It can be more endemic among people than we think.

Lowell L. Henderson, M.D.
Mayo Clinic
Rochester, MN

Dear Sir:

    Last Spring, together with my subscription to the Mayo Clinic Health Letters, I sent a copy of my view of the malpractice suit against me.
    In response, I received a letter from you dated March 13, 1987 with your observations and encouragements for me to continue to fight. It really lifted my spirit and I was grateful.
    Now, after almost ten months, and using the renewal of subscription as a pretext, I am sending you the copies of my different letters related to my suit. They will tell better than anything else my present situation.
    I hope that maybe again, I would receive a letter from you with some kind of guidance because even with the sympathy of many people, in this fight I feel alone.
    With the occasion of Christmas, I send you my best wishes.

Tadeusz Maciejczyk, M.D.
Milledgeville, December 15, 1987

The World Seen from the Distance of a Small Village

ABC Television Network
20/20 Audition
1330 Avenue of the Americas
New York, NY 10019

I am one of the addicts to your auditions, but never I was thinking to write to you and to tell you about my problems until a few days ago when, while speaking to one person, he told me that my problems and my reaction to them as well as my evaluation of them and my fight, would be good material for you. Maybe. I hope so.

I am sending to you the copies of my different papers that will explain my situation. As my collision with the "malpractice" is a fragment of a deep national tragedy, I am convinced that it calls each day more for true attention, discussion, correction and a time for healing.

I send you my papers that are dating back to my first collision with the malpractice insurance requirement. Then came my malpractice suit and my reaction. I would be grateful if you could give attention to my battle. Maybe you could send an observer to my upcoming trial. And if somebody from your team would come here for more information or explanation, I would be glad.

I will be very grateful for any help you can give me.

Tadeusz Maciejczyk, M.D.
Milledgeville, January 13, 1988

Book Two

William T. Cacciatore
Attorney at Law
Rockford, Illinois

I received your last letter that contained a number of your objections to my answers to your interrogations and I feel that now is the time for a formulation of my objections to your interrogation and your tactics in general.

To satisfy the requirement, I will send you now a sworn answer. I will do this under protest.

I object strongly to the abuse of this method. A swearing requirement at every step is not dignifying the act of confession, is not elevating the justice authorities, nor is doing such a moment more solemn to those who have to comply. Maybe that it is putting more pressure on the people, but also it devalues the meaning of this kind of an oath, making it cheap and tolerated in the same way as we tolerate the traffic jam. Such a requirement is downgrading everybody who is interrogated because it insinuates that otherwise, the trust is impossible and everybody is a liar by nature. Such training for the whole society has to be deplorable in its consequences. It creates a barrier and an instantaneous negative attitude. Without a doubt, if it would be practiced by parents in the family circle, its effect would be disruptive. It would ruin the sincerity, the communication and the trust. And I believe that the life of a society is governed by the same basic rules as the family life is. It would be interesting to calculate how much damage this requirement already produced. Anyway, those my answers to your interrogation I will repeat in the courtroom under oath.

I thank you for your explanation of the meaning of the expression "complaint" applied to my case. It is "the document I first received" in your act of accusation.

This simplified everything. I answered already those accusations with all details and as truly as I was able in my letter to the court on February 5, 1987. I will repeat them and if necessary, I will give all additional clarification when I am in court under oath.

Here, I want to stress solemnly that I will always be willing to answer all your questions that would show some evidence that you are taking your work seriously and you are doing your homework intended to clarify our conflict. Your questions should be your original and probing the case that confronts both of us. They should not be just a print.

The World Seen from the Distance of a Small Village

A year has passed already since I received your act of accusation. Until now, I didn't see on your side any sign of a desire to touch or to approach the real issue of the trial. Your questions circle the periphery of the problems in general and obviously are intended primarily to intimidate and to terrorize. I am sorry to tell you that during all the past year I saw from your side only tricks, threats and the desire to wear me out and to win not by the merits of the problem, but by the methods of a bully. It is obvious to me that the justice by itself is the last of things that you are interested in.

But, I believe that the America's justice system is much more than your collection of tricks, of gimmicks to complicate and to wash the issues out from the real content or maybe even of some kind of escape into technicalities. Those things have nothing to do with justice. They are the loopholes or travesties and hypocrisy done to justice. They frequently make an image of justice in the people's eyes.

Looking again at the first pages of your questions, I want only to assure you that I am not celebrating the visits with my patients on the streets, asking the by-passers to stop and to listen. Either I gather the gossip that those my visits with them can generate. I also believe that the consideration and sentencing of my "crime" in the case of Mrs. Macchi should not be influenced by information about the organization of my work, by my insurance coverage, my assets or the assets of my associates. That information is not necessary in a search for the truth. The judgment and the sentencing should not be affected by the size of the expected spoils. The spoils are your objective, but not the objective of justice. It looks to me that your questions neglect the real issue and concentrate on peripheral accessories that in your hands and oratory could silence what is really important.

I also consider that the judgment of my present accusation should not be influenced by a consideration whether somebody else made a claim against me or whether or not on another occasion I violated any law. This is a play for shortcuts, superficiality and a creation of prejudice. It turns the search for justice into the search for a scapegoat and for the way to bypass justice, producing appearances in place of the truth.

The same I can tell about your questions about schools I attended, certifications I obtained, or papers I wrote. My title to do my work was given to me by the State of Illinois and at that time I gave already all that information. I do not imagine how any of that information could change the weight of my crime if I am guilty. As before, I consider that such questions serve to create appearances and to obscure the real object of the judgment.

Book Two

In conclusion, I repeat that I am willing to answer any of your questions under the condition that those questions would show your homework in this case.

I want also to stress again that your interrogation, while clarifying nothing in the element or situation where I deviated from lawful behavior or from my professional oath and obligations is violating frivolously my constitutional right to privacy.

I also want to inform you that because your threats are reinforced by the authorities of Judge Rapp and the Supreme Court paragraphs, I am sending to them the copies of this letter.

> Tadeusz Maciejczyk, M.D.
> Milledgeville, Illinois January 24, 1988

cc: John W. Rapp, Jr., Chief circuit Judge
  Noel J. Augustyn, Administrative Assistant to the Chief Justice, Supreme Court

The World Seen from the Distance of a Small Village

John W. Rapp, Jr.
Chief Circuit Judge
Circuit Court of the 15th Judicial Circuit
Carroll County Courthouse

Dear Sir:

    Here I send to you the copy of my letter to Mr. Cacciatore. In this letter I formulated my objections to his method of interrogation that is concentrating on collateral, on circumstances or even curiosities with a complete neglect of the real issue of my trial. It is my view that this kind of interrogation is not leading to a search for justice.
    Because Mr. Cacciatore used your name and your authority to put pressure on me, I feel that I should send to you this my response to him.
    Using this occasion, maybe it would be of some interest to you my letter to Senator Alan Dixon where I defined my view and my objective in this trial. Senator Dixon became apparently interested after reading the copy of a questionnaire that I sent to Pete Dupont.
    I send you my best wishes.

    Tadeusz Maciejczyk, M.D.
    P.S. After finishing, I decided to send you also the copy of my letter to Pete Dupont. I am sorry that this chain became so long.

    T. Maciejczyk
    Milledgeville, IL, January 26, 1988

Book Two

Noel J. Augustyn
Administrative Assistant to the Chief Justice
Supreme Court of the United States
Washington, D.C.

Dear Sir:

I send you a copy of my letters related to my malpractice suit. In the present letter I object to the interrogatory methods of the accusing attorney.

For better information about the origin of my accusation and the present stage of my trial, I send you also the copies of my original report to the court, dated February 5, 1987 and my more recent letter to Senator Alan J. Dixon.

I hope that the present daily fear of malpractice accusations that affect negatively all active and productive America can be reduced by a new work on the problem to eliminate the abusive excesses.

I hope that you will try to help.

Tadeusz Maciejczyk, M.D.
Milledgeville, Illinois, January 27, 1988

The World Seen from the Distance of a Small Village

Meredith White
Senior Editor of 20/20, ABC News

Dear Madam:

I thank you for your prompt answer to my letter. Because you returned all the papers that I sent to you, I can consider that your decision was negative and absolute.

But I didn't ask you to put me on the screen.

I was trying to get you involved in clarifying and correcting the chaotic and enormously abuse problem of malpractice litigations. My case in this general horror picture is only a small sample. It illustrates quite well how easy a pretext for such litigations can be fabricated. There is no punishment, no price for a false, frivolous accusation, so why not try? In the last five years the amount of those litigations was growing like an avalanche and as an avalanche it was dangerous and destructive to society. It was teaching not how to be wise and constructive in life, but how to be smart. It was teaching that a solid work is only for the old fashion fools and leads to nowhere. It was deviating the dreams of many people in the wrong direction. It was defining a success as a selfish disregard for all the rest of the world.

It is my belief that if the old lady, who was opening a bottle and in the process injured her eye, received 10.5 million dollars in compensation, obviously, it was not justice. It was a camouflaged robbery of society. It was not the insurance, nor even the factory who ultimately paid the price. The price was paid by thousands of ordinary people who the next day after this parody of justice had to pay increased premiums for their insurance or an exaggerated price for the factory products. It looks like the jury, the judge and even the lawyer who defended the factory were all accomplices. It has no other explanation. And I cannot classify the lawyer of the plaintiff who "won" this "compensation" otherwise, but as an ordinary thief of the society with a law diploma. If the same act had been done by a thief with a gun in a bank, hundreds of detectives would be sent to apprehend him. The victorious lawyer, after doing the same, came out from the courtroom with a smile as a hero and created behind him hundreds of other lawyers who will try to imitate him in this kind of success.

How long can a society contemplate quietly such pseudo-justice? How long can honest people tolerate this caricaturization of their justice system? Most of them say nothing, but they feel a rising anxiety because their values of their nation's justice was in their eye publicly desecrated and their institution of trust became an arena of public dishonesty?

During the last few days of the Christmas season, I was in San Antonio, Texas, and for several hours, I silently walked inside the Alamo monastery. My impression was deep. I felt a clear message that the defenders of that place left for the generations to come, a message: that a man, when it comes time, should take a stand and defend what he considers is right. Those silent moments at the Alamo only increased my conviction that I should stand my ground in this insignificant post of mine, in my remote place and maybe in the same way as Colonel Travis did, I must call the attention of the outside world to the situation.

I include here my last letter to the accusing attorney where I formulated my objections to his interrogatory tactics.

I would like to have your answer to this letter, but if you are only annoyed by my insistence, please do not try to be polite. Anyway, I will continue to watch your program.

Sincerely,

Tadeusz Maciejczyk, M.D.
Milledgeville, January 31, 1988

The World Seen from the Distance of a Small Village

Crescent Counties FMC
4151 Naperville Road
Suite 203,
Lisle, IL

I received your letter questioning the medical necessity for hospitalization of James Adams with a feeling of uneasiness, disbelief and even anger.

It was a man whose condition was visibly worsening from one day to another. He had constant, sometimes unbearable headaches. With, and frequently without any exercise, he suffered from chest oppression and pain. He was exhausted after trying to come from sitting in a chair to the bathroom and he was walking like in a dream. Verbal contact with him was limited. He comprehended slowly and at times, he was not responding at all. He watched TV without paying attention to it and he complained that everything was dim in his right visual field. Frequently he had urinary incontinence and he was unaware of this. He had feelings of nausea and he was almost not eating. He required constant attention because he had a tendency to fall. His inability to move was potentiated by the fact that he was taking of his leg prosthesis because the stump of his leg was irritated by eczema, sometimes infection, and it was painful.

He couldn't come to the office. I went to see him in his home. Checking, and trying to understand the situation, I couldn't act differently, but to arrange an admission. I was not interested in making a profit from this admission. I was trying to clarify the situation and to help.

I do not question whether your office has a sense making your big judgments from the distance and post facto.

I only want to stress that it would be much more simple and logical to me if I could have your advice on how to proceed, not now, when all is already over, but in those hot moments of making a decision. If you are really trying to be helpful, please send me a list of your members whom I could call, or who eventually would come to see the situation and to make a decision at the spot, in real life.

If you do this, I will retain all my respect for you and my high regard for your service.

Otherwise, the next time, in a similar moment of uncertainty, I will be again alone, immobilized by your distant shadow, but forced to decide anyway. I am sorry that in such a moment, when distracted by a thought about your judgment, my decision could be paralyzed and deadly wrong.

Book Two

A society whose superiors are fearful and trying to demonstrate that nobody can be trusted, that everybody is a potential abuser and every action therefore needs to be scrutinized by bureaucratic professional judges, such a society merits pity.

I am sorry that this social degeneration is happening here in America. It is a sign of decadence.

Please inform me how I should act, when I would feel that I should admit the patient. Whom of you could I call to get permission?

Tadeusz Maciejczyk, M.D.
February 4, 1988

Paul Simon
United States Senator

Dear Sir:

I saw you yesterday evening after almost all the votes of Iowa were counted. I had the impression that you were tired, probably discouraged and worried. Nevertheless, you were promising that today you would be on your post in New Hampshire and fighting.

I am glad that you will do this. I see the other candidates concentrating their interest in one aspect of life. But the life should contain much more than the accent on the economy, advocated by Rep. Gephardt or that all Americans would be as rich as Massachusetts under Dukakis.

A true life has to have much more than this to create an atmosphere of fulfillment. It has to have warmth and togetherness, harmony, poetry and a purpose great enough to elevate the human spirit, filling its emptiness because the emptiness leads to a search for all kinds of surrogates of happiness.

On your road to New Hampshire and hopefully to the Presidency, I wish you the best.

I send you the copies of my last letters. Maybe something in them could help in your coming discussions.

Again, my best wishes.

Tadeusz Maciejczyk
Milledgeville, IL
February 9, 1988

The World Seen from the Distance of a Small Village

Kurt Waldheim
President, Austria

Dear Sir:

Reading here and there about the pressures and rejections that because of your past, you have to feel and endure, I decided yesterday that I should send to you the copies of my two letters that I wrote and I sent to different politicians and to newspapers here in the U.S. Whether they made any difference, I do not know. But I sincerely believe that every person is changing and transforming and the society should give him a helping hand.

Maybe my letters could give you some relief in the moments of darkness and discouragement. I wish you the best in your struggle.

Tadeusz Maciejczyk
Milledgeville, IL
March 1, 1988

Book Two

Blue Cross and Blue Shield of Illinois

Some time ago I signed a PPO Addendum. I didn't understand completely its meaning, but I wanted to show my good will and my readiness to get along for the sake of the patients. Now, I have been notified that I still have to sign something called MPP, without which the PPO is invalid.

This additional requirement somehow passed the point of my acceptance of a need for a security in my work and for my better feeling by "belonging." It created in me an apprehension. What really am I signing? Why this urge to form clans of the obedient and the privileged? Why those who do not sign are destined to be excluded, or maybe slowly in this way suffocated? What is the future of a society that willingly, just for privileges, is ready to put its neck into the dog collar? It reminded me of the story from the old legend about a man who signed a pact with the devil, giving his soul in exchange for the life of power and pleasure.

I do not understand well the difference between PPO and MPP. It was always enormously boring to me to read those pages of rules and small print. Maybe they contain a secret of a promise for the future of the world, but at the present, I do not see in them a good medicine for our ills.

I was trained to be a doctor. As such, I feel useful and needed. It is a great feeling.

In addition, I need to write because it obligates me to concentrate and to formulate my thoughts clearly and to the last point. I also like to paint, to catch the moments of life on canvass because it permits me to see the details that are invisible to the hurried eye. I like also gardening, because it puts me in contact with the wonders of nature and within its peaceful silence, it helps me to look deeply inside of myself. And finally, I like to read. I do not speak about medical books, because they are a part of my profession, but the books about history of men, because it gives me a better understanding of our present time and maybe even of the road to our future.

What I cannot stand and digest are the artifacts of the treacherous small print, with all its promises of golden cages, beautiful perspectives and hidden traps. It is possible that signing those PPO and MPP forms would require from me some kind of solidarity that would go against my conscience as a doctor. How otherwise can I interpret your pressure and your insistence to sign special declarations before I could be admitted to your circle and acquire the privileges related to it? Obviously

The World Seen from the Distance of a Small Village

those who resist giving up their own vision of being a doctor will be excluded and discriminated against.

Thinking about this, I send you back your declaration unsigned. I want to be free. I do not want to be manipulated as a doctor.

As a free man, free professional, I promise you my sincere efforts and my complete cooperation to help your patients. What I want to repeat again is: even at the present time of stress and scrutiny, I want to preserve my inner moral code as a doctor, the way I understand it.

I hope that you will understand my intention and let me cooperate in your organization as a willing, but free co-worker.

Until not long ago, the U.S. was a free country with a promise of freedom of conscience to everybody. Only recently this promise because gradually chopped off by pressures, frequently expressed by rules of small print and a lure of privileges to those who are ready to "belong."

A long time ago, in the Twenties and Thirties of our century, the same mentality, the same methods of temptation and twisting maybe armed with tools somewhat more radical, changed the people of Russia into the Soviet People.

We, here in this country, we all have an obligation to cultivate and to preserve the freedom of man. This is the greatest thing that the U.S. has to offer to the world.

                                        Sincerely,
                                        Tadeusz Maciejczyk, M.D.
                                        Milledgeville, March 31, 1988

Book Two

U.S. News & World Report
The Holy Land Solution

I read the editorial "The Land of Cain and Abel" (Morton B. Zuckerman, *U.S. News & World Report,* April 4, 1988) that is extremely pessimistic giving almost no chance for peace. He was telling that he senses the solution and that the solution exists and the only problem is to find it.

I think that building a new edition of an Iron Curtin in Palestine, disputing only at what points such a line would run, is hardly a solution. It would embitter everybody on both sides. It would create an environment where the hate and looking for chances to change that temporary status quo would never die. The danger of explosion and of war would hang in the air together with a persistent conflict of those immediately and distantly involved.

The solution has to be elsewhere.

I think that the solution lies in a tiny line that can be found at every point between the two nations of Palestine. This line is composed of two ingredients that can bring hope. Those ingredients are:

1. An undisputed love for the land on both sides.
2. A realization that the past decades in spite of strife created a kind of mutual dependence for both nations—a kind of symbiosis.

Whatever will be the course of negotiations for a final political picture in Palestine, it has to be built on the foundation made from that tiny line. Only such a structure can promise hope, success and permanence. Only it can give a kind of satisfaction to both sides.
To obtain such results, certain elements are indispensable.

A. It cannot be done by a conference of outsides. It has to be done by a direct negotiation of two involved sides.
B. Each side has to be completely free to choose their representation. Any hiding behind the "principle" that the PLO should be excluded, would render peace impossible.
C. In such a confrontation, all the grievances should be presented into the open and discussed to its depth in appropriate committees or subcommittees.

The World Seen from the Distance of a Small Village

D. A vision of future relations between both nations should be more and more apparent from those talks and not from the impositions from the outside.
E. The demarcation line between both nations should remain as it is now. It should remain permeable in both directions. The security of both nations should be built on the trust and good will from both sides and not on the separating walls or the number of guards.
F. A special bi-national court should be established for judgment of violations of such agreements because without a doubt, both sides will have a number unsatisfied and rebellious.

The self-government of both nations should be independent in its policy of interior, but certain problems should be subjected to the accordance of a special coordinating commission.

The relations with the outside should be free to both sides with a condition that certain part of them would be obligatorily discussed previously with the other side.

In such a scheme, the security of Israel would be based on the acceptance and special treaty by hopefully all Arab states. Such treaties should guarantee diplomatic relations with cultural exchange, economic cooperation, tourism and student exchanges and all kinds of good will missions.

Such an arrangement and its execution, in spite of emotional pressures and against all accumulated prejudices and condemnations, would require an enormous amount of courage, a courage of a completely different type that what was on display in the Middle East until now.

I do not know. It looks to me that realization of such a project would be a true test of greatness for both, for Israelis and for Palestinians.

I include here two letters that I wrote four years ago about this problem.

Sincerely,

Tadeusz Maciejczyk
Milledgeville, Illinois, April 7, 1988

Book Two

Der Bundesprasident
Wein, am 25. Marz 1988
Sehr geehrter Herr Maciejczyk

    Im Hinblick auf die Vielzahl der in den letzten Wochen eingegangenan Briefe, ist es mir nicht moglich, Ihr freundliches Schreiben im Einzelnen zu beantworten. Seien Sie aber versichert, das ich Ihre Bekundung der Solidaritat sehr geschatzt habe. Ich mochte Ihnen hiefur meinen aufrichtigen Dank zum Ausdruck bringen.
    Mit allen guten Wunschen und den besten Grusen.

                    Irh

                    (President of the Country)
                    Vienna

25 March 1988

(Translation: Very respected Mr. Maciejczyk:

    Because of large amount of letters received in the last weeks, it is impossible for us to respond to your kindly writing. But you can be assured that your expression of solidarity was much appreciated. For this, I would like to send to you my sincere thanks.
    With all my good wishes and best greetings.)

                    Yours,

                    Kurt Waldheim
                    President of Austria

The World Seen from the Distance of a Small Village

Paul Simon
Senator of the United States

Dear Sir:

I send you a copy of my letter to Secretary Schultz about a solution to the Holy Land crisis. My previous letters written about four years ago to Vice-President Bush are giving this my view a kind of background.

I also send you a copy of my letter to Blue Cross and Blue Shield. As you can see, I am not a good citizen. I complain and protest too much.

As to your last observation that campaigning is like a cold shower, I would tell that such cold showers are making us think more sharply, are giving us new ideas and an accentuation of our own originality. You will be a much better servant of society, just because of this cold shower. What will be within four years? The passing time always is our darkest moment and later the source of the best stories to tell and of some very special smile, directed not to anybody else, but toward our inside, our spirit, that due to them became deeper and more resistant to pressures, or to temptation of glamour.

In spite of everything, my best wishes.

Tadeusz Maciejczyk
Milledgeville, April 10, 1988

Dennis Maach, Ph.D.
Bruce J. Kelly & Associates, Inc.

Dear Sir:

I thank you for your confidence and distinction. I cannot accept your offer, but I am grateful.

I have been here in Milledgeville for over 20 years in my solo practice and I do not know whether I would adjust easily to the group practice. Except this, in last years, I entered here in a kind of battle that requires my presence in this my post. I have to stay here until I clear up the situation.

I send you some of my last letters concerning some of my positions and battles. Probably after reading them, anyway you wouldn't like to renew your proposition. But I am as I am.

Book Two

I would like to ask you a favor. Please send this letter and the copies of my other letters to the physician group that was interested in a new member. I want them to feel that I have a deep appreciation for this offer and that I wish them the best co-worker availability.

                              Tadeusz Maciejczyk, M.D.
                              April 14, 1988

(This is my speech made to veterans in Milledgeville. I was invited to speak to them on Memorial Day.)

Decoration Day 1988

Today we celebrate the memory of those who went to defend our country and our freedom and who didn't come back. They died for a cause and for a purpose. Their sacrifice became for us a lesson and in the same time, a testament. In this testament, those men gave us a duty and a moral obligation to know and to understand the meaning of their sacrifice and to make an effort in our daily life to act for the prevention of another such catastrophe, shaping our future according to their last will.

If we would remain deaf to this testament of those who fell, their sacrifice would become useless and purposeless and our future would be probably considerably more dark.

Then—what is this testament?

The dying men, in the fury of the battle, most likely had no times to formulate any precise recommendations. Their testament, more than this, was evident in their overwhelming longing for a better world, in their rationalization and in the sense given by them to the horrors of life that became their destiny.

This testament and its meaning was felt more clearly than ever during Armistice Day of November 11, 1918. It was not because of the ending of WWI that we celebrate this day even now. It was because on this day, there was a general feeling that the signing of that day's armistice was terminating all wars. Because of this, the millions of veterans of that war were the last veterans ever to live. This atmosphere of hope and optimism, of a new faith in mankind, is the essence of what we

The World Seen from the Distance of a Small Village

celebrate each year on November 11 and why this celebration has not become outdated in spite of everything that happened afterward.

Those expectations of the Armistice Day soon were betrayed by the realities of life. Today, the veterans of WWI are old and feeble, mostly without the strength to take part in any celebrations. But the celebrations are gong on. Each time younger men and women are joining the files. In the 20th century, each generation was forced to pay a special tribute to the monster of war.

Then, what went wrong?

What happened to this spirit of November 11, 1918?

Why did the events go this way?

The peace that followed WWI lasted about 20 years. Those years never really represented a true peace. Its atmosphere was tense. The feeling of a pending, new inevitable catastrophe and unwillingness for a frank talk were stronger than ever. The diplomacy of that time was guided more then by anything else by the book of Machiavelli on how to outsmart and how to use everybody else. The nationalist movements were building impenetrable walls between nations. The class struggles and spread of Communism were intense.

In this way, what came was inevitable. In September of 1939 a new World War started. It was crueler than the previous one. It lasted six years and it still didn't resolve grievances and tensions. If anything, it created many new ones. The realities left by that war, frequently brought the world to the brink of another global disaster and gave us in its tale the Korean War and the war in Viet Nam conflict.

Today we are living in a time of shaky peace. Another global war was prevented until now not as much by a general consent and good will as by a fear of the consequences of the atomic arms. But the race of arms with more and more destructive weapons continued as high as before the previous world wars. The gloomy prospect of a madman or of miscalculations cannot be eliminated.

It is logical and it is very important that during Decoration Day, we should speak not only about wars and its victims, but also about the chain of causes that lead to wars. It is important because there were the situations that if resolved differently could prevent the final cataclysm It is our obligation to know those causes in order to be wiser both in the present and the future.

The wars in the 20th century didn't develop in a vacuum. They had deep roots.

How deep?

Perhaps the early industrialization era set the basis for modern conflicts and wars.

The development of industry was greeted with hope and optimism. The general expectation was that it would bring improvement and new richness to life for everybody.

The society in the early 19th century was mostly rural. The new machinery improved production in the fields, but also produced an excess of population on farms and in villages. That excess of population was forced to migrate to cities with factories in order to find work and to be able to survive.

The life in the towns of those displaced and unskilled villagers was pitiful. Nobody cared about them. Their work was unpredictable. They could be forced to work 16 hours a day even the children, or they could be dismissed without any consideration or compensation. Their pay was small—just enough to survive. Nobody was taking any responsibility for the injured or sick. Striking was forbidden and was punished. The attempts to unionize were considered as a threat to the wonders of the future. Workers were living in filthy slums where life was short. They were decimated by accidents, by illnesses, by alcoholism that looked like the only consolation. But, they were producing wealth and they were increasing the power of their nations.

Those years of industrialization in the 19th century were the years of paradox.

In 1851, during the opening in London of the first big industrial exposition, the pride and joy was felt everywhere. Prince Albert was predicting that the "Progress," which that exposition was documenting, would bring to earth an abundance and a paradise-like life for everybody. Of course, because of that abundance, any future war would be unnecessary. Nevertheless, those were the same years in which Charles Dickens was writing his books about the misery of life of the working class and Karl Marx in the same London was gathering materials for "Das Kapital," a book that later became a sort of bible for the Communist movement.

A rapidly increasing strength of Western Europe was confronting in the 19th century a state of deep weakness everywhere else. India was already dominated by Britain. The Turkish Ottoman Empire, so mighty hundreds of years before, was in the process of disintegration. In the Far East, China was weak and unwilling to modernize. Industrial progress created a means to penetrate finally into the previously forbidden interior of Africa.

In this general situation, counting on the advantage of their strength and increasingly hungry for raw materials, Europe entered on the course of exploitation of the world.

The result of this new drive was probably more visible and striking in China.

In the beginning of the 19th century, China was prosperous and famous for many legendary treasures. China also contained certain numbers of people addicted to opium. England used this opportunity and organized massive shipments of opium from India. China protested. Those imports were altering the life, producing changes in the population, draining resources and spreading misery. Two times, China tried to stop those shipments with military force. In response, British and French troops shelled the open Chinese cities forcing China to capitulate and stop protesting. Those were the so-called "Opium Wars." At the end of the second Opium War, the British and the French looted and burned the Summer Imperial Palace of Chinese emperors. Together, with Germany and Russia, they imposed a state of complete take-over and exploitation. Europeans controlled commerce, custom duties and taxation. No European could be judged by the Chinese, even if he was guilty of an obvious and ugly crime.

China became denigrated and humiliated. Chinese uprisings against the "western Devils" were suppressed without mercy by the combined European forces. The last of those uprisings, the most cruel one, called the "Boxer Rebellion" was fought around 1900. China became exhausted and helpless. It was calculated that in the middle of the 19th century, China had two million opium addicts. At the end of the century, there were 120 million. The misery and the destruction of life was visible everywhere.

The veterans of the Korean War probably remember the passion and the fury of the Chinese attacks. They should understand why it was so. It was not the Communist ideology that was moving them; it was the memories.

The penetration into the interior of Africa and the news about fabulous resources of that land produced a big rush to exploit those resources. This multiplied plantations and mines in the new land. Roads were built to transport obtained goods to Europe. The local population was forced to work for almost no pay. From the miserable paychecks in some places still the head and hat taxes were collected. An escape from the working camp was punished by death; poor work was punished by cutting off the hand.

France, England and Italy were making their inroads into the weak remainder of the Turkish Empire in Asia Minor and North Africa. After the English occupation of Egypt in 1883, a frantic scramble developed to grab as much colonial land as possible. In a very few years, all Africa, except Ethiopia and Liberia, was divided and under European control. There was a strong pressure from the European states to divide in a similar way the ancient, but presently helpless China. The U.S. opposed those plans and somehow China was spared from another humiliation.

The wealth, which Europe accumulated from industrialization and from its colonial enterprises, didn't bring the expected paradise or peace.

It was true that the material progress was unprecedented. The standard of living was rising. On the surface, life was carefree and optimistic. Below the surface tensions were rising. Rivalry between competing nations was becoming each time more bitter, marked by resentments, jealousy and greed. Each state was watching every movement of others, trying to outmaneuver them. Quarrels over different rights were multiplying.

In order to act from the position of strength, each country was constantly increasing its military forces. The industries everywhere were producing a massive amount of weapons and were trying to modernize them and in this way increase the edge of advantage. When Germany, for the first time in history, established obligatory two-year conscription of all able men for military service, soon all other nations followed this pattern. When Germany started to build its own naval force, England, which until then dominated the seas, took this as a direct threat. In order to increase the power and the security of the involved nations, alliances were formed: England with France and Russia; Germany with Austria and Italy. The national selfish feelings in each country became more virulent and more aggressive. As a byproduct, it created a self-discovery of nations that until then didn't feel any aspirations for self-determination or self-government.

In 1914 in Europe, the two alliances, with their enormous armies in full alert, were watching each other. The electricity was in the air. The accumulated tension needed only a spark to explode. The general disposition of populations was like before a picnic or a big adventure. It was maybe best described by Margaret Mitchell in her novel, *Gone with the Wind* in a scene of a party at Tara at the beginning of the Civil War. Everything looked romantic and promising. The uniforms were beautiful and spirits were high. The few scattered voices of caution and restraint were rejected as the voices of pessimists and cowards.

And then, after the shots in Sarajevo, the sparks went off and the enormous armies crashed. After the initial cavalry charges and bravura, it all became immobilized in the bloody mud of the trenches. By 1916, all the enthusiasm for war was gone. Millions were dead. The new French conscripts, while going to the frontline, were making loud sounds imitating the cows shipped to the slaughterhouses. Nobody knew any more what all this war was all about, but the national pride was prevailing and the carnage was going on. The entrance of America into this war

The World Seen from the Distance of a Small Village

finally shifted the balance of forces, broke the impasse and the peace treaty was signed. Not long ago proud Europe lay in ruins.

The wealth accumulated from the progress in industrial production and from the colonial empires, didn't bring paradise to the people as was expected.

Still worse. The lesson from the catastrophe of World War I was short-lived and didn't change the attitudes of nations. It only added new intensity to the old passions and distrust and to hatred. The peace treaty signed in Versailles soon became only a starting point to a new build-up for the next confrontation.

And the question still remains: why those wars, which brought so much pain and destruction to the nations, in the final account produced only a negative teaching of smartness, summarized in the illusion: "the next time I will be prepared better, and I will get better planning." Not the wisdom, but a gambling casino attitude, remained as a high point of the leaderships.

Years later, General Omar Bradley, who led the American forces during D-Day in Normandy, explains this contradiction this way, "In the world of nuclear giants, we are ethical infants. Our trouble is, that we are becoming so absorbed in the mystery of the atom, that we are neglecting the mystery of the Sermon of the Mount."

And the scientist Charles Steinmetz brought that explanation one step further. He said, "Spiritual power is a force, which history clearly teaches, has been the greatest force in the development of men. Yet, we are merely playing with it, never have really studied it, as we have the physical forces. Some day people will learn, that the material things do not bring happiness and are of little use in making people creative and powerful. Then scientists of the world will turn their laboratories over to the study of spiritual forces, which have hardly been scratched."

And so, today we celebrate again a Memorial Day. As every year, we gather, we march, we listen to the speeches, we give the gun salute to the death, and then, we go home and we forget the ceremonial disposition of this moment until the next appropriate ceremonial day. Maybe, along the wall of the Viet Nam monument, the grief reaches deeper and the images from the past are more vivid. But anyway, as here, as in Washington, this day is made only to look backwards and to remember—never to build the projects for the future.

Maybe even that the memories are becoming less and less emotional as the years are passing and all the celebration acquires a form of a rigid ritual, devoid of meaning and leaving us free from any obligations. We are doing our lip-services, we perform the ceremonies and we organize the show, but we completely neglect the "testament' left to us by those who died. We never direct our efforts in the continuous work for the cause of a true peace that would be not false and superficial, but real and deep.

To change this, I ask now the Command of the 553 Post of the American Legion in Milledgeville and all its members to approve two special plans that could be added to this ceremony of Memorial Day.

Plan One: To establish a special scholarship from the Veterans. Each year, on November 11, the Post would ask the young people, from those in high school and to the age of twenty, to do a written work on the subject: The Need and the Role of Spiritual Strength in Resolving Today's World Conflicts.

The participants of this competition would try to present their own vision, conclusion and suggestions for such a question and under a coded name; they would enter their works before the end of April. A special jury, elected for this purpose by the Legion, would qualify them for the No. 1, 2, and 3 awards.

During Memorial Day, the authors of the rewarded works would be asked to read them to the public during the ceremony and would receive the rewards. Then, The Legion would send their original works to the Archives of the General Headquarters of the American legion to be kept there as a special documents of our time. The copies of those works would be sent to the White House, to the Secretary of State, to both Senators of Illinois, to our District Congressmen and to the State Universities.

If it would happen, that this plan of action could be accepted in many other veteran posts in the U.S., then it would be possible, and it would be useful to organize a meeting together of all those who were rewarded for an exchange of impressions and for discussion of merits of their suggestions, or of the nature of differences in their works. In such circumstances, this kind of working encounter should be kept every year nationwide.

Plan Two: The 553 Post of Veterans in Milledgeville would ask the Headquarters of the American Legion to undertake a continuous task that would also be a duty, to observe and to make investigation in order to discover those persons who have distinctive qualities for leadership, not because of their political position or experience, not because of their managerial or commercial skills, not because of their connections, race, eloquence or personal charm, but because of the spiritual strength of their spirit and their wisdom that would qualify them for public trust. Each year on Decoration Day, the General Headquarters of the American Legion would announce the name or names of such persons.

In conclusion, I want to stress my feelings that dwelling in the past, without simultaneous commitment for active involvement for the future, most likely results in stagnation, sterility and an anxiety of losing

The World Seen from the Distance of a Small Village

the grip on our destiny. Contrasting with this, when we learn from our past and we use the accumulated experience for our future planning and action, we grow.

To fulfill the testament of those who fell in action, we should remember them, but also we should explore the best ways into the future. We should involved in this task, the young and we should look constantly for the wisest and spiritually strongest men for guidance.

Tadeusz Maciejczyk
Decoration Day, 1988

Book Two

Crescent Counties Foundation for Medical Care
The Case of Mrs. Mildred Dublo

Responding to your second letter, dated June 3, 1988, requesting additional information to explain why I decided to hospitalize Mrs. Dublo on July 19, 1987, I can only repeat that the admission was appearing to me to be a more rational solution in her case in that situation.

1. She was looking sick. (She expired on August 6, 1987.)
2. She had far-advanced Alzheimer's disease that was worsening rapidly.
3. Because of Alzheimer's, it was impossible to establish with her any doctor-patient relationship. She was unable to explain anything.
4. She was brought to the office at 10:00 PM because she was restless, in her second night without sleep, complaining of chest pain that apparently was radiating to the thyroid region. She was short of breath, with wheezings and rales in the lungs. She had tachycardia of 112/minute; she had a headache and she was giving the appearance of being ready to faint at any moment.
5. From my office, I am twenty miles from the hospital. Pt. had an additional several miles to the office.
6. Pt. needed calm, objective observation and testing to find what it was. Her home was near to an emotional breakdown.

If you reject the judgment that I made in this case, you will give me also a message that I am out of touch with today's realities because if I would have a similar situation today, as a doctor, I would act in the same way. I would admit her.

In our medical approach today, we measure the human needs by the computerized rules and so, we become washed out of humanity that a time ago was supposed to be one very important ingredient and asset of a true doctor. Now, I am forced to be an automat with a rigid one button to be pushed in such or another occasion.

America is losing its humanity, its previous warmth and consequently its togetherness and its moral strength. The lack of warmth and computerization of all human needs are breaking the souls, are emptying the life and increasing an uncertainty and disregard for old values, inclining more to drugs and crime, destabilizing family life, creating increasing numbers of people, especially children, who have difficulty

The World Seen from the Distance of a Small Village

adjusting and reaching fulfillment in life. It will be very difficult to repair the damage to society done by computerized solutions imposed on people and by constantly growing armies of special commissions, inspectors, and enforcers of what to be official wisdom, or cover-up for unsolved and deteriorating crises. It is not a good substitute for a meaningful dialogue and creation of healthy environment that could feed the personal internal growth for everybody.

It is no fun, there is no merit, no pride in being a doctor now in America. I am watched constantly as a potential abuser, criminal or sucker in cases of malpractice. More and more, I am forced to use an expression of Stalin, when he described the role of people in the socialist state, as a small screw in a big engine without any room for my own individuality. In America, today the dog's collars are produced in abundance for everybody. They are supposed to be the remedies for present failures. They will be the material for the "progress' into tomorrow. That is all that bureaucracy can deliver if the genius for leadership is nowhere.

But I just do not believe in such a method of salvation. I am glad that I am getting old and I do not need to stay for long in this multidimensional swamp that in this country is becoming more and more real.

I hope you will notify me about your decision in this case of hospital admission for Mrs. Mildred Dublo.

> Tadeusz Maciejczyk, M.D.
> Milledgeville, IL, June 12, 1988

I sent copies of this letter to the Secretary of Health in Washington, D.C, to both Illinois Senators, to our District Congressman and to Presidential candidates.

Book Two

George Bush
Vice-President of the United States

Dear Sir:

I received a letter from "Americans for Bush" and I read it with a feeling of uneasiness.

I support you for the Presidency, but I hope that you will not carry on the "Reagan Revolution." I hope that as President, you will be your own man with your own ideas and your own touch with the nation and with the world.

I am not sending any money. Instead, I send you a copy of my letter to the Crescent Counties Foundation that illustrates my apprehension about present-day America and in which, maybe, I come to some diagnosis. I was writing this letter in a state of frustration.

As you are a veteran, I am sending you also a copy of my Memorial Day speech in which I was trying to understand and to find a light for the darkness.

I wish you the best.

         Tadeusz Maciejczyk, M.D.
         Milledgeville, June 16, 1988

The World Seen from the Distance of a Small Village

Editor
Robins Reader
Richmond, Virginia

Dear Sir:

    I am sending you here a copy of my Memorial Day speech.
    I do this because your last spring issue gave me an idea when I was asked to speak and I was vacillating because never before I was doing any speeches. I can tell that in this my address, I took the seeds from your pages and I threw it a little further, maybe in the ground of people's souls.
    I would be glad if you would find time to read this, my speech, maybe also to give me your opinion, or even send the copies to the local Veteran Posts, or to whomever. And I think that the two points plan from this speech, if practiced, and changed in a tradition, could add positive points into the life in the U.S.
    I do not know whether it is worth anything, but I am sending you here also a photocopy of my notes taken during a visit of an old lady, a few weeks after she was put on Reglan.
    I thank you for sending me Robins Reader and for making it as it is.

                                          Tadeusz Maciejczyk, M.D.
                                          Milledgeville, June 23, 1988

Book Two

Department of Nuclear Safety
Springfield, IL

    I do not know what is making inspection of my facility almost 100% more costly than it was intended for an average inspection, but anyway, what-a-hack.

    My countryside solo practice is becoming defenseless, is getting less and less practical and is going downhill. It cannot cope with a bureaucratic endless screw-up in this age when just handling paperwork is a very complicated task—probably more important than attending the sick.

    There was a time, when I was enthusiastic and dedicated. I never got rich because I never knew how to charge, but I had satisfaction that in no other profession was possible.

    Today, I do not fit. The work became dried out of personal interaction with the patient of its previous confidence and warmth. Patients became numbers and their illnesses became points on computer screens. Instead of being stimulated to study medical situations, I am forced to study the constantly changing rules played by government, Medicare, Medicaid, insurance companies, etc. Today, in place of previous closeness and trust, the distance and the mistrust with suspicion and a possibility of incrimination became the daily reality of work in the office. The third parties are constantly interfering and cooking something new.

    In this environment, a solo practice in a countryside cannot do more than gradually disappear. The people from the countryside will join the lines before big clinics that have the means to deal with this new reality of the practice.

    As for me, I wanted to work until I would be 100, but I am depressed and worn out by these last few years. I am trying to find some different useful occupation for me that would permit me to grow and would preserve my need for self-esteem.

    Sincerely,

    Tadeusz Maciejczyk, M.D.
    Milledgeville, IL June 26, 1988

P.S. To illustrate my point, I include some of my previous letters.

The World Seen from the Distance of a Small Village

Department of Health and Human Services
Washington, D.C. 20013

As time is passing, I feel more and more pressure that is suffocating my practice. Because of this pressure, my small solo practice in the countryside is approaching a limit of breaking down.

Here I send you some of my recent letters: my call for help. Such small isolated offices as mine, have no resources to deal with the ever-expanding bureaucracy, its creativity for new rules, it's capricious short-sightedness in patching, and its never-satisfied hunger for more and more papers. In this increasingly absurd situation, the attendance of the sick became not a primary objective, but a secondary addition.

I consider those letters that I send to you a kind of feedback from the periphery. They show my sincere reactions. I hope that these letters will be taken seriously by you. Without sincerity in feedback, all regulations can get out of hand.

Sincerely,

Tadeusz Maciejczyk, M.D.
Milledgeville, June 27, 1988

Book Two

Sister Joann Boneski
Sister of Saint Dominic

Dear Sister:

I received and I read your letter. I understand the work and the missions that the Sisters have fulfilled for centuries and I am sad many times that the change of time put in their place the so-called social workers who after learning something of sociology and psychology, are replacing your previous frontline in the fight for a better world. I am sorry because the social workers frequently care more about the exterior effect, about the hours of work, and about how to keep jobs, than about doing a real inroad into the souls of the people that is essential to succeed in this kind of frontline. They usually do not put into a necessary warmth and love. They frequently just keep the drill. For the Sisters the way to do things was dictated by heart and by faith, by a need to have a mission and this is much more than a diploma upon graduation.

I am sorry that I am not rich. I never had a talent for such a purpose. During the last five years, I have been opposing the malpractice suit craze and for over one year, I have a suit on of my own. My practice became reduced by the required malpractice insurance price and by the governmental Medicare regulations. I would like to survive on this my post until my youngest daughter, who this fall will enter DePaul University, is finished with her schooling, Afterwards? I do not know. I am discouraged.

I am sending you some samples of medicines. I do not know whether they can be of any use to you.

Meclomen, 100 mg. - one capsule ever 12–24 hours for arthritis, if necessary (take with some food in the stomach.)

Minocin, 50 and 100 mgs. For infections about 200 mgs. Daily.

Minipress and Maxzide - one tablet daily for hypertension.

Norflex 100 mgs - one tablet every 12 horus for pain (especially skeletal muscular pain.)

In other tablets you will somehow discover its use.

Maybe, that I would like to ask you for a kind of gift for me from you. I have now two special projects. I need some prayers.

I was asked to be a speaker during last Memorial Day. I did my speech a little longer than the people were expecting and I asked the people for a realization of a special plan that could be added to the Memorial Day ceremonies. I would like this plan to develop into a nationwide practice and tradition. It would require work and dedication and would go against

The World Seen from the Distance of a Small Village

the resistance of an inertia. (I send you a copy of that my speech with the medication package.)

The other plan is written in my native Polish and is about the problems there.

In meantime, I wish you the best.

Tadeusz Maciejczyk
Milledgeville, July 4, 1988

E.I. Fediay, Chairman
Americans for Bush

Dear Fellow Conservatives:

I received your letter and I am burning from shame reading it. I am sympathetic to Bush and his campaign, but I would like to see him as a man, not as a manipulated, blind and deaf puppet who speaks with a jargon of your letter and has for the people only your message that can be summarized that while talking much, is telling absolutely nothing except for the repeated and worn out slogans of professional politicians of the lowest category.

The world is full of deep problems and of causes to worry that require an urgent effort to perceive, to evaluate, to bring them into open and frank discussions and to change and correct. Those are the real objectives of the Presidency. And you are sending me here a pointless, colorless, shallow, generalized and funny, party-empty, mentally idle stuff.

I do not know whether you are really for Bush or whether, by such a presentation, you are making him to look ridiculous in the eyes of everybody who thinks and in this way you are trying to provoke doom for his campaign.

If America on both party sides, will try to flow into the future on such a profound ideology and philosophy, I can only feel pity for America and for the world.

Tadeusz Maciejczyk, M.D.
Milledgeville, July 7, 1988

P.S. I send a copy of this letter directly to Mr. Bush.

Book Two

George Bush
Vice-President of the United States and
A likely next President of this country

Here I am sending to you a copy of my letter to E.I. Fediay, Chairman of Americans for Bush. What I wrote in this letter, was my sincere, immediate reaction after reading a letter that was addressed to me as to the "Fellow Conservative."

I would prefer to be called a "fellow who cares" without the epithet of conservative or liberal that so richly decorates the otherwise empty letter of those who say they are working for your election. Such a letter can only produce anxiety, uncertainty and anger.

I write this note and send the copy of my letter directly to you because I feel a respect for you and I care.

Tadeusz Maciejczyk, M.D.
Milledgeville, July 7, 1988

The World Seen from the Distance of a Small Village

THE MAN IN THE GLASS
(Author Unknown)

When you get what you want in the struggle for self
    And the world makes you King for a Day.
Just go to the mirror and look at yourself
    And see what that man has to say.

For it isn't your father or mother or wife
    Whose judgment upon you must pass;
The fellow whose judgment counts most in your life
    Is the one staring back in the glass.

You may be like Jack Horner and chisel a plum
    And think you're a wonderful guy,
But the man in the glass says you're only a bum
    If you can't look him straight in the eye.

He's the fellow to please—never mind all the rest;
    He is with you clear up to the end;
But you pass the most difficult, dangerous test
    If the man in the glass is your friend.

You may follow the world down the pathway of years
    And get pats on the back as you pass,
But your final reward will be heartaches and tears
    If you cheated the man in the glass.

    A few days ago, I was talking with Edgar Imel through the fence of the garden. We were discussing the human nature. He told me at that time this poem. It was written by a prisoner in a prison. I remembered. And later I asked Mr. Imel to give me a copy of this poetry. He brought it to the office. Mrs. Sibley made for herself a copy also.
  July 10, 1988

1988 Republican Platform Planning Committee

    I thank you for the distinction of choosing me to answer your survey.
    I do this because if you really look for my opinion or advice, I would feel guilty if I would leave you without giving you my point of view.

If, on the other hand, your questionnaire was only a pretext to collect money, then I have to disappoint you. At present, I feel a squeeze. I do not belong to those who enjoyed the blessings of the "Reagan Era of Prosperity."

I have to confess also that during the last few years, my pride of being a part of America hit the lowest level. My friend, a life-long friend of American wrote to me, "It is a pity that the actions of such a leader as Pres. Reagan is, are appearing from here so very little clean." And I had nothing to answer him. We can multiply our military defenses, but if we fail to win the respect of the people of the world, our security will have a shaky base.

I voted for Reagan and I became disappointed. Gradually, I came to a conclusion that he cared less to build the real things than for its exterior appearances and effects. Reagan's America started to look to me like a rich man who lost his fortune, but not his habits and pretensions. Publicly, he would act with the old time splendor. Behind the scene, he would enter in secret of camouflaged debts to keep the show. He would try to avoid the pain of a fundamental re-examination and of facing the truth.

If the Republican Party intends to win in this election, it has to start to look toward the future—not to be afraid of revisions and innovations. The Reagan Era belongs to the past and is already sclerotic.

Looking at your different points under the questions Number 1 and 2, I don't understand why you asked only for a few minutes to answer them. Such answering was not worth even those few minutes. In presenting your questionnaire this way, you are clearly indicating how low your opinion is about the potential of the people to whom you directed this survey.

Those points are a repetition from the past. They are not asking for any effort or input toward a creative and refreshed platform. The platform, which can be seen through your survey, will not mobilize people. It is very true that the people are down and undecided. They are tired of the "Reagan on the stage" performance. They are hungry for something else, something real. Maybe this hunger was the secret behind Jackson's strength during the primaries.

For those reasons, instead of repeating the litany of headlines championed by Reagan that brought little success in the past, why not call for a new "openness" and open the windows to the future. Maybe for this purpose it would be useful to create a "Feedback from the Country" department dedicated to handling, evaluating and using all suggestions and propositions, selecting them evaluating their practicality and presenting it to the government or to appropriate organizations.

The World Seen from the Distance of a Small Village

Such a "Feedback from the Country" department could be an effective intermediary between the people and the centers. It could develop into a feeling of togetherness, involvement and co-responsibility. It could create a better climate. It would be an open invitation to everybody to participate. Also, maybe it could become a medicine that would have the ingredients to cure many of our present ills. It would be an open invitation to all the people to dream, to think and to grow.

I also wanted to say that the whole convention and platform should be constructed in such a way to create an image of the next President as a father to the nation, as George Washington was. He should not appear there as a partisan party chief.

Maybe my letter will be unpleasant to you and you will be inclined to dismiss it as invalid. But in this crucial time, I wish you luck. Not the amount of money, or advertisements, but the freshness of your ideas, their sincerity and value will decide who will win in this election.

Tadeusz Maciejczyk, M.D.
Milledgeville, July 21, 1988

John P. Comer
National Commander of The National Legion

Dear Sir:

I read your message in the August edition of the American Legion. You are telling there about the work done by Veterans to make the world better and to improve the life for our children and our youths.

It is logical. Veterans did much. They were fighting on the battlefields to make the world more just and more kind. And this fight really never is over. Somehow the world constantly requires a caring hand for the daily repairs and improvements. This is a continuation of a battlefield fight and the Veterans are not abandoning their posts and responsibilities.

Last May, I was asked to deliver the Memorial Day speech. My first reaction was to escape. I never was a public speaker. Then I decided to take the challenge. In my speech, I told about the testament left for us by those who died, about the causes of wars, about its deep roots, about the present unstable conditions and I asked for approval of a two point plan that I presented at the end of the speech.

After reading your message, I decided to send a copy of my speech to you in hopes that you would read it. If you find it useful and the two points plan is viable and practical, with a good possibility for realization, then I would like you to present those points to all commanders during the September convention in Louisville and spread it across the country to all posts for discussion and maybe for realization.

Such a plan in action would be something new and perhaps it could bring the promise of a good harvest.

I wish you the best in your work.

Tadeusz Maciejczyk
Milledgeville, August 6, 1988

John P. "Jake" Comer
National Commander of The American Legion

Dear Sir:

I thank you for your August 17th letter that answered the problem of my two-point program in my Memorial Day speech.

I have no talent for proper organizational proceedings. Maybe because of this, I am in a solo practice. I admire all those rules and orderly progress in decision-making. Of course, if they do not kill the element of spontaneity, which in specific circumstances can be beneficial, forceful and refreshing. Perhaps the feeling for such a need and moment to depart from a routine makes the difference between the chairman and a leader.

I am not an American Veteran. During WWII, I was in a Polish Home Army. But I spoke with Veterans and I know about Veterans' scholarships and about the Constitutional Oratory contests. About three years ago, during the period of discussion and preparations for the Bicentennial of the Constitution, I made an attempt to take part in the discussion. Naturally, nobody answered.

But the oratory about the Constitution can be done today and can be completely forgotten tomorrow. Generally an oratory is shallow and has no strength to make a lasting influence to crystallize an idea or to train a mind.

Contrary to this, a taking part in the contest proposed in my speech could make a special, maybe life-long mark, on the participants, could call the talents that otherwise would be lost to a general life-stream and could prepare a cadre of very special people with a vision and dedication. Their views would be seen, to some extent, as self-exposure in their work and would be trained and tested in the confrontations of the yearly national reunions for discussions of those views. Such public dis-

The World Seen from the Distance of a Small Village

cussions could attract attention and could do lasting influence on many persons, especially on youths and even in high places of policymaking.

I know that such a contest would not be easy and not everybody would be called to participate, but those who would do here in America and maybe also in other countries through their veteran organizations, could develop a potential to make a deep and good impact on the world.

I wish you, and all Veterans, the best.

                                      Tadeusz Maciejczyk
                                      August 25, 1988

P.S. I send you a copy of my letter about the Constitution and maybe another one that I called "Is the defense strategy = as a peace strategy?"

Book Two

1988 Presidential Issues Survey
for the National Republican Congressional Committee
Survey Number: AB-4758

Before I start to respond to each point of this survey, I want to stress that I am not an admirer of Pres. Reagan. I voted for him. I became disappointed. I would not like his "leadership" to last any longer than strictly necessary. (I include here my letter to the 1988 Republican Platform Planning Committee.)

I will vote for G. Bush, but I would like him to be himself, not just an addition or continuation of the Reagan years. In this sense, his stand on the environment was very encouraging to me.

Question No. 1: I disapprove.

A. R. Reagan was mainly a charmer, floating on the surface, avoiding the depth of the issues, leaving the people with a hunger for truly living this life, not just placing it on the stage.
B. During the Reagan years, the powerful interest groups, pressing for the advantage, created so many new laws and obligations that they are suffocating the life out of ordinary people. Writing papers became almost more important than the work itself. I wonder what an army of clerks is necessary to screen and to answer those never-ending paper giants. A feeling of something basically false and sickening from which we cannot liberate ourselves is paralyzing. (I include here some of my letters dealing with the problems of work in my field.)
C. The new laws multiplied like the weeds in my garden and there is no official institution in sight that would screen them periodically, weeding out the excess and the absurd. We are starting to look more and more like Israel in the time preceding Christ, when the scribes created laws for any function of the day and the Pharisees elevated them to be almost a substitution for religion and a relationship with God. Advocated by Reagan, decentralization and more freedom for people's initiatives became a joke. It became just the same as what he said during the convention, that thanks to him, we can walk safely on the streets. Should I consider this as his complete disconnection from life, or his complete lack of judgment?

Question No. 2: Wrong track. See above.

The World Seen from the Distance of a Small Village

Question No. 3: Disagree.

The first and more forceful element in the fight for a balanced budget should be a complete frankness with the nation. The leadership should present priorities, indicate excesses, the places of waste, and convince the people that they are the participants and not merely an object of manipulation. Such a dialogue could be done through the "Department of Feedback form the Country" that I proposed in my letter on July 21.

The politicians are clearly teaching that when the problem of votes is concerned, all the adherence to principles, to elements of judgment, or of ethic in social or national arrangements are always for sale and always have a price. Nobody even makes a secret from this during campaigns. An unpublicized, but open and widespread contempt for politicians' assurances and promises is a nationwide reality. A constitutional amendment, without breaking the commerce of promises for votes, will remain nothing more than a decoration, generating later disappointment and more ugliness of cynicism.

Question No. 4: Agree

Probably we owe to trust Gorbachev more than the previous Soviet dictators (he is initiating some changes) but with all the caution. What are the true objectives of those changes?

I include here my letter to Senator R. Dole and my article named "Is the defense strategy = peace strategy?"

Question No. 5: Disagree

I include here my article, "Cocaine Plague—Crack addition"

A) The cause of drug use is within the people here in America. The main effort, the principal battle, should develop on the home front. An action should be directed by the answers to the questions: what is pushing the people to buy drugs; what is the nature of the predisposing emptiness and anxiety? Not a military intervention, but a leadership in the homework will mark the victory. Ronald Reagan didn't touch this field.

B) The interception and the identification of smuggling and distributing chains should be kept at the high level.
C) All identified dealers, up to the top, should be punished not merely by a fine, but by a confiscation of everything that they and their families have. This money should be used to finance the rehabilitation and the efforts of identification and interception.
D) If drug usage would cause the death of a user, the identified top dealers in the chain should be put to death for a premeditated murder.
E) The identified top dealer could expect more lenient punishment for reviling the name of his superior.

In conclusion: If our leaders and our society at large have no will and are not responsible and strong enough to act with the strongest measures and determination, the mess will intensify and the history will condemn all of us.

Question No. 6: Strongly Agree.

To deny any person, a President or a simple individual, the Line-Item-Veto on any document, he is required to sign, is not a "compromise," but a direct violation of the integrity of that person. It is an immoral violation of his conscience, his authority, his ethical approach to the problem. It is a loud laughter from the authority and from the rights of the person who is expected to sign after such an act of intrusion and "smartness." It is an act of blunt contempt, of denigration and humiliation. It is an open abuse that in my opinion has no justification in any human relation. It doesn't mean any political skillfulness, but to the contrary, it is a political cowardice of a fear of an open, frontal approach. It is sneaky. It is not noble. The names of the authors of this type of action should be made public and the explanation before the nation should be required at minimum.

Question No. 7: Uncertain

AIDS undoubtedly needs funds for scientific work to find the cure. AIDS needs special institutions for its victims, as TB (tuberculosis) had sanitariums; not just a number of beds in hospitals. To fight AIDS, the government and all the moral authorities of this nation should create an atmosphere that would limit the spread of this illness. A mere distribution of condoms should be the last of the list of remedies. The moral elevation, the emotional fulfillment, the building-up of the people, the uncompromised fight with drugs, should have top priority. A surface plaster remedy is easy and cheap. This fight will be a stick with which to measure the greatness or mediocrity of our leaders and of our system.

Question No. 8: Uncertain (SDI-Star Hans)

Again, I direct you to my letter to Sen. R. Dole and to the copy of my article: "Is the defense strategy = peace strategy?" The main part of those letters retain still its complete actuality.

Question No. 9: The decline in ethical and moral values in this country. All the other factors that are threatening this nation today have the base in the decline of the ethical and moral values of people. The presidential leadership here is enormously important. Ronald Reagan left here dissatisfaction and a hunger that his beautiful oratory and his personal charm had no strength to approach.

Question No. 10: Uncertain.

The tax increase is only an invitation and permission for a continuation of the politician's commerce of promises for votes. It is also an excuse for not doing a true inventory of what we have, or what our needs are, of the best ways to remedy those needs and of the most effective ways to stimulate the inertia of those segments or people who are able, but who refuse to be productive and to contribute to a common well-being.

If such a correction would be done, if all of them would be frankly discussed with the nation through the "Feedback Department" and measured in life practice, then a temporary tax increase would be justified.

Question No. 11: Definitely No. (A visit of Pres. Reagan here)

For success of this election, G. Bush has to get out from behind the shadow of R. Reagan and except this the popularity of R. Reagan here is very questionable.

Question No. 12: My recommendations to the next President are: Be Yourself. Do not think about re-election, about the interests of the party, about popularity for today. Do just what you deeply feel is right. Only in this way you will reach greatness and the party it's strength and inspiration.

Book Two

Tadeusz Maciejczyk
Milledgeville, September 5, 1988

Rural Health Task Force
Springfield, IL

My observations:

1. Medical practice in rural areas is becoming less and less attractive to young doctors. Those areas could be completely emptied from doctors in the years to come and its population forced to travel to clinics in big towns if the present trend continues.
2. Rural doctors in solo practice are under a growing squeeze. They cannot afford the rapidly increasing list of indispensibles to make their office function. The work with the patients helping them as it was before, is not a problem. The problem is the enormously expanded and still growing paperwork, the confusion of patients who cannot understand and cannot cope with responding to the complexity of the paper loads. The problem is our own complicated relationship with Medicare and Medicaid that is exhausting. The problem is also the ever-pending threat of malpractice: its imposed limitations and high cost of insurance to practice. All those problems are making the work especially in small and isolated outposts of medicine in rural areas depressing and unattractive. I send you here copies of my letters where all those points are more clearly described.
3. The paperwork requirements are affecting all health care institutions. Not the work itself, but the perfection of charts, became the testing area for the growing army of inspectors and supervisors. Health services are getting too many generals and not enough soldiers.
4. It is now a law that nursing homes have to get all their medication from the same approved pharmacy. This requirement affects not only the Medicare and Medicaid patients, but also those who pay for themselves. The price of medicines obtained in this way is not always low. I wonder why there is such rigidity and why the interference with the citizens' right to make their own search for the best contract? This imposed rigidity is surely not

constitutional and is violating the freedom of choice principle. Who introduced such a law?
5. Public Aid, as it is in the present, is not helping rehabilitation of the needy, putting them to work again. In many instances, it helps to create a permanent and hereditary dependency and expectation for more "rights." It clearly discourages them to take partial work that would pay less than their assistance. I wonder whether social workers subconsciously encourage a permanent dependency because the number of dependents affirms their position and status?
6. The Public Aid institutions in health care and also in education, by enforcing only a partial pay for serving its clients, is creating an additional burden on those who pay for their health care or education. In reaction, it is producing compensatory, higher pricing for visits or tuition of those who strive to pay for themselves. This is a kind of additional taxation and indirect punishment of the people who struggle to pay their bills. Whether it is just, wise or moral, I do not want to judge. For sure, it creates changes in the people's character and feelings on both sides of the issue and in this sense, it will affect the future.

Those are the problems that come to my mind at present. Commenting on the letter of Carol Johansen, R.N., the health coordinator for the Head Start Program whose "generosity" is limitless, I want to say that I never refused to see Public Aid patients, and I always dedicated as much time to them as to any others, but I cannot afford to give them medicines or immunizations.

When I was giving it in the beginning, after repeated paperwork and calls, I was paid almost 1/3 of my cost for those substances, or maybe nothing at all. I was always trying to help those in a true need. Now this my gift to them is transformed into a demand from the coordinators of the Head Start Program. To some extent, I feel betrayed.

Tadeusz Maciejczyk, M.D.
Milledgeville, September 29, 1988

Book Two

Illinois Academy of Family Physicians

I feel guilty for not responding to your repeated invitations to join your organization. My attitude is due probably to the fact that once I was burned.

Until the beginning of the eighties, I was a member of the AMA. My membership finished abruptly and in an ugly way.

I do not remember exactly what year it was. It was towards the spring. AS always, I was struggling to pay three tuitions and to pay taxes. When I did this, I was ready to pay my AMA membership dues, when without any previous warning, I was notified from the AMA offices in Chicago that my membership was cancelled because I didn't pay my dues on time. The next day I received similar notification from my county medical association. Apparently the AMA sent the news to them before writing to me and I do not know why they responded with such an eagerness to condemn. To make me feel worse, the AMA forbade the insurance company to continue my disability protection.

I felt angry and I felt betrayed. I even didn't know that there was a deadline to pay the dues. I didn't like the harsh, intolerant and repressive moves of the AMA after so many years of belonging to the organization. I didn't go to any more of the county meetings. I responded negatively to later pressures from the AMA to join them again. Before that incident, I considered the AMA as a friendly and humane organization. I do not want (at present time) to be a member of a bureaucratic, repressive, cold and jumpy organization that in place of communication, established a law of striking with a stick before any effort to talk and to clarify.

At present, my isolation became increased by the effects of other problems. In 1883, I protested against obligatory malpractice insurance and I lost my privileges in Sterling Hospital.

The next aggravation in my situation came in January, 1987, when after several voices from Sterling Clinic that I would be taught a lesson, I got my own malpractice suit. In this suit I decided to be my own lawyer. I want to keep the argument of the accusation within the medical field. I do not want lawyers to accommodate and twist this problem to the ground where they are at home and at ease. I also asked for a counter suit against the lawyer. I do not know what will be the outcome of all this adventure, but I cannot just bend.

I send you the copies of my different letters where I describe my position on several situations in the present medical practice. I consider that before my admission to your organization, you should know the facts about me, so that you will not regret my admission.

The World Seen from the Distance of a Small Village

My best wishes to your organization. I understand well the need for togetherness in this uneasy time of transition and of the rapid progress into the unknown.

                                        Tadeusz Maciejczyk, M.D.
                                        October 6, 1988

Book Two

Rotary Club of Kalibo
Kalibo, Aklan, Philippines

Dear Friends,

Your letter came here a long time ago while Cristina was still at home, before her departure to the university. The delay in my answer was due to the fact that it came in the moment of squeeze: of time to pay taxes, taking Cristina to school and the fight over malpractice insurance. This was the reason that my response to your letter had to wait until a better moment—until now.

Anyway, with your letter, or without it, I wanted to write to you and thank you for taking care of Cristina when she was in Kalibo. I know you all from her photographs and also from her talks and descriptions. I do not know how you did this, but Cristina came home from her year-long adventure very nostalgic, very sorry that the year in Kalibo couldn't have lasted many more months. She liked to speak about that time, about you and about different places and moments there. She almost couldn't see her home here and couldn't enjoy the old frame in which she lived before. Her heart was there.

With the passage of time, she adjusted and she entered again into the daily routine of our lives here, but not completely. Now, in school, where the tempo of working already became very intense, she has to read a lot and to write never-ending papers, leaving her not much time to rest. When she calls home, she always asks whether something from the Philippines came for her here.

I have no doubt that in Cristina's life, if her life would be creative and rich in new thoughts, the memory of Kalibo, of your people and your islands will always have a loud resonance. Maybe one day, she will go there again to renew the old friendships. Who knows? Life is marvelous because it brings us its hidden treasures that are always there if we have the will and persistence to look for them, to recognize them and to mobilize our capacities and work to make them useful and good for us. I do not know what the future holds, but I have no doubt that in Cristina you will always have a life-long friend.

In the meantime, both my wife and I send you our best wishes.

Tadeusz Maciejczyk
Milledgeville, October 13, 1988

The World Seen from the Distance of a Small Village

The Rockford Council for Affordable Health Care
Rockford, IL

Thank you for your letter.

Truly, my first reaction was not to answer it at all. But I have to be fair and to give you my explanation as to why I reacted in such a negative way.

Your proposed services add only to a more bureaucratization of medicine, which is already suffocating. I do not wish to have another babysitter and an additional amount of paperwork to cope with.

It is amazing to me how the bureaucracy, being completely unproductive and sterile by itself, is flourishing and multiplying, creating constantly new positions of administrators, assistant administrators, directors and a new horde of project staffers, and how it gravitates not to real work, but to the command centers and artificial complications of the obvious. The money spent on you could be used better attending more directly to those in need.

The problem of health care is that it is creating too many generals with artificial assignments who consequently are enormously alienating the real workers in the medical field. The parasitic invasion of Health Care never was so acute as in the last few years.

I am sorry that my opinion about you has to be expressed in this way. If you disagree with me, I would be glad to listen to your side of the logic for your intended purpose and action.

If you give me the address of the W.K. Kellogg Foundation, I would gladly send them this, my point of view.

Tadeusz Maciejczyk, M.D.
Milledgeville, October 20, 1988

Book Two

Crescent County Foundation for Medical Care
Lisle, IL

Re: Case of hospital admission of Pearl Martha Lott

    The conditions for her admission were outlined already and it is not easy for me to add to this anything new. From experience, I know that arguing with you about these matters is time lost. You are there to deny and to save money.
    But this 92 year old lady in the ER had a hard time breathing, was anxious and had no strength to be shuffled to the hospital and back. I had to help her in her distress and to evaluate her. It is not easy to stamp an exact computer etiquette on each patient. It is necessary to be there, nearby, to feel the misery of the patient and to try to do something practical and helpful.
    I did what I thought was the most appropriate thing and you, the high priests of approval or denial, in an isolation room and not bothered by any personal contact, you are free now to pass sentence.
    I was never trying to abuse and I am astonished by what I see in this beautiful U.S.
    Please, do whatever you feel is appropriate from your point of view.

                                            Tadeusz Maciejczyk, M.D.
                                            Milledgeville, October 27, 1988

The World Seen from the Distance of a Small Village

James H. Sammons, M.D.
Executive Vice-President of the American Medical Association

Dear Sir:

I send you my response to your survey. It is only an approximation. I do not keep the record that would permit me to answer your questions exactly. I did this survey together with the nurse who fills out the insurance forms and with the afternoon clerk who keeps the finances.

This survey has limitations. It only tells the numbers. It doesn't reflect the emotional stress of the present working condition in a solo medical practice. In those conditions, the feeling of frustrations, of being helpless against abuse (approved $5 for an extended visit; no pay at all for all house calls; the repeated zeroes in the column of payments for additional services during visits, the new threat of punishment for delay in paperwork.) Consequentially, I feel that my practice is changing. The mood, the enthusiasm in the office, is not the same. Each time, more frequently a thought is coming to my mind that I could be forced to close the office because everything has its limits. The calls to Illinois Medicare center in Marion are going against a deaf wall. Nobody there takes the responsibility. Apparently, nobody there is authorized to explain and to inform. The repeated applications and reapplications are wearing my patience, are consuming my time and are costly. Marion's insistence that a computer installation in my office would resolve all differences sounds phony. Such an installation and its operation are economically impractical in a small solo practice in the country.

At the present moment, it looks that each month, each day; I am nearer to the point of giving up. Whether somebody else would come to take this medical country outpost, I do not know. I doubt it.

America has a special dark side to its soul. It destroys things recklessly just for the convenience of the moment, for putting a patch on a hole that would last until tomorrow, but resolve this moment's difficulties, for saving face after electoral promises, for a sheer act of showing that everything is moving and acting. Election realities are forcing politicians to have two faces and the consequences of such a system cannot be anything else but a deepening chronic illness for all the country. This system is entrenched, is universal in America, is acquiring new gravity with each election. To stop, to reverse its progress, would require a providential, strong man at the top who against almost everybody, would dare to make a shake up of the American conscience. I hope that the presently-elected candidate would be such a man.

Book Two

You have to forgive me that with this letter and with the copies of my previous letters, I complicated the clarity of your survey.

Tadeusz Maciejczyk, M.D.
Milledgeville, November 28, 1988

P.S. I am sorry that my writing is so clumsy. It was after the end of the day's work and I was tired.

Like for irony, two days after I sent this letter, a notification from Illinois Academy of Family Practice that I was nominated as a candidate for the Illinois Family Physicians Year Award for 1989.

The World Seen from the Distance of a Small Village

My Reaction to Letters from Washington

Today I received two letters from Washington. One was from congressman Guy Vander Jagt asking for participation in a stirring farewell salute to President Reagan. The other was from Senator Robert W. Kesten asking me to demonstrate my opposition to Soviet atrocities by donating to the Freedom Fund that would expose Soviet barbarism to all the people.

Also, today I had in my office a grandmother of a 21-year old girl, a wife of a U.S. serviceman, who when working in an all-night supermarket was abducted and killed during a robbery of about $56.00.

No.

After looking on the eight years of Reagan's leadership, I am not in the mood to join his admirers in erecting a triumphant monument memorializing the Reagan reign. Nor, after today's visit of a crying grandmother lamenting the senseless murder, one of the frequent murders now happening on the U.S. streets, do I want to speak or think about Soviet atrocities. With the present domestic situation of rising crime, mercilessly for the society tolerated by our so-called justice, we have no moral strength to point our finger on anybody else, even if everybody would agree that the Soviet crimes should not be tolerated. Except this, the Soviet atrocities are known for a long time to the world. It is not necessary to make a new collection to feed the second Columbus who would explain to us again that America exists.

I do not share the opinion of congressman Jagt that President Reagan did so much and that it made our country great again.

We borrowed heavily and we have an illusion of prosperity that induces us to relax and to take a nap. But we are in debt up to our necks. Evaluating this kind of prosperity in my way, I would have to give President Reagan one distinction: he was the one, who more than anybody else, was an effective teacher of how to live above our means, disregarding the consequences.

The borrowing was used to spend, not to invest. Subconsciously we know this and we are looking anxiously into the future, but we also receive our daily dose of tranquilizers and consequently we close our eyes; we enjoy the present and we demand, demand, demand. In a field prepared this way, the selfishness, the querulous mood in which malpractice suits are flourishing, the unfaithfulness, the each year bigger number of divorces resulting in confused and deeply hurt children, of the drug abusers, of the homeless and of crimes—are the fruits. In this field, also our Justice Department concentrates on the lucrative and on the spectacular, neglecting completely its primordial obligation to provide safety and security; to be a teacher of what is good or wrong; to give the society the condition to live, to develop and to grow.

You have to forgive me that I saw the picture of America under Reagan's leadership in such a way. He gave the country a false feeling of prosperity. He emphasized the money and the muscle strength as a virtue and a purpose and he produced a deepening spiritual and moral emptiness. His superficiality and care about the shine of the surface made our soul empty and weak.

I remember the years back to 1980. It was inflation and unemployment, but at the time I didn't feel any contempt towards America or any feeling of pity. At that time, I was more proud to be a part of America than I am today. It is true that the effectiveness of Pres. Carter was insufficient and he was too naïve in his idealism, but he was honest and his reactions to the world's events were deeply moral. I do not see as much his miscalculation in his Soviet grain embargo or in the Olympic boycott as I see the true faces of the free world's countries, of our trusted friends, who at that time of a test, rushed to take advantage, to make a business. If I would harbor any feeling of contempt for what happened, it would be towards those our friends. I see the lesson for us from those experiences in such a way. I will always bend my head before Carter's intentions and Carter as a person. He represented the ideals for which America stood years ago, nearer to our founding fathers and that are apparently not practical in today's world.

In this place I also want to stress that I voted for George Bush not because of Pres. Reagan's inspiration and success, but in spite of them. I had a feeling that after his long restraint and loyalty, he was a man ready to be himself. Bush knew how to control himself to avoid the discord of a two-headed government. I hope he will use this inner discipline wisely. I hope that he will not just be a continuation of the last eight years.

In conclusion, I do not see the parallel between the leadership of Ronald Reagan and the men of such idealism as George Washington and Abraham Lincoln. I just cannot.

But, I would not like to miss the occasion to send my farewell card to President Reagan. I will send him this letter. And as my donation, I include here the newspaper reports about the murder of Karen Hill, given to me by her crying grandmother.

The World Seen from the Distance of a Small Village

Quad-City Times
Wednesday, November 23, 1988

Karen Hill, 21

Fort Polk, Ia - Services for Karen Hill, 21, formerly of Albany, Ill. will be 10:30 A.M. Saturday at Fulton, Ill, chapel of Boema-Renkes Funeral Home. Burial will be in Lusk Memorial Cemetery, Albany. Visitation is 3–5 and 7–9 P.M. Friday.

Mrs. Hill was slain Monday near Fort Polk.

She was born in January 30, 1967 in Clinton, Iowa.

She attended Roverbend Grade Schools and was a 1985 Fulton High School graduate.

Karen Eads married James Hill in 1985 in Morrison.

She enjoyed spending time with her pets and working on her clown collection.

She was an active member of the high school track team and received the 1985 Fulton High School Most Valuable Player award, which she shared with her brother, Dough Eads.

Memorials may be made to the Fulton High School Athletic Boosters.

Survivors include her husband, Jamie; her father, Herschel Eads, Garden Plain, Ill., and her mother, Jessie (Mrs. Steven) Knepp, Bettendorf; a sister, LueAnn (Mrs. Daniel) Piercy, Fulton; brothers, Doug Eads Fulton and Jeffrey Eads, Garden Plain; a stepsister, Lisa Knapp, and a stepbrother, Steven Knepp, both of Bettendorf; and her grandmothers, Beverly (Mrs. Francis) McBride, Sterling, and Nellie Simmons, Albany.

Book Two

Quad-City Times
Clinton Bureau

Autopsy Could Provide Clues in Woman's Death

LEESVILLE, IA - Authorities are still waiting for autopsy results to provide some clues into the death of a former Fulton woman found slain near here. Hunters found the body of Karen S. Hill, 21, Monday morning in a wooded area about 3-1/2 miles south of Fort Polk.

She had been working as the night clerk at a convenience store along the road to the U.S. Army base.

Her husband, Sgt. James Hill, a Morrison native, is stationed at Fort Polk.

Authorities believe Mrs. Hill was abducted from the store sometime between 3–4:30 A.M., and that an undetermined amount of money was taken from the cash register. A newspaper delivery driver called sheriff's deputies about 4:30 A.M. to report that there was no one in the circle K Food Store.

The sheriff's department received a call about 2:30 A.M. from hunters who reported finding a body, which later was identified as Mrs. Hill.

Thad Bailes, the department's public information officer, said Mrs. Hill apparently was shot in the head. No weapon has been recovered, and there are no suspects, he said.

At this point, and looking at those newspaper cuts, I would like to speak about another problem: the problem of Day Care Centers for small children. It was such a hot subject during the pre-election debates.

Considering the generalization and standardization, as well as the government role for such an institution, I would like to consider one small fact. Between the ages of three and five, something very important is developing in a child. At this time, he develops a CONSCIENCE.

A child already knows the existence of other beings around him; he already developed enough skill to speak and he became ready to learn what is good and what is wrong. This enormous task is developing in the child by his constant testing and provocations, by his never-ending questions and a kind of sorting and putting in order all the responses he receives. To complete this work, to develop his inner judgment, he needs a special environment. He needs somebody with an infinite dedication, patience and love, in whom he would have a complete confidence and trust, somebody, who would be with him most of the time. The nature gave him for such a purpose, a mother.

The World Seen from the Distance of a Small Village

The most modern and best-equipped Day Care Centers, provided with the best toys and managed by personnel with the most qualified diplomas will remain always a very poor substitution for the role of a mother. I am already old and the memory of my mother is not vanishing in me. With the passing years, it is growing.

I would like to ask you to consider this problem during the next time of national discussion or demands for Day Care centers. Please, imagine a society that was marked by the absence of even diminished effect of the child-mother interaction during the time when their children should have a full time for the development of conscience. The increases in the strength of the police force, the increase in infinition of prisons and corrections centers will not stop the progress of nihilism or disappearance of an inner anger or frustration in many people. Those remedies are at the end of a development of personality. We should not neglect its beginnings.

                                          Tadeusz Maciejczyk, M.D.
                                          Milledgeville, December 1, 1988

Book Two

I include here my last letter to the AMA because it also shows a growing problem.

I sent this letter to: Pres. R. Reagan
Pres.-Elect G. Bush
V.Pres.-Elect Dan Quayle
Congressman Guy Vander Jagt
Senator Robert W. Kesten
The Grandmother, Beverly McBride
Both Senators from Illinois
Our District Congressman
The newspapers, *Newsweek, Time, U.S. News and World Report*
Former Pres. J. Carter
The Justice Dept.

Robert P. Luciano
Chairman and Chief Executive
Schering-Plough Corporation
One Giralda Farms
Madison, New Jersey 07940

Dear Sir:

I was notified that effective January 1st, 1989, Schering Lab. Will no longer distribute its products directly to doctors, except for injectables. Schering Corporation gave for explanation two reasons:

1. Doctors do not need this service. They can deal easier with local pharmacies or supply houses.
2. The diminished volume of direct deals with doctors made them uneconomical.

The World Seen from the Distance of a Small Village

I am one of those doctors affected by your decision and I am asking you to reconsider your conclusions. I am asking you to continue your direct deals with doctors in spite of rising difficulties because:

A. the central point of the problem is not the doctors' convenience or the company's economical losses in maintaining the direct deals with them, but the growing pressure from the generic drugs. Your retreat will only help them to succeed completely at your ultimate cost.
B. The shrinking base of direct dealings with doctors is one of the indications that the generics are winning the battle.
C. The closing of direct deals by growing numbers of pharmaceutical companies are discouraging the doctors, are making them more sensitive to the propaganda and pressures for using the generics. Just when we have an uneasy task to convince patients about superiority of the authentic drugs that makes them desirable in spite of price differences, the companies are distancing themselves from us, maybe giving us a signal that they already accepted the defeat and we should also. Why to try? Who cares?
D. The medical practice in present days is increasingly uneasy. The signals, which are coming form everyplace are trying to convince that not the quality and care, but smartness and a knowledge of the new guidelines, a complete adjustment to the new rules of the game, would open the door to the success. I am trying to fight for my viewpoint (as an illustration I include some of my recent letters) and I would like to think that you are not giving up. Increasing the distance between you and the doctors will also enormously increase the distance between your products and its ultimate receiver—the sick.

I understand your feelings. Many times I have also an urge to give up, but only for a moment.

Tadeusz Maciejczyk, M.D.
December 15, 1988

Book Two

George Bush
President-Elect of the United States

If I were to bear any responsibility for the image of the Republican Party, I would forbid such letters as the one that I recently received. (I include a photocopy.)

Such letters are downgrading the dignity of the office of the Presidency and the prestige of the Party. Its intellectual content is pitiful. This letter gives me no direction, no information, no guidance. It only spreads a panic and a feeling of the certainty of impending doom. It clearly shows that the party already lost its grip on the situation and is floating aimlessly. It gives no hope, except that we still can bribe somebody.

This letter degrades the party and the Presidency in the same way as it degrades all those to whom those letters were sent: the most trusted sympathizers of the aims of the Party, those who still are willing to sacrifice for the common good. It is a cheap policy that will backfire in a true moment of need.

Please, can I get the information on how this money was intended to be spent?

Tadeusz Maciejczyk
Milledgeville, January 2, 1989

The World Seen from the Distance of a Small Village

George Bush
President-Elect of the United States

Dear Sir:

At present the newspapers and the airwaves are filled with commentaries about the U.S. economy and the problems of next year's budget. Generally they are pessimistic and if some moderate optimism appears, it is conditional. One of my friends, a good Democrat and supporter of Dukakis, described to me the present situation in this way: "After the defeat, my only consolation is that not Dukakis, but Bush has to take over the present economic mess."

I am a layman in matters of economics and in my work, I never knew how to get rich. The money, the luxury, never were a magnetic force for me. But lately I started to think about possible solutions for America's economical and budgetary problems and I came to the following conclusions:

1. To win in the present situation would require a bilateral (government and people) effort. It never will improve if the obligations are put on one side, while the other side remains passive and demanding.
2. Your promise of "no more taxes" should not change, except in an unseen emergency.
3. Without increasing taxes, both sides, the government and the people, will have to take on new obligations:

    a. The government should stop all present urges for salary increases until the imbalances are solved and will scrutinize and correct all present excesses in contracts and in the way of doing business, and also will eliminate what is unnecessary.
    b. The people, the taxpayers, will be guaranteed no more taxes, if they in return agree to put into savings account or invest in local enterprises 10% to 30%, depending on the size of their income. I would exclude from those investments the dealings with Wall Street.

4. The requirement for saving or investment would remain voluntary, but for all those who would not comply, the tax deal would be different: they would pay normal taxes on 70% to 90% of

their income. The 10%–30% designated for saving or investment would be taxed by 60%.
5. Mitigating circumstances, such as family or business disasters would be taken into account.

Such an arrangement would give everybody a free choice. It could change the present habit of spending everything and living on the edge in a permanent worry and insecurity. After the initial shock and discontent, the next years could show an adjustment, relaxation and new confidence because everybody would have the strength of created reserves.

This arrangement could solve the present problem of the S&L.

It could also solve our chronic trade imbalance by decreasing the imports of unnecessary good that the world is trying to produce only for America because nobody else would buy it.

It could stimulate the local economy and consequently the economy of the whole U.S.

It would make unnecessary in the future, a humiliating trip by our Governor Thomson to Japan to beg them to make investments here in Illinois. It could also decrease the present accelerated sell-out of America to foreign capital.

It would create a new habit in our society, a new attitude. The present extreme selfishness of our generation that consumes all of what is possible, even at the expense of the standard of living of our children and grandchildren, and with all this, is so chronically unhappy, could be modified and America would become a happier and gentler nation.

I wish you the best in your work.

Tadeusz Maciejczyk
Milledgeville, January 5, 1989

The World Seen from the Distance of a Small Village

Internal Revenue Service
Kansas City, MO

Several days ago I received a letter from you. It looked like any of your letters at the end of the year.

I opened this letter today. It told me that I still owe the government $46.46. The letter was written in Kansas City on January 9. The last sentence of this letter told me that in responding, I should allow enough mailing time to be sure that my payment was received in Kansas by January 19. A stiff term of 10 days.

I am sorry. I am late. In my small solo practice, I have to do everything by myself: the usual work, the studying, the administration and lately also rapidly mounting paperwork. This paperwork I do at the margin of my time. I cannot sacrifice my true work and obligations to this new growing artiface.

Today I checked my books and I do not see any mistakes in my calculations. Anyway, I am sending you the required money with the hope that you will explain the cause of our differences. What can I do? Such differences can be understood among humans.

What shocked me in your letter was not the additional payment requirement, but the last sentence of your letter. Small businesses have to struggle hard today to survive. Such a pressure as yours, declared in your last sentence, can break them. I know that you are just performing the duty put on you by the law, but in doing so, surely you will not help the country in its present situation.

I admit that in the present frame, created by our lawmakers, I am guilty again and again, I should be charged with a new penalty and have it added to interest. Please send me the notification. I will not hold it against you. In paying this new obligation, I will get a special satisfaction to personally contribute again to the 50% pay increase for our beloved Congress. They really are in need. And everybody knows that those poor members of congress are tied in such a complicated knot of laws that they virtually cannot refuse to take this extra money pushed on them against their will in the time of the biggest, immobilizing national debt—in the time when our poor President is scratching his head in vain searching for a solution to our budgetary problems.

Long ago, in 1836, in another hard time, a cry "Remember the Alamo" gave strength to people and changed history. In 1990, the cry of the time should be "Remember the Congressional Pay Hikes of 1989."

Even considering the extremes of our present debt, and its potential for disaster and in the face of the cynicism of the proposition itself of payment increases by 50%, as well as the Congressional readiness for acceptance, I thought that a more appropriate reaction to this sad show would be to ask the people of every community in the country to start collecting signatures and send the lists of them to the President asking him to dissolve the present Congress and arrange new elections. The country couldn't get worse.

Tadeusz Maciejczyk
Milledgeville, January 29, 1989

Herbert R. Doggette, Jr.
Deputy Commissioner
Social Security Administration

 Responding to your letter dated February 17, 1989, I want to tell that now days, in the practice, in the effort to be independent and useful here in America, the growing paperwork is the most frustrating and frequently frightening part of our occupations. In my small practice, shattered by malpractice and Medicare limitations, I cannot afford to hire help for those paper monstrosities and the new forms, always armed with special numbers and explanations below that I can hardly understand. This growing paperwork is like a more and more urging invitation to give up, sit down and apply for public aid.
 I do not understand your questioning of my figures in my reports. Every quarter I reported them as well as I could. I explained previously that for one employee, the cleaning lady, I pay on the social security and state taxes, but not the federal taxes. This creates a difference in the reported numbers. I asked how should I do this correctly, but I never got an answer.
 I send you the sheets that I found in the books of 1984 and 1985. I hope they will solve the problem. Otherwise, I will have to admit that I am not fit to practice anymore.

Tadeusz Maciejczyk, M.D.
Milledgeville, February 21, 1989

The World Seen from the Distance of a Small Village

1989 Presidential First Term Agenda Survey
Registered Survey #Il00416521

Section I

1. In the past when the Democrats raised your taxes they never used the increase to reduce the federal deficit. Do you think there is any reason to believe that they would use a tax increase now to reduce the deficit they created?

Answer: Undecided.

I do not know this part of U.S. history, consequently, I cannot judge. Personally, I doubt that the increased taxes would be used wisely. Easy come, easy go. Certainly the increased taxes would exacerbate the appetite and fight for the "just" part of the pie. The recent congressional cry for salary increases would be like a preview illustration of what it would be like. Our representatives, entering the Olympus of Congress, very quickly forget the realities and promises left behind. At this point, I want to make it clear that in my mind I do not charge Democrats for the federal deficit. Responding to this survey, I condemn the biting, unilateral, partisan tone that saturates its every page. Such a tone and such a language is very little convincing. It doesn't invite to think and to look for new ideas or solutions. The solution suggested in this survey is only one and it is the same as in many other letters from Washington: hate the villain and give the money. Those letters, written by stereotypes, where the villain and the situation is changed, and everything else is repeated and predicted, are creating an image of our supposed-to-be leaders and that is creating a chill in the spine. What really can we expect from institutions that for communication with the nation are using such senseless shortcuts. Those letters, including this survey are not dignifying, are not creating strength. They only denigrate everybody.

2. Instead of a major tax increase, Pres. Bush advocates a "flexible spending freeze" to reduce the federal deficit. Do you agree?

Answer: Undecided.

Book Two

    a. I know what a major tax increase is and to some extent I am ready to confront it with my arguments.
    b. "A flexible spending freeze" is for me a new notion, fuzzy, undefined, unmeasured by previous experiences. I think that a good explanation of this policy and limiting this survey to its discussion would be much more productive.

3. Do you agree with former Pres. Reagan that lower taxes are the driving force behind the unprecedented economic prosperity we have enjoyed throughout much of the last 6 years?

Answer: No.

    I do not consider "an unprecedented economic prosperity" something that left behind an ugly streak of enormous debt, that already now is strangling our economy by it's interest payments and that without a doubt has to be repaid by our children and grandchildren. More than this, in the hard, serious time, it created in our leadership a false satisfaction and relaxation, adding the elements of irresponsibility and unconcern, while in the masses of the nation it implanted anxiety, uncertainty and a growing symptom of profound emotional illness: living just for today, divorce, drugs, homelessness, dullness of conscience, crime, etc. As for me? In this time of prosperity, I felt mostly a merciless squeeze. I summarized it last fall in this sentence: "Each time more frequently a thought is coming to my mind, that I could be forced to close my office, because everything has its limits."

4. Would a dramatic increase in your federal income taxes force you to cancel a major purchase such as a car, home or family vacation or make other important changes in your life?

Answer: Yes.

    It is true. A huge Federal income tax increase would limit my personal economy. For me, it would have also different dimensions. I practically lost my faith in any long-term U.S. policy. Especially U.S. economic policies are guided increasingly by an instant advantage and a promise of a quick profit. The U.S. has no patience or ability for long-range planning, for an investment that would benefit the next generation, for a building of a solid foundation necessary to create a lasting stability and confidence for years to come. In the past decade we got used to spending instantly what we earned and to borrow again and again, constantly repeating that we were in the midst of an unprecedented prosperity. We had no guts to face the truth. Still today we sing the same song and no politician dares to speak about the need for restraint, for sacrifices and a calm look on reality.

5. Do you agree that the Amendment to the Constitution mandating a balanced budget is the only way we will ever stop the deficit spending by the Democrats in Congress?

Answer: Undecided.

Personally, I doubt that a constitutional balanced budget amendment would solve our problems. The wrong is within us and a magic of this amendment and its absence is only a convenient excuse. Whenever the public anxiety and anger is rising because the carelessness, shortsightedness and budgetary mismanagement by those who love so much to be called our leaders, became more visible than usual, the lack of this amendment is brought before us as a magic formula and guiding star towards a budgetary order.

To break this game, I would establish this amendment in the constitution adding to it sanction strong enough to be respected. In case of budget failure, a special commission would investigate why. Without serious, unexpected incidents that would justify or attenuate the failure, the congress would be dismissed and new elections scheduled!

6. Many Democrats feel that even though Dukakis lost, he had a right idea when he opposed important military programs such as the MX Missile, Midgetman Mobile Missile, SDI and many other programs. Do you agree that we should reduce the deficit by making drastic cuts in our nation's defense?

Answer: Undecided

In the present world we have to have a strong defense. Nevertheless, I also agree with Mr. Dukakis that the military with its hardware and high technology should be adjusted to the changing realities of the world. Our military strength and readiness should be always alert and vigilant, but never stiff and inflexible. In the present world's games, our supreme objective should be a lasting peace that would be just and equal for everybody. For this purpose the military is only a tool that can give chances for the other work to develop, to give roots, to mature and finally give fruits. By itself, the military is not a promise for salvation of mankind. With each passing decade, its destructive power is more horrifying. For this reason, we should never stop to look for other ways to obtain peace. In our planning, in our policies, in our strategy, those other ways should have the same rank and importance as the military. They should mobilize into its ranks the best hearts and brains and the noblest characters of the nation. They should search for a universal ideal, adjusted to our time that could help to build togetherness and a common purpose in the world.

Really, we have already a pattern for such togetherness. We should take another good look at the Roman Empire, where a mosaic of nations, languages and cultures formed for over three centuries a lasting and sincere *Pax Romana*. After centuries, this world's wonder fell not from internal strife, but from the outside pressure. Even the barbarian conquerors of Rome, after understanding, defended the idea of *Pax Romana* and later, when anarchy prevailed during the dark ages, the memory of this phenomenon was as a lasting light.

I know that if we would establish such a dream as a purpose for ourselves, we would find a proper key that would help us to create a similar organism in the present time. Such a creation would free mankind from many present fears and could give us a new, happier direction for life. A strong military can guarantee for us only the present status quo and a persistence of divisions and rivalry. The other forces of peace could penetrate the military walls, break the divisions and reach the hearts everywhere.

For this reason, my opinion is that the calculated reduction in military spending is possible and can give positive effects. In such a plan the money saved from military reductions should not be used for free spending, but for a genuine search and true action toward a creation of a healthy "Global Commonwealth."

I want to observe here that Mr. Gorbachev is using similar alternatives to the military and he is winning where America is losing, even if nobody is sure of his ultimate aims.

7. Many Democrats feel that federal spending is about as low as it should ever go. In your opinion do you feel there is more waste that should be cut in the federal budget?

Answer: Very Likely

Federal spending purposes should always be viewed and adjusted to the needs. A common sense should guide us to decide until where the people should help themselves and at what point the government should intervene to preserve and to advance the life of society. For this purpose a dialog with the nation through the Feedback Department, which I once proposed, would indicate this delicate and changing line for action.

Another problem here is the waste and abuse in government management. Everybody reads about government and military wasteful spending that many times appeared not only grotesque, but criminal.

Government and military contracting should require two fundamental elements for proper function: a) a knowledge of the subject; b) a character and honesty of those who are making decisions.

Related to those two elements are the now famous Congressional visitations and speeches for fees. Thinking about them, I am not objecting to its practice, but I could attach to them two or three conditions. 1. The speech would be made and publicly acknowledged by the visitors. 2. The visit and the content of the speech would be published in the corresponding districts of the Congressman or Senator. 3. A special commission would watch those activities to assure there was no conflict of interest.

In such an arrangement, those visitations could make the members of Congress more aware of the substance of transactions they have to discuss and more informed and wise at the time of voting. In addition, the people at home would know better the extent of knowledge and involvement of their representatives what could be an asset during the next election time. Finally, the rumors about suspicious deals during those visitations could be eliminated.

8. Pres. Bush campaigned on the tough anti-crime platform. Do you support his effort to appoint Federal judges who will take convicted felons off the streets as a means of reducing crime?

Answer: Undecided.

Book Two

This question is very broad, certainly too complex to be answered by marking one of the three boxes. Without a doubt, the anti-crime platform should be respected by the criminal elements. Judges have the duty to protect society from the criminals' terror. An unjustly lenient judiciary is not fulfilling its social and moral obligations. It is not correcting the criminal. It only makes the criminal more insolent in the future, giving him an impression that he is untouchable, giving him a lesson in how to play successfully with the authorities, inviting willing imitators around him and as a byproduct of all this, such a judge is cooperating in spreading crime.

I am convinced that a judge, unwilling to be just, to sentence, and to protect society, is dangerous to this society even more than the criminal.

On the other hand, a judge should have a knowledge and instinct for human nature that cannot be well-explained in any book. There are criminals—leaders, hardliners, who hardly can be rehabilitated and who deprive and induce others to follow them. There are others who are beginners, who were passively induced, whose crimes were emotionally accidental, who entered gangs by their whatever attraction, but not by inner malice. The judge should know how to separate them and how to enact the most effective rehabilitation program in each case. Those from the second category never should be put to the same prison or correctional institution as the hardliners. They never should be pushed deeper into a life of crime because the prison becomes for them a kind of crime-academy and graduation. Anybody identified in the prison or any other penitentiary as a hardliner and an inducer for others into crime, should be immediately transferred into a completely different prison, created exactly for this type of criminal. Such a strict separation, even if costly in the long range, would help and save money. A judge who doesn't see this problem, will not reduce crime.

A judiciary should be involved also in all forms of civil activities that directly or indirectly are related with prevention of crime by helping and patronizing all social processes that can stabilize family life and a normal, positive development of personalities in children.

The World Seen from the Distance of a Small Village

As an illustration, I want to repeat here what I wrote after a visit in my office of a crying grandmother whose granddaughter was abducted and murdered during a robbery of the place where she working.

"Looking on the newspaper cuts given to me by the crying grandmother, I would like to speak about another problem: the problem of Day Care Centers for small children. It was such a hot subject during the pre-election debates.

Considering the generalization and standardization, as well as the government role for such an institution, I would like to consider one small fact. Between the ages of three and five, something very important is developing in a child. At this time, he develops a CONSCIENCE.

A child already knows the existence of other beings around him; he already developed enough skill to speak and he became ready to learn what is good and what is wrong. This enormous task is developing in the child by his constant testing and provocations, by his never-ending questions and a kind of sorting and putting in order all the responses he receives. To complete this work, to develop his inner judgment, he needs a special environment. He needs somebody with an infinite dedication, patience and love, in whom he would have a complete confidence and trust, somebody, who would be with him most of the time. The nature gave him for such a purpose, a mother.

The most modern and best-equipped Day Care Centers, provided with the best toys and managed by personnel with the most qualified diplomas will remain always a very poor substitution for the role of a mother.

I would like to ask you to consider this problem during the next time of national discussion or demands for Day Care centers. Please, imagine a society that was marked by the absence of even diminished effect of the child-mother interaction during the time when their children should have a full time for the development of conscience. The increases in the strength of the police force, the increase in infinition of prisons and corrections centers will not stop the progress of nihilism or disappearance of an inner anger or frustration in many people. Those remedies are at the end of a development of personality. We should not neglect its beginnings."

Concluding—like for everybody else in life, the judge should know his duties and responsibilities of this unique role. In the same way as in medicine, his first obligation would be not to produce unnecessary harm. When necessary, he would condemn. He should rehabilitate whoever is able to be rehabilitated. He should help in developing life condition that

Book Two

would limit or eliminate incubation of crime among the young. Only by such multiple approaches will the judiciary be able to liberate society from under the siege by crime.

In his role, the judge should be visible. He should always remember that in his duties he is a special teacher for every segment of society.

Section II

1. The Soviet Economy is stagnating from bureaucratic control centralized management and spending up to 18% of its GNP on their massive arms building. Do you think America has an obligation to bail out the South Viet Economy through loans guaranteed by U.S. Taxpayers?

Answer: No.

America has an obligation to influence Russia and all the nations living within the Soviet Republic to acquire all those qualities of freedom that were conceived by the founding fathers of the United States and expressed by them in the Constitution.

Economic help, especially such that would just bail out the present Soviet state, would only stabilize the Soviet system making it the next time around, after revitalization, much more dangerous to the world.

The U.S. is confronting here a very special situation that requires wisdom, clarity of judgment and purpose and a masterpiece of diplomacy as much when dealing with the Soviets as well as with the nations of the free world. We are living in a time of an appearance of hope, which very easy, by the temptation of quick success, or by hasty shortcuts can be changed into a nightmare.

2. Throughout the Reagan Years, not one inch of soil fell under Soviet domination. Do you feel the Reagan, and now Bush, policy of peace through strength is the reason for this remarkable record?

Answer: No.

The World Seen from the Distance of a Small Village

A "true strength" is a combination of many elements. During the Reagan years, we increased our arms and muscle strength. We mismanaged all other aspects of the true strength. Except for the liberation of Granada, we didn't improve even by one inch, the situation in Central America. We never tried to comprehend the people there. We never developed any positive, original policy for those nations. Our approach was rich in buffoonery of words, contrasted with a complete inaptitude to understand, to create new approaches and attractions, to use those people and their longings to build something, what would be their own contribution to the democracy of the world, based on their traditions and character. Our efforts in Central America were motivated not by a noble desire to help, but by a desire to break them, use them, and in this way resolve our political fears and goals. We never descended to sit down with the simple people and to develop a friendship and trust with them. We only dealt with dictators who, from their point of view, were trying to use us.

Our policy in Central America during the last 8 years, was not something we could be proud of.

The same stagnation of our imagination and failure in our policy in spite of world-wide attractiveness of the fundamentals of our culture, we can see in every other corner of the world. America's credibility, moral prestige, leadership prestige, economic base for that "peace through strength" program, a capacity to look on ourselves critically, and to undertake necessary sacrifices—all those components of a true strength, hit the ever low during the Reagan years of self-indulgence, and a leadership without one single ideal as a compass for guidance.

If not one inch of soil fell under Soviet domination during the Reagan years, it was due to the courage and sacrifice of the Afghan people, who stood up and showed the Soviets, that there was a limit to their voracity. If the Soviets would venture into other places with less or no resistance, their consequent expansion would be unpredictable, and I doubt whether Reagan would confront them.

3. Do you feel it is a moral responsibility of the President to work towards the deployment of the system such as SDI that will defend us from nuclear attack?

Answer: No.

Book Two

A moral responsibility of the President is to work for world peace, approaching this purpose with a multitude of coordinated actions, supported by convincing and mobilizing people's hearts new ideas. A moral responsibility of the President is to be innovative and flexible in ways, while never losing his sight from the real objective of our efforts. A high priority given in your survey toward the deployment of the SDI contains that nothing is expected to change and that the never predictable armament race will continue until its bitter end. Such a program and priority would be really rigid, sclerotic and narrow.

The real challenge an moral responsibility for the President is to lead the U.S. as well as the whole world into a new era of a global commonwealth.

4. Many Democratic leaders believe that M. Gorbachev reforms indicate that the Soviet Union no longer represents a serious threat to the West. Do you agree?

Answer:

The Democratic leaders and everybody else, before they come to such conclusions, should read the history of Russia. Even the pre-Soviet Russia, while under the strain, in 1870's adopted policies and developed campaigns in the western world that looked like a prototype for Gorbachev's actions and pronunciations—remained exactly as before. The Russian emissaries and propagandists' presentation of Russia to the west didn't change the Russian system in anything but façade. Then later in 1905, after another strain of war with Japan and the internal revolt, Russia established a people representation in Duma, the prerogatives of this, Congress-like institution, became restricted to practically nothing as soon as the central authorities recuperated and consolidated its power.

Gorbachev is intelligent. He has more leadership qualities than many western leaders taken together. He is good under pressure. He is flexible and he understands and uses Western people's longings to support his goals. In consequence, he is winning the confidence of the people in vital areas, where America under Reagan, was losing its convincing edge.

Maybe Gorbachev is sincere and as far as prudence allows, he should be helped, but he can be also much more dangerous than all his orthodox and rigid Communist predecessors.

The World Seen from the Distance of a Small Village

Unnumbered points of the survey:

1. Special Sponsorship Contribution
Yellow postcard to Dear Congressman to express my active support.

Answer: No.

I am sorry. I am not doing this for two reasons.

A. I never became rich practicing medicine and in the last years, my practice became severely limited by malpractice and Medicare. At present my ambition is not to fail to finance my youngest daughter through the university. This is my primary obligation.
B. I believe that the American election system became very undemocratic because of money. The best men, even with the greatest talent and character integrity, with originality of vision, and a gift for leadership, cannot now break the barrier created by the vicious escalation of the electoral cost.
Only the parties can present their candidates. But the parties are interested not as much in talents, leadership qualities or independent ideas of their candidates as in their loyalty to the party, even above the interest of the country as a whole. In this way, we have an increasing number of the "yes men" as our representatives. Maybe because of this, the congressional debates became so dull that its TV transmissions became a complete failure, repelling, instead of attracting the viewers. The present congress became the last place to look for fresh, redeeming ideas. Our Congress became self-circled, fearful of trespassing the line of popularity, I have the impression, very unidealisitic and schlerotic institution that badly needs to be reformed.
A member of Congress, who lives more than three terms in Washington, and has only a second hand connection with those whom he represents, is not representing any more his district or state. He became there an outsider, displaced into an abnormal, artificial, frequently unreal environment inside the congress and Washington as well. A limit should be established: 3 terms for Congressmen, 2 terms for Senators, after which they should spent a number of years in their districts, taking an active part in all

the aspects of life there, before they could become eligible again to be candidates for Congress.

A Congressional designation for life for many of our representatives is not an expression of the health of the system. It shows the apathy of the electorate, of the electorate's paying back for the small services received, participating in this way in a kind of corruption, in the disinterest for the need in congress for constant revival of ideas that would change the dullness and ineffectiveness of the work of routine.

Here I want also to express what I firmly believe that those members of Congress who acquire large amounts of money for re-election, are not viewed by me as the men dedicated to the country and to their mission. I look on them with a deep suspicion. If the American proverb is right telling, that there is no such a thing as a free meal, then the question arises in what a way those coffers of our distinguished representatives were filled to assure their re-election? What they were giving in exchange for those filled up with money coffers? Was it only their knowledge that was so generously rewarded by whoever it was? Or, were they giving something that belonged to all of us? How to relate the chronic and never completely explained to the public our perennial wasteful spending for government and military needs?

As for me, I would have all my admiration and I would give my vote to those representatives, who after years of serving in Washington came out from there as poor as they were before, for those who fought there their battles for their beliefs, even for those who didn't arrange so many small conveniences for their district people, because they were boycotted and separated by their "yes men" colleagues. Such men would prove to me that I could still trust and revere the institution that spiritual prestige lately became drained to the bottom.

2. Yellow postcard to "Dear Congressman" to express my active support.

Answer: No.

The text of this postcard reminds me of my distant past when after the "liberation," the unexpressed happiness descended on my country and I had this extreme luck to live under the sunshine and

The World Seen from the Distance of a Small Village

tender care of our liberator, the genial Josef Stalin. At that time, we had also prepared words put into our mouths and they were similarly servile. Their description and their judgment about those others, were also similar.

No. Thank you. If I have anything to say to "Dear Congressman," I will do it with my own words.

Tadeusz Maciejczyk
Milledgeville, February 26, 1989

George Bush
President of the United States

Dear Mr. President:

Last week I read a note in our *Daily Gazette* that, while apparently nothing is moving in our internal or exterior policies, you are actively involved in mapping the plans for actions that would prepare and would enter us into the 21st century.

Thinking about this, I decided to send to you the copies of my two letters, written several years ago. One of them was about the problem of aging, the problem, which without doubt will be with us in the future. The other letter was about my vision of Martin Luther King Day.

The main thought of what I wrote about MLK Day would remain the same. Only, that now I would change the MLK Day into "Martin Luther King's Dream Week." Such a week also would be placed in a calendar for a warm spring time. Also as I was thinking before, the ways of celebrating such a week would be left completely to the local inventiveness, dedications and needs. The central authorities would create only a necessary for such a celebration atmosphere of togetherness and solidarity, not only between the races, but between all the variety of groups that compose the society; and would give the official signal for initiation. The end result of such a week would be a sum of local expressions and actions. In this way the dream of ML King would never become a routine or a passive, immobilizing calendar day for lazy inaction.

Book Two

The suggestions in my letter about aging could also become one of the points in your mapping of the future. It could change or attenuate the anxieties of the old, or of those who are approaching old age. It could easily bring down the cost of living for those people. It could give them a new chance to be active and involved. It could give them a platform to work and to be useful. It could bring them some feeling of safety. It could diminish the gap between generations, because their many talents, their experience and more amount of a free time could engage them in many tasks of healing of our present social problems. Such living conditions would be different from the Florida vacations that are no more than an escape. It would give the old new dynamics, new fields, new objectives.

Of course, such a system would be voluntary, but it would be like a safety valve for everybody. Persons living alone could go there temporarily whenever their usual arrangements would be altered. A chain of such homes across the nation could bring completely new solutions and dynamics for visiting distant relatives or for vacations. A membership card in such homes could be valid in some exchange for all travelers.

Those two points at present are like a row material for realization and they could add to the richness of life. I hope that in your plans you would take them into account.

I wish you the best in your work.

> Tadeusz Maciejczyk
> Milledgeville, March 19, 1989

The World Seen from the Distance of a Small Village

Physician's Choice
Editor

    Thank you for sending me your newspaper.
    Responding to the suggestions given in the article, "Attacking the Deficit," I agree with Mr. Bergsten, that there is an urgency for action to correct our growing imbalance of payments and that a continuation of the present passive contemplation and our inability to decide and to carry out the necessary treatment, would bring harsh consequences.
    Maybe the increased taxation to break the present condition would be beneficial, but I think that a similar purpose could be archived by a more palatable, and in the long run, more heart-lifting measure. I wrote about this in one of my letters that I addressed to our President. A practically mandatory saving for everybody who works could be a good answer to the present situation.
    I am sending you a copy of this letter to President Bush. I would be glad if you would send the same copy to Fred Bergsten.
    After reading your newspaper, which is trying to touch us and to guide us through many of the problems of our lives, I decided to send you a copy of my recent replies to a survey that was sent to me. It could be that you could find some interesting points to develop in your paper.
    Somehow, we are living in a time when apathy changed our democracy into passivity in accepting routine solutions, in our routine voting for our representation, in a kind of boredom with our institutions and an escape into a seclusion of our small, private world. Speaking with people, many times I had such an impression. With your newspaper you have a chance to make a change.
    I wish you the best in your work.

                                    Tadeusz Maciejczyk, M.D.
                                Milledgeville, March 21, 1989

My Answer to the Message from Senator Harlan Rigney

Question No. 1: No—for two reasons.
    a. During the last election, Gov. Thomson was assuring everybody about perfect balances and the good condition of Illinois treasury. I remember him giving grants to different institutions during his campaign TV appearances. It was intended to be an obvious proof of a perfect economic situation in our state and his excellent budgetary management of all its needs.

Book Two

In scarcely three months after this skillful show, he changed the tune and he asked for a radical increase in taxation, predicting a complete economic collapse if such an increase would be rejected. I can understand different, even completely naïve and unproven views expressed during political campaigns.

I cannot but condemn and strip completely of my confidence those politicians who in order to win are consciously using and repeating pure lies. The political tricks should have its limits. A political figure without one inch of public decency who consciously abuses the confidence of the electorate, counting on weakness and wishful thinking of the people, and its lack of memory afterwards, is not building the society. By making a cheap show of such smartness, lying shamelessly to win, he is implanting a social illness that in the past brought already many nations to its fall and disintegration making them weak, unprincipled and without mutual trust.

The people in Illinois have an obligation to remember those attitudes of our leaders if we want to make this state a good place to live for us and for our children.

Because of this, as long as Mr. Thomson is the governor in Springfield, I will oppose any tax increase—even if it is justified.

b. I do not feel that the schools should be founded by the money from the victims of addictions.

Question No. 2. No—for the same reason as in No. 1

Question No. 3. No, but I am ready to consider it when Mr. Thomson is out of office.

Question No. 4. Uncertain. Welfare grants of 342 per month can only be a partial help to survive. An increase of such payments to truly disabled and those in need should be done, but only by constant elimination of those recipients to whom this help was intended to be a short term facility and of those who have the ability to be productive, but who prefer to be passive and lazy. Looking from the window of my practice, I know that such persons exist and that the social workers are not doing their work well, if they fail to mobilize and to lift those people.

Question No. 5. In the present situation of a squeeze put on small businesses, an obligation for them to provide a health insurance for their employees could be almost a kiss of death and the result would be worse for everybody.

Maybe a distribution of the cost of insurance for those people between: employer, employee, state, insurance companies, hospitals and doctors could be an answer.

Question No. 6. See No. 5

Question No. 7. No.
Creation of hysteria, of no trust, of bad blood, is not in the interest of anybody. On the other side, any suspicious situation or behavior should be discreetly, but firmly checked.

Question No. 8. I am inclined to say yes.

Question No. 9. Uncertain.
It would depend on the nature of the state mandate. The petty mandates, which are now days so frequent, should be challenged anyway all the time. The fundamental mandates, which define the mission of schools, of teaching and of the formation of minds and spirits, should be kept, whatever the difficulties.

Question No. 10. Uncertain.
I do not know the importance of all the elements that should be considered to answer this question. The big mass of such trucks, when multiplied by its speed, are producing much bigger factors of inertia and create much bigger consequences. I do not know either how to calculate the degree of the wear out of the roads and especially of the bridges by this big, fast-moving mass. From the pure convenience, I would say that a uniform speed for everybody on the road would be most practical.

Question No. 11. Yes.
Or at least make it very inexpensive. Also, in more than 25 years of premarital testing for syphilis in my practice, I didn't see even one positive test. Should it continue? And how about gonorrhea? It is spreading, but it is not being tested.

Question No. 12 Should be restricted to certain areas.

Question No. 13. No.
We have already enough tragedies and social problems produced by our careless weakening of characters. Gambling is producing no wealth. It provides only a temptation, something that was a part of the original sin. (I do not say this from the religious point of view, but from psychological evaluation.) This kind of activity will not advance the quality of life in any place.

Question No. 14. No.
   a. We want to keep our places clean and pretty.
   b. A decision and permission for such dumps here would only delay the fundamental solutions.
       1. How to produce less garbage.
       2. How to increase recycling and other use for garbage.
       3. How to ban those substances and objects of our use that are the more frequent elements of the unrecyclable part of the garbage.

Without pressure for searching for those urgent measures and solutions, America will look more and more like a big garbage place. The present saturation we have accomplished in only a few decades.

                Tadeusz Maciejczyk, M.D.
                Milledgeville, IL, March 27, 1989

Additional Comments to Senator Rigney's survey.
Question No. 1. If you were a legislator, what would be the first law you would propose?
   Answer: When I was a student, my best professor told once that in order to be a good teacher, it is necessary to know what to tell. Of the same importance however, it is mandatory to know what not to tell. The clarity of the teaching and the real impact on the students depends on those two factors.
   I imagine that the same principle applies to any work well done. It applies also to the work of the legislators. Too many detailing laws at every step and in every direction are confusing and are overshadowing the main line of the lawful behavior.
   Tacitus, the Roman senator and historian 19 centuries ago, came to the conclusion that the more corrupt the state is, the more numerous

are its laws. This observation is very real still today. Maybe it reflects the philosophy of the proverb that the fishing is best in the muddy waters.

Thinking about this and responding to your question, if I were to be a legislator who cares about life in Illinois, the first thing I would do would be to take a good look at all the volumes of present laws and I would start the task of weeding out those that make only a confusing crowding.

Question No. 2: What do you think is the most serious problem facing the state today?

Answer: The most serious problem facing the state today is not as much the different deterioration in many areas of our lives as the general apathy created by lack of communication and sincerity between the authorities and the people.

The main attribute of democracy: a participation and openness, a constant active verbal and in action dialogue between all elements of society, became substituted by disinterest, by keeping distance, by fragmentation and pettiness. Springfield is not giving any lead. It seems that it is hanging somewhere in the distant vacuum. In a mind of an average man, Springfield is far away, unconcerned and in the same way uninteresting, inhabited not by leaders, but by bureaucrats of routine.

The biggest of Springfield's ceremonies: the inaugural address and the yearly opening speeches of session, generally are like a monument for dullness, monotony, grandiosity and emptiness. It is more likely their original intention was to open a dialog and cooperation with the people. But they do not connect. They do not put together the governmental body and the minds, the emotions and the actual needs of the people. They touch nobody. They are boring and repelling. They never give the people the strength or the sense of a common purpose or a new direction or new ideas born from observation and feeling of the rapidly changing time. They serve no practical purpose anymore. It would be the same, if those pump ceremonies would not exist at all.

From here, from the periphery, it looks that we have no leaders in Springfield: only "*apparatchics*," if I may use the Soviet vocabulary to describe this kind of dignitary.

I hope that this can change; that the forces of constant renewal will come and prevail.

But, if we are too indifferent, we will continue to have only what we deserve.

Question No. 3: Additional comments or suggestions.

Book Two

The other day the TV news announced that Gov. Thomson went to Russia to develop commercial relations between Illinois and the Soviets.

In relation to this, I have several questions:

a. What are the true qualifications of our governor to negotiate any commercial problems?
b. What were the new expectations that prompted this trip at this time?
c. What preparations for this negotiation were done? What studies? What revised evaluations? Projections? Consultations? Calculations? What was done to prepare our governor for all those business contacts with the Russians that undoubtedly will require a knowledge of the subject and responsible decisions?
d. What was the expected cost of this trip for the state and what benefits can the people expect from those negotiations?
e. Why was the planning of this trip never announced before to the people? It could give additional enrichment and more relaxed flexibility for those negotiations. Why instead did this trip become another surprise, another unexpected shot from the hip?
f. Will the results of those negotiations with Russia be fully explained to the people of Illinois after the governor's return? After his trip to Japan with a similar purpose and under similar circumstances, what happened afterwards was complete silence.

Tadeusz Maciejczyk
Milledgeville, April 4, 1989

cc: Governor Thomson
    Both Senators of Illinois
    Our District Representative
    Local Press
    The White House

The World Seen from the Distance of a Small Village

Lee Atwater
Chairman of the Republican National Committee

Dear Sir:

It was encouraging for me to receive your letter. Generally my writings are followed only by a complete silence, and I am left with an uneasy feeling that by writing those letters, I am making a fool of myself because nobody reads them.

I thank you also for telling me that you want and you need my input.

At this point I want to make it clear that my input will not always be what the Party would like to hear. As an illustration of this, I send you a copy of my recent reply to a survey of an Illinois State Senator Harlan Rigney. In this survey I express my true opinion about one of the most important Republicans in our state. As you can see, my opinion is not flattering.

I am glad that you approach your work with optimism and with a willingness to take everything into consideration, and in this way face the party with the new decade and new century. You are telling me about your new message from the party to the country and to the world. Those messages would include hard work for peace and for prosperity as the key feature.

But, what do you mean by those words: "Expanding peace and prosperity?" Surely, it is an attractive invitation for everybody, but I wonder what moves and what actions you have in mind? How would you target those goals?

I ask this because "prosperity" is something that I do not know how to measure or how to define.

Years ago, when I was in Spain, I had a very good and completely gratuitous lesson about the relationship between human nature and what probably is the essence of prosperity.

It was pre-Christmas time and the mood of the people was filled with excitement. I was walking at night through a lonely street when a streetcar appeared and passed by. The car was filled with young boys and girls. They were all singing a song that stuck in my memory. The tune of the song was simple. It was like this: "*Todos queremos mas, Todos queremos mas, Y mas, y mas, y mas, y mas, y mas, y mas . . .*" (Everybody wants more . . . and more, and more. Somebody who has one, wants two; somebody who has five wants ten; that who has twenty wants forty and that who has fifty wants one hundred. The refrain started again:

Book Two

Todos queremos mas, Todos queremos mas, Y mas, y mas, y mas, y mas, y mas, y mas . . . .

Then, if it is so, if the prosperity is so ambiguous, how can we decide how much of it is healthy and at what point does it degenerate into an insatiable appetite for more and more and more? When, and what kind of brakes should be applied when the material well-being is starting to change into a dangerous illness; when such prosperity and the drive for more ceases to be satisfying, fulfilling and changes peace into war.

In this moment a thought came to me, that to illustrate better what I mean, I should send you a copy of my speech during the last Memorial Day. This speech could be titled "An Aberration of a Drive for Prosperity."

Probably there are other convincing examples of my idea.

Not long ago there lived a lady, extremely prosperous, who was publicly described as a "poor, little rich girl." And I think that Elvis Presley would be more happy and he would live longer if he would not be so prosperous.

I know that almost everybody: single persons, whole societies, all the nations, want prosperity. It is the easiest goal to think about, the more visible condition for envy and for a development of an emotional involvement. To some extent, it is the measurement of our success in life. It is a goal that excites and blinds and not always brings the best from the people. It looks to me that the drive to the mere prosperity is one of the more primitive desires of men.

It is so, that when reached, we frequently find the prosperity insufficient. Even without an obsession for prosperity, if it is not paralleled by a development of other needs of the soul and ways for fulfillment in life, it is leading into a narrow, restless and unhappy existence and a tendency for self-destruction.

For this reason, if the Republican Party is looking into the future for peace and prosperity, it would be useful to develop a good knowledge and the variations of the fundamental ingredients for a development of a true peace. We should also be prepared to recognize and to introduce to our lives those elements that we all need for prosperity to be fulfilled and happy because without them even the more prosperous are empty and miserable.

One hundred years ago the world was preparing its entrance into the new century with an illusion of a utopia of life of prosperity and peace. The result of this was the extreme of hate and destruction. We should think about this. We cannot repeat the same miserable mistakes.

If the Party wants to be a true guiding light and force, it has to reach much deeper than to the easy slogans.

The World Seen from the Distance of a Small Village

Sincerely yours,

Tadeusz Maciejczyk
Milledgeville, April 13, 1989

I include: The survey of State Senator Harlan Rigney
My Memorial Day speech
My letter to Pres. Bush about economic solutions
My letter to Pres. Bush about my ideas about Martin Luther King's Dream Week and my suggestions for the aging of America.

Book Two

Our Strange Priorities

First, I want to speak about the sudden demand for civic centers in our state. A civic center for the Quad Cities was discussed on television for months. Apparently it has now entered the state of realization.

Then, suddenly, the Sterling *Daily Gazette* informed the community about discussions of similar centers for Sterling and for other cities across the state. The Coalition for 35 Civic Centers Authorities pressed and got a State Civic Center Grant. A few days later, it was confirmed that the cap on the amount of State Civic Center Bonds were raised by 100% to create funds necessary for this project.

Perhaps 30 years ago, when the prosperity and the optimism were real, the idea of a civic center would appear to me natural and commendable. But the time has changed. Today? Today, when all across the state the schools are closing and teachers are dismissed to save the money, a proposition to spend millions of borrowed dollars for civic centers looks to me, expressing it mildly, frivolous.

To tell the truth, I didn't observe in our area any new explosion of artistic creativity or even of social life activation. Our lives in those aspects continuous as sleepy and depressed as it always was. And except this, I always was thinking that the creative spirit is free. Usually it appears far from the places where splendid centers are waiting for them to make them feel comfortable. Creativity is rather related to the fullness and restlessness of the soul that cannot but express itself, creating in the process the masterpieces of art. Only afterwards, even maybe after initial rejection, the ordinary people are starting to build temples for those creative heights, to gather, to preserve them, to put them on display and to study them.

And I wonder. What really originated this sudden craving for civic centers in Sterling and in other places? Was it the skillfulness of the lobby for 35 civic center authorities? Or maybe it was something that I would call a "spoiled kid syndrome?" The other kid got a new toy and God is the witness, that heaven and earth will crash if I do not get a toy exactly the same as he.

Here I want also to observe that if such centers would be considered useful, necessary and would be built, at least it should reflect the special individuality of each place. It never should be a product of an assembly line with the serial appearances as are the different kinds of automobiles or different burger places to eat.

The World Seen from the Distance of a Small Village

1. Not long ago, I received a letter from the Blackhawk Area Council of Boy Scouts of America asking for help in keeping the area Scouting alive. Scouting always was a good educator of the young. It developed values, character, personal fitness and citizenship. But today, the cost of Scouting is rising very rapidly. Even the insurance gives no relief. While those costs are sky-high, the sources of funding for the organization are drying up. Do we need Scouting?
2. In such a situation it is still difficult for me to comprehend the decision of our Gov. Thomson to bail out the White Sox baseball team from Chicago, using millions of state money for this.

    The White Sox became restless. Illinois appeared to them unattractive and they contemplated a move to Florida. To agree to stay, they demanded a price. And of course, what would Illinois be without the White Sox? Our Gov. rushed to pacify them. They got everything they demanded. Why not? All the self-esteem, the past, the present and the future of Illinois depended on the White Sox glories. The other problems: the schools, the Scouting, the thousands of other neglected needs were far behind the danger of the possibility of the White Sox departure from our state.

    This Governor's action should be printed with big letters to remember because his visibility during the real crisis and needs is rather insignificant.
3. Yesterday, I saw on TV the Iowa governor signing the bill for gambling on the Mississippi River. He stressed that personally he was against it, but in the face of overwhelming acceptance and pressure, he was changing this project into law.

    Previous to this ceremony, television was bringing almost daily the last moment news about the gambling situation. Important personalities were speaking explaining advantages, counting millions of dollars that would pour into area businesses, painting pictures of new developments, new jobs and new prosperity. As I know, no one calculated how many cases of personal and whole families depauperizations would be necessary for each case of success in this kind of enterprise. Gambling is producing nothing. It presents only a kind of temptation to commit a calculated robbery from the attracted victims. It leaves behind its glamorous front a dangerous array of downfalls, of self-deprecations, of tragedies in the families by disrupting their economic security. It brings more divorces, more escapes into alcoholism, more tragedies with children.

Book Two

I was stunned when I heard that originally the 18 year-olds could gamble. What a surprise it would create for the parents. How that would affect their school progress, their approach to work, their values of honesty? After raising the admission age to 21, the opposition softened and gambling became established.

I do not argue with the need for activation of depressed businesses of the area. A development of tourism always made sense. But tourism could be stimulated in other, more dignifying and elevating ways. The Mississippi area has a rich tradition of Indian past, of French colonization adventures, of so many ethnic group settlements from which could be developed tales, games, colorful presentations, competitions and festivals that would produce interest, attractions, stimulation of talent and creativity would change the area into something really exciting.

The problem is, that such a direction for development would require from everybody here much more than just a passive expectation. Such a project would demand the mobilization of all the best in the region: of vision, of imagination, of research, of courage and of dedication and hard work. This kind of development would leave on this land a permanent mark of distinction. It could bring out the best from the people, elevating everybody.

But no. Why sweat? The gambling proposition required no effort at all. It was a lazy man's choice. Everything in this project was already prefabricated by organized gambling. The area was expected only to be blinded and to be lured by the exterior glamour and by the enormous promises of the gambling syndicate and give permission for gambling establishments.

But easiness in life is not always so easy. We have to pay always the price for our shortcuts. In my understanding, gambling has nothing to do with the development of the area. It has everything with its exploitation with seeping out all the vital reserves of the place. Gambling is a parasitic institution that brings destruction, misery and emptiness.

The overwhelming vote for gambling should be a call for a deep look into our inside fabric and a signal for alarm. Why are we so anxious to get rich the easiest way, closing our eyes on the consequences? What does it mean for the future?

Tadeusz Maciejczyk
Milledgeville, April 30, 1989

The World Seen from the Distance of a Small Village

James H. Cunningham Insurance Agency, Inc.
Kelly S. Loughran

I thank you for your attention and your offer. Probably, reading your previous letter, I didn't understand well the difference between Class 1 and Class 3.

Really, my work became limited almost to the office practice. I discontinued obstetric. The last one I did in October 87. The conditions of doing only uncomplicated obstetrics are always uncertain. Last minute complications can happen and in a small country hospital, it is not easy to obtain help in such situations. And also, all my hospitalizations became almost null. Zero. Maybe after a battle with malpractice, I lost the enthusiasm. My trial still is hanging. Probably they do not know what to do with me—and so I do not return to Sterling Hospital.

With all those limitations, I think that the minimum of insurance will be all that I need.

Again, I thank you.

T. Maciejczyk. M.D.
Milledgeville, May 7, 1989

Dr. Ravenscraft
Hebron, Kentucky

Dear Sir:

Yesterday I received a notification from Mr. William Cacciatore telling me that you were called for interrogation and that in this way you were also involved in the suit against me.

I do not know what was the character of your notification, what he really wants from you, what were you told and all together what do you know about this my trial?

Because I know how traumatic such a notification can be, even if the accusation is completely unfounded and ridiculous, I send you the copy of the act of accusation against me and of my responses, the copies of statements that I did during my two appearances in court and all my other correspondence dealing with this trial.

I believe that the malpractice bonanza reached such a degree of shamelessness that it needs to be resisted for the good of any person who truly works in this country and for the future of this country.

I would like to hear from you and to be helpful in some way, if it is possible.

I wish you the best.

Tadeusz Maciejczyk, M.D.
Milledgeville, May 19, 1989

Grace Commission
J. Peter Grace, Chairman

Dear Sir:

You request to answer this survey put me in an uneasy situation. I am not well prepared to answer all those particular points. Your questions are constructed in such a way that the only logical answer to them is "Yes." Then, why bother, if the answer is already obvious?

What is disturbing me in this survey is that you are not asking for any contribution of thought, for a different angle, argument or input. Rather you are urging those who participate to make the marking automatically, in five minutes, without bothering to think. The stress was put only on contribution. I got the impression that for this survey I was especially selected not because I can express some original ideas, but because I have an M.D. behind my name and because of this I am targeted for money exclusively, for nothing else.

Probably because of this M.D. I receive many such letters daily. And many other people do. The general opinion among the people about those letters became very skeptical. When I asked them how they would respond to those questions, they told me: Do not bother to write to them. Those questions are only a cover-up to get money. Nobody will read what you write. They will look only for the check and the rest they will throw to the waste paper basket. And they will never tell you what they did with the money.

The World Seen from the Distance of a Small Village

Those remarks are a measurement for a devaluation of the dialogue between our leaders and the people. Such a barrier and such a distrust is sad and is frightening. Who is guilty?

I know that the problem of waste in the government is real and that there is a need for such a commission as yours to work out the problem and to put light on different twists and abuses of powerful special interest groups and its lobbies. But then, the President and the different governmental agencies should speak about those problems to the people. This is a natural, necessary part of leadership. Surely after such calls of the leaders, the press would be eager to look into to the matter to dissect, to explain, to create opinion. Consequently the prople would react.

Instead, you are conducting your fight by sending impressive survey sheets, calculated to get mechanical, easy answers by reflex. You directed those surveys to a limited number of "especially selected participants" whose most likely common denominator is not the knowledge of the subject or an interest in the public affairs, but their potential to contribute.

Frankly, I do not believe in such a backdoor maneuver. I do not think that the tons and tons of survey papers arriving in Washington would make any change or any impression on the lawmakers. The U.S. is an open society. Such problems should be dealt here openly and with full force, provoking discussion and resonance. Those selected groups surveys will not translate into any voting shift and will not create any popular battle cry. In my opinion except for the money collection, they are useless.

Here I want to add that the waste problem in America is not limited to those situations that can be counted in money. It reaches many areas of life and consequently is undermining the very foundation on which societies are built.

The first amendment was once a great achievement and gave America a special distinction among nations.

Today the same amendment is used to protect the spread of pornography and of implantation of vices. It is used to attack any institution or authority, to weaken character of the people and of organizations, to immobilize and to enslave. Any pressure group, which gets its wealth and power from spreading those ideas or attitudes, is getting a safe shelter in this amendment. The harvest from those activities and from its conditionings, is already very costly and its cost will rise.

Today it looks like America is losing its battle against inundation in narcotics. Having to choose between protection of our children and the bad effects that a decisive war against drug traffic chains would produce, we vacillate, we are undecided and we are inclined to sacrifice our children. Such a sacrifice is less controversial and produces less shock. But without a shock of a total war, we will have no cure, no relief. Listening to the people

Book Two

I heard, that many influential, important personalities are involved at the top of that traffic pyramid and because of this, our costly war against drug organizations is never reaching its neurological centers. Those centers are well protected. The top men are safe, the courts are ridiculously ineffective and the society goes deeper directly into drug habits and indirectly into an environment of the drug-related crimes, insecurity and general intimidation on the streets and even at homes. The numbers that could somehow illustrate the human destruction and waste are going up. The cost of this? Nobody really can calculate.

America was once a land of opportunity. And it is still today. But the true opportunities are harder to find. In its place, America became a land of pseudo-opportunities. At present, almost each state establishes a lottery to supplement its budget. Gambling places are multiplying. Everywhere the courts are busy in resolving malpractice and other querulous civil suits.

But pseudo-opportunities are sterile for creation or even maintaining wealth and they have serious consequences that we are already paying. A person involved in lottery, who buys the lottery tickets and in this way raises those enormous amounts of money for those frequently fabulous premiums, so cheerfully announced by every TV station has no emotional energy or inner peace left to be productive, to concentrate, to be creative and to look around for something real. Living constantly between high hopes and each time deeper disappointment in such a permanent emotional imbalance, he is more likely to develop passivity in action, disillusion, frustration and rebellion, maybe family break down and personal depreciation in self-respect and self-confidence.

Gambling produces the same effect with the difference that the illness is much quicker to appear; its symptoms are more sudden, more visible and more dramatic.

The explosion of malpractice suits against anybody who does something positive and can pay, is the best illustration of the mushrooming, parasitic hopes and tendencies in a large segment of our society that dreams to get rich without work. They look for a pretext and any pretext for them is good to try. Well-entrenched interest groups are cultivating and defending those hunting games and expectations. They explain that those actions are promoting safety and just recompense for negligence. And certainly such explanations would be true if those measures to compensate and to protect from neglect and abuse would be not changed into a parody, hungry for money and completely blind for any kind of proportion or even decency.

The courts responded to the epidemic of malpractice suits in a way that encouraged for litigations even the completely absurd claims. Instead of an impartial consideration of guilt, damage and just compensation, the courts allowed for the verdicts of the especially selected jurors, easily influenced and brought to a point of an emotional hysteria by the eloquence and the show performance of the accusing attorneys. The U.S. Courts became guilty of an unjust, unprofessional, completely astonishing in its irresponsible behavior, that made from the U.S. Justice and from the jury system almost a laughing joke, if it would be not for the tragedy of its consequences.

Those malpractice litigations and its unreal rewards put its long shadow on every enterprise, on every initiative and every idea ready to be put into practical use here in the U.S. It introduced a state of intimidation into every active, creative enhancing life center in this land. The cost of the now days practiced restraints, safeguards, of the loss of initiative, or even complete abandonment of projects is staggering. The burden of this cost was put on every family on every person in the U.S. As a documentation of this, I include here a copy of a statement from a pharmaceutical company. Every communication media, as well as every true leader should feel a duty to present to the people those hidden robberies perpetuated and imposed on society.

Speaking already about the court's handling of the malpractice suits, I want to add my impression from observation of the U.S. Court's preparation for the Col. Oliver North trial.

In those preparations, an enormous effort was done to find jurors who never heard about the Col. North saga, about the Iran Contra-affair and about all that loud and deep emotional storm that passed across the U.S. during the previous Congressional investigations. To find such a rarity, no consideration was given to the capacity for judgment in the people so ignorant, so disinterested in even the most traumatic national tragedy, so remote to the problems of the present world. Their capacity to judge apparently was not a problem.

Before such a collection of man-made jurors, the best representatives of America's legal complexities were making eloquent speeches to present the problem, to argue and to counter-argue. It made the atmosphere in the courtroom strange and artificial.

The Byzantine effort for arranging this "perfect" jury untouched by any previous influence, by any previous knowledge of the case, looked to me like a search for a Pharisaic type of purity and perfection. It showed more preoccupation with the exterior appearance than with the effort to bring the truth and peace to the nation. This attitude, the way I see it, was putting the judiciary itself on trial for hypocrisy.

It can be that today's work became too complex for the jury system. The number of complicated litigations have multiplied and the people

Book Two

became uncertain about their roles in being a central element to measure justice.

My concern here is that without confidence in the justice of the courts (people are expressing such doubts) life becomes more uncertain and the multiform waste in people's performance is going up. Somehow the human genius needs certainty in justice to light up and to shine.

The next arena of an enormous waste is in the education system: a waste that extends far beyond the problems easily solved with additional money. It is true that complaints about money squeezes and demands for more funding was dominating lately the discussion about school problems. But the TV program of Barbara Walters or the article in *Newsweek* about daily teaching conditions in the present day's classrooms are testifying that the crisis is much deeper than the scarcity of money. It looks to me that more than this, the soul of the U.S. education system became ill and requires a complete examination, diagnosis and treatment. The primitive schools of 100 years ago were doing a better job preparing children to confront life that existed at that time.

I have difficulty putting into words what I feel about the present day's U.S. school problems. To those who see its solution only in additional monetary funding, what I have to say will sound like blasphemy. I believe that the main source of schools' ills is an overabundance of material facilities contrasting with the softness and resistance to be involved of the human material. Primarily it is a human crisis.

Years ago, I heard on the radio about rioting in a Chicago school. It was late September. The weather became suddenly cold. The classes were still without heat and the temper of the kids exploded. They vandalized school furniture and broke windows demanding heat. To my astonishment the authorities of the school admitted their guilt and that student anger was justified.

Listening to that news, I remembered my third year of Gymnasium in Kielce in Poland. It was Feb. 1945. The front line just passed and after almost six years of no schools, our town, the teachers and the students in a common effort, opened the school classes again. The outside temperature was below 20 (Celsius). There was no heating. There was not one piece of glass in the huge glass windows. The snow was in every corner of the room. We were sitting on whatever we brought from home, making notes on our knees. There were no books. All the libraries were burned in the fall of 1939 when it was considered that we would never again have a need for books. I remember the hand of our profession, with a hole in his glove, writing on the blackboard. Many of the boys were without breakfast because bread was scarce those days. On the ashes of everything else, the spirits were strong. Almost nobody failed.

The World Seen from the Distance of a Small Village

The memory of that scene stood in contrast to the radio news from Chicago.

Why such a contrast? Apparently here, having everything, the human factor shows a very low endurance or motivation. And I do not see any direct effort to correct this phenomenon. Instead, we are trying to compensate, to create additional facilities, to oversimplify, to provide crutches in order to make the learning process effortless, easy and more attractive. The homework became almost eliminated. The continuous need to repeat and to digest what was already learned was bypassed by modern devices. We use calculators before we dominate the basics of mathematics. We teach word processing before teaching to process words in our own minds and in this way make us feel independent and creative. We forgot that "repetition is *mater studiorum*" as it was for centuries. The medium changed, but not the human mind. Every strategist knows that advancing the frontline, without constant tedious work to consolidate the back calls for trouble. Those repellent repetitions are not appearing well in the reports. So, we rush. Then we introduce the different remedial studies. Each time more costly our education system is not working as it could. Probably there are many conditions that added to this picture.

During the last decades, the authority of teachers became restricted. Of course, it was done in the name of progress. The created feeling of impunity encouraged a rise of "negative leaders" especially among teenagers. The order in classes suffered from distraction. Also suffering was the teachers' dedication, their self-esteem and professional pride. Frequently their efforts were mutilated and turned ineffective before even reaching the minds of students. The motivation factor, the center of any work well done, was getting thin on both sides.

The break in teachers' authority came in the time when the stability of American families became more insecure than ever before. Consequently the students were coming to school with the burden of their own growing anxieties and uncertainties, their feeling of guilt for what was happening at home, and their self-depreciation. In other times, when the teacher's image was high, they could console them and give them encouragement. But thanks to the eagerness of our society to expose, downgrade and destroy all authorities and institutions, we left the children within a special vacuum and loneliness in which they were expected to grow, to develop life principles and to retain enthusiasm and faith in the life's mission. With our carelessness and selfishness, too frequently nobody was really concerned about our children's state of despair. Only their growing rebellion or their acts of self-destruction were provoking an alarm.

Into this vacuum and lonely existence of our young, the different kinds of media launched a widespread attack to get their attention. The TV shows became different, the book stores, the special telephone call capabilities and the videos had less restraint and became more obscene. The First Amendment protected all of them.

During the presentation of a math teacher in our Rotary meeting, he spoke without much enthusiasm about his subject. His pride, honor and life fulfillment was elsewhere. He was also a coach of our school football team. The team's glory was his glory and feeling of greatness. A sign on the road at the entrance to our town said that our town was a home of "Missiless," the name of all the teams and sports groups of our school.

If such a sign would have an announcement that our town was a champion, for example, in the world geography in our region, the created pride would be at least the same, but it would be more proper for a school and more stimulating for the students. I never saw such a sign in any place. President Kennedy's call for physical fitness degenerated into an image of a school that is a sports center and between the sports events, also bothers with teaching.

Yes. We can pour into our schools a lot of additional money. If we do not heal first the soul of our schools, we can get disappointed in the results.

The epidemic of divorces in America, without a doubt, is a cause of enormous waste. I do not speak only about the cost that the society is paying to clean the debris left behind by the divorce trend as for example an increased number of Public Aid recipients. There are also many more subtle realities resulting from divorce.

In adults it produces not infrequently a lifelong emotional devastation. Also, divorce provides a special training ground for irresponsibility, instability, a casual approach to obligations, promises or vows. The solemn vows to the family, if once broken, opens the field for devaluation of all other values and life principles. It would be interesting to conduct a serious study in how this problem is translating into relations towards employers, towards society, towards the country. A pattern once established can work increasingly well in all other varieties of circumstances.

To this, we can add the fact that during all the stages of divorce, the emotional involvement, its pain or maybe hate, the development of unforgiveness or even of blind vengeance, the frequently experienced feeling of guilt or personal depreciation and consequently the deep self concentration, are influencing the working capacity, increasing negligence, distraction, inattention and accidents.

A divorce is diminishing its participants in other ways. A divorce is basically an escape: an escape from difficulties, from the process of a mutual adjustment, from an appearance of pain in the family relationship. In the act of divorce, we shut out communication, we preclude reconciliation. But it is a fact that a person can achieve an internal growth, higher maturity and better personality only when he confronts and resolves life's difficulties. Only at that time we are really forced to think again about the problems deep to the roots, to look for new ways or improvements, new insides, new remedies. In the process of this effort, we are changing, we are getting stronger, more self assured, with greater tolerance towards others and a new vision of things. This way we mature. This way societies, even whole nations, can improve and mature. By contrast, a person who all his life tries to escape pain, most likely will remain forever a helpless kid without a chance to grow.

It is necessary also to consider that the chill of divorce has a chain behind that lasts much longer than this person's life. It introduces a virus of an emotional illness into the souls of his children that victimize them throughout their lives and can be transmitted into future generations. The shadow of a divorce can be very long and its consequences can be difficult to heal.

Who can calculate the real cost of divorce? How much waste is it producing? How can we put a monetary value on its tragedies? What will be its projection on the future?

I do not want to prolong this letter speaking about waste in Health Care. I already passed the deadline for answering. Except this: I wrote about it many times.

I do not send you a contribution for two reasons.

1. I do not believe that your actions could be effective
2. I, myself, became a waste.

There was a time when I was enthusiastic in my work. I approached medicine primarily as a mission. A mission to help.

When our hospital in 1983 demanded from all its doctors to have malpractice insurance, I protested. Such a costly insurance would force me to increase the price for my services to my patients. As a consequence of my stand on this issue, I lost my hospital privileges. Then in 1987, after several voices that I will be taught a lesson, I got my own malpractice suit. It stemmed from a 1982 incident. AT that time I saved the foot of my patient from amputation recommended by a specialist. The patient is still walking on her two feet and I got a vendetta. Fortunately for me, the accusation is ridiculous, but it drags on. I refused to hire a defense lawyer and until now I am successful in my own defense, but I feel the strain. My practice has become limited. My previous work enthusiasm was dampened. Why

Book Two

struggle? I would like to be able to pass my youngest daughter through the University. Then? I do not know. I have no savings to retire. To go on public aid is not very attractive. I am not bitter, but I lost my faith in American common sense, sincerity, fairness and justice. To work and to be effective, I need fresh air. In America, the working air became poisoned and this process is getting only worse. I am sorry that I am making such a statement. I represent a waste. I do not know what is the number of cases like mine. Altogether they spell nothing good for America.

                                              Tadeusz Maciejczyk, M.D.
                                              Milledgeville, June 15, 1989

Cc: The White House
    The Justice and Education Departments
    Party Headquarters
    Both Senators and District Representative
    U.S. World and News Report
    Newsweek
    Time
    20/20
    Local newspapers and state authorities

The World Seen from the Distance of a Small Village

Philip M. Crane
United States Congressman

Dear Sir:

I do not remember how long ago I received your letter about the Panama Canal situation and the Resolution 47 in congress. Today is the 4th of July. My worries about my malpractice suit, for which I have to go again to Court on July 14, have somewhat subsided and I decided to answer you and to express my opinion on this matter.

1. I consider that the Panama Canal Treaty of Jimmy Carter was painful and not easy to do, nevertheless, it was the wisest and most far-reaching decision that calls for constant, thoughtful and tactful touch and guidance towards an evolution in which the U.S. as well as Panama could remain friends and equal; perhaps one day approaching a moment of a declaration of a common citizenship. (In the post-Suez Canal era, an insistence to stick to power holding in the canal, would create a condition of aggravation, mobilizing all of Central and South America against the U.S. and really giving an open field for the Soviets to take the harvest.)
2. Any annulment of the Treaty now would be a free, precious gift to Noriega because it would put the masses and the sentiment of the masses of the country behind him and against the U.S. It would be like an Iraqi war action for Khomeni. The nationalist feelings are one of the most powerful and also frequently most blind of human emotions.
3. The fight against Noriega and his conspiracy with Castro and Ortega should be fought not by sizing the Canal again, not by pressure of the material, military, political forces, but by a wise, far-reaching communication for planning of a mutual future between representatives and the people of both nations that eventually would create a sincere and durable commonwealth giving merit and pride to both sides. In such a development, the conspiratory connections of Noriega would have no consequences and eventually all of them would lose their influence. A show of a fist and action for the Canal Treaty nullifying by the U.S. Congress would give Noriega a strength and more likely would put openly or secretly the Soviets behind him.
4. Making treaties then nullifying them just because of one or another twist or whim would destroy U.S. credibility as somebody

who can be trusted. Who with a sound mind would have any confidence in any serious promises or treaties signed by U.S. Presidents?
5. If the CIS is a real major Conservative think-tank, it should start to think how to outmaneuver Noriega without breaking the previously given U.S. word. It should imagine and structure a situation of cooperation and mutual building of a common future based on friendship, sincerity and mutual growth of both nations.

To break something already existing, it is not necessary for any think-tank. A think-tank is necessary to confront a challenge for development of a new vision and new initiative, for creation of new bounds between two nations, to not to miss any occasion that can serve to reinforce those bounds and to avoid those that divide and create negative emotions. A think-tank should provide enough content to involve for our mutual good every thinking person in both of the nations. In the history of humanity still nothing noble and durable was built on a brute, blind force. It always was done by the creation of good will, new ideas and new bounds.

Writing this, I want to stress that nobody really can label me with a ticket of "liberal."

Neither do I like to be called a conservative. Those notions are rigid and somehow not proper for a thinking, receptive and reflective mind.

I always considered that to look into the future, a person has to have a firm base in the past, but not to dwell there: just to be free and when necessary, to go back a distance and to do an effective, forceful and well-directed jump forward. We always need a clear understanding of our past, not to be immobilized by its emotional feelers, but to look into the future with more open and more understanding eyes.

I wish you the best in your work.

Tadeusz Maciejczyk
Milledgeville, July 4, 1989

cc: President Bush, The White House
    Former President Carter
    Party Leaders

The World Seen from the Distance of a Small Village

Editor of *AAFP Reporter*

Dear Sir:

Today, I had my first chance to read the AAFP reporter and I got a strange impression of an intimidation, or even of an inferiority complex of family practitioners when confronted with the privileged camp of specialists. From the huge majority, as we were a few decades ago, we became a minority in the medical field and we are not sure any more, where in this field we fit. Without a doubt, not the specialist, but the family practitioners are the guardians of the main medical tradition. Yet, we are not sure whether we can survive in the present world that moves very quickly towards each time bigger differentiation and fragmentation of skills. The Family Practice goes against this contemporary world trend. It remains true to the traditional mission of medicine, which while progressing and opening new horizons, never forgets to be in the service of human beings.

Our complex and our uncertainty would be justified if we measured our status and our place in work only by monetary rewards, maybe by prestige or even in some cases by an arrogance of some super-specialists.

But those factors are not exhausting the central question whether FP will survive and attract a new generation of doctors.

It looks to me that the dividing line between FP and specializations is running through different differentiating factors.

During the differentiation time, on one side we have an influence of fascination with the new equipment with the new possibilities, even new titles with which to adorn our bare M.D.s. On the other side, there is an internal inclination of each student of medicine to decide what way he wants to go.

In medicine, as in any other field, there are those for whom an open horizon and a total approach to the problems of each patient are uneasy and frightening. They feel more comfortable when they are limiting themselves to a treatment of only a small segment of our organism, scarcely giving attention to anything else. Those doctors define their work basically as the repair of human engines. They like the predictable daily repetition of their practice problems because they feel safer and more effective this way. In such a practice they can concentrate more on the few problems they resolve. Their segmental knowledge can go deeper. They can follow more closely the rapidly advancing progress in their small field and they can master the use of the new instrumentation.

All this is giving the specialist a feeling of power and importance. They are inclined to take the glory for the progress as a personal merit.

They convince themselves that they are the practitioners who keep the pace with the time and because of this they represent the image of the doctor of the future.

But this rush into the future is producing many negative effects that are getting more visible as the time passes. It strips the patients from their personalities and wholeness. They are shifted from one specialist to another for a check-up or repair of one or another segment of their bodies. The problem of warmth, affection or personal confidence becomes secondary or not existent. In the age of glorification of computers, they become numbers. In such a practice, the face of each patient is the same: a face taken casually out from an anonymous crowd. Not those patients as persons, but patients for a coding numbers is what is becoming really important. The world that is coming is producing fewer and fewer individuals. It is busy to build and to overextend a bright rainbow of generic commodities, luxuries and facilities for a passing by, noisy, but silent and practically invisible crowd. And the world, with all its created comfort, becomes a desperately cold and lonesome place.

On the other side of the dividing line are the doctors for whom the principal objective of their medical training is a service to all human beings, to entire families, to communities. They do not look primarily for money, for a title or prestige. They look for a kind of mission to fill their lives.

A practitioner with such an approach to practice is not afraid of a variety of problems that can pop up during the working day. He welcomes them and is doing his best to solve them. To each visitor he will extend a special warmth, special personal interaction. It is probably true that such a practitioner almost never would be a good businessman and seldom will make a special scientific mark. For him the rewards will be all those special events of daily work.

I think that such a practitioner generally would have an individual mind. He would rather rely on himself, but he also will recognize his limitations and his need for specialists to supplement the care he gives.

Such an inclination among the students in the medical training places as in the medical practice, is a special gift of nature. It is the essence of medical vocation. Those doctors should not feel secondary in importance in the medical field practice whose time in the rapidly changing world has passed. The rapidly advancing medical knowledge is and should be, applied and directed to the eternally same human beings in the individual form. In this approach the GP and the FP have a special distinction: they preserve the human factor in the developing medical science that shows all the signs of overlooking the individual in order to serve the crowd.

The World Seen from the Distance of a Small Village

I have an impression that the FP will survive and will redefine himself more firmly. From the present retreat and decline, it will go forwards to regain its real place in the patients serving medicine.

It would be interesting to prepare a collective work to define this real place of FP in medicine and to make a study of human personality and character that would indicate a predisposition among future practitioners for general family practice or for specialty.

Tadeusz Maciejczyk, M.D.
Milledgeville, July 14, 1989

Book Two

Clerk of the Court of Carroll County
Case No. 87 L 2: (dated January 22/87)

Dear Sir:

In preparation for the approaching trial, I asked by subpoena and I obtained, the entire chart of Mrs. Wilma Macchi's hospitalization in Community General Hospital of Sterling on February 1, 1985, which included: history, physical examination, all consultations, all progress notes, X-rays and lab work, and a complete operating room report.

I also asked and I obtained a complete charge of similar documents from all visits of Mrs. Macchi in Sterling/Rock Falls Clinic.

Both of those documents are in my possession and they will clearly disclose a lack of support for all, and every one of the points of accusation act handed to me by Mr. Cacciatore on January 23, 1987.

I also asked and I obtained from Morrison Community Hospital a copy of the hospitalization chart of Andre O'Bosla in 1985–86, which indicates that at that time I treated successfully a patient with very extensive decubitus, aggravated by longstanding complications from diabetes, malnutrition, blindness, incontinence, adding to all this a large cancer in the right lung. The enormous decubital infected and necrotic wounds of this patient's sacral area, of both hips, both ankles, one elbow, and a large decubital opening over the mid-thoracic area of the spine, were completely closed and healed before that patient left the Morrison Skilled Care Center to enter Good Samaritan Nursing Home in Mt. Carroll.

Because of a very strange correlation with my present accusation, which really has no other logical explanation but vengeance, I asked, with the agreement of the family, for a copy of the hospitalization chart of Mrs. Hazel Edlund in November and December of 1982. During that hospitalization, I resisted all pressure from Dr. James Allen to amputate that patient's foot. I felt the intensity of anger of Dr. Allen, when 2–3 months after her discharge, during the meeting of internists, at its end, Dr. Allen left the room and the presiding Dr. Styczynski asked the doctors to condemn me for the way I treated Mrs. Edlund against the advice and insistence of Dr. Allen.

Finally, because all the act of accusation against me is based on the "expert" testimony of a doctor, who spelled twice my whole name, but failed to sign his testimony, I prepared a subpoena that I will give directly to Mr. Cacciatore or to his representatives during this session, in which I request the appearance of that expert in the courtroom for con-

The World Seen from the Distance of a Small Village

frontation and discussion. An expert who refuses or is afraid to defend his statements is a worthless authority who never should be taken seriously in any court. The act of confidentiality does not apply to him in this place. Here, he is not in danger of life or persecution. Without a confrontation with this expert, all this trial is losing is substance, and would contradict any true search for justice.

I have one thing more to say in this letter. Today I received another letter from Mr. Cacciatore in which he says that because I failed to provide him until now the list of my expert witnesses and did not disclose myself as an expert witness, Wilma Macchi prays that the court would bar me from calling any expert to testify on my behalf at the time of trial in this cause.

Today's letter was a surprise to me. In the previous correspondence there was no other term to present my witnesses except the 14th of July hearing. I want to stress that the biggest danger to life in any country is a court system corrupt enough to be guided in its decisions by tricks, instead of a desire to a constant, consistent and sincere search for all elements necessary to reach the final and just verdict. I hope that this court will repudiate such an attempt from the attorney, who apparently forgets that his primary obligation is a quest for justice.

Not long ago, in the letter to the Grace commission in discussing the waste problem, I wrote, "What is my concern here is that without confidence in the justice of courts (people are expressing such doubts) the life becomes more uncertain and the multiform waste in people's performance is going up. Somehow the human genius needs certainty in justice to light up and to shine."

Here I want to express my full confidence in this court's impartiality and mission.

Tadeusz Maciejczyk, M.D.
Milledgeville, July 13, 1989

Book Two

NOTE: The next letter is not about my malpractice case, but it is a look into the soul of the judiciary.

Editorial of the *Daily Gazette*
Sterling, Illinois

Several days ago I read in your editorial its final conclusion that the judgment of the Supreme Court about the flag desecration, even if painful, was correct.

I saw the flashes from that desecration moment on TV. The flag thrown on the floor was burning. Some young were passing by indifferently. Some in the background were yelling. One young brave approached the flag and spat in its direction. It was very instructive to watch.

The Supreme Court declared that all those acts were a sort of protest, expressed not with words, but with symbolic gestures. It is true that because of this interpretation, those gestures became a symbol of the limits of the new freedom.

I had my doubts, but I had to agree, that they are people who express themselves only with gestures. The mutes have only gestures as their only way to communicate. Then, maybe those new boundaries of freedom of "speech" were logical and were opening new horizons for a better tomorrow, in which everybody would be more free than ever.

Then today, before I opened my eyes in the morning, I got an exciting idea that the limit for our freedom, even with a permission for flag desecration, would still be insufficient. The limits for our freedom should be pushed further and further. During our daily lives, we have so many suppressed emotions and so many unfulfilled needs and wishes.

Probably only a very few of us are enjoying the moment of paying taxes and filling out those tedious forms. We should be free to protest paying our taxes by not paying them. In doing this, we should be secure that our Constitution would give us an adequate protection against those who would like to violate that our sacred right.

The same logic should apply to the act of theft. It is clearly a gesture of protesting against inequality because some have, and some no. We should have a constitutional right to steal.

Killing anybody obviously is not recommended, but the act of killing is without a doubt a gesture, which provides an emotional outlet for our indignation, anger or fear. I firmly believe that without legalization of killing, our first amendment will not be fully understood. All those special killings, which are telling about emotions behind them, should be legalized and should be protected by a modern and progressive inter-

The World Seen from the Distance of a Small Village

pretation of our Constitution. If I cannot kill, somehow, my freedom of expression is limited and it could lead gradually to other suppressions of our freedom, substituting it with an ugly tyranny.

Years ago, there was a young man in Clinton, who periodically burned houses. Another man in New York periodically shot people. Should their freedom to do so not be protected? Each time they did this, they were sending a message to society that their insides were dark and turbulent. They wanted their messages to be symbolic and clear to everybody. They fully deserved recognition and some kind of permit based on the good intentions of the First Amendment.

With such a maturity and progress in development of our constitutional freedoms, really the courts would be unnecessary and the fullness of freedom would be at the reach of anybody who would like to use it. And also, as the interpretation of the constitution would have nothing more to add, the supreme Court would become an institution of the past, without any interest to anybody in that modern day of progress.

Tadeusz Maciejczyk, M.D.
Milledgeville, July 16, 1989

Cc: The White House
The Supreme Court

NOTE: These are my thoughts about flag desecration. Freedom is a very fragile and delicate item. Its transgression easily leads to excesses and to the burial for what freedom really is.

Book Two

(This letter was written to Cristina, my daughter at such a special moment of my life. It shows my mood and my soul.)

Dear Cristina,

In a few days you will be 19. Yes, it will be a big day for you: a day to reflect, a day to see the past with some special new light, a day maybe for some conscious or subconscious decisions.

The life is such a strange mystery. It constantly mirages us with distant images and illusions. We are constantly after something, what most often remains for us not easy to define. We are in a permanent journey, constantly between hope and disappointment, between our best intentions and promises while confronted with our weaknesses to implement them; between the joy and sadness. We are forced every day to make decisions and we are uneasy to mobilize ourselves to make them stick.

Life is a span of time given to us that we have to fill up with a content. This our daily job can decide whether we can look into the mirror and smile, whether at the end we could get a fulfillment or an overwhelming emptiness and disappointment. What is precious in life can have different substance for different persons. And so, in life, we are a kind of guardian of what we consider is important. This is our lifelong task. Somehow we are marching into the future listening to the drum, rhythm, that somewhere very deep in us is marking our steps. In this march we can give ourselves completely to our most distant objectives, or we can be erratic, without aim, without true light. A life is a great fight that requires a purpose, a vision and a stubborn daily upkeep because life is not for a moment. It is by all our instincts for eternity.

And so, what can I wish you on this day of your birthday? Perhaps that your life could be always noble. Such conception of life can give sorrows, but it gives back rewards that cannot be measured by any standard.

Here at home everything is, as it always was, maybe, that in the last week I had difficulty to smile and I was in a pensive mood. On July 14, I had a hearing in court and the judge was rough on me with an accusation that is a complete absurdity. It looks like I am against an enormous wall. A justice can have very strange bendings. The final trial will be on November 13. So, at present, I am against something unknown.

It is rough also on Mama. And I do not know how to explain it to her and how to make this for her more acceptable.

Saturday, Terese will come for the weekend. So we will have all the talk about her journey and her impressions from Spain. Irka called a few

The World Seen from the Distance of a Small Village

days ago and said that everything is going well with her pregnancy and that what she expects is a boy.

After dry weather, that was threatening to create a new disaster, in the last two days we had a wonderful rain.

Best wishes for both of you. I love you both.

                            Papa
                          July 20, 1989

Book Two

John W. Rapp, Jr.
Chief Circuit Judge of the 15th Judicial circuit
County of Carroll
Mt. Carroll, Illinois 61053

Dear Sir:

After the July 14 hearing it became clear to me that the expectation for justice for me in your court is equal to zero. Because of this, I ask you to make short the preparations for the remaining formalities for the trial. It makes no sense for me to spend even five minutes of my time on the selection of jurors to whom I would have no right to speak.

Nothing was left for November 13 to be discussed or clarified. My presentation of hospital documentation from Mrs. Macchi's hospitalization, which is so fundamental to the presentation of this case, was declared by you invalid and inadmissible. The same was true of her chart from Sterling/Rock Falls Clinic, which details all post-hospitalization visits of Mrs. Macchi for her problem.

I was also denied in that hearing to be listened to and to indicate my other preparations for the trial. I had no chance to tell about my presentation of documents from the hospitalization of Andres O'Bosla and another chart of Mrs. Hazel Edlund, which put a special light on the background of this accusation against me. My intention to give a subpoena to Mrs. Cacciatore to force him to present in the court his mysterious expert, who solemnly testified against me, but failed to sign his testimony, was forbidden by you. Finally, you declared that I could not speak at the trial for myself as an expert witness.

That hearing on July 14 was cut short when you left the room in the middle of my sentence saying that you do not want to listen to me anymore.

There is not much left for the trial on Nov. 13. As you predicted, that trial will be short.

In this letter I want to explain why I resist your pressure to hire a lawyer who would speak for me.

After receiving your summons with the text of accusation, almost immediately I received different proposals to defend me. After explaining the obvious absurdity of this accusation, I received from all of them the same response, that to get me out from the deep troubles I was in, I needed not only a lawyer, but the best one. I came to the conclusion that what I was witnessing was a coordinated, shameless and abusive game of lawyers called "Justice." I felt that in my conscience, I couldn't support such a blatant farce. I include here a copy of my letter written two years ago when my conclusions were still fresh.

Over 40 years ago, I was condemned to death in the court of Stalin, when he was breaking my country to be a part of the Soviet monolith. If I would be caught, I would have the same chance for a fair trial there, as apparently is given to me here in your court. There for me would speak an agent from Internal Security, in whom I could have just the same confidence as here in any of the friends' attorneys of Mr.. Cacciatore, who offered to me their services. As here, there the accusation would be based on the denunciation of a man, whom I would have never a chance to see. (There such denunciations have a special unflattering name: a *donos*.) There I was condemned because of a drive for power and domination. Here I will be condemned for money and for a personal vendetta. The justice and ethical level of both those trials looks to me about the same.

I will be in your court on November 13 for the final display of your justice. AT the present, I feel that I have nothing else to add, if not for other factors, because I will have no voice.

It is true that on the other hand, I would like to think that all I experienced on July 14 was only your pressure on me to hire a lawyer. But I will not do this. I will go, as I intended, into this trial and I will take the consequences. I cannot go against my conscience.

What will I do after the trial? I do not know. I do not see any purpose in working under such an oppressive justice, which is something completely opposite of what America represents to the world. In my letter to the Grace commission about waste, I wrote recently that to work, I need a fresh air. In America, the working air became poisoned.

I wish you a happy conscience and true pride in yourself.

Tadeusz Maciejczyk, M.D.
Milledgeville, July 23, 1989

Book Two

Department of Nuclear Safety of the State of Illinois
Springfield

    I thank you for your second notice for X-Ray Device Inspection Application.
    At present, my situation is such that I do not even know whether I will be in practice next year, or maybe even whether I will have a home to live in.
    My use now of the X-Ray machine is minimal. I even do not have at this time any more X-Ray films. What is the purpose to work in a society whose justice system is cooperating hand-in-hand with an enormous leech laying on the body of the country and dedicated to keep all the pores of its victim open to suck its blood until the last drop? I am speaking about a large part of lawyers.
    In medical school, I was taught to inflict the minimum amount of pain that can not be avoided in the process of healing.
    Apparently, this principle doesn't concern the courts of this country. They give themselves a completely free hand for inflicting immeasurable suffering, especially to the families of their victims, not checking even and being completely unconcerned about the validity of even more absurd claims. As I was writing to the Grace Commission on waste, "the U.S. Courts became guilty of an unjust, unprofessional, completely astonishing in its irresponsible behavior in their handling of the malpractice suits."
    I understand that this letter could sound strange to you. To explain, I am sending you copies of my last correspondence for the case of my impending malpractice trial.
    I will evaluate again my situation after the trial. I want to see what will be left from this piece of the very unholy specific of this country.

                                          Tadeusz Maciejczyk, M.D.
                                          Milledgeville, July 27, 1989

The World Seen from the Distance of a Small Village

James G. Jones, M.D.
President of the American Academy of Family Physicians
Kansas City, MO

Dear Sir:

This time I write to you asking for help and for a commitment. My malpractice trial is scheduled for November 13.

I do not want in this trial to get a deal between two lawyers. I would like to give this trial against me a wider meaning. I believe that, if in this trial I would be declared innocent, but I would not move the problem of malpractice in general to some different dimension, my victory would be very illusive. I could only expect another accusation, maybe better prepared, because nobody is always completely right. For this reason, I want to defend myself, but also to attack the system.

In this trial, I have a big advantage, because in this case, there is no cause for a trial against me. I have a big disadvantage, because I know nothing about courtrooms. If you would like, I could send you the act of accusation and all the other documents. I sent you them already once, before I was admitted to the Academy.

What I want from you now is direct help. I would like the Academy to send an official observer to my trial on November 13 in Mt. Carroll, Illinois, to monitor the handling by the court of the medical part of the conflict. Your presence would give me some encouragement, because in the courtroom, I will feel very alone.

I would also like all the suggestions you can give me; not to get a lawyer, but anything from your previous experience and observations.

I consider that such an official monitoring by the Academy should be a permanent part from now on, of every malpractice suit. We have to organize a self-defense, because the aggression against the medical profession went far beyond any limit of justice or even decency. In our society, we have different organizations against cruelty to animals, but we have no one against cruelty to families of frivolously, without any official restraint suited professionals. This fact should mobilize all of us. Appeasement leads to nowhere, only to more bondage.

The monitoring if possible, of all malpractice suits should have a purpose. It should lead to a completely new approach by practitioners to this malady. It should provide rich material for serious, scientific work about all aspects of those suits and their consequences. The accumulated material could be presented to different universities and its different faculties

Book Two

for discussion and elaboration, to acquire a better pressure on politicians and the court system, and to influence, to teach the public.

I send to you the copies of my last letters related to my trial. As you can see from them, even with the obvious absurdity of the accusation, my prospects are not looking too bright. Somehow, I offended the system, and they are after me.

I would like to have some answer from you as soon as you can decide how to act in my case. I need the feeling, that somebody stands for me, and also that my stand can generate a new force.

Tadeusz Maciejczyk, M.D.
July 30, 1989

The World Seen from the Distance of a Small Village

Chief Justice of the Supreme Court
United States

Dear Sir:

I write to you because I was pushed into a situation that should never happen under the U.S. Constitution.

I am a doctor, a general practitioner in a small country village. In 1983, I opposed the obligatory malpractice insurance. In my understanding, it was an unjust, indirect squeeze on the sick and the needy. Then two and one-half years ago, I got a malpractice suit. Its reason? I challenge you to send any independent investigator to find fault on my side. The pretext is senseless. Its examination would give you a better idea about the abusiveness of these suits.

My court trial is scheduled for November 13.

My wife, in desperation, went to Mt. Carroll to investigate. She was told that there is no hope for me; that I am an easy target; that we will lose everything material, even my good standing and my good name. She was encouraged to divorce me and in this way to save some of her part. She was told that we will suffer a lesser damage if I would agree to make an arrangement, a kind of appeasement, paying a ransom.

In our home now there is silence and pain, anxiety and fear. Nobody can sleep at night. We are all before an unknown. My youngest daughter, a straight A honor student at DePaul University in Chicago, could be unable to continue. And if she could, will she have the peace of mind necessary to study? I hope that this experience would make her more mature and deep, not broken. A nagging anxiety dominates everything in our home now.

In this land, there are societies to protect animals from man's cruelty. In this land, there is no institution to protect from the cruelty of those affected by the ravages of the treasure hunters, who, armed with diplomas from law schools, are plundering society without mercy. They are sure of impunity. There is no regimentation, no restraint, no obligatory pre-screening. My family is suffering, is passing through the days of hell and again, I challenge you to investigate and to find out whether there is any guilt on my side.

The Constitution of the United States tells about the establishment of justice that would provide domestic tranquility necessary for life. But without my guilt, such tranquility was taken away from us with the cooperation of the justice system. The Supreme Court, who so tenderly defended the right to desecrate the flag, has no time to introduce any

Book Two

order in the spread of malpractice accusations where everything goes. The suffering and all the different damages done by them to the country, is not breaking the mood of happy indifference, of our highest judicial authority. The bulk of the malpractice suits have very little to do with justice, while inflicting pain, spreading a feeling of insecurity, instability, mistrust and even of partial paralysis in the minds and actions of the more active and valuable part of society. The plundering by hoodlums is not producing such devastation to life, as the plundering by the men who work in the orbit of justice.

My family is really suffering, sees no light, no encouragement from any place. And as I told you, I challenge you to check for yourselves to try to find guilt in my case. The accusations became a farce, which anyway is working.

In this situation, I do not ask for help. I accuse you for not providing me and my family just protection against abuse of unfounded assaults.

I would like to think that you would take my plea seriously, do the necessary homework and establish firm rules and order in the field of malpractice treasure hunts.

I send you my last letters that will give you some background to my plea.

Tadeusz Maciejczyk, M.D.
Milledgeville, August 3, 1989

Enc: Letter to the Court indicating my preparation for trial
Letter to Judge John W. Rapp, Jr.
A letter written two years ago about my reasons for not
trusting lawyers-defendants
My letter to the Dept. of Nuclear Safety, which maybe in
the best way illustrates our pain.
My letter to the American Academy of Family Practice.
My answer to the Grace Commission survey about waste,
where :I spoke also about the judiciary and
malpractice suits.

P.S. Because of my wife's insistence, in an effort to re-establish some family harmony, I will go this afternoon to see Attorney Robert Weismiller in Mt. Carroll, whom my wife found different from the bulk of the others.

This doesn't mean that I am ready for arrangement. My life experience taught me that such an approach to abuses and blackmailers creates only a very fragile illusion of peace. Besides, I want to look in my

The World Seen from the Distance of a Small Village

face and not to be ashamed. Maybe I should send you a piece of poetry that my old neighbor gave me across the fence when I was working in my garden. It was written by an inmate in prison. I enclose a copy of a poem named "The Man in the Glass."

T. Maciejczyk

George Bush
President of the United States

Dear Sir:

I came to the point that I am asking you for help. My problem will be explained sufficiently in my previous letters that I include. I know that my malpractice problem does not belong to your line of duty and I do not ask here for help exclusively for me.

The malpractice treasure hunts are hurting and depressing the performance of this country in many ways. Yet, for this performance, you will be judged by your successors and by history. I ask you in this letter to form a commission to evaluate the effects of malpractice frenzy since it appeared in full bloom during the Reagan era. A recovery, whatever its projection, cannot function well in the shadow of the guillotine of malpractice threats. The accusation against me is completely absurd, and it is paralyzing and destroying my work, my family, my faith in the country and in its justice. If such cases would be multiplied by its amount in each field, really, the recovery would be uneasy.

As I promised, I went to see Attorney Weismiller. We had only a friendly talk. He said that I have to have a lawyer in court because otherwise "they will crucify me." The problem is that I have not much faith in the system, which is so punitive, so destructive, if I do not go their way. I see this my case as a "judicial gang's justice," not justice. I just do not know how to bend under such pressure. I would rather take the prospect of a crucifixion than to give such a system a satisfaction.

I do not know what I will do or where I will be after November 13. I would like to be able to work, but to do so, I have to be free from the perverse effect of the shadow of the "guillotine justice." Can I work as a doctor after this experience? Can I do something different and be useful?

I am standing before an unknown.

Book Two

I wish you the best.

Tadeusz Maciejczyk, M.D.
Milledgeville, August 10, 1989

Who—If the predictions given my wife by men close to the court would be true, after Nov. 13, I will be:

1. Homeless. My home will be taken away from us to pay the "justice."
2. Jobless. A) my office will be sized for the same reason.
      B) My reputation as a doctor will be in ruin.
3. Divorced. The only way for my wife to retain some of her belongings.
4. On Public Aid because what else will be left for me?

With such a "justice," especially made in the U.S., the U.S. will be condemned to failure. A fear at every step never was stimulating and inventive.

The World Seen from the Distance of a Small Village

Meg Greenfield
Newsweek Editorial

Re: "Scandal in the Courts" (*Newsweek,* August 26, 1989)
Dear Ms. Greenfield:

I send you here my recent, personal material from the different page of "justice." It could very well be material for an introduction into a second chapter of the report of Steven Brill.

If he, or any reporter from *Newsweek* would like to come to Mt. Carroll on Nov. 13 to witness my trial, I would be delighted. My trial is also a problem increasingly pressing for awakening and a closer look at its development and consequences.

If you would like in the meantime to see the accusation act against me, and my previous responses, I will send you all the required copies.

It was encouraging to me that somebody started to speak about the question of justice.

Tadeusz Maciejczyk, M.D.
Milledgeville, August 17, 1989

American Academy of Family Physicians

Probably, I would be not the best choice for a speech assignment. In this aspect, I have not much of a talent. Except this, I have now an approaching malpractice suit, which as ridiculous as it is, nevertheless is threatening and exhausting. In this suit, I decided to face it and to go for a collision. I am before an unknown. I do not know what will happen to me after November 13. I asked the Academy for help and I hope that I will get it from you. I send you again my last letters concerning my trial.

I send you also a copy of my letter written to AAPP reporter on July 14. It deals with the problem that you are raising in your last message, a problem of how to mobilize vocations for Family Practice among young men, who are contemplating their future in the medical field.

If I can be of some more help to you, you have to tell me.

Tadeusz Maciejczyk, M.D.
Milledgeville, August 17, 1989

Book Two

Dean of DePaul University of Chicago

Dear Sir:

I need to make a special arrangement with you that was forced on me by circumstances. If you read my letters from the last several weeks, which I include, you will have an idea what those circumstances are.

Taking them as they are, I want to have assurance that my daughter Cristina, who will enter now the second year of your school, would not suffer at least from the immediate consequences.

I have not much, because I never had a talent for making money, but I would like to pay in advance, before it is too late, for the upcoming trimesters (including tuition and housing.) I would like to have an approximate estimate for the upcoming year and separate for each trimester of the years 1990 and 1991. Here I also want to pay for the fall trimester in Florence for Cristina. I hope that after that time, I will be able to put my life together again.

I would like you to send me this estimate soon, because I do not know how long I can dispose of my savings. I am standing before an unknown.

I also hope that if Cristina would take hard whatever is to come, that you would understand and help her.

I wish you the best.

> Tadeusz Maciejczyk
> Father of Cristina Maciejczyk
> Milledgeville, August 20, 1989

The World Seen from the Distance of a Small Village

George Bush
President of the United States

Dear Sir:

Today there is a change in Poland that requires a simultaneous and important action from the Western World, and especially from America. A victory in Polish experiments could mean a peaceful dissolution of the communist threat to the world: its failure—a freeze with unpredictable consequences. The present changes represent possibilities of wide range and in the struggle with Soviets, it can be of almost the same category as the NATO Alliance was and is. It can contain, but more importantly, it can cure the Communist illness of mankind.

At present, Poland needs economical aid. Poland has a spirit, has an enthusiasm and willingness. It lacks experience of an economically free society and because of this, its self-confidence in handling the transformation from a Communist economical structure to a free enterprise economy. Only the very old people in Poland remember a free market life.

For this now imminent change, Poland needs some capital. But giving Poland only money, even in big amounts, would be a mistake. Such money could easily be misused, producing deeper disappointment or even collapse of will.

More than money, Poland needs guidance and teaching at each step and at each level of the transition of its economical life.

For those reasons, to help Poland, the West should provide some initial capital, but more than this, the West should organize and get ready for action as soon as can be a "Transition Advisor Corps" that could have the same structure and function as the Peace Corps and should give the same feeling of distinction and merit, even of a mission, to its participants. It should be a corps of volunteers.

Such a Corps would provide:

A) Advice and guidance in every field and at every level from the simplest family enterprise to factories, management, banking, simple and chain commerce and corporations.
B) An independent view of practicability of each particular enterprise there.
C) It could to some extent bind those enterprises to the similar entities in the West, involving in this way the private business in this recovery and would give an assurance to the West that

the experiment in Poland is a real and lasting phenomenon with a perspective for expansion.

D) It could defend this Polish experiment from the Soviet desire to clamp and to suppress, because it could mean a bigger and more serious confrontation.

E) It would give the example and encouragement to other Eastern Bloc countries and even to Soviet population, making those changes more stable and irreversible.

F) It could win the battle with Communism not on a NATO-Warsaw Pact front line, but in an action of friendship in a common effort in helping and healing.

Tadeusz Maciejczyk, M.D.
August 24, 1989

The World Seen from the Distance of a Small Village

John M. Poindexter
Rear Admiral
United States Navy

Dear Sir:

I received your letter today.

I cannot help you with money. I am almost in the same situation as you are. To illustrate this, I am sending you my last letters that deal with my problem. As you can see, I am also facing the unknown. In this free country, there are very alive forces of special terrorism: for money, for vanity, for popularity, for self cover-up or just for a simple vengeance.

While I cannot help you financially, I do not want to pass your letter with silence. In such situations as yours and mine, a moral help is also important. I know it because I need it now very much. For this reason, I would like to reach you personally with this letter. If it sinks into some room of your office, it will remain useless.

I voted for Reagan. I became deeply disappointed with him and I told him about this publicly long before his departure from the White House.

But I believe that everybody who does a work is subject to err, to make mistakes. Only that, who does nothing can tell that he never did anything wrong.

A vengeful processing of you will not lead this country to any bigger moral or spiritual greatness.

In place of a "special prosecutor," we should have an appointed special panel of the biggest moral and intellectual authorities in this country, to analyze the events of the Iran Contra Affair in all its dimensions to draw from it a lesson and to make from it a kind of sea lantern for our voyage into the future. America's forefathers did this from their experiences and what they did was great.

If we are wise, understanding and forgiving, we can fulfill the hopes that the world is placing on America's shoulders. If we are small, vengeful and always righteous, as the special prosecution is demanding in your case, we will learn nothing and we will disappoint the world including our children and grandchildren, who will pay the price for our present pettiness.

In addition to my last papers, I send you also a copy of my letter to Sen. Simon about the importance of forgiveness.

I wish you the best in the struggle.

Tadeusz Maciejczyk
Milledgeville, August 24, 1989

Book Two

J. Jarrett Clinton, M.D.
Assistant Surgeon General Director
Dept. of Health & Human Services
Washington, D.C.

Dear Sir:

I thank you for your letter and advice.

I know. I should adjust to the rules and enter the squeezing machine as expected. This way, my punishment would be not as harsh as predicted to my wife by legal counsels.

It sounds ironic. If I were a notorious criminal, my treatment would be more lenient and more effort would be put into finding the truth.

But my problem is different. Here the real problem is the money. Here is the fight not for justice, but for the golden cow and it's free milking. My stubborn unorthodoxy could put into question the present state of this lucrative "justice game."

I feel that until now, what I obtained from the court itself and from the related legal system, was a promise not of justice, but an insistence on conditional justice. I will survive, and I will be able to continue my work if I play this game as expected. Otherwise, I will be destroyed. This fact was communicated to me and to my wife in very clear terms. No cruelty was spared by legal personnel in spelling this out.

But I do not know how to bend under such pressure, even as I am perfectly aware that this pressure can crash me.

Conditional justice is doing to society the same thing conditional love is doing to the people who receive it. It is not elevating him, not strengthening, no sublimating. It is destroying his soul, his self-esteem and self-respect, convincing him of his natural worthlessness. It is always only for pay and never for this person's uniqueness and value. Such justice is also given by the street gangs to the terrorized by them for ransom merchants, or even by the Soviet KGB that terrorizes to extract obedience. Each such tyrant established his special price for his conditional peace and justice.

From the U.S., I have the right to expect not an "ersatz," but an authenticity in justice.

The Task Force on Medical Liability established by you in 1986 made a paper that altered nothing, didn't touch the ground in any place and which in this way gave permission for all treasure hunters to continue their terror undisturbed and uncontrolled. Since then anyway, this Task Force entered in a long uninterrupted nap, and life goes on as it was.

The World Seen from the Distance of a Small Village

I hope that on a Federal level, you will really address the issue of malpractice. In the meantime, I will continue my fight for a better America and for a better world, according to my understanding.

My best wishes to you.

Tadeusz Maciejczyk, M.D.
September 14, 1989

George Bush
President of the United States

Dear Sir:

I received a letter from the Bureau of Health Professions. It was an answer to my previous letter written to you. I thank you for this your indirect answer.

This letter from BHP looked to me like another trial to put my problem under the rug where it would be invisible and undisturbing.

But the present situation of a practice of malpractice deserves attention. It became a sort of domestic terrorism. It hangs over the heads of everybody who is judged to be able to pay, even if the medical profession was hit the hardest. Like the international terrorism, this one also can be explained by some, by its noble purposes and intentions. That intended noble theory, in practice, became an ugly show of greed. It became a true burden for the country and for its economy, even for its social health. Because of this, it should be reviewed, re-studied and put under strict rules.

I am speaking about this because I became the target of such a malpractice accusation and I feel the enormous mercilessness with which such accusations operate. They inflict enormous suffering. In my case, considering the gross absurdity of the claim against me, those threats and pressures exerted by the legal personnel on my family, it nothing short of terrorism.

In my family, it produced devastation. My wife left home two weeks ago for Chicago where she found a room for herself and manual work just to survive. She said that she couldn't live under the present pressure that was put on us. She preferred to move to relative safety now than to be evicted from home during the winter time when we would have no resources at all, because all would be taken from us to pay for "justice." She demanded from me to surrender, sell what we have, pay them and retire, escape, disappear.

It was such an enormous suffering during those last months. And again, I challenge the competent authority to investigate my case just to get an idea of how this domestic terror works and what it is doing to people, to families and to the country. The American family is already under stress and is fragile. It deserves protection. For the sake of the country, the free, uncontrolled, unruly terror of the malpractice threat has to be redefined. In its present form, it is too devastating to the land.

I send you the copy of my answer to J. Jarrett Clinton from the Dept. of Health and Human Services.

I send you best wishes in your difficult work.

Tadeusz Maciejczyk, M.D.
September 21, 1989

The World Seen from the Distance of a Small Village

National Opinion Survey on Congress

1. Undecided. It would be easy to condemn, but I do not know how a model Congress should be like. Certainly the present Congress is not giving the people a good pattern or example of how to be a good citizen, or even how to be a good person, good human being. Certainly the present Congress is not a guardian of any big ideal or idea. Its biggest force, a constant eye on popularity and re-eligibility drives the members of Congress away from big ideas or ideals into a smallness with excessive preoccupation with their own advantage and a neglect or even betrayal of a wider public trust. True statesmanship and the primordial goals of the country are frequently in Congress far behind their particular big "Me"—directly or indirectly.
   The members of congress should have an image of the elders of the whole nation, but I would never call our present congress this way. They never act like trusted guides in our journey through time, or as the guardians of our most important values. I think that the congress depreciated themselves enormously during the last few decades.
2. Undecided: How to define the will of the American people? This will is passing now through a depressed low. Mostly we are passive and taking the line of the least resistance. We were put to sleep to the sounds of the beautiful perspectives of a never-ending, constantly increasing prosperity, and we do not want to wake up and face the new reality. Maybe we lost the freshness of imagination and the tenacity and endurance to be ready for the new, rapidly emerging world. Frequently, we choose an escape route and shortcuts. We are constantly speaking about our rights and we forget even to mention our obligations. Short solutions and all kinds of devices for deception are frequently the preferred confrontations for both: Congress and the nation.
3. No. The Congress has the responsibility not only to cast the votes on the issues, but also to give examples and to bear the difficulties of the nation. Congress, so much striving for popularity in all other public appearances, should also find a proper way to meet the nation's approval for their pay raises.
4. Yes. I wrote about this on another occasion. I include the copy.
5. Uncertain. I do not know exactly what are the "regulatory laws," but if other Americans must obey them, they are written also for Congress. They should be first American's then Congressmen.

6. Uncertain. With the present catastrophic situation in our repeated budget imbalances, and a growing national debt, congress should establish short and distant goals for reduction of debt and also for some kind of re-evaluation and restrictions of our "rights" for demands. Without a serious work on remedies and priorities, and a restraint on a tendency for pleasing and charming, without a serious frank discussion with the nation, the forcing of balance the federal budget is a mere game of words.

The true merit of congress would be not in making the gimmicks with the budget numbers, but in an elaborate plan for facing the whole situation in our real world after a frank, nationwide discussion of issues.

7. Yes. I include my previous writing about this problem.
8. Yes. The minimum of ten dollars.

Your estimate of 35 dollars for preparing and mailing each survey decreased my trust in your sincerity. Is this just another stroke to get money and to look good? Somebody who is doing this survey overpriced himself shamelessly. Was I chosen as a recipient of this survey just because I am an M.D. and supposedly I can pay?

The truth is, that my situation lately became very uncertain. I send you the copies of my last few letters that can explain why I am saying this. Our Congress never dared to look into the true picture of the malpractice suits. It would touch very unpleasantly the very powerful forces in the country and could jeopardize re-elections. But it is also a very important issue of national health.

Tadeusz Maciejczyk, M.D.
Milledgeville, October 8, 1989

The World Seen from the Distance of a Small Village

Tom Tauke
Member of U.S. Congress

Dear Sir:

I send to you my responses to the survey of "National Opinion on Congress." I do this because I have very little trust in the "Citizens for a Sound Economy." After reading their evaluation of the price for each survey cost, I doubted their own sound economy.

The survey by itself was not original. The mere marking of one of the three windows to make an answer, will add very little to the understanding and ways of improvement of our present congress. Altogether, it looked like another letter from the sideway moneymakers from Washington: another exploitation of the dwindling number of those who still believe and care.

Such a stream of letters of this kind from Washington should be regulated because they do the same the frequent calls by the shepherd boy about wolves did. When the wolves really came, nobody answered his cries.

I send you my best wishes.

Tadeusz Maciejczyk, M.D.
Milledgeville, October 10, 1989

Book Two

Lee Atwater
Chairman of the Republican National Committee

Dear Sir:

I thank you for considering me to be a President's Council member. It is a high honor. I wonder, nevertheless, what was the central point for this proposition? Was it that I am an M.D. and consequently I can pay contributions, or was it because my thoughts or my involvement could be helpful? A passive, nominal only, only for membership dues membership, however prestigious, is not attractive to me.

Because your survey was requested to be returned on November 10, I cannot participate in its mission. On Nov. 13 I will have a malpractice suit against me in which I will be my own attorney. All the predictions for the outcome of this trial are grim to me. I was told by the judge that my trial will be short, and by a person close to the court, "they will crucify me there." My wife was told by local lawyers after Nov. 13 we will be homeless. Our home will be taken to pay for "justice." I will be jobless because my office will be sized for the same purpose and my reputation as a doctor will be in ruin. I will also be divorced because it would be the only way for my wife to retain some of her belongings. Finally, I will be on Public Aid because nothing else will be open for me.

With such a beautiful justice system against me, you cannot ask me to concentrate now on your survey, or to think about a membership or special honors. In place of this, I send you now what I have on hand.

1. My answer to the Grace Commission survey about waste.
2. My answer to Rep. P.M. Crane about Panama and the Panama Canal Treaty.
3. My philosophy about permission for flag desecration.
4. My letter to Pres. Bush about help to Poland.
5. My answer to the survey on "National Opinion Survey on Congress" with an included letter to Rep. Tom Tauke.
6. I send you also the last few letters about my malpractice trial because it is also an issue for the nation to consider.
   I will try to answer your survey after Nov. 13, if I still exist. In the meantime, my best wishes in your work.

> Tadeusz Maciejczyk, M.D.
> Milledgeville, October 19, 1989

The World Seen from the Distance of a Small Village

Lynn Martin
Member of U.S. Congress

Dear Mrs. Martin:

I received your letter and invitation to be a founding member of your campaign. I thank you for this honor. I do not know what this term means and what would be my role in such a position.

The role I could learn, but at present, I have no time, no disposition and no energy for any new obligations. Now, even my very existence is uncertain.

On Nov. 13, I will be in court to defend myself against a malpractice accusation.

The predictions for the outcome of this trial are grim for me. I was told in an angry manner that the trial will be short. Another good person, who knows the place, predicted that "they will crucify me there." When my wife, in desperation, went to Mt. Carroll to investigate, she was told that after Nov. 13 we will be homeless, because our home will be taken to pay for justice; that I will be jobless because my office will be seized for the same reason, and my reputation as a doctor will be destroyed; that I will be divorced because this would be the only way for my wife to retain some of her belongings. Of course, after all this, I will have nowhere else to go, but on Public Aid.

What a wonderful work of justice! What a paradise is it to live here?

In this situation, I lost my faith in the U.S. Justice, and also in the sense of working here. What for? Just to be again a sucker for this or another Mr. Cacciatore, the plaintiff's counsel? If I am not over-insured, if I do not over-protect myself by thousands of unnecessary tests and repetitions, by additional consultations, by timidity to do a necessary and decisive step, I can be destroyed at any moment.

No work can be innovative, really helpful, really positive, if it is done while walking on a minefield. In the U.S. at present, with everybody trying to be rich, whatever the way, to demand and to show; with the creativity and inventiveness restricted by every place threatening suspicions and accusations; with the querulous mood of the country and lawyers instigating the people to jump one on another; the U.S. will have only one way to go: downhill. The U.S. spiral of debts is only one of the symptoms. I was never a pessimist, but I am becoming one.

In the present, so much important time of the world's transition, America has no moral leadership and its vision reaches no further than the next step. It is a tragedy.

Book Two

I wish you the best in your campaign.

> Tadeusz Maciejczyk, M.D.
> Milledgeville, November 1, 1989

P.S. I send you my last two letters to explain better my view of this problem.

The World Seen from the Distance of a Small Village

My Four Opening Statements for Trial

1. As the evidence will show, I am not guilty of any of the charges in this case. I was never asked by Mrs. Macchi to treat her bedsores. I never saw those sores. In the almost 14 years since she moved to Kentucky until she was hospitalized in Sterling, she was in my office three times, always for completely different acute problems. Those problems apparently I resolved well.
2. All, and every one of the points of accusation deals only with one medical problem of this lady: the problem of bedsores, and my handling of them, my insinuated negligence or incompetence in the treatment. Because of this, all discussions of my eventual guilt should be restricted to this condition.

    Any trail to circle around, to create general appearances and impressions, should not be considered as a pretext or evidence to incriminate. My eventual guilt should be pointed clearly, and it should be within the limits marked by the accusation.
3. I do not blame Mrs. Macchi for what she did to me. I consider her another victim in this show of justice, even if she is on the other side of the spectrum in this trial. If at any time, Mrs. Macchi would be in need, I will help her to the extent of my possibilities without even a mention of our present Golgotha for both of us. I consider that the true villain and criminal in this process is somebody else. Mr. Cacciatore surely is looking for such victims as she. Without them, he would have no chance to play his game of intimidation, intended to cash easy money from this way caught prey or sucker.

    If such a case as mine can lead in the U.S. to such a suffering and agony for the working man and his family, then I am asking the court and the people: What is the sense to work? Where will society end with such justice?
4. I was told that during this trial, I will be crucified. Because of this, I ask the court and the jury of the listening people to differentiate well between the interrogation intended to explain and to put light on the situation, in the search for the truth and the questioning and catches calculated to twist and to bury the truth and to crucify.

Tadeusz Maciejczyk, M.D.
Milledgeville, November 12, 1989

Book Two

Malpractice Suit Dismissed

Carroll County Review, November 15, 1989

MILLEDGEVILLE - The malpractice suit against Dr. Tadeusz Maciejczyk of Milledgeville, was dismissed by the court Monday morning "for want of prosecution," but the plaintiff still has 30 days to file a motion asking the court to reinstate the case.

Chief Circuit Judge John W. Rapp, Jr., explained that neither the plaintiff, Wilma Macchi of Polo, nor her Rockford attorney had appeared for the trial. The attorney told Judge Rapp that he thought the trial had been set for another time.

Dr. Maciejczyk, who was acting as his own counsel, was present and waiting for the trial to begin, as were a large contingent of Dr. Maciejczyk's supporters to filled all available seats, the jury box and even the window sills.

Judge Rapp explained that, at the pre-trial conference held July 14, the trial date was set for Nov. 13.

Since the pre-trial conference was held, the plaintiff waived a jury trial. The plaintiff's lawyer told Judge Rapp that in Winnebago County, when a jury trial is waived, the trial goes on a different docket and a different date is set. In Carroll County, Judge Rapp said, the trial still commences on the set date and would have been held Monday and Tuesday.

According to the opening statement, Dr. Maciejczyk has prepared he was asked to treat Mrs. Macchi for one condition and was then sued because he did not treat her for an additional problem (bedsores). She did not advise him or seek treatment for the bedsores, he claims.

"If such a case as mine can lead in the U.S. to such a suffering and agony for the working man and his family, then I am asking the court and the people, "What is the sense to work? Where will society end with such a justice?" the doctor asked.

The World Seen from the Distance of a Small Village

Clerk of the Court of the Carroll County
Case No. 87 L 2:

Dear Sir:

I received the copy of Mr. Cacciatore's motion to reinstate this case and his petition for the hearing on this motion, which he scheduled for December 26, 1989.

Here I want only to say that most likely I will be unable to come to such a hearing on that day.

At the present, we expect the birth of our first grandchild at any day and the Christmas time will be for us the most likely occasion for the baptism ceremony. I expect that the harassment, practiced by Mr. Cacciatore, and which lasts already for almost three years, will not go as far as to destroy this, our family event.

Because of this, I ask the court to transfer this hearing to some later, more convenient day.

                                          Tadeusz Maciejczyk, M.D.
                                          Milledgeville, November 30, 1989

Book Two

The Daily Gazette
Editor

To add to your editorials, I want to present to the readers my comments.

The almost unanimity and precision of our Congress in approving the pay raises for themselves was spectacular. No other national emergency produced such a marvelous response in our lawmakers. And one should marvel still more if he realizes that it happened just a few days after a session dedicated to increase our national debt ceiling because our Government had no money left for the current governmental operations.

Nothing could stop our distinguished representatives from their drive for more money for themselves. They did this while discussing the ethics for Congress. And what an ethical lesson it was for the nation. The Country, the people, were watching it with a sickening feeling in the stomach.

The Congress had no time to finish, or even to touch many of the urgent measures concerning the life of the country. Only this one, so very important debate was developed, was conducted, and was concluded with a precision seen only on a very special parade. The our own district Congressman deserves applause and gratitude from the members of Congress for orchestrating this operation. Whether she can expect such appreciation and gratitude from us, the voters, each of us has to decide at the time of casting our votes.

Such lessons as this should convince us that our representatives are changing in Washington. Frequently there, they are forgetting their roots in the districts and their true identification with the people and a solidarity with them.

Surely, their staff is responding to our letters and to our small petitions. This is for them a reassurance for popularity and for reelection. But their hearts, their true, non-mimicked interests, their ambitions, are directed elsewhere. Not every one can handle, as was expected, the success of election, the suddenly received special honors and distinctions, the feeling of power, and not be spoiled.

For those reasons, a Congressman should not serve more than three terms in a row; a Senator no more than two terms. If they really care about the District and their people, they would return there, getting active, giving the district their experience acquired in Washington. They would live again, but with a special inner transformation the joys and the difficulties of his homeplace. This second living in place would make them more valuable and in consequence would make them still better representatives, if after required years, they would decide to run again for office.

The World Seen from the Distance of a Small Village

Without such a safety valve, our representatives, even when giving an illusion of success in Washington, are becoming increasingly sterile and progressively alienated with their home base.

The present system, in which each party is providing not a choice, but a single candidate, selected by some distant party committee for the people's final decision in pools, gave us a succession of Congresses ineffective in their results, unimaginative, selfishly preoccupied with themselves and their re-election, whose main attribute was not an individualism and freshness of ideas, but party obedience, routine of procedures and smallness.

I would like the people to consider and to express their opinion, whether it would be useful and good, if each party would give the people not one, but a choice of two candidates for the final November election. Surely, it would express more clearly the will of the people, would assure a better access of a new blood to Congress and would be much more democratic. How many times we go to the polls without illusion because all the choices given to us are disheartening.

My final observation in this sad situation is that the nation's elite is formed not by those who accumulate material wealth, but by those who grow rich in spirit and from the fruit of this spirit are giving generously to the neighbor, to the community, to the nation and to the world.

Also, I want to add that I do not see a reason why the salaries of Congressmen and of the judges were linked together. Those are completely different categories of work. Did it happen only because of a "smartness" from one side?

Tadeusz Maciejczyk, M.D.
Milledgeville, December 1, 1989

Book Two

Edwin O. Hult, Jr.

Dear Sir:

With the approaching Christmas, I want to send you my best wishes and a sign that I remember you in a very special way.

I do this because you are not a usual, but a very special human being who radiates love—a commodity not frequent in today's world. With this quality you are giving encouragement and help to others. There are not many persons as you. It is more likely that in the same way as in my place, did you leave behind a warmth and a sunshine wherever you were.

I know that you have retired from your professional work. I do not believe that you would stop also the special activity and quality of living and reassuring with what did you saturated every moment of interaction with others during your professional life. Men as you have no right to stay in a quietness of home and in the distance from people. There is too much need for you everywhere.

To remember, I send you my self-portrait and the few things I was writing recently. My trial day didn't bring any conclusion in my malpractice suit. The other side didn't appear, but they reapplied to continue harassment. The problem is that the Sterling Clinic wants to establish a satellite station here in Milledgeville. I would like to make a peace with my wife during this holiday and I do not know how because she wants me to quit everything and to be only a family man. And I have a need for some kind of mission in my life. There is a conflict between the two. I am trying to find a solution and I do not know how.

But again it is Christmas and I wish you and your family the best.

                                        T. Maciejczyk
                                        Christmas time 1989

Newt Gingrich, M.C.
General Chairman of GOPAC

Dear Sir:

The World Seen from the Distance of a Small Village

I agree with you that the present U.S. Congress no longer represents the American people, but I am not sure whether the Democratic majority is the only origin of this reality. The cause is most likely deeper, much more widespread and because of this, it requires not a partisan, but an objective study of the offending factors.

Of course, the franking privilege is giving a big advantage for incumbents and it would be good to suspend them for at least six months preceding elections.

The gerrymandering of voting districts probably never will satisfy both parties, and should be decided not by party quarrels, but by some independent institution, if such an institution exists.

Both of those remedies are touching only the surface of the electoral malady.

The fundamental problem here is the human material selected by parties for representation. My advice here would be: Try to select not the popular and charming, already-known figures and the "yes men," but men with character and individual ideas and imagination, deep enough to integrate the needs and the aspirations of the people whom they represent, into the life and future of the whole nation. Our representatives should give us a feeling of honesty and trust, and the almost certainty that they elevate our lives.

Elections in which party candidates can win not because of their merit, but through manipulations and more or less dirty tricks, even if they would satisfy the party, they produce in the people a feeling of helplessness, of alienation and an attitude of resistance, passivity and sarcasm. In consequence, the party prestige is disintegrating in the minds of the people. If the parties are unable to select the best from us for our representation and leadership, giving us instead their preferred puppets, then why bother with such parties? How many times after election we have the feelings not of excitement, expectation and a readiness for a new start, but a disappointment and apathy? As it is at present, I am not sure whether I will go to vote during the next Illinois Senatorial election.

A search for candidates should be always a most intimate, deep and wise interaction between the party and the district's populations. Without such homework, the pre- and post-election malaise, as within the party, as well among the people, will not work for the health of the country.

I send you my previous letters that relate in some way to elections. I wish you the best in your work.

Tadeusz Maciejczyk, M.D.
Milledgeville, December 21, 1989

Book Two

The Carroll County Review
Editor:

At the end of this uneasy for me year of 1989, I want to thank the people for so many signs of friendship, which compensated enormously the hardship. I want to thank again for the birthday cards, and also for the cards that came after the Nov. 13 and for the Christmas cards, even for the cards, when the news came, that I got a grandson. Equally, I want to say thanks to all who came to the Courtroom to give me moral support when I needed it. And I thank you for the smiles and greetings, which meet me wherever I go and which are similarly comforting.

As you know already, the accusing party asked for a reinstatement of the trial. The hearing for reinstatement will be on January 22, at 2:00 P.M.

At that time, I will present to the court and to the people my response to the insistence for continuation of this trial.

Maybe you will be interested. Anyway, you are dealing with public problems. So, I send you copies of my last two letters concerning the approaching 1990 election.

My best wishes,

Tadeusz Maciejczyk, M.D.
Milledgeville, December 28, 1989

The World Seen from the Distance of a Small Village

Associated Physicians Insurance Company
James H. Cunningham Insurance Agency, Inc.
Oak Park, IL

    I received this letter from the hospital where I admit my patients. The truth is, that I reduced enormously my admissions. Those send to Morrison Hospital generally represent no risk. More often they go there and then are transferred to a nursing home. At the present time, I delegate the more complicated cases to somebody else at a different hospital.
    I do not know how much my insurance covers. If what I have is enough, I will be glad. I need this opening to a hospital for the peace of mind of many of my patients.
    If the coverage is inadequate and requires more money, I would have to think the situation over and make a new decision.
    I was trained to be a doctor, not a tax collector.
    I deeply resent the situation that forces me to increase my patients' fees to pay for this absurd and this social horror of endemic malpractice fears, which already leads to so much suffering of the innocent. I saw the anxiety of the people whose insurance suddenly doubled and who have to make a decision whether to eat or to have this security. The chain of events, spreading from the malpractice terror is frightening and is the threat of a permanent instability, or even collapse in the future. I wrote about this problem to the Grace Commission on waste. I am sending you a copy.
    Please, give me your answer for the hospital.

                              Thank you,

                              Tadeusz Maciejczyk, M.D.
                              January 11, 1990

Book Two

Morrison Community Hospital
303 North Jackson Street
Morrison, Illinois 60270

January 17, 1990

Tadeusz Maciejczyk, M.D.
444 Main Street
Milledgeville, IL 60151

Dear Dr. Maciejczyk:

    We are in receipt of notification from the James H. Cunningham Agency, your insurance provider, indicating your current malpractice insurance coverage is $100,000 per patient with a $300,000 total limit. As you are aware, the Medical Staff bylaws for Morrison community Hospital require $1,000,000 malpractice insurance coverage for the granting of privileges. This requirement has been stipulated by the hospital's insurance company.

    I regret to inform you that you cannot be granted medical staff privileges due to this lack of sufficient malpractice insurance. If, at some point in the future, your level of insurance is increased so that you meet this requirement, we will be happy to reconsider your privileges.

                        Sincerely,

                        Wayne A. Sensor
                        Interim Administrator

                        WAS/jb

The World Seen from the Distance of a Small Village

Publisher
The Daily Gazette
Sterling, Illinois

It is not nice, or maybe even not very healthy to speak about an established holy cow, but I have an urge to do so.

Frankly, I do not like what the present Martin Luther King's Day is doing to martin Luther King's dream.

The present holiday is not inspiring. It is not inviting to reflect and to act unselfishly from the best of ourselves. It doesn't have MLK's spirit of generosity. As it is now, it rather irritates, divides and opens the old wounds again. For sure, it is not healing, it is not finding any new ways for expression and communication. This movement now is not spontaneous, is not reaching the streets and the homes, where it should show its more enduring force and spontaneity. It is not revealing any new true leaders who appear generally only within the spontaneity. A sclerosis of ideas brings only colorless bureaucrats or apparatchiks.

The MLK Day now circles around church or secular ceremonies, gala receptions for the selected celebrities, different meetings, maybe manifestations and protest marches. It produces also the inconvenience of closed postal offices and closed schools. (In this last holiday custom it is closing rather, than opening the minds for the big idea of a brotherhood for everybody.) Within this way created ceremonial day, too many small people are riding, or are trying to get a free ride on the holy cow of MLK's memory for selfish destination toward spotlights, prominence, power and money. Sadly, MLD didn't leave any heir who could measure to his size. The sound of "We will overcome" in the liberation movements of Eastern Europe was inspired not by the present agenda of MLK's movement, but by its fever from the past. Today, this movement only reinstates the animosities. It has nothing to do with MLK's dream.

In 1983, when the holiday for MLK was discussed, my idea of an MLK memorial was different and I wrote:

"Another lazy day without aim. As designed, it would be a dance around a magnificient, but already cold monument. It would be a day for politicians who have nothing to offer, but speeches. In no way would it be a day of MLK's dream.

The nature of Martin Luther King's dream is dynamic, requiring action and involvement. As such, it should be a day of commitment at every level, from personal reexamination: who am I? How can I be better? Through striving for peace in the families, among neighbors, between neighborhoods. For such a day the homes, houses and streets could

Book Two

be cleaned and beautified by voluntary work to add splendor to the occasion and the disputes could be resolved in a different, very special spirit. In such a day the achievements toward realization of MLK's dream could be publicized and some kind of Oscar could be rewarded to the most outstanding. That day the authors, the artists, theater groups and film companies could present their new creations and the school children, instead of staying home, could have a day of deliberation on how the dream of ML King could be put into action and stay alive in hearts.

Because of a dynamic nature of such a day, the dream day should not be placed in the winter when the communications are limited by the weather. More appropriate would be a warm spring day. Such celebrations should be spontaneous. No official approval to hold them is necessary and if turned into tradition, it could be the biggest day in the U.S., and it could spread beyond the U.S. to the world, wherever hate and indifference make life miserable and dangerous."

I would like to invite everybody to discuss and to enrich this idea.

Tadeusz Maciejczyk, M.D.
Milledgeville, January 18, 1990

The World Seen from the Distance of a Small Village

Clerk of the Court of Carroll County
Case No. 87 L 2:

Dear Sir:

After the Nov. 13 court trial, in which the entire accusing party didn't show, explaining this by obtained misleading information, I had the impression and a hope that all this process could finish this way. I do not like quarrels. I prefer to dedicate my time to something more positive.

But again, I received from Mr. Cacciatore his usual type of letter, in which, after long explanations and justifications, he is asking for a reinstatement of this process.

Unwillingly, I have to welcome this opportunity. I say "opportunity" because this accusation and all this process, requires clear explanations, deep to its genesis and intentions. Since its beginning, I had a feeling, that pressing for those explanations was my duty, not only as the accused one, but also as a citizen of this country who cares for its future.

In this trial, should be revealed the identity of the doctor who wrote the medical denunciation without giving his name, nor signing this supposed legal document. (I include here the photocopy of this pseudo-document.) I have to know who is behind the accusations of this trial and what are its ultimate motivations. After all, the signs of a clear uneasiness and unwillingness of Mrs. Macchi to appear in court and to confront the judgment of the people, the question is, who is actually the party that is pressing for reinstatement?

In this trial, I would like to find all the names and all the facts, to gather all the evidence, because I intend to forward them to the highest American medical authorities asking them to judge them by the Medical Code of Ethics and to express their opinion and their verdict about this kind of subsurface treachery among doctors or among medical institutions.

I consider that those treacheries, those methods used by some, should be known to the wide public for their own protection because whoever is using such a cowardly cover-up tactics to advance their ambitions or interests, surely will not perform their service to the patients with more honesty and integrity.

The highest medical authorities of this country have an obligation and a duty to preserve the true integrity of the medical profession.

I feel also that I should go to the bottom of this affair as a citizen because if a nameless, faceless denunciator who acts in the darkness, avoiding responsibility to clarify and to prove, if such denunciators succeed in creating and spreading fear, uncertainty, anxiety and bring the society to a paralysis of will to act, even manipulating the justice institutions to reach their wishes, then it would mean the end of freedom for every man in the country. I lived already under such conditions. It remained in my memory as a time when I was walking through a deep, sticky and stinking mud.

I hope that this process will help to clean the air because such a cleaning in this country is starting to be more and more necessary.

Tadeusz Maciejczyk, M.D.
   Milledgeville, January 18, 1990

   P.S. I send this letter also to:
   The American Medical Association
   The American Academy of Family Physicians
      different medical journals
   Paul M. Schwab, Acting director of the Department of Health
      and Human Services in Washington, D.C.
   Both Senatorial contenders of Illinois
   Local Press
   Time
   Newsweek (both expressed interest in this case and asked for
      continued information.)

The World Seen from the Distance of a Small Village

Editor, *The Daily Gazette*

I am sending you the text of my statement during tomorrow's court hearing. I include here also the denunciation of the "medical expert," who in this document forgot to give his name or to sign it.

The subject of accusation:

Mrs. Macchi, a paraplegic from a car accident in the 1950's, was my patient since 1969 until April 71, when she moved to Kentucky. Since then until her hospitalization in Sterling on Feb. 1, 1985, she was in my office three times.

1. September of 1977 for acute sinusitis
2. September of 1983 for urinary infection
3. September of 1984 for acute arthritis of her right knee.

Now, I am dragged already for three years because according to the faceless medical expert, I am guilty of mistreatment of her bed sores, which I never saw.

T. Maciejczyk, M.D.
Milledgeville, January 1990

Cc: *Carroll County Review*

Book Two

Wayne A. Sensor
Interim Administrator
Morrison Community Hospital

Dear Sir:

Thank you for your last letter and the information about the suspension of my hospital privileges until I increase my malpractice coverage to the required level.

In my previous letter, I expressed already my opinion about this requirement. I want to repeat that I was not trained to be a special tax collector.

I want to be fair to the people and I do not want to increase their charges for office visits without presenting to them my situation created by your request. I want to see their reactions, to hear their voices and their opinions, their approval or disapproval of this artificial burden put on each of them. I need this, because the doctors' malpractice insurance is ultimately paid, not by the doctors, but by them. To me, this "tax" collection is especially repulsive, horrifying and unjust, because it is imposed with premeditation, and without even one through to those already sick. The sicker the person is, the worse his situation is, because the sicker he is, the more he has to pay for this hidden taxation.

For all those reasons, I will stop all my admissions to your hospital until I get the peoples' answer. There are many ways to impose misery and injustice. I do not want to be an instrument in this imposition. And obedient submission by them to this burden will not help them. It will only perpetuate and accentuate their exploitation.

The people will have the opportunity to judge you and to judge the system, which cares so little about them, which puts on them such hidden burdens without any reflection or conscious restraint. Such burdens are imposed on the people generally not by true leaders, but by a rigid and numbed to all feelings bureaucracy, and by politicians who have no love for the people and only are using them.

This is what I have to say about this shameful condition.

Sincerely,

Tadeusz Maciejczyk, M.D.
Milledgeville, January 21, 1990

The World Seen from the Distance of a Small Village

Dr. Marvin M. Gibson
President of the Rotary Club, District 762
916 19th Street, N.W.
Washington, D.C. 20006

Dear Sir:

Our Rotary Club is writing this letter asking you for help.

We have at present a Rotary exchange student from Belgium, Geoffrey Peeters, who expressed a wish to be able to see Washington, D.C., with all its monuments and institutions, before his return home.

Our small club would like to help him, but our resources are limited. We cannot finance his stay there or delegate him to somebody who could guide him and take responsibility for him. We would not know how to arrange meaningful visits or give him adequate explanations.

In this situation, we want to propose to you a temporary exchange between our student and your students. Geoffrey would go to Washington where somebody from your club would wait for him in the airport and take care of him during his stay in Washington. At the same time, we would receive your student in the same way and with the same conditions.

We think that such an arrangement would be highly complementary and would reinforce our idea of bringing to the world a sense of togetherness. Our clubs, by nature, and by location, complement each other. You are in a big, urban place, in a capital that gives a special perspective and view to your exchange students. We are a small, rural community lost in endless fields. We can show your students the American farm life, the spirit of our small towns, the Mississippi River and the American eagles flying free over the Savanna Bridge. We could tour with him the historical Galena where the reminders of early frontier life are well-preserved, where there is an abundance of Civil War memories and where the home of General Grant is.

If such an exchange experiment would appear to be possible and would be evaluated as useful, it could create a pattern for a more permanent cooperation between our two clubs.

Book Two

We hope that you will look into our proposition seriously and we wish you the best in your work of building a better understanding in the world of our children and grandchildren.

>Richard A. Deeds
>President, Milledgeville Rotary Club
>Acting for this case secretary: Tadeusz Maciejczyk
>January 25, 1990

The World Seen from the Distance of a Small Village

The Carroll County Review
Letter to the Editor:

The problem, which I want to present here to the people is not mine only. It affects them and indirectly is putting on them a constantly increasing burden.

In 1983, I opposed an obligatory high cost, malpractice insurance for doctors, because it was ultimately the sick, who would have to pay it. Consequently, I have lost my hospital privileges in Sterling Hospital.

During next years I was admitting my patients to the Morrison Hospital. About at the end of 1985 I had to agree to have a minimum malpractice coverage. Sine 1987, to keep this minimum, I discontinued delivering babies, even I had to stop my assistance in surgical operations of my patients, and I limited the number of my admissions.

About two weeks ago, I was notified that in order to admit any patients, I have to have a full malpractice protection of one million dollars for thee claims. I was told that the insistence on full coverage came from Springfield.

The numbers of this story are like this: Till now I was paying for my limited liability $5,260.00 annually. For this price, I had an insurance of $100,000.00 for each claim, up to three claims.

During 1989 I admitted to the hospital 17 patients, of whom no one represented any big risk. In this way, I was paying in 1989, $310 to insurance company for each admission. With the presently required coverage, I would have to pay this year to insurance Company $12,216.00, plus $3,500.00 for additional obligatory Stock purchase from the company. This would raise my insurance payment for each hospitalization to $925 dollars.

During last year the Medicare, which was covering almost all of my hospitalizations, was paying me $55.00 for admission, plus $18.00 for each visit, altogether about $120.00 for each case.

In this transaction I was losing about $190.00 with each hospitalization. I was doing this to keep the hospital doors open and for the peace of mind of my patients. I cannot absorb the presently required $800.00 loss, however.

In this situation, I want to ask the people: Should I increase the price for office visits to pay for this obligatory insurance? Is such an arrangement just and moral? Whether they know what it is doing to every one of them?

In my response to this requirement I was writing to the Director of Morrison Hospital, that as a doctor I was not trained to be a tax collector.

Book Two

I told him that I want to be fair to the people and I do not want to increase my charges for office visits, without presenting to them my situation, created by the new request from Springfield. I want to see their reactions, to hear their voices and opinions, their approval or disapproval of this artificial burden put on each of them. I need this, because the doctor's malpractice insurance is paid ultimately, not by the doctors, but by them. To me this "tax" collection is especially repulsive, horrifying and unjust, because it is imposed with premeditation, and without even one thought on the already sick. The sicker is the person, the worse is his situation caused by sickness, the more he has to pay for this hidden taxation, for which the doctors have to do the dirty work of collecting them.

I told the Director, that for all those reasons, I will stop all my admissions in his hospital, till I get the people's answer. There are many ways to impose misery and injustice. I do not want to be an instrument in this imposition. And obedient submission by them to this burden will not help them. It will only perpetuate and accentuate their exploitation.

I told the Director, that the people will have the opportunity to judge him and to judge the system, which cares so little about them, which puts on them such hidden burdens without any reflection or conscious restraint. Such burdens are imposed generally not by the true leaders, but by a rigid and numb to all feelings bureaucracy and by politicians who have no love for the people, and only are using them.

This exploitation has its consequences. It created a situation where more and more people can hardly afford doctors' or hospitals' services, where the insurance cost was rising rapidly, and the denial of insurance because of health conditions became more and more frequent.

I want to ask the people to express their opinion about this situation. This year is an election year. Each candidate for local, state or federal posts should be asked for explanation and solutions. James Reston was telling that "all politics are based on the indifference of the majority." Please, speak out now for your own sake.

And to see what the people are buying for those enormous sums of money collected from the sick, I invite everybody to watch my own malpractice accusation and trial, which will take place on May 21 in the Mt. Carroll Court.

Tadeusz Maciejczyk, M.D.
Milledgeville, January 28, 1990

The World Seen from the Distance of a Small Village

Kenneth W. Whittington, M.D.
President
The American Academy of Family Physicians

Dear Sir:

I am sending you different papers from my several months of adventure in my Family Practice. I hope they can be interesting and call attention to the present dangers not only to some particular doctors, but to the institution of the Family Practice as well.

During last summer I wrote to you about my malpractice trial. I had no defense attorney, and I was tense and worried. Nobody really wanted to speak about malpractice. Not one politician was willing to touch this taboo subject. It was beyond their competence. Apparently, for them it was not a social problem that was wrecking this country for years.

From the Dept. of Health and Human Services, I received a different, scientific explanation of my distress. It was just nothing of importance. I suffered from the usual "malpractice stress syndrome." Graciously, they sent me several articles about this new illness. In my bitterness I was thinking that the same consolation could be given by the KGB Society to Solzhenizyn when he was on his way to the labor camps in Siberia. What he suffered was of no importance. It was just "Gulag stress syndrome."

But here I want to write about different observations from my trial.

My trial was scheduled for Nov. 13. I was there. A crowd of people from Milledgeville was there. We were waiting. Nobody from the accusing party's side appeared.

Two days after that the trial director from "The Sterling-Rock Falls Clinic" called my office. He wanted to know whether I still wanted to continue to work, or whether I would prefer to retire now, because they were interested in my place for their satellite clinic. They had already established such units in some places around Sterling. I denied any desire to retire and a few days later I was notified that the attorney of the plaintiff asked for a reinstatement of the process against me. I agreed to this request. I explained my decision in my statement to the court during a January 22 hearing.

Here is the central theme of this letter. I have every reason to believe, but I have no direct proof, that this whole trial against me was manufactured in the clinic. Mrs. Macchi, the plaintiff, was nothing more than a convenient substitution in this trial.

Already in the fall of 1986 several rumors came from the clinic that I was to be taught a lesson. Shortly afterwards, on January 22, I was

Book Two

given the summons. The medical denunciation in that document had no name and no signature, but by its style and special expressions, it pointed to Dr. James Allen, the Clinic specialist in infectious diseases.

I had a clash with Dr. Allen in 1982. At that time, I hospitalized in Sterling, an 80+ year old diabetic patient with a rapidly progressing gangrenous lesion in her foot. She was toxic and in shock from septicemia. After a week in the hospital, she improved, was conscious, was eating, had no chills and her temperature became normal. Her foot wound, after debridements stopped spreading and started to heal. At that time I was told by the head nurse that Dr. Allen, a superior authority in the hospital for infectious diseases, wanted to be consulted. Why not? About three days later, on a Saturday morning, I was called by Dr. Allen to come to the hospital to sign a permission for operation because the patient didn't want to sign it without my approval. All the operating team was already waiting. What operation? To amputate the foot. I refused and I resisted all concentrated pressure and threats. I continued medical treatment and I kept the patient for two more weeks at the hospital. Then I attended her for several weeks at home. The foot of that patient healed completely and she was walking on her two legs until she died last summer. Since that battle for the preservation of the foot of Mrs. Edlund, I have had a mortal inflexible enemy.

The present pressure for reinstatement of my trial was not likely to be the idea of Mrs. Macchi. Already last summer she refused to appear in court before a jury. At least this is what was said about her refusal.

I have the impression that this trial, since its beginning, was financed and directed by the Clinic. If I would have had a defense attorney in these past three years, the cost itself would force me now to give up my practice, even without any court verdict. I have no insurance coverage for this trial. I never got rich with my work and surely, I would not be in a condition to outspend the Clinic for legal fees.

The malpractice siege of the medical profession puts a very uneven burden on medical institutions. While, because of it, every doctor has to pay in order to have hospital privileges, most likely only doctors in small private practices, with limited resources are working under a condition of constant danger and insecurity. Their activity became gradually strangulated and their work became more likely emotionally exhausting.

Contrasting with the situation of small offices, for the big clinics, the terror of malpractice created a bonanza and a golden opportunity for expansion and dominance. The malpractice threat gave them a perfect excuse for endless multiplication of consultations and numerous, repeated testings. The medical staff of the clinics expanded enormously since the malpractice became an open pressure factor. All the clinics around became staffed with all kinds of specialists and subspecialists. Because of this work arrangement, the clinics became relatively immune to the squeeze of malpractice.

If it happens, that such a clinic has a benevolent attitude and creates a good cooperation with private practices around, the medical climate could be wonderful and everybody would benefit.

If, by contrast, the clinic becomes obsessed by domination and a monopoly in their place and around, then the life in such a place becomes uneasy and unhappy. Such a pathological development of those medical institutions deserves attention and a special study.

The history of treatment of Mrs. Macchi in the Clinic probably can give some clue as to why she has turned against me. Before the time of her hospitalization, we were like good friends. The fifth point in the court summons says "the first time Mrs. Macchi had reasonable grounds to believe or learned of any possible negligence on the part of the Defendant was on February 1, 1985." It was the day of Mrs. Macchi's hospitalization and her contact with Dr. Allen.

The picture of Mrs. Macchi was a perfect one for the purpose. A poor lady, paraplegic after a car accident in the Fifties, and permanently in the wheelchair, she was a perfect subject to gain pity among the jurors.

During the hospitalization, Mrs. Macchi got all the attention and care. She was seen by different doctors: those who did diagnostic work, a surgeon, who performed debridement; a plastic surgeon, who made a graft and Dr. Allen who performed her bone biopsy, after a bone scan tested negative, to prove she had osteomyelitis. How he did this in a field so enormously contaminated? Consequently she was given an IV of antibiotics during the hospitalization and for months afterwards while she was evaluated by a G.I. tract specialist for intestinal complications.

When all this was over, she was presented with an enormous bill and a squeeze. To avoid problems, she was given an outlet: she could sign a paper putting the guilt on me. Probably she was assured that I would not suffer. All would be settled in a settlement between the lawyers and the insurance would pay all the bills, the court costs and maybe something to help her in her difficult economic situation.

With all this, a question arises. Is my case an isolated pathological aberration of a relation between medical institutions, or is it something that appears more often, with all the variation of the stage, drama and intensity. If the second possibility is true: how does it affect the Family Practice? How does it affect the private practice in general, or the whole of medical care in the U.S.? Did anybody ever do a survey to collect dates and take a picture of the situation with all its tendencies, complications and consequences? If the cases as mine are not the exception and they appear in various forms throughout the land, then maybe we are building and celebrating our "Family Practice" in the wrong time and in the wrong place: somewhere on the edge of an active volcano?

I have a need to put my house in order, to get some guidance, and to feel togetherness among the "Family" practitioners. I also feel that those doctors, who practice under the shield of "family practice" should have a special obligation towards family units that hardly can cope with the unrestrained medical costs. The Family Practice should take a stand and fight not only for their part of the pie, but for the economical availability of medical treatment to all the average and less-than-average income families across the U.S. The name of our organization defines our work, but also contains the element of a mission.

I would like to have some guidance and help from you.

Tadeusz Maciejczyk, M.D.
Milledgeville, February 11, 1990

The World Seen from the Distance of a Small Village

Editor, *Newsweek*

Dear Sir:

Several months ago I sent to you my letters in which I described my fight with the malpractice system. In response, I received from you an encouraging letter that somebody from your staff would look into my problem.

Several things have happened since then. They are described in the material that I am sending to you now.

I still believe that what I am doing is right and that an enormous good would come to the whole country if the issue of malpractice would be put under the light or under a microscope; if it would be dissected and studied from different points of view and then evaluated for its consequences.

I am aware that really I should not send to you my last letter to the president of The American Academy of Family Physicians, because it contains names, while I still cannot prove or document my suspicions. But that letter paints a better picture of the situation than any other. I send you this letter not for names publication, but to give you a special inside, which would help you to look into questions it contains and to make your own investigation, based on what I could say.

I consider that this problem that I am raising has merit. In his address, President Bush spoke about the alarming rising costs of medical care. Medical care, which has to feed richly a parasite and has to walk on the minefields to do the job, will be very expensive and very insecure. It can very well parallel to a trial to be yourself with God you see in the time of a holy inquisition.

I would like to think that you would be interested in this problem.

Tadeusz Maciejczyk, M.D.
Milledgeville, February 15, 1990

NOTE: Lilka is the kid sister of my two best friends when I was 8–12 years old. The last time I saw her, she was nine. She got my address and asked me what I was doing in such a strange place as America. Her two brothers are dead.

Book Two

Dear Lilka:

A letter from you was for me a big surprise. Those our years of childhood when together with Nick and Stach and Wacek, we were running around on the streets near to our homes, those days are appearing to me so distant. Almost our whole life separates us from them.

Those our lives. They had written in a different script for every one of us. Completely different from what we could then imagine. Those years are coming back to me as the most happy times of my life, and those segments of streets where we were playing together as the most wonderful place in the world. Afterwards, we adjust to everything and everything became usual and ordinary and losing its original freshness. For me, that small world of ours, to which I never had a chance to return, for me that world became forever "the land of childhood years, which always for me will be as beautiful and as pure as the first love" as was expressed in the poem of Mickiewicz. In general the poetry of Mickiewicz, of Slowacki or of Norwid nobody can feel and understand to such a depth as those who, as me, have to live in the foreign land and in different culture.

How do I remember that enchanted world of my childhood?

Once it came to me in a dream.

That dream put me into the center of our school reunion. The celebration was taking place in our old school building, but the building in that dream had the appearance of a magnificent royal palace.

All of my former classmates were there and all of them were dressed in a variety of fantastic attire of kings, queens, princesses, admirals and other important dignitaries. Their heads were covered with beautiful cap pieces. And under those rich caps, their faces were the faces of 11 to 12 year old boys and girls. I remembered every one of them by name. We had so much to tell each other.

And in that whole crowd, only I was showing the true me. Only I was showing my old, wrinkled face with my bald head adorned with the remaining gray hairs on both sides. And only I was wearing my old, worn-out jacket.

In that dream, from the distance of my age, I gave a special look to that enchanted world of my childhood and the memories left behind. I would like to preserve forever those memories unaltered and unprofaned, only that when once I was asked where I would like to go, if I would have a chance to visit the most fabulous places of the world, I responded that I would like to go to Wloszczowa.

You want me to tell you my story, but what can I say?

The World Seen from the Distance of a Small Village

As in any other places of the world, my life here is just a daily, usual, to some extent regulated by routine experience. From here, from this simple place, I am trying to understand what the world is trying to say and to teach me. And I am still waiting for some new, big adventure that could come to me from behind the next moment of time.

If somebody would have told me in the old days in Wloszczowa, that my children would not understand my language, I would never have believed it. In some ways, it hurts. In a certain way, my children are not entirely mine. A few years ago, I encountered different groups of people during the Rotary ceremony and I talked with them. One lady standing near to me asked how many languages I spoke. I responded that when I am in the office, I speak English. With my family at home, I speak Spanish. But when I am alone with God, I talk to Him in Polish.

How strange are our lives. What have I learned from mine? I think that the greatest lesson for me was that the borders between states are artificial. The limits of the extensions of cultures and of spiritual forces of different human groupings are natural. This should be recognized and honored. Because otherwise, the people are more or less the same everywhere. The disputes and quarrels over frontiers should not destroy the deeper truth of brotherhood of all of us. We should learn to live with one another, honor and respect the others and together build a better future.

My family now is scattered in many places. I am at home alone and so I have time to think. In some way I like this present silence in my home. Norwid, in one of his poems, wrote how silence speaks to us and reveals to us matters and truths that are jammed and deafened by human bustle.

My wife is in Spain now. Irka (my daughter) lives in Buffalo, New York. On the 24th of March, I will go there for the baptism of my first grandson. Pablo is in Barcelona, Spain where he is a physician. He will get married this year. Maria is now in the University of Ames where she is finishing her doctorate and teaching industrial psychology. Teresa finished her studies of literature and is looking for work. And the smallest, Cristina, is now in her second year of art history. The next semester, she will go to Florence in Italy. There was an old poem in Polish literature in which a young man dreamed about big deeds in his life and those big deeds are symbolized by a sword. The poem is entitled *"Sen o Szpadzie"* (The Dream about a Sword.) And I am alone at home where my dreams about the sword continue to be alive and still exploring.

My best wishes for all in Wloszczowa.

Book Two

Tadeusz
March 4, 1990

NOTE: This was translated from Polish. I never imagined that translation would be so hard and so disappointing.

The World Seen from the Distance of a Small Village

A Letter to the Editor
Time Magazine
A comment on "From Submission to Revolution," *Time*, March 19, 1990

Dear Sir:

The interview with Jens Reich, the founder of the New Forum, was interesting, was rich in reflection and in inside.

To maintain those qualities and clarity of the thought, it didn't need the support of an epithet about "those untidy Russians and Poles." The eminence of socialism created in East Germany could be expressed much more clearly in other ways.

Self esteem and the search for self, which has to downgrade the others to be seen or understood, always leaves behind suspicions and always creates bad feelings. The pharisaic prayer of satisfaction, that "I" am so much better than the other untidy guy there in the corner, was never a promise or an *avant garde* to common understanding, to spiritual growth or to lasting peace.

In these very important days for both, for the East and for the West Germans, I wish them one very important quality that will decide about the future of the world. I wish them wisdom.

Tadeusz Maciejczyk, M.D.
Milledgeville, March 18, 1990

Book Two

Howard L. Ravenscraft, M.D., J.D.
Hebron, Kentucky

Dear Sir:

Today, for the second time, Mr. Cacciatore used your name to make me feel his strength and pressure, as well as my fragility under the blow of justice. The first time I genuinely worried about you, I wanted to help you and I sent you all that I knew about my case. I was wondering why I never got any answer from you. Today I got the picture.

And today, thanks to you, the letter from Mr. Cacciatore was not so dully and dreary as usual. I read with interest your extensive testimony, your curriculum vitae and your credentials.

And I was impressed. Maybe even I was amused.

I was impressed by your overwhelming certainty in every one of your observations, conclusions and statements. Never was there room in them for the smallest doubt or for a possibility of a somewhat different scenario. Also, the synchronization between each of the questions and your answers created such marvelous harmony. Your answers flowed spontaneously and easily in a wide-open stream of sentences.

After reading this extensive document, I felt a kind of admiration for the very singular qualities of your exploring mind. In the old times, in order to clarify the unknown, the wise men looked into the darkness, searching for a flash of light that could give them some new inside and possible open a road towards the truth and knowledge. All those bothers were absolutely unnecessary for you. To you all those insides and conclusions came easily, without effort, without the shadow of a doubt, without any further need for a double check. In your interview all the charges were met with quick responses, which were obvious and were told with the tone of a born expert.

What can I tell you?

Reading your document, I felt very humble, very amused.

I felt very humble, because in this remote corner of the world, where I live and work, such an unequivocal judgment as yours, I was inclined to take not as a sign of genius and wisdom, but as an illustration of mind's simplicity and rigidity, which sticks to just a few accepted rules and does not tolerate any deviation from this simple line. The few accepted dogmas are giving such a rigid mind safety, certainty and authority—a clear right to condemn anybody else. For such a person, any doubt, any other suggestion or interpretation is breaking down that cozy place where such a person locates his whole righteousness.

The World Seen from the Distance of a Small Village

Obviously I was wrong when I tried to believe that fully alive and exploring men are never free from doubts that appear to them from every side, at any moment deviating their already made judgments to some new questions, to some other possibilities, solutions or truths. All such new questions are forcing those men to take the pains of revisions, corrections, conducting them sometimes to a complete change of their line of thinking. Those doubts and corrections for them are never effortless and never are easy.

Here, in this remote corner of the world, I sincerely believed that precisely an admission of our uncertainties, as well as our readiness for correction and change, however painful, were the only long range guides towards the truth, to wisdom, to greatness and to a personal fulfillment of life.

Finally, because of my ignorance, I am inclined to question some of your assumptions and verdicts. I will be delighted to see you in the courtroom on May 21, where we will have a chance to continue our discussion over those differences.

I assure you that under your impressive credentials and life successes, I feel my enormous smallness.

Tadeusz Maciejczyk, M.D.
Milledgeville, March 18, 1990

Book Two

Clerk of the Court of Carroll County
Case No. 87 L 2:

Dear Sir:

    I want to notify you that I was told who was the mystery expert in my case and why he was condemning me for my wrong doing. I wrote my humble letter to him, and I invited him to the courtroom on May 21 to continue our exchange of opinions.
    I am sending you the copy of my letter to:

> Howard L. Ravenscraft, M.D., J.D.
> Hebron, Kentucky

I cannot tell that I am impatient, but I am ready.

> Tadeusz Maciejczyk, M.D.
> Milledgeville, March 18, 1990

The World Seen from the Distance of a Small Village

The U.S. Census

In order to put myself in a better picture for the Census purposes, which could be a real basic tool for government and private enterprise planning, I feel that I should add to your questionnaire an explanation of events, which in a very short time could change my life completely and make my answers to this questionnaire completely invalid.

On May 21 I have to go to court for a malpractice accusation and trial. The accusation does not make much sense and is absurd, but it hangs on, puts pressure on, absorbs energy and it destroys my life and the life of my family. As you can see, my wife is not counted any more in my questionnaire. She could no longer bear the pressure.

I discovered that the candidates for my defense lawyer were playing a "justice game" instead of being frank and defend. Consequently, I decided to defend myself. The predictions for me in this situation are not encouraging. The men close to the court told my wife that after my trial (and I quote this from my letter to Pres. Bush) I will be homeless, my home will be taken away from me to pay for the "justice." I will be jobless. My office will be seized for the same reason and my reputation as a doctor will be in ruin. I will be divorced. It is the only way for my wife to retain some of her belongings. And consequently, I will be on Public Aid; nothing will be left for me.

The letter to the President was sent to the Dept. of Health and Human Services to be answered. In this answer, I received the consolation that what is happening to me is just nothing of importance. That it is a simple "malpractice stress syndrome." In their goodness, they sent me several pamphlets about this new illness. In my bitterness, I thought that in the same way Solzhenizyn, when he was on his way to the labor camps in Siberia, could be consoled by the KGB Society that what was happening to him was nothing of importance; it was just ordinary "Gulag Stress Syndrome."

What can I say? Within a short time, I could be homeless and my address will be somewhere under a bridge. I will be jobless. I love medicine and the contact with the people, the possibility of being helpful to them, but I dislike very much the frame that was imposed on my work and the marking of me as the next more convenient sucker in the "justice game." I am still not divorced, but my wife left for the safety of Chicago to work there manually without the harassment to which the medical profession is predisposed.

Book Two

I do not know what I will do when homeless, somewhere under the bridge. I do not like to be idle. In anticipation of the brilliant future reserved for me in my new condition after the trial, I imagine that I will have a hard time resisting the temptation of trying to write a possible next bestseller about the attractive, cozy place U.S. justice loves so much to prepare for those who are careless enough to dream about a private practice, private enterprise, or some other independent, sincere and creative work here in this beautiful U.S.

This U.S. is going downhill, is entering into more and more of an astonishing debt, is losing its soul and its prestige, because it harbors too many parasites.

Tadeusz Maciejczyk, M.D.
Milledgeville, April 3, 1990

P.S. I am sorry I am somewhat late, but I was away for the baptism of my grandson. I send this letter without any corrections. You are giving me no time.

The World Seen from the Distance of a Small Village

William T. Cacciatore
Attorney for Plaintiff, Wilma P. Macchi
Rockford, IL

To your request for "admission of facts," I will respond only to the first point: I did not treat decubitus ulcers of Mrs. Wilma P. Macchi.

At the time of the appearance of those ulcers, she was not my patient. She was only my former patient, for whom I felt sympathy and I was helping her acute, urgent needs when she was here in this area for whatever the reason.

Mrs. Macchi was my patient for about two years, from January 16, 1969 until February 12, 1971. In the spring of 1971, she notified me that she was going to live in the South. (I didn't ask where.) At that point we had a warm farewell.

Afterwards, during the next 14 years until her hospitalization, I saw Mrs. Macchi three times:

In January, 1977 for acute sinus infection

In September, 1983 for urinary infection

In September, 1984 for an arthritic inflammation of the right knee.

At no time Mrs. Macchi asked me to treat her decubitus, even after she told me that she had such a problem. She told me this with a kind of embarrassment, after her visit in 1983. After that visit, I walked with her to the door to help her onto the entrance steps and I asked her how she was able to do her housework. That's when she confessed to me her setback.

In February, 1984, her husband came to the office asking for something to keep her decubitus clean. It was not a visit. I spoke with him across the appointment window. To help in the situation, I wrote him a prescription for the acetic acid and Betadine, a general remedy for protection of this kind of lesion. I didn't charge for this service; I didn't put it in the chart and I didn't remember it until the interrogation in the courtroom.

During her third and last visit in my office in September of 1984, Mrs. Macchi didn't mention her decubitus. Her problem at that time was a large, swollen, red and hot knee.

In summary, Mrs. Macchi never asked me to treat her decubitus. I never examined her for that problem. I never saw that decubitus. I never felt that I was supposed to force her to submit to such an examination and to treat the lesion. She was in my office as an old time patient and also as a friend, always for a very specific, acute problem, a kind of emergency. Comparing the frequency of her visits in my office during those two years, when she was my patient, and the three visits in 14

Book Two

years, between her departure to the South in 1971, and the hospitalization in 1985, it was obvious to me that there, where she was living, she had her own family doctor.

This is all I can tell you in my "admission of facts."

I want to tell you here, that in your last letter, I noted an increased worry about the outcome of this trial, its cost and your possible promises to Mrs. Macchi. For the first time, I thought that maybe your only client in this trial was Mrs. Macchi and that your role in this trial was not a cover-up for the primary contract with Sterling-Rock Falls Clinic in Sterling. I am not completely convinced, but it could be.

The fact is, that in this tragic conflict between Mrs. Macchi and me, I see the real villain, not in Mrs. Macchi, even after she betrayed me and my trust in her, as in the Sterling Clinic policy to expand and the vendetta of Dr. James Allen.

If my present assumptions are true, if you are not in service of the Sterling Clinic, I would like to invite you to join our forces and to point the finger at the real instigator of this affair, who manipulated Mrs. Macchi and convinced her to the point that she became an instrument for their policy, and now are using our feud while staying on the side and watching for the possible worse outcome. For years, the Clinic tried to eliminate from their pass those, who wanted to remain independent and create in the area their undisputed monopoly. This trial against me was made to eliminate me from my place. The voices about this I heard already in 1986. Those voices from the Clinic were saying that I would be taught a lesson.

I have the impression that by changing the essence and the direction of our trial, you could help Mrs. Macchi; you could cover the trial expenses and most likely you could have some extra gains.

Otherwise, if you are not in the service of the Clinic, we could destroy each other, to the satisfaction only of the Clinic.

If you consider that my proposition could be of any value to you, I would like you to contact me.

Tadeusz Maciejczyk, M.D.
Milledgeville, April 9, 1990

P.S. On April 5, I handed a subpoena to Dr. James Allen for interrogation during the trial. I have a few special clues.

The World Seen from the Distance of a Small Village

Crescent Counties Foundation
For Medical Care

RE: Case Rahn, Orville, HIC#337-32-6453A/Reference 3-90/835

Two days ago, I obtained from you a "confidential" letter concerning my treatment of Orville Rahn. You are viewing my intervention as insufficient, indecisive and contributory to his death. After such a statement you are asking me for my comment.
My Comment:
Orville Rahn had many longstanding illnesses that were aggravating each other and brought him to a stage where there was no hope.

1. He had longstanding diabetes
2. His peripheral vascular system became a mess (toes amputated for ischemic gangrene)
3. Crippling arthritis, with bone degeneration and breaking down of the left knee.
4. Gout, with gouty deposits and kidney damage.
5. Gastritis or gastric ulcer from long use of anti-arthritis, anti-gout medication.
6. constant fullness in abdomen from insufficient blood supply to the intestinal tract. The distress was worse during digestion, to the point that he was afraid to eat.
7. Constant pain between blades in the back of the thorax.
8. Chest pain—a mixture of coronary insufficiency, esophageal reflux and nerve roots compression at the cervical/thoracic junction.

In September of 1988, Orville Rahn had a complete examination in Monroe Clinic and afterwards, I didn't see him until October 9, 1989. The Monroe clinic gave up on him and he was sent home to die there.
On October 9, he was brought to the office because of squeezing pain behind low xyphoid process. Nitroglycerine was not helping and was producing a headache. At home he was on Clinoril, Cardizem and Nitroglycerine patches.
The ECG done in the office showed Q waves in lead 1 and AVL, like in an old lateral infarction and S-T segment depression in V, which could mean an incomplete injury, or stress. He didn't want to go to the hospital. Altogether, I gave him Carafate to treat the gastric injury.

Book Two

I went to see him two days later in his home (eight miles) at 7:00 P.M.; he was well after the visit until the dinner of October 11. After eating he had nausea, some pain behind xyphoid and in the back between blades, and the fullness in the whole abdomen. He was conscious at the time of the visit and sitting in the chair. Laying down in bed was producing retrosternal pain, especially behind xyphoid. He showed with his hand the very limited area of pain in the low sternum. His pulse was regular, 80BPM. BP was 120/80. Lungs were clear to auscultation. Abdomen was soft.

In this situation, to help him sleep without Clinoril for arthritis, I promised him a shot of Demerol and I came later in the evening to give him this shot. It was not for cardiac pain.

He had a good night. He rested. He was in good spirits and in this condition, when he was shaving himself, suddenly he collapsed and in a state of unconsciousness, he was taken to the hospital where he died shortly after admission, apparently from a massive myocardial infarction.

The vascular break could also have been in some other vital place in the body. I wonder about the thoracic descending aorta. The hospital ECG, taken a short time before his death, was not very typical of an acute myocardial infarction.

CONCLUDING: I do not see how, as suggested by you better evaluation, a more timely hospital admission could have improved the chances of this patient, saving his life or improve the quality of his life. He was already sick and tired of his recent hospitalizations and I had only two and one-half days to make a miracle.

If, in spite of this, you see that I was wrong, please explain to me the details, because I still want to learn. I did what I considered proper in the given situation. I cannot act in medicine against my judgment of common sense or my understanding of what is human. I never intended to make my work a spectacle of surface perfection.

CONCLUDING IN ANOTHER WAY: Looking at your threatening letter, mostly a print and an added request for detailed information on who I am as a doctor, brought to my mind a scene from July 1945 when at midnight, suddenly two soldiers with bayonets on their guns entered our home. Behind them was a lieutenant from internal Security, who like your letter, pierced me with his cold, penetrating eyes without one word, and after this long, silent interrogation, extended to me his hand with "your documentation please." It was a scenario just like yours, only in a different setting. The group left, because at that time, we had

The World Seen from the Distance of a Small Village

in our home, a Russian captain in a kind of quarter and he, in a decisive moment, got up and in an insistent voice, demanded the lieutenant to inspect his documentation as well. One week later, the Internal Security surrounded my home, put my mother five times against the wall to tell them where her son, the bandit, was. And after twelve hours of terror, they took both my parents to prison for further interrogation.

The institution, which in order to function and to control their subjects, has to use a constant threat of repression, the "cold eye" of interrogation, the threat of documentation check-up and even puts the suspects against the wall, as it was in the old times of the rule of Polish Internal Security, Russian KGB, or German Gestapo, is not showing through such methods its strength or health and sooner or later will come a drive for freedom with East Europe and Russian type of revolt. Finally, in all such situations comes a loud "Enough is enough."

It was a time when I was approaching medicine as a mission to serve and to help.

The present surveillance, establishment in medicine of a police-like state, the horrors of the malpractice dragging in courts, the institutions of bribery of malpractice insurance in order to practice, which is paid ultimately by the sick, the insecurity and the fear to dare, all this transformed the previously noble vocation into an arena for smartness, escapism or responsibility, protective devices and artifacts, enormous waste and hordes of speculators and overlords, with their phony assurances to the public, dirt greed and a loss in medicine of a backbone sense of mission.

Congratulations.

Tadeusz Maciejczyk, M.D.
Milledgeville, April 19,1990

Book Two

The Daily Gazette, Sterling, Illinois
Letter to the Editor

Sorry, but I disagree completely not only with the "essence," but with the spirit and logic of your editorial of April 20, 1990.

It is true, that the U.S. has no rights or obligations to stick its nose and interfere with the internal politics of other sovereign states. But it is also true that the U.S. has a duty, if its democratic principles have to mean anything, to speak clearly and in unequivocal terms about the moral rights and moral issues of Lithuania. Voicing our conviction and our stand should not interfere with the meeting of Pres. Bush with Pres. Gorbachev, only adding to its importance. Such a voice will be, and should be, the voice of our conscience (not of our hostile feelings towards Soviets) that nobody has a right to dull, and to change by whatever the considerations into an uneasy, artificial or even indifferent smiles.

In this difficult time for Russians, when they have to swallow many bitter pills and for their own, as well as for the world's sake, come to terms in a noble way with the previous brutal Soviet excesses and Stalin's paranoia, such a clear and loud voice of conscience from American people and from our President, expressed without hostility and without false pretensions to perfection, would be an easing factor and could have a beneficial effect in this time of Russian uncertainty and spiritual turmoil when somehow, they have to reach the peace within themselves and with their painful past.

In know that in Russia noble people exist with noble spirits. I would not be alive if one of those Russians had not given me a helping hand in a critical moment. Many times, I wondered whether he paid a price for that act.

The question that I have heard, which asks how much we should go back into time to resolve the border disputes, is not an issue and has no application in the case of Lithuania.

The fact is, that Lithuania was incorporated into the Soviet Empire as a result of a secret and to this time degrading and shameful for the Russians pact between Stalin and Hitler. Once absorbed, Lithuanians suffered from deportation, execution, suffocation of all signs of authenticity and from methodical destruction of their previous way of life. The Soviets did nothing to gain Lithuanian respect or friendship and did everything to be despised. It is true that the Russians themselves were the subject of the same terror and of Stalin's madness, but this is not a point here.

The World Seen from the Distance of a Small Village

Now, in the time of "Glasnost," in the time of budding self-searching of their souls in many Russians who are confronted with radical changes and are trying to find new ways into the new approaching era, in this special time, it would not be humiliating, not one more calamity for their country, to correct the results of Stalin's treachery and the violence of his secret police, letting the Baltic states free as they were in the time of the Molotov-Ribbentrop conspiracy. Russia already admitted their guilt in the massacre of Katyn. (The Katyn Forest Massacre was the site where more than five thousand Polish military were executed by the Russians in 1940, then blamed it on the Nazis. Eventually, Gorbachev admitted the massacre was indeed ordered by Stalin.) The other places are still waiting for revelation. This admission eased the emotional tension of Poles towards Russians. The next step in this direction: the restoration of the independent status of the Baltic states, would only add to the prestige of the new, emerging Russia and the world's confidence in their constructive, future role. The independent Baltic States could change from forced to true friends of Russia and would remain connected with Russia in many positive ways. For Russia, unconditional granting of independence of the Baltic States would mean a passage from political phobias and greed, into a new political wisdom.

But if the Soviets continued their pressure and harassment to bring the Lithuanians to their knees, and to "teach them a lesson," then, it would mean that nothing had really changed in the spirit of the Soviets in spite of glasnost and in spite of Gorbachev's charm.

The Russians have to understand that while we have no intention for any intervention in their internal affairs, they have no right to impose on us a moral blackout and to force America to deny to help a world community in need, whether this need was produced by a natural disaster or by human malice.

By a clear declaration of such a position, the U.S. most likely would not risk any new upheavals, but rather would contribute to the new world's stability. It would be a voice that truly could help the Russians correct the past injustices, grow and leave more decisively the Stalinist manners behind them.

I believe that now is the time to say clearly that if the Russians will confirm and seal Stalin's act, continuing an economic squeeze and political intimidation in Lithuania, then the U.S. reserves for themselves the right to bring humanitarian aid to Lithuania, not as an act of hostility towards Russia, but as an act of solidarity of the fellow men and in the same spirit in which the U.S. brought help to Russia during the

Book Two

starving years in the Twenties and Thirties, a starvation brought on by the insane policies of the Soviet rulers of that time.

Pres. Bush, in this unusual situation, should not be bashful. Obviously, caution and dialogue between Russia and Lithuania are of extreme importance, but the timid, from under the table murmur of Secretary of State Baker, suggesting that the present Soviet behavior could harm some of our new business and commercial relations, should remain only as a measurement for Mr. Baker and nobody else in America.

On the copy of this letter sent to Pres. Bush, I added this remark:

Dear Mr. President:

Writing this letter to our local newspaper, I was intending to talk especially to you. Because of this, I send you a copy.

I wish you the best in your work.

Tadeusz Maciejczyk, M.D.
Milledgeville, April 22, 1990

The World Seen from the Distance of a Small Village

Alan R. Nelson, M.D.
President of the American Medical Association

Dear Sir:

I thank you for your letter and for the invitation to become a member of the AMA.

Long ago, I was a member of the AMA. I was a member for many years. Once, I was even an alternate delegate. Precisely shortly afterwards, came a break.

I do not remember what the year was. As always, I was struggling to pay tuitions, to pay taxes and then I was saving to pay the AMA membership. It was never easy for me. I am completely untalented at asking my patients for money.

Then, when I was almost ready to write a check for the AMA, I received a letter from the president of County Medical Association, Dr. Lambos, that I am not a member anymore of the association because I didn't pay my dues. In a few days, I received a similar letter from Chicago with an additional sanction of cancellation of my insurance that would cover the office expenses in case of my disability.

I was struck by the way this problem was handled by the organization of the most humanitarian of all professions. I even didn't know there was a set time to pay those dues. I refused to belong to an organization that uses such Draconian methods to control their members. I never again went to the county medical meetings.

Today, my situation has changed. I protested the obligatory malpractice insurance and I lost my hospital privileges. I provoked one "important" doctor and I got a malpractice trial. My practice is now small. Maybe I would be unable to afford the present AMA dues, whatever they are. I refused to have a lawyer for defense and the predictions for the outcome of that trial, which will be on May 21, are that I will be crucified there. My wife was told that after the trial we will be homeless. I will be jobless and if she would like to retain any of her belongings, she has to divorce me. The blackmail of the medical profession by the so-called guardians of justice is very special, and I do not like to bend. I asked for a counter-suit, asking for $100,000 from the accusing attorney and from the mysterious accusing doctor to be paid to the AMA to fight such a frivolous accusation as mine.

I send you the copies of different papers that I wrote. I am sorry that there are so many, but they are revealing and interesting.

Book Two

My decision about my AMA membership has to rest at least until the conclusion of my trial.

I send you my best wishes.

                                          Tadeusz Maciejczyk, M.D.
                                          Milledgeville, April 26, 1990

The World Seen from the Distance of a Small Village

The Daily Gazette
Carroll County Review

About three months ago, I wrote a letter to the local newspapers about malpractice and about the new insistence to keep the level of that malpractice insurance, and consequently its cost, at the highest level. One of my statements in that letter was erroneous and now I want to make the necessary correction.

I was told that the pressure to keep this insurance high and expensive came from the political circles in Springfield. I was informed in this way at the time, when my hospital privileges were revoked because my coverage was insufficient.

Later, I didn't find a basis to suspect the politicians in Springfield to bring such a new problem on themselves, and I went to Morrison Hospital Director Wayne Sensor to ask him directly.

No. It was not Springfield that was doing this. The pressure came from The St. Paul Insurance Co., and its local representative Gene Jost from Marus and Jost Co. in Morrison.

The fact is that the malpractice fever tempered down and the courts are showing more responsibility in giving previously fabulous rewards. Nevertheless, the St. Paul Ins. Co., is insisting on enforcing this insurance at the highest levels. The hospital director told me that even the dentist, who occasionally extracts teeth at the hospital, has to have the same insurance coverage of one million dollars for three cases. The Ins. Co., insisted that the amendment to the hospital by-laws, which established the policy, was still valid.

I remained without hospital privileges. Maybe I am a stranger or a lunatic in today's world, but I believe that obediently paying for this insurance by doctors, whatever the price, just to buy relative safety for themselves, is not virtuous for the doctor.

Malpractice insurance, which is nothing but a ransom from blackmail and harassment, is done on many levels of labor and production. Because of this, it contributes enormously to the spiraling costs of health care and of many other aspects of our lives. In a large segment of our society, health care has become more and more unaffordable.

In my understanding, the most technically-perfect doctor's performance, which produces patients near collapse and anger at the payment window, or when he is looking for health insurance, somehow misses an important ingredient of the medical mission and practice. The malpractice suits intimidation took a toll on doctors, on hospi-

Book Two

tals, putting an unusual stress on legal safety, on detailed, massive paperwork and recordings, which became more important than the real service to humans.

The medical profession was supposed to be one of the most humanitarian occupations. But the humanitarian, the human relation factors and their mission are vanishing from life in our society, leaving in its place only a business; a cold, naked striving-for-safety business, which in their special logic, in this time of need, is trying to impress and to attract with the exterior splendor: a special, luxurious entrance to the hospital in Sterling, a costly beautification of the hospital in Morrison. More and more, it serves mostly those who can afford it.

I want to repeat again that the pressure to keep the malpractice insurance high, as it was in 1985, was produced not by Springfield politicians, but by St. Paul Insurance Co. and its local representative, the Mauris and Jost Co. in Morrison.

As in a previous letter, to see what you are buying by paying those enormous malpractice taxations during each medical service, or medicine, I invite you to watch my own malpractice suit that will be at 9:30 A.M. on May 21 in Mt. Carroll, Ill.

Tadeusz Maciejczyk, M.D.
Milledgeville, May 3, 1990

The World Seen from the Distance of a Small Village

Theodore C. Eickhoff, M.D.
Chief Medical Editor of Infectious Disease News
Presbyterian St. Luce's Medical Center
Denver, Colorado

Dear Sir:

I have a problem and I am not sure at all whether I have any right to ask you for help. Nevertheless, while reading your paper and just after the pre-trial session, I got the idea to turn to you for some answers.

I have a malpractice suit against me. I send you a copy of the accusation and some of the material that accumulated over the past three years of pressures and threats.

The accusing party is trying to prove that because of my mismanagement of Mrs. Macchi's bed sores, she became a victim of unnecessary suffering and expenses. From the documents you will see that I was never asked by Mrs. Macchi to treat her decubitus and that she could not be my patient in the situation as it was, but this guilt is pressed on me with all the insistence.

Because of this, I ask you to read and to examine the pages from the hospitalization of Mrs. Macchi and to tell me the following:

1. Whether an aggressive approach of taking bone cultures during the operation of debridement of the decubitus ulcer (after neg. bone X-ray and neg. bone scan) was indicated, and was meaningful for further treatment?
2. Whether breaking periostium to take a specimen for culture was prudent or safe?
3. If the specimen for culture was taken during beveling down the sacrum, why there is no record in the lab of any, even the smallest piece of bone tissue, only this mysterious "bone culture?"
4. the bone culture showed exactly identical bacterial growth as the necrotic tissue from debridement. Was this a proof of multiple bacterial osteomyelitis, or just bone tissue contamination in that enormously infected tissue above the bone?

I understand that you have no obligation to answer my questions. I never imagined that I would be confronted in my work with such a problem. Maybe I should seek safety behind the shoulders of a lawyer,

Book Two

but I feel that here I have to defend much more than any lawyer would like to fight for.

I would like to receive your answers before May 21, if possible.

However you choose to respond, I will be grateful to you for looking into this problem.

Tadeusz Maciejczyk, M.D.
Milledgeville, May 6, 1990

The World Seen from the Distance of a Small Village

Congressman Guy Vander Jagt
Chairman of National Republican Congressional Committee

Dear Sir:

I want to thank you for the Certificate of Appreciation from the Republican Party that I just received.

From my previous experience, I know that in the headquarters of the Party, nobody really likes to read letters; nobody is interested in what possible ideas they can bring, only in the money they might contain.

As you can see, I do not send you a check. And I will try to make this letter short and clear.

I have lived for over three years under the pressure and threats of malpractice. The accusation is nonsense. The threats are real. To illustrate how wonderful is my life, and what a wonderful prospective I have for the development of my life, I am sending you a letter that I added to my official 1990 Census report. That letter is also short. If you would like any more detailed explanation of the absurdity of my life and work in today's U.S., I would be delighted to send you all the material I have. Until now, nobody showed any interest and I feel very alone in my stand.

In the meantime, I assure you that when, after my trial, as predicted by the guardians of law around the court, I will be homeless, jobless and divorced, and my consequent residence somewhere under a bridge, I will hang your certificate above my head. It will help me to dream about the wonders and joys of living in the U.S. after a decade of Republican administration.

Tadeusz Maciejczyk, M.D.

P.S. Today, when I was in church, I decided to send you a copy of my letter about Lithuania and the Baltic States. I sent it also to the President about three weeks ago.

Our moral, clear and firm stand in this problem is not an academic, or impractical question. With such a stand and commitment, we will help raise in Russia men of the same high moral standards and convictions. Our pragmatic, only for today, indifference to the moral, which would be limited to the extent of popularity and dreams about the new Soviet market, will discourage those men who could be providential. It will be a clear evidence to the Soviet's worst hoodlums that they have a good

Book Two

chance to retain power, use the West, as Lenin recommended and after invigorating their economy, change their smiles into typical Soviet grim faces, demands and threats.

We are so used to borrowing from our children and grandchildren to enjoy our present moment of prosperity and popularity, that we are ready also to misuse the present changes and opportunities in Russia, getting a short time advantage and leaving our children with the burden of dealing with an economically strong Soviet empire, which in addition would be filled with the feeling of contempt to the West for its stupidity.

Tadeusz Maciejczyk, M.D.
Milledgeville, May 13, 1990

The World Seen from the Distance of a Small Village

J. Jarrett Clinton, M.D.
Assistant Surgeon General Director
Dept. of Health & Human Services
Washington, D.C.

Dear Sir:

I want to thank you for your support in this uneasy time for me of pressures and threats and of my trial that is approaching within one week.

One year ago, I asked you to look into the malpractice problem and to help. As a final word, I received from your dept. an assuring explanation that what was happening to me was nothing unusual: just a simple "malpractice syndrome."

Now, in one week, I will be in the courtroom.

Strangely enough, I am not sorry for what I did. More than this, I am proud that I behaved this way, trying to help. Studying medicine, I was taught to help. I did what my conscience, what my understanding of a doctor's mission was dictating me to do. If circumstances were to be repeated, most likely, I will do that same. I will try to help. Medicine was supposed to be the most humanitarian of occupations. Just this element attracted me to medicine more than anything else. I do not imagine myself, when confronted with a need, that before doing anything, I would look at whether it would or would not raise the eyebrows of the watching lawyers. I refuse to read, or to study the increasingly cumbersome and clever traps spread by the lawyers for their rich fishing or hunting. They do not care for consequences. They are not only the hunters. Many times they are the highway robbers, armed with the law-scripts. The factory of this dense nest of those traps is there, near you, somewhere around Washington.

And so, I became something like a criminal in this land. Worse than this, the tenacity to incriminate and to press charges against me is greater than in criminal cases. Here is the game for money: justice here is a very distant consideration. Money became more and more the real God in America.

The government of the U.S. is protecting this hunting, those legal games for money, whatever the means. The lawyers are everyplace in government. A true fight against this destructive social gangsterism could be uneasy, could require strength and a real stand for something. And Washington is not famous for such qualities and virtues. Washington is too opportunistic, too faceless, too much made by the promoters of vices

Book Two

and weaknesses. Washington only knows how to expand itself into a bureaucratic monster, with its inertia, its waste, it astonishing creativity for new papers, and new rules, which nobody can count, remember or understand. Washington created its own logic and philosophy of grabbing whatever possible, while going the way of least resistance, no matter whether there, at the end would be a precipice.

I am facing the "justice game" against me alone.

For you, for the memory of my stand, in which you were so understanding, I am sending you some of the new material that accumulated sine I wrote to you. I have not much hope that you would pay any attention to this material and to this general problem. I know that this material could be used as one more useful tool, or witness in a search for solutions to the negative aspects of malpractice. It could be. In spite of the modern version of enlightenment, and the approaching of the 21st century, I still believe in miracles.

I wish you the best in your work.

                                        Tadeusz Maciejczyk, M.D.
                                        Milledgeville, May 13, 1990

The World Seen from the Distance of a Small Village

DePaul University
Office of Financial Aid
Catherine C. Thomas, Director
Chicago, Illinois

Dear Mrs. C.C. Thomas:

I send you now $12,500.00 for tuition for Cristina Maciejczyk for the next school year of 1990–91. My problem with a malpractice suit is still hanging and I am still going through this test alone, without a lawyer. Many people wonder why I am so stubborn in this matter. But I have to follow my logic and my instinct in my fighting for a better world. My trial will begin within a few days, on May 21. I really do not know what my situation will be after all this is over.

I would like you to send me each trimester, a note as to where I stand with my account.

And I am grateful to your university because Cristina enjoys the learning and the environment in your school. She has an enormous desire to go to Florence next fall and I am sure that she will use her time there well.

Sincerely,

Tadeusz Maciejczyk
Milledgeville, May 17, 1990

Book Two

Dear Dr. Maciejczyk,

After reading the article in the May 22 *Sterling Gazette*, I thought I would write you a letter of encouragement. When I read something like this, after going to you for most of my life, it makes me very upset! You have been the only doctor who I could really trust 100%. When I told you of a problem I was having, you would know how to cure it, and I never doubted your judgment! You have done my family nothing but good over the past twenty years. I'll support you in any way I can!

After reading the claims the woman made, I can only think that here is a person trying to capitalize on you, because you oppose malpractice insurance. I sometimes think another problem with this country is that we have too many lawsuits! It seems like everyone is sue-happy.

If I can help in any way, I would be proud to do so and I agree, "truth and justice will prevail." Thank you for being there when I needed you.

                        Sincerely,

                        Robert L. Mckenna

The World Seen from the Distance of a Small Village

Milledgeville MD Beats Odds, Attorney in Malpractice Suit

A *Daily Gazette* Correspondent
Milledgeville - June 1, 1990

Dr. Tadeusz Maciejczyk of Milledgeville fought his own case in court and won. Chief Circuit Judge John w. Rapp ruled in the doctor's favor in the malpractice suit brought against him by Wilma Macchi of Polo.

Maciejczyk first learned of the verdict Wednesday morning when Macchi's lawyer, Attorney William Cacciatore of Rockford, called to congratulate him on winning the case. Official notice did not come until Thursday's mail.

In his opinion, Judge Rapp stated that the preparation and trial were "severely complicated" by the doctor's decision to serve as his own attorney because of the doctor's lack of knowledge of court procedure.

But Judge Rapp's final conclusion was that "the defendant's conduct was not a proximate cause of the injuries complained of by the plaintiff," and he entered judgment for Maciejczyk and against Macchi.

Maciejczyk admitted that his handicap of not knowing court procedures was "enormous" and says he wouldn't advise others to be their own lawyers. It brings a lot of stress and insecurity, he said. Macchi's case against him has been pending for over three years, he noted.

But on the other hand, he said the trial created in him a strength he never suspected he had. His stubbornness also had a little to do with it, he conceded.

For years, Maciejczyk has been adamant against purchasing malpractice insurance saying that the huge settlements awarded by the courts encouraged people to sue and furnished lucrative cases for lawyers. He calls it the "blackmail of doctors." By acting as his own lawyer, the doctor said he was "refusing to feed the system."

"Citizens suing one another is a symptom of society we are living in," said Maciejczyk. "It has to be diagnosed and treated."

The doctor was denied the use of then-community General Hospital in June 1983, when he refused to carry malpractice insurance. He now carries minimal insurance coverage for a total of $100,000 each for a total of three claims a year. But since January, the doctor said he has been denied the use of the Morrison Hospital since he is not carrying $1 million worth of malpractice insurance. He now refers his hospital patients to doctors he can trust, he said.

Book Two

Malpractice insurance, Maciejczyk claimed, is paid ultimately, not by doctors, but by the patients.

Maciejczyk vows to continue his fight against malpractice insurance and to make the public aware of the "disaster" that is going on.

The doctor says he is enormously grateful to all who supported him, had patience with him in court and who gave him strength by showing him understanding.

Maciejczyk, who served as a *freedom fighter* during World War II in his native Poland, and escaped to Spain where he received his medical training, feels that, after his day in court, his implicit faith in the judicial system has been justified.

The World Seen from the Distance of a Small Village

Our View

The Daily Gazette, Sterling, IL, June 5, 1990.

It didn't exactly make national headlines—maybe it should have—but it did make them here, where it counts. And it must have sent, if not shockwaves, then certainly chills, through many of our many lawyer friends around here.

It all happened only last Wednesday when a little-known physician, a gentleman with a long name, who has difficulty articulating himself in the English language, and was totally unfamiliar with courtroom procedure, managed to muddle through it anyway.

Muddle through? That is a gross understatement. He kinda beat the system. What actually happened was that, in an unfamiliar environment away from his normal milieu, he bested a high-powered attorney from Rockford who *was* in his normal milieu.

The physician, of course, is Tadeusz Maciejczyk of Milledgeville. He successfully won a malpractice suit brought against him by a Polo woman. The verdict brought an almost-audible sigh of relief from the residents of that Carroll county city, most of whom depend upon Dr. Maciejczyk for their medical needs.

If the winning doctor is known for anything, it is stubbornness. He'd be the first to agree with that. Indeed, he evidenced it twice in this dramatic instance: In insisting on functioning as his own counsel and in doing something—or rather not doing something—that helped bring him to the court in the first place: refusing to purchase malpractice insurance.

That latter example of stubbornness, by the way, resulted in his being denied use of then-Community General Hospital in June 1983 and later Morrison Hospital, because he is not carrying $1 million worth of the insurance.

Dr. Maciejczyk, bucking the trend, long has called such insurance 'blackmail of doctors." He is convinced that the insurance, which brings huge settlements from the courts, only encourages people to sue, thereby furnishing lucrative cases for lawyers. He also suggests that such insurance is ultimately paid by the patients and not the doctors, adding to the costs of today's already exorbitant medical fees.

We all know that. We also all know that the right to sue always will be abused—but should that prevent an injured individual from legitimately using the judicial system to right a wrong? In that respect, we have a question for Dr. Maciejczyk and those of his peers who would do away with malpractice insurance. How else would an injured patient or family be compensated should carelessness or negligence contribute to grievous suffering?

Ideally, of course, it would be nice if the medical profession was comprised only of perfectionist, scrupulous practitioners and there didn't have to be any consideration of protection or insurance.

But that is not the case. Which probably accounts for the data from the American Medical Association which shows that, although there has been a leveling off in the claims rate in contrast to the increases observed in the early and mid-1980s, insurance premiums paid by self-employed physicians from 1982 to 1988 have increased. They rose at an 18.3 percent annual rate during this period, increasing from $5,800 in 1982 to $15,900 in 1988.

So we can understand how Dr. Maciejczyk and his fellow doctors feel about it.

That is not to say we sympathize with just as unscrupulous attorneys who look for any excuse to encourage clients to sue, sue, sue. But when it is warranted, why not?

As for an individual—plaintiff or defendant—serving as his or her own attorney, which doesn't happen all that often . . . well . . . Dr. Maciejczyk doesn't advise it—in spite of his success.

But we must admit that the whole idea is intriguing. It's not that we would want to take business away from all those hungry attorneys out there—heaven help us—it's just that . . . well . . . perhaps it enforces the notion held by many that it is not necessary in every case, in every instance, for an individual in court to have a lawyer.

But don't tell that to those attorneys; that could be a real ego-buster. (I can see those letters coming already.)

There was yet another surprise in the Tadeusz Maciejczyk case.

It came from William Cacciatore, the attorney representing the other side. He called Dr. Maciejczyk to congratulate him on winning the case.

That also doesn't happen very often.

The World Seen from the Distance of a Small Village

Darryl Walker
CGH Medical Center
Sterling, Illinois

Tad -

    Congratulations on your win. I am very glad for you. I know you are a man of strong principle. I hope it was worth all your time and energy to prove your point and I hope it makes some difference.
    Again, my congratulations.

                                              Darryl Walker
                                              June 2, 1990

Book Three

Involvement: Feeling of Mission

Illinois Academy of Family Physicians
Andrea L. Anderson
Membership Coordinator

 I cannot tell whether I should or I shouldn't be re-elected for membership in the Illinois Academy of Family Physicians.
 I admit that during the last two years, I neglected my post-graduation education. That means, I was studying and reading, but I didn't take any formal courses. I didn't have the necessary peace of mind to undertake this kind of steady effort.
 In the last 3-1/2 years, I confronted a malpractice suit. The accusation was ridiculous and frivolous, but the pressure and the harassment were real. In this suit, I was my own defender against a professional lawyer from Rockford and against the expert testimony of Howard L.

The World Seen from the Distance of a Small Village

Ravenscraft, M.D., J.D., from Hebron, Kentucky. The final days of the trial were during the last days of May.

I won.

Now I am in a state of decompression. I still cannot concentrate. I need some rest and an adjustment to the next phase. I think that next Fall I will be ready to start normal post-graduate courses as I did for years before.

I know that at present, I do not meet your requirements. You have to make a decision.

I am sending you photocopies of newspaper clips. I feel that I should respond to questions raised in the editorial. What do you think? What would be your response?

Tadeusz Maciejczyk, M.D.
Milledgeville, June 7, 1990

Book Three

Guy Vander Jagt
Chairman of the GOP Victory Fund

Dear Sir:

Today I received your letter and a fresh, new 1990 sponsor card of the National Republican Congressional Committee.

Today also is a day, when for the first time, I have no money on hand to pay my nurse and my office secretary. After almost 3-1/2 years of an exhaustive malpractice suit, which I won alone, without a lawyer, I am tired and disheartened. I lost my faith in the present American system, which while using the old values in the front, shows not much to cheer about behind that façade.

I am still a Republican sympathizer, but I am not enthusiastic about Party politics and I cannot vote for candidates just because the Party is sponsoring them. Particularly here I refused to vote for Lynn Martin. (I include my previous letters where I said why.) I am still not sure how to vote for a Congressman seat and I have to confess, that the Democratic candidate looks to me much better material for a responsible representative.

I write this letter simply to tell you not to spend more money for more letters to me. After years of strain, my practice has become very limited and I am not rich enough to be just a sponsor. Because my charges to patients were always low, the present Medicare reimbursement for me is not enough to keep going. I lost my faith in the American political process and I have even no more desire to try to present my point of view to the Central Party offices in Washington. It is just a loss of time. Nobody there is interested in ideas—only in contributions. It is not an institution to serve society. It is only short-sighted self-service. The partisan letters from the Party, where the issues are absent or very shallow and the epithets plentiful and poisonous, are not mobilizing me. Rather they are repelling; they denigrate the Party and somehow they contributed to my loss of respect for the Party.

I know that my usefulness to the Party is measured only by the amount of my contributions. My intentions of dialogue with the Party failed. Nobody ever answered my letters. Apparently for the Party, such a membership as mine has only one meaning and serves one purpose: pay and never tell anything off the line. I am willing to sacrifice, but first I have to believe and I have to trust.

The World Seen from the Distance of a Small Village

I am sorry that I am writing this letter this way, but I am trying to be honest.

Tadeusz Maciejczyk, M.D.
Milledgeville, July 5, 1990

Book Three

Editor
Time Magazine

Dear Sir:

    I hope "twenty-something" was read by many, especially the young. It showed well our image reflected in the eyes and in the souls of the youngest generation that now starts to enter into public life.
    Two centuries ago, America was created by the men-giants, gifted with an idea, with vision, with the capacity to achieve, to concentrate and to sacrifice.
    America of today is not producing such men anymore.
    The post-war generations rushed to material comforts and gratifications and to the instant, easy success. America's rapidly progressing decline came as a natural consequence. In politics we navigate without any distant vision or purpose. In economics we plunged cheerfully into an enormous debt. In the extreme case of the attitude, which led to such a downfall, the men responsible for the S&L criminal theft do not even show a blush of shame or repentance. In the arts, the present mediocre creations are not trying to call attention and interest of the public by its own merits, but by the spice of pornography or even sacrilege. In science we are losing our previous forestage. In the basic units of the family life, we created a mess and we raised millions of children emotionally marked for life by the childhood's lack of love, of parental closeness and guidance.
    Any greatness to crystallize and to manifest itself requires a spiritual strength, stamina, and a strong dose of Puritanical self-discipline. In present America all those requirements were by-passed in the general relaxation of manners and in the impatient expectations of glamour, of an easy success with the minimum of obligations.
    If the new generation, now approaching a public state, is looking around with caution, slowly making their own minds and their own approaches to live, without hasty splashing into the existing pool of lifestyles, then it could be that finally we can expect a renewal and a new time for greatness.

                              Tadeusz Maciejczyk, M.D.
                              Milledgeville, July 19, 1990

The World Seen from the Distance of a Small Village

Editor
The Daily Gazette
Re: "A Balancing Act by Martin"

Dear Sir:

The constitutional amendment of a balance budget always was and always will be an excuse to not even try to change the present condition. It is a debate to avoid a true debate, which nobody wants to start or to press for, because then the naked realities would put pressure on us to act, to be honest, and to show the real guts, which vanished almost completely from our political life long ago.

Mrs. Martin is right. The taxpayers are already bearing a sufficient burden and want fiscal discipline from Washington.

As everybody else, I am not for new taxes. But I can better understand the "change of lips" of Pres. Bush than the heroic stand of Mrs. Martin against next taxation.

Every thinking man has a right to change his mind after looking at mounting evidence and after careful assessment. I would agree to this new call of our President for a sacrifice, but only under very special conditions. Such a sacrifice of all the taxpayers should not give to our beloved members of Congress a new blank check to spend, and to show their sweetness to the electorate, but would be a call for a GENERAL MOBILIZATION of the nation to fight the approaching disaster. In such a call for mobilization, the causes, the purpose, the strategy, the goals and the obligations for everybody would be spelled out clearly and without ambiguity. Such mobilization would mean a total war against those elements of our present national life, which brought us the chains of our enormous debt and our continuous decline on the wide front of our life as a nation.

Mrs. Martin's hard stand against taxation looks phony to me. Less than one year ago, and only a few days after a special session to raise the ceiling of our national debt because the government had no money to pay its obligations, Mrs. Martin was presiding over an extraordinary pay raise for the members of Congress.

Was Mrs. Martin not aware that the congressional paychecks were coming from taxation? What was her logic in that legislation of Congressional salary increases while being in such opposition to the new taxes? Did she think about reductions in other obligations or services, and if so, what was in her mind?

Book Three

At this point, I would like to ask the Editor of the *Daily Gazette* to give us the names of all the members of Congress who voted for the enormous pay increase for themselves and now are against a tax increase. Could the *Daily Gazette* send them the letters asking them the same questions that I am presenting to Mrs. Martin and then to tabulate those answers for us—the readers?

> Tadeusz Maciejczyk, M.D.
> Milledgeville, July 22, 1990

The World Seen from the Distance of a Small Village

Citizens for a Sound Economy
(A survey on Congressional Pay Raises)
Washington, D.C.

Points 1, 2, and 3:

I am sending to you my letters in which I expressed my protest against the congressional pay raise. In those letters, I formulated my arguments and my points of view. Some of those letters were published in the local press.

Point 4:

The money from campaign contributions, spent or not, is public money, given in trust for certain political dreams and actions. They were never meant to be purely personal gifts. At its best, they were expressing a faith and a confidence of contributors in the integrity and capacity of the candidates for the realization of those dreams. At worst, they were the payments for bad and secret deals, contrary to the public interest, but even then, those payments were related to the power of the office, not to a person.

In both of those extremes, and between, those campaign contributions were related to the functions and to the attributes of the office. They were never intended to be purely personal, disinterested gifts or a compilation of the office salaries.

Because of this, the unspent money from campaign contributions is public money, given in trust, and with special public and common good intentions. This money should remain a public fund for realizing those or similar intentions. The public official, after his retirement, can express his views for what public purpose that money could be used best and could be a member of the trustees for those funds, but he should never take those funds for personal use.

In this sense, the act of personal appropriation after retirement of the campaign contribution, voted by Congress, is a very special measurement of the moral condition of our present Congress. It can only parallel the scandalous betrayal of the public trust by the S&L officials. The names of those members of Congress, who made use of that self-serving, selfish, and astonishingly shameless Congressional law, should be made public and put under the proper light. Legalized or not, it was an act of stealing no different from any other criminal theft.

Point 5

I consider that Congressional public appearances and consequent speaking fees are not bad in themselves. They can be useful and challenging, increasing the understanding of the matters for consideration or for voting. To be positive, those public appearances and speeches should be authentic.

Such speeches should always be a labor of the speaker showing his personal homework, his understanding of the subject, his own evaluations and conclusions, for which he takes the responsibility. They should show the maturity and the intellectual growth of the performer. Such speeches never should be just a reading of a text, already prepared by somebody else, unassimilated, and forgotten a moment after the arranged show was over.

The invitation, or the speaking fee, should never be considered payment for voting. Especially after such a paid invitation, the justification of the cast vote, or of the related lobbying activity, should be carefully scrutinized. The purpose of the visit, the lesson from such a visit, should appear in the Congressional newspaper and in the newspapers of the part of the country of the involved representative.

Only after fulfillment of those three points, the speaking fee could be considered as earned, and only in such a way those speaking arrangements could contribute to the quality of performance of our representatives.

I want to go beyond the strict limits of this survey. I am sending to you some of my other letters that ultimately deal with the basis for a sound economy and a sound quality of life in the U.S. The future of this country, and of the world will depend on our approach to our difficulties.

I wish you luck in your work.

                                        Tadeusz Maciejczyk, M.D.
                                        Milledgeville, August 9, 1990

P.S. I would be grateful if you would read all these letters and maybe tell me your point of view in all these subjects.

The World Seen from the Distance of a Small Village

Lewis K. Uhler
President of the National Tax Limitation Committee

And

Congressman Newt Gingrich
National Taxpayer Action Project
Washington, D.C.

Dear Gentlemen:

Finally I have to tell you what I think.

I receive many letters from Washington (several every week) in which, after pages of partisan and superficial presentation of the particular problem, and after a few suggestive and obvious to answer questions, I am asked for a donation for an action, which would cure, save and sooth our painful perception of Washington's dirt. The promising remedies are never clear, and no sign of any action or improvement is visible after such consultations and collections. Never are such letters followed by the next one that would explain how much money was collected and how that money was spent and what the results of the particular action were. Generally, what followed was an other questionnaire with another request for money.

This avalanche of questionnaires and surveys appears to me more and more to be a very questionable, very abusive black market business, practiced by certain Washington circles with accelerating frequency. This business is pasturing over good will and a readiness for sacrifice of many good people.

Naturally, those activities have a distant harvest. They create a growing distrust and also growing distance. They are spreading a non-involvement, suspicions and even sarcastic or cynical responses to every move in the Capital. They undermine the involvement even in good ideas or policies, because they act like a story about the boy who called wolf. It creates a feeling that the country's malaise has no cure and no hope.

The consequences of such a massive, unscrupulous and probably lucrative, but never checked Washington "industry," for the country's health is negative. As in everything, the communication with the people, the questionnaires, the surveys are good if they are used wisely, if they have depth, and if they are not abused by charlatans.

Book Three

To help you in your gathering of information, I filled up the survey page of your questionnaire. I send you no money, but I send my other letters that can increase the scope of the information for your study.

I gave you here my sincere reaction to your questionnaire and I think that is my greatest contribution.

I wish you the best in your work.

Tadeusz Maciejczyk, M.D.
Milledgeville, August 26, 1990

The World Seen from the Distance of a Small Village

William E. Dannemeyer
U.S. Congress
Washington, D.C. 20069-1075

Dear Sir:

Yesterday I received two letters from Washington: yours and another from the Republican Presidential Task Force. The content of both was similar. Both were asking for monetary support for the ongoing campaign. After different explanations, in both those letters the money, and only the money, was the center rhetoric and the answer to all challenges of the election time. The inquiry for the issues, for the best message to the people, for ideas, for tactics, for the search for possible new thoughts, were absent in both. In the U.S., more and more only the money can buy everything. The parties and the leaders affirm that everything goes, if the price is right.

In your case, in the same way as you, I am sure that the Congressman who breaks the laws should not be allowed to make the laws.

Any leadership is a full time institution. It cannot sustain itself, cannot attract and cannot grow without an obligatory uniformity of behavior on the job and at its free time. No leadership can survive if it practices one set of moral principles while on the stage and another, completely different, when the curtain goes down. Our private activities behind closed doors are a thousand times closer to our hearts in shaping our inside, our soul, our character, or fidelity and our values. It was said long ago that no one can sincerely serve two masters at the same time.

If our Congress wants to be trusted and respected by the ordinary, average American, it cannot permit itself the luxury of a double standard in behavior of its members: leading, by giving an example is the more effective way to lead.

I have no doubt that the use of dirty tricks by Pres. Nixon, as a sure way to win election, gave a practical lesson to many people. History will count and will evaluate properly this special contribution of pres. Nixon to the story of America. The dirty tricks went down to the application in our daily life by many and weakened the very foundation of this nation. The multiplication of scandals, whether they were discovered or not, at every level and in every field, made our efficacy, our economy, our internal strength, slip down.

In this letter, I would like to convince you that for your campaign victory you have a very powerful point and message. The people today

Book Three

are hungry for every sigh of decency in our leaders. They want our leaders to be not only more or less knowledgeable administrators in their office, they want them to be also the guides and the teachers in our private and national journey through time.

But, if you want to prevail with your message and win, you have to mobilize yourself completely for this fight, stand firm, and accept all the consequences of this action, including the worst. You have to be ready to lose your Congressional seat for the truth. In the struggle for what is moral and right, there is no room for a convenient accommodation. If you rise to your fight in such a way, the people will sense and will understand your aims and you will grow as a person. If you stand on this issues in this way, you will become not only the representative in Congress of the people, but also their guide and their teacher.

I do not want to present to you a mere phraseology in this very important matter. Recently I was living through a similar situation and I had to take a stand, or to shrink down. I send you some papers to illustrate this.

I urge you again. Do not put your trust in the almighty power of money. America did this and America became weaker, sicker and up to its ears in debts. Put your trust in the redeeming might of a belief. Be a knight in your fight for moral transformation in Congress.

I send you $25.00 to help in the basic logistics of your struggle.

And I send you my best wishes.

> Tadeusz Maciejczyk
> Milledgeville, September 3, 1990

The World Seen from the Distance of a Small Village

Albert E. Mitchler
Executive Director
Republican Presidential Task Force
425 2nd Street NE
Washington, D.C. 20002

Dear Sir:

I am enormously grateful to the Republican Presidential Task Force for sending me a real and free check for $25.00, for considering me worth of "special recognition," for inviting me into the Candidate Escrow Funding program and, as if all this were not enough, for giving me a place in the "Who's Who" of the Republican Party.

I am a simple person, from a distant, small place and I am not used to so many honors. Also, here we are used to speaking a simple language. Your letter is so enormously sweet and seductive that it puts a question mark on its sincerity. Your presentation of the attractions of your proposition is testing my vanity. And I was never vain.

I am uneasy, because I never borrow money for something that is not absolutely essential. If I cannot afford something, I am just happy without. And I do not understand how the expensive Hi-Tech Voter Identification, Hi-Tech Voter Registration or Hi-Tech Voter Turnout Programs can present us with better candidates and would make Election Day more meaningful and more attractive to us, the voters.

Not long ago, I was reading in our local paper, *The Daily Gazette*, that the debate between the two candidates for representative in our district, was disappointing and boring. The candidates sounded like their party automats. They showed no individuality behind the indoctrinated rhetoric.

In this situation, the need for an enormous amount of money, for trivializing and masquerading the election in the time when we, as a nation, have so many really urgent needs, looks really grotesque. It illustrates exactly the soul of our parties.

Instead of being a vibrant center for a search, accumulation and discussion of ideas, and finding solutions and new ways into the future, the parties formed a closed club, hungry for power, but empty inside. In place of intellect and honesty, the parties turned to intrigue, tricks and superficial slogans supporting them with spending unlimited amounts of public money and public trust. The effort is done not to lead in the best non-partisan directions, but to get an edge, and to outsmart the adversary.

The enormous amount of money spent during campaigns is not used for the research of the existing problems and its remedies, not for a genuine search for a talented and dedicated people, whom we have without a doubt, but to impose on society their obedient followers, who would be good rubber stamps, not even for the good of the country, but for the party.

To me, the electoral campaign is looking more and more like a carnival parade of Rio de Janeiro, where behind the face masks, it is impossible to recognize the real person. The disguise of such a campaign-carnival is costly, naturally. The result, a gray atmosphere that they leave behind after the Election Day, is depressing. Our election is not renovating and not revitalizing any more. They only procrastinate and accentuate the old ills.

It looks to me that the parties have to change and reform, eliminating their elements of stagnation and sclerosis, or they will be brushed away by an inevitable social change.

Finally, I want to thank you again for your tempting invitation. The problem is that I do not like the atmosphere of the closed clubs. I want fresh air to breathe.

Tadeusz Maciejczyk
Milledgeville, September 6, 1990

P.S. I include a copy of my letter to Rep. William E. Dannemeyer. I received your letter on the same day and both together helped me to formulate my view.

The World Seen from the Distance of a Small Village

The following letter is in regard to an interview with Ted Koppel on ABC Television's *Nightline* where Dr. George Habash promised increased terrorist activities.

Dr. George Habash
A leader of the Palestinian People

Dear Sir:

I saw you yesterday on television speaking about the present problem of the Middle East and I decided to write to you.

I know that I am only a countryside doctor here in America, whose voice in the world's arena has very little importance, but in the same way, as I wrote to Vice-President Bush six years ago asking him for proper consideration of the Palestinian cause, with the same sincere wishes for the Palestinian people, I am asking you to fight for the rights of your nation, but always in a noble open way that in the end would never depreciate the dignity of your nation and of your rights.

I know the bitterness and the desperation of the subjugated nation. I am from the country where for decades and generations this song: "whether we have to die in the field, or to rot in the taigas of Siberia, from our labor and our toil, Poland will rise to live," gave strength to endure, to fight and not to lose hope.

I can imagine also how tempting it is in your national condition to look to Saddam Hussein for leadership and for fulfillment of your hopes.

But Saddam Hussein is not the present time Saladin of the Arab world. Saladin was noble, was generous and was great. Saddam Hussein gives the impression of a bank thief who, when discovered, covers himself with the innocent by-passers to reach safety. He started his career as an assassin and morally, he never grew into anything better. He was using the people, or nations, when he needed them. He had no restraint from stabbing them in the back, if that would give him any advantage. He killed many of his previous associates; he poisoned the Kurds and he terrorizes now the people of Kuwait who were supporting him during his long struggle with Iran. He needs and he uses now the hunger of the Palestinian people for all Arabic leader and their sincere enthusiasm to believe him and to make sacrifices for him. But what can you expect from him if he will not need you any more? Judging from his past, he will use you, he will dispose of you when the world scenario suggests for him to do so.

Book Three

I do not think that Saddam Hussein has any merit to be the leader of the Arab world. The Arabs and the Palestinians within them, deserve true greatness for leadership. Terror, terror of killing the innocent, terror that Saddam Hussein practices now on his Arabic brothers in Kuwait, brings only contempt and condemnation—never greatness.

I would like to truly wish the best for the Palestinians. The years of suffering was for them, a teacher and a guide. The future will test them. I hope, that in such a test, the Palestinian people will not lose their human face and will grow in dignity.

I send you copies of my previous letter to Vice President Bush. I am also tempted to send you my special letter about forgiveness.

Again, I wish you the best.

Tadeusz Maciejczyk
September 27, 1990

The World Seen from the Distance of a Small Village

Edgar Bronfman
President
World Jewish Congress
P.O. Box 90400
Washington, D.C. 20077-7786

Dear Sir:

This week, as almost every other week, I received several letters from Washington asking for my signature on one or another petition and for generous financial help. Your letter caught my attention because of its special appearance.

As you, I also have a strong desire to eliminate hate from our life on earth.

Hate has different targets, different directions and different intensities. Depending on this, it can be called anti-Semitism, racism, class struggle, the hate of different ideas, of a neighbor, even a hate of ourselves. To diminish, to eliminate this hate requires sincerity, self-examination, and work from the ground up. Diplomacy, talking to leaders, or a massive signature collection will change little. Hate among people cannot be eliminated by decree, by leaders' agreement, or by political pressure. Tolerance and elimination of hate can grow only from our own profound transformation and the consequent change in our acts that are like seeds for the life of the future.

I do not believe that the kind of action that you are proposing would reach the souls, the feelings of those who are inclined to hate. Only our conduct, our example, our own homework can.

I am not sending you money. I am just recovering from my recent malpractice suit in which I defended myself without a lawyer and which I won. My practice is limited now. Besides, I never knew how to get rich from practicing medicine. I never knew how to charge.

But, as an act of solidarity with your general idea, I am signing your petition.

I am also sending you a copy of my recent letter to Dr. George Habash, to whom I also sent copies of my previous letters to Pres. Bush and to Sen. Paul Simon.

As an act of frankness, without which any fight against hate cannot success, I also send you a copy of my letter to "Crescent County Foundation for Medical Care," where I described one episode of my life. The lieutenant from Internal Security, who came to arrest me, was a Jew. I do

Book Three

not have any resentment for his conduct to the Jewish nation. I understand that he acted as an individual.

I wish you the best in your work. I wish the best for the Jewish nation. As a child, I had good friends who were Jewish.

Tadeusz Maciejczyk

Milledgeville, October 7, 1990

The World Seen from the Distance of a Small Village

Internal Revenue Service
Kansas City

I received your notification today and I am appalled with dismay, disbelief and frustration. What you are demanding is not an act of justice, not an act of social or political wisdom, it is not a foundation to build a future on. It is a show of destructive smartness and a practice sanctified by some artificial robbery laws. This sort of procedure will destroy the confidence, the good will and the belief in the future for this country. If this is the way to compensate for the budget deficit and the national debt, it is very shortsighted and will fire back.

I confess that I am not an expert, not a lover, not an admirer of the massive, rapidly growing paper work that suffocates more and more the true work. Just today, I was in the nursing home where in the last week a new line of offices were added in spite of that the Home has the same amount of patients and fewer nurses than previously. The burden created from the bureaucratic malignancy is thrown on the people. The cost of everything is going up. We have more and more people who cannot afford medical care. The insurance companies became more discriminative with admissions and more costly. Just now, I have a problem with a wife of a teacher who retired, lost his school insurance and the extra insurance refused to cover her costs as a result of being admitted to the hospital for a mildly obstructive pulmonary disease. The life in the U.S. is more and more devastating, dehumanized and frustrating. The simplicity of life and the effectiveness of the simplicity are more and more crashing down under the weight of the bureaucracy.

I tried to respond as well as I knew how to your previous letters and I had the impression that all the questions were answered. Apparently the hunt for pretext and for money became more relentless.

In this way, today, I received a penalty assessment for $2,573.92 for "intentional disregard of the filing requirements." I received no more specifications and no explanation. What is the "requested period?" What is the dating of my transgression? How many? How can I get the papers to fill them out?

I thought I was doing the best I could.

With your letter I am stunned and I am angered. If this is the environment in which I will have to work, then it is better that I quit working and apply for Social Security. I just recently resolved a protracted and nerve wracking malpractice suit in which I defended myself and I won. At present, my practice is diminished. I feel that I am necessary here; that I am helping the people, but with this additional stone thrown on me, when the work situation becomes increasingly ugly, why try?

I cannot pay you this amount of the unexpected penalty in ten days. I am sorry. I never knew how to get rich from my M.D. degree. The patients always look to me as victims, not as sacks of money. I have always had difficulty paying the employees. And I have an aversion to borrowing. I will pay you this new squeeze money as soon as I am able to gather it.

Because your action pushed me into the prospect of forced retirement, before I make this decision, I will send a copy of your letter and this answer to Pres. Bush asking him for his advice.

The problem is that I wanted to work at least until the university graduation of my youngest daughter. I do not like to retire. But either I like to work, if I do not see a point in working when I do not know when I will be pushed behind the next corner or after another day. The realities of life in the U.S. are changing. I never was a pessimist, but I am becoming one.

I wish you a big harvest from this new trick. What will be next? Who care?

                                    Tadeusz Maciejczyk, M.D.
                                    Milledgeville, October 1990

The World Seen from the Distance of a Small Village

Congressman Guy Vander Jagt
National Republican congressional Committee
Washington, D.C.

Dear Sir:

I couldn't remain deaf to your many letters and appeals written in the name of the Republican Party and for the sake of the effectiveness of the rest of President Bush's presidency.

My letter probably will not fulfill your expectations and maybe even will not be read at all. So many of my previous letters were followed only by silence and then, by another, disconnected, un-answering print-letter. Why would this my letter be different?

I am not sending you money for this campaign. I do not feel like being a part of it. In this campaign I am used only as a potential money donor. Of course, I am an M.D. What I was trying to say never was counted, never was considered. The party reaches to the periphery only for donations and for votes. Otherwise, the party behaves like a closed circle of insiders, a kind of perpetual royalty, distant from the reality of life of the ordinary person to whom it directs occasional smiles, expecting from them adherence, faithfulness or even adoration. In such an arrangement, there is no room for a common experience, togetherness or mutual understanding.

It looks to me like both parties became increasingly isolated, distant institutions, dwelling in the glories of the past, unable to evolve, required by the rapidly passing time. The parties because of this have very little to offer for today and still less for tomorrow.

The parties were supposed to lead our society towards the future, to discover, to select the best leaders, to cultivate and to test a common vision, to renovate constantly, giving the necessary new frames for changing life situations. The people are willing and are waiting . . . but the parties are empty, providing us only with shallow slogans, avoiding issues and risk-requiring stands. They force on us their old, worn-out tags and cronies, masquerading the elections to the point that nobody knows who is who. The old honesty that breeds confidence and true adherence, does not exist any more. The pre-election propaganda is filled with dirt and shows little courage, reality or constructive thinking. Each candidate is presented to us, not objectively, as he is. Candidates are shown to us behind two different masks. One, put on by his party, paints him in wonderful colors, another put on him by the opponent, is ugly and filled with dirt. Those changing masks are flaring constantly before our eyes on every TV screen, disorienting, discouraging, depressing and making us wonder whether to bother to participate in such a denigrating show.

To keep this special circus going, we, the voters, are expected to give generous contributions and to smile with admiration. We are losing our orientation because we are intentionally blinded and misled. By such propaganda, we are discouraged to think. We are expected not to be individuals, but a party partisan and an enthusiastic nameless crowd.

In the vacuum of thought and character, both parties are turning more and more toward an unexciting popularity contest. The meaning of the parties already lost its previous qualities, content and substance. What remains from them is only a frame. The parties are not elevating the nation any more. The parties are only trivializing what before was considered noble and worthy of living.

The approaching elections are not exciting me. They are not exciting many people around me. Frustration prevails. For whom to vote?

In such a situation, spending money to push the people to the voting places only increases the bitterness. The Republican party didn't make true preparation, made no effort, did no homework, no search for candidates, for new characters, new talent. The party went the easy way, giving us no choice but to confirm the old, unappetizing candidacies and party's rubber stamps.

In my local situation, in our state and district, I cannot vote for the Republican candidates.

I will not vote for Lynn Martin. If her readiness to sacrifice for her country was illustrated by her role in the Congressional pay hike just a few days after a special session to increase the debt ceiling because the government had no money for its daily operations, then I do not want to see her in any governmental position for making decisions. Except for this, she can be witty and graceful, but I do not see her in a size or character to be a U.S. Senator.

I will not vote for Mr. Hallock. His personal and his family life are not very exemplary. During all this campaign, I did not see in him anything convincing. I do not want him to represent me.

My reservations in voting for Mr. Edgar are different. He represents the continuation of the Thomson administration and this is enough to make me think twice. If Gov. Thomson lasted to long in his post, it was not because of his merit, but due to the Democratic disarray. All the state wants a change.

It looks to me that in the Nov. election we should have not one, but two candidates from each party. This would give the people a stimulus

The World Seen from the Distance of a Small Village

to think, to be a factor, not just a manipulated mass. It would rejuvenate and renovate the party and would give a better chance to select more accurately those, who would like to be our leaders.

Finally, not a number, but a quality of the people of the party in Congress, or elsewhere, will help to elevate the image of the presidency and of Pres. Bush. The exemplary minority will give the President a better chance to govern than a mediocre mass.

I am sorry I was forced to write this letter.

Tadeusz Maciejczyk
Milledgeville, October 16, 1990

Book Three

Francis A. David, M.D.
Publisher of *Private Practice*
Oklahoma City, OK

Dear Sir:

After reading your editorial about a doctor who received an extremely upsetting letter from his state board of medical examiners, I decided that maybe it would not be too late to send you the copy of my letter to such a board, after a similarly upsetting letter from them.

Last Spring, after previous many sharp notes from the Crescent Counties Foundation for Medical Care, because I hospitalize different times "unnecessarily," I received from them a cold and brief letter threatening my license to practice because at that time I didn't hospitalize a patient. That patient collapsed then at home, was taken to the hospital by ambulance and died shortly after admission.

It is good to have conditions that stimulate extra effort, extra attention, extra sacrifice in dedication. All this goes together with good inspiring leadership.

It is very destructive, if those, who are in a position to be the leaders, use this position not to elevate, but to suppress, to police, to spread uncertainty and distrust and to create, in order to work, an anxious need to be surrounded by a costly wall of protective insurance.

The tyranny of the present siege put on the medical profession is far beyond the need for elimination of incompetence or excess. Those measures are implementing legally safe medical conduct, but without warmth and washed of the human approach to those who suffer.

The medical profession shaped in this way will be morally weak and will never provide for the true health needs of society. The cost of this kind of medicine will always be staggering. Such medicine will always be infested by parasites, ready to suck the last drop of blood from the medical professionals and from society. And we are on the way to such a situation.

I send to you my last letter to the Family Practice Assoc. as well as the copy of my letter to the Counties Board.

I wish you the best, especially because it is Christmas time and because your articles are checking well the pulse of medical work.

Tadeusz Maciejczyk, M.D.
Milledgeville, December 9, 1990

The World Seen from the Distance of a Small Village

John W. Rapp, Jr.
Circuit Court Judge
Mt. Carroll, IL

Dear Sir:

For some time I walked with the idea that at the end of the year, when all the echoes and emotions related to my trial had died out, I would send you copies of all my papers that were inspired by that trial. In those years, I wrote to many places, trying to get support or solidarity with my stand. I tried in them to explain the reasons why I was confronting the accusations differently from the other doctors in my situation.

If those letters apparently were in vain, because they didn't bring me help, or even sympathy, they had a different effect on me. Writing them helped me to clarify my own ideas, to formulate my answers to the premises, to have a peace within me in spite of the exterior turmoil.

I do not know. Maybe the volume of all those letters will be worthless to you. Some of my thoughts and beliefs can be naïve. But, my trial was different in many ways from others' malpractice suits. For sure, I am not a lawyer, and I do not think like a lawyer. The situation in which I was put was completely unfamiliar to me. My thinking, my actions therefore, were different, were truly original. Nothing in my reasoning or in my conduct could be dulled by routine. There had to be some kind of freshness and authenticity in my understanding of the problem, in my conclusions and in my responses.

Precisely because of this, I am sending you those papers. Maybe somehow they can be useful to find a more human, more just approach to the avalanche of malpractice accusations that leave behind them so much pain, so many tragedies, so many somber consequences for the particular person, for society, for the whole nation.

Because it is the time of Christmas, I wish you the best in your life and in your work.

Tadeusz Maciejczyk, M.D.
Milledgeville, December 20, 1990

Book Three

Dear Friend - American G.I.:

I want to send you my best wishes.

I know that it would be better if there would be no need for you to be there. A peace is wonderful. I would like to prevent, avoid war.

But my anxiety would be much bigger if this present conflict would be resolved only partially, or not at all. If Saddam would retreat, would retain his strength, even at the price of retreating from Kuwait, the future of the world would become uncertain.

He would be hailed as a hero who stood up to America and the whole world. The Arab masses would flock to him. No present Arab government would hold for long. The opposing resistance would not last long. The Saddam Hussein domination would extend across the Muslim lands. For the oil money he would easily acquire weapons and within not long **he** would dictate and would blackmail America and everything else. He would know how to revenge, how to humiliate, how to show his omnipotence. Who then would dare to risk the destruction?

This present war is not a war for gas and its price. It is a fight for existence that has no precedence in world history. In the present moment, in this conflict, I do not see a place for diplomacy. The world is on the crossroads, whatever the dove would tell. In this way I understand the need for your presence there. I pray for you.

Tadeusz Maciejczyk
December 29, 1990

The World Seen from the Distance of a Small Village

Sen. Paul Simon and Family

Dear Friends:

I thank you for your Christmas card. I wanted to respond to you immediately, but somehow I became distracted by different problems and I am writing to you now, during the New Year's Day. But, in the same way as it was before, I send you my best wishes for your personal life and for your public work. I am glad to see you were reelected. And also, I understand your joy of becoming a grandfather because last December, for the first time, I ascended also to this family rank.

Your Christmas card was a surprise to me because for a long time I didn't keep any contact with you.

During these last few years, I was confronted with a malpractice accusation. Against this accusation I stood alone. Except for the local people, I didn't get any help or even signs of solidarity from anybody. The threats against me were real and were ugly. After three and one-half years of legal maneuvering and without any lawyer on my side, I won in two days of courtroom arguments.

After the trial, I felt a sensation of relief in the first few days. But then, I felt empty. The summer appeared to me like a convalescent time after a long illness. I looked with apprehension upon my life and work here in the U.S. I felt empty inside. I am sending you some of my letters from that time.

Now we have the situation in the Gulf. I have the impression that you and I are looking at the situation differently. My experience with the Hitlerian type of behavior was more immediate than yours. The long-range plans of Saddam Hussein are frightening to me. If he is not stopped drastically, if he retains his power, he will be in a condition to completely change the world's order. To do this his way, he will have not the slightest moral restraint. The clue as to how it would be can be seen are in the history of his peace talks with the Kurdish representation in 1971. The survival of the Kurdish leader Barzani was due only to a special fate, or Arabian kismet. The story of that peace diplomacy of Saddam Hussein is very instructive. It should be read today with special interest. As I see it, the present confrontation in the Gulf is not for the price of the oil. It is for the order of the world that we will leave for our children and grandchildren.

Again, I wish you the best in your work.

Tadeusz Maciejczyk
Milledgeville, January 1, 1991

Book Three

George Bush
President of the United States

Dear Mr. President:

I am sending you the copy of my letter to some G.I. in the Persian Gulf and a copy of my last letter to Senator Paul Simon, in which I was trying to explain why the negotiations with Saddam Hussein in the long range can be deplorable and dangerous to the U.S. and to the world.

In the present days, when the diplomats from many countries are rushing to Baghdad as years ago, they rushed to Hitler, it is time to put into question the values of the diplomatic promises and of the moral standards of Saddam Hussein. His past record of his diplomatic maneuvers should be scrutinized and made public.

It would be a good time to remember and to seriously take into consideration the Saddam Hussein methods during his diplomatic talks with Kurdish leaders in 1971. At that time, one of the mullahs of Hussein's delegation was persuaded to put into himself a subcutaneous microphone to record exactly the decisive concluding words of Kurdish leader Barzani. In such a decisive moment, he was supposed to come close to Barzani and to press the button. He was not informed that what he was activating was not a microphone, but a bomb. He was killed. Barzani survived because a servant stepped between to put tea on the table.

How much has Saddam Hussein improved since that time? What is the real value of his assurances? What are the dangers of letting him survive the present conflict, retaining his prestige? These considerations are really frightening.

I want to wish you the best in your work.

Tadeusz Maciejczyk
Milledgeville, January 3, 1991

The World Seen from the Distance of a Small Village

Lee Atwater
Chairman of the Republican Party
National Headquarters

Dear Sir:

I thank you for your letter in which you called me "a very special American and an active citizen with the strong interest and knowledge of American politics." After this introduction, I was asked to become a sustaining member of the Republican National Committee. "The President needed me on his team."

I received that letter just after Pres. Bush's inaugural address to the joint Congress. I was still under the impression of that great speech that moved me deeply and enlarged my image of the President. I was ready to cooperate, to give the maximum of myself.

In spite of this, I didn't sign your membership card. The problem is that, against your advice, I read your letter before signing. That letter cooled my enthusiasm completely.

In this time of enormous change, with multiple crises and challenges at home, with the Persian Gulf War going on, with the unquestionable need for a new look on ourselves and for the fundamental reshaping of the world's present structure—at the entrance into the next century, I expected to see in your letter new ideas, new depth, new horizons and new spirit.

In that letter, I found only the same old small battlefields of Washington filled with blaming somebody else and worn out slogans. That letter, with only small corrections, could be a perfect copy of any other similar letters from the last decade. That letter was not uplifting, not moving. It was washed of any noble emotions, of any intellectual elaboration, or any sense of responsibility. It was truly a very depressing lecture. Whoever wrote that letter is not a growing person. He permanently stays in a dead span of time, inside the small world of Washington's politicking. His vision is not reaching any open horizon and his labor will not build the future.

I would like to be involved, to be drafted into the world or realization of our best vision for the life of the world of the next decades and centuries. I would like this work to be intense, wise and worthy of whatever sacrifices are necessary. I would like to feel that such a work would elevate me and would elevate all those around me to a higher inner life. The 19th century Polish poet Cyprian Norwid, in his poem about human labor, finished it with this sentence: "Do you want to know how

Book Three

important your work is? Consider how quickly your thoughts turn back to God from that labor." [1] From my experience I know that a good work is bringing us always nearer to God, is giving us special dignity, special strength and a special inner peace in spite of outside dangers. Pres. Bush, in his inaugural speech to Congress, told of this with different words.

And so, whenever you consider this kind of work, I will be more than happy to give the best from me. I will not join your present structures or programs. Pres. Bush, America and the world deserves more. Much more.

In your life, I wish you the best.

Tadeusz Maciejczyk
Milledgeville, February 10, 1991

P.S. To make my intentions clear, I am sending a copy of this letter to The White House.

The World Seen from the Distance of a Small Village

Editor of *Time Magazine*

Dear Sir:

I want to read to you my letter to an American G.I. that I wrote to him at Christmas time through Roger Clapin G.I. Gift Pac. in Washington. I would like to ask you to send this letter to Rev. Richard Landsale, a correspondent to *Time*'s Letters to the Editors, February 18, 1991.

I wrote the following in that letter:

I know that it would be better if there would be no need for you to be there. A peace is wonderful. I would like to prevent, avoid war.

But my anxiety would be much bigger if this present conflict would be resolved only partially, or not at all. If Saddam would retreat, would retain his strength, even at the price of retreating from Kuwait, the future of the world would become uncertain.

He would be hailed as a hero who stood up to America and the whole world. The Arab masses would flock to him. A present Arab government would hold for long. The opposing resistance would not last long. The Saddam Hussein domination would extend across Moslem world—about half a billion people. The opposition, the resistance would not last long in any place. For the oil money, he would easily acquire all the weapons, even the most destructive ones and would blackmail America everything else. He would know how to take revenge, how to humiliate, how to show his omnipotence. Who then would dare to risk the destruction?

This present war is not a war for gas and its price. It is a fight for existence that has no precedence in world history. At no time has any person with desire for grandiosity and with no scruples or morals had a potential for such an extensive domination and such horrible weaponry at his disposal. The present moment, in this conflict has no place for diplomacy, whatever the doves would say. The world is on the crossroads.

If you would like to put any part of this letter in your Letters to the Editor column, please do it,

Tadeusz Maciejczyk
Milledgeville, Febr. 14, 1991

Book Three

Daniel J. Ryan
Navy Officer Programs
Glenview, IL 60026-9989

Dear Sir:

I thank you for your second letter suggesting to me to consider medical service in the Navy. Of course, I would like to have such an experience and such an adventure.

I have no sea experience. Once, I crossed Gibraltar on a small vessel. The water was rough. Everybody on the vessel was sick and vomiting and I was among the very few who enjoyed every minute of that trip. I have either military discipline training. I was in the Underground in Poland during World War II. The discipline there existed, but it was different, affecting the exterior less and more the commitment to the cause. I would be ready to go anyplace the Navy would send me, except submarines. Claustrophobia would break me.

Against all these desires for acceptance of the offer, I have two outstanding problems. The first is my age. I was born November 1, 1923. I am now 67. I am in good health. Daily, I take one tablet of Vasotec - 10 mg., which controls my mild hypertension. I do not smoke; I do not drink. I feel healthy. I like to paint and I do not need too much entertainment to be happy. In my office, with the patients, I create a relaxed atmosphere of confidence in the people. It comes to me naturally.

My second problem is that I committed myself to be here for at least one more year. I never made this official, but during my last malpractice trial, which lasted over three years and in which I refused to have a defense attorney, yet I won in the final two days of courtroom debate, I mentioned to the people that I would stay here at least until the graduation of my youngest daughter from DePaul University. She will be a senior next year. Then I will be free from this special commitment.

I do not know whether my chances after 68 would be very great. The navy would not suffer from my acceptance. I do not feel that old; I would like to work still for a long time while being free from bureaucratic strangulation at every step.

I am sending you copies of my letters where you can better see my rebellious character. Maybe my character doesn't fit into the structural requirements of the Armed Forces. I do not know.

I wish you the best in your work.

The World Seen from the Distance of a Small Village

                                Tadeusz Maciejczyk, M.D.
                                March 24, 1991

Enc.   Letter to Judge Rapp, "Expert to Expert" - March 18, 1992, Letter to Physician Assoc. Family Practice, December 3, 1992

Commonwealth Edison
P.O. Box 286
Chicago, Illinois

    Today I received your threatening, completely unrestrained note demanding immediate payment or else you will discontinue your service to me on April 4.
    I was your customer for over 26 years. I always had the same address and I always paid my bills on time. Last month, I received from you only one statement, instead of the usual two: one for home and one for the office. As time passed and the other statement did not appear, I left it all for the next month's readjustment. I paid the whole bill, for both months, on March 23.
    I understand the need for firmness in conducting business. I also feel that there is a big difference between firmness and the uncouth, vulgar jumpiness of your note. Whoever formulated the policy expressed by that note and whoever sent that message should not hide himself behind the noble name of Edison. The name of Edison should never be denigrated by this kind of public relations conduct.
    If American companies behave with such manners here at home, as well as in the world, it is a small wonder that we have problems. Churlishness and jittery unrestraint in resolving small situations were never a good road to success and to greatness.

                                Tadeusz Maciejczyk, M.D.
                                P.S. I am sending the copy of this letter to my Congressman.

Book Three

Time Magazine
Letter to the Editor
RE: "Keeping the Hands Off" - April 8, 1991

Dear Sir:

The euphoric enthusiasm and glory that I felt after the liberation of Kuwait are disappearing each day under a ticker feeling of uneasiness, embarrassment and shame when I watch the present carnage in Biafra and Kurdistan.

The ashes of the Warsaw ghetto were already cold for over a year when in August and September of 1944 the Red Army watched passively for 63 days the agony and slaughter of the people of Warsaw, just from the other side of the Vistula River. It was not the Soviet policy to help. It is not our policy now. History will be the judge.

When the political artifacts prevail and permit the giant crime to go on, the world takes a practical lesson in humanity and in solidarity. After this lesson, the world will not be better. The indifference to someone's cry will get deeper roots. With this lesson we will make our streets no safer and we will not raise the will of the people for an economical recovery. With this lesson the prospect for the 21st century will be enormously darker. Somehow the spirit of Vietnam will be alive and will eat us.

It is a pity that the enormous moment of Kuwait liberation was wasted by the smallness of political selfishness.

> Tadeusz Maciejczyk, M.D.
> Milledgeville, April 3, 1991

The World Seen from the Distance of a Small Village

Is It Too Late?
Letter to the Editor of *Newsweek*

It is very painful to read about the enormously tragic consequences for those, who inspired by Desert Storm, dared to rise up against Hussein. Our magnificent military, but above all moral victory, fell into a vacuum of our post-war policy and degenerated into the present monumental calamity. We didn't have any working vision for the future and we had no sense of destiny. We reduced that war to a passing episode in history that didn't stabilize or change the bases for similar future sickness of the region.

This epilogue of the Desert War was still harder to take because when we were already clearly confronted with the developing gigantic human tragedy, we behaved like the two very important men who were passing the road before the Good Samaritan did.

Now we are starting to react. It is better than nothing, but for many it is too late. Probably it is too late also for many of the opportunities in the region we had. The Desert War was an investment that became mismanaged.

Tadeusz Maciejczyk, M.D.
Milledgeville, April 18, 1991

Book Three

George Bush
President of the United States

Dear Mr. President:

I received your letter answering my doubts and my anxieties related to the post-Desert War situation. I thank you for this kindness. Writing today, I include for you another of my letters to *Newsweek*, in which I expressed my feelings in a somewhat different way.

The Desert War was a magnificent victory that moved up and united the whole country. The post war time shocked everybody by its unpredictable consequences and our complete inertia to make that war's effort fruitful and lasting. Suddenly, from the extasis of a great, noble action, we were submerged into chaos and an absence of any positive post war policy. It is still time to initiate creative and positive moves that would give full sense and value to the effort of the Desert War, but the time for this is running out very rapidly. At the present, we cannot close our eyes, abandon action half-done and for consolation jump into different world's scenario, maybe only to finish it also in such an inconclusive way. We have to find strength and inner discipline to finish what we started with the Desert War mobilization.

The steadiness and constancy in this effort to continue to battle for a lasting peace we owe to all those men and women who were there and in the time of a growing tension were telling us simply and gallantly that they were ready to do their jobs right, and to die if necessary. For all of them, for the spirit of all of America during the time of the test, the Desert War causes and consequences cannot remain lost, unfinished or neglected. Even the most spontaneous and enthusiastic welcome home for the returning troops would not cover up the bitterness of the failed cause. Above all, the failure to proceed and to press for finishing well all the open ends of the postwar problems, could be very costly within a few years.

Already now, Saddam Hussein is acting not as a defeated man, who weeks ago was only one step from a complete collapse, but as a victor who puts conditions on the winners and acts in his home in the old way of uncorrected, pathological brutality. The lost war became for him only a minor inconvenience and delay and gave him a very precious lesson. He sees himself not only as a survivor, but as a winner. Within a few years, frustrated Arab masses, increasingly will look to him with new admiration. Nobody will be able to enforce on him the U.N. Resolutions that already now falls into complete silence and the weapons pushers will find their way to overcome all restrictions and embargoes. Within a few years Hussein can be strong enough again to be a real danger. The lesson of the Desert War will teach him to be smarter in preparing his strikes and I have no doubt that the humiliation of the Desert War will be for Hussein a permanent strong call for revenge. Within those years probably it would be not easy to organize a second crusade against Hussein.

For all those reasons, America cannot turn away leaving the work half done.

What was done calls for organized, unlimited planning and probing to obtain not a temporary truce of diplomatic negotiations, but a lasting peace of souls of all the involved nations. The experience of the Desert War has to give a clear message and direction. All the involved nations have passed through very deep emotions and are not the same any more. What was appearing to emerge from that transformation and now seems to disappear and vanish rapidly has to be caught again, discussed, and elaborated into a reality that would not be forgotten.

It was always so that the road to greatness was not easy and always required us to overcome the loss of stamina of will, of the interference of all those who deviate attention to something else, easier and more "rewarding." Cyprian Novid said in his poetry, "No—the first labor of any work is the mind's constancy."

It looks to me that the conclusion of the Desert War that brought for a moment a great sublimation of the world's spirit, should be planned to obtain by a convocation of two, special international bodies:

1. One, to judge the lawlessness and crimes.
    a. Those, responsible for the crimes in Kuwait.
    b. Those, who killed indiscriminately the civilian population in Biafra and in Kurdistan.
    c. Those responsible for the precedent-making, ecological crimes. Those crimes, the real precedence, cannot be forgotten and left with silence. It requires a new legislation, created, admitted and signed by all the nations of the world.

2. A Dialogue. The Creation of a body that would organize and preside over a dialogue of all involved nations (not exactly states), that would show their feelings, emotions, dreams and aspira-

Book Three

tions. These dialogues should be honest, but kind. They should be free from politics and from discussions of all dividing problems. They just should show the soul of each disputing nation. It should create an atmosphere in which later, all those problems could be dealt more effectively.

A dialogue between Moslems, Christians and Judaism conducted in the same spirit of openness, of honesty and kindness that could lead to eventual reconciliation. Just today, in this Sunday of Pentecost, St. Paul told us that "there are different ministries, but the same Lord." The Desert War has shown that we can act as brothers.

After those works, maybe the true fruits of the Desert War could emerge, be embraced and be protected from being spoiled by all of us.

Tadeusz Maciejczyk
Milledgeville, May 19, 1991

The World Seen from the Distance of a Small Village

Clayton Yeutter
Chairman of the Republican National Committee
Washington

Dear Sir:

I thank you for your letter (May 2). While reading it, I had an illusion that it was not the usual, impersonal print from Washington that generally kills any dialogue and originality, numbs the voices from the periphery and by its generally not very elevating monologue, makes Washington more and more isolated, self-centered and out of touch with the countryside.

If, as your letter says, I could be considered as a truly active member of the Republican National Committee, it would be not for my monetary contributions. I am sorry, but I have no talent for the business part of my M.D. office. I have a hard time charging.

Just today, I was talking with my youngest daughter, Cristina, a junior at DePaul University in Chicago, an honor student, and on the Dean's List every semester for the past three years. She would like to do a post-graduate study at Northwestern University and she is worried that the school is so expensive. I feel that she is my first obligation.

In this letter I wanted to say that in the same way as you, I think that getting started early in the preparations for the 1992 campaign is crucial.

But I am not convinced at all that the main job for such a preparation would be the candidates recruitment and training or a new voter registration. Those methods were used in the past and really, the people are already tired and sick of such an approach to the electoral dialogue with the country during the election year. This method should be put into the grave, together with all the remnants of the unholy Nixon discovery of the effects of the dirty tricks.

In my understanding, in those early stages of the preparation for the campaign, the truly important work would be a fresh and deep re-evaluation of all possible campaign issues. It would require a critical look at ourselves, on the country, on the world, rejecting any previous stereotypes or routines and a new best approach to every one of the mounting problems. Those studies should be done with the spirit of honesty, sincerity with the people and should include a continuous communication with the people for gathering and scrutinizing all of the perceived ideas. Such planning should be done and based not on the wishful thinking or to outsmart the adversary, but to truly solving the country's problems and in spite of the bitterness of some of the measures, retain the sympathy, the cooperation and the understanding of the population of the whole country. After such preparation, I would not worry too much about the intentions or the resourcefulness of the Democrats. We would speak, we would have a dialogue not only with the party's faithful, but with the nation.

Only then, after such a work, and not before, the rep. Party would have to choose proper man for each post. Of course, you can start the election campaign from the other end, adjusting the world to the men already chosen and trained in the campaign's rhetoric, training that would convince the people. But this will not work.

The last election showed very clearly how disappointed, how dispirited, how alienated, how plainly offended the people felt when they approached the voting places. The common *vox populi* was that the election was a fake. How long such a political circus can be repeated, I do not know. In 1990, the candidates and the people had almost nothing to tell each other. In the atmosphere of that election, a feeling of a lack of purpose and of an inevitable doomsday was in the air.

This time, we can prepare the election in a completely new refreshing truthfulness and sincerity. The simplicity and the sincerity are the most difficult objectives of any mental, emotional work. Did we grow enough to dampen the routine and to show the people our true soul, our true capacities and our true faces?

In this letter, I include a copy of one of my last responses to a survey that to some extent can be illustrative.

I also am sending the copies of my impressions from the post Desert War developments. About this, same lack of sincerity is hanging in the air. Everybody feels this. Everybody's face changes into something depressing and embarrassing when talking about that problems. Nobody wants to bring this to the surface, but within one year it can explode. The Rep. Party should be prepared for such an eventuality.

Because today is Decoration Day, I am sending you the copy of my speech for that day three years ago. I send you that copy, because at the end of my speech, I made some suggestions on how to look for our future leaders.

Again, I thank you for your letter and I wish you the best in your work.

                                        Tadeusz Maciejczyk
                                        Milledgeville, May 27, 1991

The World Seen from the Distance of a Small Village

K. Johnson
Medical Review Auditor
Medicare Part B
Marion, IL

Dear Sir:

I thank you for your letter with the explanation of your "reasonable charges" for me. My mind, used to small places and rural simplicity, cannot grasp easily your complex formulation for payment, even, when I am convinced that your highly trained and impartial hearing officer has a clear and ready formula for the enormous variation of human sufferings that you are required to express with the same dry and naked code number. The time spent for the same in this way defined diagnosis can be a quick application of something, or a long, time-consuming, tedious and patient job.

I have not the time, nor energy to argue with you. Except this, like reading your codings, I can predict your answer.

But, I will use this occasion to send your answer and all this problem to the Republican Presidential Advisory Committee in Washington, to whom just now I reported my views, and I will ask them to study and to evaluate the future of the rural medical services in the United States. Under the whip of your complicated formula of payments, those rural services are condemned to die and will not last too long.

Under your formula for a just payment, I just cannot keep my office functioning and certainly, I cannot afford the each time your more loudly required a special electronic connection with your central office.

Being a doctor at present in the U.S., especially an independent, starving to serve in the country-side doctor, the so-called provider, is a prescription for self-destruction. The bureaucratic monster has no soul. It has only an enormous stomach and teeth.

I wish you the best in your wonderful service for mankind and for this increasingly poor country.

Tadeusz Maciejczyk, M.D.
Milledgeville, June 6, 1991

Book Three

Republican Presidential Advisory Commission

There is another reason why I do not send the money. Economically and psychically I was beaten down in the last years to the point that I lost faith in any success of a small, independent honest enterprise in America.

In my small, solo, countryside medical practice, almost every day I wondered whether it made any sense to fight for my independent work. The burdens on my office became frustrating; the mounting, suffocating paperwork, the never-ending collisions with Medicare, the constantly changing expensive, increasingly complicated coding books, the threats, the denials, cuts, delays of payments, the increasing insistence that only an electronic connection by computers to the central (that I cannot afford, nor do I like) would give me an advantage and the same deal as the clinics have. Otherwise, I can justly expect only more difficulties, more unexplained denials or cuts that would be impossible to correct by a usual telephone message saying someone will be with me soon.

I like my work as a doctor. I like the contact with the people. I enjoy helping, explaining, teaching; I am dismayed by the bureaucratic interference and its growing inhumane rigidity.

America, it looks to me, has no talent for creating anything simple that works. Everything born from our legislators or from governmental bodies shows a genius for complications. Those complications create hordes of new officials and also hordes of abusers seeding and planting a general uncertainty, caution to start, or to proceed, anxiety, loss of energy, loss of individuality and creativity in a good, normal population, but increasing the numbers of those who strive and flourish in the developing murky waters. As a result of this, we have a general atmosphere of mutual distrust and suspicion between people and officials. This atmosphere brings more complications, more supervisions and restrictions leading to some dreadful dead end.

With my character, to work enthusiastically, creatively and effectively, I need independence, my own assessment of how to deal with what is moral and what is humane. I do not like to give those attributes to the whims or to the calculating minds of somebody else.

In America, increasingly, only the big institutions can flourish because they know or they can afford the knowledge of the necessary deals and tricks. Americans more and more are becoming the soul-less robots of the big giant institutions that within the law can operate with complete lawlessness. Those robots, selling themselves to the giant, can increasingly sell themselves in other areas, becoming empty inside and to

The World Seen from the Distance of a Small Village

compensate the emptiness becoming more and more bulimic in their needs or pretensions for today with a complete disregard for others or for tomorrow. (The typical Reaganite spirit of prosperity.)

I consider Reagan as one of the most notorious villains in America's history. I cannot believe now that I voted for him.

As Stalin in Russia changed the dark side of the Russian soul into an enormous caricature of the Soviet People's Paradise, so Reagan accentuated the American tendency to luxury into an unrestrained bulimia, the shine of the surface pose, the idolatry of the rich and famous. He created his unprecedented prosperity by borrowing, by plunging the country into enormous debt, asserting that the appearance was more important than the real life, like in a movie. The results were wonderful for the day and catastrophic for tomorrow. It brought not only debts, but also many scandals, very costly for normal people and to the whole country. It formed also a generation in which the American "pursuit of happiness" changed into the present American drive to get rich from the lottery, from gambling, from lawsuits, from completely unrestrained destruction of others, or of the riches that belong to all of us. Reagan is guilty of popularizing selfishness, ruthlessness and superficiality that the money and luxury, not that virtue or character, are the most effective ways to live, and a real god in America.

If this tendency is not changed, I see the future of America in a very dark and bitter tone.

To illustrate how I came to such a conclusion, I am sending you different copies of my previous correspondence.

SECTION II
1. See my introduction to this survey
2. Pessimistic
3. Wrong track

SECTION III
1. I approve and I disapprove. To explain this controversy, I am sending you some of my letters about this matter.
2. Yes. The world has no other way to go, but to closer and closer unity, hopefully retaining all of its richness of diversity. Whoever is trying to argue against this truth is arguing against the time constantly marking by all the clocks. Instead of hiding our heads in the sand, would it be better to calculate how we can help our neighbors and how much we can gain for both of us?

Book Three

3. No. The sooner the Soviets come to a complete break, the better. Every help to them will go mainly to preserve and to re-establish what there was. Their small gestures of some arms treaties are calculated as a fishing nest to get money and help. The present establishment will never stop dreaming about power and domination. The present establishment has no other values, qualities or alternatives for their own self-esteem and a life without self-esteem is very bitter. All the authorities before and during the czars, and now, were always playing the long distance planning games, patiently giving up or waiting, if necessary, but with the unchanged distant objectives: a domination with the help of one or another ideology and of the whip of the police and the army.
4. I disagree. We cannot go back and pretend to live in the global circumstances of the 19th or 18th centuries. In spite of all the weaknesses and miseries of our structures, nobody else but America is destined to lead the world somewhere to some Commonwealth of the 21st century.
5. Disapprove. The armed forces have a different purpose and should preserve different spirits. Except for this: the drug influx will never be stopped by a blockade of borders. It will be won only if we use every caught trafficker or pusher and we soften him enough to tell who his superior is and in this way reach the centers of importing and distributing drugs here, inside the country.

Each case in which somebody dies because of drug use should be treated as a murder during the martial law time, with the death penalty. This penalty could be reduced if the condemned person would reveal the name of his superior. Then his superior would have a chance to save himself in the same way. The executions should be carried out. We have to make a clear choice whether to be nice to the drug dealer or to our children and our future.

SECTION IV

1. What can I say? My preparation for economical questions is not the best in the world. Reading your headlines of remedies, I imagined a scene in which the very busy, first-class tailors were in a constant hassle of preparing a magnificent garment for a known, great king. The garment had that distinctive quality that could be seen only by the eyes of the absolutely innocent. All

The World Seen from the Distance of a Small Village

those remedies are a bluff, if nothing really meaningful is done. The goal should be not a choice of the best plaster, but a diagnostic work and a true treatment.
2. I include my previous assessment of this problem.
3. Similar to No. 1. Your projected choices are like walking in circles during the time of a snow blizzard. Without marking the distinctive points, without establishing direction, it can be a deadly walk.
4. yes. But only after a clarifying, sincere discussion with the nation. Those discussions should be done by the President and detailed by different departments of the Government. The present Congress, after raising their own salaries, in the face of a clear economical uncertainty, has no moral authority to put any additional burden on the nation.
5. No.
6. No opinion. It is one of the plaster to cover an infected wound, just to make it look better. Would it be better to identify the infecting bacteria and then make an appropriate treatment? Otherwise, sooner or later, the pus will weep down from below the edges of the plaster.
7. Numbers? No. Motivations? Yes. Those who are persecuted fighting for freedom—yes. Those who dream about an easy life here—no.
8. Doing it drastically by answering yes or no, would collide with life. The conditions of balance should be studied, discussed and enforced. Without such work and such discipline, the life of our children could be downgraded severely. Such greedy attitudes, for example, as cutting the Redwoods should be condemned.
9. Yes. Not for a crime in a moment of passion and anger, but for murder with premeditation, for dehumanized tortures, for the depraved and abusers of small children—yes. It would be good to given them time for repentance, but limited. The civilized justice of soft punishment produces a growing intolerable injustice to society.
10. No opinion. The problem is so complex, so entangled, that I do not know. First, should be provided a safety from criminals, a safe walking on any street at any hour of the day or night. Only that in this problem, I do not know what is first: the chicken or the egg.
11. Yes. See Section III-1.

Book Three

12. Declined? From what moment or from what height? Education is increasingly hampered by the American family situation that more than before is producing in children self-depreciation, feelings of guilt, negativism and escapes. Our schools became the first line defense against those crippling consequences. Maybe because of this, the administration of schools became big, complicated and costly; remedial teaching more frequent, with escape from tedious basics to what is more fancy and more attention-worthy. But without the basics, education is walking on weak legs, producing not only droppings, but also the present tendency to a massive escape into the very narrow fields of lifework. This narrowness of education is producing in the people a tunnel view of the world, an effect of blinds on the horses. The society of such individuals will be always anxious about possible changes in their narrow fields, insecure, uneasy for new adjustments and most likely will not feel an inner fulfillment.
    In conclusion, the costly fancy will never compensate for the solid and wide basics in preparing for life.
13. Yes. AIDS has a nasty potential, especially in societies where the morals are lax. A puritanical society would probably be safe, but our chances to become puritanical are very slim.
14. Yes. I know that the school prayers are most likely just automatic, without concentration or thinking. But every one of us has moments of special sensibility when God's presence catches by surprise. If school prayer would produce such an affect in a fraction of a the thousands who pray this way, it would be wonderful. Those who oppose prayer can enter the class after the prayer is finished. The First Amendment practiced just to satisfy the minority pressure groups are leading to devastation and injustice.
    Speaking about absurdities that can be made from the good and wise First Amendment, I include my letter to the local newspaper in 1989 during the flag desecration crisis.

SECTION V
1. Yes. I am sending you a copy of my first letter about this problem.
2. Yes. They are corrupting our officials from their start in the public service, or even before that. They made the entrance into public office economically prohibitive for the incorruptible. They

The World Seen from the Distance of a Small Village

are making a mockery from the democratic principles of free elections. Only the biggest beneficiaries (the most used to agree to conditions and to be not themselves) have chances to succeed. This special advantage for the chosen, is putting the American elections not very far from the elections in Communist countries. There are many ways to twist democracy and it is one of them.

3. Yes. Not only negative. During the last elections, they were also dishonest, false, abusive and shameless. The last elections advertisements produced a sickening feeling in the people and an impression of a big, but cheap, organized, or maybe disorganized political farce. The people had no choice. Frequently they voted only to prevent the worst. I didn't see any enthusiasm or joy during that, unworthy of America's idealism elections. I am sending you a letter from that time reflecting my feelings.

4. News magazines and TV. Newsletters from elected officials are generally self-serving, trying to impress, not to communicate or explain.

5. Somewhere between mostly accurate and biased.

6. I never know.

SECTION VI

1. None of them. A control of one or another of the places of power can and should be only the end result of our priorities scheduled for the work of today. A priority for today has to be a clear plan for frank communication and issues discussion with the people. Somehow the people feel the bias and the emptiness or lack of sincerity. The good rule is that you should not be a better speaker than you are a man. The work should be done to clear our minds and to open our eyes to as many problems of today as possible and during the election not to be just a loudspeaker for the party's slogans.

2. My feelings about Republican candidates and office holders are not expressed in any of your three eventualities. In candidates I look for the quality of character, for his depth of vision, for wisdom, for his originality. The party ticket of the candidate comes after those characteristics, not before. The party has an obligation to elect and to present to the people the best. If the Republican party would fail to do this, I would have to look for the best somewhere else.

    a. Voting only on the basis of loyalty, without pressuring for selection of candidates, would produce a loyal, rubber stamp, a Soviet type Parliament. I always thought that before loyalty to party, we have to be loyal to ourselves, to the country, to God. By manifesting this, we can prevent the party from decadence, from stagnation and from sclerosis. The party membership has to be a living, feeling and thinking organism. No, I am not an automat.

    b. The ideas of the Rep. Party, how to organize the life in the country, at its best are only schematic and ambiguous. They should be a subject of a constant adjustment, complementation, clarification and confrontation in order to be alive and vibrant in the ever-changing realities of life. Whether they are the best for America? I am still trying to see and to understand.

    c. A reluctant support indicates that our elaboration and explanation of Rep. basic ideas were insufficient or that those ideas are losing their attractiveness and because of this require a new touch. Generally, I do not like to be just a reluctant supporter.

3. Maybe, but not automatically. During the Desert War time, the Republican's status of minority was completely unimportant. The idea and the action, a new mobilization of minds and wills, nullified the importance of numbers. That moment in history showed clearly the importance of an idea and of a vision. The aimless, visionless, yes-man majority will never be the biggest asset. It also shows how much we have to work in this early stages of the preparation for a campaign, for the preparation of ideas, for vision, of the purpose, and how important will be the finding of the truly matching candidates.
4. To answer this point, I am sending you a copy of my very bitter letter from the last campaign where I explained why I couldn't support the candidates of the Rep. Party.
5. No. No position can be clear permanently. It needs a special body to adjust and to define. I hope that it will be one of the works done by the Party to introduce us and the nation into the election time for decision.
6. I do not know. I was never very good at gossip.

Tadeusz Maciejczyk, M.D.
Milledgeville, June 6, 1991

The World Seen from the Distance of a Small Village

Jim Coyne
U.S. Congress for
Americans to limit Congressional Terms

Dear Sir:

I thank you for the membership card.

I want to stress here that I identify myself very deeply with your effort to introduce changes in Congress.

The present situation of almost perpetual representation through practically automatic re-election systems when confronted with the present decline of morals, of self discipline and of a driving sense of duty to society and to the country, with the general increase of selfishness and multiplication of scandals, cover-ups, games of tactics and words in place of dedication and constancy of minds—all those factors give you a very special mission and a special title for your work. This work has to be expressed, organized, made public and it has to penetrate every corner of the country. This work, if done, will give you a place in history.

To increase the effectiveness of your action, the drive to limit the terms for the members of Congress has to be combined with a special definition of the new type of personalities whom the present time requires for the people's representatives. The people, while they are called to change their election habits that until now were made for an easy, path of least resistance, have to have a new supply of ideas and inspirations in how to look and how to search for new and better representation. Such a search has to be not just a last minute, confused and embarrassing marking of the most easy name to remember from the pre-election propaganda, but a result of a year round observation and evaluation that would bloom and ultimately mature in making the final decision.

Presently, the selection is made mainly in Washington, far away from the people, who should be primarily interested in such appointments. To confirm those appointments in the present system, the people are approached, not by an honest presentation and discussion, but by an avalanche of propaganda, expensive, confusing, shallow, frequently distorted and malicious. The people instead of being elevated to vote, are brainwashed, degraded, confused and helplessly depressed by indiscriminate manipulations. In consequence, they approach the voting places with an almost indifferent attitude, like something that should be a sacred duty, but is pointless and can change nothing.

Book Three

For this reason, it is not enough to call the people to change their voting habits and every certain time look for a new name, new face. Such a change would still not improve the value of the people voting, or even the quality of representation in Congress. It would still not make an emotional union between the countryside and Washington. Such a change could be done only if the search for the best representation would become a perpetual passion of districts, would be a constant challenge to spot, to involve and in some way to train the people with character, with talent, with vision, with wisdom, honesty and knowledge. Such an atmosphere would change completely the present gloom of voting and the quality, the resonance, the vibrancy of the U.S. congress.

Writing to the Republican Presidential Advisory Commission and answering the question as to whether PAC contributions should be prohibited, I responded:

Yes. They are corrupting our officials from their start in the public service, or even before that. They made the entrance into public office economically prohibitive for the incorruptible. They are making a mockery from the democratic principles of free elections. Only the biggest beneficiaries (the most used to agree to conditions and to be not themselves) have chances to succeed. This special advantage for the chosen, is putting the American elections not very far from the elections in Communist countries. There are many ways to twist democracy and it is one of them.

I am sending you a copy of my Memorial Day speech in 1998. At the end of that speech, I indicated one way to look and to find people with the qualities for leadership.

I wish you the best in your work.

Tadeusz Maciejczyk
Milledgeville, July 4, 1991

The World Seen from the Distance of a Small Village

Clayton Yeutter
Chairman
The Republican National Committee
Washington, D.C.

Dear Sir:

I received your survey; I read it and I became uneasy and disappointed. This reading gave me the impression that in Washington's Republican high circles nothing really changed. In this survey, I saw the same making in circles, the same vague, imprecise language, the same unrestrained partisanship that blames everything on the other, without giving any sign of self-examination or self-discipline. I see in such a public letter only living proof that the Party cares very little about the people and is only using them in the most selfish way, in the same way as described by you Congress.

A true love for the people, or for the country, sounds and appears differently. A true love would give in such a letter a feeling of sincerity and clarity and would show more originality. True involvement is always stimulating for minds, is daring, and is refreshing. It is also contagious and mobilizing. Years ago, in the countries behind the Iron Curtain, the local Communist dignitaries talked to the people with language similar to yours. They had an audience because the presence at such meetings was obligatory.

I do not see any purpose to filling out this survey. I responded to the same, or similar questions many times already and I do not see any sense in marking the same points again and again if those points are not digested and developed one or more steps forward. A place in leadership requires concentration and constant homework. Only then can it create strength and attract attention. Without them, any leadership very soon finishes in stagnation and worthlessness.

I am not sending any contribution. This survey didn't give me anything worthy of sacrifice.

Tadeusz Maciejczyk
Milledgeville, July 14, 1991

Book Three

Al Jourdan
Chairman of the Illinois Republican Party
Springfield, IL

Dear Sir:

After strong vacillation, I am accepting your invitation to be a 1991 Sustaining Member of the Illinois Republican Party.

My vacillation came from my observations of our Party in the past. The long reign of Gov. Thomson was absolutely uninspiring to me. I include here my letter to the *Sterling Daily Gazette* written after his last election.

The presidency of Ronald Reagan didn't bring elevation to the life of this country. In my letter to the Republican Presidential Advisory Commission, I wrote this about him: "I consider Reagan as one of the most notorious villains in American's history. I cannot believe now that I voted for him.

As Stalin in Russia changed the dark side of the Russian soul into an enormous caricature of the Soviet People's Paradise, so Reagan accentuated the American tendency to luxury into an unrestrained bulimia, the shine of the surface pose, the idolatry of the rich and famous. He created his unprecedented prosperity by borrowing, by plunging the country into enormous debt, asserting that the appearance was more important than the real life, like in a movie. The results were wonderful for the day and catastrophic for tomorrow. It brought not only debts, but also many scandals, very costly for normal people and to the whole country. It formed also a generation in which the American "pursuit of happiness" changed into the present American drive to get rich from the lottery, from gambling, from lawsuits, from completely unrestrained destruction of others, or of the riches that belong to all of us. Reagan is guilty of popularizing selfishness, ruthlessness and superficiality, that money and luxury, not that virtue or character are the most effective ways to live and a real god in America."

The memory of the 1990 elections, on the Democratic as well as the Republican side, gave me a feeling of deep moral and ethical crisis in our state and in the whole country. Those elections degenerated into a denigrating spectacle that while wasting enormous amounts of money, showed nothing but empty slogans and plenty of dirt. I wanted to vote Republican in that election and I couldn't. In the same way as many, many people around me, I voted without hope for the future and with no pride. Obviously, there are people of character and leadership qualities among us, but both parties are apparently afraid of them, avoiding renovation or true selection. Both parties prefer to look for the gray, unexciting "apparatchiks" (obedient, unimaginative, gray party members) with a quality of an obedient stamp.

What really are those "Republican principles of government" endangered by the Democrats? They are always proclaimed in very vague, imprecise terms, but in those early stages before the next election, I would like the Party to explain those principles to the people with clarity and firmness. This would do more than all those costly tricks.

And what are those "our views and values?" I read this characterization so many times and still I didn't hear any clear answer devoid of empty phraseology and without ambivalence.

Then? Why should I support a Party candidate if their life's philosophy is anything that I would admire? Or in whom I would put my trust? The last elections in this aspect were horrifying.

I do not feel that the liberal leaders who are determined to embarrass the president, have no value and are not useful for the Republicans. They are giving us a useful contrast and are preventing us from political sleepiness. They are the elements with which we can sharpen and clarify our ideas making our ideals more palpable and more convincing to the electorate.

I do not see any attempt in the Rep. Party to use the opportunities those liberal leaders are giving us. And this would be an occasion for deepening and crystallizing our goals, making them shiny and durable. During the last election I had the impression that the Party was avoiding and was afraid of light. The Party was giving the impression that it is preoccupied with hiding and is not willing to pass through the process of purification. Now, in this early pre-election time, our party should explain what mysterious "responsible Republican program" really is.

Speaking about my membership, you tell me that after acceptance "I may enjoy the benefits of membership." Exactly what does this promise mean? I do not know either, and I was not told in your letter what my duty would be. I know that the Party is looking for money and needs as many milking cows as possible and wants those cows not to ask questions, but really, I want to know what plans the party has for me beyond the passive role of a happy sucker. In what other way can I hope to make the 1992 a Republican year?

An assurance that virtually every day the Republicans are making a difference in government and I, as a sustaining member, will make a

Book Three

difference too, is at the same level as a similar phraseology in the Communist party's in every Soviet satellite about a decade ago.

As a member I feel that my obligation would be to ask, to express sincerely my views and to see the Party growing not only in membership, but especially in spirit, in wisdom, in character, giving the people an example without which any talk about leadership is nothing more than a masquerade.

I wish you the best in your work.

Tadeusz Maciejczyk
Milledgeville, July 28, 1991

The World Seen from the Distance of a Small Village

George Bush
President of the United States

Dear Mr. President:

Your speech to the people of Kiev was for me like a blow to my faith in justice. I tried not to think about it, but finally, now, I need to tell you what I feel. I do this because I do not want my faith in America's mission to be undermined.

In Kiev, Mr. Gorbachev used your friendship, your authority and with this, the myth of America, to silence the voices, and to extinguish the desires of the Ukrainian people to be free.

Years ago, for the same purpose, the Soviets used their KGB and the Gulag network.

I never expected that now, Mr. Gorbachev would ask you to pay for his smiles and for his carefully measured gestures with a repayment that could substitute and sanctify their previous oppressive practices of tyranny. In Kiev, Mr. Gorbachev used you to preserve the dirty laundry of the czarist and then the Soviet's imperial policies.

In Kiev, did you pay for Gorbachev's "friendship" or maybe for his part in the present Mideast peace conference with the money that never belonged to American and that never should be used in such a deal by any representative of the Free World? Nobody has a right to suffocate someone's desire for freedom just to pay for the short-term compromise or convenience.

Just now, on my desk, I see the certificate of recognition sent to me from the Republican National Committee for my "commitment to helping America to remain the land of the free and the home of the brave."

But we will not remain free for long if we engage ourselves in selling or suppressing the dreams of freedom of other people. Doing this, we will not remain the home of the brave. This country's greatness was founded on their initial understanding and fight for its freedom. We should never betray this heritage.

I hope that your pronunciations in Kiev will never be confirmed or repeated. In the same way as the Baltic States, Ukraine deserves to be free. I am sure that being free, the over 50 million Ukrainians would contribute enthusiastically to the future peace in the world. Imperial Russia, with or without Gorbachev's smiles, will always represent a threat and a permanent potential for the world's disaster. The ethnic Russians can be best helped by distancing them from their imperial past and by involving them in the normal and healthy life of the present world's community.

Probably I should add here that I am not Ukrainian.

I wish you the best in your uneasy and with responsibility-overloaded work.

Tadeusz Maciejczyk
August 11, 1991

The World Seen from the Distance of a Small Village

Medicare Administrator
Part B News RSVP

Dear Medicare Administrator:

I thank you for your insistence to help me get every Medicare dollar I am entitled to.

I admit that today, not the medical knowledge and doctor's dedication to human needs, but the virtuosity in juggling the coding numbers is the number one issue for all medical institutions to navigate and to survive. The coding books, the letters about coding and their constant changes, as frequent as the changes in ladies' fashions, together with its increasing complications and added threats, with their enormous bore, are creating an atmosphere of anxiety and uncertainty, invite to defensive postures, to the inside anger and frustration. Those books are costly. In spite of their cost, they are insufficient, rigid in expressing the enormous variety within the same coding entity, and even they are incomplete. Just yesterday, I spent a long time trying to find a number for something as common as plantar calluses. In such a situation, this coding system is creating a temptation to stretch and to exaggerate. Can it be that for such a purpose, the bigger medical institutions are hiring the coding experts or jugglers? From the other side, the Medicare centers become vigilant, suspicious, increasingly prone to accusations, additional threats and the creation of an expensive, complicated system of control.

The climate that this system created for the medical practice, for receiving medical care, for escalating its cost, for its secondary impact on every industrial and productive institutions, cannot be easily measured.

The young doctors are escaping to clinics where they can isolate themselves from the ugliness of the general frame of the present day medical practice. There, they can close their eyes on all the effects of the system and secure by the costly malpractice insurance, they can cling to a narrow medical field in which they scarcely see a human being in their patients. They delegate the hassle imposed on medicine to the clinic administrators and to the coding experts.

But they have to pay a price for this convenience and safety. They have to become only a screw in a given institution. They have to give up much of their own individuality, of their own approach to the art and mission of healing. They become just employees, robots, providers. In such a condition, a cynical understanding of medical work can start to

Book Three

develop. Why not? The system is still young and its fruits will be best seen years from now.

In this system, the small, solo practices, where the impact of today's artificialities is more direct and crashing—those small, independent practices are disappearing and most likely will be extinguished. The crutches with which Medicare can operate in clinics are less available in such isolation. The present Medicine became crippled and the necessary crutches you support have to be corrected and adjusted 24 times a year. For a solo medical practitioner, it is frightening.

Again, I thank you for your offer.

If I really intend to be a truly effective doctor, healer, counselor and guide for my patients, I would have no time to read your "Part B Survival Guide" 24 times a year.

By nature, I am an optimist, but I have no illusions. I will try to keep my office open as long as I can. I realize that one day the mounting oppression from Medicare will pass the limits of my resistance and I will be forced to give up and to close my solo countryside practice.

In this field where I work, in medicine, the U.s. is not the land of the free any more and neither is it the home of the brave. It is increasingly an imitation of the well-known "Workers Paradise."

I wish you the best in your unending work to improve the Medicare crutches.

> Tadeusz Maciejczyk, M.D.
> Milledgeville, September 1, 1991

The World Seen from the Distance of a Small Village

Clayton Yeutter
Chairman
Republican National Committee
Washington, D.C.

Dear Sir:

Probably now, especially after the unexpected telephone call from your headquarters in Washington, it is time for me to speak clearly.

If the Party has no other use or designation for me but a sustaining membership, please scratch me off your list. I am an M.D., but I am not rich.

Worst than this. I completely lost my faith in the value of honest work in the U.s. or in any security in life that such work could provide. I was forced to reduce my work. To some extent, here, I am a waste.

In 1983, I opposed obligatory malpractice insurance because its heavy price was transferred immediately to patients, making the health cost escalate out of proportion. As a consequence, I lost my privileges in Sterling General hospital.

For some time, I admitted my patients to the more distant, small hospital in Morrison. Pressure was put on the hospital. In 1987, I stopped to deliver babies. In 1989 the hospital was forced to demand from me full malpractice insurance. Since that time, I work only in my office, without malpractice insurance and without rights to hospitalize patients. And I keep the office visit prices as low as possible.

In January of 1987, I had a malpractice suit filed against me. The accusation was ridiculous. Most likely it was a vendetta from one doctor. After realizing the legal ploys of lawyers who rushed to defend me, I decided to defend myself. I didn't want to compromise. For almost three and one-half years, my family and I lived under constant pressure and harassment. I was told that in the courtroom I would be crucified. My wife was told that after the trial we would be homeless because our home would be taken to pay the costs; that I would be jobless, because my office would be seized to pay the cost, and my reputation would be in ruin; that we would be divorced because if my wife wanted to retain anything personal, she would have to divorce me.

I looked for help every place, including the party and the President. In response, I received a letter from the Department of Health and Human Services with a tranquilizing assurance that what was happening to us was nothing unusual. It was just "malpractice stress syndrome." Graciously, they sent me several booklets about that new illness. I answered them that

Solzhenizyn, when he was on the way to the Gulag, could be similarly assured by the KGB society that his anxiety about that trip was nothing more than "Gulag Stress Syndrome."

During the entire year of 1990, the year of my lonely stand in the courtroom, where against everyone's predictions I won the case, my whole income was $27,000.00. For an M.D. it was not bad. From this I had to pay the taxes and the University costs for my youngest daughter.

At present, I live in my home here alone. My wife went to live and work in Chicago. She worries that at any time I might get another malpractice suit and she doesn't want to pass again through such suffering.

An honest and creative work in the present U.S. is not very practical or attractive. It can lead at any time to "crucifixition" or destruction. A present work has to be done from behind the barricades and fortifications of special, costly insurances and a special protection of special new protectors and always in a climate of uncertainty and caution. The bold moves forward are getting very scarce. Such a climate for work will never create a successful or happy society.

In the next election, the echoes and the forces of that climate will be louder than ever. Your election plan, secretly revealed to me, was floating far above all those domestic illnesses. This plan was just a copy of the usual. But a bluff cannot substitute forever a true revision of the existing problems and a true and sincere communication and dialogue with the nation.

I am sending you a copy of my last letter to the Medicare Administrator—Part B News RSVP—and my letter to Al Jourdan, Chairman of the Illinois Republican Party.

I wish you the best in your work.

> Tadeusz Maciejczyk, M.D.
> Milledgeville, October 3, 1991

P.S. Sorry for distractions while writing this letter. The flies were impossible. They enter with ever opening of the door. I want to add also that I received the photographs of Pres. Bush in good condition. I will not display it in any prominent place. Since the 1940s, when behind the iron Curtain school children were handed as something exciting a picture of a smiling Joe Stalin, with a recommendation to hang it above their beds, I lost the inclination to such shows. Several days later, in an equally happy atmosphere, the children were asked how their parents reacted after such a display. What they told them or to other members of the family?

The World Seen from the Distance of a Small Village

Guy Vander Jagt
Chairman
National Republican Congressional Committee
Washington, D.C.

Dear Sir:

I write this letter to confirm that I received your official, registered, Congressional Rating Survey letter No. 073-27 and also to make it clear that contrary to what the pollsters say about me, I am not satisfied with the Congress and the job it's doing. Contrary also to your insinuations, I am skeptical not only about the Democratic majority, but also about the Republican minority as well.

Lately, I stopped responding to the increasing amount of different surveys. I see no sense in bothering. They all are about the same in content, in tone and in their intellectual level. The same questions, which I already answered many time, without any sign of evolution, without any calm report of progress, are repeated there over and over again. Some of them are showing something that the Germans call *Schadenfreude*, because the adversary was wrong, but very little of a clear correction. Altogether, those surveys are not building, not leading, not teaching. They are only showing in a more naked way a squabbling smallness, a humiliating emptiness, and a complete absence of vision, of leadership, or responsibility. They are only a pretext to ask for money from which nobody ever gives any account. With that abundance of different "surveys," congress, with the whole Washington political establishment, are casting over all the country a gray, colorless, tasteless, depressing shadow, absent of any positive force to really rise or mobilize.

In spite of the nothingness of those messages, this Washington establishment still has the pretension to involve with them and to lead the nation. No leadership can work in such a vacuum of ideas.

And the country is responding accordingly. The gloom, the apathy, the non-involvement, the keeping hands down, the growing selfishness, the increasing lack of spirituality and spiritual strength are multiplying. The people are uneasy about moving forward or even opening themselves. The short upsurge of idealism and energy during the Desert War is dying and the negativism is taking over, increasing the distancing and even the contempt toward the "accomplishments" of our Washington aristocracy.

For all those reasons, Mr. Chairman, if instead of sending me another "personal," almost secretive survey, with the same set of ques-

Book Three

tions, instead of going to another Bermuda business party, if instead of this you rise publicly to the podium and fight to clear the atmosphere of our national life telling things as they are and drawing out the necessary conclusions with really workable suggestions, then I promise you I will stand behind you and I will fight on your side for the better future of America and the world.

If instead, you, with all the congressional factions, continue your merry-go-round, just to make for today and to be again re-elected, then, Mr. Chairman, do not bother me with your surveys or letters. Looking on the congress as a whole, I am in the same way as many around me: dispirited and pessimistic. If nothing else, the future history will judge appropriately your small games while the country is agonizing with the true problems and declines.

I am sorry for the content of this letter, but I am serious. I have not two faces. I say what I think.

         Tadeusz Maciejczyk
         Milledgeville, November 2, 1991

cc: Clayton Yeutter, Chairman, Republican National Committee
   George Bush, The White House
   Al Jourdan, Chairman, Illinois Republican Party

The World Seen from the Distance of a Small Village

George Bush
President of the United States
Washington, D.C.

Dear Sir:

I received your letter with an invitation to be a party of your 1992 campaign.

I thank you for this expression of confidence in me.

In my evaluation, I see in you a dedicated leader, driven by a dream of a peaceful and safe world for decades to come. In this effort, I will always be on your side.

In your Vice-President Quayle, I see a man open and receptive to the needs of the time, a man with the capacity to grow on his job where he is showing a clear mind, common sense and freedom from destructive pride or vanity. I think that he has all the qualities to be a good President when his time comes.

Within those dimensions, you can count on me.

But in your letter, I see also that you are living in a different world, different from the one in which the average American, not just the privileged are living.

Contrary to your experience, from my point of observation, I do not see around me a "vision of renewed national purpose," or an "optimism in the future." As a real sample of what I see here, was an anxious face, with tears in the eyes and a deep emotional outburst. "In what kind of a country are we living now?" of my patient Burton Temple, who has his mother in the nursing home, pays for her maintenance there with a sacrifice to his own living standard and who was notified that the price of keeping his mother there soon will go up? He was already stretched to the extreme.

Also, I see no spirit in the young, who are approaching the working age. There, I see the prevalence of anxiety and uncertainty, frequently even escapism and suffering from the absence of a great, mobilizing purpose. AT present, there is nobody on the horizon to lead by comprehending and breaking this special vacuum in which so many are submerged. The emotional inertia in any individual, by rolling downhill, is spreading vices, maintains flourishing drug business, and produces recruits for crimes. By no means are you identified by the people as one who cares to change this inner illness of the country.

In this letter, I have to tell you that I will not enter the club of "six membership levels." I do not feel that I belong there. My life saga was different. Like a true club of snobs, this membership proposal differentiates no other merit, but money. I am not good for collecting and I would feel no pride wearing a pin that puts such an accent on money, just money. I can imagine the pleasure Mr. Harkin could get by describing this club with his usual picturesque oratory to middle class America that now is really hurting and that will be the biggest force during the election time. The pins of such a snobbish club could bring only a feeling of distress and distancing to the widest spectrum of the electorate.

If, for a change, you would like to establish a special membership arrangement for those who would distinguish themselves by contributing time and energy to the true quality of your campaign, whomever they would be—rich or poor, with global vision, or with vision restricted to their locality—if in this way you would open the door to participation and to building together, to those who would give their time to your cause, to those who would come forward with new, useful ideas, to those who would present new approaches to our mounting problems in different fields, to all those who would show the necessary new spiritual leadership for our inside emptiness that so often cannot be deafened even with drugs or kicks, if you would open such a canal, receptive to everybody, then I would like to be a part of it.

Such a window, widely open for fresh air would catch attention and could become a force much more useful to your re-election than the present boiling infightings for the boundaries of the new electoral districts, infightings that nourish the spirit of nobody, but create bitterness and general shrinkage of perspectives.

If the creation of such an open door for participation of the people's minds and spirits in the process of shaping our life would pass the examination during the pre-election time, maybe it could remain permanently open in the form of a special secretariat in our government.

Yes. For all distinguished in such participation, a special pin could be presented—a pin of the same level category, if anything, with a note of the field of distinction.

Such a pin should be given not now, but later, around Labor Day, the hottest, the decisive time, for the people to make up their minds. The echo of the rewarding ceremony surely would be strong until the moment of voting.

I know that if I were to receive such a pin, I would consider it a high honor and I would wear it proudly. I also think that such a pin could have the power to change, to elevate, even to sublimate the lives of many. It could create even a kind of a breaking point in a fight with our emptiness, our drug dependence, or devastating tendency to value only the material.

The World Seen from the Distance of a Small Village

I wish you the best in your work and in your approaching campaign.

                              Tadeusz Maciejczyk
                              Milledgeville, November 10, 1991

P.S. I am sending you a copy of my recent letter to Guy Vander Jagt, Chairman of the National Republican Congressional Committee.

Book Three

Clayton Yeutter
Chairman
Republican Party
Washington, D.C.

Dear Sir:

    I am sorry, but I am not putting a "Yes" sticker on my reply.
    The tremendous new opportunity of enormous gain in redrawing the Congressional and the state's legislative maps produces no excitement in me. Just a feeling of sadness and disappointment.
    My impression is that this opportunity is deviating attention from the real and difficult problems of the country to the noisy infightings of Party strategists giving them the impression of enormous activity and merit, while correcting nothing. Your "opportunity" can be very attractive to politicians. To normal, working people, it is only boring, disturbing, or in the best case, indifferent entertainment for the professionals. It is disturbing, because it is giving an early signal that the upcoming campaign will produce the same costly miserable show as it did the other times.
    Our politicians do not want to realize that the time of the successful old tricks is over. The country became devastated by them enough and now the country cries for a new, creative, far-sighted approach to elect their representatives. The issues and the ideas, not the voting districts, or even the parties, will attract the attention of the people.
    Yesterday, I wrote to Pres. Bush telling him about alternative new approaches to prepare campaigns, able to call attention today. The old stereotype became too obsolete, too sclerotic, too sterile.
    Here, I want to thank you for sending me a sign that somebody in the Headquarters was reading my previous letters. Your response to my problems was the same as everyone else when I asked for help in the time of stress, a finger pointed to others who surely should help.
    I wish you the best in your work.

                                           Tadeusz Maciejczyk
                                           Milledgeville, November 12, 1991

The World Seen from the Distance of a Small Village

Al Jourdan
Chairman
Illinois Republican Party
Springfield, IL

Dear Mr. Chairman:

I thank you for your special certificate.

I would like to feel that it was sent to me sincerely only because of my merits. I know, nevertheless, that it is not so. My merits for the Party, especially for the Illinois Party, are less than minimal. I know that the only purpose of your letter was for a collection.

But I have memories from the previous campaigns. I do not want to repeat what I saw time after time, a similar uncaring for quality, for sincerity, for new ideas, new spirit. Until now, I saw no signs that any kind of renewal in campaign preparation is underway.

And in the politics as usual: shallow, egoistic, deceptive and short-sighted, I have no desire to participate.

I hope I could see a promising change, and soon.

I wish you the best in your work.

Tadeusz Maciejczyk
Milledgeville, IL, November 17, 1991

P.S. I am sending you a copy of my last letter to Chairman Yeutter and Chairman Guy Vander Jagt.

Book Three

Time Magazine
Letters

In your otherwise very good article about World War II in Europe, the last sentence is misleading and needs clarification. "The methodical extermination of millions in the six Polish death camps," was done on occupied Polish territory and entirely by the occupying German authorities and forces. In those six "Polish death camps," and in others outside Poland, nearly three million Poles died.

No. Those death camps were not Polish. Or they were Polish only to the same degree as would be Philippine the American prisoners camp after the Bataan Death March.

Tadeusz Maciejczyk
Milledgeville, December 1, 1991

The World Seen from the Distance of a Small Village

Sandy Gelston
Treasurer
Americans to Limit Congressional Terms

Dear Lady:

I agree that the defeat in Washington State calls for a new attention and a continuation of efforts.

If we learn from Washington experience and analyze all elements that played a significant, or even marginal role, if we screen all the arguments and take a good look at all centers of counteraction, including forces and motivations of their background; if we study those backgrounds strengths and weaknesses, and its nerve centers; if we do a good study of the process of transformation of the minds of Washington voters; if we try to find which arguments touched and convinced them most, and why anyway 45% stayed with their conviction; if with all those preparations, we observe intelligently and analytically all future moves of the forces that like to keep things in Congress as they are, in this way protecting their investments in the particular members of the present Congress; if we keep vigilant and persistent, then the battle in Washington will be precious to us, not to them. It will be only a school ground that prepared us for real labor in life.

I send you my contribution of $40.00 and I send you some of my last letters that had some connection with the 1992 campaign. Maybe they can also contribute to your efforts.

I wish you the best. Within my possibilities, you can count on me.

Tadeusz Maciejczyk
Milledgeville, December 5, 1991

Book Three

Republican National Committee
Membership Office
Washington, D.C.

    I confirm that I received your renewed card for 1992 membership in the GOP

    After receiving your reminder letter, I have to clarify my situation. I do not like and I am not excited about a "Sustaining GOP Membership" for me.

    I do not understand well the difference between normal and sustaining memberships. What are their prerogatives or limitations? And altogether, why is there such a tendency to subdivide members into different categories? Why can't the memberships be uniform and democratic? Whom is this system protecting? And whom is it just using?

    As I do not approve, and I do not like any human segregation in categories within a party or within a society, I ask you to remove my name from your membership list.

                                      Tadeusz Maciejczyk
                                      Milledgeville, December 29, 1991

The World Seen from the Distance of a Small Village

Clayton Yeutter
Chairman
Republican National Committee

Dear Sir:

I thank you for your invitation to take part in your 1992 Rep. Senate Majority Survey, as well as for your highly complimentary opinion about me.

I agree with you that powerful forces exist in this country that are pushing America in a wrong direction, leading it not only to material, but also to moral and spiritual bankruptcy. An assault on fairness is one of the components of the deepening decay.

I will answer this survey the same way as I usually do—not by marking the "Yes" or "No" or "Undecided" spaces. Any survey marked only this way is rigid and superficial. It hardly reflects the reality. In my understanding, such surveys are practically worthless. Responding to this survey I will try to answer each question the best I can and I beg your pardon, if I do not fulfill your last requirement of "Please, be brief."

Questions Nos. 1–4

I think that the public hearings and judgments of Mr. Thomas were far more damaging to participating senators and to the whole Senate institution than they were to Mr. Thomas. They brought to the surface the hypocrisy of Senatorial dealings. As a result, they produced a deepening estrangement and alienation in many. I heard the question: "Are those, those our venerated leaders?"

That trial showed all the negative faces of phariseeism: "Listen all the great country of ours—look how good we are, and how miserable is that creature whom we judge!"

That trial denied the most accepted law of human life and ridiculed the teaching of Christianity.

We, the humans, we are learning and acquiring wisdom not from our perfection, but from our mistakes from failures. Through our miseries and blunders we are growing from childhood into teenaged mentality, finally to a full maturity. With such trials as the one against Mr. Thomas, St. Augustine would never have become a Saint and more than this, a theological father and guide for Christianity.

To complement my opinion, I am sending you my two previous letters about forgiveness.

Question No. 5

Book Three

My knowledge of economy is very limited. As many others here around, I am skeptical about the effectiveness of treatments of our economical maladies with just manipulations of taxes. The illness is much deeper and requires much more imaginative and a more farsighted approach. Just today I received a circular E correcting the taxation circular edited two months ago and bringing a tax relief. But how will the circular look for 1993, after the election?

Question No. 6

Yes! Without a doubt.

True representation has to have a living and fresh connection with the district. It cannot be limited to occasional or second-hand contacts, compensating a prolonged absence and acclimatization to a completely different, highly artificial atmosphere and lifestyle of the members of Congress. Such conditions are producing not a representation, but a PSEUDO-REPRESENTATION that leads into estrangement and grandiose complexes. ("Send me $50 for my campaign because I am worth it!" This was written to me by my Congressperson not long ago.)

For those who practice such a pseudo-representation, their districts are necessary only for one necessity: to be re-elected and for the preservation of their status everything goes, except sincerity and love for the district, or even for the country.

Our representatives in Congress, if truly they want to represent, they should be enormously excited about coming back to their districts as normal citizens, enriching there their knowledge by a second look on their territory and their constituency after their Congressional experiences and then, run again after an appropriate length of time and if elected, to show a true excellence in what representation should be.

Question No. 7.

Both of those methods of intended healing of economy are only a testimony of superficiality and shortsightedness. I do not see in them a policy. They produce only an endless and aimless patching, practiced since the beginning of time by all the losers of the world. Nobody should be paid for presenting to the country only such choices.

Here I would like to suggest that all our representatives should be scrutinized before elections for their ability to handle their own domestic finances. Somebody who there proved to be financially irresponsible, practicing lightly spending and borrowing, should be excluded from running for Congress. How in the world should he be trusted to handle the finances of the country?

The World Seen from the Distance of a Small Village

Question No. 8.

I would have to have more information to make a judgment. Why? For what purpose? Could this be accomplished in other ways without hurting not as much the rich, as the poorest who need gas to reach the work place? It looks to me that with such a remedy, we could start a vicious circle. Many of such vicious circles were already produced in the last decades and we still didn't learn.

Question No. 9.

The most important issue facing America in the Nineties should be the rebuilding of our nation's infrastructures.

By this, I am not talking about roads and bridges. I am talking here about our actions, big or small that added one to another could heal our wounds, put us more together and permit us to appreciate life more.

To start:

A. I would cut short glorifications of the rich and famous and I would direct all the lights and glory on the honest and on the responsible. The glorification of the rich brought too many scandals and produced temptations. And the want of the riches never has a bottom, frequently goes together with greed and is guided by ethics rather infrequently. I tell this because people need fresh patters to follow and to direct their lives accordingly.
B. I would re-define, re-examine and search for a new realization and cultivation of an atmosphere of trust. Today this trust is very low in America. Suspicions and accusations appear everywhere, poisoning the air, distancing people, paralyzing actions, killing spontaneity and incubating abusers who are increasing the vicious circle.
C. I would increase awareness of the difference between being kindhearted or good-natured and being good. These two completely different human behaviors are frequently confused, are taken for the same, but their consequences, their fruits, are completely different.

    The kind-heartedness requires no effort, permits everything just to look good, have peace and not to be bothered. It gives satisfaction to everybody for a short distance. It spoils, it breeds unhappy, unadjusted adults and sometimes human monsters.

Book Three

Being good requires vision, purpose, wisdom and self-discipline. It directs, corrects, creates physical and spiritual growth and helps to reach fulfillment in life.

The differentiation of those two notions is of enormous importance in the life of any family, any society or nation. Maybe the difference between those two approaches to life can be illustrated best by remembering what happened to Helen Keller.

D. I would never stop to stress the enormous need for sincerity in our private and public life. The protracted, proverbial insincerity of politicians created a wide spread distrust of them. We need, we want to see in them a whole person with a perfect soul. When sincerity fails, we suffer. The last State of the Union was spoken with a very benevolent voice, was adorned with an almost constant smile, but in all its length, it didn't mention the central problem: our enormous debt that every day grows bigger. That speech put our President in a false situation and already is producing for him difficulties in the primaries. Nobody really believed in his repeated assurances that "we will . . . ." That speech didn't mobilize. It was paralyzing, increasing anxiety and alienation. Whoever wrote and put that speech together didn't help the President, nor the country.

E. I would do everything to relax the strangulating bureaucratization of everything we do or do not do. The detailed laws, the mounting paperwork, became at least tenfold in the last few years. The proper work became secondary to papers and its readiness for the crowd of controllers whose demands became each time more stringent, frequently more distant from a common sense, even ridiculous. Those detailed laws, born from our "leaders" good-heartedness are immobilizing, are increasing anxiety and defensive postures, are enormously costly and are breeding legions of "experts" and advisors who for high pay sell their advice, teaching how those laws can be by-passed or ignored, or even how to profit from them. The proliferations of such laws is almost as dangerous to society as the Aids virus is. And its volume is growing. About 19 centuries ago, Tacitus, the Roman senator and historian wrote that the more corrupt the state is, the more numerous are its laws. His observation is especially alive in today's America

F. Avoid practicing "croney-ism"

The nomination of Lynn Martin to be a Labor Secretary in the time of radical changes in the field of the labor force was a clear example of "croney-ism" and had no justification. It was felt here with a deep uneasiness. Bypassing the interests of the country, the President did this for a friend and to look good to the women's movement. The Congress confirmed this nomination without making one question, obviously to repay Lynn Martin for her role in increasing Congressional salaries. The Congressional salary hike, as the nomination produced a very depressing and discouraging show for the country.

G. Curb the malpractice rash.

From a search for justice, malpractice degenerated into massive "justice games" that are terrorizing not only doctors, but every action born and held in this country. It is very difficult to work, to make decisions, to be responsible or compassionate or creative under the terror of this very special "justice."

Who can count how many job possibilities went from this country elsewhere to escape the axe of this pseudo-justice? How much more expensive became the products made under the constant threat of this new inquisition? Who knows how many present days' blues grew from those justice games?

It is almost a national emergency to take a good look on the size, on the substance and on the consequences of this serious national malady. I include here several of my letters written in the heat of the struggle, during my malpractice suit in which I defended myself and I won.

Also, because the malpractice explosion in a certain way, is a measurement of a new freedom and of a new justice, I include here my letter about flag burning and flag spitting.

H. Change the present competitions in schools, especially in high schools from completely one-sided sports shows into true competitions in all the fields in which those schools are preparing their students for life. In the same pattern as the sports championships, the schools should organize championships in English, in knowledge of literature, in history, in geography, in mathematics, in physics and chemistry, in creative arts, etc. As the schools are supposed to be primarily institutions for formation and training of minds, the scholastic competitions should mean the biggest merit for students and for schools. Only with these organized and active competitions, the schools should be permitted to compete in sports. In our schools the boys who kick the ball should not overshadow the potential Einsteins or

Book Three

Shakespeares. America is already suffering from the present sports priority in its schools.

I. Re-establish and make popular handcrafts. With the present trend, America is becoming a nation of factory's, office's, institution's employees who are reduced just to small screws in a big engine without chances to show their own individuality, creativity or dreams. Handicrafts would give such chances. Surely there are people who would be attracted to them, feel comfortable there and succeed.

    i. While massive factory products are overflowing markets, those markets surely would have still plenty of room for objects made by hand. Each of such objects would be more unique and would bear signs of love put into their creations.

    ii. Every year, expositions of those products could be organized in on the county, state and national level, stimulating them and permitting them to grow in numbers and in excellence. A special department could be established to guide, to cultivate and organize those works. Surely, reviving those skills and those productions could provide a buffer zone for our recessions.

J. Use national holidays not only to provide ceremonies and parties for politicians and political activists, but to create through them new involvements, new windows into the future, new understandings and cooperation between groups. In relation to this point, I send you my letter about my version of Martin Luther King Day.

K. Create new approaches and new ways to deal most constructively with the problem of the permanent, hereditary dependency.

L. Create new ways to discover and train our leaders. In relation to this I am sending you a copy of my speech for Decoration Day and my last letter to President Bush.

Probably, this is enough. I wish you the best in your work.

Tadeusz Maciejczyk
Milledgeville, February 25, 1992

The World Seen from the Distance of a Small Village

Clayton Yeutter
Chairman
Republican National Committee

Dear Sir:

I am sending you my answer to your letter and survey. As you predicted, I did this according to my convictions. And also because I was selected to represent this area of Illinois in this survey, I was trying to take into account what the people from here were telling me.

O.K. They were telling me politely that I am a fool believing that writing to Washington would make any difference. "They want your money, not your opinion," was a general consensus. I believe them. Nevertheless, I wrote once more.

Taking into account the general sentiment, I am writing a check for $35.00 to our local Salvation Army, one dollar for every Senatorial race. Below the skin here is an uneasy feeling that soon we will need more Salvation Armies than we need politicians.

I also want to say that if I am not advised otherwise by you, one week from today, I will send the copies of this letter to national magazines, then to local newspapers and of course to the Salvation Army, to explain my third contribution to them since Christmas.

I hope that this survey will add and mean something to you and to the Republican Party.

I send you my best wishes.

                              Tadeusz Maciejczyk
                              Milledgeville, February 27, 1992

P.S. I an including a photocopy of my check to the Salvation Army.

Book Three

Thomas Rhodes
Assistant to the Chairman
Republican Presidential Advisory Commission

Dear Sir:

About one year ago, I received from you and your organization, a letter that sounded exactly like the one that I obtained from you today with the same sentences, the same appeals, the same promises and practically the same points or questions in the survey.

At that time I took you seriously. I was trying to respond to all your questions as well as I could.

I do not care much about your certificate, duly or not duly authorized.

I was disappointed because not even once did I receive the promised special issue briefings or classified, national survey results. Since that time, I didn't see even a trace of your activity, any sign of your life. And today, I received from you exactly the same letter with the same requests and the same questions, the same renewed need for money. My life changed significantly since your last letter and you are where you were one year ago.

Considering your hibernation, why should I worry about your implementation of a variety of sophisticated programs necessary to run your Commission? President Lincoln said long ago that nobody can fool the people all the time.

My impression is that you are not doing anything good for President Bush.

I am sorry that I had to write this letter.

Tadeusz Maciejczyk
Milledgeville, March 21, 1992

The World Seen from the Distance of a Small Village

Sally Webster
Sustaining Membership Director
Republican National Committee

Dear Sally Webster:

I am responding to your letter because it was completely different from most such letters that I received from the Republican Party. Your letter showed talent. It had a freshness and the strength of somebody who really believes in his work and its mission. Those are the qualities that I appreciate and I hope your bosses will not only preserve, but reinforce them by their own actions and conduct. So many times in such letters as yours from the Party, I have seen only shallowness, arrogance and dullness of routine.

I would like to have your faith. I would like to believe in the intentions, wisdom, vision and clarity and strength in the implementation of those Republican principles you are talking about and in the merit of the selected Party candidates.

Years ago, I had such a faith as yours. I lost it.

I didn't like the atmosphere of the time of elections. I didn't see wisdom in candidate selections. I didn't like the boring, rigid, indoctrinated speeches or disputes of our politicians. They were not elevating. They were degrading the nation. The challenging country and world changes were not touching the candidates. Those candidates were after positions, prestige, privileges, not after true labor of shaping the future. During the last elections in 1990, I voted for the Democratic candidates, not because I wanted to. They were less damaging.

I also have to say that never in my life in the U.S., I felt so victimized, so much harassed, so much dispirited as in the Eighties and now, during the Republican Presidency. One year ago, in my survey for the Republican Presidential Advisory commission, I wrote this about President Reagan:

"As Stalin in Russia changed the dark side of the Russian soul into an enormous caricature of the Soviet People's Paradise, so Reagan accentuated the American tendency to luxury into an unrestrained bulimia, the shine of the surface pose, the idolatry of the rich and famous. He created his unprecedented prosperity by borrowing, by plunging the country into enormous debt, asserting that the appearance was more important than the real life, like in a movie. The results were wonderful for the day and catastrophic for tomorrow. It brought not only debts, but also many scandals, very costly for normal people and to the whole country. It formed also a generation in which the American 'pursuit of happiness' changed into the present American drive to get rich from the lottery, from gambling, from lawsuits, from completely unrestrained destruction of others, or of the riches that belong to all of us. Reagan is guilty of popularizing that selfishness, ruthlessness and superficiality that money and luxury, not that virtue or character are the most effective ways to live and a real god in America."

During the Bush presidency, except for the short period of Desert Storm, I never felt the President's touch to inspire the people, to motivate them, to lead them. During those four years in the U.S., the wolves had an almost completely free ride among the population. The shepherd was absent. Only the new election year shook his apparent indifference, but his remedies, his leadership, are surface deep, are non-inspiring for the people, are not elevating, not mobilizing. To change the present marasm is done nothing, is visualized nothing, is dreamed nothing. Most likely after the shakeup of the election year, the events will continue their sleepy, hollow way in the Republican White House until the next election of still deeper frustration and suffering among the ordinary, unprivileged people of this country.

In the P.S. of your letter you are sincerely hoping that everything is all right with me and my family. I do not know. The last years were not easy for us.

In 1983, I refused to pay malpractice insurance because it was ridiculously exaggerated, very expensive and its cost was immediately transferred to the bills of the patients, the sick and already suffering. Consequently I lost my hospital privileges.

In January 1987 I got my own malpractice suit. Its accusation was ridiculous. Its pressures were enormous. I defended myself without a lawyer and I can tell you that nothing was spared by the judiciary to break me and to break my family. My letters to Washington were mostly unanswered. In that suit I won.

Now my practice is reduced to the minimum. I do not have hospital privileges; I stopped doing X-Rays in my office; I do not do surgeries. I do not deliver babies. In 1990, the year of my last stand in the Courtroom, my total income for the year was $27,000. From this, I was paying still tuition.

Also, now I am at home alone. My wife couldn't cope with the present realities of my medical practice. She went to work in Chicago. She doesn't want to live through the terror of another trial again. And I work with a constant uncertainty. What will happen tomorrow? I like to work for

The World Seen from the Distance of a Small Village

the people. I hate every workday now. The last year's bureaucratization made nauseating what before was simple and natural.

History will judge the Bush presidency not only for the surface appearances and manipulations, but also for the abandonment, for neglect, for the careless contribution to the decay of a moral and spiritual makeup of society.

What can I say?

As I told you, I lost my faith. I do not like to be s sustaining member in the Party. In my last letter to the Party in 1991, I asked to be removed from sustaining membership.

I respond to this letter because you asked me to and because I saw in you a difference from the usual. I hope that this letter will not discourage you or break you. I wanted to be frank and to make you see the need for change.

To make you see better a different reality, a reality of life as it is, I am sending you my last letter to the Chairman and I am sending you all the additions to that letter.

I wish you the best in your work and for your future achievements.

                        Tadeusz Maciejczyk
                        Milledgeville, March 26, 1992

Book Three

Al Jourdan
Chairman
Illinois Republican Party

Dear Sir:

I received your membership dues statement.

But I do not intend to renew my sustaining membership. Why should I belong to such a passive structure where even the name "sustaining" precludes my input or any influence of my point of view.

I know that the time for action is now. But the problem is that I do not see any movement in the Party that would testify to its renewal. Either I see any visibility, any declaration or pronunciations of the Illinois Senatorial candidate for the Rep. Party. Who is he? What are his qualities for leadership in this uneasy time of expected fundamental changes? In my opinion, those qualities should be already made known. Only the particular points or planes should be left for the true debates. The newspapers surely would write about him, his past merits, his character, his philosophy of life and it would come without expense. There is a hunger in the people for such news, for discovering those whom we can trust and be proud of.

To belong, I would like to be convinced. I would like to feel the desire to dedicate all my energy to the cause. At present, the sleepy atmosphere of the party is not exciting, not inviting to me.

I am sending you the copy of my last letter to Sally Webster, sustaining membership director in Washington. I explained there my feelings and my objections. I am sending you also my answers to the last survey of Chairman Yeutter where I responded to some fundamental questions.

I send you my best wishes in your work.

Tadeusz Maciejczyk
Milledgeville, April 2, 1992

The World Seen from the Distance of a Small Village

J. Fannin
Tax Examiner
Internal Revenue Service

Dear Sir:

I thank you for the explanation of my penalty. My note, attached to payment, was just an outburst of bitterness and of my growing pessimism.

No, I have no justification for a delay of my payment. I just forgot it. I paid it the day I discovered my omission.

It is not easy nowdays to strive to be independent. In my small countryside medical office, the rapidly increasing paperwork is killing all the joy and satisfaction from the true work. That paperwork, their artificiality and the constantly changing coding system, the more and more frequent new rules, new directives, each time closer terms to remember to pay taxes, all with the attached imminent threat of penalties, are destroying the soul of the working man.

Big institution can afford to have special offices and special personnel to watch and to handle those problems. In my office, I have to deal with them after the daylong assistance to the sick when I am already tired. The administrative norms are changing and are growing and with them grows the anxiety, the confusion, uncertainty and depression. More and more times I ask myself why work in such conditions? How many times can I pay the penalties—penalties that in other, more healthy environments would not exist—and not break down?

The young doctors are escaping to clinics where they are protected from all those harassments. But the clinics are enormously more expensive to patients and to the whole health system. The clinics are organized with the business mentality. How many of my patients told me that they cannot afford to go there any more?

Such fools as I are still operating their places on the old principle of primarily helping the people and the sick. They are more vulnerable to the bureaucratic hammer. They cannot cope. They feel more and more the approaching complete strangulation.

The truth is that when the working force gets dispirited, driven up to the ceiling or completely destroyed, the lawmaking institutions and the bureaucratic system goes down with them. Or maybe that is what is necessary for a renewal of America.

Book Three

I know that you are doing what you have to do. I am sorry for getting bitter and telling what I feel. Maybe it is time for me to retire. Anyway, America is not what it was.

I am sending you a copy of my answers to one of the latest surveys where this my growing uneasiness is expressed in a somewhat different way.

I sent you my best wishes in your work.

Tadeusz Maciejczyk, M.D
Milledgeville, April 12, 1992

Letter to the Editor
Newsweek Magazine

RE: Robert J. Samuelson's "I Am a Big Lawyer Basher"

Dear Sir:

I am very grateful to you for the initiation of a public discussion about the growing abnormality of our civil justice system and the emergency needs for its reform.

A society so tempted to litigate and so prone to resolve all its emotional conflicts in the courts without any trial to develop an alternative, positive approach in order to live together in justice will always be emotionally sick and dissatisfied and ultimately will deviate into increasing destabilization, disintegration and decay.

Litigations are producing mostly bad blood, intimidation of many, loss of initiative, stagnation, progressive loss of self-esteem with growing anxieties and depression. In addition, and above all, they produce an enormous overgrowth of parasites in society.

We see already an alarming increase of all those factors in our country. It is high time to do a good Spring-cleaning of our home.

Tadeusz Maciejczyk, M.D.
Milledgeville, April 23, 1992

P.S. I am sending you my last survey response where, among other things, I talked about litigations and my own experience in Court.

The World Seen from the Distance of a Small Village

Letter to the Editor
Time Magazine
RE: "The Fire This Time" (May 11, 1992)

Dear Sir:

During the L.A. rioting, among many of its horrors, one episode reached the bestial level parallel to the beating of Rodney King. For the sake of the future, that scene should not be forgotten or unanswered, just because of the present touchy and delicate relationship between races.

I am talking here about the senseless beating of Reginald Denny. Those men, who participate in that spectacle of hate, should be brought to justice.

But the trial against them should be different from usual. Besides the punishment, the secondary, but the most important objective of that trial should be a special and deep look at all the elements that led finally to the explosion. I think that such a trial should create a base for a breaking of those barriers of hate and lead to eventual true reconciliation and peace.

To make such an outcome possible, those black men should be judged by black personalities known for their character and wisdom. Those judges should be elected especially for this purpose by the whole community of African Americans in this country.

The inferiority complexes, the accumulated bitterness will never be shaken only by giving the blacks special opportunities, by desegregating schools, by the forced desegregation of neighborhoods, etc. The effort to grow, to cultivate character, to be able to forgive, to grow spiritually, has to come from inside. Such a growth is not easy. It is much more easy to hate and to be proud of being a hate hero than to pass the difficult process of self-examination, to understand deeper and to make new decisions that since then would shape life. Martin Luther King was especially demanding for blacks. He dreamed not about surface deep, forced equality, but about new growth, new maturity among the followers. Without such an inner transformation, all facilitations given to black communities would not bring them the true peace of the soul and the hate would constantly prepare the future situations for the new explosions.

It looks to me that today's black leaders prefer to keep the blacks in the pit with all their stigmas and complexes inflamed while playing their non-inspiring, uncreative "leadership" mostly by extending their hands

Book Three

for contributions. They do absolutely nothing to change the self-image and to create a true pride, based on daily conduct and general achievements of the blacks.

If the explosion in L.A. would help to create such a change, the results would be much brighter for all of us, and the dream of Martin Luther King could be truly alive.

Tadeusz Maciejczyk, M.D.
Milledgeville, May 10, 1992

Betty Stanton
PDDA Coordinator
Scott-Levin Associates, Inc.

Dear Lady:

I looked at the forms to be filled for each patient and I gave up. I am sorry. Here in this countryside office with one nurse and one half-day clerk, we are already exhausted, not from seeing and helping patients, but from the paperwork. We already cannot bear this any more.

The sterility and the nonsense of this paperwork explosion are demoralizing and killing all the previous enthusiasm for medical practice. The daily stress of coping with the ever-increasing avalanche of papers is inviting each time louder to retire, to escape, to start to do something else, something where the nonsense is not dictating and is not bending the real work.

At present I am taking voluntarily a course in ambulatory medicine that will last for one year. The usefulness, the need for constant study in the constantly-changing medical field is obvious to me. The artifacts put on medicine by the continually mushrooming of bureaucracy is an aberration from normal. It is a kind of malignant growth in the body of medicine.

I am sending you back your report forms. I have no energy and no motivation to do this work. The energy that I still have I want to dedicate to something positive, beautiful and useful.

Nevertheless, I wish you the best in your enterprise.

Tadeusz Maciejczyk, M.D.
Milledgeville, May 25, 1992

The World Seen from the Distance of a Small Village

Tom Luce
Chairman
Perot Petition Committee

Dear Sir:

I received your letter today and I wanted to tell you and Mr. Perot that I see in him a hope for the country and maybe even for the world. I listened to Mr. Perot and I felt his strength, together with a simplicity, openness and a special gift for leadership, not in normal times, but in the uneasy and stressful times.

Simultaneously with this letter, I am sending you a packet of my previous letters that maybe can be of some use to Mr. Perot in the approaching debates.

Also, because I read about this today, I want to indicate here my stand on the problem of abortion.

I am a doctor and I know that abortion is nothing less than murder of an incipient human being. I know also that the rights to abortion are not making women free. On the contrary. After such an experience, women are left with the lasting, frequently disabling or even destroying scare in their self-esteem, an open wound in their conscience and a self-condemning feeling of guilt.

I also realize that abortion is not a primary social disease, but a last chain of moral conditioning that is shaping the living climate, preparing the ground, inviting and pushing the young. The government effort to clean this kind of situation is almost non-existent. Rather the trend continues like an undisturbed avalanche.

Forbidding abortion while doing nothing to clean and heal the circumstances that make abortion so endemic is hypocrisy. As long as the present conditioning exists, the rampant abortion problem will not disappear by an act of prohibition. It would only go underground, making the situation infinitely more tragic.

The fight against abortion has to start somewhere else, not by blocking abortion clinics. A true fight with this problem is enormous and could really be a true test for us.

I think that a true stand against all the causes that lead to the endemic abortion problems could also resolve almost all problems the country is facing now.

Book Three

If I can be of any help to you, please tell me.

Tadeusz Maciejczyk
Milledgeville, IL, June 8, 1992

Richard N. Bond
Chairman
Republican National Committee

Dear Sir:

I received your invitation to serve as an Illinois Delegate to the Presidential Trust of the Republican Party. I thank you for this distinction and honor, but I have my objections.

1. If this invitation is just an honorary fiction, I am not interested. If, on the contrary, you have work for me to do, I would like to have more specific directions.
2. Over one year ago, I received a questionnaire from the Presidential Advisory Commission. At that time, I took it seriously. I responded to each question as well as I could. I never heard from them again until last spring when I got from them an identical questionnaire with exactly the same questions. Only the dating of that questionnaire was changed. I came to a conclusion that the Presidential Advisory Commission was not a working institution, but just another pretext to ask for money.
3. I am not an admirer of the legacy of President Reagan's Presidency. Looking on the consequences of his "reign," I see each day more clearly the seeds of destruction he planted in the American soul and in the American life. From President Bush I expected a new vision for America. All the people around here are waiting for a change, for new directions. Here, the continuation of Pres. Reagan's heritage is perceived as a direct road into an increasing gloom. Behind Reagan's shiny frontal façade, the foundations were crumbling or were absent.

The World Seen from the Distance of a Small Village

4. I do not understand well your persistence to keep me within the Republican Party. I am an M.D., but I said clearly that my material means were limited. In the atmosphere of the 80s and 90s, my work and even my family, disintegrated. After my opposition to the obligatory malpractice insurance, I lost my hospital privileges. Then, because of a vendetta, I had a malpractice suit against me that lasted for three and one-half years. I defended myself without a lawyer and I won. But my family life and my practice collapsed. My wife left. She couldn't bear any more of the terror of that trial. At present, my work is reduced just to office visits. At home I am alone and I live very simply. I just want to provide still for the two tuitions for my youngest children. In Reagan's America, and still after him, an honest work was not giving any assurance, stability or satisfaction. As I already said, during those last years, the wolves multiplied and ran loose in America producing devastation. The shepherd? The shepherd didn't care.

I would like to see the Republican Party as a center of a vigorous life with a knowledge and strength to do what is right with a discipline to renew and to provide true leadership.

What I really see is a closed circle of old Party activists whose main preoccupation is not to serve the nation, but to retain their positions, their privileges and their power. I do not see that the party is interested in new ideas, in freshness of thinking and in renewal. If the Party is reaching to the periphery, to the so-called "sustaining membership," its main objective is only the money.

Those members are measured only by one stick: by the size of their monetary contribution.

And so, the Party is aging and is becoming sclerotic. The croney-ism is becoming more frequent. Slogans and tricks have a priority. The vision of tomorrow and the real work for tomorrow became neglected and was substituted by vague promises and assurances. Advantage for today became the center for all moves. Popularity became the goddess and the popularity is always shallow and frequently frivolous.

By such a mentality, the Republican Party is losing its connection with the actual life, with the true people and with the true issues. The Party is reducing itself this way to an anemic existence in the sphere of the old memories and habits of the people, maybe in their need for belonging or for prestige from the old glories.

Book Three

I have an impression that I will not receive a medal for my feedback from the periphery, or to say it in a different way, from the real breathing and working America. But I can console myself that what I said here was sincere and was filled with the care for the truth and with the love for the country and for its people.

I wish you the best.

Tadeusz Maciejczyk
Milledgeville, June 28, 1992

The World Seen from the Distance of a Small Village

Richard A. Viguerie
Chairman
United Senior Association, Inc.
Chantilly, Virginia

Dear Sir:

I received your urgent invitation to stress the problems of the Seniors now in this election year when the conditions are the most appropriate to extract concessions and promises from politicians by insinuating that we would not vote for them if they refuse. We should insist that our causes should have a priority among all other problems of the nation.

This petition is symbolizing present-day America. The multitude of pressure groups have only themselves in mind, demanding and threatening while refusing to elevate themselves by positive and creative programs.

In this petition we are no better than the present Negro leadership that prefers to keep their constituency in the pit with all the stigmas and complexes inflamed while playing their uninspiring, uncreative "leadership," mostly by demanding and extending their hands for retributions. "Give us compensation for our past and present sufferings, because otherwise, the flames of the L.A. riots will appear in every corner of America."

It is enormously sad that practically every group in America at present, is playing such a game. Sure. In this election year we can press for special priorities for Seniors. The campaigning politicians will agree to everything, then after the election, not one of them will remember what and to whom they made promises. Life will go on as usual. Only the bitterness, the insecurity, the bigger than ever isolation of every one of the striving-for-priority groups will take a new toll on the living conditions in America.

It is true that America is now not only in an another election year, but also in a very special, precedent-making, soul-searching, multi-dimensional transformation. To direct this transformation wisely, to make it fruitful in the future, the narrow look, the selfishness, the "what is in it for me" attitude of the pressure groups are not the best tools to carve the future.

Now is the best time to make a good inventory of all the forces and potentials that we, the Seniors, are representing and what we can offer to society. Happiness generally comes more from giving, than from receiving. What, and in what way, can we, the Seniors, give to the nation?

A few years ago, I saw on TV a wealthy, well-dressed Senior on an expensive golf course saying that he demands for himself Social Security benefits because this was his right. I got sick looking at him. Such men will not help America in a time of crisis. Most likely, they are the cause of America's downfall.

If we, the Seniors, if we would define our active (not just parasitic) role in society, our position to negotiate, to defend our true needs, to defend the integrity of the Social Security Trust Fund, the price of Medicare's monthly premiums or the kind of services Medicare should provide, the defense of our needs would be much easier. Remembering the man on the golf course, I understand that the "means Testing" has a justification.

Best wishes.

Tadeusz Maciejczyk
July 12, 1992

The World Seen from the Distance of a Small Village

Richard N. Bond
Chairman
Republican National Committee
RE: Platform Advisory Tabulation Code 310182

I do not consider myself as a "sustaining member" of the Republican Party. I do not like this name and this category. By only its name, those members are excluded from true participation and they are set apart from the privileged circle of the Republican priesthood and their Saints.

Nevertheless, I was asked to participate and to contribute to the ideas gathering for the platform that would shape and direct the political actions of the Party. I feel that I cannot refuse such a call and remain silent.

In this answer I do not like to just confirm your leading questions.

I will not respond to the whole question. 1. About the points it contains, I have already said many times and I do not like a mechanical, senseless repetition. I saw those questions already many times in all the surveys of the last four years and its formulation until now became completely frozen without any sign of change or maturation. No new thought transformed them into something more specific or more precise.

In Question 2, I am completely skeptical about the capacity of this administration to direct the health care issue or to control its cost.

The evidence of the past ten years in this aspect is not encouraging. In order to take care only of the Senior citizens' health, this administration created enormous bureaucracy that operates from a rigid frame and is inclined to terrorize the health care workers to stress its authority.

The newest flower of this bureaucracy, the OSHA, can be the perfect illustration of this bureaucratic bumbling and puffing. It created pages of new orders and requirements, with new considerable expenses that have to be added to the already existing. It added also a new line of threats, creating a new heaven for the malpractice lawyers. With disbelief, I saw that the previous threats of a few thousand dollars for each transgression was elevated to a bombastic $70,000.00.

This Administration has no capacity for an inspiring and energy-mobilizing approach to the ever-increasing critical urgent health care issue. It created only doubt, insecurity, perplexity, confusion, disinvolvement and a need for multiple, expensive devices for self-protection. It opened the field to a legion of profiteers and abusers.

Never until now was the ownership of health insurance so costly and so uncertain with so many hidden traps and small print. Never before were malpractice accusations so common and abusive, so destructive to the material and to the moral tissue of society. Never before was the cost of medicine spiraling upward so much. Never before were so many games played in the health care field to take advantage, to satisfy greed, to catch the biggest part of the pie. Never before was a patient reduced to be a number without a name and the health care so much a business without a face.

In the last ten years, the Rep. Admin. Practically destroyed the medical private practice in America. The uncontrolled and abusive malpractice threats, the increasingly bigger burden of dealing with the regulations of the Health Care Admin., the absurd paperwork, the general atmosphere of work's uncertainties and tensions, all those created defensive moves by the doctors.

To work, the doctors now look for a refuge and safety in the big medical clinics that have their own administration and offices to play games with the Washington Health Admin. while they perform their work relatively undisturbed. The true private practice, all those who still defend their independent spirits are pushed into the corners and are condemned to a slow death.

And so, the private practice that is the most elastic, most practical, most inexpensive and most responsive to the needs of the people, became practically swallowed into the obscurity of the enormous, never satisfied and always extending bureaucratic stomach.

The games between the government Health Admin. and the clinic's admin. are not cheap. In the clinics, under today's pressures, the historic spirit of medical service, even of the Hippocratic pledge became more and more dislodged and routed out. In the hands of their own bureaucracy (always very well paid) the clinics became the usual American business places where the principal objective is mainly the money. The doctors in those clinics became pampered employees if they went along smoothly with this new medical philosophy or emptied down from their idealism and gradually changed by different kinds of pressures, or purged, if they would remain too independent.

Altogether, I have no hope that this Administration has the capacity or guts to create a just, inspiring and healthy Health Care system.

Turning to another problem:

I read with uneasiness your unspecific, generalized condemnation of Democrats and elevation with self-pride of Republicans. Such a partisan, blind, party-loyal chauvinistic approach is good for no one. It is not good for Republicans. It invites not to think, not to change, not to act with responsibility. It is enormously cheap and tasteless. It never will convince or mobilize. It always will seed doubts. It will not touch those who could be the true potential leaders in the future.

Speaking about leaders and leadership, I disagree completely with the President's and the Republican Party's persistent excuses that they visualized, acted upon and investigated practicality or importance of problems; that they then presented them to the congress and only the obstinate treachery of the Democratically dominated Congress prevented the realization of those plans.

The President, if he is a true leader and if he had clear vision and clear plans for realization, always would have a great recourse to speak about them publicly to the nation to gain the support of the nation and together with the nation press the Congress to do what should be done.

As I know, never during his presidency, did President Bush use this recourse. So many times I was ready to give him credit, to see in him a spark of true caring, of clear concepts, of true originality. I prayed for such a testimony of leadership in him, as well as in the Republican Party. After such expectations, generally I heard only the same excuses. I saw the same disinterest for true labor necessary to be aware, to be creative and disciplined in his work for the country, for the good for us, for our children and grandchildren, for the world.

Never did the nation see in this President a true builder for the 21st century. He never showed a continuity of action already done. The great promises, if they were pictured during election time, or at some other occasion, always hung somewhere in the sky without any evidence that they were taken seriously for realization here on earth, in life as it is.

In his administration, we saw only the daily patching, the desire to not reveal the shortcomings, or potential dangers, but to cover them up. The ideas to govern the nation were coming not as much from the Administration as from the omnipotent lobbies. Nobody in the government cared for the nation or for the true working man in America. This abandonment was felt very deeply in the past decade and it created the present lack of confidence, the present need for a change, for renewal, for Perot.

To this overwhelming hunger for leadership, for vision, for sincerity, for a constant true dialogue between those who govern and the governed, for the need to be the same body in hardship and in prosperity, this Administration and the Republican Party is responding with a self-exaltation together with blaming everybody else for failures and is washing constantly their hands as proof of innocence.

The nation is watching.
The nation is waiting.

Book Three

Will the next Republican platform present the life and the facts as they truly are? Will it give the right direction we should take? Are this Administration and this Party really capable of performing a truly farsighted work for the benefit of our children and grandchildren? Until now the grandchildren became the main victim of our behavior today. Can the Republican Party platform truly identify itself with the nation's needs and eliminate its tendency for egotism?

Whatever it is, 1992 is a very special time for soul searching and for change. Can the Republican Party be trusted again? I hope so, but I have no special illusions.

I include here copies of my recent letters about my view of the Pro-Life vs. Pro-Choice dispute and a letter to one of the presently abundant pressure groups: to the United Senior Association.

I wish you the best.

Tadeusz Maciejczyk
August 2, 1992

The World Seen from the Distance of a Small Village

Theses H. Stoica
Deputy Director of Medical Operations
Illinois Department of Public Aid
Springfield, IL

Dear Ms. Stoica:

The treatment of Public Aid patients has become complicated again by new rules and requirements. I didn't apply for a waiver certification for lab testing because I couldn't believe that even those simple urine testings would require special permission and certifications. Here in this office in the countryside, we do only those simple tests if they are logically required to identify problems.

I was notified that since September 1st, those tests would not be paid in the absence of an attached waiver.

In such a situation, my work to help P.A. patients becomes hopelessly impaired. I cannot make a responsible diagnosis and consequent treatment decisions without on the spot examinations of the necessary specimens by available means. I cannot see the patient, send his specimen to the lab, see him again after two or three days, then maybe send him again for another test because the lab pointed to something else and finally, after such delays, make up my mind about how to treat his problem. This is nonsense!

All this absurdity can make good sense for jokes until they pass a certain line. From that point on, they are strangulating and destroying.

With the present requirement of the waiver, I realize that I cannot help P.A. patients any more. I will be forced to deny them my services, explain to them why and send them to some other medical office. Please send me the addresses of such medical offices where I can refer my patients.

When a bureaucratic twist requires complicated and costly absurdities, I have to give up. I can only feel pity when our elected men in order to prove themselves, instead of simplifying things, make from problems a masquerade and complicated labyrinth.

Again, please send me the names of the offices for my referrals of the P.A. patients.

Because I stopped laughing when looking at the performance of our dignitaries, I will send copies of this letter to the Health Administration in Washington and to the Illinois Medical Family Practice Association.

Book Three

I wish you the best in your wonderful administrative leadership performance.

                        Tadeusz Maciejczyk, M.D.
                        Milledgeville, September 15, 1992

HCPA CLIA Program
Baltimore, MD

In this new pressure and taxation imposed on such "laboratories" as mine, I can hardly see a useful purpose. It has no justification. It creates only a new bureaucracy, eager to show its importance and to develop a new feeding ground for themselves. This new creation of yours is not helping to care for patients, is not easing the necessary work and surely is not limiting the cost of health care.

It also creates a new antagonism and a deepening feeling of one more unjustified abuse by those who pretend to serve.

When the working circumstances are repeatedly poisoned by bitterness, the fruits of the work acquire an increasingly unpleasant taste. I am sorry.

I am sending a check for $100 to your offices in Dallas. I pay this new taxation under protest.

I include here my previous protest directed to the Public Aid offices in Springfield, IL and send my letter to the Platform Advisory Committee where I wrote about health care problems.

                        Tadeusz Maciejczyk, M.D.
                        Milledgeville, November 13, 1992

The World Seen from the Distance of a Small Village

Richard N. Bond
Chairman
Republican National Committee

Dear Sir:

I received your Nov. 27 letter and its call to reaffirm my Rep. Party commitment and membership and to rejoin the battle for the Party's goals, principles and values.
I expected this call.
In this call I expected a new seriousness, an analysis of the defeat and a tentative plan for rebuilding and for renewal.
In the changing world and with a changed tapestry on the Washington scene, a somber study of all the factors of the past and a renewed formulation of the Republican points of view should be clearly presented in this letter.
That letter should stress the need for concentration, for new homework, for new ideas and for the party's goals and principles. After the last election, the old ways of proceedings should be suspended, re-examined and scrutinized for the clues to necessary changes. New personnel should be called in to enforce the new strategy, new methodology and new approaches to each controversy. Leaving the old staff members to do the presently necessary work would only assure that nothing would change and the possibility of bitterness or of recrimination would accelerate stagnation and decay.
Also, this time is clearly not a time for contemptuous phraseology directed toward Democrats. All the plans, purposes and procedures of Democrats should be presented and discussed with serenity and dignity. Every hatred, aversion or contempt directed toward the Democratic actions will work against the long-term success. They are giving a clear permission to not concentrate. They are providing a good pretext to escape responsibility and neglect the introduction of changes. They will surely give an OK for a shabby, worthless groundwork, which at the present time, should be done to the point of excellence. An underestimation and contempt for the adversary and consequent laziness to do the best preparation for the upcoming confrontation were the causes of many defeats throughout the centuries of history. Those pages of history also show how often even the clearest and the most obvious lessons were ignored, teaching nothing, correcting nothing.
A claim in your letter that the Republican Party is still the home of the highest ideals and the brightest hope for America is at the least an unearned self-glorification.

Book Three

Those Republican ideals became diluted, abused and distorted by the Party's leadership. During the last decade that process led the country to an almost strangulating point economically and emotionally. The ethics of the party elite frequently became embarrassing and catastrophic in consequence. The old Party ideals remained only for propaganda, for rhetoric intended to impress. The party's messages to the periphery (those that I received) seldom were elevating. Frequently they were degrading. They were a perfect illustration of the Party's emptiness, decomposition or even death.

In your letter, you present "the finest, the most visionary statesmen and leaders in the free world who are Republicans." I can hardly see such qualities in any of them.

I have a great respect for Senator Bob Dole. He is an excellent Senator and a great figure for the whole country, but I do not see in him a special "spark" or touch of a true leader.

Lynn Martin surely is not a leader. She is an opportunist with great ambitions. She flows on the surface and with the current. When I saw her giving the nomination speech during the last convention, it became clear to me that after the elections, nothing would change in the Republican leadership; that the same neglects and failures would continue for the next four years. It added one more point for the reasons why I voted for Ross Perot.

Ronald Reagan had a spark and charisma. He had no character and no standard for morals.

What can I say about George Bush? The wounds are still too fresh.

After reading your letter, my first impulse was to accept your new membership chard. Nevertheless, after thinking it over, I decided to send this card back to you. In your letter, I didn't find any signal for change. I saw in it the same Party jargon, the same self-glorification and the same shallow and cheap characterization of others as always. I found in your letter the same vacuum of ideas, the same general tone that so many times in the past sounded to me detestable and unacceptable.

The Party that appears from your letter, in spite of the last lessons of history, is not attractive to me. I will wait for a change.

If nevertheless, in spite of my decision, you ask me to respond to some of your questions, to some new surveys, I will always try to do my best.

With Christmas approaching, I send you and the Republican Party my best wishes.

Tadeusz Maciejczyk
Milledgeville, December 6, 1992

The World Seen from the Distance of a Small Village

William Clinton
President of the United States

Dear Mr. President:

I am sending you two of my letters written nine years ago, but still very real today.

In one of them I expressed my reaction to Martin Luther King Day. The other dealt with a different solution for the elderly.

At the present time, the circumstances are pressing for change and for a renewal in the country and you are committed to such changes. Perhaps my letters could contribute to such an effort.

I think that not a person of MLK's and consequently his "Day" has to be venerated, but MLK's dream and it's message to the world. His "dream" contains solutions that are necessary and priceless, not only in this country, but everywhere else. This "dream" has the potential to be an instrument and a tool to sublimate a single person or to lift a whole society. Similar "tools" for shaping life existed in the past and always helped. One of them was a Scouting movement in the beginning of this century; another was the Peace Corps in the time of Kennedy, just to mention a few.

The present ills of our society cannot be healed with money or with bureaucratic dispositions alone. The spirits have to be healed first. The providential men of dedication and action have to appear and the people have to have a chance to lift their eyes to something greater and more redeeming. Only such a transformation can produce a change in the soul of men. And this transformation has to be the centerpiece of any true domestic recovery.

If the "Week of MLK's Dream" could be declared, giving the people time for fermentation of thoughts, if such a "week" could be open officially in Washington, but the expression, the initiatives, the inventiveness would be left entirely to localities, untouched by the central planning, the eventual results could give an enormous variation of actions, rich in shapes, colors, tones and dimensions. In addition, it would reveal the new true leaders, born from action and spontaneity.

The present "Day of MLK" as it is, is a completely empty event with many negative consequences. It gives importance to "leaders," who in reality are the worthless, ambitious showmen. In the winter, it condemns children to be attached to the TV entertainment whose principal motivation is not to build children into strong and spiritually healthy adults, but a pursuit of popularity and of profit. It also closes many institutions, disorganizing the work of the normal people. Such a "lazy" day, as it is now, is entirely the opposite of the idea of Martin Luther King's dream.

Book Three

The other letter I am sending to you was about my version of care for the elderly and the disabled who are still mentally and spiritually alive and vigorous.

Such an arrangement, if realized in practice and spread across the country, could correct many painful problems of the present time. It could calm the general anxiety about growing older. By this, it could increase the self-confidence and make the expectations for old age more real and more optimistic. In the elderly it could liberate a new wave of activities. It could even decrease the need for medical visits, or of use of medicines.

During the last decades, fundamental changes appeared in our society. Families became dispersed and loneliness became a common condition. This loneliness, compounded by a worsening economy and uncertainty with its additional stresses and hazards, was never completely addressed or solved. Nevertheless, it made a permanent mark on the whole society. I know that the remedy that I described in my letter would never be satisfactory for everybody, but if 50% would get assurance and peace of mind by their presence, the idea would be worth a trial.

I did not intend to write in this letter about the third problem, but just today I saw in my office a man with a never-ending headache. He is a worker in a nearby steel mill where the workers change their working hours in three shifts and they rotate the eight hours work every week.

Such a shift change arrangement is destroying those working men, is affecting deeply their autonomic nervous systems, is decreasing their attention at work, makes the work unenjoyable and unproductive and the products probably poorer in quality. It also breaks the morals of those men making them querulous, angry and unhappy. They speak about their working place as a stinking hell. They are aging prematurely in those conditions.

It would be better to make the shift changes every two to three months minimum, with a stipulation that only 1/3 of the working shift would be changed at one time. In this way the newly changed workers, still with the effect of the eight hour jet lag, cold be protected by others who are already adjusted.

Considering everything, it looks to me that the last two problems could improve the health care by decreasing stress and improving prevention and the establishment of the Martin Luther King's Dream Week could be helpful in our fight with crime and drugs.

And really, I wish you the best in your work. I voted for Mr. Perot, but you are the President and after all, you can be a good one.

Tadeusz Maciejczyk
Milledgeville, January 24, 1993

The World Seen from the Distance of a Small Village

P.S. As of today, everybody talks about Pro-Choice and Pro-Life questions, recently reactivated. I include here my letter with my opinions about this serious problem.

Congressman Lane Evans
Congress of the United States

Dear Sir:

    I received your Congressional Update letter and I want not only to thank you, but also to make my comments.
    This was your first letter that I obtained. I live in the territory that only recently became included in your district.
    Your letter was reassuring and optimistic. It radiated with energy. The present difficulty can be overcome. The new priorities should be translated into action.
    The first priority of your letter was to overhaul the present health care system and to develop health care reform.
    But reading your recommendations for reform, I had difficulty comprehending them.
    I am not an economist and my mathematics became mostly lost during decades of neglect. I would like to see more clearly your numbers and your system of calculation. I do not comprehend how the cuts in the administrative waste of the health care could provide funds for everybody's health care rights, give to everybody an expanded health coverage, cut the deductibles, provide long term care, assure to everybody preventative and restorative care and after all those services, still preserve funds sufficient to increase our medical research.
    Is the Health Care Administration really such a colossal flop?
    If the present Health Care Administration is such a pit of waste, then maybe the best for the system would be to remove completely the primary care from the Medicare Program because by its enormity of small claims, it creates an administrative nightmare. Without coverage of the primary medicine, Medicare could concentrate more efficiently on the medical needs that really are breaking families and filling the lives of everybody with an anxious uncertainty. The Medicare without the burden of the primary care could concentrate more

efficiently on the problems of the catastrophic illnesses, on the long term care of the disabled and of the care of the very elderly in their final stages. Such a mission for Medicare would target fewer cases, would eliminate the enormous bulk of the present system and would represent a truly helping and saving hand in a moment of real need. Such a certainty would represent a real blessing for every family and for every social group.

The Primary care generally is affordable for average Americans. Of course, the jobless would be helped and the primary doctors surely would cooperate with helping.

The Primary care should remain within the sphere of individual family management for many reasons. In general, people can handle their family health problems more efficiently. Without rigid frames of central arrangement and with the appearance of competition, it would be less expensive. The enormous administrative cost could be brought to some manageable dimensions. The priorities would be seen and dealt with more clarity.

The psychological effect of making the primary medicine a family problem, in the long run, would turn beneficial.

Every person, every family, every society, needs the feeling of togetherness that gives them strength. The togetherness never grows well when everything becomes easy and free. When the element of sacrifice is devalued the togetherness becomes diluted and may die.

Besides this, the temptation for more rights, as every other temptation, never has enough. Such is human nature. And, by a paradox, those "rights" are bringing no happiness. The true element that holds together societies, is vanishing in places where the "rights" without sacrifices become an obsession. They are always divisive and personally debilitating.

It is well known that the overprotective mothers who are trying to remove all the obstacles from their children's passway, are creating very maladjusted, very confused and very unhappy adults.

We, as a nation, are increasingly sensitive to our "rights," claiming them even in the more absurd situations. Those 'rights" are justifying and sanctifying our own selfishness and negligence. They are absolving us from our duties. They weaken the families. They are making us inside more empty and more resentful. With them, we can put the whole blame on anybody else but us.

In this letter I am trying to express my belief that the primary medicine should be left free from the state or from the federal manipulations and political maneuverings because their "goodness" is bringing to families and to society more harm than good.

The World Seen from the Distance of a Small Village

I also believe that every average American needs a certainty to get help and protection in case of catastrophic situations, in the long lasting, exhaustive illnesses and in the unpredictability of the last years of our existence.

Medicare in those situations can become a true blessing and give enormous peace of mind to most Americans.

I wish you the best in your work.

Tadeusz Maciejczyk, M.D.
Milledgeville, February 17, 1993

Patty Luther
Sustaining Membership Director
The Republican Party

Dear Patty Luther:

Thank you for your letter, for your desire to win me back to the Party and for telling me that "there are just a handful of members like me who are clearly the heart and the soul of the Republican Party."

To say that I have been very generous in the past is a clear exaggeration. I really wanted to belong, to participate, to contribute. And I found that my only usefulness to the Party was in my monetary contributions. That was always the beginning and the end of my role and my assignment. For me, it was proof that my "membership" was nothing more than the useful for the Party fiction.

I am sending you some of my last year's letters to the Party that will explain to you better the reasons for my frustrations and withdrawal.

I send you my best wishes.

Tadeusz Maciejczyk
Milledgeville, March 25, 1993

Book Three

U.S. News and World Report
Letter to the Editor

Dear Sir:

M.B. Zuckerman's plan for how to deal with the never-receding nightmare of drug addiction in the U.S. could be a wonderful remedy if the nature of the problem were primarily only an addiction.

But it is not. It has deep roots in many dark aspects of the present life.

Because of this, I am afraid that Mr. Zuckerman's remedy, after another number of years, could lead only to another costly disillusion. Fighting the drug war without fundamental work to cut the roots of the monster will bring no victory, only a deeper feeling of hopelessness.

The original cause of the epidemic of drug addiction is the people's need to calm the pain of spiritual emptiness that brings to the surface a state of anxiety, instability and an emotional hunger for redeeming change. Drugs are the loud cry for relief, for any kind of soothing for the soul.

Where the daily life is dominated by such a spiritual emptiness and there is not strength to make true change, drugs are attractive as an instant escape from frightening reality. They provide a cover up; they give plaster to put on an ugly and painful wound; they tempt with the desired hiding place from the world.

Drugs attract because an escape into them requires no commitment, no act of will, no internal mobilization to face the problem. Those drugs act like a wonderful mirage on the thirsty traveler in the desert. They create a hope and an illusion. But they have no life-saving water. They only deviate from the proper route and in this way they can be fatal.

Our country became ripe for this plague of addiction long before the proper addiction appeared.

We became drawn into a pursuit of materialistic rewards and an instant satisfaction. To make this happen, our moral makeup became gradually relaxed and increasingly porous.

Divorce became commonplace. Responsibilities too frequently became somebody else's problem, not mine. Popularity, whatever its nature, opened the doors to the world. God and prayer were eliminated from schools and public places to satisfy sensitivities and "constitutional rights" of a microscopic minority. It became OK to desecrate the flag. Ordinary gambling became ennobled with the respectful new name of

481

The World Seen from the Distance of a Small Village

"gambling industry." TV shows as they are, became a very important, but not very elevating teacher of life. And so on.

All those changes brought consequent pains and scars, disorientation, loneliness, alienation and misery to the soul.

Into this picture came the flow of drugs. The new condition of the country became a paradise for all kinds of drug dealers and pushers. They organized, they developed strategies and they have no desire to leave their heaven.

Then, what can be done?

A long time ago, I was told a ridiculous, but sharp popular wise dictum that those who are not taking risks are not going to jail.

Maybe, in our desperation, confronted with the unyielding drug offensive, we should take a true risk.

What would happen if against all existing apprehensions, we would designate those twenty square miles for opium poppy cultivation and fill the market with a satisfying amount of heroine and cocaine, legally open to every body to buy?

Anyway, those substances are on the streets in abundance. The costly vigilance of traffickers didn't change the supply a bit. At least the new arrangement would eliminate the foreign producers, together with all the dealers and pushers. Precisely they are those who are the most interested in sustaining and spreading addiction. It could be that such a move would also decrease crime because forbidden drugs and crime are complementing each other, creating an accelerating, moving wheel.

Of course, this act alone will not make a miracle. The rehabilitation will continue to be important. But the most important way to win the drug war would have to be a general life renewal in which everybody would be involved.

On this front, the family stabilization would be a must. The responsibilities, especially towards children, should be scrutinized and enforced. TV would have to clean some of their programs. God and prayers should be put back into schools. This restitution should be done not by another court order, but as it should be in a true democracy, by the majority vote of all parents of each school unit. God and prayers should not be removed or imposed on society by a chosen few, as it happens in every dictatorship. By the decision about God and prayers, the Supreme Court satisfied the influential few and violated the wishes of the vast majority. At the beginning of this century, Lenin and Stalin, making their interpretation of the spirit of Marxism, eliminated God from life in Russia and we all saw the results.

Book Three

To fight the attraction of drugs, the whole nation should be involved. Everybody's good ideas should be precious because all of them combined could create a new environment in which the drugs would lose their appeal. In this way, and it looks to me only in this way, the scourge of addiction could be reduced. To this struggle, everybody should be mobilized; everybody should have an occasion to be creative and innovative. The reward would be a feeling of merit and of the optimism that we lost for so long. In this renewal, everybody should have a chance for fulfillment.

Tadeusz Maciejczyk, M.D.
Milledgeville, April 27, 1993

The World Seen from the Distance of a Small Village

Ruth Cohen
Editor
The Hudson Monitor

Dear Ms. Ruth Cohen:

Responding to your letter of May 5, 1993, yes, I won the malpractice trial against me. Counting in money, I didn't pay one cent for all those court procedures.

Counting in other ways, this trial gave me much more than could be bought with money. It gave me a deeper insight into myself. With it I grasped better the true values in life. By passing through its rigors, I even understood better the meaning of Christianity. If that trial was traumatic, it paid abundantly for all the bruises it produced.

In the interview I said that I would not recommend to anybody to defend himself. I was tired and I was not given enough time to formulate completely my thoughts.

Summarizing all my experiences of that trial, I have to conclude that I suffered less than those who, protected by their lawyers, have to wait endlessly in the darkness and in a complete passivity for the results. At least I had constantly my hand on the pulse. I was living the battle. I was developing the strategy. I was building defenses and I was attacking when it was handy. In no moment of those three and one half years was I a defeated man. If anything, I was growing and finally I won. This trial gave me a kind of new dimension. I was tested. The experience was painful, but I never felt broken. At times I had the impression that this trial liberated me in a special way and prepared me for even greater battles.

Judge Rapp was complaining that the procedure was severely complicated by my lack of knowledge of court procedures. Yes, I didn't know the ceremonies, the routine, but I added to the procedure the element of freshness and spontaneity, of a completely new approach or tactic that overall made my trial not such a ceremonial rigid bore. I would say that even for the judge, and without a doubt for the accusing attorney, that trial was a refreshing new experience.

I observed also how anxious all the parties were in that trial to play it as a usual game in which not exactly the proper medical issues would be centrally discussed. The pressure was to make a judicial dance in the center and its medical issues were just a periphery ready for exploitation. When such a cozy arrangement was impaired and the medical is-

Book Three

sue remained as a central problem to be discussed, the accusing attorney became insecure and soft.

My trial convinced me that the only way to finish forever with all the abusive accusations of malpractice in medicine is to stand up and to force the accusing party to talk directly, in medical terms, about the specific fact that created the accusation. Such a change will happen if the doctors stop hiding and in the cases of abuse, continue to pay the ransom called reconciliation. Only such a stand will stop the "justice games." Such a stand would not destroy medical practices. On the contrary, it would add to its true recognition. It would also bring down the medical cost and in this way benefit the majority of patients.

Any person, any group, any society that rather pays ransom, then risks a confrontation with an abuser, is losing face, dignity, integrity and will not fulfill its mission well.

I send you my two last letters that were published here in the local *Daily Gazette*. Both of them have some connection with the medical work.

I wish you the best in your work.

Tadeusz Maciejczyk, M.D.
Milledgeville, May 23, 1993

The World Seen from the Distance of a Small Village

Francis A. Davis, M.D.
Medical Action Committee for Education

Dear Sir:

I continue to be interested in matters that are adding soul to our work as physicians. A medical treatment without this invisible, but permeating everything backbone of medical service is losing enormously its effectiveness and ultimately is leaving the help seeking patients half-unrelieved, anxious and hungry for that special additional gift from the doctor.

I believe that the arranged by a third party overwhelming business oriented medical industry with doctors kept as the employees will be too dry and too sterile to generate this special soul-reaching element of the medical practice. For this reason I will always oppose subjugation of medical services to any political or business intermediaries. A truly effective medicine should remain, as far as possible, a private contract and intimate in its relation with patients.

I will not come to the June 18–19 meeting of the Medical Action Committee for Education. I am here alone in this small countryside, solo practice. I do not feel important or really prepared for such a meeting.

As a doctor, I reduced my practice. I lost my hospital privileges after I opposed the obligatory, high-priced medical malpractice insurance. This high price has to be paid ultimately by the sick. Also, after my own experience of being tried for malpractice (I defended myself without a lawyer and I won.) when I felt no help and an uneasy, condemning indifference from the medical circles, I feel still more isolated and on the side.

Using this occasion, I am sending you a copy of another of my letters that lately was published in our local *Daily Gazette*. I would be happy if you would read this letter. Also, I want to ask you to give a copy of this letter to William J. Bennett, PhD, the former drug czar who will be an honored guest at that meeting.

I wish you the best in your work.

Tadeusz Maciejczyk, M.D.
Milledgeville, May 23, 1993

Book Three

Ross Perot

Dear Sir:

    A few days ago, on my day off when I was sitting alone in my office doing paperwork, a representative (and an old friend of mine) of one of the pharmaceutical companies came in. We sat in the waiting room. The initial professional talk about medicines quickly became replaced by a conversation about the present problems of the country: the health care, the crimes, politics and about life in general and its meaning and the future of the world.
    The conversation was long and at its end we talked about your appearance on the political stage and what that brought to the country. When we shook hands to say good-bye, my friend recommended that I ask you a somewhat solemn question: are you the one, or should we look for somebody else?
    I know that such a question exists in the minds of many. And I understand that such a question is not easy to answer honestly for anybody. Even the present timing is not helping to decide.
    We are living in the time of enormous change. This time, more than ever, needs a leader with true greatness. Somehow, the world is uneasy and the world is looking at the horizons in a search for a man.
    With this letter, I am sending you many others that could be of some importance in finding the road to the future. I divided them into four groups.

    a.   The first group is letters sent directly, or as copies to President Clinton.
    b.   The second group is letters written to the Republican Party during 1992.
    c.   The biggest bulk was sent in such a form to respond to the 1992 Republican Senate Majority Survey.
    d.   In this last group I put my pronunciations where I tried to formulate my suggestions for the betterment of the future.

    I would like to think that you would like to read all those letters. They reflect the conditions and the feelings in this part of the country as they were filtering through my mind. I know that you have many other priorities and not enough time, but anyway, I hope.
    I send you my best wishes.

                                        Tadeusz Maciejczyk
                                        Milledgeville, July 5, 1993

The World Seen from the Distance of a Small Village

Time Magazine Letters

Dear Editor:

After the bitterness and agony of the court battles, it would be good if both sides would genuinely try to help Jessica. Jessica already wears the scars from her mother's anxieties during pregnancy. The fetus is reacting to the special uterine contractions during such uncertainties and retaining them in the subconscious for a lifetime. To add new blows to this condition, would not be an act of love or justice. Its purpose would be only to calm the guilt feelings of the natural parents and their present scruples considering Jessica as something distant, as a self-rehabilitization gain.

What Jessica needs now is an unselfish, unlimited love, peace and security to develop her own feeling of being loveable and to be able to love others. In her age now, she started to process of a development of conscience: a lifelong perception of what is right and what is wrong. By the age of seven, she will show her basic personality, fundamental to all her later life.

Those processes should not be disrupted lightly. As John Powell once said, "we are not the masters of our fates and captains of our souls. The truth of the matter is that we are largely shaped by others, who, in an almost frightening way, hold our destiny in their hands."[2] Each of us is the product of those who loved us or used us or refused to love us.

Considering all this, the best way to resolve the dilemma would be to create a new, special relationship between the two families with Jessica in the center of those relationships.

In such an arrangement, Jessica would remain with De Boers in Michigan where she would have her home, but she will know that she has another set of loving parents in Iowa who she could visit and love. In the same way, the children of the Schmidts would know that they have a sister in Michigan and whenever they go to see her, they would be welcomed as they would be in their own home, receiving there equal loving, trusting and guiding care.

Also, both sets of parents could and should become true friends knowing each other better, trusting and helping each other, developing new ideas together that could enrich the life of each member of this new big family.

In the atmosphere that would develop, there would be no place or need for jealousy, for guilt feelings, for scruples or hostility.

Book Three

The only unequivocal measure of love is the capacity for self-forgetfulness. If this would really exist, all other positive solutions and developments would be almost spontaneous.

Would it not be wonderful to build such a relationship on the ashes of the old feud?

My best wishes go out to both families.

Tadeusz Maciejczyk, M.D.
July 18, 1993

The World Seen from the Distance of a Small Village

Time Magazine Letters
Re: "A City Without Hope" (*Time Magazine,* July 26, 1993)

Dear Editor:

It takes a soul of a real coward, ridden by many painful and dark complexes to be so merciless to anybody who is already lying helplessly on the ground, exhausted to the limit and practically without the means to defend himself. A true man, with a sense of dignity and justice, behaves differently.

I think that the sons and grandsons of those Serbs, who at present are displaying so vividly their "heroic" spectacle before the audience of the paralyzed world, will live with the feeling of guilt and shame. The rest of the world will also. The rest of the world has no moral strength that could be taken seriously and have a power to restrain.

It was almost yesterday, I remember, the beautiful dance made together by different regional groups of Yugoslavia during the Winter Olympics of 1984. That beauty could flower and prosper in togetherness. It was killed by the preachers of the Serbian edition of *Mein Kampf* philosophy and the consequent madness.

And the world is washing their hands like Pilate and Chamberlain.

Tadeusz Maciejczyk, M.D.
Milledgeville, July 25, 1993

Book Three

Responses to the Republican National Committee Issues Survey

Explanations:

1. As the population increases, the environmental damage acquires a more ominous significance for the future. The present moment's economic advantage and prosperity just for today, is not an excuse. A special science and special faculties should be established for theoretical and practical studies of environment guided by a clear vision, common sense and avoidance of hysteria. Criticizing Brazil for destroying the tropical forests while destroying forests here just for today's profit or employment will not convince Brazilians and is making us hypocrites.
2. Adoption of the second option is like opening the door to all kinds of stretchings. The acceptable line would always change, mostly down, and as in the case of the national debt, our children and grandchildren would pay the price.
3. When government starts to be very benevolent, assuming responsibilities for all needs and desires of citizens, it kills their self-reliance, self-pride, their own initiative, and even their capacity to grow. As a paradox, it even suppresses freedom. When government acquires functions that should not enter into its scope, only the bureaucracy grows more voracious, the regulations become more strangulating and the citizens more cranky, more demanding, more passive and more helpless. The Soviet experience in the Communist utopia should be a lesson.
4. Do well, what the government should do well. Delegate all other functions to private initiatives, supervising only its efficiency and honesty.
5. Spending cuts, as well as the reasons and wisdom of eventual tax increases should always be well discussed with society. Society should never be an object of passive manipulations, but a partner in building together.
6. I marked 5 for problems, in which I do not understand sufficiently its mechanics. Implementation of NAFTA is a logical way for a development into the future. But it should be gradual, by certain well-defined steps. The difference between Mexico and the other two partners is too enormous to make from it instantly a complete economical unit. The effects of indigestion would be too painful. Such a commonwealth should be realized step by step. The experience of each step in realization should be the

base for the next one. The extent of changes with its possible positive/negative consequences should be discussed in depth with the nation before implementation. Such a commonwealth should not be just a treaty between the governments, written in official jargon incomprehensible to the common man, but an adventure in which all people would participate adding their input.
7. A protection of domestic industries would be an invitation to get sleepy and enter into stagnation. Free trade requires more effort, more input, more discipline and understanding for planning. Protectionism is tempting, like closing one's eyes in the face of danger. It always brings a shock of awakening.
8. Consequences of immigration can be positive or negative. It has to be controlled, but not closed. Some emigration, such as seasonal workers, is necessary and should be permitted, but the U.S. cannot become a dustbin for those who only burden social services.
9. Our borders are not in danger.
    a. Each act of terrorism is different, was born and nourished differently and has to be calmed and neutralized by a different formula. I include here my article written a long time ago as an answer to Mr. Zuckerman's call for all-out mobilization against terrorism ("Freedom vs. Terrorism," *U.S. News and World Report,* June 2, 1986) and a letter to George Habash, a Palestinian leader, who during the Desert War, in a conversation to Ted Koppel, was considering the use of terrorism. I am also sending you my two letters to Vice-President Bush in 1984.
    b. Promoting democracy has to mean something else besides simply giving money or sending troops. I do not think that we really have any plan for promoting democracy or justice. Most likely even, we already lost the moral strength necessary and fundamental to succeed in such an effort.
10. We cannot buy friends. We can help friends in their unexpected need, but we should not give anybody a permanent and expected subsidy. I would prefer to have friends who become friends by conviction and good will, without bribing them. A wealthy man or nation generally has no friends, only clients. And the U.S. is now not as wealthy as it used to be. Our clients conveniently prefer not to know this and continue to ask or to require.

Book Three

11. We should put Vietnam, as well as Cuba, in our orbit. The way to do so should be worked out actively. Not just by waiting for a complete collapse of the adversary. The long range planning somehow should have a priority.
12. Once I wrote a letter to Rep. Martin about a different way to conduct elections. She considered it unnecessary. She already had a better script. I am sending you a copy.
13. An illustration: About 500 years before Christ, there was a riot in Rome. An angry crowd gathered around the Senate buildings shaking firsts and arms. They were protesting a new tax increase. To confront the crowd, the Senators delegated one of them to talk to the people. He started: A long time ago, when the human body was still not integrated and each of its members were autonomous, all the members rebelled against the stomach. What does he think? He sits comfortable and warm inside and all of us have to protect and serve him. And so the arm refused to bring food to the mouth, the teeth to chew; the brain to think how to provide, the legs to walk and so on. And this gave the members satisfaction and euphoria. But after a time, the members became weak and shaky; the teeth started to decay; the arm had no strength to rise and the brain to think. Finally they concluded that while the stomach directly gave them nothing, without him, they could only perish. The crowd listened, calmed down and dispersed. I would only add to this story that to do its function properly, the stomach should be watched for gastritis, peptic ulcers, perforations, neoplasms and other maladies.
14. I am the victim of a malpractice suit and I know first hand how malignant it became. It was a goldmine for the lawyers. The lawyers swarmed to it like flies to honey. Their greediness and loss of all respect for true justice or common sense intensified each month and each year. In indignation, I defended myself in court without any lawyer and after three and one-half years, I won. But in the process, my family life was destroyed and I lost a feeling for creative enthusiasm to work in America. As I wrote to the Grace Commissions, to work, I need fresh air. In America, the working air became poisoned by the explosion of the farce of the malpractice suits. The original noble intention of protection against abuse and careless, criminal neglect that would be like a life-giving blood, degenerated into poisonous, malignant leukemia, a killer of all daring in action, an immobilizer of each fresh under-

taking. I limited my medical work to the basics in the office. I refused to have medical malpractice insurance and I have no hospital privileges. The working atmosphere in America became too poisonous, too demanding of expensive briberies to do even the ordinary. With the malpractice institution, as it is now, America is condemned to decline and slowly to suffocate. If you wish, I will send you my correspondence from the time of my trial, written in the heat of the struggle.
15. I am sending you my letter to Rep. Evans. This letter of mine about health care reform was published in the local paper and had a good response among the people.
16. 1 and 2 are true and that sets a somber perspective for the future of health care.
17. I am sending you a letter where I explained my position.
18. Boot camps for young offenders would create perfect conditions where the worst of them would influence everyone else. Suppressed anger and frustration, any inadequate move of guards, would help to push them into the worst of choices for life. Such camps, I feel, would be a school for hard core criminals in the future. Each young offender should be not only judged, but first of all, studied for the origin of his offensive tendencies. The judges should have at hand a wide range of rehabilitative measures for the soul and for the emotions, engaging them in labor of restitution that could have the power to redeem and change the offender. The work to prepare those different solutions, to create all the spectrum of different rehabilitative measures, is urgent. This work could be started with a special questionnaire.
    a. Also, I consider that a special law should be created through which a parent, who disappeared from the life of his child, should be considered equally guilty in the juvenile crimes, be subpoenaed to court and really feel the sentencing. A parent who clearly neglected or abandoned his child committed a crime against society. What we are witnessing now is just a harvest from previous years and if not truly corrected now, can turn towards much more in the years ahead. It would be good to keep in mind that a child during infancy needs all the amount of love he can get. This will be stored in his subconscious for life and will permit him to shape his life with love for himself and for others. From the ages of three to five, a child learns what is right and

what is wrong. In this time, he has thousands of naïve questions each day and only a loving person can answer them with patience and true care. A child will not get those answers even in the best of day care centers. We neglected this aspect of childcare. Mothers too frequently had no time for their children. How can we correct this situation?

    b. We have enough jails to lock up people convicted of violent crimes. But we fill them up with drug offenders. Prisons will not correct those drug offenders. They are going there to get a new seminar in how to organize their drug business better and how to get new contacts and all this is done at the expense of the taxpayer. The drug offenders should be punished the way that would hurt them the most. They go into their business for the love of easy big money. All their money, all their possessions should be confiscated without mercy, leaving them practically out on the streets. To earn a living, they would get an obligatory work sentence for several years at minimum wage in places that care for their victims. Also, it should be clearly established that those drug dealers whose sales resulted in the death of someone, should be put directly onto death row where they would wait for eventual mercy. I am not cruel. Only the situation became increasingly critical and the old methods of fighting crime as leading nowhere.

19. Too many civil rights leaders, advocates and believers degenerated into an easy-for-them and nice-to-their-listeners demagogue creating a very unhealthy relationship with everybody else, interfering with a positive growth of different persons and different groups of people, forming bigotry and intolerance, creating distancing, impairing mutual understanding and a sincere exchange of views. Only a very few, very unusual people can continue to be civil rights leaders and keep free from its ugly residuals. I do not believe professional civil rights leaders are a positive force in society.

> Tadeusz Maciejczyk
> Milledgeville, September 23, 1993

The World Seen from the Distance of a Small Village

Finally:

1a. Define the direction for the nation and for the world.
1b. Restructure and motivate its leadership, its brain centers and its executive system to be alert, honest and responsive to ever-changing times (eliminate routine and smartness.
2a. The Party, which liberates the best from each individual, creating for him ways to grow as persons, citizens and performers of a creative work.
2b. The party that will not manage, but guide and patronize positive individual enterprises.

These points in opposition to the Democratic Party, which in their "goodness" makes magnificent gestures, trying to give things away for free, to collectively eliminate life's problems and by all this crippling individualism, a true personal self-worth, self-discipline, with all this making men more passive, more weak, more cranky, more helpless and more relying on "his rights."

Tadeusz Maciejczyk
Milledgeville, September 26, 1993

Book Three

Editor
The Daily Gazette
Sterling, Illinois

Dear Sir:

The letters in your column about leaf burning were of many kinds. Some were emotional, some scientific, others diplomatic, angry, and lately, even nasty. After consideration, while working in my garden, I decided to add my opinion to this whole problem. My letter, for a change, will be a pseudo-scientific one.

I vote for granting the falling leaves complete autonomy. Let them fall. Let them be a beautiful testimony for the changing time, the way nature intended.

Here, in the American prairie land, those prairies never would develop if during those unnumbered years of formation, the armies of human beauticians would hunt the falling leaves, raking them and burning them mercilessly.

Nature had a different intention for those leaves. At the end of the year, when the life of the plants was coming to its end, those leaves gave the earth a warm cover for the winter and a natural fertilizer for the next growing season. Those leaves contained the necessary minerals that only roots of trees could reach in the depths of the earth. When mulched, they gave life to the next generation of plants.

But we humans have a tendency to manipulate Mother Nature in an unwise way. We want to make in our yards a reception room order. We cut the grass short, even a day before it freezes. We persecute every falling leaf that makes the yard a little less spotless. And then in the spring, to compensate, we poison the earth with fertilizers and other conditioners to correct the growing sterility of its soil. We have a special drive to transform and to break nature, to adjust its appearance to our particular taste or fashion.

I am painting a picture of my daughter sitting on the ground covered by a colorful carpet of autumn leaves. If the readers would like, when I am finished, I could bring this picture to *The Gazette* to demonstrate once more the beauty of nature.

Consequently, at this stage of the leaf burning debate, I ask and I vote for a ban for every intervention in the natural sequence of leaf falling. Let them fly freely in the air after each passing car. Let them find for themselves a quiet place somewhere in the corner for a winter sleep. Let us consider those leaves as friends, not as an enemy to be destroyed.

The World Seen from the Distance of a Small Village

They are the symbol of passing time, a coronation of all the good things nature gave us during the year.

And I, a fellow who never liked to rake and who is too frequently waiting for a convenient wind to solve the problem, I will sleep with a cleaner conscience and even more than this, with a feeling of merit because I helped our old Mother Nature.

And who knows? Maybe the people from the plastic, artificial, spotless places would flock to us as tourists to see the enchantment of fall unspoiled by human "progress."

Tadeusz Maciejczyk, M.D.
Milledgeville, October 4, 1993

The distant, small Milledgeville Country
Fall

Book Three

The distant, small Milledgeville Country
Winter

The distant, small Milledgeville Country
Spring

The World Seen from the Distance of a Small Village

The distant, small Milledgeville Country
Late Summer

Book Three

James Edgar
Governor of Illinois

Dear Sir:

I would like to ask you a favor.

I know a young lady who impressed me with her special gifts. She is simple. She likes people and approaches them easily and naturally. She radiates happiness. On top of this, she has an enormous need to help others, passing to them her optimism and her goodness. Physically she is strong and healthy. She could be a miracle worker for the old and for the disabled.

This lady is also retarded.

Her retardation is a special combination of innocence, simplicity, inability to calculate her own advantage or to face the rigors of school education. Her parents are protecting her and are trying to keep her in a kind of safety zone because outside she could be hurt or ridiculed.

But, if she remains too long in the safety of her parents, she will not only be relatively retarded, but also wasted. She will never explore her talents; she will be deprived of the wonderful feeling of giving herself and seeing herself in the eyes of those she could help.

Thinking about this, I went to one nursing home administrator to talk about her. She could be such a blessing in such a place. My hopes were cut short very quickly. "We cannot do this," the administrator responded. To employ her, or even to use her as somebody to help take care of patients would be against the law and could bring malpractice consequences.

Her special gifts for such work were not a factor. The law forbids her to even help feed somebody who cannot hold the spoon or who needs help to walk around. To do this, a special category of nursing helpers was created. To be one of them, it is necessary to have 150 hours of special training and a diploma.

What can I say?

With the same logic, the law should forbid any woman to become a mother if she does not show a similar diploma demonstrating competence in diaper changing.

It looks to me that the capacity to be a good nursing aide or to be a mother, should be measured by a different stick. The biggest factor to be considered here should not be a scholastic diploma, but the amount of love such a person is capable of giving and the richness of her soul.

But we are living in a time of prescribed and required perfection. A multitude of laws are defining more and more what such a perfection should be. Special guardians are watching. Any deviation form the prescribed formula, any different or common sense approach to problems could be the cause of an accusation of malpractice with the consequent torment of court drugging, a ruin of reputation and financial death. The guardians love their mission. In their explanation, in this way, they protect society from abuses. And they are eager because their reward can be fabulous.

Never mind that perfection is impossible for any normal human being or society and those who pretend to be perfect are condemning themselves to failure. If anybody is perfect he has no need, no room for any improvement, or for any further effort to revise. He cannot learn from his mistakes because theoretically he doesn't have any. A presumption of perfection is a dead end for life. It leads to tragedy. Perfectionism is explained in books as an obsessive, compulsive disorder not recommended for anybody.

And so, for us, the normal, usual human beings, the standard or the model to follow is not to be perfect, but to mature and to grow. We should have room for mistakes and we should learn from them. We should be free to dare, to discover new ways. The present abundance of laws becomes strangulating.

In other, not so perfect times, Helen Keller was permitted to break the limits of her safety circle and to reach for new experiences. In spite of her enormous handicaps, she became a sort of First Lady of her time. Today, with all the proliferation of claims for special rights, Helen Keller would be condemned to her initial nothingness. The ever-present malpractice threats would immobilize Ms. Sullivan, her teacher. Today the liability, like inquisition in the old times, is enforcing on everybody his zone of safety and every person with drive and initiative can feel this.

Really, is the present system of diplomas selecting the best for the nursing aides?

Not so long ago, visiting a patient in one of the nursing homes, I asked her why she had so many bruises on her forearms. She told me the nursing aide attending to her had whispered to her, "And now, you old bitch, turn around or I . . . ." For sure that nursing aide had passed a training program and received a diploma.

The other day, as I was leaving a nursing home, an old lady extended toward me her thin arm. When I approached, she murmured, "Give me a kiss."

She didn't care whether I had a diploma to do this. She needed a testimony of love to give sense and meaning to her existence in that stage of her life. Love . . . this is the factor that really matters at the end.

Book Three

I know that this letter is long and your time is limited. I wanted to explain why I am asking you to help that young, retarded, enormously gifted lady fulfill her dreams. With her as a worker, we will not denigrate the care for the elderly. On the contrary, we will add to it a new dimension.

Tadeusz Maciejczyk, M.D.
Milledgeville, October 19, 1993

The World Seen from the Distance of a Small Village

At times, it looks to me that if Rotary had existed at least fifty years before it was born in 1905, maybe the wars of the 20th Century could have been avoided.

Those wars created another meaning for the month of November. Tomorrow we will remember Armistice Day. It will be its 75th anniversary.

Armistice Day brought to the sufferings of that time high hopes and expectations, but no plan and no vision to make them a reality. For the sake of all of us, we should understand why we had those wars and why the hopes of Armistice Day died.

For this purpose, I will repeat now my speech from Decoration Day, 1988.

Concluding now, I want to establish a scholarship that would put requirements on the receiver and also would give him or her a life-long challenge.

The receiver will make a written work about the "Need and the Role of spiritual Strength in Resolving Today's World Conflicts." This work would be read on Decoration Day and Rotary would give the reward.

For this purpose, I include here a check for $300.00 that will be kept in the treasury of Rotary and I will do this every year as long as I am here. I hope maybe other organizations or individuals will also contribute by adding to this amount and in this way, stress the significance of this challenge.

Tadeusz Maciejczyk
Milledgeville, November 10, 1993

This is a speech giving during a special meeting of Rotary International

The month of November is called Foundation Month in Rotary. During these days, special attention should be given to those actions of Rotary that are healing the wounds of the world and are exploring different ways to live together on this planet.

Book Three

Editor
Physicians Financial News

Dear Sir:

I read your article about a likely crackdown on fraud, a consequence of the health care reform, and I felt uneasy. Not about the vigilance against abuse and fraud, but the methods described made me feel a chill in my bones.

It reminded me of a similar methodology of vigilance after our "liberation" by a state, famous at that time for its social advancements, worker paradise and of course, a womb-to-tomb coverage for all the needs of its citizens.

Like in your script, at that time, people were also getting invitations to do their weekly reports about their friends, co-workers and superiors. The effect was seen very quickly. Like magic, in a very short time, everybody felt very alone and very insecure. And the method probably was effective because every night people were disappearing. Later, when I crossed at night the borderline between the Soviet and the English part of Germany and I found people to whom I could talk publicly and freely, at that moment I felt like an ecstasy of freedom. Freedom appeared so real to me. I could almost touch it with my hands. Never before and never after, in such an intense way, did I feel what freedom meant.

Remembering this, I wonder what price we will pay for this kind of enforced honesty in health care? A society in the grip of a mutual distrust, anger, antagonism or malice is not creative any more. It is rigid, cautious, taking heed and is shrinking in itself. Is it some kind of a rule that when a government promises such a wonderful goodness to everybody, an ugly tale follows? It looks to me that our society has already enough problems.

With the occasion of this letter, I am sending you my previous letter to Governor Edgar. I would like you to read that letter and to tell me what you think about its problem. Is there a helpful positive solution for this lady whom I described in that letter?

I wish you the best in your work.

Tadeusz Maciejczyk, M.D.
Milledgeville, November 21, 1993

The World Seen from the Distance of a Small Village

Subject: The Need and the Role of Spiritual Strength in Resolving Today's World Conflicts. (Guidelines for writing the essay)

Before starting to write, take two months to try to discover a spiritual strength within you. Those are the introductory points that you should read, digest and absorb.

a. Learn to be happy about who you are. Here are ten signs apparent in those who truly and joyfully accept themselves as they are:

   i. Self-accepting people are happy people. They have good company twenty-four hours a day.
   ii. They go out to others. If you like yourself, you can presume that others will like you too. They enjoy and savor the moments of solitude. For those who do not accept themselves being alone means painful loneliness.
   iii. They are always open to being loved and complimented. They will not wrestle with regret. If you really knew me, you would not love me.
   iv. They are empowered to be "real." Everybody has to accept himself before he can be himself. They do not need to carry around a set of masks to hide the true self behind.
   v. They accept themselves as they are right now. They are not filled with anticipation of theme they will become. If you love or allow others to love only the potential you, this love is useless and destructive.
   vi. They are able to laugh at themselves often and easily.
   vii. They have the ability to recognize and attend to their own needs. Charity begins at home.
   viii. They are self-determining people. They take their cues from inside themselves, not from other people. They do what they think is right and appropriate, not what other people may think or say. They can resist the mob psychology. They are not afraid to swim upstream.
   ix. They are in good contact with reality. They engage themselves with life as it really is.
   x. They are assertive. They assert their right to be taken seriously, to think their own thoughts, to make their own choices.

Book Three

I accept a) my body, b) my mind, c) my mistakes, d) my feelings or emotions and e) my personality.

b. You must accept full responsibility for your life.
    i. We are not completely free. Our habits hold us captive. Our yesterdays lie heavily upon our todays and our todays will lie heavily upon our tomorrows. Full responsibility is something in me that determines my responses to various stimuli and situations in life. An emotion is a perception that results in our physical reactions. Our behavioral and emotional responses have only two real choices: a) we "own" them and b) we blame them on someone or something else. If you take responsibility you will get to know yourself. If you shift the responsibility to something or someone else, you will never know your real self.
    Remember, growth begins where blaming ends. If your emotional pattern is self-destructive or socially alienating, look at the perceptions or attitudes that are writing your life's scripts. Take "full responsibility." Happiness is an inside job. A blamer, like an active alcoholic, does not grow up. He searches for peace by shifting the responsibility for his own life and happiness to something else.

    III. You should fulfill your needs for relaxation, exercise and nourishment for all three parts of you: your body, your mind, your spirit. No one can be truly happy unless the needs of all three are provided.
    Stress: It can be positive or negative. Stress can impact our bodies, our minds and our spirits.
    ii. Our body: adolescence, aging, illness, accidents
    iii. Our minds: we can perceive ourselves as inadequate, unloved, underdogs, unworthy; reality can be threatening.
    iv. Our spirit: it gives us the security and comfort of faith and its overview. Without it we soon experience painful loneliness and anxiety. The spirit registers stress when we cannot find meaning in life.
    Our response to stress is fight or flight. Prolonged stress causes everything to loom out of proportion. A healthy body contributes to a happy mind and a healthy spirit.

The World Seen from the Distance of a Small Village

I. Resentment: remember when you resent others you put your happiness into the hands of that person. You give him real power over you. The only true solution is to forgive and in this way you release yourself from the high price of continued resentment.
    You must make your life an act of love. Love is not a feeling; it is not a temporary emotional attraction. It is not a falling in or out of love. Real love is a decision and a commitment. It is the only life principle that can bring us happiness. Other life principles are: How can I make the most money? Where can I have the most fun? How can I achieve influence and power? Love begins at home. We must first love ourselves. To the extent that I fail to love myself, I will be unable to love others. I must balance my needs with the needs of others.
    i. A frequent fact is what is really good for you may not be what you would prefer. If you love, you will not join others in lies or deceptions. You will not satisfy the emotional bully. You will not permit anyone to manipulate you. Love is definitely not for those who seek the course of least resistance.
    ii. God asks us to love one another. He gave us talents. He wants us to use those talents, to stretch as we find and use them. Have you ever given a gift to another person and then noted that the other person never used your gift?
    iii. There are three parts of loving. Love is an art. I have to decide when it is time for kindness, when encouragement is needed and when the other person is ready to be challenged.
        a. Kindness—make it clear you care.
        b. Encouragement: Loving is not keeping the other weak and dependant on you. You must help him to use his own strength, think and choose for himself.
        c. Challenge: I must challenge you to put your goodness and giftedness to work.
    iv. Love has to be unconditional. Conditional love is not really love—it is barter. A lot of anger we see in the world is the result of a conditional love. We feel used and treated as a smoker treats cigarettes.
    v. Unfaithfulness: This is not easy to address. You have to preserve your own self-esteem. At certain points I would

have to ask you to choose between faithfulness with me or unfaithfulness without me.
    vi. Affirmation is an act by which we help others to appreciate their own goodness and giftedness. No one can believe in his or her unique worth unless there is some recognition of that worth by others. The greatest contribution love can make is a sincere affirmation. It is life changing. It can be world changing.

II. We must stretch by stepping out from our comfort zones. There is no one road for everyone. In our rendezvous with destiny, we have to take chances, run risks, get rejected and be hurt, be knocked down and get back on our feet. Our comfort zones lie in certain emotions, actions and even in the clothes we wear. One of our obstacles to growth is that we tend to rationalize those comfort zones and remain within its safety.
    i. Stretching: a deliberate stepping out of our comfort zone. We try something that is right and reasonable from which we have always been inhibited by fear. Repeated stretching will usher me into a new and larger world. I will be more free. I will develop a "stretch mentality."
    ii. Expression of Emotions: Bottling up our feelings inside is self-destructive. We need to tell others how we truly feel. The penalty for refusal is unhappiness.

III. Personal authenticity or "realness" calls for listening to what is going on inside us and laying it on the line in a mature way. When I know that I am gifted at doing something and my talents are needed, I must step forth. I am nothing if I am not real.

IV. Relationships are essential for a full and happy life. Starting relationships is difficult. Stretching to initiate relationships challenges us to open up. To extend an invitation, to risk rejection, to take chances. Most stretching requires time and repetition. If we stay with it, we will get a growing sense of ease and peace in doing what we could never do before. By stretching we give up the pleasure of safety. We are stepping out over the fences and ditches of our inhibitions. We are acting against our crippling fears and this is liberating. There is no such thing as a strong or a weak will. What is making the difference between strong and weak is motivation.

V. Underachievers: They have all that is needed except the drive or incentive to use their gifts. They sit on the curbstones of life having one identity crisis after another. Who am I? What am I worth? Who cares anyway? They can get out from this limbo of half-existence by stretching, by overcoming inertia, by gradually becoming self-motivating.

VI. We must learn to be "good finders." A scientific study of the 100 most successful and contented people found only one quality that was found in all of them. They were all good finders.
   i. Good finders look for and find what is good in him or herself, in others and in all situations in life. There is a lot of goodness waiting for us to discover. It all depends on what we are looking for.
   ii. "Two men looked out from the prison bars. One saw mud and one saw stars." Looking for what is good in ourselves is not in any way conceit or vanity. You can conclude it with a humble act of gratitude. It is the only reasonable thing to do if you want to be happy. To be a true good finder, you must set your own sight on the many gifts of God to you. We have to look beyond the weak and foolish things that cover the goodness. To go in search of the beauty that no one else has ever looked long enough or far enough to discover.
   iii. Function of Crisis in a human relationship is really a challenge to look deeper and to think. You will find the other at a deeper level. It can mean a new beginning in the relationship. Our biggest opportunities will probably come into our lives disguised as problems. In the end, we probably profit more from suffering than we do from success. We must be ready to look for and to find good in all the situations of life. Try to "reframe" your difficult experiences. Many psychotherapists ask their clients to repeat a story of misfortune.

VII. We must seek growth, not perfection.
   i. Unrealistic rhetoric: reach for the top! Give it your best. Don't settle for your second best.
   ii. Perfectionism leaves us room only for failure. The end result of such failure is discouragement. We act out our discouragement or anger in obnoxious ways, but they are always buried in pretense. Others would never suspect.
   iii. Semiperfectionists are impatient with the mistakes and oversights of others as well as their own. They find it hard to laugh at their own

mistakes and weaknesses or those of others. A real perfectionist cannot admit that unrealistic hopes or expectations bedevil him or herself.

iv. Perfectionism is humanly unhealthy. A healthy person can control his or her life. The perfectionist is controlled, is driven by compulsion. He is not free. He or she has to, must succeed and be perfect. Perfectionists believe that their worth is measured by their performance. The only way to impress others is by being perfect. Perfectionists fear the displeasure and the punishment of others. Their emotional groundswell results in loneliness, sadness and depression, stress. They are the people pleasers. They work hard to meet the expectations of others. They overpromise. The penalty for failure is the loss of self-esteem. They see others only as watching and ready with pen and paper to grade them.

We learn by trial and error. Failure is only a learning experience. All failures can be educational. Learn from the mistakes of others. You will not live long enough to experience all of them. *If you set out to enjoy, you will do a better job than if you are determined to make it perfect.*

With this last statement as a motto for your work, you can start now to write. Reading these preparatory instructions did you feel that nations might have similar problems in coping with life as do individuals?

You cannot help others or the world if you didn't look deeply into yourself, trying to understand, to be yourself, to be real, to grow, to stretch out for new experiences, to challenge the present you with new vision and a new plan for life.

Tadeusz Maciejczyk
Milledgeville, December 16, 1995

The material for the preparatory points I took from the book of John Powell, SJ. *Happiness is an Inside Job.*[1]

The World Seen from the Distance of a Small Village

Haley Barbour
Chairman of the Republican National Committee

Dear Sir:

Early in December I received from the Republican National Committee's 1994 Membership Drive, an invitation to become a sustaining member. I already said before that such a membership is not attractive to me. I do not see a purpose nor a place for me in such an arrangement.

The objective of the drive, as I was told, was to elect the maximum number of Republicans to public office. In my understanding such an aim should be a consequence of being prepared and a by-product of party reform, of its clarity in planning for the future and of the power of a moral standard applied to all its undertakings. In my understanding, only such a basic work can give the Republican Party a title to preside over national or world problems. Without this work, the ping pong game of more or less elected officials will be only the function of the failure of the others, will be a result of depreciation and will accelerate the downhill process.

Being in power with only a fraction of a comprehension of what do with this power will condemn the governing party to the game of patching, to be constantly one step behind the events and never shape them. Such would be a pitiful situation for the government, for those who are governed, for the nation and for the world. As I can see, a desire for power without the hard work of preparation would be a dazzling testimony to irresponsibility.

I was told that now the Republican Party will return to the roots of Republicanism and that this switch will be the device and mechanism for a victory in elections and for future governing. To me, such a program clearly indicates a complete lack of program or even of the will to truly create one. Such a program is imprecise, hanging somewhere in the sky. It is one of many slogans that never obligated to anything, never changed events positively, never archived anything memorable. A power mixed with emptiness and hypocrisy was always frustrating and tragic.

I would like to belong to a party that would make me proud, that would elevate me to my most noble dreams, that would mobilize the best in me, that would help me grow as an individual and as a member of society.

Instead of this, I see the Republican Party that is planning just another game of deception, that is anxious to be put on the stage instead

Book Three

of being ready to enter into a workshop with a clear, creative disposition of genius, whose guideline for work would be a love for all of mankind and not just a particular desire to succeed in election.

About 150 years ago, the Polish poet Cyprian Norwid wrote about successes:

> A success became a God now
> It spread its sorcery over the Globe stretch
> Before it retreated even the old victory
> Which always is worth effort
> Till this crowd comprehends at the side of its grave
> Till this insane gang will get aware
> That the victory liberates human potential
> While the success—oh yes—wonderfully intoxicates.[3]

I wish the Republican Party not a success in the upcoming elections, but a victory over the existing and future problems. A success can be cheap. Victory never is. It requires honesty, work and guts.

As my present contribution, I am sending you some of my last writings. It can call your attention to some problems existing here in the backwaters.

I also want to say that I established a special scholarship, different from other existing scholarships because it has to be earned. Five years ago, I made a speech to the Veterans on Memorial Day. At the end of that speech, I asked for the creation of a program that would permit discovery of those who want to think and to understand more deeply. I asked for scholarships for those who would write about "The Need and the Role of Spiritual Strength in Resolving Today's World Conflicts." Nobody was willing.

This year, during a Rotary meeting, I repeated that speech and I founded one scholarship. I would like to have more money for the second, third and fourth places. I hope that somebody will help.

I am sending you the copy of that speech and my introductory preparation for candidates before starting to write. I would like you to read those papers and to tell me your impression.

On the occasion of today's New Year's Day, I wish the best for you and for the Party.

                    Tadeusz Maciejczyk
                    Milledgeville, January 1, 1994

The World Seen from the Distance of a Small Village

P.S. I wonder what would happen if this contest declared here would penetrate into every locality of the U.S. or even of the world? Would it have an influence? Could it product strength and force necessary for a change?

Harold B. Smith
Chairman of the Illinois Republican State Committee

Dear Sir:

Again, I received your letter with an invitation to become a sustaining member of the Illinois Republican Party.

I do not know well what would be the limit of my input to the Party in such membership. From my experience I think it would be reduced to an obligation and expectation to support the Party generously with money. Yes, I am an M.D.

I received a similar invitation from the Republican Central Committee and I responded to Chairman Haley Barbour explaining to him my restraints and apprehensions. I am sending you the copy of that letter. I explained in that letter why a sustaining membership is not attractive to me. The history of previous Party performances didn't make me proud or attached and until now, I do not see even an attempt to do any of the work of reform.

Last September, I responded to Chairman Barbour's Republican National Committee Issues Survey. He asked for ideas and opinions and promised a continuous work of search for new ideas. That survey was supposed to be followed by several others, exploring in depth every field of present life realities and possible remedies. The battle cry for the new election is here. The search for ideas? Apparently we can go forward carried by the waves of changed feelings. Why to think?

I am sending you some of my letters where I tried to speak about problems. I would like to belong, but as I see the Parties at the present time, I prefer to remain independent.

I wish you the best in your work.

Tadeusz Maciejczyk
Milledgeville, January 9, 1994

Book Three

Lane Evans
Congress of the United States
Washington, D.C.

Dear Sir:

Today I received your second Congressional update letter in which again the health reform problem appears to be the more persistent, more difficult to solve properly and with the biggest gulf between the wonderful everything-for-everybody and the realities of true life.

I responded to your first letter writing about this problem and I include here the copy of that letter.

My general idea about the best role for government in the health care area can be summarized in two main points.

1. Whatever would be the government's program in the national healthy system, it should not remove the basic responsibility of everybody to take care of themselves. The usual, not catastrophic sphere of health should not be the subject of a national health plan. This area should remain free from political games and up to every family, every adult preferences.
2. The dreaded catastrophic illnesses, which destroy families economically and emotionally, should start to enter into the scope of the National Health Care System at a predictable level.

The government's health coverage, as it is intended, would alter the tradition and the source of the most basic strength of the U.S. It would undermine the healthy individualism and the pride of Americans. It would kill those aspects of the present health system that shows excellence. It would start an era of experimentation with all the upheavals and uncertainties with all the mistakes, losses and patchings of the emotionally loaded and explosive unknown.

I do not think that the present plan would bring relief or satisfaction. Rather it would create general ill feelings. It would deny the creativity, the resourcefulness and the strength of the people. The psychological difference of the two parts of the same Germany that became apparent after reunification, should be enough of a warning and restraint for the government in pushing their "goodness" on society. To explain the difference between the show of goodness and being good, I am sending you a copy of my responses to one Republican survey about a year ago.

The universality of the coverage for the catastrophic illnesses certainty would be welcome everywhere in the nation. It would give to everybody a greater sense of security and of belonging without a restraining jacket that would be presented to everybody with a complete universal coverage.

With such help from the government, our private insurance would become much less expensive and less subject to insurers anxiety or malice. Such help would not denigrate, but would elevate the people feelings about themselves, mobilizing them to do their part the best way.

Taxation for the coverage of catastrophic situations and for the unpredictabilities of our last years' existence would be surely accepted by the people.

I consider that such an arrangement would be just, would be helpful and assuring and would not produce a psychological impotence as its byproduct.

I wish you the best in your work.

Tadeusz Maciejczyk, M.D.
Milledgeville, January 20, 1994

Book Three

The Editor
The Daily Gazette
Sterling, Illinois

Dear Sir:

Last July, responding to the article about the life in "A City Without Hope," (*Time Magazine,* July 26, 1993) I wrote to the editor of *Time Magazine:*

It takes a soul of a real coward, ridden by many painful and dark complexes to be so merciless to anybody who already is lying helplessly on the ground, exhausted to the limit and practically without means to defend himself. A true man, with a sense of dignity and justice, behaves differently.

I think that the sons and grandsons of those Serbs, who at present are displaying so vividly their "heroic" spectacle before the audience of the paralyzed world, will live with the feeling of guilt and shame. The rest of the world also. The rest of the world has no moral strength that could be taken seriously and have a power to restrain.

It was almost yesterday, I remember, the beautiful dance made together by different regional groups of Yugoslavia during the Winter Olympics of 1984. That beauty could flower and prosper in togetherness. It was killed by the preachers of the Serbian edition of *Mein Kampf* philosophy and the consequent madness.

And the world is washing their hands like Pilate and like Chamberlein."

Today after reading about the new massacre in Sarajevo, I asked your *Daily Gazette* not only to publish this letter, but to send it to the present Olympic Committee in Norway in order to arrange one minute of standing up and silence every day as long as the Olympics lasts. This minute of silence will be dedicated to the Spirit and the memories of the Winter Olympics of 1984, to the people who were such a wonderful masters of the house there, to salute all those there who suffered and died to resist aggression and to condemn the aggressor. This act of Solidarity, of the moral support and moral condemnation should be shown on television all over the world.

If the *Gazette* would consider it appropriate, it could be useful to ask the people for signatures on a specially prepared list to express our solidarity with those who suffer now in Sarajevo. Such lists of signatures should be sent to the Olympic Committee in Norway as soon as possible.

I thank you for your help.

Tadeusz Maciejczyk, M.D.
Milledgeville, February 8, 1994

The World Seen from the Distance of a Small Village

The Olympic Committee
Lillehammer, Norway

I wrote my letter to the *Daily Gazette* after reading in *Newsweek* about the new massacre in Sarajevo. I did this between my normal work and this afternoon I took it to the *Daily Gazette* building 15 miles away.

The editor was in agreement with me that my letter should be published without delay and he promised me to do his part. He asked me nevertheless to send my letter to you separately and immediately. His gathering of writings and gathering signatures can take a few days.

A minute of standing in silence at whatever spot each athlete or any other person would be at the moment of a special signal, all this shown on all television screens of the world, could impress, could create a necessary moral force for decisions and could finally bring peace to Bosnia.

Such a moment of silence would express the true spirit of the Olympiad in ancient Greece and would give the modern Olympic Games a very special and beautiful tradition. Such an act would add to the Winter Olympics of 1994 a special meaning, a meaning that the present world needs desperately.

I wish you the best and I will watch.

Tadeusz Maciejczyk
Milledgeville, February 8, 1994

Book Three

International Olympic Committee

M. Tadeusz MACIEJCZYK
Box 788
444 Main St.
MILLEDGEVILLE IL 61051
USA

Lausanne, February 13th 1994
Ref. No 1994/bar

Dear Mr. Maciejczyk,

I acknowledge with thanks receipt of your letter dated February 8th 1994 and your kind consideration regarding the situation in Sarajevo and your suggestion for a minute of standing in silence.

As you may have seen on television we have held a minute of standing in silence during the opening ceremony of the XVIIth Winter Olympic Games in Lillehammer as a special signal of peace and solidarity in honour of the victims of Sarajevo, the Olympic City.

Yours sincerely,
Juan Antonio SAMARANCH
Marquès de Samaranch

The World Seen from the Distance of a Small Village

Haley Barbour
Chairman of the Republican National Committee

Dear Sir:

I received a letter from the Republican National Trust in Washington with an urgent request to respond to a very important questionnaire called the Republican Strategy Survey.

I looked at this letter with interest and illusion. I wanted to participate and to reach the depth of the discussed subjects as far and as deep as my capacity would permit.

The letter of the Chairman, Rodney A. Smith, after a small introduction, became the usual Party rhetoric that could be almost a copy of thousands of other similar letters from the past. I looked into the survey and my arms fall down; my eagerness to cooperate disappeared.

That survey was completely worthless. More than this, it was harmful and degrading to the Party and to the Nation. It was not an invitation to think, to collect the wisest and most realistic thoughts from the participants, thoughts that could bring new light to the GOP's mission for the nation and for the world.

It was a voice of a more than ordinary agitator who is trying to create mob hysteria and lead such a mob nowhere. Or it also could be the voice of a very dull salesman who is trying to be wise and sell his worthless product to the blind and brainless listeners.

I hope that the next GOP survey will not be such a cheap hoax, made up in five minutes from abundant slogans everywhere in the midst of a drinking party, but a serious study giving the participants different ranges of choices, reasons behind them, consequent discussions or additions of new ideals.

This survey I got will give no category, no argument, no enlightenment to your candidates. It will not give them a necessary status of greatness. It will make from them mob agitators, shallow-minded users of slogans, an unattractive meeting of high personalities who like in previous years would make from a high opportunity time a nauseating and depressing show of degradation of the present political life and a dreadful omen for the future of leadership of the nation.

Yes. It was not once or twice. Many times in the last years, I saw people approaching the Election day in a state of depression and resignation. The preceding display of quality of political aspirants left them com-

Book Three

pletely dispirited and pessimistic, betrayed and robbed of all illusions, of all their readiness to give themselves and to grow in this self-giving.

I am returning your survey unmarked. It is not worth the effort of marking on the line of a "very important" grading. I am not sending any money to promote this survey. I do not want such mediocrity of political creation to be sent to people in the GOP's name.

This nation today is facing mounting consequences of previous slogans of nonsense and stupidity that at one time or another were attractive in their simplified form to the electorate.

This nation is witnessing everywhere petrification, rigidity and brain sclerosis of different branches of bureaucracy that should be shaken to its baseline and breathed in a new spirit and a little humanity. We see the public institutions that were supposed to help and redeem and that became a bastion of social nonsense, refusing normal renewal, perpetuating inertia, forcing the honest in need to be dishonest and giving premiums to smart abusers or those without scruples. We as a nation, are standing before an enormous task of finding meaning in life for every individual, every community, for the nation and for the world, and in such a time, the highest offices of the Republican Party are sending me thirteen slogans giving them the name of a Republican Strategy Survey and still expecting me to pay for this affront to the minds of those who want to be Republicans.

I expect to receive another survey made by somebody who thinks, who knows, who cares and who really can lead.

I send you my best wishes.

Tadeusz Maciejczyk
Milledgeville, February 25, 1994

P.S. In my previous letters, I included my letter to the Olympic Committee. A few days ago, I receive an answer from its president, Juan Antonio Samaranch. I am sending you a copy.

The World Seen from the Distance of a Small Village

Nancy Kerrigan

Dear Lady:

Even yesterday I would never predict that I would be writing to you. It came to me suddenly this morning when I was thinking again about your appearances on ice. In those appearances I saw a special grace and charm combined with solemnity and dignity. Your movements had a fluidity and strength of the best poetry. I wanted a gold medal for you and I felt anger against the judges who decided differently.

After thinking again this morning, my anger melted away emerging into a completely new idea. We never know our destiny. An invisible hand directs us into new directions and new discoveries. At least I had such feelings several times in my life.

It came to me that this your "defeat" could become a starting point for a completely new life and mission for you that could be thousands of times more precious than the Olympic Gold Medal.

I thought that all those years of effort and determination to acquire excellency in your skating led you to the probably uneasy moment of standing on the second place stand for the Olympic Medals and thanks to this special turn of events, an opening of a gate into a completely different calling.

Your disappointment and sorrow, to which you had to present your best face, became an almost life-saving gift to an old nation that only recently became free and at present is struggling with thousands of new experiences, anxieties, failures with the feelings of their loneliness and a continuous pressure from inside and from outside.

The Olympic gold medal for the Ukraine is your uneasy gift to them and gave the Ukrainian people a new focal point for pride and unity, for a new confidence and optimism, for a new energy, new believing in themselves.

And the issue is of enormous importance. With the loss of the Ukraine, Russia will not be strong enough to present a renewed threat to the world. Domination became a passion to Moscow during their constant expansion from a small principality in the 15th century. They used for that expansion different watchwords. In the beginning it was an idea of unifying all Russian-speaking people. Then they felt a right to interfere everywhere that Orthodox Christians lived. Especially in the 19th century, it was the idea of Panslavism and in our century it was Communism that permitted them to infiltrate and find their believers in every corner of the globe. The Russian dream of domination still burns below the surface and can explode under some different pretext.

Book Three

A free Ukraine, in alliance with its neighbors can be an effective shock absorber for such expansion liberating the world from the nightmare of previous decades.

Thanks to your narrow second place, a special opportunity was given to you and only you can act to make it fruitful.

What would happen if one day you decided to visit Oksana in her homeland, embrace her, together visit many places of that land and maybe even together act on ice? Nobody now has such a special chance to reach the hearts of Ukrainians but you. I think that in the Ukraine, you would be greeted as a queen like a symbol of something enormously important like a new chapter in history. You have the power to give the people there new smiles and new strength. And you could continue to use skating as a background to your new role and place in the world's events.

I realize that such a task could be intimidating and discouraging to many, but I looked at you and I knew that you have enough personality, character, toughness and goodness to not melt away from such a call. Nobody else in the world now has such a chance. Only you. A destiny is something strange that only a few people experience. Responding to destiny leads to a new meaning, a new enlarged view of life.

I should add here that I am not Ukrainian. I am a Pole from Poland. I had some good Ukrainian friends years ago.

I wish you the best.

Tadeusz Maciejczyk
Milledgeville, February 27, 1994

Department of Health & Human Services
Health Care Financing Administration

I can only smile with a feeling of sadness and resignation when you declare that the dipstick for urine, hemocult for stool and finger pinch for blood sugar represent a laboratory that requires your special control and your paid permission. Those tests are performed widely by patients themselves and by everybody who cares to perform them.

Lately, the practice of medicine in the U.S. gave a bitter taste to many and became a wide field for abusers, always in the name of purification. Not otherwise, but in this way, I see the need for your control of my "laboratory" a control reinforced by threat of reprisal.

The World Seen from the Distance of a Small Village

I opposed the forced malpractice insurance payments because it added disproportionate costs to medical treatments and I lost my hospital privileges. Then I was accused of malpractice. In its course I had a chance to see that the trial was not in the name of justice, but for a "justice game" of lawyers. Because of this, I refused to have a defense attorney. I defended myself and I won the struggle after three and one-half years. It destroyed my family life. My wife was told by lawyers that in the courtroom, I would be crucified; that after the trial we would be homeless and I would be jobless because our home and my office would be sold to pay the costs and my good name would be destroyed. They told her also that if she would like to retain something, even something very private, she would have to divorce me and that after a trial there would be nothing for us but public aid. The terror of the official U.S. sometimes hardly can take a second place behind the Soviet Gulag.

After that trial, I reduced my practice. I do not do surgery. I do not deliver babies. I cut the outlet of the X-Ray to prove that I am not involved in the X-Ray taking. I eliminated the lab except for those few standardized things.

And that nothing you are elevating to the rank of lab work that you should regulate. I believe in regulation, but in this case, my only conclusion is that you are degrading yourself for money.

Years ago, responding to a survey of the Grace Commission, I wrote that to work I need fresh air and that this fresh air in which to work became poisoned in America. This poisoning is deepening with each passing year. A policeman placed behind every working person never enhanced the work. It only created thousands of abusers and thousands of new needs to control.

Please tell me how much you want this time for tolerating my "laboratory."

Tadeusz Maciejczyk, M.D.
March 6, 1994

Book Three

Editor
The Daily Gazette
Sterling, IL

Watching the Olympic Games was interesting and exciting. The events of competitions in television reportings were complemented by the spotlights on the host country and on its people giving those reports special charm. Watching the people of Norway in this way, two facts caught my special attention:

1. During those games, Norwegians showed to the world their deep attachment to their past. They showed their love for tradition for the old ways of living, for old beliefs, old customs, old ways to live, to work and to celebrate.
   By contrast, here in our country the old is constantly under pressure. We rash constantly for new rights, new freedoms, new morals, new relationships and for whatever another new would come into the focus on the moment. We are tearing apart what still yesterday was normal or even sacred. Every day new slogans catch our attention. Caring just for today, we refuse to sit calmly as the founders of this country did over 200 years ago and to make a solid plan for our future. Bigger mouths, not bigger characters or minds have the best chance to assume leadership. And so we leave behind us for our children no solid ground to stand on but a confusion of ideas, doubts about morals, breakdown of values into which they could put their trust.
2. The other factor that struck me while watching the Lillehammer Olympics was the ease with which the Norwegian people sing. Their spontaneous singing in small groups or in big crowds had harmony and strength. It filled for them the time of waiting, calmed passions and gave them special joy. That attitude of the people contrasts sharply with the absence of song or singing here in the U.S. I do not remember anybody singing here just to relax and enjoy. Many people pass with auriculars on their ears, apparently listening to some music. But such an approach is passive and by a strange twist, it becomes one factor more to isolate and to estrange the individual.

I know that the known signers or singing groups here attract big throngs of enthusiastic listeners, but I wonder whether it is the music or

The World Seen from the Distance of a Small Village

the bizarre and exotic of those shows where there is the main attraction because as a rule, the melodies of those "concerts" have been reduced to a rhythmical ritual noise and the lyrics are generally pitiful.

In talking with young people, I got the impression that for them singing appears to be something that's sissy, something they are not comfortable with. And I know that singing is anything but sissy. It lifts the heart. It helps to communicate. It gives a new frame for relationships. It gives relief from accumulated burdens of daily life. It has the power to bring a smile and optimism from the shadows of hopelessness.

When I was small, in our school there was no hour without a flow of songs from one or another window of the building. I remember those classes of singing with special affection. They gave special tones to those years of my life. And later, during the darkness of war and occupation, those songs or an echo of those songs, gave hope and optimism in spite of the surrounding madness. They helped not to bend, but to raise and to look into the face of true danger.

No. Singing, singing with spontaneity is not sissy. It adds to the femininity or masculinity of each of us. It helps us to enjoy good times. It helps to endure adversity. It helps to find the right way of life. As I see it, it would be a wonderful remedy and antidote for many afflictions and problems of our children.

And to do this would not require raising taxes.

Tadeusz Maciejczyk, M.D.
Milledgeville, March 10, 1994

Book Three

John Greenwald
Editor
The American Legion Magazine

Dear Sir:

In his article "A Day for Remembering," Gary Turbak narrowed the content of that day to just remembering the past and enjoying the present. Really, this is all that the fallen friends, history and the future ask from us? When I approach that day, I see in its inside an enormous material to ponder and to search for conclusions for our part in the continuous effort to make the world a better place to live.

The wars of the past, their emotional echoes, the values they defended, the innumerable lines of graves they left behind, the lessons they taught us—all of them are calling us to understand more deeply, to make commitments and to work accordingly for the future.

History never stops marching. We are always in its center. We are always between the enormous experiences of the past and the enigma of the future. The past should be for us a powerful teacher. The ground on which we are walking during Memorial Day is challenging us to think, to understand, to be responsible and to be involved. Six years ago on Decoration Day I made a speech with a similar message.

Last November 11th, I repeated that speech during the Rotary meeting and I established a scholarship for those who would listen to the testament left for us by those who died defending our freedom. I asked them to write an essay about the need and the role of spiritual strength in resolving today's world conflicts. Last December, in order to help, I composed the introductory points to consider before starting to write.

Now, I am sending you my speech, those points and the responses from two seniors from our school. By responding, they demonstrated something inside them that somehow calls upon them to be leaders. I am grateful to them and I wish them the best.

I have hope that you will publish some of this material.
I wish you the best.

> Tadeusz Maciejczyk
> Milledgeville, May 1, 1994

The World Seen from the Distance of a Small Village

My presentation of contestants during Senior Honor Recognition banquet on May 5, 1994.

Six years ago, during the Decoration Day ceremony, I talked to Veterans about the testament left for us by those who went to defend our country and who didn't come back. I told them that the dying men, in the fury of battle, most likely had no time to formulate any precise recommendations; that more than this that testament was evident in their overwhelming longing for a better world; in their rationalization and in the sense given by them to the horrors of life that became their destiny. At the end of my speech, I concluded that to fulfill the testament of those who fell in action, we should remember them, but also we should explore the best ways into the future; that we should involve in this task the young and that we should look constantly for the wisest and spiritually strongest men for guidance.

Last November 11, during Armistice Day, I repeated that speech during a Rotary meeting and I established a scholarship, different from all others in the sense that it was not given freely, painlessly. The volunteers were asked to write an essay about "the need and the role of spiritual strength in resolving today's world conflicts."

To explore their own spiritual strength, I recommended to participants to read, to digest and to absorb some introductory points that showed the essentials of spiritual life within us. It is my understanding that to lead, to be a leader, the most fundamental quality is the spiritual depth that is something that never comes free and that requires voluntary discipline. A true wisdom comes to men through such preparation.

I talked about my project to many people. One of them responded in a special way. I want to tell you about this. Without being asked, he gave me money for the second prize in the contest. This man was Orvill Williams. Here and now I want to express my gratitude to him. His response was heartlifting and encouraging to me.

This year two students responded to my challenge. They are: Stephanie Bogot and Amanda Erdman. The scholarships, as they now stand, are $300 for first place and $200 for second place, will be presented to them during this year's Memorial Day ceremony after they read their work to the public. I would like to invite everyone to that Veteran's Ceremony.

After the reading, both those essays will be sent to the headquarters of American Veterans, to the White House, to both Senators from Illinois, to our Representative and to all state universities in this state. I hope

Book Three

that both contestants: Amanda Erdman and Stephanie Bogot, will continue their daily preparatory work to someday be ready for true leadership.

May 30, 1994
To the people of the town during Memorial Day.
    Precisely today is the appropriate moment and the right ceremony for the presentation of the two special students from our school who dared to take a challenge.
    That challenge required time for concentration and preparation, time for rethinking the basics of leadership, especially of leadership necessary for direction in the present confusion in the world. They had to give up time for rest and relaxation in order to write an essay about the need and the role of spiritual strength in resolving today's world conflicts. The failure to resolve those conflicts in the past created the need to defend our values with arms, paying the price of millions of deaths and an enormous amount of suffering.
    The two students who chose to take this uneasy task, who felt that the task was worth their efforts and that it could be necessary preparation for their future battles to shape a better world are Stephanie Jo Bogot and Amanda Erdman.
    I hope that this first step into true preparation for the burden and privilege of leadership will be for them not the last one. I hope that they will build inside of themselves necessary wisdom, knowledge and spiritual strength to take their places in shaping the world's future. I would like to think that in doing this, they would look not for success, but for true victory in their mission. About the difference between success and victory, the Polish poet Cyprian Norwid wrote this about 150 years ago:

> The success became a God now.
> It spreads its sorcery over the stretch of the world.
> Before him retreated even the old victory
> Which always was worth the efforts.
>
> Till this crowd comprehends at the side of its grave,
> Till this insane gang will grasp the truth
> That the victory liberates human potential,
> While the success—oh, yes—wonderfully intoxicates.[4]

    I wish the participants in this contest not success in their life's purposes, but victory over the problems they will confront during their

The World Seen from the Distance of a Small Village

lifespan. Success can be cheap. Victory never is. It requires honesty, work and guts.

The works of these two students was read and evaluated by three members of our Rotary Club for first and second place. In my mind that placement has secondary importance. The important fact was taking the challenge, starting the work and bringing it to conclusion.

Those works will now be read in alphabetical order of the participants and the Commander of the American Legion in Milledgeville will give them the rewards. Afterwards, the works will be sent to the White House, to our Governor, to both Senators, to our Representatives and to Illinois State Universities to be a testimony and a flashlight for the emergence of leadership that the generation behind us will pursue.

I hope that this program will continue for years to come, assuring a special selection for talent, personalities and dedication in those who want to build a better world in the future.

I also want to again thank Orvill Williams who in a special way helped to realize this project. And I thank all of you for your participation in this ceremony.

>Tadeusz Maciejczyk
>May 30, 1994

Book Three

This letter was sent together with the essays of the two students to the President, Senators and universities.

Last year a special scholarship and a special opportunity was presented to our senior class students. This scholarship was different from all others because it required participants to take on a challenge. To be eligible, students had to write an essay about the need and the role of spiritual strength in resolving today's world conflicts. Five students volunteered. Two of them finished the work. They read their essays during our Memorial Day ceremony, at which time they received their premiums.

Because those two students took this difficult and unusual task, did the necessary preparation, completed it and presented it to a large public, they showed special qualities within them that differentiated them from all others. They didn't shrink before the challenge. In taking it, they grew. They showed an interest and a power of will necessary to succeed. It is very likely that after this experience, they will take other challenges stored for them in the future more naturally and with more ease. They will look towards those challenges with the same vision and clarity.

These are the reasons why I want to present these two students to a larger audience. With this letter, I am sending copies of their work to the President of the United States, to our Governor of Illinois, to both our Senators and our Congressmen and to all Illinois State Universities.

It is most likely that from such students as these two, will come our leaders in the future. We in Milledgeville are planning to present similar challenges to our seniors every year.

> Tadeusz Maciejczyk (in the name of our Rotary Club)
> June 12, 1994

The World Seen from the Distance of a Small Village

Editor
The Daily Gazette
Sterling, IL

Dear Sir:

In reading today's newspapers, including *The Daily Gazette*, an atmosphere of uneasiness, dissatisfaction and resignation mixed with a longing and searching for some kind of correction in our daily lives appears on almost every page. What is happening, if not modified can lead to something unpredictable.

Really, I do not understand how we can expect to get the best from our democratic system, to make this system vigorous and creative, to be stimulating and inspiring, to be helpful in developing inside of us a healthy self-esteem or a greatness of a free spirit while at the same time this democracy is mutilating itself by the endless trials to be nice and to accommodate every whim of the vocal and extremely emotional pressure groups. Those groups prefer to play the role of being deeply offended and not understood; of being unprotected in spite of their constitutional rights. For justice, they turn to the highest courts.

And those courts accommodate them. After doing the newest interpretation of the Constitution for such matters, they dictate new laws that give those groups satisfaction by restrictions imposed on the rights of the abusing majorities. The vocal minorities are triumphant, but never satisfied, always vigilant and always pressing to further extend their rights. All other potential minorities are watching and are taking note. They also begin to protest, to condemn and to demand.

The society as a whole is taking those restrictions with dismay, then with resignation, respecting the courts decisions and making adjustments to those new laws. The ever-present threat of liability and costly lawsuits becomes a very convincing enforcer.

Liability suits were almost unheard of even two decades ago. The blackmail of malpractice erupted suddenly in the early Eighties and changed the climate and the life in this country. Everybody became jittery, uncertain, and doubly cautious. Even the universities, which for centuries were the centers of freedom of speech, introduced an obligatory "correctness" on their campuses.

All this created a new America. The element of sincerity evaporated. The art of communication, the desire to find a common ground and mutual understanding through serious public debates lost its attractiveness. Faith and trust in public institutions became eroded. Blaming somebody else became a fine art and the best weapon in the general elbow fight for more concessions and more rights. In the vacuum created by the lack of positive stimuli, the negative became more dominant, entering in the character and in the souls of the people, especially the young.

Human nature abhors a vacuum.

Those court dictates are causing discomfort, fragmentation of society, costly cautions, mutual distrust, general apathy, negativism and sarcasm. With those negative reactions on the rise, something very important in the life of any society is getting moribund and is dying. Sometimes it looks to me, that those pressure groups are acting in the same way as the Palestinians in their terrorist attacks years ago. Yet, the long lasting effects of their tactics can be more damaging to the future than the explosions of the terrorists' bombs.

With this, I do not want to say that the grievances of those minorities are negative. They are useful. They have the potential to clarify our hidden problems. They can breathe new air into the life of our communities. But they should not be regulated by court decisions. Until now the courts' rulings in those matters only fragmented and shallowed the nation planting into its soul a deep-rooted discord.

The nation would gain much more if those problems arising from the co-existence of all fragments of our society would be studied, debated and searched for solutions by a special body convocated for each problem differently. Those debates should have an open participation. They should be open-minded to all aspects and sources of frictions. They should learn from life and at the same time they should clarify, make conclusions and teach. It would be useful if the moderators in such debates could be persons trusted and respected by everybody for their character and their wisdom. Also, it would be good if they would have some judicial experience.

Such debates would clarify the differences, would bring more good will and more mutual understanding. They would not fragment and separate. More likely they would bring unity and would elevate the spirit of everybody creating a better climate for true growth.

Not long ago, *The Daily Gazette* brought the letter of Aaron Mathes about his desire to have a prayer at his graduation that was denied by a law-abiding school principal. Pegi Sofola told about the emptiness in the souls of our children. "Young people are looking for something in which to hang onto and after looking around, they find such an element in gangs." Kevin Lyons in his prospective explained why the U.S. District Judge could not consider Good Friday to be a holy day. Its mining

The World Seen from the Distance of a Small Village

was not attractive for commerce. The public schools are walking on tiptoes for fear of lawsuits. School books have become sanitized from any meaningful mention of religion.

All these problems have a common denominator. The true meaning of life that can elevate and give the best frame for life experiences were washed out from life spirituality and reduced to values of material utilities. The notion of God and holiness was erased from public life to satisfy one of such minorities.

And yet, a human being needs an ideal, a notion of holiness, a feeling of a presence of God. We all have moments when we need to raise our eyes up and confront our miseries with something eternal and redeeming. Good Friday, used well and according to its meaning (meaning valid even for the atheists) can give the country more riches and more strength than all the commerce done on such days. What would happen if Good Friday would be declared as a day to consider the need for personal sacrifice for a common good or for the truth? Such a day could give common ground for believers and unbelievers.

The riches within every community, society or nation have many dimensions. The material well-being is only one of them and maybe it is not the most fundamental. It is sad that we have to spend so much of those material riches on building prisons and on calming our fears and anxieties.

I feel that the country at present has an enormous need for change.

Tadeusz Maciejczyk, M.D.
Milledgeville, June 30, 1994

Book Three

Trustmark
Lake Forest, IL

    I am sending you a check with some delay. I am sorry.
When I received your statement I was dismayed. Last year I paid $3,177.21 for three of us (full premium for my wife and my daughter Cristina and a supplement for me.) This year, for only two of us, my Christine and me, it was $3,531.71.
    I was astonished by this increase in such a special timing when the life of the insurance system and of the whole healthy care is at stake. Such an increase will surely multiply the number of those who will decide that the cost of health insurance went up and out of their reach. They will help Mrs. Clinton to get her wish.
    A smart move for today only, without a vision for tomorrow and such a clear display of greed, never indicates wisdom and frequently only foretells self-destruction.
    I hope you can correct your desire to get rich quickly. Your action in addition to helping the Clinton administration impose their public health program will give a clear signal to everyone of the branches of health care to also raise prices. The circle will go around and your gain will not be as fabulous.
    I am paying and I wish you luck. I asked for motives behind your radical price increases and I still didn't get an answer.
    I am sending you my two letters written to our Representative about my idea for health care structure.
    Again, my best wishes.

                                          Tadeusz Maciejczyk, M.D.
                                          Milledgeville, July 1994

The World Seen from the Distance of a Small Village

Robert Gurnitz
Northwestern Steel & Wire Company
Sterling, IL

Dear Sir:

News from Sterling says that you are planning to open your own Northwestern Steel and Wire clinic and in this way attend to the medical needs of your workers and their families.

I am a general practitioner in Milledgeville. I have been here for 30 years and during this time I provided medical care to many of your workers. It appears to me that to your workers who live here, a continuation of my care for them would be truly convenient. Your clinic, especially in its initial stages, would be overloaded with patients. If my office could be considered as part of your clinic, it would be the most practical solution for your workers from around here. Some loose association could be arranged if you consider such cooperation useful and convenient.

In making this proposition, I have to inform you that all my medical work is limited to work in my own office. I lost my medical privileges in the Sterling Hospital when in 1983 I opposed obligatory malpractice insurance for doctors. I saw this sudden requirement as blackmail of the medical institutions that in the long range would make health care very costly and the environment, the working climate for treatment, very strenuous. I include here my correspondence with the Hospital Administration during that time.

I survived and I defended my practice against all pressures. I have many patients here and in Sterling who consider me as a trusted friend. I arranged hospitalization for them, when necessary, through other doctors.

One convenience of my association with your clinic is that I never abused anyone. I never overcharged for my services. I still do housecalls and I see patients if necessary, at any time, even on my days off.

If you are interested in my cooperation with your clinic, please contact me.

I wish you the best in your work.

Tadeusz Maciejczyk, M.D.
July 28, 1994

Book Three

Russell F. Coats
East Jordan United Methodist Church

Dear Sir:

I thank you for your letter. It is stimulating to have an echo to our views from somebody else's observations, doubts and questions. It leads to deeper exploration of the problem, a search for new discoveries, arguments and the natural laws governing such events.

Your letter had a stimulating effect on me. And after thinking it through, I am more certain than ever that the courts, the traumatic confrontations and verdicts, are not the answer to the colliding social issues. Even if the court ruling is just and right, those rules are not healing. They are deepening the abyss between the winners and the losers. In this way, they are perpetuating a climate of confrontation. The triumphant side usually shows its triumph, humiliating the other and jealously watches their gains, contemplating further movers to consolidate what they got.

The losing side has to accommodate and to recognize the fact, but seldom gives up. As time passes, something very pernicious rises in the souls of such losers in court. They start to be resentful. Once begun, such a process tends to grow and dominate all feelings, creating negative conclusions and negative energy that is boiling under the surface, leading to unpredictable actions or explosions. Hurt feelings are not easy to calm. They twinge with each piece of news, every fact that in other circumstances would have no meaning or would produce completely different conclusions.

Court hearings are in fact ongoing collisions. In social matters such collision evokes deep emotions that have an appeal to the masses and in those masses can grow to unexpected proportions. The court confrontations in such matters open wounds that never heal easily, enter into the souls and the genes and can last through generations. Looking at the pages of history, we can see clearly its tragic seeds: the intensity of hate in Lenin, whose older brother was hanged as a result of a court verdict for his activities against the Czar; the rise of Hitler, whose anger and hate against the system created by post WWI rulings, mobilized in hate all the otherwise great nation; the recent massacre and madness in Rwanda.

People can get free from destructive resentments only by forgiving. Such forgiveness is impossible in court confrontations. It can be reached through a wisely conducted debate. It can come from the goodwill found, created and nourished in such debates. Such debates could be used at

The World Seen from the Distance of a Small Village

every level: in world discords, in the problems affecting the nation, the town, the village. Slowly the skills of debates would take root and human life would find a new climate and new dignity.

Again, I thank you for your letter and your sympathy.

Tadeusz Maciejczyk, M.D.
August 18, 1994

Book Three

Harold B. Smith
Chairman of the Illinois Republican Party

Dear Sir:

I want to tell you that I understand the need for a united action against the mirages and temptations placed before the nation by President Clinton and his spiritual co-believers. I refused to renew my membership in the Republican Party to protest the status quo in our politics.

The present time is a special time. The voices for change are rising. There is a growing uneasy feeling about the present mediocrity of our leadership. An underlying hunger for greatness in resolving this country's and the world's conflicts can be detected everywhere. In talking to people, I feel their longing for a special redeeming change in our lives. The momentum is always precious because it is an opening gate for action. The present politics as usual, playing the Washington small games without a distant vision can only bury that momentum. The arms, raised for action out of disillusion, will fall again into passivity.

I said this and it was also the idea of Chairman Barbour that this time should be dedicated primarily to gather the best ideas and to organize them into the best arrangement that would be appropriate to meet the needs of the rapidly approaching new world.

The present acceleration of technological knowledge very quickly will change the structures and the life on this planet. This technological pressure calls for new vision and bold changes in the life of the global human family.

This new world that emerges so rapidly before our eyes, more than ever before, will need spiritual content intense enough to parallel those technological changes. New approaches to the togetherness of life will have to be worked out to give relief to the accumulating anxiety and to give rise to a liberating optimism.

Those changes cannot be the result of a last minute reflex correction. They have to be wise and just, generous but strict. They have to permit flexibility and have room for all new surprises. They have to inspire and reach the soul of mankind.

The alternative, a lack of such groundwork, could be restlessness in that highly technological world with an emptiness of spirit, explosions and even possible self-destruction. To usher us wisely and safely into that new world, a special leadership will be essential. That leadership will need a ready array of possible options and a framework in which to act. The time to work on that is now.

The World Seen from the Distance of a Small Village

I am sending you $30 for my dues.

My practice is limited now. After my opposition to an obligatory malpractice insurance, I lost my hospital privileges. After my malpractice trial, I lost faith in creative individual work in this country.

At the present time, I have my own project on which I want to concentrate my rather small resources.

I am sending you copies of my last letters.

I send you and Governor Edgar my best wishes.

Tadeusz Maciejczyk
Milledgeville, September 4, 1994

Book Three

Dick Cheney
ACU Advisor

Dear Sir:

I filled out your survey and in order to define more clearly my understanding of government's place in health care, I am sending you two of my letters to my district Congressman and maybe one, not very nice one to my insurance company.

The true root of the present malady of medicine is not limited to government intrusion. The backbone of medicine was broken by the massive blackmail of malpractice suits. Without clarifying this aspect of medical care derangement in the U.S., medicine as a service and as a mission will always be sick. Really, if the malpractice blackmail continues, the government's takeover of health care will not make much difference. Both trends are destructive.

To illustrate this, I am sending you some of my letters from my own struggle with the inquisition of malpractice. I also want to tell you that at present, I have my own project on which I would like to concentrate my resources. Last year I created a scholarship that was given the nickname of "Scholarship Challenge" by others.

I am sending you the history of this scholarship that started with my speech to veterans during Decoration Day 1988. To assure its' continuation this summer, I painted eight oil paintings of flowers from my garden. With the help of our Rotary Club, if those paintings were to be sold, we would have some base to continue and to extend this scholarship for years to come.

As an advisor to the ACU, I am sending you my letter to Nancy Kerrigan. In that letter I talked about a project that certainly would have a positive significance if realized. If the ACU could find a sponsor for such an adventure and somebody could convince Nancy, it would be wonderful. Or maybe I should send to you all my letters related to the last Olympics in Norway.

In my last two letters I wrote, I talked about the negative aspects of court verdicts in social issues. Maybe they would be of some value for discussions in the ACU.

Finally, for you, the Secretary of the Armed Forces during the Desert War, I am sending you my two special letters from that time. Maybe they would be interesting to you.

The World Seen from the Distance of a Small Village

I am sending you $25 for the ACU needs. Sorry. My practice is limited to the minimum since my trial and I was never famous for charging too much for my work. I love medicine and I love people, but I hate the frame that was imposed on medical work.

I send you my best wishes.

Tadeusz Maciejczyk, M.D.
September 22, 1994

Book Three

Harold B. Smith
Chairman
Illinois Republican State Central Committee

Dear Sir:

1. The most critical issue facing Illinois and the whole country is apathy and boredom. This is in spite of all existing facilities for entertainment and excitement. They calm for a moment. They never reach deep. They prevent us from really getting to know ourselves, intensifying the shallowness of life. We have no exciting ideas around, no personality who could mobilize, move and transform. A good bureaucracy is not exactly the same as good leadership.
2. Immediate steps should be only provisional and temporary. To control crime, a foundation should be laid for a long-range strategy.
   a. No more prisons. This represents a completely negative, typically panicky and defensive way to react to crime. It certainly would bring the very painful and costly consequences to the more distant future. About this, I wrote one year ago:
      a. We have enough jails to lock up people convicted of violent crimes. But we fill them up with drug offenders. Prisons will not correct those drug offenders. They are going there to get a new seminar in how to organize their drug business better and how to get new contacts and all this is done at the expense of the taxpayer. The drug offenders should be punished the way that would hurt them the most. They go into their business for the love of easy big money. All their money, all their possessions should be confiscated without mercy, leaving them practically out on the streets. To earn a living, they would get an obligatory work sentence for several years at minimum wage in places that care for their victims. Also, it should be clearly established that those drug dealers whose sales resulted in the death of someone, should be put directly onto death row where they would wait for eventual mercy. I am not cruel. Only the situation became increasingly critical and the old methods of fighting crime as leading nowhere. Their sentence could be

reduced by identifying their superior who would take their place on death row.

Prisons and even boot camps for young offenders would create perfect conditions where the worst of them would influence the more innocent. The suppressed anger and frustration, an inadequate move of guards would help to push them into the worst choices in life. The issue is very delicate.
Each young offender should be not only judged, but first of all, studied for the origins of his offensive tendencies. The judges should have at hand a wide range of rehabilitative measures for souls and for accumulated in them emotional destructive material. They should be engaged in a labor of restitution that would have a power of redeeming and changing their lives.

Also, I consider that a special law should be created through which a parent who disappeared from the life of his child who then became an offender should be considered equally guilty in the juvenile crimes and especially he should fee the weights of justice. A parent who neglected or abandoned his child, committed a crime against society and the consequences for him should be heavy.

In the same way, any gang-type crime offender should be put into rehabilitation, required to pay restitution for damages and sentenced to soul changing service. The one who really should be punished in such cases should be his superior, preferably the superior's superior. As long as justice only spanks the most peripheral offender leaving the nucleus of madness untouched, the rise of crime will never be stopped.

To fight crime, a heavy fist of justice will make a small difference. Imagination and diversity of actions can bring change. Those diverse actions should be made for the human soul, its needs and hungers as they are now, at this moment in time. The Scouting organizations (Boys and Girls), so wonderful and dynamic at the beginning of this century, became sterile, almost invisible and without power to conquer and to inspire. I was a Boy Scout and I see the difference.

Book Three

What would happen if some organizations or some authorities established a kind of competition to create "noble gangs" attractive to kids not because of money or facilities given to them, but because they filled the inside emptiness and created a real sense of belonging and of growth that gave these kids the pride they need?

A true helping hand to such institutions as the Mercy Home for Boys and Girls in Chicago at 1140 W. Jackson Blvd. would be a much better investment for the future than all the prisons we could build. In our society there are resources to be used to win the battle with crime that have never been used efficiently. Considering only the people in the Golden Age category. How many of them would volunteer, would give time and enthusiasm if a field and frame for such a mission for them would be created and diversity, common sense, imagination would be encouraged and hailed before all the nation. Maybe even this kind of war on crime that truly could have a chance to win after counting everything would be enormously less expensive and would put society and the nation together.

3. States, counties and localities should have the greatest role in deciding the ways, the substance and the conditions for welfare. This would give elasticity and better uses of funds. The Federal government should coordinate and supervise the local activities.

4. Freedom was the greatest treasure of America for two centuries. Freedom imposes on individuals a sense of responsibility. Destroy the notion and the internal need to be responsible for our lives and America will never be the same. The health care reform should control the spiraling costs and the uncertainties of insurance coverage during the time of an individual's difficulties, but never should be automatically given to everybody as a right. By making such virtues as individuality and responsibility unnecessary in such a vital and emotional area of human life as the health problem is, a foundation will be put on weakening of characters and removal of one of a very important factor in the family togetherness. We need health care reform, but not of such a kind and not for such a prize.

5. I was thinking and writing seriously about balanced budgets ten years ago. After repeating this as a slogan for so long, with-

The World Seen from the Distance of a Small Village

out seeing any change, without deepening, without serious studies of this subject, without even partial implementation, with all the continuing quackery and abuses of common sense in budgeting, this slogan became not a force that could move, but a symbol of duplicity, smartness and dishonesty. This slogan became one more point to create general apathy and uninvolvement. Whoever makes such a point to shine and omits any actual explanation is losing face and credibility. This is a common feeling among the people in the countryside.

6. and 7. These are the games of the Party, a special show of cleverness that I do not like and I would not spend five cents for it.

Make a solid plan, capture with this plan the general attention, wake up with them, involve with them and all those cheap and degrading moves behind the scene, all those tricks will be unnecessary.

My recommendation here would be: use as a guide the five fundamental ingredients of mind that the leader should have 1) common sense; 2) imagination; 3) capacity for abstraction; 4) memory of history's lessons; 5) a fantasy; and add to it a knowledge of realities.

I assure you that the leader or the party that would display a policy based on such points would have no problem winning. The people are hungry for such leadership. And, because I am not excited about the present Republican Party stand that takes it confidence not from its excellence, but form the failure of the other, I am not sending you any money. The money I have, I prefer to reserve for my own project that can do better things for the future than the present Republican Party.
I wish you my best.

Tadeusz Maciejczyk, M.D.
Milledgeville, October 9, 1994

Book Three

Members of Rotary International, Milledgeville

As one year ago, today I want to announce a call challenging the willing students to a work that can give them new meaning in their lives. I want them to search for the qualities in leadership necessary for today's complicated, confusing and uncertain world.

As one year ago today, I will announce the subject of this year's homework for them to volunteer. It will be similar to the previous one, but also it will be different. As one year ago, it will be equally demanding for dedication and concentration. Those who will decide to take the hardship of this work by the same will declare that they are willing to serve and to guide their generation into the future.

This year's theme for the essay will be: "The Need and the Role of Spiritual Strength for Leadership in Today's World."

Adding to this general theme, the participants will be asked to explore the mind of a true leader. A leader obviously has to show character in his life; he has to be convincing in his mission; he has to be open-minded. But together with this you will try to illustrate the five special qualities of his mind:
1. for common sense
2. his gift for imagination
3. his ability for abstraction
4. his capacity his prudence evidenced by learning from the reading of history
5. his willingness to accept fantasy that is a forerunner for imagination, the most advancing scout between dreams and reality.

As one year ago, each applicant will be given a preparatory text to help them look inside themselves. The essays should be returned to the Milledgeville Rotary Club. The three selected works will be announced during the banquet for the honor students in May and the authors of the selected works will be asked to read them to the public during the Memorial Day ceremony in Milledgeville where they will receive their rewards from the Commander of the American Veteran's Post in Milledgeville.

Later, those three selected essays will be sent as a special document form our time to the White House, to both Senators of Illinois and to all state universities of Illinois. They will also be sent to the leading newspapers in the U.S.

I want to stress that this challenge is not limited to Chadwick-Milledgeville schools, but to all students from outside who would like

The World Seen from the Distance of a Small Village

to participate. They will be welcomed. They can apply for instructions and material at our school or to the Milledgeville Rotary Club. I want to encourage all eligible students to make a decision and to participate.

I am depositing my check of $300 to initiate the funding of this scholarship. The profit from my painting will be added to it. I hope that this scholarship and the tradition it can develop will continue for years to come.

> Tadeusz Maciejczyk
> Milledgeville, November 11, 1994

Book Three

The American Academy of Family Physicians
Kansas City, Mo.

This year I am late with my dues.

I wanted to do this long ago but with the occasion I wanted to discuss with you my point of view on the health care system. I wrote to my Congressman two times about health care and he never responded. Anyway, I consider that my plan has merit and should be considered seriously.

During the last years several serious problems were developing in the U.S. President Clinton placed the health care issue to the front. Senator Moynihan contradicted this, saying that not the health care but the welfare system acquired the proportion of a true crisis. My impression is that the biggest problem facing America is the Family Crisis that became a focal point and the source of many other maladies. Family crisis is continuously increasing and is producing a destructive impact on many, especially on children and by this, on the future of this country.

Family stability and health calls for a good and deep look at what it means and is becoming a priority.

The family is strong if it preserves and develops a sense of a mutual responsibility and the care of one for another. Not anything else, only the example of parents making sacrifices, caring sincerely providing what they can, can implant values into the souls of children and serve them as a living lesson that would last for their lifetime. No school, no Day Care institution or any other organization can do this, can take their place.

If the role of parents as such caring providers is diminished, is made pointless and hollow by the good intentions of government or any other institution that could provide all those things playing the role of a big, wonderful provider, the family institution is weakened. Those good actions are taking from the family the instinct of duty; are depriving them from the healthy pride of good ambition, are providing permission for neglect.

Those good services are changing parents and are changing children too. Created emptiness and worthlessness changes   personalities. Resourcefulness is less and less a challenge. In its place develops an expectation of more convenience and easy solutions or rights. With the decline of an instinct of providers, a self-deprecation develops, then selfishness and anxiety and feelings of guilt.

For the best upbringing of children there is no substitution, no escape from sacrifice. Prince Charles had the best medical care. He had the best toys, best entertainment; he had all the facilities and privileges in schools and yet today he seems to be not only unhappy, but miserable. He had everything. He never saw in his parents a true sacrifice, which means true love, given to him.

The automatic medical care provided by government, a special "goodness" of different organizations (at this time of the year they give toys to children), all those good intentions are undermining the family institution and structure.

The element of sacrifice, the show of true care in spite of difficulties, the real appreciation for the humblest thing the family can have, is giving the children a practical and lasting lesson of responsibility and of common sense, is creating a mutual estimation within the family, is teaching how to develop a genuine resourcefulness. And something more: it gives the family a feeling of pride and merit.

In talking about giving, I want to stress that there is an enormous difference between "good" and between so-called "goodness." The difference between the two apparently same qualities is of enormous importance in the life of every family, every society, every nation. Goodness comes from the desire to be seen as wonderful, to be popular, or from the wish to not be bothered. The goodness is giving satisfaction to everybody. It spoils. It breeds unhappy, unadjusted adults and sometimes-human monsters.

Being good requires vision, purpose, wisdom and self-discipline. It directs and corrects. It helps to develop physical and spiritual growth and it leads to fulfillment in life. Maybe the difference between them can best be illustrated by remembering the life story of Helen Keller.

Her parents were so loving and so compassionate. They permitted her to grow like a pig, without any rules, messing everything everywhere. What else could they do for that poor creature? The teacher whom they hired, appeared to them a monster, cruel and inhumane. But it was that teacher, who from that "pig" made an almost First Lady of the 19th century and whom Helen loved until the end of her life.

If a child is given a wonderful toy by a stranger because the parents cannot afford it, with this toy the child receives a powerful lesson, that beyond parents, somebody else is much better, who gives without asking for merit. Such a child learns to be unhappy with what he has at home. His parents and everybody at home are losing authority.

If the parents, or any adults are given health care or anything else for free, the lesson they get is that the responsibility, the taking care of family needs are not required from them any more. That neglecting pays more than effort; that complaining provides more than self-reliance. This kind of giving is crippling and destroying individuality. It places into souls the seeds of discontentment. It ends not in happiness and progress, but in dependency and decadence.

Any giving requires wisdom and sincerity, selectiveness and discipline. It can produce wonders or can serve as an invitation for indulgence and a hindrance for self-development. Either way, its consequences can grow out of proportion in extension and in time. It is something everybody should think about.

In this letter I am trying to express my belief that the primary medicine should be left free from the state or from the federal manipulations and political maneuverings because their "goodness" is bringing to families and the society more harm than good.

I also believe that every average American needs a certainty to get help and protection in case of catastrophic situation in the long lasting, exhaustive illnesses and in the unpredictability of our existence in our last years.

Such a health care program in those situations would be a true blessing and would give an enormous peace of mind to most Americans.

It would not spoil. It would encourage and build.

Tadeusz Maciejczyk, M.D.
Milledgeville, December 1, 1994

P.S. I want to tell you about my special scholarship that I would like to extend to many places in the U.S., I am sending you copies of my writings related to this.

And because of present situations in Bosnia, I am sending you copies of my special correspondence about that.

Merry Christmas to everybody.

The World Seen from the Distance of a Small Village

CGH Medical Center
Mammography Reporting System

Dear Dr. Maciejczyk,

I have worked at CGH in the X-ray department for 17 years. I remember many years back how I enjoyed seeing you, taking a call from you or talking to you in the department, however brief it was. There are times my thoughts return to physicians I seldom or never see anymore. You are among my enjoyable thoughts.

When I read your story in the *Gazette*, it pulled at my heartstrings and made me realize how little we know of someone else's life.

I do not want to let the chance go by without thanking you for sharing a part of your life with the area communities. I personally thank you.

Wishing you a happy holiday season. May the angel, who has been with you this far in your life, continue to walk with you.

Sincerely,
Cynthia McCombs

Note: Cynthia wrote this after reading an article in the *Daily Gazette*, describing how and why I left Poland—about my life.

Book Three

William Clinton
President
The United States
The White House
Washington, D.C.

Dear Sir:

Just a short time ago, I received a big envelope from one political organization (with which to some extent I sympathize) asking me to sign their formulation for health care that consequently would be sent to you. I didn't sign it.

I do not like this kind of pressure. They are always strong in numbers, poor in quality. I always prefer to walk my own way even if it would not be attractive or popular.

This doesn't mean that I am for your plan. I always opposed it and I explained why in my two letters to our district Congressman. I sent copies of those two letters to the White House at the same time.

This month I wrote again about my view of the more proper health care system to The American Academy of Family Physicians. This letter was published in the *Daily Gazette* of Sterling, Illinois. As I know, the general reaction to this letter of mine was very positive and confirming. I do not know whether this carries any meaning in the brain centers of the White House. But it should.

I am sending you now those three letters. Before your next State of the Union address you should take into account all the possible views on that subject. It is hot.

Now, during this time of Christmas and with the approaching New Year, I wish you the best.

                                        Tadeusz Maciejczyk, M.D.
                                        Milledgeville, December 22, 1994

The World Seen from the Distance of a Small Village

Editor
The Daily Gazette
Sterling, Illinois

Dear Sir:

It was already a long time ago when somebody asked me what I thought about Mr. Vallez and his "View in Color," I responded that he was my inspiration.

I didn't answer then to the long look I received because at that moment I was too busy. Today I have more time and the last publication of the "View in Color" was especially stimulating. Then maybe I should tell you now about my secret ambitions that were awakened within me by Mr. Vallez's column.

The cause of my responsiveness to Mr. Vallez's call was within me. For years, when I shaved I was a witness of a sad fact that I had fewer and fewer hairs on my head. Of course I could not think about this. I could find a consolation to my ego in a Spanish proverb that says, that *"El hombre y el oso cuando mas feo, mas hermoso."* (A man and a bear, when more ugly are more beautiful.) With such a consolation, I could dedicate my energy to sharpen my skills, to discover new talents within me, or to make from me a man with stronger character.

But after my new enlightenment, I will not do this. Doing those works I would lose a golden opportunity and maybe even a golden cow.

Instead, I will organize a new minority. This will create a new place for me. I will be a leader. I will have power and maybe with this, I will make a fortune. Every ruler since the Stone Age knew the formula of dividing and governing.

My minority will be a very original one; it will be innovative. My minority will be a minority of the Bald and I will be counted. I will have something to say. The local newspaper will give me a weekly column that will be called "The Bald View."

In our publications we will fight for our rights. For our cause we will fight on the beaches, we will fight on the streets, we will fight in our homes and we will fight wherever Churchill wanted to fight. He was one of our own. He was also bald.

While on the streets we will march in throngs chanting that, "Bald is beautiful. Bald is smart. Bald is sexy."

We will go before the White House where we will demand special rights for our minority. We will complain about thousands of years of

Book Three

our sufferings. Just promises will not calm us. We will demand an establishment of a new department that would serve us exclusively and that would be called "The Hair Care Department." We will formulate a wording of a new amendment that would guarantee our special privileges during the length of the next century.

On Capitol Hill our demands will be different. Congress should designate for our cause 3 billion for research of baldness as a national priority. Without a doubt. We are entitled. Baldness is genetic. We have no guilt. But it interferes with the equal opportunity act for us. We never can have the same chance to become the movie stars. And more than this, we never have the same chance to see a glimpse of admiration in the ladies' eyes.

To even partially mitigate those experiences we will ask on Capitol Hill another different act of justice. We will ask for a government paid toupee for each member of our minority. Even if some of us would have the misfortune to live in the world of sophistication, he would need at least two toupees. And as Mr. Turk once explained this to the government referring to the entitlement of a free health care for everybody, we will not be satisfied with the second class toupees. We want only the best, of the latest fashion and made in Paris.

Manifesting before the leading universities of this country, we will demand an absolute correctness in speeches, in conversations, even in the facial expressions. Any transgressions in our demands should be punished by denial of the rights for education for the offenders. Once I tried to explain to one such fellow that baldness helps to ventilate the brain and in this way improves the quality of thinking. He answered that on the stupid head even the hair doesn't like to grow. It shows the lack of sensitivity and a clear prejudice.

Our activity will be directed also to influence the minds and the hearts of the youngest. We will distribute to the kindergarten children illustrated pamphlets about the life of the bald. They should know and should be prepared. It is never too early to educate.

We will never stop with our efforts.

I will talk to the public, but I will keep my distance. I will talk to them from the height of a pedestal. My speeches to them will be enigmatic to sound great and will be fuzzy to intrigue. Except for this, I would never remain as a leader of our minority if I tried to really clarify problems.

But I have a good trick to compensate for that fuzziness.

The World Seen from the Distance of a Small Village

While talking behind me in the semi-darkness of the scene, I will put in line famous personalities from the past, depending on my needs, I can put Socrates or Jesus Christ there or Marx, whoever.... When I finish my sentence, I will make a gesture with my hand inviting those personalities to the full light where they will applaud me warmly and approvingly. When that makes an effect, I will ask them to step backwards to the semi-darkness. On the stage only will I be king. Nobody else.

What a triumph it will be for me. Reading a good lecture can create such wonders. I am so grateful for the "View in Color."

Tadeusz Maciejczyk
Milledgeville, December 29, 1994

Book Three

Embassy of Norway
Washington, D.C.

As 1994 is closing and in remembering the events of this year, I want to thank you for your gift to the world in the Winter Olympics in Lillehammer. It showed us not only the world's best sport competitions, but also your country.

With this letter, I send you my observations and reactions influenced by the Olympics. I will be glad if they can show to you a kind of special reflection in our eyes of that time and of that event.

This year I started a special project that to some extend parallels the spirit of the Olympics. Maybe some day this kind of competition can spread also throughout the world and consequently make this world a better place to live.

With the approaching New Year, I wish you and your country the best. Watching the Olympics I was impressed by your country and by its people.

Tadeusz Maciejczyk
Milledgeville, December 28, 1994

The World Seen from the Distance of a Small Village

Illinois Republican State Central Committee
Springfield, Illinois

I am sending you my membership pledge card a little late. I was distracted by other problems and by work and I forgot.

Along with sending this pledge, I am sending you a copy of my letter to the American Academy of Family Physicians. It deals with the present family crisis in America with the art of giving in general and specifically with the government health care program. Health care given by the government appears to me as another kind of welfare system, this time extended to everybody.

Recently I read a report about the incredible difficulties in initiating a private enterprise in agriculture in western Bielorussia and even in Lithuania that before 1939 was free. 55 years of Soviet-type welfare created a situation of passivity, of enormous difficulty, and at present a complete impossibility for personal independence and capacity to work, to make a break through. This conditioning of the mind and will is not easy to comprehend. I do not see anything promising for the future of humanity in the governmental goodness of resolving all life's problems for everybody.

Also, because I want to be a faithful member of the Republican Party, I have to report that recently, after long conditioning by reading a certain weekly column in our local newspaper, I decided to create a new minority in the U.S. Sorry. Finally I will also be a leader. The membership drive is open. The political consequences of the existence of this minority cannot be properly evaluated in this moment. The sad story is that my letter initiating creation of that minority is only a caricature of the realities of life in today's America.

I also include my letter indicating this year's theme for the Scholarship Challenge.

My best wishes to everybody.

                                          Tadeusz Maciejczyk, M.D.
                                          Milledgeville, January 26, 1995

Book Three

Newt Gingrich
The United States Congress
Washington, D.C.

Dear Sir:

I am sending you a collection of my letters because all of them give a special vision of today's America, not easily seen from the height of Capitol Hill. I am sending you these letters because you are a leader with a vision, with the understanding, with the dream and with the courage to stand up for what you believe.

This collection contains letters about my opposition to buy obligatory malpractice insurance, also, letters from my malpractice trial in which I represented myself and won. They were written in the heat of the battle and probably represent a unique document of such an experience. In my letter to Blue Cross, I summarized my view on managed health care.

All these problems are enormously important and waiting for decisions. I hope that my letters will contribute an additional view for you during your decisions.

It was originally my idea to send you these letters. Now I decided to also send you a collection of my letters related to the last Olympics in Norway and the letters about a special scholarship that has the nickname of "Scholarship Challenge." In my last letters I responded to the worries and anxieties of people from around here as expressed in the "Your View" column in our local newspaper.

A special place should be reserved here for a letter that came to me only two days ago. It connects to the problems described in the beginning of this collection. The hospital that suspended my privileges in 1983 and to some extent collaborated in the fabrication of my accusation, wants to get me out of my place of work and put in the village an obedient, hospital-dependent doctor. As I explained, it is a part of a war between hospitals for the territory.

Life is changing. It is more and more difficult to stay as an independent factor. It looks like it is the end of America as it was known in the past.

I wish you the best. I didn't know you before. Today you appear to me as a very special phenomenon, a lonely leader with a frame big enough to sit on the side of Lincoln.

Tadeusz Maciejczyk, M.D.
Milledgeville, March 5, 1995

The World Seen from the Distance of a Small Village

Letters to the Editor
Newsweek Magazine

Re: "Sex in Sacramento"
Spring, 1995

Dear Sir:

    Strange flowers are growing with increasing frequency in our society and in our culture. They, like the lectures of Professor Joanne Marrow of California State University, are not opening and building minds and souls.
    They poison them.
    If such flowers are blooming in schools, they kill the spirits in their development stage and they spread desolation at the entrance of life. They act as one more branch of terrorism. As such, they are more dangerous to the future of humanity than those other acts of terrorism that use poison, bullets or explosives. Its deadly effects are reaching deeper and have a longer effect on life.
    I include here a copy of my letter to our local newspaper, *The Daily Gazette*, that for a long time carried a weekly column called "View in Color." It defended minorities of different kinds and degenerated becoming more and more bizarre.
    I do not know whether it was because of my letter, but one week after it was published, the column of "View in Color" somehow vanished.
    I wish you the best.

                                        Tadeusz Maciejczyk, M.D.
                                        Milledgeville, March 30, 1995

Book Three

The World Seen from the Distance of a Small Village

Editor of *Time Magazine* Letters
Re: "The Message of Miracles" (April 10, 1995)

Dear Sir:

The scholars' rush to debunk and doubt the greatness of God, shrinking Him to human proportions and to their own image is nothing new. Such was the sin of the fallen angels. This special pride and haughtiness of those scholars represent no merit or the greatness of their minds, but their pretense.

I would imagine that those scholars would not have an easy task to explain modern telecommunications or travel to even the most prominent men who lived 1000 years ago. Yet, between God and humans the difference is much bigger than those 1000 years of human progress.

Personally, I need God to raise my eyes and my spirit to Him, to find my way in my daily life and to consolidate my strength against my weaknesses. The "God" of those Christian scholars offers me nothing of that.

I have one moment in my life for which I have no human explanation. I live with the memory of that moment and until now nobody could help me to solve the puzzle it represents. Maybe those scholars could explain to me, with their exploring minds, the true meaning of that special moment.

It happened in 1945. After the passage of the front during the winter offensive, another occupation started in Poland. For years I was in the Underground. I belonged to units that didn't give up after the change.

The events started at the end of July. One evening, at about midnight, a lieutenant and two soldiers from Internal Security entered our home. The soldiers had bayonettes on their guns. That was the usual way many people were disappearing at that time. It was a continuous process.

In my case, on that evening the work of that unit of Internal Security was complicated by something they didn't expect and that was truly unique.

For several days at that time, a Russian captain was coming to our home. It was lasting each evening for about a week. He was the Army medical doctor. He was appearing at about 8 P.M., sat with us around the kitchen table and was starting conversation that usually lasted until after midnight.

In those chats we talked about the ordinary life of people in Poland before the war, how they worked, what the customs were, about schools and literature. More than this, it was obvious that the captain was absorbed by one special problem. How could he believe that God really

Book Three

exists? He was from Orel. During all his years in school, he took the obligatory classes in atheism. He didn't look merely for an expression of faith or posture of piety. He wanted contra-arguments to those lectures in school. This theme was repeated several times each evening during his visits.

That night, when the Internal Security entered our home, that captain sat at one end of the table and we, as usual, sat around. The Internal Security lieutenant was visibly surprised and uncomfortable seeing a Soviet captain sitting in the midst of us.

He changed the usual scenario of such visits. He kept complete silence. Since his entrance, he sank his eyes into mine. It was a long strange and deep silence. He interrupted it extending his arm to me while still looking into my eyes and said, "Your documentation, please."

He looked with great attention at my card, still from the time of Nazi occupation, then he gave it back to me with the same slow movement with his penetrating eyes fixed on mine. Again, there was a long silence. In the room, everything was motionless. The Russian captain sat in his place alternatively looking into my eyes and into the eyes of the lieutenant. The lieutenant vacillated. Suddenly he turned to my father asking for his documents. He looked at them briefly, then he went slowly around the table looking at everybody from behind. He went back to take his position between his soldiers and his face changed. It was clear that finally he had made his decision. He started to talk when the captain rose to his feet. He was tall and his voice was commanding He took out his documents from his chest pocket and thrust it before the eyes of the lieutenant as he said, "Your obligation is also to investigate who I am. These are my documents. Please check them. It is also your duty."

The lieutenant didn't look at them. He only said, "We are here just as a patrol." And they left.

That was the last evening the captain was in our home.

I also have to say that at that time, after six years of war vacations, I was again in school. I was in the third class of gymnasium.

Almost immediately after the "liberation" in voluntary work, we cleaned and we prepared our old building as well as we could. On Sunday, February 19th, all the young people gathered in the cathedral to start the school with prayer and the next day we had our first class after six years. The days became very cold. There was no heat in the building. More than this, there was not one piece of glass in the big windows of our room. There was no window glass in the entire town. We sat on the floor. There was no furniture. Some of us brought something from our

The World Seen from the Distance of a Small Village

homes to sit on. We had no books. The school library was burned in a jubilant ceremony in the autumn of 1939. We were not supposed to have any need for books during the next 1000 years. Those days we were almost always hungry. There was no such thing as school lunches. But our spirits were high. Almost nobody failed in learning. We finished that class at the end of July.

The new school year was scheduled to start in September. And in that time, I had a special problem. My only pants were falling apart and it was becoming more and more difficult to repair them. I needed to go to some less destroyed place to earn money to buy pants before the new class in September. That was the driving force for me to leave my town. The obstacle was that I was of age to be called into the army and I could not get out. But I got permission. Those lousy pants helped convince the administrative captain. My school grades were good.

So, on August 1st, at 4 P.M. I waved my hand to my mother and two sisters who were standing before our house. "I will see you within a month," I called to them.

That was the last time I saw them.

Twenty hours after I left, at noon on August 2nd, my home was surrounded by Internal Security. During the next twelve hours of hell, during which my mother was thrown against the wall five times with a gun to her head, they searched and turned everything upside down. In the evening my father came from work. At midnight, both my parents were taken to the Internal Security prison for interrogation. The neighbors brought something to eat to my sisters.

I received the news about what happened at home three weeks later. A special man came to the place where I was to tell me the story, bringing me letters form home. Fortunately my parents had been freed. My orders were never to come back to Kielce.

It was a shock. I decided to organize my place in now western Poland, where everything was still in a state of confusion and slow organization. But soon I learned that staying in Poland would not be easy. Letters were sent after me. For one month, I never was sure whether the next day I would still be free. Finally I decided to go west.

I went alone. Friends made documents for me. One said my mother was somewhere north of Berlin and was sick. I was going to meet her and bring her home. The document was in Polish and in Russian. And so, I left my place again.

I didn't know where exactly the new boundaries were. I came to the last station on the Polish side wondering what to do next. It was almost evening. Around the railroad, a company of Russian soldiers waited for

Book Three

the train to go to East Germany as the occupation unit. I approached them and started a conversation. I told them the story of my mother somewhere north of Berlin. They were very friendly. "We will help you pass the border," they told me.

It was night when the train came. For the soldiers there were only standing places. There was not much room to move. During more than three hours of searching during the passage from the Polish to the East German side, I stood in the center among the soldiers. Not one of them moved. They covered me very efficiently. In the morning the train got to Cotbus on the German side. I said good-bye to my soldier friends and I took a train to Berlin.

I knew that in Berlin I could go to the Occidental sectors. On the train I listened to conversations of passengers and in this way I got some idea where those western sectors were.

I came to Schlesien Bahnhof in Berlin at about 5 P.M. I had no address to go to. On the street before the station for the first time, I saw a group of English or American soldiers. I stood looking at them. I wanted to approach. I remembered my only sentence in English, but Russians were everywhere. It would not be safe. Finally, I started to walk towards the town.

On the streets, the inscriptions said that anybody on the street after 8 P.M. would be shot. Others said what the penalty would be for somebody who took a stranger in for the night. When the streets were less crowded, I approached some old ladies asking them where such a refugee as myself could find a place for the night. One lady told me about a bunker a few blocks away where the passing soldiers were given help. I went there. After a small time of questioning, I got a room and bed there. I was the only one there not in uniform, but I slept there as an angel.

In the morning, I started a long walk through East Berlin toward the English sector. I got there at 4 P.M. With the illusion I was ready to tell my story to the English Gendarmery only to learn that they were sending such people as me back to Poland. I had to escape from them.

Again on the streets I asked bypassers how to get to the American sector. I could go there taking the train at the nearby Lehrnte Bahnhoff. It was on the Russian side. I went there.

I needed some rest and so I sat on the floor against the wall behind the newsstand. I was deep in thought when a young man approached me asking whether he could sit beside me. OK. We started to talk in German. Later it became obvious that both of us were Poles. We were both going west. He spent the war in Germany. In 1939, their farm in Pommern was taken by Germans and he with all his family, was taken to

The World Seen from the Distance of a Small Village

forced labor to German farms in Germany. When the war ended, his family sent him back to Pommern to see what happened to their property. Now he was returning. He knew the place and how to pass the border. After my checking of him, I decided to take a chance with him.

It was about 10 P.M. when we left Berlin, going west.

Somewhere in the middle of the night our train stopped in one station. Someone on a loudspeaker ordered everyone on the train to get out and to gather on the big plaza before the station building. The train was checked to be sure that nobody was hiding inside and then it was removed from the place. The huge crowd on the plaza was surrounded by soldiers who pointed their guns at people. There was only one outlet from this circle through which everybody had to pass to show their documentation and permission to be on this train.

The night was very black. There was only one light over the place, a single glowing lamp above the name of the station written on the wall. The place was called Stendal.

My friend and I we stood in the crowd trying to be on the most distant edge from the check point. We were looking for some way out, some cave to hide in, some spot without soldiers where we could slip away. But the soldiers were everywhere, the place was completely unknown to us in the middle of a country that not long ago was so hostile to us and at that moment suffered from the same indignity as we.

The hours passed very slowly. The idea of panicking and running was not practical. Our run would be very short. Finally, the crowd before us became thinner and the inevitable was approaching. It came a moment when I lost all my hope. In resignation I decided that however it would be, tomorrow would be another day to measure the possibilities.

It was then at the end of all our hopes when we heard a voice from the other side of the railway. "Come with me!"

Without one moment of hesitation we went. We crossed the railroad line and in the darkness of that night we followed the silhouette of the man who called us. Nobody else responded to that call. Only the two of us. The soldiers who were making such a thick line, somehow didn't pay attention. We passed them. We followed the shadow of that man who walked in front of us. We walked between the ruins of houses, then we entered a long tunnel. That tunnel was without lights, but I remember that we saw the shadow of the man walking before us. When we emerged from the tunnel, I remember the daylight was starting to appear on the east side of the sky. When we finished walking, the day was already clear. We approached a plaza in the street. That man stopped, extended his arm before him and told us, "Go there!" We went and there we found all the people who had already passed the checkpoint. At 9 A.M. the train was put back on the line, we got in and without any more problems we came to a final station before the border, a village called Bischop that was about 3 km from the border.

We spent all that day in the bushes behind the village.

When night came and the stars were in the sky, we started to walk from our hiding place northward following the star. We passed small fields. Then we entered into pastures divided into small quadrants by small ditches with water and with wire lines above. As we were going we became more and more uneasy. Where was that border? We had to be near, but we were lost. We moved another quadrant forward when a sudden noise pushed us to the ground. There were horses that approached us from every corner of the place touching us with their noses and with the big noise were jumping back. The situation became really uneasy. Russian soldiers, the border guards could be anywhere near.

In this situation, we decided that on that night we had no chance so we went back. Walking through the field we saw a pail of potatoes on the ground covered with straw. We went there. We entered under the straw and we had an excellent night of sleep. The next day was Sunday. Nobody came to the fields. All day we spent under that straw watching the nearby road and Soviet soldiers passing by. We had plenty of time to study the distribution of the place and to plan our next night's moves.

From our place we saw a line of thick woods on the north. The woods were on the English side. Between us and the woods were the meadows divided into small quadrants. On the right and on the left scattered trees were growing. In the middle the space was completely open without any trees. We decided to go through that open space. It gave less possibility for sudden surprise.

That night was completely black again with cloudy skies. When the traffic on the nearby road stopped, we started to move towards the border. We had to take our shoes off. With the water from the ditches, they were too noisy. In the middle of our crawling, we had to stop and lie on the ground. There was a big fire in Bischop and a shooting. The light from that fire reached our place in the field.

Finally when all the noises and lights subsided we moved forward again. We heard already the rush of the trees in the woods. We were near. Then we heard the Russian solders calling to one another. It gave us enormous relief. We were going just between them. We knew where they were. A few more movements on the ground and we got up and ran. Reaching the line of the trees of the woods we saw all the material accumulated to make barricades. Probably we had here our last chance to pass in this way.

The World Seen from the Distance of a Small Village

In the woods we ran for awhile, then we stopped. In this darkness in the woods it was easy to be lost. We sat on a small hill with our backs against each other so we could get a little warmer. The rain started to fall. Finally the day cleared the darkness. Slowly we approached the edge of the woods and we saw a man. We asked him. Yes. Thank God. We were on the English side.

That man advised us to look for English patrols. They were returning refugees to the Soviet side. By noon we had gone the distance of 20 km. And we came to Ulzen. Here I had a different, very special experience. I met Poles and I could talk with them without any fear. After several months in "liberated" Poland, in that moment, I felt with all its intensity what it means to be free. Never before, never afterward have I had such an appreciation for freedom than at that one moment of passage from one world to another. I could almost touch that freedom with my hands. I cannot describe that feeling with words.

This is my story of escape. In this story I can explain many moments as special coincidence, special luck, maybe even by my special ability to use situations to my advantage.

In that story I have no explanation for what happened in Stendal. Really, what happened there? Who was that man? Why did he help us? How could he know in that black night that we were in such distress.

In the last years, that memory comes back to me with more intensity than ever. I didn't even say "thank you" to that man. I do not remember in what language he spoke to us. Why was I saved while so many perished? What can I do to repay?

I do not know what those wise scholars who transformed God almost to an old Greek vision of gods, would say about my event in Stendal.

Really, I do not care what they would say.

Once, in the past, a man called Popper, speaking about intellectuals who so eagerly adjusted great truths to the needs of contemporary political or other tendencies, described them as intellectual asses. For me this description fits those scholars very well in this case.

Sorry for making this story so long. And I am tired.

Tadeusz Maciejczyk, M.D.
Milledgeville, April 9, 1995

Book Three

Scholarship Challenge 1995

This year, as one year ago, I asked senior students to make their own search into the enigma of birth and of functioning of true leadership and a true leader.

The volunteers, willing to undertake such a task were given as a help a description and a study of the ingredients of a personal maturity without which any leader would be standing on nothing more but legs of clay. With this as a base, the candidates were asked to write an essay about the need and the role of spiritual strength for the leadership in today's world.

This year, I asked the candidates to pay special attention to such qualities of a true leader as:

1. his capacity for common sense
2. his gift for imagination
3. his ability for abstraction
4. his prudence evidenced by learning the lessons from history
5. his willingness to accept fantasy as a forerunner for imagination, and as the most advancing scout between dreams and reality.

Three candidates responded to the challenge this year.

My observation is that every challenge produces resonance and stimulation only in those who selected themselves by discipline and self-preparation. To undertake any challenge and to bring it to fulfillment, it is necessary to listen, to decide, to dare and to persevere. For this, I am enormously proud to present to you this year's three students who dared.

They are: Sue Johnson, Mandy Koch, Erin A. Ritenour

Those students will read their essays during the ceremony of Memorial Day that provides a proper stage for a deliberation about leadership. This year, circumstances happened in such a way that the senior students will be on a graduation trip at the end of May and they will not be able to read their essays personally. Each of them will assign a substitute to do so. Reading those works, sharing their content with the public on that day, is an integral part of this scholarship reward.

After the conclusion of reading of those essays, I will make my personal observations about their merit, about the strength and the weaknesses of those works and then I will announce the theme for the next year's contest for deliberation about the need of spiritual strength in leadership.

After the ceremony the originals of this year's works will be sent to the Veterans Headquarters, and copies to The White House, to the present Speaker of the House, to the governor of Illinois, to both Illinois Senators, to our representative and to all universities of Illinois as special documents to our time.

At this point of experimentation with this scholarship, one question became startling. Why for the second year did no male students respond to my call to comprehend the inside personality of a leader? Without a doubt, with such work they would be preparing themselves for eventual future leadership.

Such an indifference cannot be explained by their excessive burden of the school curriculum or their less than expected interested in the future of this country and of the world.

Is the involvement in the school sport competitions a factor because by its disproportionate prominence, by its glory, glamour and public admiration, it is overshadowing everything else?

But the school sports competitions are not helping to prepare young men for the requirements, special rigors ultimate solitude in decision making of the present day, not phony, but true leadership. Preparation for such leadership requires a continuous dedicated lifelong cultivation of minds and especially of souls.

In 1837, the greatest poet Russia ever had, Alexander Pushkin, was killed in a duel when he was 37 and at the height of his creativity by the army official because Pushkin, in his writing, in the officer's understanding, offended the honor of the army. The official who grew within a myth, that army by its discipline by its coordination of action, by its creation of strength, that by this, the army was preparing men for every task and every assignment, for dying Pushkin had only one epithet filled with contempt: a poet.

Three years ago, responding to a Senate Rep. Majority Survey and within it to a question: what is the most important issues facing America in the Nineties? Among ten suggested responses, I said that as the schools are supposed to be the place primarily for a formation and training of minds—the scholastic competitions between schools should mean the biggest merit for students and for schools, the school sport competitions remaining behind them. I said that in our schools, the boys who kick the ball well should not overshadow our potential Einsteins, Shakespeares or Lincolns.

Book Three

I hope that next year, this challenge to create their own vision of body, mind and spirit of a leader will be taken seriously also by men.

Tadeusz Maciejczyk, M.D.
Milledgeville, May 4, 1995

The World Seen from the Distance of a Small Village

Memorial Day

Those are the three essays about spirituality in leadership that reflect the image of the present world's problems in the eyes and minds of our seniors. What have those essays told us?

They all stressed the need for development of spirituality in our lives because spirituality is the backbone of our stability and strength. Spirituality is an essential part of a feeling of dignity in whatever we are doing. Spirituality can give us inspiration and stamina to transform our sufferings and failures into a new foundation for growing. Spirituality has the power to defend us from despair in our hard times when temptation to look for consolation in alcohol or in drugs would be hard to resist.

The participants say that today's world is producing an excess of noise, a multitude of distractions, and a general haste without clear design or direction. It confuses. It creates shallowness and impatience. In the midst of all that bustle, the young have not an easy task to approach and to direct their own life adventure.

As a consequence of all the pounding turbulence from the world, the young have a very special difficulty to develop roots into spirituality. The absence of spirituality is created behind a vacuum that is painful and easily leads to rebellion, kicks and tragedies.

All participants stressed the importance of prayer and faith in our development. Everybody needs to communicate with someone who unconditionally is his friend and advisor. We all had an experience in which we had to decide against all odds.

I remember reading how Lincoln paced the floor of the White House during nights when he was alone and had to decide and stick to his decisions. In that pacing, Lincoln was not alone. At those moments he was engaged in the very intense dispute and arguing with his unconditional friend and advisor, God.

I think that for Stalin or Hitler, in their moments of similar pacing the floor, their confidantes and advisors were somebody else, the fallen angels.

But with whoever it would be, such communication, in the decisive moments of our lives, makes a difference. The inability to communicate in such moments, being at such times completely alone, can be suicidal.

The other subject is the role of dreams and fantasy in the formation of our lives. Almost all our labors begin with them. To transform those dreams into constructive reality, we need imagination, common sense, a reflection upon them and of course strength and guts.

Book Three

I do not agree with the romantic song that compares our dreams to a river. Our dreams provide only a spring from which a river is born. Its further shape and size depends on us.

In conclusion:

Evaluating the works of our three outstanding students, I see in all of them a need for a spiritual force in every human being and especially in those who are to become our leaders. The world as a whole also needs spirituality. All three contestants are saying that spirituality has the power to transform us, to help us grow and to find deeper meaning in our lives.

The weakness of those works is that not one of them identified and described the elements that we should cultivate and which by its byproduct help us grow up to the tasks and into fulfillment.

Also, practically no one touched the problem of the five qualities in a leader that were supposed to give a special accent to this year's work.

Those two minuses decided that all three essays were put into third place and received the third premium. In this problem, I feel here my guilt. During the whole year I never made contact with the contestants to discuss and to clarify their difficulties. I will try to correct this in the future.

The subject of next year's essay about the need of spirituality in leadership, will be a description of elements of greatness in a man, in a leader.

In the 1850s Cyprian Norvid described such greatness in one of his poems. It was over 20 years after the defeat of the Polish war of liberation in 1830–31. That emigration, after that defeat, mostly in France, in Polish history was named a "Great Emigration," because of the extraordinary men it contained. They created an effective government in exile in the time when in the country a revengeful Russian military rule destroyed and suppressed everything. They fought in every war of liberation of their time. They created the literature of the highest class. In music, Frederic Chopin described in his special vocabulary the last stand of the struggle of 1830–31 in his Great Polonaise.

In the 1850s a dispute appeared who in that emigration was truly great. Norwid explained it in this way:

Great is a man for whom it is enough
To bow his head
And without a spear in his hand, without shield,
to win decisively.
Becoming inferior he avoids envy

The World Seen from the Distance of a Small Village

And the envy in full gallop
Runs behind and hangs on him the stigma of a cross
Exclaiming: He is small
And is lying to itself, as was lying before,
While he with a calm understanding
Accepts the grace and disgrace with nerves
But the truth with the conscience.
In this way the people are boasting that they knew the great.
Only to prove,
That the small will not recognize the great
Before he passes away.[5]

Sorry that I am not a poet and I cannot make a better translation. I hope I expressed the intention of Norwid.

I hope also that next year's seniors will respond to this my call.

Tadeusz Maciejczyk
Milledgeville, May 29, 1995

BOOK FOUR

"My Sen O *Szpadzie*" (*My Dream* About a Sword)

In my public service, a growing feeling of being burned out. Escape into a diary.

Explanation:
An old Polish song about young man, who dreamed about big deeds in his life.
Exact Polish translation of "sword" is MIECZ.
While material appearance of MIECZ and SZPADA is similar, their meaning is different.
MIECZ kills.
Proverb: He who fights with MIECZ
              From MIECZ perishes.
SZPADA symbolizes a fighting for, or defending something, elevating, which touches the soul.

The World Seen from the Distance of a Small Village

Time Magazine
Tampa, FL

How strange it is.

For years I received from time to time similar envelopes with promises of big money. I didn't pay attention to them. Without opening them, I put them in a pile for paper collection.

This time I almost started to do the same when, after reflection, I decided that for a change, I would look at the mechanism to see how those sweepstakes worked. I never believed that I would have any luck with money. In so many other areas I was lucky.

But this time a thought passed into my mind that maybe I would have a chance to repay my debt for the good things I received from others for free, when I wasn't even asking.

Late in the evening, I opened the envelope and for the first time I saw that it was not a usual sweepstakes. It was from *Time Magazine* and it somehow sounded real and concrete.

What would I do with such money?

I would continue working. I need contact with people and I need a basic scheme for my days. A base from which to generate ideas and projects.

I didn't jump from excitement reading your announcement. I became very serious and grateful. I asked to be given enough wisdom to handle the new situation. This premium would create and help not to overlook the signals for special tasks, which somehow I always expected.

I thank you again.

And, if I really would win your Grand Prize, I would tell you about my project that consolidated in my mind after reading your message and maybe about my other small project that now is entering its third year of special calling.

Again, I thank you.

Tadeusz Maciejczyk
Milledgeville, June 4, 1995

To: The Government of Illinois,
the Government of the U.S. and State Universities

This year, for the second time, the senior students from our school were confronted with a scholarship proposition that was imposing on

Book Four

them an effort to imagine, to acknowledge, to study and to write an essay about the need and the role of spirituality in leadership.

This challenge was responded to by three students who read their works during our Memorial Day ceremony.

This theme reflects to some extent the longings and the needs, the world's vision and the reflection on the present time by the growing new generation in a very special moment of their lives when they are about to leave behind the routine and the safety of their homes and of local school looking toward a bigger, exciting and frightening world beyond.

This by itself is making from those works a special document of our time. As such, I send you their works together with my evaluation and with the theme for the next year's "Scholarship Challenge" contest.

My dream is to extend this context to other places and if miracles happen, arrange a more or less national, or even international encounter of all the winners of local contests to discuss, to deliberate and to draw conclusions from their talks about the essence of good leadership and about the qualities of a leader.

I thank you for your attention to this message from Milledgeville's students.

> Tadeusz Maciejczyk
> (in the name of our local Rotary)
> June 8, 1995

The World Seen from the Distance of a Small Village

P.P. Report
Editor

Reading about the enthusiasm of young doctors to enter into the field of sports medicine because it opens so many wonderful opportunities, I cannot but express my reservations.

I agree that physical fitness is helping to develop a healthy personality. I also believe that exaggeration of the importance of school sport games and competitions is making a mockery of school purposes and the unique missions of schools. It signals wrong directions and gives false assurance to the young.

Dr. Rice is right in saying that exercise can stimulate more mental energy, can reduce stress and can improve relationships.

Exercise is increasing the adrenaline flow and adrenaline, like drugs, can create the post-exercise high with easiness in talking, relating and being optimistic.

The problem with adrenaline is that it has a short life span. It can also bring a low afterwards.

A young person in school, who consciously or unconsciously is looking and searching for his future place and role in life, needs a different, strong basic build-up to be able to develop a healthy personality, good self-esteem, and eyes-open, mind-open to reach a life fulfillment. Concentration on athletic activities during school age frequently closes other developments and ambitions neglecting the other aspects of life's preparation and leaves behind a wasteland.

Our schools, in their rush for cheap effects, put the athletic performance on a pedestal and are guilty of making shallow the life purposes of the young, of narrowing their field of interests, deviating from, or even barricading other, more essential roads.

Rushing to sport competitions, our schools even didn't develop a kind of gallantry and gentlemanship in players. Too frequently sports became an arena, not for relaxation after studying, but of the fierce, "kill the other" mentality, to show that you are a man.

This way today's schools sports are not reducing stress or improving relationships. They are not elevating spirituality in players. They are making from them the old-time gladiators to induce local pride, consolation or anger.

As far as my observations can see, the school sport has almost only one lasting effect on students. It produces legions of "sports fans," who after their school years, review the old triumphs on the Easy Boy chair watching sports shows. The professional sports should be enormously

Book Four

indebted to our schools for making them so enormously rich for their astronomical salaries, for their popularity. Our schools could ask the professional sports for a generous back pay. It would be completely justified.

I think that schools, in order to regain their prestige and their role in the life of society, should reduce the present sports drill to its healthy proportions.

School sports should not create the post-school passive, partisan, self-depreciated fans, but assured adult people who starve to discover their true vocation in life, who can consider their work not as a burden, but as a means to grow, and who know enough and appreciate school sports hours enough to actively continue such sports relaxation after their working hours in their adult life. Such actions happen sporadically. They should appear all over the country.

(I also believe that the Easy Boy Chair is not the most happy and glorious addition to American life.)

Tadeusz Maciejczyk, M.D.
Milledgeville, June 22, 1995

The World Seen from the Distance of a Small Village

Editor
The Daily Gazette
Sterling, IL

I received a letter from a political party with an urgent message to become a generous sustaining member and send the money without delay.

That party needed the money to prepare strategy for the general election in 1996. The letter painted a gloomy picture for the whole nation if that strategy would have no chance to develop just because of not enough funds.

I wanted to see the core of that redeeming strategy. As I read the letter, the bitter taste in my mouth grew.

That money would go for the mass mailing to voters to teach and to convince them how to vote. This party needed an unlimited amount of money for volunteer phone banks to identify voters supporting their candidates.

The letter claimed that such a strategy would succeed in providing our nation with leadership of greatness, goodness and wisdom.

That letter, and that strategy left me sad and empty. I was expecting that party to develop a plan that would invite public discussions of all the issues, from the smallest and local to the most important for the state, the country and the world.

The themes would be prepared. The new ones would appear in the process. Everybody willing would participate. Such discussions would not be rigid with the division between the stage and the rest sitting in their seats.

Those discussions could be organized as picnic-like reunions with a central area, but otherwise everybody mixing freely. The party would provide not as much speakers as coordinators of discussions and clerks to gather and register materials that would then be studied and later discussed in the following rounds of meetings. The cold or hot drinks and some food could be brought by participants like in another kind of picnic.

Such meetings could be located anywhere, minimizing the expenses, maximizing fun and good spirits.

Such meetings surely would call the attention of the press, of the radio or even of television. All this would increase interest and involvement in each next round of discussions. It would create an emotional involvement in the upcoming elections and in consequence those elections in 1996 would make not such a blind, stagnant, boring and dispirited ceremonies as it usually was in the past.

Book Four

Each round of such meetings would provide material, would create new questions and new answers for the next round. Spontaneity and openness of those meetings would show a new crops of talents, would create a deeper understanding, greater willingness and involvement. Elections prepared in such a way would have an element of fresh air, so necessary for every time of new growth.

For such an approach to the electoral process and practice, I would be willing to contribute.

For the plan described in the party letter, I will not give one cent. Such bureaucratic, secretive, corrupt and always suspicious methods are not leading to a brighter future or to greatness. They always give birth to mediocrity, general disappointment, uninvolvement, bitterness and stagnation.

Those methods are good for some pseudo-democracies, but not for America.

Tadeusz Maciejczyk
Milledgeville, July 30, 1995

The World Seen from the Distance of a Small Village

Editor
The Daily Gazette
Sterling, Illinois

Dear Sir:

The UN conference on women in Beijing started to debate today. On the Valley Living page, your paper mentioned the lives of women in different countries. Whatever the differences, whatever the personal needs and aspirations, one demand should be made clear for women, as well as for men. They should face their responsibilities and put their priorities in order.

Men and women have the same mental capabilities, but nature gave them different main tasks in life and consequently different body builds and different emotional structures.

The primordial task for women is motherhood and because of this, her first responsibility is to her child. This responsibility starts with the moment of conception. Already, during the pregnancy, an emotional torment of the mother, the non-acceptance, anger because it could interfere with her other plans or dreams, has an influence on the baby. Without a doubt, the baby's life and development starts with conception.

Then, during the first two years of life, the most essential need of the baby is the mother's presence and love. At that time, the baby feels like being a part of the mother. Nobody can remember those first two years of life, but everybody carries through life the consequences of the amount of love received during those days and nights.

A human being, who received all the love at that time will grow into age with conviction that he or she is worth true and unconditional love. Also, it is most likely that only she or he could give such unconditional love to somebody else.

A person who didn't receive such love at that age, even if he would be very successful or even if he would conquer the world, inside he will always have a painful doubt as to whether anybody could truly love him. For him, a love affair will most likely be a barter-like transaction.

At about two years, the baby is changing. He is trying to find out who he is. He says, "No," he tries to escape, to impose his desire on others. The kind of love given to children at this stage has to be adjusted to those changes. A simple love can spoil now. The love given to the baby has to have now elements of guidance and discipline; it has to start to educate. But in spite of those changes, it cannot be less loving.

Book Four

Children between two and five are constantly asking questions. Those questions can be silly and repetitious. The child will not ask them to a stranger, and only the mother can respond to them most convincingly.

It is very important to answer those questions. Through them, the baby is learning about the world around him, about the rules he has to obey, about what is right and what is wrong. This is the way in which a baby is developing his conscience.

That amount of conscience, the baby will develop in those years before school, in close contact with mother and the rest of the family, will be like a rock for the conduct of his life. Even if such a person went wrong, he will retain the inside judgment about his conduct and the strength to correct himself.

Later in life, the development of conscience will be less penetrating and much more easy to shed.

Those talks with the child, those conversations, have no substitutions. Not the most wonderful toys, not the best and most entertaining care centers, no company of other children to play with, can take its place.

As the years pass and the child grows, he never stops to ask questions. His questions are changing. Each day, each new encounter, each school day, brings them new experiences that they have to understand, to put in order and to assimilate. Children look for those clarifications to those with whom they have the most closeness and who have the strongest authority over them. This is mostly likely to be the mother.

But, if the mother is not there, or maybe she is, but her attention is elsewhere because she is watching a soap opera on television and the child is silenced impatiently, the normal, healthy personality growth of the child will be impaired and if such dismissals repeat themselves, that growth can be hampered forever.

A child neglected in such a way can close and isolate himself. He can become moody, depressed, hyperactive or restless. He can alter his previously good progress in school and he can start to dislike himself and blame himself.

Everybody, whether child or adult, needs to feel the reflection of himself in somebody else's loving eyes, in communication with others close to him. Without such a constant support, the energy for good development vanishes; negatives grow out of proportion and an emotional crippling develops.

If the growing child, after repeated trials, is not getting answers to his questions, after a time of vacillation, he will start to look for those answers somewhere else. He will be attracted to gangs. He can try to escape from home. He can turn to kicks, to vandalism or to other anti-

The World Seen from the Distance of a Small Village

social activity. He will feel the need to protest silently or loudly. Depending on the company he keeps, he can become a criminal.

The girls, without strong ties to their mothers, complicated by unexemplary images of a father, can become easy prey and look for understanding and affection in unhealthy ways. She can become pregnant causing a shock to the family, maybe their wake up, or maybe anger and condemnation.

A good image of a father has enormous importance in those restless teenage years for the girl's feeling of stability, self-confidence and self-celebration. It gives her peace inside and also a clue for what to look for in relating to boys.

Good child rearing can be wonderful and most rewarding in the poorest of places and can become a failure in the most affluent places, equipped with all facilities and helps. No money spent, no best social circles, not even the education is the main factor. The factor that counts is the true love given to the child and the time spent on true communication.

Those are our responsibilities and it has to be our priority because the situation is getting more critical with each year. Are we really ready to take such a stand and truly confront the problem?

Tadeusz Maciejczyk, M.D.
Milledgeville, September 8, 1995

Book Four

Julie A. Logan
Administrator
Polo Continental Manor

Dear Ms. Logan:

I am sending you a copy of my current professional license.

I do not carry liability and malpractice insurance. After my experiences, I refused to pay for it. (I am sending you copies of my letters form the past that explain why I feel this way.)

Not having malpractice insurance, I was denied hospital privileges and I limited myself to an office practice that frequently is very busy. If hospitalization is necessary, I refer my patients to wherever they want to go. I believe in freedom with a sense of responsibility and I feel that I serve my community well.

I know that Sterling Hospital has tried for a long time to force me out of my practice in Milledgeville and to put in my place a hospital-paid and hospital-obedient doctor. The hospitals are fighting for territory and in this way for money. It is not exactly my impression that their main purpose and main commitment is to serve the people.

But I will stay here, whatever the pressures, maintaining independence in my practice.

Please notify me whether I can continue to care for Mrs. Kunz, my only remaining patient in your facility.

Tadeusz Maciejczyk, M.D.
Milledgeville, September 12, 1995

The World Seen from the Distance of a Small Village

Bob Dole
Senate Republican Leader
And
Haley Barbour
National Chairman

Dear Gentlemen:

Three days ago, I received a letter from you in which you pressured me to accept my 1995 RNC Membership card and immediately write you a check.

I know that I am an M.D. and I should have plenty of money. That money was the only objective and a focal point of your letter. Pay! And we will direct you and all of the nation into the next century.

Yes, I am an M.D., a countryside solo practitioner who for years, struggled to maintain freedom in my work. I never tried to get rich. I worked during my life. All my five children finished university educations. I have no retirement arrangements or capital. Today, I live alone. My family disintegrated under the pressure of a malpractice suit against me, in which I defended myself without a lawyer and after three and one-half years of struggle, I won. My income in 1994 was $41,763. Because I am alone, my taxes are high. From what is left, I pay full tuition and maintenance in the university for my youngest daughter who studies architecture after four years of art history and two years of high math. This doesn't bring any relief in taxes. So, my living is austere. But I do not complain. I am happy when I am able to work and to serve.

Of course, I can still pay for my RNC membership fee. But before I do, I want to ask you a question. I have a right to ask whether, under your leadership into the 21st century, I would be able to work productively as an independent medical practitioner, or whether I would be suffocated, silenced and nullified?

The voices are that in order to reduce the cost of Medicare, your inclination is to put the whole medical profession into the bondage of managed care organizations. I am in private practice and I want to keep my work this way. I want to be dedicated, responsible and never abusive and I want to be free. Only freedom with conscience and responsibility produces the most creativity, the most compassion and the best results. I do not want to relate to my patients under pressure from administrators who for one or other reasons could demand I obey their mandates.

In 1983, I opposed the suddenly obligatory malpractice insurance for doctors because, as it exploded, it was not based on true needs, but on blackmail. That suddenly, the ever-present malpractice threat produced enormous economical damages, shaking prices and an air of insecurity in every enterprise, but also something that we will never be able to calculate. It changed the souls of very many people. The true work value became undermined. Creativity in work became dangerous. Work responsibilities became something for old-timers, for birds.

The new whisper felt across the country was persistent and convincing. Do you want to get rich? Then Go! Accuse somebody. Find any pretext. You are risking nothing. And for those who felt uneasy: You will harm nobody. Insurance will pay. And if you cannot find such a pretext, then try gambling. Or cheat. Look around. So many are getting rich this way.

To make gambling more palatable, the ordinary, wasteful, character destroying gambling, ascended to something noble and productive. It was named "the Gambling Industry." Every town tried to get a license for such a wonder. The consequences were not important. The immediate revenues for the cities was.

In 1987, I was accused of malpractice. The accusation was ridiculous. The pressure and the blows were real. (I am sending you some of my letters from that time. I can send more if you wish. They are like a special documentary. They can help to find a better road toward the future.)

I won that trial without the help of any lawyer.

In the Eighties, the omni-present malpractice threat changed the nation and changed the medical practice forever. Suddenly, everything and especially any spontaneous action became treacherous, more complicated and enormously more costly.

That was the time when the independent medical practices started to disappear. Constant intimidation, insecurity, and rising costs became unbearable. Ever-expanding clinics took their place.

A new breed of administrators transformed those clinics into business places. Profit, new expansion and more profits, were the chain objectives for each good administrator. They were well prepared for the occasion. They knew how to turn every move of Medicare, any new development or change into more money. The danger of malpractice became a very convenient excuse for chain consultations and unlimited testing. Every clinic became stuffed with always increasing amounts of specialists and sub-specialists. Any panic alarm about some health hazard was a wonderful opportunity to make all those big clinics busy. Common sense was downgraded becoming almost a four-letter word. Calls for preventive medicine had no limit for exploitation.

The World Seen from the Distance of a Small Village

Those practices reached the point where nobody could afford the cost. A fierce fight developed. Stronger clinics tried to bankrupt the weaker and to extend into new territories. The remaining private practitioners were pressed to give up, join the clinics or disappear. I felt such pressure and behind the back maneuvering to kick me out many times. And probably those pressures will reappear.

Those remaining private practices get help from no one. The government builds more and more obstacles for them. The paper work increases with each month. The rules, the codes are constantly changing without reason. Harassment by OSHA and other institutions of perfection are choking and appearing more and more like ordinary extortionists. All kinds of speculators who knew how to fish in muddy waters, have to be added to this sad picture.

The holydays of clinics with their ruthless exploitation of situations brought consequences. The health insurance prices doubled every year. The people, the employers couldn't afford them and started to look for alternatives. In our nearby town, the biggest employer, the steel mill, in desperation, decided to build their own clinic for their workers.

In such an uneasy climate, managed care became a tempting promise. But is it a safe, good and a lasting promise?

The idea of capitation can be a sample of what to be expected. Everything will be controlled by the distant powerful magnates, who in time, with all alternatives destroyed, with doctors in the role of servants, insecure in their place, because any day they could be dismissed if their idea of providing care would differ, with patients without any other place to go, in such a condition those magnates will dictate. Our government couldn't control smaller and more vulnerable clinics. Surely, it will not control those giants of managed care. It is incredible.

In the Twenties, the Soviets destroyed peasantry and put peasants into *kolkhozes* controlled by distant Communist bosses. In the 90s, the Republican majority in congress intends a *kolkhozation* of doctors in managed care. Both of them were intended to create a predictable and affordable human Communist or Republican paradise. All private practices will disappear. There will be no way for them to exist. Yesterday, I saw on television that the private corner store pharmacies are also condemned to die.

I cannot believe it. The Republican Party that was proclaiming itself as a bearer of tradition, a defender of freedom, an advocate of private enterprise, is now, in its rush to patch today's ills, is destroying what was traditional and delivers the nation into the hands of managed care businessmen for unopposed, not easily correctable exploitation.

Book Four

The people expect from the Republican Party not to be guided by their 94 electoral successes and act hastily, but to be wise and in their moves look far into the future. They want from the Party more dialogue and more true communication.

Managed care will not be a cure for the health service in the U.S. The health of the people will be served best if primary care could be given back to independent practitioners with their work free from killing pressures, not trampled by capricious policy makers or deviatated from their original feeling of mission into a business arrangement by administrators of managed care magnates.

In my life I had one moment that looks like a miracle and almost in the same time a moment of a true ecstasy when I reached freedom. (See my letter to *Time*.) In the rest of my life, I want to work, to be responsible and to be free.

Tadeusz Maciejczyk, M.D.
Milledgeville, September 22, 1995

The World Seen from the Distance of a Small Village

Congressman Phil Crane
American Conservative Union
Washington, D.C.

Dear Sir:

    Because you wrote in your letter that the ACU helped lead the defeat of the liberals' medicine plans, I am sending you a copy of my letter to Sen. Dole and to Chairman Barbour, in which I expressed distress and reservations felt by me and by many other people from here about how Republicans dealt with medical care.
    I think that the idea of simplification of taxation would stimulate the economy and would enormously help the nation to grow, but after what I saw in your wonderful arrangement for medicine in this country, I do not trust you.
    I would appreciate very much any good explanation of the basic philosophy of your solution for the medical care in America, especially for its long-range consequences.
    I would like to expect from our leaders not surrogates, not a substitution of one disastrous situation by another, similar or enormously worse.
    I would like to wish you the best.

                                    Tadeusz Maciejczyk, M.D.
                                    Milledgeville, September 28, 1995

P.S. I am sending you a letter in which already in 1988 I told why I distrusted and why I do not want to participate in any managed care.

Book Four

Vincent D. Keenan, C.A.E.
Executive Vice-President
Illinois Academy of Family Physicians

Dear Sir:

I received your letter from which I can deduce that you were really reading all my letters that I sent to you. I am grateful because so many times, on such occasions, I was left with the impression that my letters were thrown into the garbage basket even before taking a glance at them.

The same day I received an invitation from IAFP to come to a conference in Oak Brook to learn how to succeed with managed care in a primary care setting.

To tell the truth, I have no ambition to be used as a gatekeeper and either I am interested in winning the favors of the big managed care bosses and their eventual patting on the back, by becoming an outstanding servant in the per capita arena.

In my life I was never for sale.

As a doctor, I have a strong respect for the mission doctors take when entering this profession, to downgrade it in such a way. I also had my own life experiences. I lived for a while in a so-called people's paradise. I saw how men were manipulated there, used, or thrown out when the need for them was no longer there. I was condemned to death in the court of Stalin for being a "bandit." And I had one moment in my life when I felt with enormous intensity what it means to be free.

I want to preserve my freedom.

I am sending you copies of my last two letters. The first of them was published in its entirety in our local newspaper. The second will be, I hope. I am adding also another of my letters, written in 1988 where I explain more clearly why I do not wish to participate in manipulated and distorted medicine. I am sorry that I have to write this letter in such a way. I would be grateful if you would send those other three letters to the Board of Directors.

I wish you and the medical profession in the U.S. the best.

Tadeusz Maciejczyk, M.D.
Milledgeville, September 30, 1995

The World Seen from the Distance of a Small Village

N.M. Camardese, M.D.
President
Freedom in Medicine Foundation

Dear Sir:

I thank you for your letter and for an invitation to join your movement.

I see that like in any other organization, your main preoccupation is with the membership and with the amount of money that membership would provide. What I do not see is how you intend to fight for that freedom. What would be the content and the meaning of such freedom? What would be the duties and responsibilities? What is the strategy? What risks would you be ready to take and what pains to endure?

To some extent, I distrust those who, from such calls for freedom, are making mostly a business structure and arrangement for fee collections. I would like to understand better what your organization is doing practically to promote your call for freedom.

I am sending you now my last letter to the Republican Party and one old one, in which I explain better my opposition to managed care.

I wish you the best in your work.

> Tadeusz Maciejczyk, M.D.
> Milledgeville, October 1, 1995

Book Four

Thomas J. Self
Department of Nuclear Safety
Springfield, IL

Dear Sir:

I received your letter, written on September 29, 1995.

Yes, I have X-Ray equipment. I didn't use it since my malpractice trial that finished in 1990. At that time, it was rendered inoperable. Mr. Benjamin cut its cable. In such a way it stays now, covered with dust in a place where I keep the garbage. If you have any use for this equipment, you can take it at any time.

After my malpractice trial, I reduced my work just to office visits. Under the present condition, the U.S. is not a good place for an independent worker, for an independent small medical practice.

I am sending you my letter written recently, where I explain the reasons of this belief of mine.

Tadeusz Maciejczyk, M.D.
Milledgeville, October 8, 1995

The World Seen from the Distance of a Small Village

Haley Barbour
Chairman
Republican National Committee
Washington, D.C.

Dear Sir:

I thank you for your letter with its additions to explain the need to reform medical care in the U.S. I understand that the present condition of this problem has to be changed. With this, your letter ignored completely my fundamental question that I asked.

Will, under your plan, will be considered some help, some stimulus to preserve or even to encourage private, independent unrelated to managed care, or any other business arrangement, medical practices, especially those related to primary care?

Will the Party make such an indisputable announcement?

As the situation is developing now, the remaining independent practices in the U.S. will be destroyed in a very short time. Each day the prospect for them to remain free is getting more gloomy. The managed care is squeezing them each day more aggressively. The government's capricious changes in rules, codes, payments or special considerations are added to it.

And yet, those remaining private practices are still preserving some stability and still are giving the soul to medical care. The present attraction of managed care will wear out and disappoint one day. It would be sad if all alternatives would be destroyed in the meantime.

I see leadership in any society, nation or world in a different way. True leadership is not the same as the money management. True leadership takes strength from an idea, big and deep enough to give hope and meaning for active lives and is bringing fulfillment for the searching soul of individuals.

When the spirit, under such leadership, is growing, the money somehow is made and it is spent wisely. Contrary to this, when the spirit vanishes from a society, no amount of wealth satisfies. All evils enter into the empty space and the down-rolling is the only direction to go.

Our nation, at the present time, needs leadership that could touch every individual human soul.

Everything else is less important.

I wish you the best in your work.

Tadeusz Maciejczyk, M.D.
Milledgeville, October 12, 1995

Book Four

Michael C. Menzel, PSA
Illinois Department of Employment Security

Dear Sir:

I thank you for your letter. In that letter you did not tell me how I should finish this year's payments for your taxation. Because of this, I will pay them as usual, as until now, and with the new year, I will pay according to your formula.

But I will make those payments the way you indicated, under protest.

No Federal, no State taxes are collected in a similar manner.

Your new requirement is more than unjust. It abuses. It permits you to tax the whole year amount for short term, or for changing work workers.

This, your requirement also is making a bad teaching for all of us. It teachers that whoever has an opportunity or a power to dictate "laws," can twist them according to his own convenience.

What really is a "law" if it is stretched and unjust? Francis the First, king of France, made a law that gave him the right to have a first postnuptial night with any bride of his nation. Yes. It was a law.

As I promised, I am sending you some of my letters.

I wish you the best.

            Tadeusz Maciejczyk
            Milledgeville, October 29, 1995

The World Seen from the Distance of a Small Village

Le Donna Witmer

I read your article about your dream to change the world, transforming it into a better, warmer place to live fully.

I put your article into a place where I keep things that touched me deeply. I like to have them, to read them in a changed situation and to reflect. I am sure your article caught the attention of others too.

We are living in the world filled up to the top with superficial talk and trivia. With them, the simple human being frequently is hungry for sincerity expressed in a simple way and for a touch that could penetrate the surface and reach the soul.

Your articles about teenage drinking or the people with disabilities were timely and were necessary.

If you do not stop, if you continue your journey towards your dream, you will make a difference.

Of course, you will have disappointments. You will have times of emptiness when you could think that nothing else you can do because everything you say is falling on deaf ears, but you will also have scores and triumphs.

But above these things, you will have something very wonderful. You will have a deep feeling of meaning in your life and a peace inside. This way you will never stop growing as a person and in spite of predictable disappointments, you will be always open and eager to new tasks, to new insides, to new opportunities to share yourself with others. You will have no need for different facemasks to cover your insides, because inside you will feel free.

And what you are writing, those words will be like the grain particles thrown to the ground. You will never know where they will start to germinate, to grow and to give fruit. How much fruit, where and when—that you will never know.

I wish you the best in your journey. I also had similar dreams in my life.

> Tadeusz Maciejczyk
> October 26, 1995

Book Four

Jody Johnson
C.M.E. Coordinator
Trinity Medical Center
Rock Island, IL

Dear Sir:

In previous years, I attended the "Medicine for Today" courses in Rockford. This year, as Rockford changed to Wednesdays, I switched to Rock Island.

I enjoyed your two seminars that I already attended. They were very well done and they were prepared in every detail. In a background of both of them was an atmosphere of good open arms.

But I have to say that I was distressed by the last lecture of the first day of those conferences. It was a lecture about dangers and never-ending targeting of doctors by malpractice lawyers.

That lecture, in my judgment, was not even intended to help doctors. In every extent, in its whole structure, it served the cause of the prosecuting lawyers. To increase this paradox, the doctors paid the bill for this pseudo-service.

That lecture was not helping the doctors in their work or in their life. That lecture was presenting a scenario that the accusing lawyers would like to engrave and to repeat over and over again in a mind of every doctor. That lecture was a master display of ordinary blackmail. It was conditioning doctors to be paralyzed, to hide, to look for protection and safety. It sounded like an expert preparation of the field for an abundant harvest of lawyers.

Your last announcement of the conference, "Can Your Office Withstand an Audit?" was like another push of doctors into the open arms of the businessmen from managed care.

That lecture and this new conference, are spreading an atmosphere of gloom and of helplessness. They urge escape, looking for cover and protection. It discourages independent work for doctors. It puts the dignity of being a doctor into a strange limbo.

About this problem, about dignity and independence in medical work, I wrote to Senator Dole and to the Chairman of the Republican Party. I am sending you a copy of that letter.

With this occasion I am also sending you copies of my other recent letters related somehow to medical service. And, if I can bother you more, I would like to send you a description of my special project from this and next year.

The World Seen from the Distance of a Small Village

I send you my best wishes.

> Tadeusz Maciejczyk, M.D.
> Milledgeville, November 12, 1995

Lieutenant Governor Bob Kustra
Springfield, IL

Dear Sir:

I understand the importance of a balanced budget for further healthy development of this country.

I am sending you a check for $25. I am not sending you back your survey. I do not like to just sign such obvious generalities.

Instead, I am including here my letter about problems with the medical care in this country, about the roots of its present situation, the dangers of its present tendencies and about the best and more sound, most economical road in medical care to follow.

I include also my letters about women, parents and about raising children. It can be of help in formulating your program to prevent juvenile emptiness and crime.

Maybe, together with those letters I should send you my letter about the excess in stressing the importance of sports competitions in our schools.

I could send you more of my letters, but probably you would not read them anyway.

I send you my best wishes in your decision to break the old patterns in performing public service and for your intentions to take the true hardship in bringing responsibility and a common sense to our public offices.

In these your efforts, you will have my best wishes.

> Tadeusz Maciejczyk, M.D.
> Milledgeville, November 16, 1995

Book Four

Letter to Editor
Newsweek Magazine

I read the article of David Kaplan about lawyers inference and suppression of publication of your report about the tobacco industry in the *60 Minutes* report on CBS.

Understanding your frustration and the devastation of this country made by malpractice suits and by malpractice threats, I am sending you some of my letters from the time of my refusal to pay a malpractice bribe in order to practice medicine, about the malpractice trial against me, in which I defended myself without a lawyer and won, and also about my protest and reasons for it against managed medical care.

I can send you more of my letters if you would wish.

Our country is looking more and more like the story about one small town that was a wonderful place to live in, was prosperous with its people helping each other and happy. That town had only one lawyer who was starving and miserable.

Then, that lawyer had a fantastic idea for himself. He brought another lawyer to that town. In the time afterwards, they both became rich and dominant in the life of the town and the people became agitated, hostile to one another, poor and miserable.

This country has an enormous need for somebody who would examine well the tragic harvest in the U.S. from the lawyers playing their "justice games."

Also, I am sending you my letter to a local newspaper about parents and raising children. It also became an issue of high priority.

I wish you the best.

Tadeusz Maciejczyk, M.D.
Milledgeville, November 19, 1995

P.S. Please send this letter, together with the enclosed material to Mike Wallace.

The World Seen from the Distance of a Small Village

The American Academy of Family Physicians
Kansas City, Missouri

I am late with payment of my dues because together with my check, I wanted to tell you what I think and what my anxieties are about the approaching takeover of medical services by managed care systems.

I entered the general practice residency (Family Practice didn't exist at that time) because I considered it to be a center, the essential part of all medical services. Only the general practice was giving me the most complete contact with people, with families and with problems of life.

Choosing the countryside for my practice, I didn't look for importance, affluence or appearances. All I really wanted was to be necessary, to be useful and to work according to the code of my conscience.

Last year's euphoria within AAFP because of the approaching managed care would need more family practitioners and would make them more important, made me sad and uneasy.

As a general practitioner, or family physician, I do not want to be a "gate-keeper," or a kind of a medical handyman for everything the managed care bosses would like to have. I do not consider such a role as proper or dignified for our profession. Such a role looks to me inappropriate and pitiful.

To me, general or family practitioners were always much more. To me it was always a kind of medical ministry or priesthood requiring special vocations. Its extent is reaching far beyond the mere care for the body. It should have the strength and the purity to be able to reach the souls of people.

Such a performance never can be realized if the family doctors work in situations subservient to any kind of businessman from managed care of from any other makeup. In order to protect such a standard for family practice, its practitioners have to be free.

A long time ago, somebody very important, somebody who changed the appearance of the world, said very clearly that nobody can serve two masters at the same time. This statement applies in all its depth to the medical professionals, especially those in primary care.

I believe that medical services, subservient to businessmen from managed care or to any other kind of managers will mark a dark period in medicine and will not serve the people well.

Book Four

I would like the AAFP to lead the struggle to free the medical profession and especially the primary care from any business managerial arrangement.

Tadeusz Maciejczyk, M.D.
Milledgeville, November 26, 1995

P.S. I am sending you copies of my other letters that deal with this problem.

The World Seen from the Distance of a Small Village

Mr. A.G. Hulvey
U.S. Chamber of Commerce
Washington, D.C.

Dear Sir:

I thank you for your invitation to be a member of the U.S. Chamber of Commerce. I know the importance of participation in active public life. I know how critical the situation of our country is.

I know the importance of going upstream while defending the fundamental values in the life of society.

Right now I am fighting for my survival as an independent medical practitioner. I do not know how long I will be able to survive. I will try to survive and to endure the present squeeze on independence in medicine by managed care.

I am with you on the need for a balanced budget. I am sending you no membership fee now.

Just today I was told that the local teachers cannot be my patients any more. From now on they have to go to managed care doctors. I am preparing myself to resist the hardship. In my fight with the "giants," I will look for your help.

I am sending you some of my letters that explain why I am not going with others in the same direction.

I send you my best wishes.

> Tadeusz Maciejczyk, M.D.
> Milledgeville, November 26, 1995

Enc. Letter to Senator Bob Dole
      Letter to Haley Barbour, Chairman
      Letter to Blue Cross/Blue Shield
      Letter to Judy Johnson

Book Four

Time Magazine
Letter to the Editor

Dear Sir:

Ann Landers is 100% correct. Pope John Paul is a Polak. I am Polak and millions of Poles in Poland call themselves Polaks.

This name acquired a very specific, offensive contemptuous meaning only after the beginning of the German pre-Nazi grandiosity complex and aggressive transformation.

Prior to that moment in history, the German-Polish relations were good. The borders between the two countries were the most peaceful in 400 years of the history of Europe. German immigration to Poland assimilated very quickly and completely. A son of such an immigrant, Wilhelm Pohl, wrote his name Wincenty Pol and in the 1850s he was known as a great Polish poet. In the time of the post liberation war of 1830–31, during the most destructive reign of the Russian military rule, he wrote his wonderful "Song from our Land." The veterans from that war, while passing through Germany to France were greeted there as the heroic defenders of freedom. People were coming from towns with flowers and with their flags to meet them. The books from the explosion of creativity of different writers from that immigration were printed with extreme care in Dresden and in that time Breslau.

This spirit changed radically after German reunification under Prussian leadership. A victory over France in 1870 added to that special megalomania. Suddenly, the fact that two hours of the train ride toward the east from Berlin, the capital, marked the point where the people did not understand German annoyed the German pride. After Bismark's remark about this in the Reich, a plan was created to change this. A large sum from the ransom the French paid for German withdrawal from their soil after 1870 was used to finance a *kulturkampf* and create a *drang nach osten* (push to the east) spirit.

That "Push to the East" was a very special way to deal with the problem. Multiple new laws were created, frequently conflicting with one another and were published for that territory in German. Large amounts of policemen were sent to observe the obedience to those laws. They were putting into books every breaking of the rules, every inattention to those new rules. For each of them, a special monetary penalty was attached with typical German precision. When the time was ripe, an official was coming to many households. Those households were not

The World Seen from the Distance of a Small Village

more theirs. The penalties put together were bigger than all they had. But the government was benign. It didn't put them into jail for those unpaid penalties. They packed them into cattle wagons and shipped them to Hamburg from where they were given German government-paid transportation in the bottoms of ships to New York. There they were left, those villagers who spoke only Polish, on the streets of New York, without any direction, any help. In New York, they were presented as Polacks, adding to this name all the poisonous flavor and creating a wide variety of the so-called "Polish jokes." Apparently uneasy consciences needed such a presentation of the victims to a kind of self-justification.

Later on, during the Nazi occupation, the present Pope and everyone else in the country, we were the *Verfluchte Polacks* (cursed Poles). At the time of the progress of Germany paranoia, we became worst than that. We all became *untermenschen* (below human.)

The name *untermensch* disappeared together with the Allied victory in 1945. The American connotation related to the name *Polak* is still alive and opens wounds.

It is high time to put that symbol of hate and injustice into a peaceful grave. We should be grateful to Ann Landers for brining this chapter of human inhumanity into full light. Clearance, explanation, reconciliation after such exposure, can make one small addition to a true peace of heart at this Christmas time.

Tadeusz Maciejczyk, M.D.
Milledgeville, December 6, 1995

Book Four

Republican National Committee
Bob Dole, Senate Majority Leader
Newt Gingrich, Speaker of the House
Haley Barbour, Chairman, Republican National Committee

Dear Gentlemen:

Again, I received from you a call to accept the 1996 membership card and to pay generously for the upcoming Party's expenses.

And again, in that call you did not even mention my question, which after two months still remains without an answer.

I am sorry that I am insistent in this matter, and I ask the same question again.

Will I, under your leadership into the 21st century, be able to work productively as an independent medical practitioner, or will I be suffocated, silenced and nullified?

Will, under your leadership, be considered some help, some stimulus, to preserve or even to encourage private, independent, unrelated to managed care or to any business arrangement, medical practices, especially those related to primary care?

Will the Party make such an indisputable announcement?

This question is important not only to me (because it relates to my work) but also to many people from around here because the takeover of the country's health care by businessmen from managed care, represents an immediate threat to every independent workshop. Whom will the Party put on sale next?

The fear is that if the trend, which started with medical care, will go on, the giant economical magnates will become the lords of the U.S., and everybody else will shrink to an employee or servant level. A medical gate-keeper can be paid abundantly, but he will only be a servant whom their bosses will be able to manipulate to their advantage. He will sell his soul to those omnipotent lords. This will mark the end of the U.S. as it was known until now.

Until now, the greatness of the U.S. came not from huge monopolies of a few, but from millions of independent-minded enterprising people, each of them having the field open before him to go as far as he could reach. They, by their variability, inventiveness, free energy created harmony and balance, not only in the economy, but in all other aspects of the life of the country.

The World Seen from the Distance of a Small Village

In such an arrangement, the role of the government or of the Party would be to preserve that harmony and to direct its energy towards growth.

But, if the Republican Party, taking the lesson from Mrs. Clinton, sold its soul to the magnates from managed care, who then ruthlessly acted to eliminate every intent of different approaches to medical care, to eliminate all remaining independent practices, then such a Party is not what I was looking for when I gave all my confidence to the Republican leadership.

Going this way, the Republican Party will lose all its credentials in the eyes of many people who around here are becoming increasingly uneasy with what is happening in Washington.

Because of all this, before I accept my membership card, I ask you again for a clear, unambivalent non-evasive answer to my question.

I wish you sincerely everything good in your work and I wish you a Merry Christmas.

> Tadeusz Maciejczyk, M.D.
> Milledgeville, December 9, 1995

P.S. In order to facilitate, I am sending you my first letter written to you concerning managed care. Also I included all other letters about this problem written afterwards.

Because now is a special time of Christmas, I send you my "Almost Christmas" story, my response to a *Time Magazine* article about the possibility of miracles in the present world.

Book Four

Illinois Academy of Family Physicians
1101 Perimeter Drive, Suite 730
Schaumburg, IL 60173

I hope that Dr. Lee B. Sacks was not speaking for all Illinois doctors when he made the statement that, "Managed Care is the future, regardless of how we feel about it. If we don't make it work for us, someone else will come and take it over."

Who is that someone else?

Why do we have to be so obedient and capitulate, giving the greatness of free medicine into the hands of profit-minded businessmen?

Yes, a danger exists. But panic, surrender and short-sightedness are not the answer.

I am sending you copies of my letters and I would like to ask you not to close the discussion on this subject, but on the contrary, accumulate all arguments, make appropriate studies and strategies and establish a defense line. The freedom of medicine will be lost only if the doctors decide that "peace at any price" is the best way; that washing the hands is the best policy and selling themselves to the new bosses represents smartness and life wisdom. Only then will Dr. Sacks be completely correct.

As for me, I was under tyranny once in my life. I know how tyranny enters and how it acts after consolidation. As I already said, in the remainder of my life, I want to work, to be dedicated and responsible and to be free.

Last spring, *Time Magazine* published an article about the possibility of miracles in our present world. I experienced a miracle once. I told my story to *Time*. With the approaching of Christmas, I send this, my "Almost Christmas" story, to you.

I hope that medicine in America will remain free. I hope that you will contribute to it.

Tadeusz Maciejczyk, M.D.
Milledgeville, December 10, 1995

The World Seen from the Distance of a Small Village

Mr. Burgermeister and
All the people of Stendal

Dear Gentlemen:

I was vacillating. Should I? Really, I know nobody in Stendal. To whom do I write?

But Stendal is deeply engraved in my memory. In my mind, it associates with something that I cannot explain, I cannot forget, and that is changing my life.

Last spring, after reading in *Time Magazine* an article about miracles in the present, modern world, about the presence of God in the life of the contemporary people and about what the modern scholars were saying about God, I wrote to *Time* my story, in which I had one special moment and a special touch of God's care.

I have no other explanation for what happened during those anxious hours of my life. It happened in Stendal.

A few days ago, with Christmas approaching, suddenly I felt a deep need to share that my moment with you.

I want to send my best Christmas wishes to all the people of Stendal.

                                        Tadeusz Maciejczyk
                                        Milledgeville, December 17, 1995

Book Four

Dr. M.N. Camardene, M.D.

Dear Sir:

With Christmas approaching, I want to send to you my best wishes and also the copies of my last letters related to our struggle for freedom in medicine in America. The present situation could give the impression that all these efforts are in vain.

Managed care is gaining momentum and preparing its cadre, is squeezing out all who appear disturbing to its purpose. The government doesn't know what to do and is under the strong influence of lobbyists and those who can best afford them.

The "Justice Games" of lawyers never stop. They are now more sophisticated, more scientific or pseudo-scientific and more hungry for big rewards than ever. The medical community in general is as passive as it always was. It is ready to go with the wind, wherever that wind happens to blow; the doctors looking primarily for what is there for each of them separately. The expectations for material rewards and for prestige overshadows a true medical vocation.

The public, the people are disoriented by invisible manipulations, by different kinds of proclamations and promises. They are worried and they are increasingly intimidated by life's insecurity and hardships.

In this situation, a sporadic, lonely opposition to those winds has an appearance almost of Don Quixote's fight with the windmills. And yet, it looks to me that our fight has to go on. I am convinced that in the end, freedom for medicine will win.

Together with those reports about my input to that fight, as Christmas is approaching, I send you my old "Almost Christmas" story—a story of a miracle.

I wish you the best.

                                        Tadeusz Maciejczyk, M.D.
                                        Milledgeville, December 17, 1995

The World Seen from the Distance of a Small Village

6 January 1996

James R. Black
Office of Stewardship and Planned Giving
The Brethren Church
524 College Avenue
Ashland, Ohio 44805

T. Maciejczyk, M.D.
Box 788
444 Main Street
Milledgeville, IL 61051

Dear Dr. Maciejczyk:

Several times I have started to write, and each time some interruption prevented my good intentions. This time I am determined to finish the pleasant task.

First of all I want to thank you again for your kindness toward me the last time I was in Milledgeville. It was an imposition on my part to request assistance on Sunday, but your willingness was greatly appreciated. But then I remember many times when, in a very unselfish way, you were willing to help myself, my family, and others. It is a sad commentary of life that the "family doctor" has almost become a thing of the past. I believe "we the people" are the losers.

I remember also with great affection your family. My daughter, Barbara, had dinner in your home with one of your children so many years ago, and still recalls the happy event, though she is now 30 years of age and has two children of her own. And my son, Bob, who died in Milledgeville in 1976, always spoke with such appreciate of you and your family.

I have "officially" retired, but am really more busy than ever. I work a 2/3 time position as Director of Stewardship and Planned Giving for the Brethren Church denomination and also serve part time (the other 1/#) as pastor of a small church in Canton, Ohio. I have always loved serving people as a pastor, and am thankful to God for the opportunity of doing so again in the twilight years of life.

I have appreciated so much the editorials you provided me. I just completed the study of the subject: The Need, and the Role of Spiritual Strength in Resolving Today's World Conflicts. One with your experience would know first hand of the folly of conflict that comes from a lack of love and appreciation of others.

Once again, my friend, I thank you. I would pray that if ever I am in your little town again we will have opportunity to talk once more. If you happen upon any of my old friends, including the Pastor Ken Sullivan family, please greet them for me.

May God richly bless you now and always, and bless and prosper your loved ones.

In Christ's great love and service,

Rev. James R. Black

The World Seen from the Distance of a Small Village

John A. Swanson
Director, Health Care Services
The American Academy of Family Physicians

Dear Sir:

I thank you for your letter, your discussion of the problems with managed care, its mixed acceptance by doctors, its explanations in the included monograph. Nevertheless, all those explanations are not convincing to me.

Managed Care in theory can be a completely different thing than in practice. The stories painted in the survey in the last medical economics are not especially rosy.

Also, Managed Care in this time, when it is in the process of gaining acceptance and strength in the territory, in this present situation the Managed Care has to show its nicest face. When this phase will be over, after consolidation, after the free medicine will not be counted any more, at that time that managed care will not have a need to pretend. It will show its true face of medicine reduced to business.

To some extent I can understand that the high technology, the expensive instrumentation medicine, could require some amount of general planning and management to eliminate costly maintenance of only partially used competing among them services.

Such planning is not required for the Primary Care Medicine. The Primary Care will show the best, will be the most economical, most human, most in touch with the needs of the people, if it remains free and by this flexible, adaptable and spontaneous.

With this occasion I send to you my letters written in December.

And also, because in each of them, I mentioned my special, "Almost Christmas" story even if Christmas is already over. I am sending a copy of that letter to you now.

I wish you and the AAFP the best.

Tadeusz Maciejczyk, M.D.
Milledgeville, January 11, 1996

Book Four

Editor
Medical Tribune
1000 Avenue of the Americas
New York, NY 10013

Dear Sir:

I just read your article about a need for patients advocacy in an era of third-party control. My impression is that the mere advocacy will do very little, if anything.

I think that Dr. Glass is right when he calls for resistance to any compromise in patient-physician relationships. I believe that medicine will fulfill its mission only as a free force.

I am sending you copies of my recent letters in which I explain my point of view.

Please send the copies of those letters to doctors Cristine Laine, Frank Davidoff and Richard M. Glass.

Your Tribune looked to me very interesting.

Tadeusz Maciejczyk, M.D.
Milledgeville, February 5, 1996

P.S. After all those references to my special "Almost Christmas" story, I should probably add it to this letter.

The World Seen from the Distance of a Small Village

Medical Economics
Continuing Survey 1996

To clarify my responses to your survey, I have to say that as a doctor, I cannot be considered as typical for any group. My biggest need in order to work well, is to be free and responsible only to my conscience in my work. I never had any ambition to be rich, to show, or to pretend. I never knew how to charge. I always was uneasy taking money for helping.

I never was practical in conducting my life. I opposed an obligatory malpractice insurance and I lost my hospital privileges. When I got a malpractice suit against me, I refused to hide behind a lawyer who would defend me. I didn't want to contribute to what I understood was not a search for justice, but a lucrative "justice game" of lawyers. After three and one-half years of struggle, I won that trial and I paid not one cent for its cost.

At present I have a practice limited to my office visits. I continue to work without malpractice insurance and consequently I have no hospital privileges.

I do not belong to any kind of managed care system. I know that I am losing patients to a system that frames people by contracts with employers and somehow I am resigned to limit still further my income. I do not need much to be happy. What I really want, what I really believe, is the preservation of my medical practice from business or political disfigurations.

In my life I was taught how precious freedom is, how easily it is lost and how hard it is to recover it.

I believe that a well-understood freedom that I need to work, is my biggest gift to my patients, to the community where I live and to this country.

Tadeusz Maciejczyk, M.D.
Milledgeville, February 11, 1996

P.S. to explain this letter, I am sending you copies of some of my previous responses to pressures that destroy freedom in practicing medicine.

Book Four

Dan Ludwig
National Commander of the American Legion

Dear Sir:

    As much as I was shocked by the scandalous, public and for all of us, humiliating act of desecration of our flag, I do not feel that a special amendment to the Constitution is the answer or the remedy to solve this problem. Such an amendment would be toothless and only would invite certain elements to act and to show.
    Instead of an amendment, I would rather call for a scrutiny of the conclusion and the verdict of the Supreme Court after the 1989 flag desecration.
    Not the offenders, not the hooligans, but those Supreme Court Judges made a public declaration that the miserable, ugly and stupid show of threading open, spitting on and burning of the flat, was admissible and should be tolerated because it was equivalent to the freedom of speech.
    That declaration of the Supreme Court Judges was unwise, was cowardly and was cynical. It was like a public washing of hands to avoid taking a position. That declaration should be subjected to scrutiny, to public discussion and to redefinition.
    The American Flag Protecting Act, included in the Constitution, leads nowhere. It would only create a temptation to stage a new show for those, who feel a need for publicity, whatever the form or cost. It would also create a new mine of gold for certain categories of lawyers.
    I cannot imagine how our courts, which fail so miserably in providing safety to citizens, how those courts could confront that new problem and enforce such a constitutional amendment. In the show, in a confrontation that could appear, the prestige of all the Constitution would suffer. Each trial for those offenders could create solidarity of others and give new twists to the spectacles.
    The cause of such nihilism, of such disrespect, of such a need for kicks to cover painful emptiness inside and despair, the deepest cause for such acts is elsewhere and no constitutional amendment can change it. To treat those wounds in the souls of the offenders would be a challenge and solution.
    A gesture of a new amendment, a creation of a legion of new types of criminals to fill our already overcrowded jails, a new prohibition attached to the Constitution, is not an answer. It has nothing to do with

The World Seen from the Distance of a Small Village

leadership. It would only create new complications while doing nothing to heal the hidden wounds of our society.

> Tadeusz Maciejczyk, M.D.
> Milledgeville, March 3, 1996

P.S. I am including my letters to the local newspaper after listening to the conclusion of the Supreme Court and another letter about possible help, a letter about raising children.

Book Four

Republican Party Planning Committee
The 1996 Delegate Survey

SECTION 1.

All these points should be addressed.

SECTION 2.

- a. Raising taxes:
  Rigidity always is suspicious and frequently breaks down in times of testing. Taxes can be increased in a situation of a true crisis. The circumstances should be well explained to the whole nation. Before such a move, the Governor should consider all alternatives:
  Will introduce projects for saving and special measures for correction.
  The burden will be put equally on everybody.
  Never again will arise a situation when taxes were raised while Congress voted for themselves increases. Would be encouraging to the nation if Congress in such circumstances would bring down their salaries and special privileges.
- b. Balanced budget amendment to the Constitution? No
  A leader of recognized honesty and integrity with the ability to motivate could do this without putting the prestige of the Constitution to such a test. If we lack character and wisdom, no constitutional amendment will make a miracle for us.
- c. Line Item Veto YES!
  The President should have a right to exclude from documents he is signing those items he is sincerely opposing and present them to the whole Congress or even to the whole nation, for another public consideration, discussion, clarification and second voting. If such an item would pass such a test, the President would sign it, eventually with a remark about his personal view of the problem.
- d. Flat Tax: YES
  After all consideration, I came to the conclusion that it would create a clear situation for everybody. I remember two elected Presidents who were embarrassed by a finding that in using loopholes, legally they didn't pay one cent of taxes. In the present

system the experts of loopholes, or those who can afford them can avoid taxation. The average people, the middle class, the practically poor, but honest, bears the burden.
  e. Primary causes of economic problems:
  Those on your survey are not primary, but consequential.
      1. Our national myopia. Long range planning with some sacrifices is unpopular. We want the satisfaction, the profit, and the commodities all today. And we are selfish about this.
      2. Our inclination for surface goodness. Character, wisdom, true goodness requires looking far beyond instant satisfaction. Being spoiled is much easier.
      3. Chaotic regulations: jumpy, expensive, wasteful, frequently immobilizing and inducing inertia. In my office, even the coding books can be a clear show of such recklessness. It gives a feeling of instability, provisionality, insecurity, and a doubt about leadership that shows such immaturity. It invites to passivity. It kills the spirit.

SECTION 3.

Limit the numbers of terms in Congress: YES!

As everywhere else, some men in Congress are growing in experience, wisdom and abilities for good decisions. Many learn to be smart and to swim, catch the routine and adjust themselves to all the seasons. They are learning best how to please, how to buy and how to be re-elected.

For those best the limited numbers of terms will be not a problem. Serving in Congress they acquired status and true authority. They always will be necessary in different positions and they always will make the life of the nation and of the world richer and more fruitful.

All those others will do everything to stay in Congress indefinitely. They know that they are not good for anything else. Political action Committees can be good or bad, depending on how it would be made and used, or abused.

SECTION 4.

Welfare for immigrants? In general NO!

Book Four

But the problem is more complex than the surface of this question shows. Those lost in the process, helpless and suffering should be helped. Here an appropriate study should lead to some more specific rules and solutions.

More effort to prevent illegal immigration? YES.

I do not see clearly how. It is a game of many stages and actors. Military force on the borders is not the answer. It would destroy the basic military spirit and purpose. It seems to me that the strictly closed and guarded borders are obsolete, reminiscent of the past, the worst time between the first and second world wars. The world is going in a different direction. New ways of stabilization have to be looked for, experimented and put in practice.

English—official language? YES

Maintenance of ghettos is serving no good purpose. They will appear always as long as new immigrants are coming but also the modern media are speeding assimilation. Fragmentation is not always the same as diversity.

Right to keep and bear arms? I am not sure, but most likely, YES.

Not this right is the central problem in controlling crime. The absurd abundance of arms, combined with a moral breakdown, the family crisis, lack of positive, inspiring models for life, are creating the truly explosive mixture. I do not see any cheap and easy solution for this problem.

Is gun control needed? YES!

But gun control alone will disappoint.

Constitutional amendment to prohibit desecration of the American flag? NO.

I explained this opinion of mine in my recent letter to Dan Ludwig, National Commander of the American Legion. I include for you the copy of that letter and a copy of my letter to our local newspaper about the Supreme Court decision about desecration in 1989.

SECTION 5.

Does our criminal justice work fairly and efficiently? Surely NO!

Somehow in the U.S. Courts the justice is very expensive and money can buy in them a lot. My impression is that a lucrative justice game became more important than the search for justice. As I know, the prestige of all of our justice system came to a lowest low.

Our jails are not redeeming offenders—especially the young. Frequently they make from them hard criminals. Idleness and overcrowding are producing an explosive, dangerous atmosphere and the worst of criminals are using it, in the process pushing everybody else down.

The justice system should create a new scope of solutions aiming at rehabilitation, redeeming compensatory works, and introduction into normal life. This should be especially mandatory for the young offenders.

SECTION 6.

Government in health care? NO.
I send you the copies of my letters from the last few months in which I tried to explain my point of view.
Malpractice lawsuits are increasing the cost of health care? YES!
I am sending you copies of my letters from the time when I refused to pay that malpractice bribe and I lost my hospital privileges and some of my letters from my malpractice suit.
Medical IRAs? YES!
It would be a move in the right direction.

SECTION 7.

Merit scales for exceptional teachers? NO
Who would be the judge? It could create a very unhealthy, ugly game, would divide and could create bitterness. For the selected it would create a strange, uneasy limbo. There should be other ways to reward excellence and dedication.
Parental control? NO!
But constant dialogue with parents and mutual cooperation would be enormously positive.
A voucher system? NO!
It would help to escape, leaving worsening conditions behind. A way should be created for such parents to define their grievances and to initiate remedies.
Eliminate Dept. of Education? NO!
A central authority to promote standards in education is necessary. If the central authority would abuse their position mandating petty demands and demagogue—such pressure should not be obligatory. A mechanism should be created to discuss those differences. A line should be found between the competence of an Education Department and local authorities.

Distribution of condoms? NO!

Book Four

It would do more harm than good. It is not promoting a healthy development of character or responsibility. It is a very negative kind of "goodness" that gives its blessing to the weaknesses, desires and whims. It gives an official permission to take the worst road in life.

Voluntary prayer? YES!

I do not see any harm in this. If voluntary, it will not interfere with anybody's rights.

Preaching homosexuality, teaching its acceptance? NO!

True tolerance has a limit. Declared homosexuals who promote and agitate about their lifestyle should have no place in schools. I include here my letter in which responding to one champion of minorities, I promoted myself to the leadership in my special minority group.

SECTION 8

Should the U.S. be a leader? YES!

Whatever weaknesses we have, the U.S. is the only force in the world that can push the world in the right direction. If we hide, other pretenders for such a leadership will appear (China, any radical Muslim country, Russia) will assume such a role and it surely will hurt us, hurt the prospect for the emotionally healthy world.

Foreign Aid Programs? Yes!

But every year each of them should be reevaluated, redirected, adjusted or finished. They always should be only temporary and the purpose of each of them should be made very clear. They should not be done in secrecy.

Maintain military readiness? YES!

Wisdom and justice should be the primordial strength of our influence and of our shaping of the world, but a stick has to be kept in hand as the ultimate authority in some cases. Sorry. Such is the world.

Tadeusz Maciejczyk, M.D.
Milledgeville, March 14, 1996

The World Seen from the Distance of a Small Village

Christopher Cox, Chairman
House Republican Policy Committee

Dear Sir:

I received your one-dollar check with a letter suggesting I return that check with an abundant donation. I would love to receive such a call to help in a letter truly leading toward a better future, a letter that would be a testimony of wisdom, vision, prudence, boldness and leadership.

Instead, your letter was the usual showpiece of political prattling in its shallow, empty unconvincing building-nothing, painting-your-greatness-and-goodness-by-blaming-the-other-side-for-everything content.

Such letters, coming from Washington, from the center that claims the leadership for us, are depressing, creating gloom and apathy. They give an impression that all the big titles and the big calls coming from them are nothing but a farce with the quest not for duties, but for power. They are leading to the next circle of disappointment. They will be followed by another litany of blaming.

I believe that blaming others is the most important obstacle to growth, to be responsible and to be a leader in a true life.

I am sending your check back. I am not sending any of my money. To do this, I am waiting for somebody who without childish blaming the others, would help me to be a true participant in a new vision of a new era.

In this letter I am not against the Republican Party. I am against any kind of smallness in leadership, especially in this very important moment of history.

Tadeusz Maciejczyk, M.D.
Milledgeville, March 27, 1996

P.S. I was told that Al Salvi, who was the Rep. Nomination for the Senate seat from Illinois, as a lawyer, became rich from malpractice trials. I was a victim of this kind of abuse. I am sending you copies of some of my letters from that time. They are very illustrative.

Book Four

Newt Gingrich
Speaker of the House
RE: Speaker's Survey

Dear Sir:

My answers are tentative indicating my inclination only. Here, in this far away countryside, we do not follow very closely all the events in Washington.

It looks to me that in an international peace keeping expedition, one central command is essential for coordination and effectiveness. What is necessary is to establish the rules and the limits that would satisfy American concerns for efficacy, safety, common sense and all the other objectives related to the cause. Those assurances should be established in a very clear way.

Really. I do not know what taxations should be decreased or eliminated. Generally, I put very little attention to this problem.

This attitude changed very intensely, in the moment, when I received my last tax return. I explained it in my letter to Gordon H. Mansfield, Executive Director of Paralyzed Veterans of America.

In that letter I asked several questions and I would be very grateful if you would answer them. I would also like to ask your office to send me addresses of officials and candidates of both parties to whom I could send the same questions.

I have not enough knowledge about nature and function of those institutions to speak with any kind of authority about their need and their true usefulness for the country.

Within No. 11 of your survey I sent you different letters in which I talked about different problems. I hope they will be useful in your work.

I will send you some donation when I know what my financial situation is. I have impression, that in Washington you are one of the few who are true MEN. Maybe because of this, many around here are afraid of you. Part of the leadership is to contact, to explain, and to convince.

                                    Tadeusz Maciejczyk, M.D.
                                    Milledgeville, April 10, 1996

The World Seen from the Distance of a Small Village

Sweepstakes Authorities

Dear Gentlemen:

I wanted to write this later, after winning, but apparently the time for it is now.

Already now I should tell you about my intentions regarding the money that I could get from this reward.

About one year ago, at the beginning of this game, I wrote to you that your invitation gave me the impression that I could realize with such help something that was inside of me for a long time and what at that moment somehow took a concrete idea. I do not want this reward for my personal improvement and security.

With this money and with the help of *Time Magazine*, which at that time appeared to me as a main sponsor of this sweepstakes, I want to finance a plan of scholarship for two Americans and two Spanish students to study at the University of Lublin in Poland. I would like *Time Magazine* to help me to run this scholarship until the resources are exhausted.

The students selected for this task should have special qualities and show an interest in the objectives of this scholarship.

I would like those students to go to the University of Lublin to study for five to six years all about the territory, the conditions, the tendencies, their resources of all kinds, the possibility of complementation in mutual growth of the regions of five countries: Poland, the Ukraine, Bielorussia, Lithuania and Latvia. I would ask those students to develop an independent look at what emotions divide those countries and what, in spite of everything, is making from them a family with a common purpose and interest.

In recent years, the University of Lublin became a focal point where the students and the intellectuals of those countries meet, exchanging ideas that have the potential to shape the future.

I would like those students to have the freedom to move and to participate to feel the pulse of all countries separately and to be present in the important events of them, to be presented to the authorities. I would like them to grow into that territory and to give that territory a look from a distance, an independent opinion, advise or guidance, if necessary, to present their impressions to the people there and to the world. *Time Magazine* could have from them their exclusive reports.

Book Four

I understand that the creation of such togetherness of those countries would give stability and a new potential to the region and it would create a very important defense of the world against Russian dreams and ambitions to dominate and to expand. As such, Lublin in the last few years became one of the most interesting focal points and laboratories of the world.

And I, with the realization of my dream would feel like a true millionaire, regardless of whether I had one cent in my pocket or not.

I thank you for the opportunity of participation in your sweepstakes.

Tadeusz Maciejczyk
Milledgeville, April 28, 1996

The World Seen from the Distance of a Small Village

Scholarship

This year's scholarship for interest in the nature of leadership was given to two outstanding students who gave their time, thoughts, and a personal touch to this important subject. They wrote essays about the needs for good leadership, especially in the present time. They will read those essays during the Memorial Day Ceremony when they receive their rewards.

Those two students are:

Wesley J. Isenhart

Tammy Diane Schell

The disturbing fact about this project was that it was presented to students very late.

I asked to start this work in November. It takes time to comprehend all the elements and the dimensions necessary to build up the personality of a true leader.

It was April when I was asked what I really expected from the students in their writing. They had more important things to do before, I was told.

A call to be a leader requires an enormous work and transformation.

Leadership obtains its strength from the inside life of the individual. He has to know himself. He has to put in order his priorities for life and to take a good look on his responsibilities. He has to develop courage to get out from his safety dwellings and reach the unknown. He has to develop wisdom to make his ultimate decisions.

I have to add that no leadership can last and become a source of strength for others without the fundamental ingredient of love. Leadership without love corrupts and degenerates easily. The essence of true leadership was defined best about two thousand years ago with a short sentence: A good shepherd gives his life for his sheep.

For all those reasons we should look for future leaders in all our schools. They can appear in the humblest of places. It should be the school priority and one of its very important tasks to look for them and to give them chances to grow.

The shortcuts in this matter are not the answer. The few days camping for leaders can create only false pretension. It could change into tragedy if somebody started to believe and develop expectations for leadership positions just because he was very wonderfully charming during such camping.

To be a leader requires a long, lifelong inside job.

Tadeusz Maciejczyk
May 2, 1996

Book Four

As Memorial Day arrives, I present to you again those two students from our school who gave their time, thoughts and effort to describe true leadership so much necessary in our difficult and uneasy time in which not the idea and taking responsibility, but playing the righteousness and blaming the other became the center of the oratory of our candidates to be re-elected or elected.

During the coming years, these two students will go to the bigger world to continue their studies, but I hope that the need of leadership that entered into them while writing their essays will permeate within them, will grow and will guide them to take the lead when the moment for that comes. I hope that in such a moment, they will not shrink, escape or deviate from what a true and inspiring leadership requires.

To listen to those essays and to look inside ourselves for a vocation, for true leadership at every level, is the most appropriate thing we can do during this day dedicated to those who died defending freedom.

To preserve that freedom and to inspire in everybody the conduct of mutual responsibility and togetherness, we need not circumstantial or opportunistic dignitaries but the wise, committed and inspiring leaders who would have the spiritual strength to give us meaning for life and would give us an example of how to go through life with dignity and with a bigger purpose.

The essays will be read first by Wesley J. Isenhart and then by Tammy Diane Schell. Then their work will be sent to the General Headquarters of American Veterans, to The White House, to both our Senators, to our Representative, to the governor of Illinois to state universities and to main magazines: *Time, Newsweek* and *U.S. News & World Report*.

(After the students read their essays)

In this moment I want to thank not only in my name, but also in the name of all who came here, to stress the importance of this day and to pay special appreciation to those our special guests and speakers. To Tammy Schell and to Wesley Isenhart. I want to thank them sincerely.

In their essays they expressed their expectations and their perceptions of what a good leadership should be.

Clear formation of those ideas and a realization of what we should see in our leaders, is especially important this year as we are approaching Election Day and because of this, all the doubts, frustrations and hopes are raising in us a new high.

Precisely because of this, this year we have more than ever a moral obligation to elaborate and to realize what the qualities, what the character and what the virtues we should expect from the candidates in whose

The World Seen from the Distance of a Small Village

hands and hearts we will put our destiny, our trust and because of this, our votes.

We should make this very clear that the fundamental element, the baseline that we will require from those candidates will be their sincerity, their being themselves, their authenticity as persons, as human beings.

We should distrust those who above all are trying to please everybody and to promise everything. We should distrust those whose main talk would be the blaming of others, who are avoiding and are afraid to speak about true and uncolored realities and who are reluctant to take their responsibilities for them.

All this means that it is our obligation to clean our leadership from those pseudo-leaders who are hiding their true faces behind different sets of masks that they put on when in public, changing them depending on place, audience or occasion.

Those obligations we owe to those who gave their lives to defend freedom and to create a better future for our nation and for the world. Our effort, honesty and foresight will be the best way to honor those who died and who desperately needed to believe that their sacrifice was not just a worthless, nameless, purposeless waste.

And looking into the future, I hope that the tradition of writing and reading the essays about leadership by the students of this school will continue.

I hope that each year a new crop of young men and women will volunteer to think about the need for good leadership, for the self-preparation for an eventual leading role in society and they will write their essays giving a special touch to the Memorial Day Ceremony. It could be that by doing this, they could return the true meaning to the presently devalued and indiscriminately abused merit it takes to be a leader.

Next year special attention in writing about the need of spirituality in order to be a true leader will be used to develop the theme, "Leadership, not in an ordinary, average time, but in the time of cataclysm, danger and pain." What qualities would be required from emerging leaders in order to meet that challenge?

To illustrate such a situation, I will look to the history of Poland, which I know the best.

It was the time of the mid-19th century. The Russian oppression after the war of liberation of 1830–31 had become more and more unbearable. An escalation of events led to a desperate general uprising in January of 1863.

Book Four

It was a cruel, partisan type of war led with very inadequate resources and mostly without hope. Like here in the battle of the Alamo, the Russians didn't take prisoners and the wounded were slain. During those years and the years after, thousands were hanged, including the highest commanders of that war. Even the Russians nicknamed the governor of Poland at that time "Vieshatiel" meaning somebody who hangs people. During those years thousands lingered and died in prisons that had no similarity at all to what here we call a prison. Day after day thousands did a long walk in chains towards Siberia. Thousands were expropriated from what they had. All the upper class of the nation was more than decimated. The economy was shattered. The schools were closed for decades. The police were everywhere and the present human rights were non-existent.

In such a grim and almost hopeless condition because help or even consolation came from no where, Jan Kasprowicz, in one of his poems, paid a tribute to many women and men who in the extent of their possibilities showed a spirit that didn't break and a guidance to do everything to save what was possible and preserve whatever was possible, especially the sorrowful spirit.

This was the beginning strophe of that poem.

Blessed are those, who in the time of thunder
Didn't lose the equilibrium and strength
    Of their spirit
Who in the sight of devastations and ruins
Are not pouring from their hearts a song
    Of deaf despair,
Who during the night of impenetrable gloomy
    Shadows
Are not losing faith in the shine of the
    Morning's rays
They are blessed.[1]

Next year's essay will try to comprehend the strength and the spirituality necessary to take charge, responsibility and command in a similar situation.

P.S. We never can entirely foresee all the consequences, immediate or distant of any situations we are living through.

That Polish war of 1863–64 that engulfed the territory of most of present-day Poland, all of Lithuania, Bielorussia, the Ukraine and

The World Seen from the Distance of a Small Village

part of Latvia exhausted Russian resources, ruined the agriculture in the main breadbaskets of what at that time was Russia and brought the Russian economy to a critical low. In less than three years after suffocating the last resistance of that war, Russian was forced to make a unique decision in the whole of Russian history, to sell the territory of Alaska to America for 38 million French francs.

For Poland that war was a tragedy. But, when I look at all this tangle of events, maybe even for Poland it brought some blessing.

It could be hard to imagine the Cold War of the past decades if the Russian missiles directed against the U.S. were located not in Murmansk or Siberia, but in the rocks of the Rockies around Alaska's Petersburg or Ketchikan.

> Tadeusz Maciejczyk
> Milledgeville, May 27, 1996

To the more distant future, please, think about the leadership necessary to confront the danger of the offensive, of the cheap trash culture that in the name of freedom poisons the young and kills the higher culture in men, in societies, in the world. The danger is alarmingly enormous.

Book Four

Beverly LeHaye
President
Concerned Women of America

Dear Lady:

The tragedy of our time is that we are looking at every aspect of life not for the real things that life gives, but for generics.

In this way we created a monster of touchy-feely "goodness." This goodness became almost a religion with its priests, their dogmas and oratory to reach the masses and by this, those who want to be the powerful. It makes gains because it is easy; it is suggestive and is able to make a good show. The organizers using it can get position, influence and power and it doesn't require any merit.

This pseudo-religion, in the vacuum of spirituality, is penetrating, is convincing, is winning. But this "goodness" has no similarity to the true way of being good. It has not the fundamentals of love and with this commitment and responsibility.

The scholars of this kind of religion are everywhere. It requires no wisdom. Only cleverness and a capacity to be loud and shameless. The rewards for such generic leadership are abundant. Our society loves to be blinded. Seeing the truth requires some mobilization, profound changes in our habits in our expectations. Being good puts too many requirements on us. Showing goodness is easy. It leaves behind a mess and mounting problems in the future. But who wants to care about the future? For decades we got used to enjoying only today. We have a fear of tomorrow. Sometimes we even feel a kind of guilt, but we are not ready to give anything from our today.

And so, we created generics in medicines, in our air flights, in our family life and responsibilities, in our TV shows, in our expectation to get rich by not exactly working hard.

And so! Viva generics! Our scholars in generic society, generic family, generic diplomacy and politics are triumphant, are winning, are blinding us, and are leading us into a precipice, into an abyss. Who cares about this? Surely not our politicians. Their only preoccupation is to be re-elected.

                                          Tadeusz Maciejczyk
                                          June 2, 1996
                                          P.S. I am sending you some of my quarrels and observations, disappointments and battles.

The World Seen from the Distance of a Small Village

Veterans of Foreign Wars
Post 5418
Rock Falls, IL

    I was reading about your Flag Day ceremony celebrated for the memory of those who paid the ultimate price of their life so we can live as free men and women.
    In our place in Milledgeville, during the Memorial Day ceremony, in order to remember those who died and to make their sacrifice more meaningful, we started a tradition of inviting graduating students to write an essay about the need of spiritual strength in order to be a true leader.
    The legacy and the fruits of freedom printed in blood by those who died defending them, can be wasted and be lost so easily now, in the peacetime if our leadership loses its spiritual strength and richness.
    I send you the texts of those special inclusions in our ceremony. It contains also the theme for the next year's program.
    I also include a copy of my speech to Veterans in 1988 in which the idea of writing those essays started. I made also a few pages of a special preparation for them, to help to know themselves, which I also include.
    And in the last moment, I decided to put in my letter to Mrs. Beverly LeHaye where I worry about the direction our nation is taking.
    I wish you all the best.

                                          Tadeusz Maciejczyk
                                          Milledgeville, June 25, 1996

Book Four

To our Representative
United States Congress

Today in our church, the problem of the partial birth abortion law was raised. We received cards directed to our representatives in Congress to ask them to vote against the approval of this procedure.

I didn't just sign and return this card. I wanted to add to this action my own opinion and observations as a doctor and as a man old enough to be a witness to similar barbaric laws and actions in Hitler's Germany. The distance between this procedure and the gas chambers for the UNDESIRABLES is very short.

Morally, I do not see the difference between the doctor who performs such criminal acts in the name of social cleansing from the so-called "kapos" in the Nazi concentration camps.

During the war I was an *untermensch* (below human) and my legal rights were reduced to zero.

In this procedure, a living fetus is killed in cold blood without any remorse just in the last moment before the Constitution allows him the rights of a human being.

The nastiness of this procedure, the enormous nastiness and moral degradation of those who would allow such a crime to be permitted and lawful in the name of a special "goodness," and the so-called freedom of choice, is beyond the comprehension of any person who can look straight into his own eyes.

In my medical practice I have a few patients for whom the feeling of guilt destroyed their whole lives making them miserable, making the life of their whole families miserable as well.

Just two days ago, to one such patient who already was treated in all the best clinics around, who got no help from them and was clearly deteriorating, I recommended to her to go to church. (She hadn't gone there for years.) And to stand before God, to discuss the problem with the priest and to start to live again.

Those social cleansings of "undesirables" will plunge society into similar disabling guilt chains. Such escapes bring no freedom. They bring a lifelong moral torture.

Please, vote against this shameful law. How can we face the criminals of Bosnian atrocities if we legislate here for our internal consumption equivalent acts of cleansing.

Tadeusz Maciejczyk, M.D.
June 30, 1996

The World Seen from the Distance of a Small Village

Editor
Sports Illustrated

Dear Sir:

I thank you for the invitation to see and to appreciate "The Best of *Sports Illustrated*."

I have to confess to you that I am not the biggest admirer of the organized sports shows. About one year ago, I wrote about this in one of my letters and I even received a wonderful applause from one of the readers. I am sending a copy of that letter to you now.

I agree that sports and games related to them, are enormously valuable and should be an important ingredient in the life of every person. For the teenagers, it is like a prolonging of childhood play and dreams. For adults it helps to live a healthy life; it helps to relax, to relieve anxieties, to meet and to relate to others and above all to have illusions and to feel young again.

Such sports for everybody are very necessary complements for our mostly sedentary lives. Such sports should be promoted, should be kept inexpensive, available to everyone and in every place.

The organized, big sports didn't try to help people. It only used people in order to promote their own growth and wealth. It made only one kind of move toward people: to make them dependent fans. It didn't care to make those fans more healthy, more active, or even more friendly one to another.

Organized sports became a business.

As tall, this sport is interested in a physical stagnation of the public. Only such a public is eager to become a generic sport enthusiast, sitting and watching the big sports shows, becoming silly, very patriotic fans of certain teams, perceiving a substitute as something real; worshipping the otherwise unattractive, but over paid and over bullying idols of that sport as a kind of hero.

This generic sportsmanship for the masses, is not elevating, not activating, not improving those masses. On the contrary. It accentuates its passivity creating behind a vacuum, loneliness and stagnation in human souls.

I am sorry that I have such an opinion about the social ministry of our big sports industry.

But I know that the true, authentic sports are good for everybody.

Sports were created to promote physical and spiritual health in the society.

I would love to see a change in dealing with the problem of sports in our national sports magazines. I would like to see a magazine about sports that would not be one more business to exploit the misery and

Book Four

the emptiness of human beings, but a conscientious builder of positive personalities in every one of us.

For such a sport and for such a sports magazine, I would always do everything possible to increase its influence and to enhance its effects.

For the selfish, exploitation motivated, effectively strangulating and immobilizing the people commercial sports, I have no sympathy.

Tadeusz Maciejczyk, M.D.
Milledgeville, July 2, 1996

The World Seen from the Distance of a Small Village

Explanations to a Policy Survey from Concerned Women for America

Question No. 2: I do not know how to rank those problems. All of them are Number 1. All are interrelated; all of them have the same roots: the erosion of moral principles. Healing those roots could bring a spontaneous recovery in most of those problems.

Question No. 4: My opinion about Pres. Clinton is that he is speaking much, but is shallow, theatrical, opportunistic. Inspires no trust.

Question No. 5: I respect Senator Dole as a person. He was in his right place in the Senate, but he is not a leader. This country and the world at this time, needs inspiring leadership marked by greatness.

Question No. 6: General Colin Powell was a good military leader. Leadership required from a President is different. A candidate for the Presidency should have a vision, a sense of mission and a feeling that the time for his service is now, is urgent. General Powell didn't show such qualities. It was still not his time.

Question No. 7: Mr. Gingrich certainly is an exceptional man. He is controversial and polarizing. He is sufficiently persistent. He is a good tactician, but to inspire and to lead, he still has to grow.

Question No. 8: Al Gore definitely is not a leader. I do not sense in him the necessary strength, vision or direction. He was a good boy who entered his father's shoes. He is still trying to find his special place.

Question No. 9: Hillary Clinton has leadership capacity, but I would be afraid of her leading. She is ambitious, manipulative, secretive, using situations to serve herself. Most likely she doesn't like herself and she doesn't like anybody else. She is using people. She discards them afterwards. Probably she has no lasting friends.

Question No. 10: The United Nations can be a very important instrument in making the world better and safer. But even the best instrument needs a hand of the master to produce excellence. It is an instrument that requires a special care from every nation. It would be good if every nation would send their best intentions and talents to the United Nations.

Question No. 11: Education needs a unifying center. Look for my answer in the Rep. Committee survey.

Question No. 14: Every society has its segment of the population that is truly needy. The present welfare degenerated into huge bureaucracy, not redeeming, but perpetuating problems.

Question No. 15: None of those options can give any guarantee. If it is not directed primarily by true love, as a primordial force, it will fail.

Book Four

True love is not just a show of goodness. It requires vision, strength, and self-discipline. It needs Mother Theresa at its helm. How to do this?

Probably it is time to send this survey to you. The Republican Convention started and yesterday I listened to the speech of Colin Powell. Yes, he can be a great leader when he decides that the time for him is right.

To complement my survey, I am sending you some of my previous surveys or letters that will explain better some of the questions.

I cannot give you much money now. My practice is not what it was. In 1983, I refused to pay obligatory malpractice insurance and I lost hospital privileges. In 1987–90 I had a malpractice suit that I won without a lawyer's help. And now I have to concentrate to pay tuition. This is a priority.

I wish you the best results in your work.

Tadeusz Maciejczyk
August 13, 1996

The World Seen from the Distance of a Small Village

I.D.E.S. (Illinois Department of Employment Services)
Northern Region
260 East Indian Trial Road
Aurora, IL 60505

For some time I tried to make sense of your calculation of the employer's contribution and I am giving up.

For several years, since you devised your special formula that requires one year's advance payments of your taxation, I was required repeatedly to pay higher taxes, penalties that were 2–3 times bigger than those contributions, interest from those penalties and so on. A simple formula for evaluation that I used for decades became enormously complicated, became an excellent place for dirty fishing and continuous harassment.

In your letter from the 1st quarter of this year after my previous protests, you concluded that I have $27.01 credit in your account.

In your statement dated May 7, 1996, your demanded contribution was $50.78 (almost twice as much as calculated for trimester) with a penalty of $22.99 and interest of $3.08. There was no mention of the credit that I was given from last year.

It is very sad and very tragic that in this crucial important time when the confidence in our government is getting very thin, in this time our authorities lost their previous ability to communicate with their people using clear English language, substituting it with a convenient, incoherent mumbling of computer terms, numbers and shortcuts.

It is a pity that now, even a simple problem when coming form your agency, requires a special expert to calculate, to explain, to translate and by this requiring an additional lawyer's fee from your victims.

I am using this term "victim" very consciously. The honest was always very outstanding for its simplicity and clarity. Honesty doesn't need to hide behind your bizarre present communication. Trying to make sense of your statement, my conclusion was that you are playing a deceptive game for your special dark purpose.

As your game has been going on for years and it affects not only me, but thousands of other small employers who cannot afford special help in dealing with you, I have a right to ask:

1. Who exactly authorized you to make such a complicated puzzle from you collections, creating conditions that look like a very suspicious fishing ground?

Book Four

2. Why did it happen that from all the state agencies, only you are demanding that your contributions should be paid not quarterly, but in advance for a year.
3. To whom are you reporting the amount of money collected in this ingenious way of yours, including strange evaluations, penalties, interests and the special group designated as "other"?
4. How was this money spent and by whom?

The small employers who struggle to keep alive should have all the help from the state, should be dealt with special clarity should never become an easy victim of the smart, dirty tricks from such offices as yours.

If I am offending you with what I say in this letter, I am sorry. I want to make my communication clear.

I am sending a copy of this along with a certificate to Governor Edgar asking him to explain to me your special way of making bureaucracy mysterious and nauseating.

Also I am sending the copies of this letter to the Small Business Administration and to different places in Washington.

I am sorry that I was forced to write this letter.

Tadeusz Maciejczyk, M.D.
Milledgeville, August 18, 1996

The World Seen from the Distance of a Small Village

Letter to the Editor
Time Magazine Letters

Dear Sir:

Looking and listening to the images from the last Convention, I had a strange impression that those who were talking were not our most distinguished dignitaries, but small braggarts who were trying to tell wonderful stories about themselves, about what they did and what they still would do.

Doing so, the small braggarts want to call attention to themselves. They want to cover up their tortuous feeling of inadequacy and low self esteem and they want to convince everybody around them and also themselves that those inflated self-boastings were the truth.

Such small braggarts can be forgiven and helped.

When our highest dignitaries are using bragging and self-boasting to be loved, I feel uneasy.

And the society, which needs such bragging as a dope to get amused and in this way to decide to whom it wants to be its leader, such a society will not pass the test of history.

Tadeusz Maciejczyk
Milledgeville, September 7, 1996

Book Four

Illinois Department of Revenue
ITR - Taxpayer Notification
Document No. 96135-177-80-000
Tax year ended December 1995

To tell the truth, I do not know what you are talking about in your letter. My taxes were prepared by the Certified Public Accountants Lindgren, Callahan, Von Osdol & Col, Ltd. And I assumed they knew the rules.

Indeed those rules became very cruel for me last year.

Two main problems made from them a true showcase.

In June of 1995 I was forced to buy a car because my old one just stopped on the road. I bought a used car for $8,000. In my countryside practice a car is indispensable. I am still doing house calls and I have patients in four nursing homes in four different counties. That car was not considered for any tax discount. I had it only for my personal use and pleasures, I was told.

The second problem: My youngest daughter entered now the third year of architecture school. I pay for her tuition and maintenance that is about $22,000 with different pluses a year. For this, I didn't get even one cent of discount in taxation. She is over the age of twenty-three and it would be against the law, I was told.

Previously, my daughter finished four years of History of Arts at DePaul University in Chicago obtaining higher than a "cum laude' evaluation. Then, she entered two years of high mathematic college and finished it with straight A's. In the last two years she studied architecture and at present she is doing her third year there. Her results are excellent. Her architectural project s distinguish themselves with their elegance, simplicity and beauty. Her studies in different schools have a logical consequence and even for the future of this country, they should be finished.

The government, in its hunger for money, gives her no chances, not a minimum of help. As I was told, such an investment would be against the law. The last Convention's very loud pitch about education was just a fishing device to catch voters. The criminal laws suppressing excellence of education are on the books of tax accountants.

Against all odds, I decided that I will help my daughter to finish and to reach her dream.

If we shallow the educational standard even if we assume the two yeas of a diluted college for everybody as President Clinton promised with such a wonderful smile on his face, and we downgrade the quality and the perseverance to reach the excellence our place in the 21st century will be not the most glorious.

The World Seen from the Distance of a Small Village

And so, after paying your bleeding taxation and after helping my daughter in school, I am left with much less than $10,000.00 to live on for the year. By the grace of our wonderful, compassionate, taking-care-of-everything-Government, working as a doctor, I became a social pariah with below poverty levels means in which to live.

Life in the U.S. became a bitter experience for those who starve to be honest and independent. I can imagine that I am not the only parent pushed by the government into such a situation.

Probably thousands of other parents struggle with the same feeling of impotence of being castrated and downgraded and unable to fulfill their obligation because the taxation became a killer.

I do not want to relegate my responsibility. I do not want to teach my children how to be irresponsible in life.

The government, by forcing such attitudes on the parents, is making them feel helpless, growing bitter and frustrated. A frustration, if intense, is destroying, is diminishing. It can push into different ways of escape, into alcoholism, into passivity and self-deprecation or even domestic violence.

Our leaders are prone to such wonderful proclamations. Their squeeze on the middle class especially, in this case, what they are doing to the education of my daughter is nothing less than criminal.

I never wanted to be rich, but what is happening, what the government is doing, is beyond decency.

A government that suffocates normal life, that teaches irresponsibility, that induces frustration in families and consequently breaks family togetherness, stability and pride—such a government will bring America to disaster.

Tadeusz Maciejczyk
Milledgeville

P.S. I will ask the accountants for an explanation. If you are right, I will try to pay you before October 2. I just have no money to pay more penalties. And if this letter has a bitter tone, this bitterness is authentic. This protest of mine I will send whenever I can.

Book Four

Concerned Women of America
Washington, D.C.

Dear Ladies:

I thank you for your invitation to become a member of your organization. As you clearly explained in your letter, my participation will be very simple: I will just pay the bills.

I read your newspaper. I found it interesting and I put it in the waiting room for patient's information.

With all my positive evaluation of your work, I am not in very good shape to help you with money. I tried to explain this to you in my letters. With all my provincial naiveté, I believed that somebody there would read what I was trying to tell you in my story. Apparently what you saw in those letters was the M.D. behind my name with the conclusion that I have money and I should be a target.

I will not try to tell you again why I am not rich. After all my fights, that resulted in my medical work becoming restricted just to office visits for those who resist Managed Care, the taxes imposed on me became absurdly high. After paying tuition and maintenance of my youngest daughter's university, I was left with below poverty level means to live. Sometimes I have just enough of all those strangulations that more and more are put around the neck of all those who fight for an independent work and are not big or rich enough to push forward with the lawyer before them to break the ground and to watch.

In the first century of this era, Tacitus, the Roman Senator and historian made an observation that "the more corrupt the state, the more numerous the laws."

Our lawmakers made this country a paradise for lawyers; a paradise for every type of abuse, discouragement and torment for those who sincerely and honestly want to work.

I am sorry. I cannot help you. I tried, but apparently it was not enough. In responding to your survey, I considered that:
1. Women will never have a comfortable place in the military where, however it is calculated, each woman has to be in close contact with about 1000 sexually starved men. No law and no disciplinary procedure can make any satisfactory or viable situation from this. A woman's presence in such situations will always be disruptive.
It is always sad when somebody, instead of developing his natural potential tries to play somebody else.

The World Seen from the Distance of a Small Village

About 150 years ago, Cyprian Norwid, the great Polish poet, responding to violent Russianization of the country that created cries for armed resistance, said in one of his poems, "Not the sword, not the shield are defending the survival of the language, but the literary masterpieces."

No laws made in Congress, or in any other place can defend the moral strength or health of the nation. This can be defended or even be won by the personal conduct of the leader and the masterpieces of communication between him and the people.

Unfortunately we have an enormous abundance of those who talk and we have no communication. No one rises above the noise and confusion of those little men talks into which is submerged the population. The game of those talks is to obscure the uncomfortable truth and to win the popularity contest.

Already for a very long time, we as a nation, have no leaders. Only an abundance of politicians and of self-proclaimed "experts."

2. To respond to your third question, I am sending you a copy of my letter in which I declared myself a leader of a brand new minority. To proclaim my rights I used all the tricks that I learned from the author of the weekly column in our newspaper, the stout defender of every imaginable minority group.

My conclusion was that you cannot talk seriously with nonsense. After my letter that champion of minorities disappeared completely from view.

I see now that you have many more questions on the other side of your survey. I am not sure whether I haven't already passed the limit of your patience with me. What did you expect from your survey to make a fishing bait asking for an effortless marking of one of the three choices of every question and to send money? Such communication, in my judgment, only multiplies the superficiality of our proceedings. I consider it useless and harmful. It is one more lesson in how to avoid decisions, how to swim on the surface.

I intended to send you more of my papers, but I will limit them to this one that I promised in responding to question no. 3. It can make a good answer to different other positions.

I send you my best wishes.

Tadeusz Maciejczyk, M.D.
Milledgeville, January 22, 1997

Book Four

Newt Gingrich
National Republican Congressional Committee
Washington, D.C.

Yesterday, I received a letter from your headquarters. It was written on February 13 and it contained a membership card for me.

Reading that letter, I wondered how it could happen that such a monstrosity was permitted to be sent and to speak in the name of the Party.

Reading that letter I felt humiliated and degraded.

That letter was humiliating and degraded the whole Republican Party at least 100 times or more. It was humiliating also to the whole two-party system in America.

To me, when dealing with anybody, the most important aspect of that relationship is its sincerity and integrity.

Your letter was entirely phony and contemptuous. It treated the recipients as idiots, ready to jump into your embrace for the mixture of hypocrisy and flattery.

That letter will not increase your membership from among normal people. It was repelling to anybody with a minimum of dignity. Except this, that letter was completely empty, without any thought, idea or preparation for planning.

That letter showed clearly a stupid arrogance and contempt of the people from Washington who should be considered our elite to the primitive folks from the countryside.

Previously I had some ideas about Republican programs for the future, but after your letter, I felt that it would be pointless. Whatever the importance, whatever its value for eventual improvement, my letter would go to the waste paper basket even before giving it a glimpse.

If you really want me to write about my ideas, please notify me and tell me to whom I should direct such letters.

In the meantime, I am sending you my remarks from last year's scholarship ceremony in which I told my version of what true leadership should be and a letter to Concerned Women of America where I said what I think about our present "leadership."

In spite of the harshness of this letter, I wish you the best.

Tadeusz Maciejczyk, M.D.
Milledgeville, February 19, 1997

The World Seen from the Distance of a Small Village

P.S. I am sending a copy of this letter to local Rep. Authorities. Also I reserve for me the right to send my ideas to *Time Magazine*, *Newsweek* and *U.S. News & World Report*, including the copy of this letter if I do not hear from you.

Patrick B. Harr, M.D.
President
American Academy of Family Physicians
Kansas City, MO

Dear Sir:

I read your letter about the "Tar Wars" that would make young people more resistant to the temptation of smoking. To reach such an effect, Tar Wars created a program aimed at explaining to the 5th graders the dangers and consequences of smoking. Your letter did not convince me that such a program could have a good and lasting affect and decrease smoking addition among teenagers.

More than this. I worry that bringing such special attention to the enigma of cigarettes into the minds of 5th graders, even if it prompts them to make declarations and promises that at that moment would be entirely sincere and enthusiastic, will leave in the back layers of their minds special memories, a ready to touch and explore pattern, a dormant curiosity and the temptation of forbidden fruit. They will wait there for the right moment.

The tactics of the Tar Wars would be an excellent weapon against smoking if human behavior were exclusively rational and obedient to the conclusions and guidance of our thinking.

Buy this is not happening in real life. In our daily life we react to different situations and conditions not mainly with our brains. Mostly we react to them through different hormonal reactions, our emotional disposition of that moment, our different self-protective devices and many other very subjective forces.

We cannot escape from the powers of our emotions. They are especially forceful or even explosive, very frequently blind or even self-destructive during the teenage years.

The greatest factor for starting to smoke at that age is not the lack of knowledge about the consequences of additions. The age or 40 or even 30 seems to be very distant and not a primary concern for 5th graders.

Book Four

I have a strong feeling that those conferences for 5th graders will not decrease smoking addiction among teenagers. The greatest trigger factor for smoking during the growing years is a mixture of many factors. When I was young, during the war, it was an assuring invitation of the older man, "But man, smoke! You will look like a man."

The passage from childhood to the maturity of an adult man is marked by an abundance of moments of crisis, doubts and insecurities that desperately look for a cover. A fear of being unloved, unappreciated, unworthy, anger and rebellion that they cannot confess to anybody, the painful self-deprecation affects every teenager in a very personal way.

In our present time, the instability of family, the constant erosion or breakdown of values and traditions, the greater than ever abundance of temptations and stresses are the additional factors to break the best resolutions.

And so, I wonder whether it would not be better to not talk at all to the 5th graders about cigarettes and smoking. Instead we could concentrate our talking to them in a colorful and understandable for them explanation of what it means to grow, about different ways and dimensions of growing, what changes they can expect and how to cope with different stresses of those changes and how to even enjoy them and have a fun. It would be important to explain to them how a growing person can start to like himself and to be proud of what he is and of what he is trying to accomplish, how he can start a dream of achievements in his future.

It would be wonderful to implant into them a feeling of responsibility and what it means to be responsible at their age and in every age and situation later on.

Already in 5th grade it would be good to gently explain and to discuss with them what love really is. Already it would be useful to convince them that love is not only an attraction and feeling, but especially a commitment and care. Such an explanation could give them some base to think and to make decisions years later when the hormonal changes start to transform their lives.

In those talks to 5th graders, it would be very useful to explain what it would mean to their lives if they develop a habit and the strength to stretch and to get out from their hiding corners where they are immobilized by complexes, fears and inhibitions. Already then, they can learn to look for qualities that are not easily seen at first glance. Already then it would be good to warn them not go to after unrealistic rhetorics so frequent in our society as "Reach for the top! Give it your best! Don't settle for second best!" Make them seek growth, not perfection.

The World Seen from the Distance of a Small Village

Such a conference to the young would be much more proper and in my opinion much more necessary, creative and fruitful, much more challenging for a talk between doctors and teenagers.
My best wishes,

                        Tadeusz Maciejczyk, M.D.
                        February 27, 1997

Colin Powell
Chairman
President's Summit for America's Future

Dear Sir:

I listened to your interview on *20/20* and I read in *Time Magazine* about your plan to be a social shaker and mobilizer.
This includes a delicate area of life with many hidden emotions and complexes. To build harmony on such a field will require special leadership, strength and touch. And it can easily be spoiled and robbed from its freshness and purity by the ambitions of some.
Because of this, some kind of strong spirituality has to be injected into this movement to obtain the best and lasting harvest, durability and harmony. I listened to your speech during the Republican convention and I have faith that you can inject such a special spirit into this movement.
To obtain the best results all available ideas should be taken into consideration and deliberation before action. Gathering those ideas should fill up the first stage of your mobilization.
Thinking about this, I am sending you some of my letters from previous years. If they contain something useful for your plans, I will be glad.
I wish you the best in your work.

                        Tadeusz Maciejczyk
                        Milledgeville, April 16, 1997

Book Four

Presentation of my awards during Senior Honor Student Recognition Banquet on May 1, 1997

This year five students responded to my call to write an essay about the need of spirituality in any effective leadership. I am grateful to all of them.

It was not an easy task, but it was a work with potential to give a special touch and a special personal growth to those who responded.

To make classifications, I applied three criteria:
1. Natural leaders—what singles them out for leadership?
2. How does spirituality develop and enrich the gift of natural leadership?
3. What is the call for leadership, not in ordinary, average times, but in times of cataclysm, danger and pain? (How to generate strength, purpose and wisdom to lead the people in such circumstances.)

With these as a guide, I asked different people for separate evaluations on a scale from 1 to 10.

As a consequence of those evaluations, a premium of $400.00 was given to Ann Gertz and Janelle Janssen. The premium of $100.00 for daring to feel and to think as leaders and to respond was given to Talisa Hartje, Callie Surber and Charlotte Vos.

I am sorry that not one man made an effort to write about leadership. If they prefer effortless scholarships, then really they should never be leaders. We already have too many so-called "leaders" who only look for prestige and glory without original thought and sacrifice.

I firmly believe that giving effortless scholarships in the long range is not good either for those who receive, nor for those who give.

May 1, 1997
The first two works were sent to Veterans Headquarters with copies sent to The White House, Governor of Illinois, both Illinois Senators, District Representative, *Time Magazine, Newsweek, U.S. News & World Report*, all Illinois state universities.

The World Seen from the Distance of a Small Village

An Explanation to My Patients Who Were Under Stress

How Can I Cope with Stress?

The first principle in handling stress in my life is to know WHO I AM. If I do not know who I am, somebody else may try to tell me who he thinks I am. If I do not know me, the other people will manipulate me, pressuring me to be somebody I am not. I will feel stress when wearing masks, being unreal with others, living a double life. Insecurity always produces pressure in our lives and when we are insecure, we feel pressured to perform and conform. We try. Tension and pressure occurs as a result.

I have to know who I am by knowing WHOSE I AM.

The second principle of stress management is to know WHOM I AM TRYING TO PLEASE. I cannot please everybody. Even god couldn't do this.

But when I do not know whom I am trying to please, I will cave in under three things.
   A. Criticism - the concern of what others think about me.
   B. Competition - worry about somebody else getting something better than me.
   C. Conflict - I will be threatened when anyone disagrees with me.

We love to blame our stresses on other people, but when we get under pressure, we are choosing to allow other people to put us under pressure.

The third principle of stress management is ORGANIZATION. I have to know what I want to accomplish. I have to plan my life and set priorities. If not, I will be pressured by what other people think is important.

Every day I have to live either by priorities or I will live it by pressures. There is no other option. Either I set priorities in my life, or I will live by pressures, I will live under the tyranny of the urgent.

Preparation causes me to be at ease. Procrastination produces pressures and stress. Having CLEAR GOALS greatly simplifies lives.

The fourth principle: CONCENTRATION. Focus on one thing at a time. When I diffuse my efforts, I am ineffective.

The fifth principle: DELEGATION. Do not do it all yourself. Why do we not delegate? Why are we trying to do it all ourselves? For two reasons.
   A. Perfectionism - nobody else will do this as well ass I. But we simply have no time to do everything.

B. Insecurity - what if I give this to another and he does a better job? This is threatening to us.
But in order to be effective you must get other people involved. I cannot focus on more than one thing at a time and do it effectively.
The sixth principle: MEDITATION. Make a habit of personal prayer. Prayer is a gigantic stress reliever. It is a God-given tool for letting off our anxieties. A quiet time, getting alone with God, can be a decompression chamber for life's stresses. Many of our problems come from our inability to sit still. We are too busy to be quiet and think.
The seventh principle: RECREATION: Take time to enjoy life. It is the principle of relaxation and recreation. WE have to know when we need to relax. Rest and recreation in life are not optional. Our physical, emotional and spiritual constitutions demand periodic breaks. Balance in life is a key in stress management.
The eighth principle: TRANSFORMATION. Give your stress to God. I will never enjoy complete peace of mind until I have a relationship with God. Without a doubt. When I get in harmony with God, an inner strength will be given to me.

Make it a habit to consider these points when you start to feel pressured and tense.

This material was taken from a book of Richard Warren: *Answers to Life's Difficult Questions.*

Tadeusz Maciejczyk
May 25, 1997

The World Seen from the Distance of a Small Village

Letters to the Editor
Newsweek Magazine

RE: My impression of "A Physician's Lament"
Newsweek, June 9, 1997

Dear Sir:

This lament is more than justified.

Labeling every health care worker as a provider is nothing less than stripping them of their identity from their pride in what they became in life, from their self-image and their feelings of stability. It takes away from them the basic element of professional self-esteem.

The objective of such labeling has nothing to do with democracy or with work efficiency.

It helps to dominate and to nullify individuality. It degrades and it confuses. It permits manipulation and pressure; to use such "provider" when convenient, or to throw him away when it is not. Such a "provider" starts to doubt who he is and whose he is. The fundamental question of any human relationship if WHOM I SHOULD PLEASE starts to be blurred. Should this be a patient? The boss? My own conscience? In such conditions a normal work becomes increasingly stressful.

Looking into history, there is no doubt that the greatness of America was not built on the labor of "providers." The Soviet might was. I cannot imagine the existence of the Soviet system without equalizing everybody's label to *tovarish* (comrade)—the equivalent to our "provider."

America's greatness was created by people who knew who they were, who were proud of being themselves and who had a sense of dignity and of personal worth.

I think that in America the objective of the best possible medical care can be reached according to American tradition, not distorted by models transplanted here from the Soviet Paradise.

Best wishes to all.

Tadeusz Maciejczyk, M.D.
Milledgeville, June 4, 1997

Book Four

General Fred F. Woerner
Chairman
American Battle Monuments Commission

Dear Sir:

I received your letter in which you tell about your project of the World War II Memorial.

For several years I tried to create a kind of memorial for those who died defending freedom. My memorial had no geographic place. I wanted to implant it into the hearts of our high school graduates. I do not know whether my memorial will leave any bright light behind.

But, to answer your question:

Yes, Probably I am a veteran. Not American. During the Second World War, I was in Poland. My story from that time is different from yours.

On September 1, I was ready to go back to school. I was fifteen and I was about to start my third year of Gymnasium. Instead, that day started with the early morning thunder of bombs falling on the town. Two days later, dressed in my Boy Scout uniform and riding a bicycle, I was a messenger in our town hall.

On September 5 our troops were retreating through the town and in my uniform I went with them. That chapter of my life came to a close on September 21. It was a day that I will never forget.

I remember the night before. I was walking between soldiers in their ditches. Some of them were sleeping; others were vigilant. To the north of us, the noise and bright explosions didn't stop for a moment. The fortress of Brzesc didn't give up. Before us everything was dark and quiet.

That order and the will to defend was shattered completely the next morning. With disbelief I saw the same soldiers throwing arms. "We cannot defend this place any more," they said. For four days the Soviets were entering and advancing from the east in accordance with the Ribentrop-Molotov pact. The lines of the two invaders were almost closing. With the wide-open eyes of a fifteen-year old boy, I saw other soldiers digging deeper ditches, throwing arms into them and covering themselves with the earth. They will not get them. Or maybe we could use them later. I saw small groups searching for the best short arms. They planned to pass the Soviet line, enter Romania and from there go to France.

For me, that day looked like the end of the world. My emotional despair put me into a trance-like state. I entered an empty barn and there I had my first direct talk with God. I do not remember how long I was there in that barn. When I finally got out, the place was completely empty. The day

The World Seen from the Distance of a Small Village

was warm. The sunshine was wonderful. From the north the same thunder continued uninterrupted. In spite of everything, I felt changed. In place of previous turmoil, I felt relaxed and at peace. I looked around and after some vacillation, I started my long walk home.

Two years ago, I wrote to *Time Magazine* responding to an article of the scholars in theology that asked whether we still can believe in miracles. In that letter, I described my final chapter of my war adventure. I wanted those scholars to explain to me a special moment that I lived in that adventure. Until now, nobody could do this.

Your story about your entrance into the wartime was only a deviation from the main objective of your letter. You told me about the need for another World War II monument in Washington.

I tried to build here in this small place something that could also be called a monument to those who fought and died in that war. It was structured differently. In 1988 during Memorial Day, I made a speech to local veterans in which I suggested how to honor those men who died for us to be free. It fell onto deaf ears. Nobody was interested.

To break the silence, five years ago, I established my scholarship that here has been nicknamed "Scholarship Challenge."

That scholarship demanded form candidates a special work. They had to write an essay about the need for spiritual strength in order to be a leader. Those candidates were expected to read their essays to the public during the Memorial Day ceremony. Then they received the prize from the commander of our unit.

That project lasted four years. It didn't survive. It was messing up the normal course of the ceremonies.

I am sending you a copy of my speech to veterans in 1988. I wonder whether that project could have enough merit to create some positive influence in the souls of our present school age generation.

When I was small, my mother told me that a man never stops being a soldier in his lifetime. He always should be ready to defend his convictions and his beliefs. And I was trying.

I am not sending you money. Maybe later. At present I have to concentration my not very big resources on my immediate intentions.

I send you my best wishes.

Tadeusz Maciejczyk
Milledgeville, June 22, 1997

Book Four

July 10, 1997

The American Academy of Family Physicians
4736 Main Street
Lisle, Illinois 60532

Tadeusz Maciejczyk, M.D.
Milledgeville, IL 61051

Dear Dr. Maciejczyk:

Thank you for sharing your letter to the editor of *Newsweek* in response to the June 9 article, "A Physician's Lament." Your dislike for the word "provider" as a label for physicians is shared by many of your family physician colleagues. They too feel that it denigrates the profession and wounds their pride.

I was interested to see the information you shared on the scholarship for students on the need for spirituality for effective leadership. I am pleased to see that you are actively supporting the development of your town's young people.

                            Sincerely,

                            Vincent D. Keenan, C.A.E.
                            Executive vice president

The World Seen from the Distance of a Small Village

America's Promise
The Alliance for Youth
909 North Washington Street
Suite 400
Alexandria, VA 22314

I read about Oracle 100 millions commitment mainly to place a network computer on every child's desk in grades K-12 in the United States and I was stunned.

I do not consider such goodness of heart as progress.

More than this! I consider that it is an attempt for a glamorous, but criminal and irresponsible shortcut in the always serious and not easy task of educating.

It will create a generation that will be unable to use their own brains and skills for basic mathematics or for basics of any other subject.

It will create a sedative and accommodating assurance that cheating hard work and common sense is OK; that hard work to create a strong and healthy foundation for later developments is foolish and outdated; that what really counts in life is a smooth surface without any worries about what such a surface can cover up.

Eliminating the understanding for the need for a solid foundation work in every aspect of life will create a generation that will have a disregard and aversion for hard, solid work altogether. They will have no satisfaction of truly growing and understanding. They will be unhappy. They will suffer from boredom and from inside emptiness. They will need more entertainment, more kicks and more drugs.

Boredom is the biggest enemy of any human being. It takes away the building of true self-esteem that convinces us of our inner worth.

It will deviate the learning timetable from work of mind, character, discipline formation into games to satisfy curiosities and searching for fancy.

It will not help to develop a healthy lifestyle.

It will alter the normal childhood development.

It will produce eye and vision complications.

It will give children many bad lessons for which they have no life experiences to evaluate, to judge and to experiment. Consequently it can open a completely new book in criminology. The warnings about this are already multiplying.

Being good requires more than just providing facilities.

I sincerely believe that computers have no place in primary schools. It can be considered only for the last semester of the last year in high

Book Four

school. That would be a reasonable educational timetable to explain computers.

>Tadeusz Maciejczyk, M.D.
>Milledgeville, August 2, 1997

The World Seen from the Distance of a Small Village

Letters to the Editor
Newsweek Magazine

I am sending you a copy of my letter to America's Promise in which I express my point of view about their project to put a network computer on every child's desk from Kindergarten to 12th grade.

I imagine that in such a way the computer providers would create a wonderland for our kids. They would practically eliminate the present, already-outdated education system. The teachers, the present education providers would be unnecessary and out of fashion. Computers would educate and would produce much more up to date citizens for the 21st century.

And a strong possibility exists that education provided by computers would create an additional boom in the economy and in well-being. The entertainment providers, the kicks providers, the drug providers, the leisure and every kind of satisfaction at every level providers would be in high demand.

And if that happens, the growth in the economy would pass all expectations. We would employ more justice providers. More law and order providers, more prison care providers. I am sure that providers of our legislature would work extra hours and solve all those problems. Also the public image authority providers with the president as the highest authority provider would explain everything and would promise all the funds necessary for new advances or new solutions. And of course the tax providers (us) will be delighted to provide for all that would be considered necessary.

Speaking for my profession, we, the health care providers, will try to stick out from below the Managed Care giants' boots and help. Some of us still remember the Hippocratic oath.

I would be grateful to you if you would distribute copies of this letter of mine to all news providers working for *Newsweek*.

> Tadeusz Maciejczyk, M.D.
> The Health Care Provider
> Milledgeville, August 4, 1997

P.S. It is very sad if somebody is forced to use crutches before he knows how to walk.

Book Four

Beverly LeHaye
Chairman
Concerned Women for America
Washington, D.C.

Dear Lady:

I agree that teaching sexuality to children before the natural timing for this, is interfering with the normal childhood logical, mental and emotional formation. It robs them from their natural true childhood and creates future problems.

Teaching them, introducing them into the world of homosexuality, whatever the excuse, is criminal. It uses the innocence of children for their own games and interests. It is dishonest, dirty and ugly.

In spite of my beliefs, I will not write or send your card to my representative about this. They usually go where the wind blows. To build a future on such a foundation will disappoint. A mobilization of public opinion, a public outcry, more surely would show to our representatives how to vote.

Except this, I do not like to call our representatives "honorables." Somebody who behaves in an honorable way doesn't need such servile bows. Somebody who loves them, doesn't deserve them.

In the absence of really caring for what is right among those who decide, well done ridicule can still be the best weapon. Those who are so preoccupied with their own sexuality or homosexuality are using mercilessly the children to promote their own place and weight to be counted.

I am sending you a copy of my letter to our local newspaper with which I silenced the local stout defender of all imaginable minorities. It did more than all previous persuasions of others.

With this occasion, I am sending you also my last letters about teaching computers in grade school that I consider to be wrong.

My best wishes to your organization.

Tadeusz Maciejczyk, M.D.
Milledgeville, August 28, 1997

P.S. I am not sending you money. I am trying to be independent in my medical work and I feel all the pressure by local clinic and to some extent by the hospital to break me down and put here a satellite. Such a satellite will start to work just at my nose in October. Freedom in the U.S. is getting thinner every year.

The World Seen from the Distance of a Small Village

Diane M. Komisky
Journalist
The Journal-Standard
Freeport, IL

Dear Lady:

I read your article about Milledgeville to get a new medical clinic. Why not? America is a free country.

In your letter I want to clarify one of your sentences. Did you say that now I am in my seventies and I have no hospital privileges?

Without explanation, that sentence remains open to negative interpretations and represents only half of the truth, which is never very honest.

Yes, I am in my seventies, but I am healthy and I do not intend to retire.

I have no hospital privileges, but this represents no negligence or misconduct on my part.

I lost my hospital privileges when in 1983, I opposed the obligatory, costly malpractice insurance for doctors in order to practice. That demand was based not on the need, but on blackmail. If you do not pay, you will be destroyed. That insurance was a request for a bribe. It was not good for medicine, not good for people, not good for the country.

I made my stand on that matter and I took the consequences. Still now I would not do this differently.

Talking about hospital privileges for family practitioners, I want to inform you that a new trend exists in different parts of America in which those doctors voluntarily limit their practices referring patients with special needs to specialists, or to hospital based doctors.

Such an arrangement gives the family practitioners more time to dedicate to their patients and to develop skills required in the immediate contact with average medical needs of the people.

Hospital obligations are not helping to develop such a contact.

This arrangement goes into the right direction and has a future.

I am sending you some of my letters from 1983 and my recent one about my view on Managed Care.

I send you my best wishes.

Tadeusz Maciejczyk, M.D.
October 15, 1997

Book Four

Illinois Department of Revenue
Withholding Adjustment Unit
Springfield, IL

I received your "notice to withhold" letter with a request to pay $11,113.69 for IL 941 taxation of the 4th quarter of 1997 and I was truly amused.

My small, countryside, solo practice is severely limited in its true potential because I refused to pay malpractice insurance and consequently I lost my hospital privileges and in spite of all this, my practice is able to generate such wonderful taxation for the State.

My office is employing one full time nurse, one clerk who comes only in the afternoons and one cleaning lady who comes in twice a week. Should I increase their salaries to the height that would make your "notice to withholding" reasonable?

Reading your letter, I got the impression that in that request you are a prophet of the future of the medical profession in America. You are a visionary as Jules Verne was about 150 years ago when he wrote *Around the World in Eighty Days* and other similar books.

If the collectivization of medicine continues, it will reach the effects of farming collectivization in the Soviet paradise. Soon I will need in my office not only a nurse, but computer specialists, coding specialists, OSHA safety specialists, malpractice protecting specialists, a special stuff to read and memorize all new directives and bulletins that with each month becomes thicker and more threatening and so on, and so on.

The absurd surrounding medical services at the present time is growing more spectacular, more unreal and more grotesque each day. It is suffocating, paralyzing, restraining, making an artificial dance in order to look well to the public and to make doctors slavish subservants.

The present collectivization of medicine, creating legions of supervising commissars and infiltrating it with security agents who create each time longer lists of condemned medical field workers is not an American way to deal with obvious problems. It is an ugly escape and a show of goodness for our timid and hungry for applause politicians.

We, the medical field workers work in shame and bondage.

Only free medicine and freedom to act can bring the best from men. Slavery creates only parasitic commissars and security agents.

I hope you will be able to correct this obvious nonsense.

Tadeusz Maciejczyk, M.D.
Milledgeville, February 18, 1998

The World Seen from the Distance of a Small Village

National Republican Congressional Committee

I read your "Dear Friend" letter and . . . I am so sorry. You can consider me as burned out. I do not want to belong. I lost my faith.

During the years of my enthusiasm, I was sensitive to issues. I wrote. I was responsible and I took my responsibility as a citizen seriously.

From those years, I learned from you one very clear reality.

For you I was never more than a convenient toy to play with: to inflate me with enthusiasm when the timing was convenient to you and to squeeze for money with any pretext.

My letters written to you were practically never answered. And if sometimes I got an answer, it was written in special, characteristically Washington jargon that with many pompous words says nothing.

No, I have had enough.

I have no trust or confidence even in the slightest sincerity of any party. They never help people grow. Their love for anybody is conditional. Their messages to us, the ordinary mortals contain only an enormous self-glorification and unending blame of everybody else.

In this aspect everybody around here agrees with me. In such a situation I want to be free and guided by my own views and choices.

Sincerely,

Tadeusz Maciejczyk, M.D.
Milledgeville, March 4, 1998

Book Four

1997 Economic Census

I was trying to fill out your census.

It is very general and it tells very little about the many changes that are developing in the health care industry. Those changes in many aspects are not very good indicators for the normal and healthy future of the health care situation in America.

From many others I am sending you three of my letters that can say more about my work here and about the trend that is appearing more and more unhealthy, unwise and each time more aggressive and tragic.

The hospitals' fight for territory and domination is going in such a direction.

Sterling Hospital's satellite clinic here in this small village of 1200 is already made up and soon will be ready to function.

In the Sterling-Dixon war of attrition, Sterling hospital made its clinic on the side of the Dixon clinic. The Dixon hospital made its clinic in Sterling.

In Sterling the Steel Mill built its own clinic for their workers because the Sterling Clinic became enormously expensive to them. Now in front of that clinic of Mill Dixon and Sterling have their satellites.

Can a general study be made of such a situation all over the country to measure the extent of that costly confusion? Can some common vision and common sense be established in this field?

The primary care medicine should be free from managerial manipulations and ambitions. That would be the simplest and the most liberating; it would be the most sensitive to the needs of patients and much less expensive.

I wish you the best in your work.

Tadeusz Maciejczyk, M.D.
Milledgeville, April 17, 1988

The World Seen from the Distance of a Small Village

Charles Grassley
United States Senator from Iowa

Dear Sir:

Yesterday I saw you on television. You were worried, discussing the growing danger in the spread of drug addiction in our schools and you were anxious to find a remedy for those increasingly dangerous infestations in our society.

Looking at you on TV at that moment, I decided to send you some of my letters in which I discuss the roots of this and other maladies. I hope they can be helpful.

I also want to tell you that in my judgment, drug dealers, when arrested, should never be sent to jail. Jail can never redeem them.

More than this, jail sentences give them a free-of-charge seminar in how to improve their trade and how and where to look for new connections.

And still more than this. Jail time gives those dealers very close contact with other prisoners who are very vulnerable, but still uninvolved in drug dealings, who can be mobilized for such activities after finishing their sentences. In this way the infestation with drugs can only increase.

I think that the proper punishment for drug dealers should be logical, should be strict and should be truly painful to them. Most dealers enter the trade for money. The most logical and most painful consequence in those problems should be a complete confiscation of everything they have both directly and indirectly.

Then they should be placed into special housing that is under constant supervision and given the appropriate length of work to make restitution to society. The pay for that work should be just enough to survive.

In cases where drug dealing results in death, the person who sold the drug should be charged with murder for monetary reward. For the good of society, such a sentence should be enforced. The only way to reduce such a sentence for the arrested person would be if he reveals who his supplier was. Then this supplier should take his place on Death Row.

Such general procedures would help to reach the highest centers of drug trafficking in the U.S. and break their structure.

Book Four

If our leaders respond timidly to this pandemic destruction of society by drugs they would be unworthy of the trust given to them. I send you my best wishes.

Tadeusz Maciejczyk, M.D.
Milledgeville, April 19, 1998

William Melvin Price, M.D.
Belleville, IL

Dear Sir:

I received your letter with a call to help to turn back the growing governmental intrusion into health care.

I do not know what your plan is and your agenda to promote more market-driven health care reforms, to force the government to regulate less and to dismantle the powerful health care bureaucracy.

My observations are that the doctors did very little at the beginning of the bureaucratic takeover of health care services and I do not see them doing anything effective at present. Accommodation, surrender, what in those changes would be for me, adjustment, giving up the principles for the promises, were easier, more preferable.

If I see that you are doing serious down to earth planning, that you have an idea and you are entirely committed, I will support you. In the meantime I am sending you some of my papers about my past battles and about my present stand on the issues.

If you would read them, perhaps my papers could give you some new insights. They represent a true experience in a true head-to-head confrontation with different forces that added and effectively killed the system of free medical practices and subdued it to a rigid bureaucracy with its increasingly numerous despotic commissars and secret security agents.

I wish you luck. If you win and you are faithful to your mission, your work will not be easy.

Tadeusz Maciejczyk, M.D.
Milledgeville, April 26, 1998

The World Seen from the Distance of a Small Village

Merck & Col, Inc.
P.O. Box 4
West Point, PA 19486

    I saw your advertising of Propecia on television and as a leader of my minority, I have no choice but to protest and to condemn your intrusion into the inner life, togetherness and common stand of our members.

    Our minority is the "Minority of the Bald." This minority was established toward the end of 1994 with my letter to our local newspaper. We wanted to be as vocal and consequently as important and powerful as all other minorities were at that time in history.

    We wanted the same special rights, special privileges and similar access to dignitarial positions as other minorities. And we were determined to keep those our special rights, even if everything around us would collapse.

    Your introduction of Propecia into the market interferes with the pride, the principles and the growth of our minority. It can be disruptive and debilitating for us. It threatens our whole minority movement.

    Because of this, we are determined to defend our Constitutional rights. Your shameless announcement of Propecia could destroy our movement, could cause defections from our ranks and could put into question our common ties.

    Because of all this, we, in order to compensate for our anguish, demand satisfaction. We demand from you no less than 100 million dollars paid in cash.

    To explain better our feeling of tragedy caused by the appearance of Propecia, I am sending you a copy of my original letter in which I spelled out the purpose and the methods of calling public attention to our movement.

    And I warn you not to treat our determination lightly. We are ready to do anything for such money.

    Yours truly,

    Tadeusz Maciejczyk
    Established leader of our minority
    Milledgeville, April 28, 1998

Book Four

Along with diplomas, this letter was given to the 50 graduating students from Milledgeville High School in 1998.

Love - what is it?
Some suggestions according to St. Paul in his First Letter to the Corinthians:

> The love of which he speaks is slow to lose patience.
> It always looks for a way to be constructive.
> Love is not possessive.
> Neither is it anxious to impress,
> Nor does it cherish inflated ideas of its own importance.
> Love has good manners
> And does not pursue selfish advantage.
> Love is not touchy or fragile.
> It does not keep an account of evil,
> Or gloat over the wickedness of other people.
> On the other hand, love is glad
> With all good people whenever truth prevails.
> Love does not give up on others.
> Love knows no end to its trust,
> No fading of its hope.
> Love outlasts everything.
> Love is in fact the one thing
> That will still be standing when all else has fallen.

(Paraphrase of 1 Corinthians 13:4–8)

One of the greatest needs of every human being is to love and to be loved. This need we feel during all our lives, from infancy, until old age. This need is especially powerful at the end of the teenage years and the beginning of adulthood, when we unconsciously engage ourselves in an active search for somebody special to love.
Maybe these few pages could help you to find what to look for and what to avoid.

The World Seen from the Distance of a Small Village

What L-o-v-e Does

Love
Accepts you wherever you are.
Affirms your goodness and giftedness.
Cares about you, wants you to know that you are okay.
Challenges you to be all you can be.
Empathizes—knows what it is like to be you.
Encourages you to believe in yourself.
Is gentle in its way of dealing with you.
Keeps confidences—your secrets are safe.
Is kind—is always for you, on your side.
Laughs a lot, always with, never at you.
Looks for goodness in you and finds it.
Makes you feel glad that you are you.
Overlooks your foolish vanities, human weakness.
Prays for your needs and your growth.
Sees good things in you that others had never noticed.
Shares itself with you, by self-disclosure.
Speaks up when you need someone to defend you.
Is tactful even when confronting you.
Takes responsibility for its own behavior.
Tells you the truth always and honestly.
Thinks about you and your needs.
Is tough or tender, depending on your needs.
Understands your ups and downs, allows you "bad days."

What Love Doesn't Do
Love doesn't abuse you, or take you for granted.
Ask you to march to a different drummer.
Blame you or carry angry grudges.
Bully you by anger, a loud voice or tears.
Get you into win-lose arguments.
Give you unsolicited advice.
Judge you or tell you "what your whole trouble is."
Just tolerate you as a condescending favor.
Make you prove yourself again and again.
Needs always to be right, to have all the answers.
Pout or refuse to talk to you.

Book Four

Punish you vindictively for being wrong.
See and call attention to itself.
Show off—just to let you know where you stand.
Undermine your confidence in yourself.
Use you for its own purposes and then discard you.
Ventilate its emotions on you as a garbage dump.
Write you off because you did not meet its demands.[2]

This material was taken from a book, *A Life-Giving Vision* by John Powell, S.J. In your special moment of graduation and dreams, I wish you the inner fulfillment in your life.

I felt that the content of those papers from the book *A Life-Giving Vision* by John Powell, S.J. would have no chance to influence, to reach those who would benefit most from this wonderful eye-opening advice for healthy life planning, if that advice would be permanently locked up in a book that seldom reaches the hands of those who surely need such guidance the most.

Since 1988 I gave those lines probably to more than 1000 mostly young persons. I saw in them sudden interest, concentration and an internal involvement. I had a great feeling that I was helping and for this I am enormously grateful to John Powell.

Tadeusz Maciejczyk, M.D.
Milledgeville, 1998

The World Seen from the Distance of a Small Village

U.S. News & World Report
Letter to the Editor

RE: "Jesus and the Hustlers" by John Leo, June 15, 1998

True art is an expression of the human spirit and has the power to elevate and to give special vision on life, on the riches of nature and on human longings.

"Art" that slanders and spits indiscriminately on everything is not art. An "artist," who needs such devices to be seen and to impress, sooner of later will be completely ignored and forgotten.

Terrence McNally's creation, rather than art, looks to me like vomit from his sick stomach. He has to feel very miserable inside in spite of his three Tonys. For him I feel only pity and compassion. It looks to me that such monstrous "creations" as his, are nothing more than desperate, nasty and ugly cries for help.

Those "creations" do not deserve any violent reactions from those who feel offended by them. They should be ignored. The souls of those "artists" should be given a helping hand.

Tadeusz Maciejczyk, M.D.
Milledgeville, June 11, 1998

Book Four

Letter to the Editor
Newsweek Magazine
New York, NY

Dear Sir:

    I read "The Parent Trap" and I couldn't believe my eyes. According to Judith R. Harris, since the moment when sperm meets ovum, a new assembly of chromosomes takes place, the newly formed life enters into a long emotional, mental, spiritual and formative slumber until the next distant moment when such a creature meets its peers.
    A few years ago, after another such public explosion of unfulfillment, I wrote to our local newspaper about the healthy child-parent interaction that leads to mutual growth and joy.
    I am sending you a copy of that letter. I finished that letter with a general summary that good raising of children can be wonderful and most rewarding in the poorest of places and can be a failure among the most affluent. Not the money spent, not the social circles, not even education are the main factors. What counts is the true love given to the child and the time spent on true communication.

Tadeusz Maciejczyk, M.D.
Milledgeville, September 2, 1998

P.S. I was giving that letter to some of my patients who one way or another needed an explanation. I put this letter together with two more about sports in high school and about our sports for adults. So, I am sending you these three letters together. Maybe they could be of some interest to you.

The World Seen from the Distance of a Small Village

Dear Ann Landers:

I am reading now your book *Wake Up and Smell the Coffee* and yesterday I was reading a letter from Colonel B. McD. about his special moment when he really felt what freedom is and what it means. I also read the story of Roger Doub who fell from the surge tank and was saved by a stranger, who was working in the same place only that one special day.

I have a similar story.

I described it in my letter to *Time Magazine*. I wrote that reacting to *Time*'s article entitled: "Can We Still Believe in Miracles?"

Today, the 27 of September, makes exactly 53 years since the day in which my story began. On that day, I started my unique journey to freedom.

I took the most feared, dangerous, untested route across East Germany. Practically I didn't know anything about its dangers. If I succeeded and I passed through, I have to say, it was not because of my merit, but something I wonder and cannot comprehend until now.

It looks to me that even if it was my adventure, and it was I who took the risks, it was planned and executed to the smallest detail somewhere high above me. In that journey, I was only a pawn transported safely from one place to another. In every moment of danger there was someone or something to help, to guide, to advise, to warn. It was almost a jet trip with swift smooth passage through all obstacles. In five days I was safe and free.

That day, 27 of September, 1945, I was preparing my rucksack. Those days I was living in a house of one German lady. I was afraid to stay with my friends. The police were after me.

In one moment of that morning, when I was rolling bandages, putting them into places easy to reach, that lady was standing in the door of my room looking in silence at me. Then she left for a moment and came back and brought me two shirts of her only son who was killed on the Russian front. She handed them to me and said, "Wherever you go, this maybe could be of some use to you."

This was a goodness in practice that entered deeply into my soul.

I am sending you a copy of my letter to *Time Magazine* as one more testimony to the goodness of the human heart, to the priceless feeling of freedom and to the guidance from above that we cannot explain nor comprehend.

My best wishes to you.

Tadeusz Maciejczyk
September 27, 1988

Book Four

Addition to *Time Magazine* Survey

1. Because it is always important and because at this time it became such a burning issue, I would like to add two topics to your list. It should not be a one-time event, but a continued debate with the nation.

    a. Present expression
       (Behavior Determinate of Morals and morality in an actual American ways of life.)

        1. Awakening to, assimilation of what is moral, development of conscience in early childhood.
        2. Growth and expression of moral principles in adult years.
        3. Importance of the moral for stability and inner happiness.
        4. Unchanging moral rules that cannot be bent by cultural or civilization advances or by wealth or social status.

    b. Responsibility

        1. How it enters into the soul at an early age.
        2. How it makes or breaks men, families, societies, nations and the world.

I tried to express what I was thinking in the best way I could. I hope you can make sense of this. I include a few papers of mine that could further illustrate what I mean.

I hope you have enough patience to read all my papers. Every one of them is touching real life.

> Tadeusz Maciejczyk, M.D.
> Milledgeville, October 8, 1998

The World Seen from the Distance of a Small Village

Larry Dossey, M.D.
223 N. Guadalupe #169
Santa Fe, NM 87501

Dear Sir:

I read your book *Prayer is Good Medicine* and I am answering your request from the last page of that book. I am sending you my stories that could be useful or interesting in your research.

I want to add another story of mine because it relates very well to the content of your book. It happened during the first winter of World War II.

I had a toothache. It was intense and without any relief. It lasted all day, through the evening and deep into the night. My face was swollen. I couldn't swallow and most likely I had a fever. I felt enormously tired. There was nothing to help the pain or infection. I couldn't sleep and I was restless.

It was maybe 3 A.M. when suddenly I realized that I didn't do evening prayers. I was too weak to get out and pray on my knees at my bedside as I always did at that time. Also the room was very cold. The precious coal was only for cooking and not for heating.

And so, remaining in bed, I started to pray, "Our Father," saying it in a loud voice, maybe in a whispering voice through my swollen mouth. I cannot say at what moment of that prayer I fell asleep.

I woke up the next day without a toothache, without a fever, without swelling of my face. I felt great. During the next almost six years of the war and post war, I never had any problem with my teeth.

Only many years later, I started to wonder what really happened during my prayer that night.

I am sending you my best wishes for the continuation of your work. We never know who can be touched.

Tadeusz Maciejczyk
Milledgeville, November 12, 1998

Book Four

Susan M. Peterson
Provider Recruitment Associates
Wellmark Health Network, Inc.

Dear Lady:

I received your letter with notification that I was rejected from your health network PPO provider list.

I understand and I do not ask you to change your mind.

I am writing to explain why I decided not to have malpractice insurance, even if because of this, my hospital privileges were denied to me. I want to speak loudly about my convictions and my stand.

I am sending you some of my letters from the time when I had to decide in my conscience what to do to respond to the massive blackmail of malpractice litigations. I am sending you:

1. Some letters from my fight against obligatory bribes in the form of malpractice insurance in order to be permitted to practice medicine.
2. Some of my letters where I explain why medicine in America should not be herded in business-minded managed care, but should remain free.
3. I am sending you a copy of my letter to *Time Magazine*.
4. I am sending you a photo of my oil painting of myself. It is called "The House Call."

If you are interested in reading my letters from the time of my malpractice suit, please, give me a ring. I am sending you my best wishes for your work to contribute to the creation of a better, more fulfilled, happier America in the future.

Tadeusz Maciejczyk, M.D.
Milledgeville, November 15, 1998

The World Seen from the Distance of a Small Village

Time Magazine
My response to your five-question survey

In answering your survey, I want to tell you about three problems that could change and improve if you would put your effort and prestige behind.

Problem 1
I am thinking about the working mothers of very young children. A mother of preschool children should have the official recognition and status of a full time worker and consequently for those years she should obtain Social Security benefits. New prestige and recognition should be given to dedicated mothers. Guidance and help should be available to those who need them. The right approach to this problem and an envisioning of needs and remedies could create a better future for all.

Problem 2
It is a paradox of extremes between the intensity of sports education, sports drills and sports competition during school years and an almost absolute lack of even the minimal available facilities to continue that sport the next day after graduation. Is such a situation normal and emotionally healthy?

Could you explore the possibility of creating effective remedies for this problem? Can motivation, a spirit of spontaneity, creativity, pride from achievement, accomplishment and management of such needs be seeded into society?

Problem 3
Smoking, drinking, use of drugs by teenagers. Is the Tar War the answer to this problem? I wrote about this to the president of Family Practice Physicians, but he considered my point of view unrealistic. What is the opinion of the experts? What are your conclusions? What can be done about this persistent, dangerous problem?

I am sending you copies of my letters in which I talked about all those situations. With this occasion, I am sending you my observations about medical practice in the U.S. and to make my presentation to you my painting of myself. It hung in my waiting room and people nicknamed this picture "A House Call."

My best wishes in your work.

Tadeusz Maciejczyk, M.D.
March 3, 1999

Book Four

Letters to the Editor
U.S. News & World Report

Re: My comments on "Melancholy Nation" (March 8, 1999)

    I vacillated about whether to write to you about my sudden realization about what melancholy could be. It came to me when I read your article.
    The human body is a composition of three elements: the physical body, the mind and the spirit. Without harmony between those three elements, we enter into a state of stress.
    We know where in the brain are the centers of our body. We have a fairly clear idea which parts of the brain are necessary for our mind to operate.
    Could it be possible that somewhere in the autonomic centers of the hypothalamus exist material structures of our spirit?
    Could it be that those organic spiritual centers could produce some kind of pre-neurotransmitter that affects the known neurotransmitters and changes our moods?
    Is it possible that when we increase to the extreme our preoccupation towards our body and mind, and in this way neglect or silence the spirit, the disharmony can start to grow, reaching the dangerous point when we lose the meaning of our lives?
    Can a search for the spiritual center of our brain be a realistic part of medical research? Can a rediscovery of our own very personal for everybody spiritual life practices be a part of healing? Can the researchers make inroads into such secrets in our lives?

                                      Tadeusz Maciejczyk, M.D.
                                      Milledgeville, March 8, 1999

The World Seen from the Distance of a Small Village

Time Magazine
$833,337.00 Entry/Survey

This is the third time I am entering your survey. Again, I would like to present to you three different suggestions:

1. Looking at the people of Norway during the 1994 Winter Olympics, I made two special observations. I described them in my letter to our local newspaper. Could those two observations be further developed and presented in your magazine to the people of the U.S.? Do they have merit? Could they produce some kind of echo?
2. In 1988, I made a speech to local veterans during a Memorial Day ceremony. In that speech, I tried to find and to explain the true meaning of that day and its hidden power that could inspire and influence. Could you dedicate your issue at Memorial Day to this special message of that celebration and to the testament of those who died defending freedom for us, the beneficiaries of their sacrifice?
3. In our time, the big business institutions are changing our society, molding it into a society of easily manipulated employees. In such an environment true individuality has less and less ground to develop and by this to add its special creativity and character to our lives. I am sending you some of my letters in which I fought for the right to be free to work as a physician and as a member of our community. Can such a theme be presented and discussed in your magazine?

Again, I am sending you a packet of my papers as material necessary to understand my suggestions.
My best wishes.

Tadeusz Maciejczyk, M.D.
Milledgeville, April 8, 1999

Book Four

Time Magazine Survey

1. A study to what "mature living" are steering using many of our TV programs. How far has that image become distorted? Then, what does "maturity" really mean? How do we build it up?
2. I would like you to make a special study of countries between Europe and Russia. All three Baltic States: Bielorussia, the Ukraine, Poland and others. What could their eventual potential in the future be? How can they help contribute to, not temporary, but lasting peace? I would still like to find funds necessary to create scholarships for future experts in English and Spanish languages for that part of the world that at present is one of the most exotic spots on the map. And one day, it could be very crucial.

                                Tadeusz Maciejczyk
                                May 9, 1999

The World Seen from the Distance of a Small Village

Illinois Ad Hoc Committee to Defend Health Care

Dear Friends:

I support with all my heart the idea that a living spirit inspired to serve the people should guide true medicine. Medicine should never be primarily a business.

The businessmen who jumped into the medical service arena didn't do this because of a genuine desire to serve. They did this motivated by a sentence that I heard many times; that big money exists in "health."

For politicians, the "health" difficulties created a convenient and attractive area where they could play, making promises, appearing caring and generous, giving them all the chances to be elected or re-elected.

With those two distortions, with the addition of multiple other practices guided by "what is there for me" and by greed, medical service became a sick side of the nation's life.

The businessmen and the politicians certainly could be helpful in the functioning of the health care institutions, but their role should never be central. It should be peripheral and advisory only.

I firmly believe that primary medicine should be liberated from all artificial frames. Their offices should be private and freely scattered through the country located in accordance to need. Such freedom of medical work by itself would be competent in its quality and cost. I also believe that patients should have complete freedom to choose their doctors. Such doctors would know them, adding continuity and human touch to such relationships. The healing process is not only physical, but to a large degree also emotional and spiritual.

Specialized medicine, especially that which requires specialized equipment, should be organized and guided to gain a clear overview of changes and advances. Such a supervising body should not be directed by business or politics, but by the highest medical, pharmaceutical, industrial as well as insurance authorities that would meet regularly to guide toward the best healthy and human course of the mission of medicine.

Such an arrangement would not be rigid and immobilizing; it would not be abusive and never expand into a sterile and cumbersome bureaucracy. It would not lose energy and money in ugly, sterile and expensive infightings in order to expand, to eliminate competition to impress and to get control by any means. Surely it would eliminate a costly, arrogant and ruthless intermediary who sees not the mission and beauty in helping, but the money.

Book Four

I am sending you again some of my previous letters about this subject. Medical service is not an industry. As with everything that is creative, it needs freedom.

I am sorry for the delay in writing to you. Suddenly I had to face a personal problem. I am at present on radiation and chemo. The prognosis is good, but in the meantime, it has sapped energy from me.

My contribution is not big. I am sorry. My income is reduced now. In this town of 1100 people, I have now a satellite clinic from a nearby hospital with managed care affiliations.

I send you my best wishes.

Tadeusz Maciejczyk, M.D.
Milledgeville, May 11, 1999

The World Seen from the Distance of a Small Village

William Clinton
President of the United States of America

Dear Mr. President:

After returning home from the radiation and chemotherapy I am undergoing because I developed a Squamous cell carcinoma of my parotid gland, I tried to eat something while I gave a long look to a page of *Newsweek* from May 17, 1999 with your photograph expressing deep thinking and rethinking and above that photograph in bold letters was the inscription, "What do we do now?" (The problem of Kosovo.)

I feel your concern and inside pressure. I also understand that this question is not for me to answer.

I only want to send you some of my letters written in similar circumstances after the massacre in Sarajevo in 1994. The Winter Olympics were about to open in Norway and I wrote those letters to the Olympic Committee at that time. Maybe you could find time to read them and then to ponder.

I am also sending you a painting of me while doing my duties as a countryside medical practitioner.

I send you my best wishes.

Tadeusz Maciejczyk, M.D.
Milledgeville, May 17, 1999

Book Four

(The following letter is written to the younger brother of my wife who became a priest by vocation. At the time the letter was written, Aurelio was seriously ill with an abscess of the brain and his prognosis was not good.)

Dear Aurelio,

    Today I received your letter and I want to respond without delay. I didn't know about your condition and I am concerned. I thank you for writing to me. Reading your letter I saw what I always knew, that you are a man of character.
    Recently I read a book about Spain, its roots and the flowers. This book gave me a lot to think about and also it gave me a deeper understanding of the soul of Spain.
    In the chapter about main currents of Spanish thought, the author, John A. Crow, wrote about Unamuno. That man of wisdom, at the end of his life came to the conclusion that wisdom is to science what death is to life. Science says we must live. Wisdom says we must die and seeks a way to make us die well. He insisted, "I need the immortality of my soul—the indefinite persistence of my individual conscientiousness." He added that the man of passion, the arbitrary man, is the only real rebel.
    As I look on you, your whole life, you are the personification of Unamuno's final statement. You are the true rebel. A docile life, an easy life was not for you. You were too big for such an existence.
    In this letter I have to tell you that at present, I also have a problem. For over a year, I noted a growing tumor on the right side of my face. It appeared at an uneasy time for me. The hospital was building a satellite clinic here in my little community, clearly to squeeze me out. In this situation, I was uncomfortable saying anything publicly about my potentially serious problem. The doctors who evaluated my problem told me that if I do not undergo excision of that tumor, I would not survive two more years. I asked whether they would cut the facial nerve and they said yes. I answered that in such a situation, I would take those less than two years. I did not want a life of hiding with a paralyzed face.
    The satellite clinic opened last August and I was surviving. My position was difficult because I lost my hospital privileges when I opposed the imposition of malpractice insurance and I didn't belong to any Managed Health Care network because I wanted to be free in my work. In spite of those limitations, I felt that I belonged here, that I was needed.

The World Seen from the Distance of a Small Village

Something else happened. Last Easter, the Sterling-Dixon newspaper did a special edition about "unsung heroes." It included profiles and praise for 50 people who make the Sauk Valley a very special place. I was included in those 50 people and among them I was the only doctor. A complete paradox.

Now my immediate problem is the treatment of the squamous cell carcinoma of the parotid gland. I am now on chemotherapy and radiation. The prognosis is OK, but in the meantime, I do not feel as well as I would like.

Best wishes. I am sure you will overcome your problems.

Tadek
Milledgeville, May 17, 1999

Book Four

Jim Nicholson
Chairman of the National Committee
The Republican Party

Thank you for my selection as a voter in your survey.

Judging from your limit of five days to respond, I can imagine that you are not looking for an input of ideas, but rather only for money. But I am not rich. I cannot give much. Consequently, my answer will make no difference.

As I see how politics is evolving, how health care is managed and how education is administrated, I got the impression that the wrapping of those problems is getting enormously expensive while the product inside of those wrappings appears mediocre and has a tendency to spoil.

Looking at the list of the Republican candidates for President, I can only say that it is still too early to make a definitive choice.

People here do not like to talk about the problems of politics or elections. They are not interested and they are rather indifferent. Surely the prospect of the election of the millennium is not producing any excitement, polemics or discussions. Elections become boring to most people.

Speaking for myself, at present, I do not see the front-runner G.W. Bush as a President. I do not see in him character or depth. If he got the biggest contributions for the campaign, for me it is only proof that he already sold himself out. He will not serve the country. He will serve those special contributors.

As of now, I would vote for John McCain. He demonstrated that he has character. I do not know how much knowledge of public affairs he has. That, he will show during the campaign. But for any leadership, character is much more important than know-how.

Together with my $25 I am sending you some of my papers related to elections. Maybe you will read them.

My best wishes.

Tadeusz Maciejczyk
Milledgeville, September 29, 1999

The World Seen from the Distance of a Small Village

Reader's Digest

Poor me. I was never a perfect cook.

When I was young, after the war and I came to Spain on a scholarship for students from behind the Iron Curtain, I had a hard time deciding what I would like to study. I wanted to be an engineer because I was good in mathematics, but there were no openings in such schools. So I looked for an alternative.

My good friend, who was older than I, walked behind me trying to convince me that I should be a doctor because I have the character for this. But I was not convinced. More than this, I was afraid. I remembered all the horrors from the war. To live in such a surrounding day after day would be torture, I thought.

And so, I looked for something else. I thought about chemistry, but here I stopped over an attitude impossible for me to overcome. I had the impression that chemistry is like something that is one step further from the "perfect kitchen." For this reason, I eliminated chemistry.

Finally, after all my soul searching, I became a doctor and today I cannot imagine being in the job of an engineer.

And now you are giving me a proposition of studying a perfect kitchen textbook.

Now I have lived alone for the last ten years. I cook for myself. My cooking has this advantage that nobody wants to taste it and in this way everything is there only for me. And I eat my dishes mostly not even knowing what I am eating. Generally my attention is not on the food, but on reading at that moment.

After thinking hard today, I made a decision. I promise that I will make one chicken dish according to strict instructions from your book and I will eat it without reading anything.

Maybe this would be a turning point of my life.

> Tadeusz Maciejczyk
> Milledgeville, November 6, 1999

Book Four

First Health
West Sacramento, CA

    Last July, when I received your letter, I was undergoing radiation and chemotherapy for squamous cell carcinoma of the parotid gland. At that time, while not stopping my office work, I had no energy to respond to your questions. Now, when the cure is successfully completed, and I am the old me again, I received your decision and verdict.
    I would like to continue to be a primary physician for your customers. I can promise to be honest and effective in my work.
    As a doctor, I never abused or neglected anybody who came to me for help.
    But at the same time in my work, I need to be free and responsible only to my conscience. I do not want to be bound by the provisions of the preferred provider. I was never good in the role of the screw in a big engine.
    At this point I have to add that I have no hospital privileges and I do not keep malpractice insurance.
    In order to explain better these facts, I am sending you copies of some of my letters from the past in which I explained why I took my positions in these matters.
    And because we are approaching the Christmas season, I am sending you a story from my life that I sent to *Time Magazine* in response to their article about miracles because I had in my life a happening for which I have no human explanation.
    As a Christmas card, I am sending you my self-portrait that is known here as "The House Call."
    Again, I want to tell you that I would like to see your patients, but as a free co-worker in your organization.

Tadeusz Maciejczyk, M.D.
Milledgeville, November 29, 1999

P.S. Last April *The Daily Gazette* in Sterling, Illinois did a special supplement to hail the "unsung heroes" in this corner of the world. They published a volume of profiles and praise for 50 people who make the Sauk Valley a very special place. Among those 50, I was the only doctor on their list.

The World Seen from the Distance of a Small Village

Letters to the Editor
Time Magazine

    I read in your column a letter from Anthony M. D'Agostino responding to the theme "We Forget Hitler at Our Peril," and I was shocked.

    He wrote in his letter that Hitler didn't do the Holocaust alone. He was aided by people in Germany, Poland, Hungary, France and other countries.

    I was in Poland during the length of the German occupation and I know that Polish people didn't collaborate with the occupant. There was no Polish Quisling at any level of our society. If Mr. D'Agostino has a trace of integrity and honesty, he should document to me and to all Polish people that what he said about Poland is true.

    The same goes for *Time Magazine* that published such an irresponsible letter without a comment and without a blush.

    Slander requires explanation and public correction if we are to be honest and live together in peace. Whoever practices slander in this way shows who he really is. Sooner or later the truth will come to the surface.

    I am sending to you some of my letters about wartime and some in which I related to the Jewish problem.

    Maybe you would read them.

> Tadeusz Maciejczyk M.D.
> Milledgeville, January 19, 2000

Book Four

Jim Nicholson
Chairman
The Republican National Committee

Dear Sirs:

I am grateful to you for remembering me and for sending me a new membership card, but to tell the truth, I do not care any more.

I lost my faith in U.S. democracy. This democracy became a commodity for sale. No honest man in this system has any chance to be elected. Certainly in such a system, there would never be room for a new future Lincoln in the life of the U.S. Only puppets, liars and those who know how to sell themselves, will succeed in this kind of election. I am sorry that the progress of democracy in the U.S. is going in such a direction.

Really, at the present moment, I already do not care who of the two marionettes we have should be elected.

I have every right to complain and to be discouraged, disappointed and bitter. At the time of voting in the primaries I will have no chance to vote for the best of the candidates who entered the race. My right to fully participate in this election has been violated and stolen from me. Why should I go to the voting place on March 21 or in November? I do not approve of any of the candidates who were left for me to vote for.

I do not call it a democracy when I vote for the leftovers from the system of the primaries. Such voting is not showing the search for truth or greatness. It serves only to perpetuate a reign of mediocrity in America.

And America should be great.

Tadeusz Maciejczyk
Milledgeville, March 14, 2000

cc: *Time Magazine*
    Newsweek
    U.S. News & World Report
    The Daily Gazette (our local newspaper in Sterling, IL)

The World Seen from the Distance of a Small Village

Dear Lilka,

Thank you for your letter.
What can I tell you about my life? Last winter I started a new project. I painted portraits of my three sisters. I had their small, done-for-documentation photographs. On them, they looked the way that I remembered them. Generally they were lost in the drawers. I seldom saw them. Lately I felt the need to be nearer to them. And now I see them every day. I can talk to them; ask them how to go forward.

Eugenia was older than me. She was a good companion. Before the war she finished two years of gymnasium. She had a perfect singing voice. She was good in poetry. Then the war changed our lives completely. You know how it was during the occupation. Misery, hunger, diseases were everywhere. One day toward the end of 1940, Gienia told me good-bye and she entered the convent of Albertinas that helped the sick and the needy. She died in 1950 from tuberculosis. I think that she behaved like a soldier and she died in battle. I never found her poetry after she left home.

Irene was three years younger than me. She was your age. Her life was changed during events that also completely changed my life.

You know my story. I left home on August 1, 1945 at about 4 P.M. My mother and my two sisters were waving their hands in good-byes and I shouted to them that within one month I would be back to start my next year in school.

The next day at noon, the Internal Security surrounded my home starting twelve hours of terror. At midnight, my parents were taken to prison for interrogation.

Only recently Marilka told me the continuation of that story. My parents remained in that interrogation for two weeks. Interrogations again and again were happening at any time of day or night. The food was difficult to swallow even in that hungry time. They slept on floors. For entertainment they listened to the screams of those who were interrogated in the basement.

After their release my parents wanted to notify me of what happened and to warn me about coming back. If I returned, I would be taken directly to that interrogation basement. When it appeared that the surveillance was lifted and nobody was watching our home any more, they sent Irka to bring me the story, the letters and juice made by my mother.

The police, watching from a distance, followed behind her. Irka was arrested in Wroclaw. How her interrogations looked, she never told. After returning home, she told my parents how she found me, how she told me the story from home, warned me and put directly into my hands the letters and the juice. As proof she showed them the golden earrings that apparently I gave her. She never changed her story. She had to protect those who from that very unlikely place brought to me those letters from home, the juice and the stern warning. In the prison cell in Wroclaw, she was put in a small, unventilated space with somebody with open tuberculosis. The illness started to appear in her soon afterwards. She died in March of 1949.

I was a student of medicine at the University of Madrid when I received the news about Irka's death and I, a grown man, cried like never before and never afterwards in my life.

Irka died and left behind a mystery that is hard to comprehend or to explain. I know well that it was not she who brought me the news, the unopened letters from home and the stern warning, "Do not dare to go there!"

How it happened that there, in the very center of madness Irka could put her confidence and almost faith in somebody who would take an enormous risk to try to save me when I was unknown to them? What happened there will remain a mystery forever.

In the meantime I can try to give those events a different look from happenings that before were not looking as important.

That day, on August 1, 1945, I came to the railroad station and I presented my documentation together with my special permission to leave the town. A special clerk for that purpose, a lady, looked at my papers, checked them and then she gave me a long look up and down and she declared that from that moment I would lead a group of 60 refugees to Wroclaw. Without expecting such an honor, suddenly I became a leader, a trusted man.

I took my new function seriously. During those three days of our journey, I tried to help those people as well as I could. I fought to provide for them with necessary food and some covered space to sleep at night. I tried to solve their problems. I became their friend. During those days I was the last to eat and the last to sleep. It was a wonderful experience for me.

In all those works, I had help from one lady who was almost at every moment somewhere next to me. She was about 30 years old and she was good looking. She was very convenient and very effective in all my battles with the local authorities. She knew how to handle the problems and she was to me a good friend.

At our destination in Wroclaw, I wished good luck to everyone from our group finishing with that lady who was so helpful to my leadership and I took a long detour to reach the place of my work.

The World Seen from the Distance of a Small Village

I was happy in my new place and in my work. Everything was so normal and relaxed until the day when the unknown man brought the news and warnings from my home. I still didn't comprehend the seriousness of my situation. I just decided not to go back to Kielce. But the uneasy feelings within me started to grow. Signs of danger started to appear.

It was about three weeks later when I got the next clear warning.

It was a hot Sunday in mid-September. In the afternoon, I went for a walk on the streets to ponder what to do next. While walking I became thirsty and I entered a bar to drink a lemonade. I was sipping that lemonade when somebody touched my shoulder from behind and I heard a voice. "So, you are here?"

I turned. It was that lady who was of such help to me during those three days when I was a leader.

She was looking into my eyes in a strange and intense way and she told me that she wanted to tell me something very important. She took me to a distant corner of the room where nobody could listen and she said, "I work for the Internal Security. I cannot tell you everything here. Come to such and such a place at 7 P.M.

She left and I do not remember whether I finished that lemonade. I wandered until evening through the most remote streets and at seven, I approached the place of my appointment.

It was already getting dark. I looked at the spot from behind the distant corner. The street was empty. The building into which I was supposed to enter looked like a fortress. It had thick stone walls. Its windows were small and covered with iron bars. The entrance was big for trucks, but the gate for humans was very small. I looked at that building for a long time and then I retreated into the darkness of the streets. I was not brave enough to show up there.

Since that evening, I started to think about going west. I didn't know how. I heard about contrabandits who passed people to Czechoslovakia, but I had no money to pay them and I suspected that those places were infiltrated. Finally I decided to take the most untested, most unpredictable route across East Germany and to go alone.

It was about one week later, on Monday, September 25 when I saw that strange lady again. I was sent for some supplies. We were coming back. I was standing on the platform of the truck and we were rolling slowly through the crowded street when I saw her. She was standing on the sidewalk. She noted me. She pushed to the roadway. I saw her arms raised, a special terror in her eyes and I heard her exclamation, "Are you still here?!!!"

I understood that my time was running out. They were closing in on me.

Book Four

Two days later on Wednesday afternoon, I took the train toward the border between Poland and East Germany. I had no idea how I would pass that border. My friends were waving their hands. Then I was alone. In my rucksack, I had some cigarettes and a bottle of alcohol to use as an eventual bribe and in the pocket a kind of recommendation letter written in Polish, German and Russian that said my mother was somewhere near Berlin, that she was sick and I was going to bring her back home. You already know about the continuation of my journey.

Since the last letter from Marilka in which she told me Irka's story of her trip, I thought many times about the enigma that her story covered.

Who was that strange lady from the Internal security? Why didn't she arrest me there in Kielce when I presented my documentation to the traveling controlling clerk? Certainly my name was on her list. She could only give the signal. The guards were everywhere. Was she restrained by my unexpected nomination and didn't want to make a spectacle in front of so many people?

I do not know whether she had to go on that trip with our group, but she did. And for sure she kept a close eye on me. But why didn't she arrest me at the end of that trip after I said good-bye to everyone from the group and finally only she was left and I was shaking her hand expressing my gratitude for so much helping? Why did she permit me to go away free?

And then, was she involved in helping Irka and then in sending that special, apparently very trusted messenger to warn me and to bring me those still unopened letters from my home? How did she convince Irka that she could trust her? And then why did she take the pains to go on that special trip to warn me and to tell me in front of a crowd of people that my days of freedom were numbered?

For all this, I have no explanation. This lady will remain for me a mystery forever.

How strange our lives can be. Irka is following me with her eyes from her portrait wherever I move, but she keeps her secret.

This letter already has become too long and it is late in the night. I send you my best wishes.

Tadek
Milledgeville, April 20, 2000

The World Seen from the Distance of a Small Village

My father
Franciszek Maciejczyk
1890-1968

Józefa Jachowicz-
Wróblewska Maciejczyk
My mother in 1950 when she
was 60 years old

Eugenia Maciejczyk
1922-1950
She responded to the call
to serve, she dedicated her
life to this, and she died
doing what she considered
was necessary to do.

Irena Maciejczyk
my sister
1927-1949
She went to save my life,
and because of this,
she died.

Lilka born in 1927
from photograph
made for passport in 1960

Book Four

Department of the Treasury
Internal Revenue Service
Kansas City, MO 64999

I received your letter and I cannot claim that I was not shocked and enraged.

I send you here the documentation that you are asking for. If you wish I can send you also the photocopies of all the related concealed checks.

Probably around here I am the only doctor who still wants to be independent in his work from all the intrusions of big clinics or managed care overlords. But each day it becomes more difficult to defend my independence in understanding how to be a doctor, how to serve the patients.

What, years ago, was a hallmark of forces that made this country great, now mercilessly crashed by threats from every direction, by the flood of new rules, new codes, time consuming each time more complicated paper work, wonderful political promises on the front stage, and a special terror and squeeze behind the scenes. Only those who can afford the know-how to play in this strange dance can survive, increasingly dominate and eliminate everybody who would stay on their path.

And so, everybody now is becoming merely an employee in this wonderful USA. The individuals have no time to develop. Everybody becomes subservient, compromising his dreams and convictions. This will not fulfill the life of an individual, nor of a nation.

Because now is the time of the Republican Convention, I am sending you a letter to the Rep. Presidential candidate five years ago and two other of my letters that show the flashes from this "New America."

If you need more documentation, more papers, please let me know.

Tadeusz Maciejczyk, M.D.
Milledgeville, August 3, 2000

The World Seen from the Distance of a Small Village

The American Center for Law and Justice
The Office of the Chief Counsel
P.O. Box 90940
Atlanta, GA 30364-0940

Dear Chief Counsel:

Today I received your reminder of my pledge.

During your telephone call, I was listening. I understood the need for religious freedom and its expression, but I was undecided.

Under pressure, I agreed to contribute, but later, listening again and again to the memory of your pronunciation, its special tone, with all its holy, theatrical indignation, I concluded that I didn't want to contribute to the growing discord and bitterness in America that is deepening each year in spite of all the remedies dictated by the courts.

Those conflicts are fueled frequently by even small, but loud unrestrained by the conscience, attention or profit-seeking pressure groups. Of course, this is creating a wonderful heaven to many special lawyers.

The justice system and the courts should know and should accept its limitations in emotionally loaded social, religious and moral issues. In those areas, courts are not creating peace and reconciliation, but rather intensified, deeper-rooted, more uncompromising and inflamed confrontation.

The means healing the soul of America has to be different.

Observing the spirit of the different moments of the opening ceremonies of the Olympics in Sydney, I felt still more acutely that peace and harmony in the high courts squalls. The abundance of those court confrontations created new, unknown before, divisive inner tensions.

No, I will not contribute to your crusade. As you told me, you would need for this holy war about half a million dollars. How many other similarly holy wars can be created? What a business!

I deeply believe that God doesn't need the courts to reach the human soul.

Tadeusz Maciejczyk, M.D.
Milledgeville, September 17, 2000

P.S. I am sending copies of my previous letters that were touching these problems.

Book Four

Donna Shalala
Secretary of Health
Washington, D.C.

Dear Ms. Secretary:

I write to you because I need your advice and help.

I am an M.D. I have been a general practitioner for 35 years in a small village. During the time of change in practicing medicine, I rejected the pressure to enter into Managed Care. Because of this, I lost many patients and my practice became small and reduced in many ways.

In my work, I tried to be for the people. My charges for visits were small. I had the feeling I was doing a mission by serving. Getting rich, or attaining a special social status never was my preoccupation.

At present, I came to the point that I am not sure whether I can survive. The frequent, capricious changes in billing and in coding are the death sentence for such a small, starving and struggling to maintain its independence establishments. Thank God I have a dedicated and resourceful nurse who until now coped with all those blows. But it cannot be enough now.

The bill from the computer business for one day of work of installing the now required new window for billing was more than my whole monthly income. A few months ago, they charged $50/hour for consultation. A few days ago, it was $70. Now it is $90.

In this artificial, new situation, if I am permitted to survive, I have to charge more for visits for all my patients on Medicare and Medicaid, about five dollars more for each visit.

I will not increase my charges to those patients who pay directly. They are not producing those spiraling costs to keep the office going.

Please tell me, give me your suggestions how to survive.

Tadeusz Maciejczyk, M.D.
Milledgeville, September 17, 2000

The World Seen from the Distance of a Small Village

Ralph Anthony
Sweepstakes Director
American Family Publishers

Again I received an urgent statement from you about my "delinquent" debt. After a few times of such harassment, it is time to respond to this insolent and abusive attitude of yours.

For years, I dealt with you and our relations were good and cordial. I responded to your propositions and I always paid in advance for everything I asked for, including deliveries. I imagined that our relationship could be harmonious forever. Instead it ended suddenly with your change in dealing with me.

Last summer without much explanation, I received from you several small cards notifying me that what I was asking for was no longer available. The money paid was not returned. Instead, I received five times the same cassette of "Country Love Songs."

I didn't ask for those songs and sending me five of them was not only absurd, but insolent bad manners with added nastiness, a stupid and shortsighted something that in Spanish I would call *Cara dura*. (Hard-faced)

I do not remember what the items were that were denied to me. I believed in your reliability and integrity. I only know that one of them was a video about the greatest natural parks in the world. I wanted this video because last winter, my daughter was in Costa Rica and she visited such a park there. I wanted that video for her.

I wrote to your service department about dumping on me those apparently not-in-demand cassettes. I received an answer that this was the disposition that they received from your central office.

I hope that you will send me that video about parks and also a slip to send you back those five cassettes.

I am sorry that your good relationship suddenly degenerated to being so dirty from your side. It would be interesting to investigate and to dig out what was the trigger in this sad affair.

And I assure you that I know how to be persistent.

Tadeusz Maciejczyk, M.D.
Milledgeville, October 15, 2000

P.S. About my persistence, I am sending you a copy of two of my letters from the time of my malpractice suit. I also am sending you my self-portrait.

Book Four

Editor
The Daily Gazette
Sterling, IL

Dear Sir:

The result of the Presidential election is maybe entertaining and providing a lot of material for political jokes, but it is tragic and traumatic to the nation and maybe even to the world. Whatever the settlement is, the verdict of the court or of any other institution, it will not stop the bitterness and bad blood and in such an environment at the backstage, no government would be able to govern.

In the situation that was created, I see only one good remedy.

As the two main candidates eliminated each other, and every passing day is providing proof that they would be unable to function whatever would be the final choice between the two, the third party candidate should be named and assume the honor or the burden of the Presidency.

In this way, the quarrel between Democrats and Republicans could continue for the next four years without harming the nation. The nation would have the necessary stability and the two parties would have enough time to settle their problems and to find a better way to elect their next candidates for the Presidency.

Another of my impressions is that the judges should not be elected because they are Democrats or Republicans. They should never be on the ballot. Here some other criteria for nomination should be applied.

According to this consideration, the next President of the U.S. should be Ralph Nader who got the third biggest number of votes.

I send you my best wishes.

Tadeusz Maciejczyk, M.D.
Milledgeville, November 24, 2000

The World Seen from the Distance of a Small Village

Time Magazine

Please do not talk to me about my delinquent subscription payment. On June 17, 2000, after another clear insinuation that Poland and Poles have cooperated with the Nazis in concentration camps and in the Holocaust, I wrote to protest to you and conditionally, I have extended my subscription sending only $51.57.

That letter of mine, like the letters before, was completely ignored by you. I never received any explanation and I never found any corrections on the pages of your magazine.

Why should I subscribe to a magazine that lies without any blush that doesn't keep a standard of truth and that is offending me?

Please, discontinue my subscription.

Tadeusz Maciejczyk, M.D.
January 29, 2001

(After this letter, *Time Magazine* came to me regularly and I noticed that my subscription was extended to December 2003. Since then, I haven't seen any incorrect statements about Poland.)

Book Four

Republican National Committee
Washington, D.C.

    I responded to your survey, but please do not consider me a member. I do not wish to belong. I prefer to be free and to formulate my own opinions. Years ago, I thought that I was a part of you. It was a long time ago. Since then, I have learned and I suffered from burnout.
    A sustaining membership is an especially offensive and repulsive kind of invitation.
    It implies that I should be voiceless, manipulated at will, always obedient and admiring, preferably a blind, but rich object that provides money and votes.
    I wonder why I couldn't be just a member like everybody else in the party? Why am I destined only to be used in the Party?
    At the present time, my primary objective, where I have to concentrate my attention and my resources, is the publication of my book. I do not think that you are interested in such a caprice of somebody from the proposed sustaining membership, but I include here my presentation letter for that book. Because of my old connection with the Party, after publication, I will send you a copy.
    I wish you the best in your work.

Tadeusz Maciejczyk, M.D.
Milledgeville, April 8, 2001

The World Seen from the Distance of a Small Village

Pat Simpson
National Republican Congressional Committee
Physician's Advisory Board
Washington, D.C.

Thank you for the unexpected award. I am not used to receiving them, and really, I do not know what to do with them.

As I see it, any great work for the benefit of people has two very important components:

Primarily, it is a mission filled with purpose and commitment.

Secondarily, there is an administrative side that with dedication and common sense, as well as with honesty, provides that mission with a material means to flourish.

Such an order applies in the health care system, to problems of education, to social structuring, to the law and judicial aspects of a well-functioning society, to the cultural life of the country and, to everything else that touches life on this earth.

This general order became distorted and twisted in America and the consequences of this degeneration are mounting in every field of life, becoming increasingly poisonous and suffocating.

In medicine the primordial element of mission still exists in the phraseology of the filled-with-"GOODNESS" politicians, but otherwise it became marginalized to some fools who still in this time of smartness, remember the Hippocratic Oath and the Ten Commandments.

Big business became the king. Games to outsmart one another became the acceptable rules of proceedings. Calculated action in how to get the maximum today's profits, even stripping tomorrow, is getting acceptance and destroying whatever or whomever would be in the way became the obvious "normality."

In this system physicians became managed employees. In the footsteps of the glorious experiences from the Soviet Union, they now became "providers"—something that can be compared only to the nameless, faceless, easy to be manipulated or kicked Soviet "*tovarish*." The Soviet Union became bankrupt and putrid, but it is still an excellent teacher for our new "kings" in how to manipulate, to use or to dispose of the independent-minded.

The patients were reduced to objects of financial calculations, how to use them and how to maximally squeeze them. The honorable idea of assistance to seniors became a field in which the smartest administrators became the most valuable assets in games for money and dominance.

Book Four

This costly, smartly shortsighted, extremely damaging malady is not limited to medicine. It corroded every aspect of life in this country producing on the surface a prosperity, but thickening underground of uncertainty, anxiety, destructiveness, anger and malady. This is at least what I can see around here.

And so, I wish you the best in your dedication to improve the health care system in this country.

Personally, I have no faith in truthfulness, integrity or meaningful leadership of any party. They all became reduced to what we call today a political science, an ideal of a perfect politician.

I am sorry that my assessment of life in America of today is so pessimistic.

I am sending you copies of what I wrote previously about medical care. My working experiences became very unique, and as such, they could represent a good material to review the health care system, and to formulate a vision and strategy for the future.

                                              Tadeusz Maciejczyk, M.D.
                                              Milledgeville, May 31, 2001

The World Seen from the Distance of a Small Village

Republican National Committee
2001 Annual Survey

1. I do not understand what "needs of students first" means. Schools should do their proper part in preparing the younger generation for the tasks of life. The schools should do this without diminishing or downgrading the primary role of the family. Schools should try to improve the family life of children. Society as a whole should create a proper environment for this. Responsibility should be the key word for students, for schools, for family and for society. If this cooperative responsibility fails, the result will be a failure whatever the monetary investment would be.
2. Greater flexibility to experiment and to find what works locally would be good, but only with a central coordination that more than anything would have moral authority. Federal red tape most frequently shows a lack of moral purpose and true elevation of educational standards, but a lot of low-minded pettiness.
3. I have no clear idea what "real accountability through school choice initiative and charter schools" wants to say. Using such enigmatic formulation in surveys is not helping to clarify the problem.
4. I have very little preparation to responsibly take part in a discussion of the across-the-board tax cuts.
5. "Marriage penalty" is damaging to the institution of marriage, to society and to the country. It creates consequences that are not only costly, but also painful and weakening. It is a testimony to the government's sarcastic, abusive, thoughtless approach to the fundamentals of society. It is ugly.
6. Taxation after the death of the owner, or the death penalty is another example of the government's gluttony and voraciousness. It misses the fundamental creative and emotional forces in man. It downgrades the family as a positive unit of healthy society.
7. Provide affordable prescription drug coverage. I do not understand the mechanism of this selective action of mercy. Who is paying the difference? Who is victimized by directly or indirectly paying more? In the same way I do not understand the enormous rise in the cost of medicine, even for the old-timers. How much more do we pay for the malpractice fear of blackmail? For out of hand TV advertisements? For stockholders?

Book Four

For smartness and greed? How much should the honest, real prize increase be? Or how much are we blindly self-destructive?

8. Primary medicine should be free from all manipulators. Independence of doctors would create the most responsive, most sensitive and most economical service to all people. Doctors never should be reduced to the "provider" status. The greatness of America was built not by providers. The Soviet might was created this way. America's Greatness was created by men who felt free.
9. Payments for Social Security were collected during the years of work of every individual. Manipulating this now to escape obligation would be, to say this mildly, dishonest. How could you still want anybody to believe?
10. Option to individual partial investment of Social Security is a wonderful idea for a special type of people. It would not work for me. I paid tuitions for five children, and I was always under economical stress. Except this, I have no talent, no patience, no temperament for investing. For me attention to money was always somewhere in the periphery, and I suspect that in such an attitude, I am not alone. A supervised Social Security is a wise idea.
11. Allowing faith-based organizations to provide community-based service programs could be very good. But, if there would be money in this, soon it would be infested by all kinds of well-doers, phony social savers. America of the last decades has a special tendency to such twists.
12. Partial birth abortions should not be considered medical service. It is a calculated murder with the nice excuse. Its moral standard parallels the Auschwitz macabre.
13. I am not an expert in deployment of a missile defense system for protection of nuclear blackmail. Surely it would go only in one direction: Escalation. There has to be some other way to decrease or eliminate aggression. It would be an interesting subject for serious studies, in created for this purpose international universities. Multidisciplinary, in depth understood concepts of conflicts old and new, and of the appropriate remedies would have there its best outlet.
14. Present campaign finance laws are very convenient to those who have no objection to sell themselves. Unrestrained spending for election is not a mark of honesty. It feeds corruption. It doesn't

The World Seen from the Distance of a Small Village

elevate. It does not clarify issues. It confuses and blares. It creates distrust to politicians. It gives them a bad name. The orgy, the ugliness, the enormously low intellectual level of costly political TV ads create no betterment, but nausea and apathy.
15. Increase in military spending without wisdom in purpose of spending, has not a promise of a better future.
16. In my area, people do not like to talk about politics. Nobody here is proud of our politicians and political issues became devalued by propaganda ads.
17. Top priority for next year? Stop being a politician and start to be wise.

Tadeusz Maciejczyk, M.D.
June 8, 2001

Book Four

The Observer
Rockford, Illinois

I read the "Polish Bishops Apology for Wartime Atrocities Draw Praise" [3] and I became very uneasy.

A partial truth is worse, is more poisonous than the total lie. I would prefer to read in *The Observer* the exact text of the Polish bishops message without coloring it by Israeli Ambassador Weiss or anyone else.

The statement that the atrocity in Jedwabne was perpetrated during the Nazi Holocaust is incorrect. The explosion of anger in Jedwabne happened in 1941, not long after the Germans entered that territory. It was not influenced by the Nazis. It was not an act of cooperation with the Nazis. It was an accumulated anger, a settling of scores for what was happening in that territory during the Soviet domination.

The true Holocaust started in 1943.

The Auschwitz became the symbol of the Holocaust, but Auschwitz was not created for this purpose. It was made to kill Poles. Over one million Poles died there. Father Maksymilian Kolbe died there long before the so-called Final Solution was enacted. It was also a place of almost complete extermination of the Gypsies. Here were dying also Ukrainians, Russians and even Germans. Auschwitz became so efficient in killing, so organized and prepared for such purpose that when extermination of Jews began, it became the most convenient place for such a plan.

No. The atrocities in Jedwabne was not a part of Holocaust. It was a local, spontaneous explosion.

The Soviets entered Eastern Poland to fulfill the Riebentropp-Molotov pact of common intervention in Poland signed in Moscow on August 25, 1939.

The Soviet occupation there became a horror story.

Hunting for those who at any time expressed criticism of the Soviets or for those of any eminence was going on day and night. The prisons were overflowing in spite of constant executions. In December of 1939, during the harsh winter, the deportations began. Over two and a half million. Knocking on the doors at night, 15 minutes to get out; they were convoyed to cattle wagons without heat. Starving and cold decimated them before they reached the destination somewhere in Siberia in the labor camps and the dying was going on there.

During those traumatic years there, the Jews wrote a very special chapter of their history. In many places they became the commissars, the informers, the finger pointers for the Soviets. Definitely not all be-

The World Seen from the Distance of a Small Village

haved in this way, but it was enough to create a hate in reverse when the scenario changed, the Soviets disappeared, the long suppressed anger exploded.

It would be interesting to have and to hear the whole story of Jedwabne.

Until now the noble gesture of Polish bishops to condemn violence whatever the cause, became used by the special Jewish need to appear pure and innocent and to blame everybody and everything.

Nobody has a right to judge the cases like Jedwabne without living through such hell. We can only put those memories to the light, to remember them as they were, to learn from them, to forgive and to pray that we would not experience and live through such horrors again.

The Observer has no right to repeat what the Israeli propaganda made from such an occasion. I was never in Eastern Poland, but during the war, I lived in Kielce and Kielce became well known because one day a mob lynched a Jew there. I was not in Kielce when it happened, but I know the general conditions there that could create a moment of a blind explosion.

After "liberation" the countries of Eastern Europe, Stalin broke them to be part of an obedient, loving the system, Soviet monolith. Internal Security was installed in every locality and was very busy. Internal Security is the equivalent to the Soviet KGB. People were disappearing. The loudspeakers on every corner prized everybody who was servile, smearing everybody else. Lies were repeated over and over. People were asked to denounce the enemies of the people. There was no communication. No dialogue. Only fear and uncertainty. In such a time the minister of Internal Security was General Radkiewicz, a Jew. The colonel, a commander of Internal Security in Kielce, was a Jew. The lieutenant who came to arrest me was Jew. In that time of scarcity, the Jews had special privileges. There is nothing more explosive than growing anger while your mouth is gagged. I do not know what was the spark that produced that lynching, perpetrated maybe on an innocent bystander.

In August and September of 1945 I was in a small town of Lower Silesia called Rychbach. I do not know how many Jewish survivors were there. A representative of them was coming to the offices where I worked with the lists of abandoned properties demanding that all those properties would be given to them. When he didn't get all he was entering into a hostile, loud anger.

At that time once, on the market place of that town, I had a long conversation with Jew who was in the Polish Army formed in Russia and who lost one leg in the battle at Lenino. He was complaining to me

Book Four

how the Jews from Auschwitz ridiculed him, called him bad names and kicked him out. He didn't belong to their circle any more.

When I was a child I lived in Wloszczowa and our house was on the corner of two streets. One of those streets had a name of Berek Joselewicz. Berek Joselewicz was a Jew who, in the war of 1830–31 volunteered to be in the Polish Army and he rose to the rank of a captain. After that war, he returned to his home and there he was killed by his fellow Jews because he cohabited with Goyes and he did not eat kosher.

The honorable Elie Wiesel, winner of the Nobel Prize for peace, made for himself an occupation from complaining, from blaming, demanding apologies and money.

What can I say?

The old wisdom says that the growth begins when the blaming ends. The blamer, like an active alcoholic, searches for peace by shifting the responsibility for his life and happiness to something else. The Jews, during their long pilgrimage through foreign lands learned to live with two faces and this is still a problem for them.

One of the lyrics of one of the songs from the *Sound of Music* says, "Nothing comes from nothing. Nothing ever could."

Maybe the Jews need to look more deeply into themselves.

Tadeusz Maciejczyk
June 12, 2001

George W. Bush
President of the United States
Dear Sir:

I write this letter to you because I do not think that the immediate big stick has to be our answer to affirm our indignation, to relieve our pain, or to search for the solution.

Our biggest strength in this moment of crisis and testing should be a moral strength.

We were attacked in a not noble way, because the victims were the civilians, but we should rise above our more natural instincts, and instead of punishing, we should confront the idea that is moving those men to the point that they are ready to die for their beliefs.

The World Seen from the Distance of a Small Village

We should call the leaders of movements who provoked this, by any standard not a holy war, to step forward and before the whole world audience spell out all the grievances, pains, injustices done to them, and the aims of that war.

In the name of the Great God of every denomination, the God of the highest authority of every human being on earth, we should call those leaders to appear and to speak.

The place for this direct communication could be any neutral country agreed upon by both sides.

The discussion panel would be made not by politicians, military men, or anybody who has a governing power, but by men who distinguished themselves as the best minds in religious, moral, social, international problems, in philosophy and in any other tool of mind that would help to understand ourselves and to understand each other.

There would be no restriction in participation. The discussion should be open to anybody who can contribute to this enormous work of marking the future course of human history. Such a discussion should last all the time it could need to develop a new foundation for the new era of time.

We, who are the injured, we who are coping now with our pain, anger, frustration, anxiety, we are calling the leaders of those who ordered that attack to have the courage to appear before such an audience and to talk like a man of integrity and inner dignity should.

If those leaders would refuse to open such a dialogue, if they would ignore this call, continue to send their brave believers into a suicidal expedition while themselves hiding in safety, then we, and the world would have no choice but to consider them dangerous psychopaths and cowards who deserved to be questioned by their believers and by the world.

Then the other steps would have full justification.

Tadeusz Maciejczyk,
Milledgeville, September 14, 2001

P.S. I am sending you a copy of my article, "Freedom vs. Terrorism—Differently" written fifteen years ago. It has still many good points worth considering.

Book Four

Dear Dr. Harner:

Now I am home for dinner. I gathered the papers that I promised. It was easy. I had them already prepared.

About today's events, I worry about the very warm feelings of Pres. Bush and Russia's Putin. The price of those "warm feelings" can be staggering in consequences.

Putin was elected to the presidency after his promise to the Russian people that Russia will still be Number One in the world.

His generally mask-like face of a KGB man who was directing the espionage of the West and was ordering executions if convenient—now is smiling so beautifully to our naïve President.

Sorry that I worry.
Best wishes.

> T. Maciejczyk
> Milledgeville, November 14, 2001

Illinois Academy of Family Physicians
4756 Main Street
Lisle, IL 60532

I was involved many times with men, women and teenagers in more or less serious talks about smoking. I do not know how to translate those encounters into numbers or into percentages for a survey.

My impression is that talking about smoking or drugs to teenagers should be made very slightly from books, from making a show of knowledge or science.

If such talks are expected to touch and to motivate, it has to have the quality of a special dialogue in a very special moment when it can reach the soul. A distant, mass preaching can produce an effect contrary to the intended.

Each person, young or old, has different pains and scars imbedded deep into his life and personality formation that cries for relief, to be quenched, to be covered up.

Addressing scientifically the consequence, the remedy, the way to ease those pains and wounds that in this situation is smoking, without a special

The World Seen from the Distance of a Small Village

healing touch of those wounds, too many will sound like an added cruelty, like an irony, like a voice from a different planet.

Talking to addicts about smoking or drugs should not be a science. It is and it should be an art that should have its secret and strength primarily from a demonstration of care and love. At the same time, it has to open some new visions, new horizons; it should create a new fascination with something worthy. Without this, without love and new vision, talking from books only, will not transform and will not produce a miracle.

With the occasion of this letter, I want to inform you that soon my book will be published: *The World Seen from the Distance of a Small Village*. I am sending you a copy of my presentation of this book.

I am also sending you a copy of my letter sent to the President of the U.S. after September 11.

I still maintain that facing the idea that caused the attack of September 11 is the main issue and main challenge we have to face. Anger and fists will not solve the issue.

I was especially offended by offering blood money for killing Bin Laden. It was ugly and cowardly in the past and it remains low today. Do we have no moral strength to look directly into the eyes of that man?

Creating martyrs is dangerous. Martyrs have a long life and can create new forces, completely unexpected.

Tadeusz Maciejczyk
Milledgeville, November 29, 2001

Book Four

George W. Bush
President of the United States

Dear Sir:

I thank you for your confirmation of my writing to you in our dark days after September 11. Your letter summarizes our reactions, our goals and our ways of dealing with the problems created by terrorism.

My letter of September 14 concentrated mainly on the confrontation of the idea behind this terrorism that is giving spiritual strength to its believers to the point that they are ready to die for this special vision of reality.

Until now we didn't do anything to understand that idea. A simplistic, superficial, contemptuous snapping at what it is will not help to create harmony in the world.

Military operations, bombing the suspected enemy until they're extinct, will not create conditions for lasting peace. It will only force the true enemy to hide, to regroup and to wait for a better opportunity. It will not eliminate the illness.

History teaches that an idea that touches the soul of people always was a power not to be ignored or dealt with a fist.

The present terrorism we are facing still has such a powerful idea and ideals that convince and mobilize millions. With all our actions in Afghanistan, we didn't destroy it. We did nothing to comprehend it. We gave a crashing beating to a small part of its believers and we already created martyrs who will have a long, inspiring and mobilizing life.

A long time ago, the all-powerful Roman Empire couldn't destroy the then still small and physically weak congregations of Christians. Each wave of persecution, cruelty and scorn was only fortifying in Christians their faith and was providing new converts ready to die for their convictions. The martyrs of persecutions did not die. They acquired new life, more durable and more fascinating than any living human being could have. They were transformed into a kind of banner for the advancing and growing church.

Nearer to our time, within different circumstances and a different content of beliefs, the revolutionaries of 19th century Russia were opposing the rule of the czars by acts of terror. Alexander the Third during all his life was obsessed with a paralyzing fear of assassination. The police were everywhere.

In such a situation and with such a background in the 1870's, police arrested a young man for belonging to the terrorist group. He was condemned and hanged.

The World Seen from the Distance of a Small Village

The spirit of revolution was not destroyed by all the power of the czarist police. About 40 years later, the kid brother of that hanged young man led the Bolshevik Revolt that abolished and eradicated completely czars and their system. Wladimir Lenin even after his death gave strength and legitimacy to the new order.

Martyrs always acquire a power beyond the limits of reason. And we are creating martyrs for the enormous masses of the Muslim population. We do not know what is happening below the surface of the present calm. Maybe the new explosion of violence in Israel can serve as an indicator.

And at this point I want to raise another problem.

The highest American authorities declared several times that we want to get Bin Laden and preferably we want to get him dead. We offered 25 million to anybody who would do the killing for us, because we really do not want the publicity of judging him.

But a payment of blood money is always demeaning and leaves behind a stain resistant to any kind of washing.

The offering of blood money always says that the one making the offer has no moral strength to look directly into the victim's eyes, to truly confront him. It was a clear testimony to everybody around that the inside of the one making the offer was murky, weak and cowardly, even while he tried to impress. It was never a testimony of dignity and true inner self-respect. A crude vengeance was never the signature of a noble spirit. Magnanimity always was.

I write this because I would like the U.S. to pass the present test of building a new environment for the post-September 11-world order with the highest grades.

We have now a unique chance to create from our tragedy a true example to the world in how to behave in a noble way when confronted even with such a tragedy.

It would not be degrading to our President to look directly into the eyes of Bin Laden as into the eyes of an adversary and ask him, "Why did you do this? Explain this to us! Explain this to the world!!!" I truly wish you the best in the not an easy task to lead the world into a better future.

With the occasion of this letter I want to inform you that my book is now in the publication stage and will appear in the next few months. Its title is *The World Seen from the Distance of a Small Village*.

I am including here my presentation to this book.

I send you my best wishes.

Tadeusz Maciejczyk
December 5, 2001

Book Four

Governor James L. Gilmore III
Chairman
Republican National Committee
Washington, D.C.

Dear Sir:

I thank you again for writing and for inviting me to join your party again. Probably I should say here that I am not a grassroots leader as you define me in your letter.

Long ago, I wrote frequently about how problems appeared differently here than in Washington. Finally I became frustrated because I never received any genuine answers to my letters. I never even got the impression that anybody from the central committee ever read my writings. Following them, I was only getting another printed letter from you and a request for more money.

In this letter I have to tell you that lately I have not been one of President Bush or the Party's most loyal supporters. During the last election, frustrated with both main parties, I voted for the third party.

I also want to emphasize here that I am not convinced and that I became critical of the way "the President is concentrating on eliminating global terrorism and keeping Americans safe at home."

I tried to describe my understanding of the post-September 11 situation in my letter to the President dated September 14, and another written on December 5. I am sending you copies of those letters.

In this letter I want to stress the importance of the present moment in which the Taliban is crashed and Bin Laden, with remaining of his soldiers, are still trying to make their last stand.

These present moments, depending on what we do next will be crucial for calming emotions and diminishing or eliminating terrorism or for prolonging and exacerbating madness.

After our great military victory over ragged Taliban defenders, we are left at home with the depressing feeling that the true issues were not eliminated by this war. They still remain to us as mysterious, undefined and incomprehensible as they were before conquering Afghanistan and the destruction of the unlucky scapegoat of our anger—the Taliban.

We never did a solid work to define what and who our main foes are and what the force is that is moving them. With all our attempts to conquer Afghanistan, we didn't even touch those ideas and beliefs. They are still there, everywhere in the Muslim world. We only added to them a magnificent legend and a myth of a heroic resistance of the defenders

The World Seen from the Distance of a Small Village

of those ideas that stood up until the end to our enormous military superiority.

Those each-time-bigger craters and hollows on Afghan soil made with our each-time-bigger and more sophisticated bombs will long be forgotten while a fantastic legend about the Taliban's struggle will have a lasting life in the souls of every next Muslim generation.

And this legend has all the potential to grow. With time it will be more romantic and more compelling for the imagination and for dreaming.

At present, our priority should be to counteract the development of such a legend. To find the most compelling answer. An antidote.

Costly political treaties with friendly Arab regimes will not do this. Even rebuilding Afghanistan will not help.

The fundamental and indispensable element for a convincing and neutralizing answer to this legend would be a recognizance, understanding and a kind of working together in harmony to find out the forces that created this conflict since its beginning and increasingly poison the souls of the Muslim masses.

This would be a more proper and more difficult task than military crusades against the evil of present eruptions. Only such labor would give us a true title to greatness in the pages of history. After our very convincing show of strength, a turning of our cheek surely would not be interpreted as a sign of weakness. It would only be a sign of our inner and innate goodness and of wisdom.

For sure such a turn-around to the problem would not win the popularity contest for many, but now is the time in which when standing before an unknown, taking a less frequented road could make all the difference.

I have no illusions, but if I would get a genuine answer to my letter, I would be more inclined to join your organization again.

And on this occasion I want to inform you that in a few months my book will be published. Its title is *The World Seen from the Distance of a Small Village*. Its subtitle is *A Chronicle from the Time of Change*

I am sending you here a presentation of this book that was requested by my publisher.

I wish you the best in your work.

Tadeusz Maciejczyk
Milledgeville, December 17, 2001

Book Four

Warren A. Jones, M.D.
President of American Academy of Family Physicians
Leawood, KS 66211

Dear Sir:

I was reading your letter about present extraordinary time that requires from us, as family physicians, to face the enormous task of healing American and to serve as leaders if the terror would turn into biological madness.

I live and work in a small, countryside place.

Here the effect of September 11 was not so direct and immediate; the wounds not as painful.

Nevertheless the shock was overwhelming.

In such shock, I wrote on September 14 a letter to President Bush. In that letter I tried to find a way to solve the present global illness by making a proper diagnosis, to understand its roots, the way this illness was spreading and to find the most appropriate, the most healing remedy that would not look for an immediate satisfaction in responding, but for a deeper understanding and a new and lasting harmony among the people of this our world.

I am sending you the copy of that letter and the copy of another letter that I wrote to the President on December 5. I am also sending you a copy of my letter to the Republican Party in which I developed further what I meant by the healing work.

I also want to tell you that soon my book will be published. Its title is *The World Seen from the Distance of a Small Village*. Its subtitle: *A Chronicle from the Time of Change*.

I am sending you also a presentation of this book that I wrote at the request of the publisher. I hope that this my presentation will be interesting to you.

I am sending you my best wishes in your work and also I wish you all the happiness in this Christmas time.

Tadeusz Maciejczyk, M.D.
Milledgeville, December 20, 2001

The World Seen from the Distance of a Small Village

Dear Dr. M.,

    I think of you so often and of the kindness and love you have given to my family and me. You have always been a great role model for me in my life—a person of love, spirituality and compassion.
    May our God bless you—

                                    Becky Valadez (Daughter of Dorrance
                                    and Bette Hawkins)
                                    December, 2001

Book Four

Dear Dr. Maciejczyk,

　　How wonderful to hear back from you and receive all your writings. I am so happy to hear that you are still fighting the good fight and doing things that I believe all humans with a conscience should do. I too had great difficulty accepting that violence against violence in regards to the terrorist attack was the only answer. I, like you, hope that humans still would have the desire and ability to meet face-to-face and talk about things and hold each other accountable for our actions. It troubled me greatly to hear that we would be at war and risk the lives of our young people and those in Afghanistan who are innocent of these unspeakable acts. I told my husband and others that I am glad I am as old as I am, because the world seems to be getting crazier with each passing year. I applaud you for speaking out and I feel privileged to call you a friend. As you mentioned in one of your papers, your writing and your painting strengthens and centers you, so it does with me too. I am back in school trying to finish my undergraduate work and then on to my Masters degree. I am majoring in psychology and have a double minor in art and religion. My hope is to work with people to help them with the many troubles that we can all have in this life. My husband and I both know and can empathize with you on taking a stand for your beliefs and how it makes you an outsider. We both try to do things in our community to empower those populations that have no voice: the poor, minorities and children. It is not an easy or popular road to take, but I believe it is why God put us together. We make a great team! Please keep in touch and tell the other folks in the village that I say hello. We will stop in for a visit when we are out that way again. You made my Christmas by sending your card and your letters!
　　With much affection,

　　　　　　　　　　　　　　　　Becky Hawkins-Valadez
　　　　　　　　　　　　　　　　December 21, 2001

The World Seen from the Distance of a Small Village

James B. Gilmore
Chairman of the Republican National Committee
Washington, D.C.

Dear Sir:

I thank you for your personal letter in which you are calling me to give my support to President Bush, to our Republican leaders in Congress and to RNC. This way we would put our principles into action.

But so frequently, looking on our political scene, I had a problem to find out what those our principles really were or are.

I do not like to be a disturbing voice in our present atmosphere of celebrating our great victory in Afghanistan. I am uneasy to speak frankly what I think about our response to the September 11 day of horror. But yes, I will do this, because nothing good and far-reaching can be attained and achieved in a society in which a frankness of opinion would be suppressed by the pressures of a shallow patriotism.

The attack on us on September 11 was an event that by any circumstances could be left unanswered with a forceful, dignifying and constructive response, which would aim to build a better harmony and a lasting peace and more happy future for the whole world. Such a response would concentrate on a far-sighted creation of an atmosphere of general understanding, reconciliation, and joining hands to go into this future together.

Our response to that attack didn't go this way.

We chose to make a show that would illustrate abundantly and clearly to everybody our indignation, our anger and our military might that can truly strike back.

On the home front the reaction to the Sept. 11 tragedy was a spontaneous and beautiful togetherness of people. It was a kind of liberation of the spirit to do something, to help, even to sacrifice for the common good. Suddenly the fear of a watchful eye of the trial lawyers was forgotten and people were showing again a trust to one another and a good Samaritan way of mutual interaction.

The government, at that time Republican, responded to this tragedy by a mobilization of hurrah patriotism. This attack became for the government a wonderful occasion to get popularity and to get a complete 100% acclamation. A revenge and an instant satisfaction became a center of our policy. No effort was made to understand the undercurrents for that attack. This was not even considered.

Book Four

Only a blind anger, indignation, a crude vengeance and "teaching them a lesson" became our strategy. We had to hit somebody, and to hit him hard to prove our manhood, to show our might, and to confirm that the might is right.

And here comes something that was humiliating to me and for which I felt ashamed. We didn't know where to direct our anger. Considering different options, we choose to hit the Taliban. It was the most convenient target. It had opposition within the country. Its army was primitive. It was not forming any state structure. It was just an extremist religious sect that was trying to impose on the population of Afghanistan the original 7th century Muslim rules and rigors for the daily life in the present, not still quite 20th century society.

It was not restraining to our government that Taliban was the least involved in the Sept. 11 attack. What was important was that the Taliban was a perfect target to hit. And hitting the Taliban with all our might and fury was not compromising our relations with other important Arab countries, for whom the Taliban and its trial to live according to old Muslim rules was an uncomfortable accusation, step backwards and plain pain in the neck.

This choice of selecting the Taliban as a perfect target just because it was the easiest way to show what we can, and where we stand, did not make me feel proud. I felt the humiliation.

Apparently we didn't feel man enough to go openly and to raise the whole issue calling to the summit everybody from the Muslim world. For our wrath we chose the weakest, and we declared him a "war" completely out of proportion.

And in this "war" we were not restrained by any human considerations.

The Sept. 11 attack was a semi-premeditated murder that came together with the destruction of the symbols of our economic and military omnipotence. To this we responded with a calculated, completely premeditated murder of the whole Taliban.

The wave after wave of concentrated bombardments with the strongest and most deadly explosives of every place where the Taliban could be spotted, by any standard cannot be considered a war. It was the old time, merciless hunting of a public outlaw before judging him, whether he was guilty or not. It was our free self-given permit to kill. To revenge.

I still remember the joyfully smiling face of our war secretary, who with a gleam on his face was explaining on TV how the newest smart

The World Seen from the Distance of a Small Village

bombs would penetrate into the tunnels and kills there everybody sparing the trouble to go after them.

It was ugly. It was not a dignified show for the U.S. It was not a way on which a future peace and a common good can be built. The might is right law never in history had lasting life.

Consequent to such a policy was our treatment of the Taliban war prisoners. It is hard for me to find logic in this, but taken as prisoners in war, they were declared terrorists who dared to shot in our direction.

The photographs of those prisoners in line, in the kneeling position, with the hands strapped backwards to their ankles, and with their heads pushed down to the ground, if they were revolting to me, how were they seen and assimilated into the minds and souls of the Muslim masses? In other photographs the prisoners were wearing heavy, impenetrable hoods on their heads.

I lived through the horrors of Nazi occupation, but even those Nazis did not humiliate their prisoners in such a way. Humiliation creates more lasting, more soul-changing wounds than any physical cruelty. If those prisoners were afterwards completely radicalized and dangerous, there is a small wonder. Who was the "hero" who ordered such a treatment for the prisoners of that war? It is not difficult to imagine what will be the fruit of this our making of a new order in the world. It can be felt bitterly later on by our children and grandchildren.

The world can be poisoned in many ways, not only by air pollution.

I do not know what are the causes of the confrontation between India and Pakistan, and why just now Palestinians were expecting a big armament shipment. But we gave the precedent. We resolved our pain and our indignation not by communication and dialogue, but by a massive, murderous, annihilating blow. If we did this, why can they not do the same? We didn't show much restraint in our wrath, then why should they?

It is strange how we are isolating and incarcerating those "war" prisoners. Do we want to hide something that is bothering our conscience? Just now I was looking at the news and I saw that England was protesting our treatment of Taliban prisoners in Cuba. I saw the picture. It is really incredible that we committed this. Our government is committing something of which American will be deeply ashamed.

Book Four

Sept. 11, however painful it was, could represent an enormous opportunity for goodness. In the hands of our government it was transformed into a punitive expedition, shameful treatment of prisoners and a very uncertain future for everybody.

I wonder what will be the process of John Walker will look like?

I do not know how you will judge this letter of mine. Sincerity is not always welcomed now days.

As you see, I am not a very good fellow for the Party.

I wish you the best and I wish America the best.

Tadeusz Maciejczyk
Milledgeville, January 20, 2002

The World Seen from the Distance of a Small Village

George W. Bush
President of the United States

Dear Sir:

One week ago, I wrote a letter to Gov. Gilmore, Chairman of RNC, in which I wrote about the present war and to where this war is leading us.

I am sending you a copy of this letter because during this week I was surprised at how many people feel uncertain and uneasy about our present situation of a war without an end. What we did until now satisfies practically nobody and such doubts and such worries will have their influence.

Nothing was explained and made clear, expect that this war and constant vigilance, its cost and redirection of resources, the general uncertainty, will be with us for the next one hundred years.

Everybody is watching and waiting.

I wish you the best in those difficult problems.

Tadeusz Maciejczyk
Milledgeville, January 28, 2002

Book Four

C Alix Timko, MA
Department of Clinical and Health Psychology
MCP Hahnemann University
Mail Stop 626
245 N. 15th Street
Philadelphia, PA 19102-1192

Thank you for sending me your survey. I am glad that finally somebody is doing something to bring to some kind of sanity the health and drug commercials on TV.

I am in a rural general practice and my contact with psychiatric problems is limited. Problems of psychology always have their appearance in any medical practice.

Sorry, but I cannot answer your questions with the percentage of precision that you are demanding.

In my practice the most frequent mind-altering problems are anxiety, depression, chronic pain, stress, insecurity, simple fear of the future and pretending.

The people who are influenced by TV advertisements are maybe 10% those who really have something; they get the clue, look for more information on the web and then decide on the next step. But the majority of those who use the advertising are those who spent their life before the TV, are unsatisfied with themselves, are sedentary, already with many diagnoses and treatments.

Those TV drug advertisements are very suggestive and convincing. Such patients can appear in my office, but the next day they go to a specialist. If those advertised drugs are paid for in one way or another; they become restless and persistent.

Age? It can be any, but most frequently this problem appears between 40 and 70.

Here I want to tell you my impression about two problems that with the passage of time are becoming more and more visible. One of them is the problem of Viagra.

It looks to me that Viagra becomes a very addictive drug. They say: "Come and we will give you six tablets free." What they do not say is, "Then you will be ours. You will be hooked."

Viagra is not bringing fulfillment or happiness that promises to be so impressionable. Viagra is tempting insecure men with a mirage of sensual success while in reality it destroys their good self-images and to a high degree their feeling of dignity. It bypasses the need for closeness, caring one for another and love. Can it be that it produces erosion in their character and even in their personality? What is your school saying about this?

The other problem about which I would like to ask you is even more serious. Can social or national traumas provoke social or national psychopathic responses and if so, to what can it lead?

Our September 11 tragedy is turning into a nightmare of perpetual suspicions and vigilance, into the creation of a second shadow government and into the development of small nuclear arms with which we would hit hard whomever we suspected or disliked. What kind of peace are we supposed to preserve in this way? Are we entering into a stage of a national insanity? Development of those small nuclear arms could turn into our most unwanted surprises.

I am sending you my letters written to Washington about this war.

Could you give me your, or your university's opinion about this problem that is calling more and more urgently for some kind of true healing?

May I have your answer?

I send you my best wishes in your work.

                         Tadeusz Maciejczyk, M.D.
                         Milledgeville, March 13, 2002

P.S. I am sending you a description of my book that should be published this year.

Book Four

Colin Powell
Secretary of State
Washington, D.C.

Dear Sir:

I started this letter a few days ago after watching the news.

I looked at the devastation of Jenin and the despair of its remaining people there. As a Christian, I felt indignation seeing the Israeli soldiers breaking the door of the Basilica in Bethlehem. Until now in the civilized world, the rule was observed that in the time of war those who were looking safety in church could stay there safe. Apparently now the world is going into a different direction.

Immediately after those grim pictures I saw you in a safe, nice room, smiling in a cordial conversation with Sharon. In the background of the room, flags of Israel and America were put in a very visible place stressing togetherness and unity.

And I was wondering.

You were there in the Mideast on the peace mission searching for solutions. There, Israelis prepared for you a stage and the convenient for them music, inviting you to dance the way they wanted. And you did this. I didn't see from your side any creative move, or thought or action. You permitted to be manipulated.

What can I say?

Looking at that display of unity between Israel and American, I thought about old pictures of receptions in the Kremlin for dignitaries from the Soviet satellite countries. The arrangements, the presentation, the symbols, the special meaning for the words that would serve the intentions of the bosses of the Kremlin and the whole purpose of such shows were almost identical with what I was seeing now. A long time ago, the Chamberlain visit to Hitler had similar circumstances and was played with a striking similarity by all players.

It bothered me that while American reporters were risking their lives trying to find the truth what was happening in the forbidden areas of Israeli activities you, being on a search for a peace mission, you didn't go there to see by yourself what was happening there and make your own independent judgment. You saw only the effect of suicidal bomber shown to you from helicopter. The Israeli operation was clean, military and because of this admissible and honorable. The suicidal bombing was a despicable terrorist attack against the innocent.

The World Seen from the Distance of a Small Village

But, as I know the human nature and human spirit, I can assure you that nobody can offer his life in sacrifice just out of hate. The military operations can have such a core in its moving force.

The self-sacrifice can be done only out of love for something great and revered in the soul, when the hunger for such a spiritual value persistently were tramped under feet by a deaf, unapproachable power. Only such a circumstance and life condition can prevail over the human need for self-preservation. Those are the supreme acts of love.

A contempt and scorn, condemnation and brutality of the material mighty powers never in the long run won a battle with such a power of the spiritual.

It would be better for the next generations in America, in Israel, and elsewhere in the world, if this fact could be accepted. No armies, no tanks, airstrikes will win such a convulsions in a final account. Only the togetherness of minds and of spirits can.

Finally, as you preferred not to see what was happening in Janin, I am sending you some photographs from Warsaw done in the Spring of 1945. Warsaw was leveled to the ground by order of Hitler. It also was harboring terrorists, including the terrorists who were fighting in the ghetto of Warsaw, opposing the military might of the Nazis.

I write this letter because America has a real mission of leading the world into a better future.

Such a mission cannot be accomplished with a pre-fixed rigidity, double standards, and twisted for convenience meaning for words.

Also, I am sending you the copies of what I wrote about the Middle East conflict almost twenty years ago.

And, in spite of the appearance of this letter, I truly wish you the best in your uneasy work.

Tadeusz Maciejczyk
Milledgeville, April 21, 2002

Book Four

Senator John McCain
Citizens Against Government Waste
Washington, D.C.

Dear Sir:

    I responded to your survey.
    At this point I have to confess that my knowledge of present-day military needs is very limited.
    Neither am I sure what in the Congressional spending can be considered frivolous and self-serving and what in the long range could have a positive influence on the economic, cultural or emotional growth of the country.
    With all those uncertainties, I can only say that I trust you more than anybody else in politics.
    I recognize that our military readiness has to be adequate to meet the challenges of our time. There are and always will be in the world ambitions that can be restrained only by the presence of such a force.
    At the same time, I believe that order maintained only by the power of the military is very fragile. Military can calm the surface and force true issues to hide in the underground burying them there.
    But those unresolved ideas, needs, beliefs or longings will be buried there in the underground not dead, but very alive. They will boil under the surface until the moment of a new eruption, more emotional, more violent than ever before.
    The military has no arms and never will be equipped to control the spirit of those who feel injustice and subjugation.
    Our greatest treasure that can give strength and wisdom to resolve even the most violent conflicts are not the military forces, but our minds, our hearts and our goodwill that, looking into the future, should be strong enough to forgive, to understand, to unite and to build that future together.
    To help us in this endeavor we have a magnificent tool; we have a Constitution that in this undertaking can give us guidance. Our Constitution has already passed the test of time and is as convincing now as it was 200 years ago. It passed the reality test differentiating clearly the real approach to problems from egocentric delusions of being powerful and dictatorial.
    It also passed the test of generosity, approaching human problems with love. Not the panicky and defensive measures of protection against an unpredictable reign of terror, but the solving of the

real issues without looking for excuses that talking to terrorists leads to nowhere, will give us peace and a condition for everybody to grow.

The effective army against unresolved grievances that while suppressed by force, are boiling under the surface of an apparent peace should be different from the military.

To win such situations, such an army should be equipped and prepared to find solutions to those boiling, torturous soul issues giving them recognition, legitimacy and open, down-to-its-roots discussions without any pre-established taboos.

Such an army could be organized like the present time National Guard. The enlisted men of such an army should be equipped not with guns, but with the special skills and talents of enormous diversity necessary to reach the very center of the roots of each conflict. They should be able to engage all sides of such conflicts in discussion, in dialogue, in down-to-the-gut-level talks of all involved.

Those men in such an army should be armed with the deep knowledge of a man as an individual as well as of a man who acts as a member within his society. They should be an authority in psychology, in philosophy, in history, customs, religions and beliefs, in the regional ways of life, economy, resources, the power of the spirit and the stresses of longing.

Such an army should be divided in different branches. It should have its own line of command, from regional to national, even to international.

They should have their training and preparedness opportunities for the expected and for the unexpected. Those soldiers, while registered and at home, should be ready to be called to active duty when necessary. To be called for duty in such a corps, should mean a special honor and a special recognition.

Such a corps should have its own name that would define its vocation and its mission. It should have its own code of truthfulness, impartiality and dedication that would distinguish them. They should stand above politics.

The creation of such a corps surely would not be a waste of money and time. Such a corps could be transformed into the soul of life on this our, not-any-more big globe.

Together with this letter, I am sending you articles that I wrote after September 11, an article about "Freedom vs. Terrorism—Differently," my addition to the survey of the Grace Commission about waste in the 1980's and an announcement of the publication of my

Book Four

book this year. The title of this book is *The World Seen from the Distance of a Small Village*.

I wish you the best in your work. If you run for the Presidency again, I will vote for you.

                        Tadeusz Maciejczyk
                        Milledgeville, June 4, 2002

Russell F. Coats
Sterling, Illinois

Dear Dr. Maciejczyk,

This article reminded me of the times I met you when I brought Rev. Clark Moushon and his wife, Louise, over to your office on occasion. We had a couple of conversations in the waiting room.

I admire someone like you who has seen so much of the not-so-good aspects of life and yet not let it get your down. Someone like you is an inspiration to the rest of us.

It was a good article, and I appreciated having known you at least a little bit.

                        Russell Coats
                        East Jordan United Methodist Church
                        Sterling, IL
                        August 1, 2002

The World Seen from the Distance of a Small Village

(The following was I think a 5th or 6th grader in our school who was required to write a composition and she dedicated this literary work to me. Apparently the kids from here are looking at me this way.)

Dr. Maciejczyk

Dr. Maciejczyk is a doctor. He has brown eyes, white hair and is short. He has glasses and is skinny. He has lots of children. He is very energetic, thoughtful and friendly. He has a soft voice. He is always keeping busy in the office and other places. He also is from Spain.

Dr. Maciejczyk works in a doctor's office in Milledgeville. It is on Main Street and the building is brick. Dr. Maciejczyk is self-employed. He has two ladies that work for him. Dr. Maciejczyk works all week long except Thursday and Sunday. His hours are 8:00 A.M. until 5:00 P.M. At his job he does a lot of things. He gives medicine to people if they are sick, checks their pulse, gives shots and draws blood. When he is at work, he enjoys helping people, seeing them smiling and being happy, not sad, and having contact with the people.

His favorite hobby is painting and drawing. He has a huge garden that he loves working in the summer. In his garden he has tomatoes, peppers, carrots, onions. He draws pictures of everything.

In the summer he paints and works in the garden and other things. It is so fun working in the garden in the summer.

He really doesn't admire anyone, he just doesn't know why. It is really odd that he doesn't admire anyone, but you know we are all different, not alike.

His thoughts about Dr. Maciejczyk is he is always busy, happy and lots of other things. He makes you feel better. He is nice to everyone. He has a heart so big everyone can fit and he loves us all.

Hillary Hartman

(NOTE: Hillary handed me this her work personally and very proudly through the window of the waiting room in my office.)

Book Four

Editor
The Daily Gazette
Sterling, Illinois

Dear Sir:

    I want to thank you for writing about me and about my book, adding to that article an excellent photograph that was calling attention to all the page of news.
    I want also to thank all those, who after reading that article sent me letters, generally confirming that a man always should be ready to defend his convictions and his beliefs.
    And also, I want to thank all those, who after reading your paper were greeting me with a special smile and a sign of friendship.
    At this point, I want to stress the importance of *The Daily Gazette* in the development of my writing and consequently in the appearance of this book. Everybody needs to feel the reflection of his work and action in the eyes of others.
    Your *Gazette* gave me so many times a welcomed place for me to express my thoughts and my ideas, helping me in this way to understand myself and to grow. That help represented an enormous stimulus to me to continue writing and in this way to participate in the life of this our place and of the country.
    For all those helping, I am grateful.

                                          Tadeusz Maciejczyk
                                          August 11, 2002

NOTES

Publisher's Note: Not all references made by the author were found in their entirety.

Book One

[1] *Robins Reader,* Spring-Summer, 1983.
[2] "Dziady," Adam Mickiewicz. Adam Mickiewicz, considered the greatest poet of Poland and Lithuania, lived from 1798 to 1855.
[3] John Powell, *Why Am I Afraid to Tell You Who I Am?* (Allen, Texas: Argus Communications, 1967).

Book Three

[1] Cyprian Norwid, *Selected Writing Volume I*, (Warsaw: State's Institute of Publishing, 1968) p. 298.
[2] John Powell, *Why Am I Afraid to Tell You Who I Am?* p. 29.
[3] Cyprian Norwid, *Selected Writings*, p. 318.
[4] Ibid.
[5] Ibid., p. 312

Book Four

[1] Jan Kasprowicz, "Blogoslawieni," *Selection of Poetry of Young Poland*, (Krakow), 1903, p. 4.
[2] John Powell, *A Life Giving Vision*, (Allen, Texas: Argus Communications).
[3] *The Observer,* (Rockford, IL), June 8, 2001.

To order additional copies of

The World Seen from the Distance of a Small Village

Have your credit card ready and call
Toll free: (877) 421-READ (7323)
or send $39.95* each plus $7.95 S&H** to

WinePress Publishing
PO Box 428
Enumclaw, WA 98022

or order online at: www.winepressbooks.com

*WA residents, add 8.4% sales tax
**add $2.00 S&H for each additional book ordered

Printed in the United States
23535LVS00001B/73